Evolutions in Budgetary Practice

ALLEN SCHICK
AND THE OECD SENIOR BUDGET OFFICIALS

OECD

ORGANISATION FOR ECONOMIC CO-OPERATION AND DEVELOPMENT

The OECD is a unique forum where the governments of 30 democracies work together to address the economic, social and environmental challenges of globalisation. The OECD is also at the forefront of efforts to understand and to help governments respond to new developments and concerns, such as corporate governance, the information economy and the challenges of an ageing population. The Organisation provides a setting where governments can compare policy experiences, seek answers to common problems, identify good practice and work to co-ordinate domestic and international policies.

The OECD member countries are: Australia, Austria, Belgium, Canada, the Czech Republic, Denmark, Finland, France, Germany, Greece, Hungary, Iceland, Ireland, Italy, Japan, Korea, Luxembourg, Mexico, the Netherlands, New Zealand, Norway, Poland, Portugal, the Slovak Republic, Spain, Sweden, Switzerland, Turkey, the United Kingdom and the United States. The Commission of the European Communities takes part in the work of the OECD.

OECD Publishing disseminates widely the results of the Organisation's statistics gathering and research on economic, social and environmental issues, as well as the conventions, guidelines and standards agreed by its members.

This work is published on the responsibility of the Secretary-General of the OECD. The opinions expressed and arguments employed herein do not necessarily reflect the official views of the Organisation or of the governments of its member countries.

Foreword

This book commemorates the 30th anniversary of the OECD Working Party of Senior Budget Officials (SBO). It brings together a collection of documents, articles and extracts from publications written by Professor Allen Schick for the SBO over the years. Allen has been associated with the SBO since its inception, and we believe there is no more appropriate way to commemorate the SBO's anniversary than by reprinting this collection of his work. Over the years, Allen has made fundamental contributions to the art of public sector budgeting, and his work continues to be an inspiration for budgeting reform around the world.

Table of Contents

Tables

Introduction:

Budgeting as Dialogue

by

Allen Schick
Distinguished University Professor
University of Maryland, United States

Since its launch early in the new century, the *OECD Journal on Budgeting* has been a vehicle for dialogue between those who make budgets and those who study them. This relationship has been a productive one: scholars have gained knowledge of contemporary issues and innovations in budgeting; practitioners have gained understanding of the concepts that define their work. But the relationship has often been asymmetric. Most of the grist for dialogue has been provided by budget officials. They – not academics – have been the principal designers of new budget practices; the processes they manage have been laboratories of budgetary experimentation and innovation. This is as it should be, for modifications in budget methods usually arise out of an impulse to make the process less fractious and more rational. The conduct of budgeting is fertile ground for reform, not because scholars know a better way to allocate public money, but because the allocators are dissatisfied with the tools at hand. In fact, when reform is motivated by an idealised model of good budgeting, it is likely to leave little imprint on budget practices. But when the aim is to improve the way budgets are compiled and implemented, changes may be lasting.

The *Journal* is an outgrowth of the meetings of the OECD Working Party of Senior Budget Officials (SBO) that have been convened each year since 1980. The SBO has been the wellspring of multiple dialogues that have become institutionalised during the past 30 years. The SBO has evolved into a network that extends dialogue well beyond the annual meeting of OECD country budget officials to regional SBO meetings around the world, workshops on contemporary issues, and publications including the *Journal*. Wherever the SBO has spread its wings, the formula has been the same: practitioners learning from one another by discussing practices and developments in their countries, and scholars eavesdropping on their conservations and contributing some conversation of their own. Dialogue – not dictat – has been the operational norm of the SBO and its successful offshoots.

This approach sets the SBO apart from some organisations which, armed with rules and prescriptions, try to dictate how budgeting should be practised. The SBO, by contrast, is built on the open exchange of ideas and experiences among budget officials who draw their own conclusions and often apply what they have learned in their own countries. The SBO and the *Journal* testify to the significant improvements in budgeting that have been spurred by dialogue.

I have been privileged to participate in many of the discussions, both at the SBO and in the pages of the *Journal*. My comprehension of budgeting and my admiration of those who practise it have been greatly enhanced by the opportunity to join in the conversations. A fair assessment of my role is that I have rarely told budget officials what they should or should not do. Instead, I have sought to make sense for myself and others of the challenges facing budget officials, and of the ways they have adapted to new situations and opportunities. I have sought to facilitate dialogue by serving as a broker between scholars and practitioners. Both personally and professionally, this has been a rewarding role for me.

The texts and articles published here show that certain matters are perennially on the minds of budget makers. Foremost has been the recurring focus on performance and on expanding budget horizons beyond a single fiscal year to the medium term or longer. Rereading the texts leaves me with the impression that budget officials are caught between the need to complete budget work on schedule and their yearning for better-informed decisions that take account of substantive results and future conditions. The deadlines of budgeting and the need to dampen conflict impel them to simplify the process, often by disregarding the future implications of current decisions or by focusing on the amounts required to purchase inputs rather than on the outputs or results that flow from budget allocations. Working at the crossroads of reason and expedience, budget makers restlessly tinker with the process, orienting it more to the future and to performance, but not quite enough to quell the urge to innovate. The evidence from the texts and articles in this book is that budgeting has lengthened its time frame and that officials are much better informed on the substantive results of past expenditure and the projected results of future expenditure.

Yet there is another reason, rooted in the very concept of dialogue, why budget makers have not stretched the time boundaries far into the future or shifted wholeheartedly from inputs to outputs. In their natural habitat, budget participants discuss what is on their minds – what matters to them most. In ongoing bilateral discussions between line managers and budget people, the talk inevitably zooms in on the year immediately ahead. That is the budget that must be decided, and the year's activities are the ones that must be funded. Striving to settle the annual budget shortens the time span, even when determined efforts are made to consider the medium or long term.

The same behavioural pattern pertains to the line items in the budget. Participants focus on inputs because they need this information to decide how much to allocate. Regardless of the volume of performance information inserted in the budget, spenders in line ministries and budget guardians in central agencies have difficulty deciding expenditure levels without recourse to data on staffing, salaries, supplies, travel, the cost of accommodation, and other line items. Dialogue would be blunted if they were denied the freedom to exchange information on these inputs. Participants also discuss programmes, policies and activities and, in many countries, outputs and outcomes as well. As much as they care about results, they deem it essential to consider the cost of inputs in determining the amounts to be allocated. For them, good budgeting means tallying the cost of inputs in the light of the outputs to be achieved. It does not mean purging the budget of input data.

Much the same can be said regarding the budget's time horizon. In their conversations, budget officials want to reckon with the future fiscal and programme implications of current decisions. But they are mindful that it is the budget for the period immediately ahead that has to be decided, and their dialogue inevitably revolves around this period. Eavesdropping on budget dialogues, this writer has observed significant enlargement in the number and variety of participants. In a growing number of countries, parliamentarians and their staffs have actively joined in the discussion, as have journalists, non-governmental organisations and interest groups. The world of budgeting is no longer as closed as it once was, and the dialogue is less bounded by the internal routines of governmental budgeting. In many OECD countries, expanded dialogue has led to both greater transparency and more conflict over budget priorities and allocations. Legislators adopt more amendments, groups and NGOs proffer more alternatives, and the media find more shortcomings in the government's spending plans.

At the end of the day, however, the budget gets decided. No matter how deep the fissures or how difficult the choices, dialogue in budgeting must produce a decision. This action-forcing quality distinguishes budgeting from other governmental policy processes. It means that dialogue in budgeting is not mere chatter, but rather a means for a government to set its course for the year or years ahead. It is this quality of budgeting that has made eavesdropping so enjoyable.

ISBN 978-92-64-06087-6
Evolutions in Budgetary Practice
Allen Schick and the OECD Senior Budget Officials
© OECD 2009

Chapter 1

Budgeting for Entitlements*

---

* This paper was originally issued in January 1984 as part of the SBO project entitled "Resource Allocation and Control". At the time of writing, Allen Schick was Professor of Public Affairs at the University of Maryland, United States. An afterward was written in 2009.

During the past three decades, there has been a progressive enlargement in the relative size of the public sector in most OECD countries, as well as significant changes in the composition of public expenditure. Public expenditure averaged 28.5% of GDP in the 1955-57 period, 34.5% in the 1967-69 years, and 41.4% in 1974-76 (OECD, 1978, Table 2; these are unweighted averages). This enlargement has persisted in recent years, though the rate of growth has been slower and more erratic (OECD, 1982, Table 4-A-C). According to a 1982 OECD study for Working Party No. 1 of the Economic Policy Committee, "except for Australia, Austria, Luxembourg and Iceland, the most buoyant source of public sector growth during the reporting period as a whole [1960-80] has been the increase in transfer payments. ... Transfer payments are now roughly equal to public consumption expenditure in an increasing number of OECD countries" (OECD, 1982, p. 6). Data from a number of countries illustrate the growing importance of these payments. In Denmark, income maintenance expenditures climbed from 7.5% of GDP in 1954 to 19.7% in 1978. They rose in France from 11.2% to 17.9%; in Germany from 11.5% to 18.2%; in Japan from 2.9% to 7.3%; in the Netherlands from 6.4% to 19.4%; in the United Kingdom from 6.4% to 11.7%; and in the United States from 4.1% to 9.8% (OECD, 1982, Table 4-A-C).

These trends, the causes of which have occasioned much study and controversy, have been accompanied by a substantial increase in the share of public expenditure accounted for by entitlement programmes. The bulk of transfer and income maintenance expenditure is for pensions, unemployment and disability compensation, and other entitlement schemes. In most OECD countries, entitlements have been the principal growth area of public expenditure in recent years.

This paper discusses budgeting for entitlements under two rather different conditions: the expansion of this category of expenditure during the quarter century after World War II; and cutback and "status quo" budgeting during the decade since the first oil shock. Before discussing these conditions and the factors accounting for them, the paper provides an overview and definition of the entitlement problem.

1. The definition and budgetary status of entitlements

Despite their importance, there is no standard definition of entitlements nor, therefore, reliable means of measuring the fraction of the budget accounted for by them. Nevertheless, the budgetary characteristics of entitlements are sufficiently distinguishable from other forms of public expenditure to warrant separate analysis. Budgeting for entitlements is not the same as budgeting for the purchase of goods and services or for other discretionary expenditures. The differences between entitlements and more traditional expenditures account for the basic problem of expenditure management that besets most OECD countries. The methods of budgetary decision and management developed for traditional expenditures might require adjustment when applied to entitlement programmes.

An entitlement is a provision of law that establishes a legal right to public funds. The right might be accorded to an individual, to a household, or to any other designated beneficiary. The law usually sets forth eligibility requirements and either a schedule of payments or a formula by which the payments are computed. The law usually does not specify (or limit) the total expenditure for the entitlement; the total is simply the sum of individual payments.

Social security, unemployment compensation, family allowances and disability payments are entitlements because they accord particular classes of the population rights to money from the public treasury. The right to a social security benefit, for example, is based on age and (in many countries) prior earnings, and the money value of that right is determined according to law. The government (or the social security fund) is obligated to pay the amount to which recipients are entitled whether or not sufficient funds have been set aside for this purpose in the budget . In many countries, a permanent appropriation finances social security and various other entitlement programmes. But even when the entitlement is financed by annual appropriations, the government must provide the benefits mandated by law.

The concept of entitlements can be explicated by contrasting them to other types of expenditure. Programmes which are not entitlements entail either discretionary expenditures or mandatory expenditures. The former are easily distinguishable from entitlements because expenditures are incurred only if they are authorised by appropriations. There is no substantive law requiring the government to spend the funds and no right of recipients to payments from the treasury. If no appropriation is forthcoming, no expenditure is made. Discretionary expenditures are common in the purchase of goods and services. However, in instances where suppliers have a legal right to sell their goods to the government and the government is obligated to purchase those goods at a price determined according to law, then an entitlement would exist. Thus, agricultural programmes which require the government to acquire surplus crops at a price set by law would be entitlements. But when the government spends an appropriation to purchase agricultural products to feed persons in its care, the expenditure probably would not be an entitlement.

The second category consists of mandatory expenditures which are not entitlements. In these cases, the requirement to incur the expenditure arises out of a contractual obligation entered into by the government. Thus, the obligation to pay interest on its debt stems from a contract between the government and bondholders; a government's obligation to pay for goods and services derives from a contractual commitment to suppliers. Without these contracts, no payments would ensue. But the obligation to pay for entitlements derives from law, not from contract. Indeed, many entitlements are unilateral commitments by the government which do not require any reciprocal commitment by beneficiaries.

The distinction between entitlements and other expenditures is not so clear-cut as to rule out all ambiguity. Some programmes may have characteristics similar to entitlements but still permit a measure of discretion in determining expenditure. In the United States, for example, the food stamps programme entitles low-income persons to cash assistance for the purchase of food. Because the law establishing the programme limits the total cost and makes expenditures conditional on annual appropriations, some budget experts do not regard food stamps as an entitlement. Yet Congress always appropriates sufficient funds to pay for all required benefits and raises the limitation on total cost whenever necessary to ensure that all benefits are fully paid. For this reason, some experts classify food stamps as an entitlement.

Ambiguity about the status of some programmes does not impair the analytic usefulness of the entitlement concept. Most expenditures can be clearly classified as entitlements or non-entitlements. The marginal cases make it difficult to tally the full cost of entitlements or their share of national budgets. But to examine how the practice of budgeting has been affected by the growth of entitlements, one need not possess an authoritative listing of these expenditures.

The critical distinction between entitlements and non-entitlements is that expenditures for the former are determined by law and for the latter by budgets and appropriations. When entitlement legislation is being formulated, its future cost can only be estimated; once the legislation has been enacted into law, the government must (unless it changes the law) bear whatever cost is required by the entitlement. In these circumstances, the budget process is more a means of accounting for past decisions than of making new ones. Moreover, the budget may not be the process by which year-to-year changes in entitlement expendures are determined. These changes are more likely to result from changes in the number of eligible beneficiaries and from inflation than from discretionary budget actions. As a consequence, budgetary control of the "increment" – the portion of expenditure over which the budget organisation historically had greatest influence – has been weakened. In extreme cases, where indexation is widespread and entitlements are highly sensitive to economic performance, expenditure growth is on "automatic pilot" and the procedures of budgeting have little sway over the trend in expenditure.

In some countries, entitlement expenditures are classified as "uncontrollable". This label should be interpreted to mean that the level of expenditure is not determined by a budget decision alone. That is to say, if the budget and appropriations do not provide sufficient funds, the government still is obligated to make the payments prescribed by law. But entitlements are controllable through changes in law; in this sense, the "uncontrollable" label can be misleading.

The fact that entitlements now constitute a much larger share of public expenditure than they did 10-30 years ago has important implications for budgeting. For one thing, unless it changes the law, the government must incur the expenditure, regardless of the condition of the economy or of other claims on the budget. Moreover, as noted above, year-to-year increases in expenditure are likely to be decided independently of the budget process. In fact, variations between budgeted and actual expenditures are likely to be greater and less predictable for entitlements than for other programmes.

Entitlement issues tend to draw wider participation both within and outside government than do conventional budget decisions relating to consumption expenditures. Conventional budgeting has been described as "government talking to itself", as ministries communicate their spending wants to the budget organisation. Taking decisions for entitlements is likely to be a more open process, for the affected beneficiaries have a direct stake in the outcome and strong incentives to make their interests known to public officials. Furthermore, the distributive effects of entitlements are more visible than are those of consumption spending.

This "politicisation" of budgeting poses few difficulties when the economy is growing and resources are available to finance increased entitlements. But when the economy is weak and cutbacks are sought, the budget process may have difficulty coping with political conflict over entitlements.

2. The establishment and growth of entitlements

No single factor accounts for the prominence now accorded entitlements in public expenditure. Budget officials attribute the growth in entitlements to economic conditions, political pressures, demographic changes and other factors. In sorting out these factors, it would be useful to distinguish between the establishment of entitlements (including changes in law expanding eligibility or benefits) and the growth that occurs after the entitlement has been enacted into law.

2.1. *The establishment phase*

In most OECD countries, the great upsurge in entitlement legislation occurred during the sustained period of economic growth in the decades after World War II. There is widespread agreement that the two conditions were closely related. Economic betterment provided the means of financing entitlement programmes, as well as expectations that the state would shelter its citizens from the fluctuations of the business cycle. Protracted growth legitimised the role of democratic regimes in economic stabilisation and management, and entitlements provided built-in stabilisers against cyclical downturns. Because the post-war growth occurred while memory of the Great Depression and its harsh effects was still strong, it stimulated demands for "safety nets" to assist less fortunate citizens. Widespread affluence (and the expectation of sustained improvement in the standard of living) generated political acceptance of income redistribution schemes, for it now was possible to improve the welfare of low-income persons without lowering the economic quality of life for the more fortunate sectors of society. Governments did not so much redistribute income as distribute the rewards of economic growth. They gave some of the benefits of growth to the elderly, the unemployed, the disabled and others who were cut off from it, but the living standards of workers and businessmen continued to improve.

Economic growth relaxed budgetary constraints on programme expansion and desensitised governments to the costs of their new obligations. Often, entitlements were inaugurated or expanded with little solid data on their future costs and without subjecting them to rigorous budgetary review. Insensitivity to the cost of new entitlements was partly a function of the manner in which these programmes were developed. Entitlement schemes were frequently devised by special task forces or commissions which operated outside the regular budget process and whose proposals garnered a great deal of attention and support before the ministry of finance was called upon to review them. The legislation formulated in response to these political expectations addressed the needs and rights of the persons who were to receive the entitlements. Unlike appropriations, money usually was not mentioned at all. Attention thus was deflected from costs to needs, and there was a parallel shift in the effective locus of decision making from the budget organisation to other centres of political power. It was difficult in these circumstances for budget officials to make their case in terms of costs. As a result, budgetary power gravitated to those who could point to the public good that would be accomplished by aiding the aged, the poor and the unemployed, and away from those who worried about whether the government could afford the obligations it was assuming so willingly.

Inattention to future costs was encouraged by a number of factors. First, the expectation of sustained growth bred confidence that an expanding economy would be able to pay for expanding benefits. Second, some major entitlements, particularly social security, had self-financed funds which accumulated surpluses to pay for future benefits. These surpluses encouraged the notion that, despite demographic trends, the funds would be able to pay for the obligations which they were accruing. Third, during periods of economic weakness, the prevailing view was that spending on entitlements would spur recovery and lead to still greater improvements in living standards.

The spread of entitlements was fueled by peer pressures among the industrialised democracies. While the pattern and level of benefits varied from country to country, most were swept along by the rising expectations about their role in providing for the elderly, assisting the poor and protecting workers against recessions. A senior budget official of one less economically advanced European country suggested that its membership in the EC impelled it to upgrade the entitlements accorded citizens.

If economic growth was the wellspring of the entitlement state, then one should find entitlements to be less extensive in OECD countries that had low growth rates in the post-war era. There is reason to believe this to be the case in some southern European countries. But some of these countries have undergone rapid democratisation in recent years, opening them to intense pressures for enhanced living standards. One response has been to entitle citizens to various benefits. The Spanish government, for instance, recently enacted legislation entitling veterans of the Civil War (and certain of their relatives) to pensions, a programme which has turned out to be more costly than expected. This is due to the difficulty, common to many such benefit programmes, of establishing reliable estimates as to the number of persons who will claim and qualify for benefits.

Once started, entitlement programmes tend to be expanded. Programmes targeted for particular beneficiaries are broadened to cover additional groups. In the United States, for example, a programme designed to aid coal miners disabled by black lung disease was expanded by legislation to cover virtually all miners. In Sweden and other countries, programmes aimed at impoverished regions were expanded to other areas which did not meet the original eligibility requirements. These examples suggest that even if eligibility is narrowly defined, political forces may be set into motion to expand the entitlement beyond its intended scope. In this way, targeted programmes are incrementally transformed into universal ones, and entitlements which entail modest costs at the outset grow into costly undertakings.

Because the process of expansion is incremental, it is easy to lose sight of the entitlement's original purpose and of its future cost. Each proposed enlargement is considered in isolation, without examining why the programme was cast as an entitlement. At the point of expansion, the issue is often framed in terms of equity: why should one group be denied benefits which are already provided to another similar group? The affinities between those receiving and those denied the entitlement are accented, while the differences are downplayed.

OECD studies show that the expansion of entitlements entails both the extension of coverage and the improvement of real benefits (OECD, 1983a). Between 1960 and 1980, the percentage of the civilian labour force covered by unemployment insurance programmes increased in five major OECD countries and declined in only one. Coverage expanded from 63.6% to 89.6% in Canada; from 38.2% to 58.8% in France; from 38.2% to 47.7% in Italy; from

33.5% to 50.4% in Japan; and from 66.5% to 89.5% in the United States. There was a decline in the United Kingdom. During the same period, real benefits paid to unemployed workers increased in all of these countries (OECD, 1983b, Tables 16 and 17).

During the growth era, there were frequent adjustments in nominal payments to protect recipients against an erosion in their benefits due to inflation. Inasmuch as economic growth was robust, there often was widespread support for these adjustments, but public officials also were pressured to increase real benefits as well. Typically, therefore, inflation adjustments opened the door to other improvements in entitlements and, as a result, many OECD countries experienced a "benefits creep" with entitlements claiming a progressively larger share of state budgets and national income. In response, some countries turned to indexation as a means of dampening pressure for improvements in benefits. With payments automatcially linked to the inflation rate, there no longer would be need for periodic discretionary legislation. Beneficiaries could no longer use the occasion of inflation adjustments to obtain real improvements. Indexation protected politicians against programmatic pressures that they might not have been able to resist.

In addition to serving as a control mechanism, indexation was welcomed as a means of ensuring that the redistributive features of entitlements were maintained. In a few countries, benefits were linked to wages, thereby ensuring that recipients would partake of the expected economic growth.

2.2. *Growth without legislation*

The initiation and expansion of entitlement programmes through new legislation slackened after the first oil shock, as most OECD countries attempted to adjust to adverse economic conditions. But the cost of existing entitlements continued to rise because of factors over which governments had little or no control. Demographic trends, in particular the rising portion of the population eligible for pensions, contributed significantly to increased expenditures. The changing age composition of the population meant that even if real benefits and eligibility standards were frozen, entitlements would consume increasing shares of public budgets.

Indexation – which (as noted above) was introduced to strengthen budget control – had the opposite effect during the stagflation that persisted from the mid 1970s until the early 1980s. The confluence of high inflation and high unemployment had a devastating effect on budgetary balance in countries where indexed entitlements were widespread. High inflation automatically raised public spending on these programmes; high unemployment diminished the resources available to pay for them. Because the price level was the most commonly used index, beneficiaries of entitlements often were able to maintain their standard of living at the same time that the real income of workers declined.

Not only did low economic growth and high unemployment erode the revenue base of OECD countries, they also added to entitlement spending. Governments were obligated to provide the unemployment benefits they enacted during the growth years. But now that stagnation took hold, they found themselves locked into much higher expenditures than they had expected. One reason was that unemployment was much higher than in previous post-war recessions, compelling industrialised countries to spend much more than in the past to meet their commitments. Moreover, unemployment did not recede to the pre-recession level during recovery. Much of the unemployment was structural (due to the loss of jobs in declining industries and the incapacity of the economy to absorb large numbers of new entrants into the workforce) rather than cyclical. Structural unemployment burdened contemporary governments with high expenses with little prospect of relief from economic improvement.

If any of the three factors (demographic trends, indexation or unemployment) had occurred alone, the effects on government budgets might have been modest. But all three occurred in tandem during the past decade, greatly overloading the budgets of OECD countries and impelling them to seek means of moderating the rise in entitlement expenditures. The statutory basis of entitlements means, however, that governments cannot limit spending simply by budgeting and appropriating lower amounts for them. To cut back on entitlements, they must make substantive changes in law.

3. Curtailing the growth in entitlements

Economic malaise and dire forecasts of protracted budget crisis have virtually halted the establishment of entitlements. But OECD countries have not reduced actual spending; rather, they have sought to curtail the growth in entitlements. Entitlements are likely to remain prominent components of government budgets for many years, and the major income support programmes are likely to retain their basic features. Benefits might not be as high as they would be without cutbacks, and coverage might be narrower, but fears that governments will abandon their role in stabilising incomes have no basis in fact. Yet fear of abandonment is very real, and it has inhibited some governments from coming to grips with the entitlement problem. When small cuts in existing programmes spawn protests that the government is retreating from long-established commitments, the better part of political discretion may be to do nothing.

The conclusion that entitlements are here to stay (though not necessarily as prominent as they became during the growth era) is based on more than political considerations. Over the years, dependence on income supports has spread to most sectors of the population. Entitlements are costly because they are broadly available. Indeed, it is the middle class that garners the lion's share of the benefits in most industrialised democracies. It would be unthinkable to cast those who have become dependent on regular paycheques from government entirely onto their own means. There would be enormous economic dislocation, and the possibility of collapse could not be ruled out.

Thus far, the governments of OECD countries have sought marginal cutbacks in the growth rates of entitlements. While more far-reaching retrenchments might be attempted in the future (especially if economic crisis persists), marginal adjustments are likely to be the near-term objective of most budget and finance organisations. The reason is that these organisations are not motivated by long-term efforts to redefine the scope of government, but by an immediate need to redress the imbalance between resources and expenditures. Small cutbacks can produce visible and significant savings in the current and forthcoming budgets and can narrow the gap between revenues and expenditures. These small adjustments might not appear to aggregate to significant redirections in government policy. Transfer payments might still be the largest (and fastest-growing) component of public expenditure. But from the standpoint of budget officials, the marginal savings will be sufficiently large to make the effort worthwhile.

The marginal character of these cutbacks has generated a great deal of political confusion and budgetary opportunity. In many cases, a reduction in entitlements is accompanied by an increase in expenditure for the programme. This anomaly is due to the fact that the reduction often is calculated not in terms of past expenditure (the way reductions are normally computed in budgeting for consumption expenditures) but in terms of what the expenditure level would be without the cutback. Thus, if spending for an entitlement were above the previous year's level, a change in the programme could still be regarded as a cut. This situation can breed confusion and controversy over the size of the cutback, but it also enables politicians to take credit for both programme reductions and increases. They may thereby respond more easily to the conflicting pressures confronting government: to cut spending and to increase programmes.

3.1. *The tactics of cutback*

It is relatively easy to mobilise opposition to cutbacks. Because entitlements provide cash (or equivalents), cutbacks are more directly felt than when services are curtailed. Reductions in transfer payments have the same financial impact on beneficiaries as reductions in pay have on workers. In both cases, there is a visible loss in disposable income. Accordingly, governments have found it necessary to implement cutbacks with great care and sensitivity to the potential responses of beneficiaries. In this environment, tactical aspects of budgeting – such as how the cutbacks are presented to the public and the position of the budget organisation *vis-à-vis* spending ministries – have become quite important. The tactics vary from one budget season or political situation to another, their commen element being an opportunistic assessment of what is more appropriate for the objectives of the moment. In one year, the government might act without advance warning in the hope that the shock treatment will overwhelm opposition before it can be effectively organised. In another year, the government might try to build political support for its moves by consulting with affected groups or by openly discussing the problems that compel it to make cutbacks.

The tactics are likely to reflect each country's political culture. In Japan, where consensual budgeting is the norm, efforts have been made to gain support by spreading the burdens of cutback among the affected strata. In Denmark, where coalition governments have fragile majorities in parliament, there is extensive intra-party negotiation within government but, once decided upon, the cutbacks are implemented "by storm". In the United States, Congress has an extraordinary degree of independence, and the president has felt it necessary to appeal for public support through the mass media.

Because of the shifting and opportunistic character of these tactics, governments have made few structural innovations in budgeting to deal with the entitlement problem. Canada's far-reaching Policy and Expenditure Management System (PEMS) is principally designed to deal with discretionary resource allocations, not with expenditure mandated by "statutory authority" (a category comprised mostly of entitlements), though the new system can affect the latter. Yet there have been two significant patterns in budget practice that might harbinger future structural changes. One is the tendency noted by Daniel Tarschys to rely on "packages" rather than on standard budget submissions to propose and implement important changes in expenditure policy. The other is to restore to budget organisations and finance ministries some of the power yielded to programme innovators during the growth era.

Packaging has a number of advantages for those who seek curtailment of entitlements. One is that it enables the government to group together a number of cutbacks and to thereby demonstrate that the burden of restraint is widely (and fairly) distributed. Another advantage is that packaging enables the government to insist that all the cutbacks be acted on as a unit, thereby weakening opposition to individual reductions and making it easier for politicians to support the whole package. In coalition governments, formulation of the package has become the focal point of negotiations among political parties and the test of the government's strength and durability. In the United States, a packaging technique known as "reconciliation" has been effectively used to enact huge reductions in entitlements and other programmes.

Packaging has been used in the Netherlands and the United States to make multi-year reductions in entitlement programmes. Unlike the regular budget process which is geared to annual decisions, a package can schedule cutbacks to take place over a number of years. The ability to phase in reductions can make them more acceptable to affected parties while ameliorating the disruptions which might occur if all were implemented at once. However, multi-year packages tend to "age" as the government continues in office and opposition has time to mount an effective campaign. The initial perceptions or conditions which gave rise to the multi-year reductions may change or be proven incorrect, making it necessary to revise the package. Thus, one-year-at-a-time cuts imposed by blitzkrieg are likely to have a higher success rate than multi-year cutbacks implemented over several years. The Danish government obtained 90% of the cutbacks it proposed; the Netherland and the United States had lower rates of implementation.

Whatever its advantages, packaging can be disruptive of budgetary routines. The budget cycle can become irregular when big, controversial packages have to be negotiated, adjusted and implemented. It can become difficult to maintain the timetable for the various actions to be taken in the course of a year. But this problem, which has afflicted a number of countries, may be due more to political instability, fiscal stress and tactical considerations than to the packaging technique itself.

The determination of governments to curtail the growth in expenditure has led to potentially important shifts in the balance of ministerial power. Just as the impulse to expand programmes once enhanced the influence of spending ministries at the expense of the budget organisation, retrenchment has recently induced governments to rely more heavily on the recommendations of finance officers. Both the pro-spending shift during the growth era and recent curtailments were accomplished largely through informal changes in budgetary practice, such as in the access of ministers to the head of government or in the influence exercised by various ministers in the cabinet. But there have been some formal changes such as legislation requiring all ministerial spending proposals to be reviewed by the ministry of finance before submission to parliament. In fact, sensitising government officials, politicians and other interested parties to the prospective cost of entitlements has been one of the tactics used by budget organisations to bolster their own position and to constrain spending demands.

Expectations about the future course of spending are an important element in the contest between budget and spending ministries. If it is taken for granted that spending will continue to rise or that higher expenditure is legitimate and sustainable, then budget officials will be in a weak position to resist the demand emanating from spending ministries and from interest groups. A key task of a budget organisation bent on curtailing expenditure growth is to alter expectations about the future. One means of doing this is to disseminate "bad case" scenarios of the budgetary imbalance that the government will face unless it cuts back the automatic growth in entitlements. Multi-year projections have led to multi-year retrenchments in some countries and have been formidable inhibitors of expansion in others. In virtually all OECD countries, expectations of future growth are significantly less buoyant and less legitimate than a decade ago.

If fiscal stress and expectations of future shrinkage become entrenched, modifications in budgetary practice may become more structural and systemic than has been the case thus far. Rather than relying on tactical and behavioural features of budgeting to constrain expenditures, governments might seek more wide-ranging adaptations. The fact that this has not happened thus far might be due to: i) uncertainty about the future course of budgeting; ii) the persistence of growth expectations despite recent cutbacks; or iii) attention to short-term tactical problems. In any case, no consensus seems to be emerging on the types of structural change that might be appropriate.

3.2. Types of cutbacks

Mention has been made that the cutbacks implemented thus far have tended to be marginal and that their aim has been to curb the rate of growth, not to reduce actual spending levels. Although they may be marginal relative to the total volume of expenditure, these cutbacks can incite a great deal of political strife. Hence, budget officials have sought cutbacks which can save money without generating intense conflict. They often have curtailed expenditures in ways that do not cut programmes directly. That is to say, although financial cuts have programme implications, they can hide programme effects.

Examples of these types of cutbacks can be drawn from various countries. Denmark froze benefit levels for two years and did not adjust them for inflation. Finland engineered delays to postpone expenditure; the United States did likewise by delaying inflation adjustments for three to six months. It also saved an estimated USD 3 billion over a five-year period by rounding benefits down to the next lower dollar. Ireland established a waiting period for eligibility and reduced real benefits in some entitlements from 45% to 25% of employment pay. These financial modifications saved money without making structural changes in the affected programmes.

Financing modifications can be a form of across-the-board reduction in which all beneficiaries suffer some loss regardless of their particular circumstances. Like across-the-board cuts, they veil the effects on programme levels and convey a sense that the burden is being fairly borne by all affected parties. But like across-the-board cuts, they might actually be very unequal in their effects.

Marginal changes have been made in eligibility requirements to curtail expenditure growth. The duration of eligibility can be shortened (or limited), standards for determining eligibility can be narrowed, some groups can be excluded altogether, or a waiting period can be established before recipients become eligible for benefits. The Netherlands excluded some young people from unemployment benefits; the United States purged the disability lists of persons judged capable of working. From the perspective of government, these marginal changes are attractive because they save money without impairing the eligibility of most beneficiaries. As with the financing changes described above, the savings are realised but the basic structure of the programme remains intact.

Governments have sought to curtail expenditure growth through marginal adjustments in entitlement formulas. One such adjustment is to change the index – for example, from wages to prices, or to the lower of the two. Another is to shift from full to partial adjustment for inflation. Yet another is to lag the adjustment behind increases in inflation. However, little progress has been made toward complete de-indexation, perhaps because the propriety of compensating dependent groups for inflation is now widely accepted.

Marginal cutbacks produce marginal savings. It has already been noted that these might suffice for narrowing the revenue-expenditure gap to a politically acceptable range. Some observers believe that more drastic measures which would alter basic contractual and statutory commitments might be necessary in the future. This expectation has more to do with demographic trends (especially the ageing of the population) than with economic conditions. The argument is that, despite current trends toward economic recovery, the ratio of dependent to productive population will increase to such an extent as to make continuation of the entitlement state in its present scale untenable. If this outlook proves to be accurate, OECD countries will be tasked with much more difficult political and budgetary challenges than they have heretofore faced.

Afterword

In assessing the huge costs of entitlements, it is appropriate to step back from the particulars of the budget process and to focus instead on the social purposes served by these expenditures. After all, budget control is not the only value that governments must consider in designing public policy, nor is it always the more important. Governments purposely weaken the budget's capacity to determine expenditures because tight control clashes with other salient objectives. Most governments of OECD countries have weakened annual budget control by giving workers assurance about their financial wellbeing when they retire. The governments have established payment programmes to assist workers who lose their jobs, health care programmes to provide medical services or financial support to persons afflicted with illness, income support programmes for dependent people, and numerous other transfer programmes.

The values that underlie public entitlements are widely shared by citizens in all OECD countries. Of course, there is political controversy about payment levels and eligibility requirements, but these are marginal issues that affect the amounts spent, not the legitimacy of entitlements established in permanent legislation. Citizens may not favour every entitlement programme, but the bigger the programmes are, the more support they garner in public opinion polls.

If governments had perfect budget control, each year's budget would be unencumbered by past entitlement decisions; no legal commitments would carry over from one year to the next. Governments would annually decide how much to spend on pensions, low-income support, medical care, unemployment compensation and other forms of assistance. The budget would be restored as the means of allocating public money.

However, a world of perfect budget control would not be a perfect world. Social insecurity would be widespread. Workers and households would face an uncertain financial future. Pensioners would have to wait for each year's cycle of budget decisions to find out what their disposable income would be. A strong case can be made that society is better off because of the entitlement regime in place. These pre-decided payments cushion households against the cyclical shocks of recession and the secular shocks of old age and disability. They ease anxieties about inflation, unemployment, illness, and the affordability of health care. Entitlements should be seen as the pooling of financial risk in the largest pool that a country can construct on its own – the whole of society.

Yet, arguing that entitlements do much social good does not mean that all such spending is equally worthwhile, or that all features of these spending programmes are worth the cost. Governments can restore some budget control by periodically subjecting entitlements to scrutiny and by adjusting benefits. In fact, some national governments with the most sustainable fiscal positions have made significant changes in benefit schemes to reduce their long-term exposure.

In principle, entitlements are not compatible with budget control; in practice, the two must be reconciled. The first step in harmonising the need for budgetary discipline and the social need for financial security is for governments to be cautious in undertaking new entitlements. This is especially critical for the newly emergent economies that do not yet have full Western-style entitlement regimes. The second step is to make marginal adjustments that enlarge the increments available for allocation through annual budget decisions. It must be recognised, however, that even marginal changes can stir up political opposition. The third task is for governments to undertake an assessment of which risks can be transferred to private hands through various risk-sharing mechanisms. If governments fail to take these steps, they may be compelled by demographic pressures to move even more boldly in the future to curtail entitlements.

References

OECD (1978), *Public Expenditure Trends*, OECD Studies in Resource Allocation No. 5, Economic Policy Committee, OECD, Paris, ISBN 92-64-11796-2.

OECD (1982), "The Role of the Public Sector", CPE/WP1(82)4, Working Party No. 1 of the Economic Policy Committee, OECD, Paris.

OECD (1983a), "The Growth of Social Expenditure: Overview and Main Issues", SME/SAIR/SE/83.09, Directorate for Social Affairs, Manpower and Education, OECD, Paris.

OECD (1983b), "Consequences of Public Sector Size and Growth", CPE/WP1(83)8, Working Party No. 1 of the Economic Policy Committee, OECD, Paris.

ISBN 978-92-64-06087-6
Evolutions in Budgetary Practice
Allen Schick and the OECD Senior Budget Officials
© OECD 2009

Chapter 2

The Control and Management of Government Expenditure: Comparing Country Experiences*

* This text was originally published in 1987 as Chapters 1-7 of the full OECD publication *The Control and Management of Government Expenditure* (ISBN 92-64-12995-2). At the time of writing, Allen Schick was Professor of Public Policy at the University of Maryland, United States.

1. Summary

The word "budget" conjures up images in many people's minds of thick documents crammed with obscure jargon and thousands of numbers, and of debates over accounting conventions and performance indicators. These are manifestations of budgets, of course. But this is not what budgeting is all about; it is about the interplay of people and their ideas and goals.

Budgets are statements of the limits and allocation of financial resources which governments will use in providing assistance and services to improve the social and economic well-being of people. Budgets are the result of a compromise amongst alternative views of the desirable size and composition of government activities. Budgeting is a reconciliation process whereby people – ministers, members of the legislature, public servants and others – engage in a debate on the relative merits of these various views and arrive at the allocation of resources. Budgeting is also a process which governs the behaviour of public servants in actually managing and delivering assistance and services to the public, and in the subsequent accounting for public monies used and results achieved.

This report offers a glimpse of the world of budgeting as seen through the eyes of senior public servants in the central budget offices[1] of 19 OECD member countries.[2] The report does not offer rigorous assessments or prescriptions of "best" practices. The focus is on a description and comparison of some budgeting practices which form part of the "tools of the trade" for these officials. International comparisons are often fraught with difficulties in assessing relative performance. These difficulties are particularly acute when comparing "rules of the game" intended to influence the behaviour of individuals and the outcome of their interaction in diverse social, economic, political and administrative environments.

1.1. *The budgeting environment*

Budgets, as instruments of economic and social policy, are of course affected by and intended to affect economic conditions. Similarly, budgeting practices are influenced by and designed to influence the decision-making environment.

During the 1950s and 1960s and to some extent into the mid-to-late 1970s, the size and role of the public sector expanded substantially; the combined expenditures of all levels of government almost doubled on average as a share of gross domestic product in OECD countries. Economic performance was strong, and government expenditure policies could generally be characterised as activist, interventionist and expansionary. Budgeting was often focused on choosing amongst a variety of ideas for increased spending on new programmes or enhanced services. This period saw the increased role of governments in the direct redistribution of incomes, and the development of collective responsibility of the welfare state for the costs of individual financial risks associated with economic fluctuations, old age, and illness.

Following the mid 1970s, governments increasingly became net borrowers. By 1982, the combined government sectors of virtually all the countries participating in this study were in a deficit position. Concerns began to emerge over the consequences of the escalating debt burden; the large and steadily rising share of debt interest costs in total spending was crowding out other spending options and limiting government flexibility. Economic policy prescriptions began to emphasise the need not only for deficit restraint or reduction but also for a stable fiscal environment encouraging private sector growth. Some governments began to question the merits, let alone the cost, of a large public sector.

Spending restraint continues to be a central element in economic policy, as indicated by the following excerpts from the conclusions of the April 1986 meeting of the OECD Council at ministerial level:

> The control of public expenditures and budget deficits is essential to establish a stable domestic financial environment and to promote a durable reduction in real interest rates which will help private investment to expand and thus promote sustained growth worldwide. In countries where deficits are large and public debt is rising strongly – and this is still the case in most OECD countries – further deficit reduction cannot be postponed. Deficit reductions should be pursued in ways consistent with the objective of improving growth. Such reductions are best achieved through stronger control over public expenditure, rather than by raising taxation which would damage incentives. Where the trend of rising public debt in relation to GNP is being reversed, and budget deficits have been reduced sufficiently to restore fiscal flexibility, further deficit reductions may be less urgent. In this case, continued progress in containing public expenditure creates room for tax cuts. In addition to appropriate control of budget deficits and the overall scale of government spending, budget policy must also be directed to improving the efficacy and efficiency of government programmes. This implies flexible reallocation of resources to priority needs.

1.2. Budgeting strategies

Governments, and particularly budget ministers and their officials, have of course always been concerned with the allocation of (somewhat) scarce resources, promotion of economy and efficiency, and elimination of waste and fraud in the management of public monies. What has transpired since the mid 1970s, however, is a more widespread acceptance, albeit not universal, of the need to clearly recognise and control the financial implications of all public sector activities. This changing attitude led to reassessment and reform of budget processes, and a closer integration of taxation and expenditure policy formulation.

The resulting budgeting practices described in this report are designed to respond to this budgeting environment, and to influence the formulation and implementation of budgets. These practices can be grouped under three main strategies:

- imposing, in the early stages of budget formulation, "top-down" limits whereby the government sets a goal for total spending within which subsequent reallocations and detailed decisions about programme changes, cost increases, etc., should be accommodated;
- ensuring that spending outcomes adhere to plans and that unanticipated developments do not force an undesired overrun of the spending limits; and

● increasing value for money – always desirable in its own right, but essential in a period of restrained or shrinking overall resource limits.

1.2.1. "Top-down" budgeting

The central review and assessment of the requests for funds presented by individual ministries and departments remains the key annual task of budget offices in providing advice to budget ministers and Cabinets. However, over the last decade "top-down" financial limits have been gradually imposed on these "bottom-up" demands of individual ministers.

Virtually all countries taking part in this study now formulate and stress publicly some form of high-level target which sets a limit on total spending. In virtually all countries, these targets are specific quantitative goals usually covering a specified time period. They are intended to condition behaviour and constrain demands for more resources. They can make for more readiness to accept restrictions on spending, and help to reduce the tensions in budget negotiations.

Time is required to permit the formulation and resolution of the choices between alternate objectives and needs for public funds. In keeping with this, and the need to define limits within which individual spending needs must be accommodated, the regular cycle for formulation of sectoral or departmental budgets begins a year or more before the fiscal year begins. This long lead time may increase the uncertainty of cost estimates. But it is necessary particularly when governments seek to integrate, into the annual budget process, all decisions on new policies with financial implications.

In part because of the rigidity of some elements of budgets and the sometimes long lead times required to effect change, most countries develop multi-year projections of the financial consequences of some, if not all, expenditure programmes or investment plans. A few countries develop detailed, annually updated, multi-year expenditure and financial plans, providing targets for the preparation of future-year departmental or programme budgets. Some form of multi-year perspective is now clearly recognised by governments as an essential element of budgeting and effective expenditure control.

A few countries now formulate, early in the budgeting cycle, an overall limit or block budget not just for total spending but for individual departments or spending groups as well. This extension of targeting and top-down practices is complemented by a stricter, decentralised responsibility for adhering to agreed financial limits, and by measures to increase the flexibility available to individual units or managers, as noted below. These block budgets, which in some countries are focused on administrative or operating expenses, often reflect top-down targets designed to force productivity gains.

1.2.2. Adherence to financial limits

Budgets are not rigid expenditure plans to be blindly implemented regardless of developments in economic conditions or other changes in circumstances between the time they are formulated and the end of the fiscal year in question. All countries allow for supplementary budgets to be brought to the legislatures. In some countries, expenditure changes can, in certain circumstances, be authorised by the government without prior reference to the legislature. All countries reserve the right to change their overall plans and "top-down" spending limits should they judge such changes to be desirable. However, budgeting practice in most countries increasingly emphasises the need to manage within previously approved spending limits to the greatest feasible extent.

Countries have adopted a variety of practices to ensure that the government's targets for aggregate spending are respected during the implementation phase of budgeting, when monies are disbursed and services delivered. Some countries rely on an unallocated reserve, within the global expenditure limit, to provide a contingency to deal with unexpected expenditure requirements. Most countries do not have such general reserves, in part because of concerns that their existence encourages spending departments to transfer their financing problems to the budget office rather than finding solutions themselves.

If there is to be confidence in the usefulness of a general contingency reserve, it has to remain at a credible size. Even countries with such reserves have tended to reduce the size of contingency provided and to ration access to it more strictly. Increasingly, budgets set in advance of the operating year are strict limits, with a presumption that they will not be adjusted for unexpected needs. In some countries, cash limits are imposed, which means that individual departments also have to cope with wage rate and inflation changes; other countries, however, maintain central provisions for such adjustments. In both cases, the emphasis is on making individual spending units or ministries find offsets as required and, in some cases, adjust policies and priorities if necessary.

Most countries have information systems that enable the budget office, and frequently the legislature, to monitor the actual flow of spending or use of budget authority throughout the year. In many countries, the budget office actually controls the pace at which authority or funds are released over the year. This control is intended to provide maximum short-term spending flexibility at the centre of government and to enable very tight commitment, cash and debt management practices.

Such detailed control does, however, reinforce the attitude that the budget office, rather than spending departments, bears primary responsibility for ensuring that budgets are adhered to and that offsets are identified and implemented if required. Central control is further extended in some countries by separate limits or requirements for pre-authorisation at the commitment stage of spending. Again, such constraints are imposed to control the extent to which the government is committed to cash outlays in future years.

The philosophy of expenditure management implied by these centralised controls is in contrast to some of the recent moves towards block budgets. The extent and nature of central controls, and the information and monitoring needs of the budget office, are also being changed by initiatives in some countries to increase the accountability and authority of ministers and individual programme managers, in order to achieve continuing spending restraint and increased value for money.

1.2.3. *Value for money*

All countries seek to promote economy, efficiency and effectiveness in their programmes. In some countries, a common tactic is simply reducing the budget each year to reflect expected improvements, as noted earlier. Some countries rely on various review mechanisms – external groups of experts, reviews conducted with direct private sector involvement, value-for-money assessments by the government's external auditor, etc. – to ensure that an assessment is made and options defined for increasing efficiency or eliminating or reshaping ineffective or low priority programmes.

These review procedures are seldom closely integrated with the timetable and decision points in the budget formulation cycle. Budget offices do, however, strive to be aware of such studies and to use the findings in the course of budget negotiations as appropriate. Reviews tend to be carefully targeted on potential problem areas.

A further development in practices in some countries arises from a concern to relieve some of the strain imposed on decision makers by continuing expenditure restraint, to focus attention more on outputs or results, and to increase the incentives for programme managers and ministers to achieve savings and live within increasingly limited budgets. For example, some countries are delegating much more authority to departments to shift resources between various inputs to programmes – salaries, capital, travel, consultants, etc. In some countries, arrangements have been developed which break with the tradition of annuality in budgets; to promote effective use of public monies and encourage responsiveness and innovation, departments are allowed under certain conditions to carry unused funds forward to future years. In other cases, multi-year agreements on resource levels are being implemented, rather than the traditional annual review and determination of all individual budgets. In addition, some practices allow individual ministers much greater independent authority to adjust priorities and rearrange the mix of policies and programmes delivered.

Efforts are being made in a number of countries to enable more decentralised expenditure management by upgrading management skills and ensuring a clearer statement of the goals and objectives of individual managers. One of the key concerns in many countries is the development of adequate performance measures and of effective accounting and reporting systems for monitoring spending and results. Budget officials seek effective means to allow increased flexibility and freedom of choice for individual departments and managers, within the framework of the collective priorities of government, while ensuring that the desired level of overall expenditure control is maintained and that sufficient knowledge is available at the centre of government to provide informed and effective budget advice to ministers and the Cabinet.

1.3. In conclusion

Budgeting is about the management of ideas and people. It is not simply a matter of rationality, dispassion, logic and analysis. The determination and implementation of government budgets is often conducted in an environment of tight deadlines, competing or indeed conflicting objectives, scarce resources, and tense negotiations within a political milieu. Recent innovations in budget practices in some countries are an attempt to moderate or redirect some of these pressures while sustaining or reinforcing goals of restraint, optimal allocation amongst competing demands and value for money.

Obviously there is a wide diversity of environments and issues shaping the consideration of budget policies in the countries surveyed. There is, similarly, a variety of budgeting practices reflecting and attempting to influence the differing public management environments. In many countries, while budgeting practices evolve, they continue to stress the traditional requirements: comprehensiveness, annuality, centralised control and collective accountability.

Budgeting is not a static art. Budget officials are concerned to ensure that practices are effective in assisting governments to meet their public policy and expenditure goals. There is a continuing need to assess and adapt procedures and "rules of the game" to changing circumstances and decision-making environments. Adaptation and reform of budgeting systems is usually partial and evolutionary in nature, although the selective changes can be quite radical. International exchange of information and experiences amongst budget officials can help to inform and improve this ongoing process in individual countries. The intent of the information in this report is to illustrate the richness of current budgeting practices, as well as to note themes that are common across countries and highlight emerging issues meriting further attention in the future.

2. The scope of central government budgets

2.1. Introduction

This report deals with budgeting practices, problems and possible solutions from the point of view of practitioners in the central government office or ministry responsible for the overall control of expenditure. What is included in central government spending varies to some extent from country to country, but the main issues of control and management of spending are much the same.

In all countries the services directly provided by central government include defence, external relations, most tax collection administration and planning, and administrative support services. However, the extent of central government involvement in the direct provision of other services – such as health, education, social security, law and order, transportation or support to industry and agriculture – varies greatly among the countries surveyed. Thus, all central government budgets include substantial funding to state or local authorities, and many also include funding to separate social security funds and to public enterprises.

This report does not examine the specific ways in which central governments try to control or influence the local government or public enterprise or social security authorities, nor does it examine the budgeting practices of these authorities themselves. This exclusion from this particular report should not be taken as a measure of the importance of such issues. The social security funds, public enterprises and local authorities account for a very large proportion of public sector activity and raise some very significant issues concerning expenditure control practices, meriting further attention.

Sub-section 2.2 discusses relations with state and local authorities, sub-section 2.3 notes the variation amongst countries in the financing and administration of social security payments, and sub-section 2.4 touches on relations with public enterprises. The final comments concern three financial instruments – loans, loan guarantees and tax expenditures. The latter two are often only partially, if at all, integrated with the processes for controlling expenditure.

2.2. The tiers of government

Four countries in the study (Australia, Canada, Germany and the United States) have a federal structure. In these cases, the focus of this report is on the federal government. The other participating countries are unitary states. The importance of regional, as distinct from local, authorities varies and is changing. In some countries – notably France, Italy and Spain – there has been "regionalisation" or "decentralisation" of some hitherto central government functions.

In comparing countries, there is no common or simple division of functions and responsibilities between the tiers of government, and this gives rise to a variety of financial relationships with the central governments. In some cases, lower tiers may act merely as an agent of the central or federal authority, which not only controls funding but also closely directs or regulates the activities and services provided by lower authorities. In some instances, the central government may offer grants limited to a specific purpose, to cover part or all of the costs of a service, in order to influence what the local tier does while permitting some local discretion. Sometimes a general (block) grant may be provided, with or without indications of how the central government would like it to be spent, or some centrally levied tax revenues may be shared in pre-determined proportions, with or without guidance on the use of these revenues by the regional or local authorities.

The degree of autonomy of other levels of government differs considerably. The proportion of general grants, as distinct from grants tied to specific activities, is one indication. Other indications are the extent to which lower tiers can levy their own taxes, charge for their services and determine their own borrowing requirements. Local taxes on dwellings (and some other real estate), sales or income are significant sources of local revenue in countries in the study.

2.3. Social security

Social security is usually defined to include state pension schemes, unemployment compensation and other income maintenance programmes and social assistance grants. Its prominence in public expenditure is described in Section 3. Social security programmes are often in the form of entitlements and can be characterised as demand-led. The unemployed, the sick, and pensioners, for example, are entitled to certain benefits or grants, as determined in each case by the specific rules in governing legislation or regulations, irrespective of the "state of the budget". While the parameters of the programme can be changed, once they have been set the overall social security spending levels are determined by demand. In general, control on total expenditure in these areas can only be exercised by changing the underlying regulations or legislation.

Institutional arrangements differ markedly between countries. In some (e.g. Australia and Denmark), all or most payments are made from the consolidated pool of revenues, and appropriation is sought from Parliament. In others, some benefits are paid from a separate public fund financed wholly or mainly by specific earmarked contributions. Such a fund may also receive a grant from the central government and income from an accumulated surplus. The extent of government involvement in such funds varies. The German Social Insurance Pension Fund, financed largely from compulsory premiums, receives an indexed annual grant from the federal budget. In the United Kingdom, the National Insurance Fund, covering the main state pension scheme and short-term unemployment benefit, is administered by the central government and its transactions are included gross in the central government budget. In some countries, benefits may be paid from special funds but the central government may have to intervene if the fund gets into difficulty (for example, if unemployment rises suddenly) or may contribute towards the costs of certain elements of the fund, as is the case in Germany as regards unemployment insurance.

In some countries, lower tiers of government administer social assistance grants on behalf of central government. In the Netherlands, each authority normally has some discretion in the detailed rules for eligibility and rates of grant that it applies, and are thus expected to provide some of the financing required, with the balance coming from the central government.

Whatever the institutional arrangements, a central government is usually involved in determining rates of benefit and contributions and the terms of eligibility for social security funds, and is also likely to provide other direct social assistance payments.

Contributions to social insurance funds are generally integrated into assessments of taxable capacity and tax burdens, even in countries where such contributions are regarded as significantly different in nature from taxation. In the Netherlands, the key concept of the "collective burden", in which one of the fiscal targets is expressed, includes the sum of tax and social premium payments (and some other non-tax revenues). In Germany, one strategic budgetary goal is reducing the "*Abgabenquote*" which is the combined impact of taxes as well as pension contributions and health and unemployment premiums paid by employers and employees.

2.4. *Public enterprises*

The definition of the borderline which separates public from private enterprises is not straightforward nor easily formulated. The degree of direct public control of activities and the extent of a firm's reliance on public financing are both important elements in defining the borderline. Within the framework of the internationally agreed standard national accounts, each country has developed its own attributions.

In Australia, Germany and the United States, the central government tends to be involved with relatively few public enterprises, generally confined to such public infrastructure activities as communications and postal services and transportation. Links between the central government and public enterprises are more common in unitary states, and the government may exercise its influence in various ways. In budgetary terms, government expenditure includes any grants or subsidies paid to such enterprises. It normally also includes any loans (net of repayments), although such loans are sometimes made from an investment fund distinct from the government's general budget.

In the United Kingdom, the operational definition of public sector expenditure for control purposes includes all net external finance of the nationalised industries and most other public corporations. Most such financing is from the government but some may be raised directly from banks or overseas, in which case only the grants and loans made by the government are included in the central government's budget. In Ireland, the operational definition of public capital expenditure includes capital spending by state-sponsored bodies financed from the Exchequer, the company's internal resources and non-Exchequer external sources (*e.g.* borrowings from capital markets).

2.5. *Other financial instruments*

2.5.1. *Loans*

Loans made to others by the central government, to implement its policies, are normally accounted for in the budget and included in any overall expenditure target. In some countries, there are additional specific targets and controls on such loans by all levels of government. Generally, loans have to compete with other, non-repayable expenditure in the decision-making process.

To some extent, the decision to lend may be handled in a separate forum or presented separately to the legislature. For example, Japan budgets for loans in the Fiscal Investment and Loan Programme which is prepared and reviewed in parallel with the general budget. The United States has a credit budget that includes direct federal loans and loan guarantees, although it does not include transactions of government-sponsored credit agencies because they are privately owned. This credit budget is developed in parallel with the regular budget, which also includes the direct loans. In the United Kingdom, lending from the National Loans Fund is included in the central government budget.

2.5.2. Loan guarantees

Since cash payments by government are required only if the borrower defaults, the general practice is not to include loan guarantees in expenditure plans or budget requests. However, many governments in the study have expanded the information made available to Parliament and the public about such guarantees. The United States includes guarantees in the above-noted credit budget. In the Netherlands, some provision for anticipated defaults on loan guarantees has been included in the target for the budget deficit, and the government aims to end guarantees that are obviously a substitute for direct government action, especially in the housing sector. In Canada, reference to loan guarantees must be specifically included in the budget spending estimates in order to obtain parliamentary authority for the guarantee; however, the expenditure levels would only include cash payments resulting from a default. In Germany, the financial plan and the budget approved by the legislature include provision for the expected cash requirements arising from defaults on guarantees. In Sweden, the government proposes limits for the use of each loan guarantee programme and these limits are decided upon by Parliament. In a special section of the budget, all changes in loan guarantee limits and cash payments are reported yearly to Parliament. In the budget, realistic assessments of expected cash payments during the fiscal year are included.

2.5.3. Tax expenditures

Tax expenditures are defined as a departure from some generally accepted benchmark of the tax structure (see also OECD, 1984). They can be thought of as assistance or subsidies given through the tax system. While the budget financial statements (*i.e.* revenues) obviously reflect the impact of such subsidies, the general practice is that the determination of tax expenditures is not included in the regular process of making expenditure decisions. Tax and direct expenditures are treated relatively separately. Nevertheless, countries have put some efforts into integrating tax expenditure analyses more fully with the budgeting cycle or, at least, improving related information presented to the legislature and the public.

In France, Spain and the United States, consolidated tax expenditure statements are now required by law and are presented to the legislature, although these statements are not voted on nor approved explicitly as such. In Canada, the government has undertaken to report on the estimated value of tax expenditures on a regular basis. Decisions regarding adjustments to tax expenditures can be traded off against new spending initiatives – that is, they compete with direct spending at the discretion of the Minister of Finance. Australia, Germany and the United Kingdom also provide regular estimates of tax expenditures for information to the legislature. Some examples of tax expenditure statements are included in the OECD publication *Tax Expenditures: A Review of the Issues and Country Practices* (OECD, 1984).

Several factors – including the difficulties in determining which elements of taxation legislation are tax expenditures and which are part of the benchmark tax structure, the extent to which tax authorities wish to retain sole control of taxation policy, and the technical difficulties in costing – tend to reinforce the exclusion of tax expenditures from the regular expenditure decision-making process. However, tax relief is a means of resource allocation and may be considered to compete against other financial instruments of government policy.

3. The growth and composition of expenditure

3.1. Introduction

Over the past two decades, general government expenditure (*i.e.* spending by central, regional and local governments and social insurance funds combined), expressed as a percentage of gross domestic product (GDP), has on average increased by 21 percentage points to 50% – that is, expenditures have grown on average about 2.9% per year faster than the value of economic output. Over this period there has been marked change in the composition of public expenditure, with a growing share taken by interest payments on rising public debt and by transfer payments to households and the business sector.

These changes testify to the significant increase in the role of the public sector and, in particular, governments' greater role in the redistribution of income and the collective welfare state responsibility for the financial risks associated with economic perturbations, old age and sickness.

The following sub-sections offer a very brief overview of the changing economic and fiscal context and the variations, amongst countries and over time, in the nature of public expenditure.[3] As noted, the object of this report is to review budgeting practices and processes, not to focus on nor assess expenditure or fiscal policies. Thus, the intent of this section is simply to provide a rough sketch of the environment in which emerged a growing concern over practices to ensure the effective control of government budgets.

3.2. The economic context

As very general background, Table 2.1 provides a summary of three indicators of economic performance: the rate of real output growth, consumer price inflation and growth in employment. The data distinguish between the period before and after the first oil crisis in 1973.

The dramatic decline in these performance measures in the latter period is apparent: economic growth was cut in half, inflation more than doubled and employment growth was slower in most countries.

3.3. Aggregate revenue and expenditure trends

Table 2.2 illustrates the evolution over the past 20 years in general government expenditure, revenue and net lending, expressed as percentages of GDP. In 1965, the simple unweighted average expenditure percentage for the countries was 29% and by 1984 it had reached 50% – an increase of 21 points. The significant jump in expenditure relative to GDP in the two-year period 1973-75 illustrates, of course, the combined impact of a sharp deterioration in economic performance and the consequent upward push on government spending following the first oil shock. Over the past 20 years, the revenue share also increased, but not nearly as sharply as spending: the average revenue share rose from 29% in 1965 to 45% in 1984 – an increase of 16 points.

As shown in Table 2.3, there is substantial variation between countries in the size of general government expenditure relative to GDP, ranging from about 33% in Japan to about

Table 2.1. **Economic indicators: average annual percentage growth**[1]

	Economic output		Consumer prices		Employment	
	1960-73	1975-82	1960-73	1975-82	1961-73	1974-82
Australia	5.3	2.2	4.2	10.1	2.8	1.2
Belgium	5.0	2.1	3.7	6.5	0.8	−0.4
Canada	5.6	2.3	2.9	9.5	2.9	2.2
Denmark	4.4	2.4	6.5	10.2	1.3	−0.2
Finland	4.9	2.9	5.9	10.2	0.2	1.0
France	5.6	2.6	4.7	10.7	0.7	0.2
Germany	4.4	2.3	3.5	4.5	0.1	−0.5
Greece (1963-82)	6.8	2.6	4.2	18.5	−0.6	1.0
Ireland	4.4	3.5	6.0	15.3	0.1	0.8
Italy	5.3	2.7	4.8	17.2	−0.6	0.7
Japan	9.9	4.7	6.1	5.5	1.3	0.8
Netherlands	5.0	1.5	5.2	6.1	0.8	0.7
Norway	4.3	3.4	4.9	9.3	1.1	1.8
Portugal	6.9	4.4	3.4	21.7	0.2	1.6
Spain	7.2	1.6	6.7	17.3	0.9	−1.5
Sweden	4.2	0.9	4.6	10.8	0.5	0.9
Turkey	5.7	3.8	8.8	46.9	0.9	1.1
United Kingdom	3.1	1.2	4.8	12.6	0.2	−0.5
United States	4.1	2.5	3.1	7.5	2.1	1.7
Mean (unweighted)	5.4	2.7	4.9	13.2	0.8	0.7

1. Annual averages are calculated as mean compound growth rates.
Sources: OECD (1985), *The Role of the Public Sector: Causes and Consequences of the Growth of Government* (Table 39); OECD, *Employment Statistics.*

Table 2.2. **Aggregate budgetary trends (percentage of GDP)**

	Total revenue	Total outlays	Net lending
1965	28.8	29.1	0.2
1966	29.6	29.6	0.4
1967	30.7	30.9	0.4
1968	32.1	31.9	0.5
1969	32.9	32.1	1.1
1970	33.5	33.0	1.0
1971	34.4	34.1	0.9
1972	34.3	34.3	0.6
1973	35.0	34.7	1.0
1974	36.0	36.9	−0.3
1975	36.6	40.2	−3.0
1976	37.9	40.7	−2.1
1977	38.6	41.4	−2.1
1978	38.5	42.3	−3.2
1979	38.9	42.6	−3.0
1980	40.0	43.2	−2.3
1981	40.9	46.3	−4.1
1982	42.1	48.2	−4.9
1983	43.3	49.4	−4.8
1984	44.8	49.5	−4.3

Source: OECD, *National Accounts* (unweighted mean of all countries in this study when data available).

Table 2.3. **General government total expenditure (percentage of GDP)**

	1965	1970	1975	1980	1984
Australia	25.2	25.5	32.2	32.8	37.4
Belgium	32.3	36.5	44.5	51.0	55.4
Canada	29.1	34.9	40.0	40.4	46.8
Denmark	29.9	40.2	48.2	56.2	60.9
Finland	30.8	30.5	36.1	36.5	39.9
France	38.4	38.9	43.5	46.4	52.7
Germany	36.6	38.6	48.9	48.3	48.0
Greece	20.6	22.4	26.7	30.5	40.2
Ireland	33.1	38.6	46.5	50.9	56.3[1]
Italy	34.3	34.2	43.2	46.1	57.4
Japan	18.8	19.4	27.3	32.1	33.1
Netherlands	n.a.	46.0	52.8	57.5	61.2
Norway	34.2	41.0	48.4	50.7	48.8
Portugal	20.1	21.6	30.3	25.9	n.a.
Spain	19.6	22.2	24.7	32.3	n.a.
Sweden	36.1	43.7	48.9	61.6	63.5
Turkey	20.6	21.9	n.a.	n.a.	n.a.
United Kingdom	36.1	39.8	46.3	45.1	47.8
United States	27.4	31.7	34.6	33.9	37.2[1]
Mean (unweighted)	29.1	33.0	40.2	43.2	49.5

1. 1983.
Source: OECD, *National Accounts.*

64% in Sweden in 1984. However, all countries experienced significant, and in some cases quite dramatic, increases in these percentages over the past 20 years, including the sharp rise in 1975. In the period since 1975, there are marked differences amongst countries in the evolution of these ratios, reflecting more varied economic performance and the fiscal and expenditure policy responses of governments.

Trends in general government financial balances are shown in Table 2.4. It was following the mid 1970s that governments more and more became net borrowers. In 1960, only Canada, Ireland, Italy and the United Kingdom were in deficit positions. By 1982, 14 countries were in a deficit position, ranging from 0.4% of GDP in Finland to 13.2% in Ireland.

3.4. *The changing composition of total expenditure*

In 1960, consumption expenditure – a measure of government direct provision of goods and services – accounted for about 45% of total government expenditure, on average, while transfer payments and investment accounted for 40% and 15% respectively. By 1982, transfer payments represented over half of general government expenditure (52%) while consumption and investment shares had fallen to 40% and 8% respectively.

Based on data developed for an OECD study (OECD, 1985a, Tables 8 and 9), Table 2.5 summarises the changes in the 1970s in various categories of general government expenditure as a percentage of GDP, for eight of the countries participating in this report. Expenditures in five major categories are distinguished:

- public goods (defence and general government administrative services);
- merit goods (education, health, housing and community services);
- income maintenance (*e.g.* pensions, family allowances, unemployment compensation);

Table 2.4. **Trends in general government financial balances[1] (percentage of GDP)**

	Average 1965-69	Average 1970-74	Average 1975-79	Average 1980-84
Australia	1.4	0.7	−2.3	−2.2
Belgium	n.a.	n.a.	n.a.	n.a.
Canada	0.9	0.8	−2.2	−4.2
Denmark	1.4	3.6	−0.9	−6.1
Finland	2.3	4.6	2.5	0.0
France	0.3	0.8	−1.2	−2.1
Germany	−0.4	−0.1	−3.3	−2.9
Greece	n.a.	n.a.	n.a.	n.a.
Ireland (1965-83)	−3.6	−4.4	−8.7	−12.0
Italy	−3.1	−6.0	−9.6	−11.4
Japan	1.4	0.9	−4.1	−3.5
Netherlands	n.a.	−0.2	−2.8	−5.9
Norway	4.0	4.5	1.0	4.5
Portugal (1965-81)	0.6	1.1	−6.1	−2.0
Spain (1965-82)	0.4	0.3	−0.9	−3.5
Sweden	4.0	4.0	1.1	−4.4
Turkey (1965-72)	0.3	3.0	n.a.	n.a.
United Kingdom	−0.8	−1.0	−4.1	−3.6
United States (1965-83)	−0.5	−0.8	−1.5	−2.8
Mean (unweighted)	0.5	0.6	−2.7	−3.9

1. Net lending. A negative sign on net lending indicates net borrowing or a financial deficit.
Source: OECD, *National Accounts.*

Table 2.5. **Changes in the structure of general government expenditure, 1970 to 1981**

Changes in the per cent of GDP represented by a given item

	Public goods	Merit goods	Income maintenance	Economic services	Public debt interest	Balancing item	Total expenditure
Australia	0.2	3.4	3.6	−0.7	0.9	1.0	8.4
Denmark	1.1	1.7	5.6	−0.7	3.9	4.9	16.5
France	0.3	0.6	4.3	0.0	0.9	−0.4	5.7
Germany	−0.4	4.3	4.1	−0.3	1.2	1.7	10.6
Italy	1.2	3.6	5.2	1.7	5.4	−0.1	17.0
Japan	0.9	4.5	4.5	1.1	3.0	1.1	15.1
United Kingdom	−1.2	0.8	1.8	−1.6	0.6	3.5	4.1
United States	−2.7	1.5	1.5	−0.7	0.4	0.5	0.5
Mean (unweighted)	−0.1	2.6	3.8	−0.2	2.0	1.5	9.7

Source: OECD (1985), *The Role of the Public Sector: Causes and Consequences of the Growth of Government.*

● economic services (*e.g.* capital transactions and subsidies);
● interest on the public debt.

Expenditure on defence and administrative services has been relatively stable in Australia, France and Germany, increased in Denmark, Italy and Japan but dropped off in the United Kingdom and United States. All countries experienced a rise in merit goods expenditures relative to GDP, the largest increases coming in Japan, Germany, Italy and Australia, in which this spending category had the relatively lowest shares in 1970. In virtually every country, income maintenance expenditures have risen more than any other element, much of this due to growth in expenditure on pensions. The unemployment compensation share also rose rapidly in Australia, Denmark and Germany, considerably less in Japan and the United Kingdom, while in the United States it remained constant.

Concomitant with their rising share of government expenditures, transfer payments increased considerably in importance in family incomes, rising from an average of 9.8% of gross household receipts in 1960 to 15.3% by 1980 (OECD, 1985a, Table 15).

The growth in transfer payments or social benefits is not simply due to economic and demographic trends over this period. Recipients have enjoyed real improvements in their benefits. An OECD report estimates that, between 1960 and 1975, average real benefits per person covered under each programme rose about one percentage point faster than the growth of real GDP (OECD, 1985b). Even over the period 1975-81, the growth rate of average real benefits kept pace with the growth rate of real GDP per capita. Even when more generous rules were abated, it was rare for benefits to individuals to be increased less than roughly the rate of inflation.

A characteristic of many income maintenance or social support programmes is that they are open-ended entitlements, at least in the short term. As discussed in Section 2 regarding pension benefits, once conditions of eligibility and rates of payment have been set, the total budgetary cost is determined by the number of eligible claimants who come forward. Their number is not always easy to forecast, even for short periods ahead. In addition, such entitlements impart a momentum to expenditure levels via the automatic changes caused by their underlying economic and demographic parameters.

Such cash payments, as well as being demand-led, may also be more precisely visible to recipients than services they receive in kind, or indeed public goods from which they benefit collectively rather than individually. For example, a change in formal or informal rules for increasing cash benefits in order to offset rising prices may be more sharply perceived by recipients – who are also voters – than, say, a correspondingly marginal squeeze on resources for hospital services.

To the extent that this point is valid, it adds to the difficulty in changing at least the one-third of government spending accounted for by social security benefits. The point may not be a strong one, however, because every spending programme has its customers and its advocates. In the above example, the professionals of the health-care community may well be extremely aware of and vocal in protesting any such squeeze.

The increasing amount of total government expenditure which is pre-empted by the interest costs of accumulated public debt is also a potential source of concern over the inflexibility of expenditure. More generally, the increasing share of government expenditure which is in some sense predetermined by the weight of existing contractual obligations – such as public debt interest or entitlements based on separate legislative authority – imparts a certain measure of structural rigidity to expenditure budgets. This rigidity – or inflexibility, to use a strong word – can to some extent impair the abilities of governments to alter spending allocations to respond to changing circumstances or meet emerging priorities.

In Denmark, it is estimated that spending arising from standing laws or entitlement programmes, contracts, etc., increased from just over half of total expenditure in 1970 to about three-quarters by 1983; this spending included national pensions, unemployment insurance, general grants to local governments, child allowances, disability assistance and housing subsidies. The United States describes about three-quarters of total federal expenditure as relatively uncontrollable under current law in 1983, compared with about

60% some 20 years ago. In the United States, relatively uncontrollable outlays include payments from past, irrevocable contracts and interest on the public debt. Similar patterns emerged in other countries participating in this report.

In part because these structural rigidities and the implications for automatic expenditure momentum highlighted the need for governments to take a multi-year perspective, countries have developed medium-term budgetary targets and strategies. Section 4 deals with the development of targets and limits that give direction to a country's fiscal policy. Section 5 discusses the relationship between such targets, medium-term expenditure plans and the annual formulation of budgets.

4. High-level budgetary targets

4.1. Introduction

The growth of the public sector, the changing composition of expenditure, a changing view in some countries of government's role in the economy, and concern over the consequences of continued increases in the costs of deficit financing contributed to a change in the attitude of governments and the public towards government spending. There developed, over the late 1970s and early 1980s, a recognition of the need for more awareness of the financial consequences of government activities and public policy objectives. This changing attitude led in turn to the development of new instruments of expenditure policy and management, both to give voice to, and to contribute to the realisation of, governments' objectives.

Determination to check deficits and reluctance to add much to tax burdens led governments to develop high-level budgetary targets, often spanning several years ahead, to which spending plans were to be accommodated. Regardless of the precise links, if any, of these targets with the budgets appropriated by the legislature, such targets help to constrain demands at the start of the annual budgeting process. The last ten years may be summarised as the decade when "top-down" constraints were gradually imposed much more effectively on the "bottom-up" demands of spenders, their clients and supporters. The present state of development and widespread use of such high-level targets is the subject of this section.

All countries taking part in the study now publish some form of summary objectives or targets for fiscal policy. These usually include a target for expenditure. Many governments publish their budgetary targets to stimulate public discussion. Often this is seen as a way to further build consensus about fiscal policy goals and means to meet them.

Sub-section 4.2 briefly discusses the various definitions whereby budgetary targets are formulated or expressed, and compares current country practices. Sub-section 4.3 reviews the evolution of these targets on a country-by-country basis, and presents the particular objectives operative in 1986.

4.2. The formulation of budgetary objectives

A government's high-level target reflects both its view of how the public sector affects the economy and its priorities for levels of taxation, borrowing and expenditure.

Such a target has to be expressed in simple terms, though it is likely to ensue from a variety of complex considerations regarding fiscal and monetary policy options, the size and role of government, taxation policies and, possibly, future sectoral policies. Targets that cannot readily be grasped by politicians, civil servants and many in the general public stand little chance of influencing decisions.

In virtually all countries – the exceptions being Japan and Norway – current budgetary goals are expressed as specific quantitative targets, rather than simply as a general qualitative statement of intent. Such precision does provide a strong unambiguous message as to a government's financial objectives to participants in the budget process and to the public, and at the same time more narrowly restricts the ability of the government to subsequently adjust its aggregate revenue and expenditure levels. This restriction is increased if targets are specified for each of several years forward, rather than as a level to be achieved by the end of a future period. The latter formulation permits some flexibility and "adjustment of course" in a given year, without the government having to call into question its publicly announced target.

The ability of a government to meet its high-level target while avoiding unexpected short-term disruptions in budgets, and the budget process, depends in part on the amount of direct short-term control which the government can exercise over the components included in the target variable; for example, an expenditure target which includes public debt interest payments raises the possibility that a government might have to intervene and take decisions (possibly expenditure cutbacks) to offset an unanticipated rise in interest rates during the course of a fiscal year.

The formulations of high-level targets which are used in the countries surveyed can be grouped into three categories:

● A ratio, usually expressed as a percentage related to GDP or some similar indicator of aggregate economic activity: the ratio may relate to the level of accumulated public debt, or budget balance or government borrowing, or revenue or expenditure, or a combination of these.

● A rate of change for expenditure: a guideline could be zero real growth over the stated period, some rate of increase or a real decline. Alternatively, the target growth may be expressed in nominal terms, i.e. after taking price increases into account. Such growth rates may be published alongside target ratios for the budget balance or revenue burden.

● An absolute value for the target variable in "nominal" terms: targets in money terms can be expressed as either the future level of expenditure or the deficit, or as the amount of desired change from some baseline level.

Table 2.6 provides a synopsis of the form in which current targets are expressed by countries. A more detailed description is provided in the following section. It is important to bear in mind the simplifications which are implicit in presenting the comparisons in Table 2.6. What is being summarised is simply the form of target which a government is highlighting in its public statements of budgetary objectives. The table does not summarise all the targets which are implicit or operative in a government's budgeting process – in some sense, for many countries one could then put an "x" in all the columns of Table 2.6 – but rather the table synthesises only the publicly explicit targets generally emphasised by the government.

In light of the comments above regarding the budgeting and expenditure volatility which might arise from choosing target variables which include elements beyond the direct short-term control of government, it is of note that nonetheless virtually all of the countries have an explicit numeric target for the deficit as a ratio to GDP. This raises two sets of issues: the nature and extent of the links which are drawn with these high-level

Table 2.6. **Synopsis of current announced budgetary objectives**

	Ratio to GDP			Growth rate of expenditure		Nominal amount of expenditure	
	Deficit[1]	Expenditure	Revenue	Real	Nominal	Expenditure	Deficit[1]
Australia	X	X	X				
Belgium	X		X				
Canada	X				X		X
Denmark	X			X			
Finland	X			X			
France	X						
Germany					X		X
Greece	X						
Ireland	X	X	X			X	
Italy	X		X			X	X
Japan							X[2]
Netherlands	X		X				
Norway[3]							
Portugal	X	X				X	
Spain	X	X	X			X	X
Sweden	X		X				
Turkey					X		X
United Kingdom	X	X				X	
United States							X

1. Deficit or borrowing requirement or accumulated public debt.
2. As noted above, the objective in Japan is not formulated as a specific numeric target.
3. Norway does not formulate medium-term targets.

targets in the formulation of specific departmental budgets; and the expenditure monitoring and control practices (such as use of contingency reserves) during implementation of budgets. These issues are addressed in Sections 5 and 6 respectively.

The following paragraphs describe briefly the recent history of budgetary objectives in each country, including the particular goals operative in 1985/86.

4.3. Country practices

Australia. Beginning in the mid 1970s, fiscal policy has been geared to reducing the federal budget deficit by restraining real growth in outlays. In the early 1980s, expenditure and fiscal policy was somewhat less restrictive in order to fuel economic recovery and meet social welfare commitments. In 1985, the federal government adopted a medium-term strategy with the target that the ratios to GDP of outlays, tax revenues and the deficit should not increase from 1984/85 levels in 1985/86 and over the life of the present Parliament. This so-called "trilogy" was strengthened by a commitment to reduce the size of the deficit in nominal terms in 1985/86.

Belgium. The public sector deficit has been a major preoccupation of governmental authorities for several years. The level of public debt and its growth are such, especially since the oil crisis, that they are leading automatically to a growth in interest costs, despite the adoption of many financial restructuring measures. In May 1986, a new financial restraint plan was established with a view to reducing net borrowing requirements to 8% of GNP in 1987 and to 7% of GNP by 1989, from a level of 12% in 1985. In reducing the financial requirements of the public sector, the results of this plan should lead to a reduction in interest rates which will be favourable for economic activity.

Canada. The 1975 White Paper "Attack on Inflation" declared that "the federal government shares the view that the trend of total spending by all governments should not rise more quickly than the trend of the gross national product". The government made itself accountable for this new policy by announcing the target ceiling for outlays in advance of the fiscal year. While the policy's stated objective was to hold federal spending to the trend in GNP, in practice it was applied through year-over-year comparisons of growth rates in government outlays and GNP. Since the inauguration of Canada's "Policy and Expenditure Management System" (PEMS) in 1979, the enunciation in the budget presented to Parliament by the Minister of Finance of a multi-year fiscal plan, within which expenditure priorities are set, has been a key element of the budget process. The present government has shifted from a total outlay target to a budgetary expenditure target (*i.e.* excludes loans and advances), with primary focus on the budgetary deficit as an important fiscal indicator. The medium-term strategy is deficit reduction.

Denmark. In 1980, a medium-term strategy of gradual elimination of real growth in public expenditure was adopted. When the current government was formed in late 1982, it tried to implement maximum cutbacks in expenditures for 1983. The main fiscal objectives adopted in 1983 were the elimination, by 1990, of the central government deficit and zero real growth after 1983 in public expenditure, exclusive of cyclical changes in expenditure on unemployment benefits. Mainly due to a rapid economic recovery, the central government finances are expected to balance in 1986 and the total public sector to record a substantial surplus.

Finland. Since 1977, the government has set targets for gross tax rates and limits on state borrowing as part of its medium-term economic policies. In its economic policy statement of May 1985, the government stated that the tax burden should not exceed the 1985 level at the end of the decade, and that the ratio of state debt to GDP should not increase. Furthermore, public expenditure is permitted to grow only at an average annual rate of slightly more than 2% in volume until 1990; the real growth rate of central government expenditure has to be clearly lower than 2%.

France. Following a brief period of expansion in the early 1980s, the government moved to a more restrictive posture. Recent budgets have been guided by two fiscal constraints rolled forward from year to year: that the central government deficit is not to exceed 3% of GDP; and that the tax and social security contribution burden is to be lowered by 1% by 1985. A medium-term setting for fiscal policies has been provided by national economic plans since 1946. The ninth economic plan (1984-88) is more closely linked with the national budget than its predecessors. The economic plans contain targets for economic aggregates and indicate priority areas for public expenditure.

Germany. Formulation of recent budgets has been influenced by efforts to reduce federal deficits, keep the growth in federal expenditure to approximately half the nominal growth rate of GNP, and increase investment-related expenditure while restraining public consumption. At the same time, the government is attempting, as noted in Section 2 above, to reduce the "*Abgabenquote*" by a lowering of taxes. The current federal financial plan covering the years 1984-88 is based on a "consolidation strategy" applied since 1982 which is aimed at reducing the federal deficit to about half the level of the early 1980s. This will be achieved by holding nominal growth in federal government expenditure to a maximum of 3% a year.

Greece. Since October 1985, a two-year stabilisation programme has been applied, targeting a reduction of the public sector borrowing requirement as a percentage of GDP by eight percentage points (four points each year). To achieve this target, the growth rate of public expenditure must be kept below the expected rate of inflation, and the tax system must become more efficient to combat tax evasion and increase tax collection.

Ireland. During the period 1973-80, the government accepted big deficits to mitigate the consequences of two recessions. Since 1980 there has been a broad political consensus that the restoration of fiscal balance is essential for promoting long-term growth of the economy. Toward this end, government policy has been aiming to reduce the deficit as a proportion of GNP and to move to budgetary balance by curtailing expenditure. In the years 1981-84, the government was committed to eliminate the current account deficit over a four-year span. This proved difficult to achieve, and in 1984 this objective was dropped on the grounds that rapid elimination of the deficit would have too great a deflationary effect. The 1985-87 planning document "Building on Reality", published in October 1985, contains the objectives for 1987 of: reducing, or at least stabilising, foreign debt and foreign debt servicing, both as a proportion of GNP; halting the growth of the overall national debt/GNP ratio; reducing the Exchequer (*i.e.* central government) borrowing requirement to less than 10% of GNP (12.9% in 1985); reducing the total public sector borrowing requirement from 17% to just over 11% of GNP; and reducing the budget deficit on current account to 5% of GNP (8.2% in 1985).

Italy. Current policies are aimed at reducing the total borrowing requirements of the state to about 7-8% of GDP by 1990. This is roughly one-half of the current ratio and equates to levels existing prior to 1973. The target envisages reducing borrowing needs to almost zero, excluding interest costs on accumulated debt. The policy also envisages no increase in overall tax or contribution burdens, excepting those required to finance new services, and the redistribution of the fiscal burden between direct and indirect taxes. The targets take into account the achievement of real GNP growth of about 3%, a reduction in inflation to about 4% and achievement of a viable balance of payments in the medium term. Under these conditions, the borrowing targets imply no real growth in current expenses and real capital spending growth somewhat less than GDP growth.

Japan. The government has sought to slow the growth in the public sector but has not adopted specific expenditure targets. The 1982 report of the Provisional Commission for Administrative Reform urged that the growth rate of the expenditure general account budget should be kept below the nominal growth rate of the economy and that the ratio of total expenditure of general government to nominal GNP should be kept at almost the present level. The Commission noted that although the tax burden will have to be increased, it should be kept much lower than that of European countries.

The government's "Outlook and Guidelines for the Economy and Society in the 1980s", presented in the summer of 1983, endorsed the objective that the tax burden and the social welfare burden should remain much lower than in European countries. It also called for phasing out deficit-financing bonds during the decade. Recent budgets have sought to reduce the central government deficit by limiting expenditure growth. Guidelines call for freeing government from the characteristic of being dependent on deficit-financing bonds and lowering the overall dependency on government bonds by 1990.

Netherlands. From the early 1960s, the Dutch government worked to a norm for the annual budget deficit calculated by reference to the assessed growth of the productive potential of the economy. In 1976, the actual deficit was expected to be nearly double its trend rate. Fiscal policy then focussed on restricting the actual budget deficit, at least to its then accepted trend-based value of 4% of net national income (NNI). There was also an agreement on the appropriate growth of the "collective burden", which would allow the ratio of tax and social insurance payments to NNI to rise by only 1% a year. It was felt that these ratios were more meaningful to economic development than simply a target for government expenditure. In 1979, a more restrictive target for the collective burden was introduced: it would be held constant.

The coalition agreement on which the present government is based includes the aim of reducing or at least stabilising the collective burden and reducing the government sector deficit to 7.4% of NNI by 1986 (as a step towards a longer-term goal). These targets imply a progressive fall in the ratio of public expenditure to GDP, especially as the collective burden has substantially declined as well. Medium-term projections of budgetary prospects are used to help decide what changes should be made in each annual budget.

Norway. No agreement exists on the appropriateness of fiscal indicators for medium-term fiscal policy determination. Such indicators are only considered useful for short-term budget formulation purposes. Among the general indicators presented in the budget documents are the central government budget balance (before taking account of loan transactions), the balance excluding direct effects of the oil sector, and central government total spending.

Portugal. Since 1981, the general aim has been to stabilise or reduce the central government budget deficit. This has been given effect by expenditure cutbacks and the imposition of special direct and indirect taxes.

Spain. Since 1983, the medium-term objective has been to control the public sector deficit and curtail current expenditure. The deficit is to be reduced to 3.5% of GDP in 1988. In October 1984, a tripartite agreement was reached between the government, the Spanish Confederation of Entrepreneurial Organisations and the General Workers' Union. This Social Economic Pact encompassed fiscal objectives of reducing the deficit from 5% of GDP in 1985 to 4.5% in 1986, and of increasing the state fiscal pressure. The government's current expenditure growth is to be slowed by deceleration of public sector wage increases and slowed growth of current transfers.

Sweden. In the late 1970s, the government set a target of reducing the budget deficit as a proportion of GNP by an average of at least one percentage point per year during the five-year period covered by the medium-term budget. Specified quantitative goals for expenditure cutbacks were also presented. In 1984, the government adopted a medium-term policy of reducing the central budget deficit/GDP ratio from 13% in 1982 to 4-5% by 1990, which would result in no net borrowing by the public sector. At the same time, the tax/GDP ratio should be kept approximately constant. This implies a reduction in the expenditure/GDP ratio.

Turkey. Budgets are prepared within the framework of a Five-Year Development Plan. The Plan specifies targets for economic performance and aggregate targets for public finance, *e.g.* total public sector current and capital expenditure, transfers to other sectors, revenues and fiscal balances. The Plan also specifies annual target ratios of total public expenditure to GNP and corresponding real growth percentages.

United Kingdom. The government has published medium-term public expenditure plans each year since the late 1960s. Since 1980, it has also published, with the annual budget, a medium-term financial strategy (MTFS). This sets out its projections for the growth of money national income which are consistent with a continuing reduction in inflation while permitting sustained economic growth. Objectives are set for the growth of the monetary aggregates and for the path of the public sector borrowing requirement. The government is also seeking to reduce the burden of taxation. The objectives for borrowing and taxation jointly imply restraint on the growth of expenditure. The targets for expenditure alone are expressed in money terms (cash) at levels which imply that expenditure will be held broadly constant in real terms to 1988/89. A declining path for the ratio of public expenditure to GDP is implied. No separate targets are set for the total of central government spending alone.

United States. Recent administrations have emphasised their determination to lower the ratios of future taxes, deficits and expenditures to GNP. These fiscal policies are reflected in the annual budgets submitted by the President to Congress. During the 1980 campaign, for example, then-candidate Reagan announced a target of lower taxes and far lower spending relative to GNP, ending with a balanced budget by 1984. It has proven far easier to reduce taxes than spending and deficits. The 1986 budget set targets of a federal deficit/GNP ratio of 2% by 1988. Targets were subject to adjustment as part of the negotiations with the Congress with regard to the President's budget proposals. Late in 1985, Congress passed a Balanced Budget and Deficit Reduction Act (the so-called Gramm-Rudman-Hollings Act) which sets specific targets for deficit levels in each of the years 1987 through 1991, requiring elimination of the deficit by the latter year. Should the President and Congress fail to establish a budget which meets the targets in any year, then automatic pre-specified procedures for expenditure reductions are imposed via this Gramm-Rudman-Hollings legislation to ensure that deficit goals are met. The 1987 budget, submitted by the President to Congress in February 1986, proposed a package which met the deficit targets.

5. From high-level targets to the budget

5.1. Introduction

The expenditure budgets for a given fiscal year are the result of a process of reconciliation between a government's high-level budgetary targets and the competing claims for resources to meet existing programme needs as well as further policy developments in various sectoral fields. This section briefly explores a few aspects of this stage of budgeting and reviews country practices.

Sub-section 5.2 offers some perspectives on the annual budget cycle which leads to specific proposals to be presented to the legislature; the timing and nature of the opening decisions; the extent of any direct linkage of sectoral or departmental budgets with high-level targets; the role, if any, of multi-year projections or plans; the starting point, or baseline, from which expenditure changes are negotiated; and the level of expenditure detail at play in the negotiations. Sub-section 5.3 describes the budget formulation process in each country participating in the study.

5.2. Some observations on budget formulation

A common characteristic of contemporary budgeting is that the process for developing sectoral or departmental budgets for a given fiscal year begins up to a year or more before these budgets are presented to the legislature. This long lead time is in part a reflection of the size and complexity of public sector activities. But also – and perhaps more importantly – sufficient time is required to reconcile competing programme needs and priorities within the limits imposed by a government's high-level budgetary targets. Budget offices, spending departments and ministers need sufficient time to settle priorities and to identify and agree on cutback options if required to contain total spending within the agreed aggregate target.

In most countries, budget offices seek to integrate all decisions on new policies with financial implications into the annual cycle for formulation of the budget. This arises from a belief that it is necessary to establish priorities amongst all competing demands and from a concern that allowing new policies to be considered and implemented outside the timing of the decisions on the budget will inevitably lead to an erosion of overall spending targets. In a few countries, Canada being a notable example, reserves are specifically provided, within the budget presented to the legislature, in order to accommodate the costs of specific policy initiatives not yet agreed or implemented.

This emphasis on the annual budget formulation cycle as a mechanism for integrating programme and policy choices is changing somewhat. A number of countries are shifting emphasis to formulation of a total financial frame or block budget for a given ministry or spending department, within which the responsible minister and officials have greater freedom to reallocate funds and adjust programme priorities. This decentralisation and deregulation, which is briefly explored in following sections, can be seen as an extension and reinforcement of "top-down" budgeting; in return for greater policy or managerial flexibility, departments are expected to live within the previously approved budgets.

One example of increased emphasis on ministerial block budgets is Denmark, where the overall expenditure target is broken down into specific spending targets for each ministry almost one year before the start of a fiscal year. Another illustration is France, where a "lettre de plafond" is sent to each minister from the Prime Minister about six months before the fiscal year begins, setting out the spending targets in large categories. In the three countries which annually review and approve comprehensive multi-year expenditure plans – Canada, Germany and the United Kingdom – the starting point for the deliberation of a programme's spending level in the upcoming fiscal year is, in principle, the levels for that year most recently approved in the multi-year plan. All changes are treated as new bids (or savings) by the budget office. Those changes which cannot be denied raise the question of how they are to be accommodated – whether by raising total spending, by funding from any available reserves, or by making offsetting savings in the same or other programmes.

Practices differ amongst countries with respect to the use of multi-year expenditure projections or plans. As noted, in Canada, Germany and the United Kingdom they are detailed, annually updated, articulated plans providing disaggregated targets to guide the preparation of future-year departmental or programme budgets. Most countries, however, develop projections of the financial consequences in future years of some elements, if not all, of the current stock of expenditure programme decisions or investment plans. These projections are sometimes updated annually, or more frequently, and influence the government's decisions about the level and distribution of expenditures to be incorporated in upcoming budgets. The coverage, time frame, degree of detail, frequency of updating, publication, etc., vary among countries. More details are provided in sub-section 5.3.

As might be suggested by the relative size of the blocks which are the focus of budget decisions, countries vary in the level of detail at which negotiations are conducted between budget offices and spending departments. In Denmark, the focus is on the large ministry frames, and while there inevitably is an exchange of views on particular detailed requirements, the concern is on defining options for keeping spending within a specified limit for a ministry. The focus of discussions is more traditionally detailed in some countries: in Germany, for example, the budget office works at the level of changes to the roughly 7 000 items to be voted in the budget bill, although of course there is an emphasis on the 100 major items accounting for nine-tenths of total spending. The same level of detail is followed for the future years of the financial plan in Germany, but it is aggregated into about 40 large blocks before being published and presented for information to the legislature.

Practices are changing in some countries, particularly with respect to departmental administrative or operating expenses. In a number of cases, these are increasingly determined by top-down targets which reduce real budget levels to reflect, and to force, productivity gains. Section 7 discusses this aspect of some countries' budget formulation practices.

Table 2.7 attempts to summarise the timing and nature of the key opening decisions in the annual budget cycle, and to note the next phase in that cycle.

Table 2.7. **Opening stages of the annual budget cycle**

	Decision taken by	Nature of decision	Months before budget presented to legislature	Next step
Australia	Cabinet	Total outlay and portfolio targets	6	Ministers prepare budgets addressing targets, for negotiation with budget office and Minister of Finance.
Belgium	Ministers of Budget and of Finance	Budget norms and guidelines	6	Ministers prepare budget proposals for review by Department of the Budget.
Canada	Cabinet Committee on Priorities and Planning	Total spending and broad sectoral targets (envelopes)	6	Ministers submit detailed departmental bids, for approved programmes, for negotiation with Treasury Board.
Denmark	Cabinet	Total spending and a limit for each ministry	6-8	Ministers present draft budgets to finance minister.
Finland	Cabinet	Total spending and broad guidelines	6	Ministers submit budget proposals to Minister of Finance.
France	Prime Minister	Broad guidelines in "*lettre de cadrage*"	9	Ministers prepare and negotiate requests, leading to a specific ministry target in "*lettre de plafond*" three months later.
Germany	Minister of Finance	Total spending and broad guidelines	9	Ministers submit detailed departmental bids, for negotiation with Minister of Finance.
Greece	Minister of Finance	Broad guidelines on total spending	6	Ministers submit budget proposals to Minister of Finance.
Ireland	Cabinet	Targets for current deficit and borrowing requirements	6	Ministers submit bids for negotiation with budget office and Minister of Finance.
Italy	Treasury Minister	Changes required in total and by department	6	Ministers submit budget proposals to Treasury Minister.
Japan	Cabinet	Policy guidelines on budgets	6	Ministries submit proposals to Ministry of Finance.
Netherlands	Cabinet	Changes (usually cutbacks) required in total and by department	6-7	Ministers prepare proposals to meet targets.

Table 2.7. **Opening stages of the annual budget cycle** (cont.)

	Decision taken by	Nature of decision	Months before budget presented to legislature	Next step
Norway	Cabinet	Preliminary spending limits for each ministry	9	Ministers submit draft budgets to Budget Department.
Portugal	Cabinet	Minister of Finance sends general and specific departmental targets	9	Ministers prepare proposals and submit to Minister of Finance within three months.
Spain	Cabinet	General budget guidelines	6	Ministers prepare budgets for negotiations with central budget office.
Sweden	Cabinet	Broad guidelines and changes (i.e. cutbacks) needed, in general	9	Ministers prepare proposals to meet targets.
Turkey	Prime Minister	Broad statement of budget goals	4-5	Ministries prepare detailed budget proposals for negotiations with Ministry of Finance and (for capital spending) with State Planning Organisation.
United Kingdom	Cabinet	Planning total set for three years forward	9	Spending ministers submit bids, if necessary, for amounts in excess of previously agreed baseline.
United States	President	General fiscal and budget guidelines; sometimes department-specific	15	Spending agencies submit bids to the Office of Management and Budget (OMB).

5.3. Country practices

Australia. To start work on the budget, the Department of Finance in October/November asks spending departments for minimum estimates of outlays in each of the three years starting 1 July next (i.e. the budget year plus two out-years). These projections are usually at constant prices and include only the likely costs of approved ongoing expenditure programmes in the absence of policy changes. The costs of expiring programmes which are likely to be renewed and whose exclusion would therefore bias downwards the estimates are separately identified. Bids for new proposals are called for separately, depending on the likely level of resources expected to be available. When the Department of Finance assembles its overview, it adjusts all the projections to a consistent (budget forecast) price basis. The projections cover all estimates of total budget outlays including lending and debt interest payments.

The Cabinet then indicates broad aggregate targets for the budget year. Separate outlays targets are set for each portfolio which are consistent with the broad expenditure guidelines. The method of setting targets is still evolving in order to better reflect the priorities of the government as a whole. Each portfolio target provides a benchmark against which individual ministers canvass options which reflect the target. Detailed consideration by ministers collectively follows, to yield expenditure figures for the budget year which form the basis of the outlays side of the budget brought down in August. A summary of the figures for the budget year plus two out-years is published shortly after the budget, together with some analysis of, for example, their sensitivity to alternative assumptions about key economic variables.

Belgium. The preparation of the annual budget begins with consideration in Cabinet, generally in February or March, of technical guidelines recommended jointly by the Minister of the Budget and the Minister of Finance. Agreed guidelines are then provided to spending ministries, which prepare estimates by May based on unchanged policies. These estimates are reviewed during June and July in bilateral meetings with the Department of the Budget. Cabinet decisions on the total level of spending and any desired changes or cutbacks are made on the basis of an assessment report prepared by the Department of the Budget following the bilateral reviews. Capital projects, including associated three-year cost estimates, are reviewed by a Commission on the Orientation and Co-ordination of Public Markets which drafts a report for decisions by Cabinet.

Canada. A top-down fiscal planning system for establishing overall and sectoral fiscal targets expressed in cash interacts with a detailed bottom-up multi-year operational planning system, initially expressed in constant dollars, which deals with each element of spending. The Secretariat of the Treasury Board manages these bottom-up operations, in conjunction with the Privy Council Office which supports ministerial committees and Cabinet and the Department of Finance which deals with the top-down fiscal planning system.

Each year, the federal government reviews and rolls forward its fiscal plan containing the current financial year, the next year and the two following "planning years". Using the Policy and Expenditure Management System (PEMS), initial projections of federal expenditures, revenues and economic conditions are evaluated in the light of the government's priorities. The result is a planned path for total federal expenditure in each year, divided between an "envelope" for each policy sector, which may include policy reserves to fund new initiatives. Provision for the costs of public debt and centrally held reserves are dealt with separately. These figures are published as part of the fiscal plan in the budget documents.

Each spending department develops its multi-year operational plan (MYOP) each year. These plans are then the subject of negotiations between the Treasury Board Secretariat and spending departments, leading to decisions by Treasury Board ministers on the resources needed to continue existing programmes over a three-year period – namely the next year (for which appropriations will be sought from the federal Parliament) and the two following years.

The estimates presented to the federal Parliament approximately one month before the beginning of the financial year, seeking appropriations, reflect financial and authorities' requirements of the first year of the approved MYOPs, but are based on a recognition of the multi-year costs involved.

Denmark. Unlike Australia and Canada, where the main focus is on the federal budget only, the high-level expenditure target in Denmark relates to the whole public sector. It is expressed as an ongoing target (zero real growth in total public spending, excluding debt interest costs and excluding cyclic changes in unemployment benefit) rather than related to a particular future year. For work on the central government budget, this broad public sector target has to be converted into a limit for all central government spending, including its grants to lower tiers of government and trend unemployment costs.

Multi-year expenditure projections have been an integral part of the central government's annual budget since 1965. An appendix accompanying the annual appropriation bill shows figures for expenditure items for each of the three years following the budget year in the same degree of detail and at the same pay and price level as the votes. The assumptions underlying all the numbers are published in another appendix.

When the budget is passed by Parliament in December, the projections generally reflect decisions taken so far. Work on the next budget starts at once. The first step is to announce the target for next year's expenditure. The budget department in the Ministry of

Finance then adjusts the published projections to the assumed pay and price levels to be used in the next budget. A view is formed of the likely bids for new expenditure programmes, and of the necessary and possible cutbacks from the published programmes. In February, the Minister of Finance proposes to Cabinet a set of net spending limits or "frames", one for each minister, consistent with the new target for the total. The limits decided by Cabinet, and any general measures that may also be agreed, set the framework for the drafting of budget proposals in the various ministries. In effect, the spending limits deliminate an expenditure block for each ministry, leaving them significant freedom in how to arrange the budget proposals. This means that further negotiations within the administration and at a political level in the following months are focused on the development of cutback options for those ministries that find it difficult to keep budgets within the agreed limits.

Finland. Since the late 1960s, the ministries have been required to prepare multi-year plans and estimates of expenditure and non-tax revenue every autumn and present them to the Ministry of Finance. The plans are usually based on ones which the ministries obtain from the executive agencies. Every second year, the previous plans are only updated by means of the same process, without adding a new final year. The forward period covered in these intervening years is four years. The plans consist of two sets of figures: first of a base estimate of existing commitments and, second, of development plans which include proposals for new investment, development projects and drafts for new legislation. They are formulated at the price level used in the budget proposal for the coming year.

When these multi-year expenditure plans reach the Ministry of Finance in December, it organises, summarises and scrutinises them, following internal procedures quite similar to those used in the annual budget work. The Ministry of Finance prepares macroeconomic assessments for fiscal policy guidelines for future years and detailed comments for each ministry on expenditure in the medium term. Fiscal policy goals are approved by the government in the early spring and usually given to Parliament in the form of an economic policy statement. Letters are then sent by the Ministry of Finance to the ministries commenting on their expenditure plans. The detailed comments represent the view of the Ministry of Finance on what the level and development of expenditure should be in every major programme category in the next year's budget proposal and, more indicatively, over the medium-term projection period. This process ends in March so that it may influence the ministries' spending proposals for the next budget year, which are submitted to the Ministry of Finance at the beginning of May.

France. Work is in hand to clarify the linkage between the five-year economic plans and the annual finance act. It is done under the terms of the 1982 act to reform the planning process.

Among other changes, the government undertook to publish indicative reviews of central government finances covering three years to help clarify the linkage and as background to other new proposals about expenditure. The Ministry of Economy and Finance was made responsible, drawing on projections prepared by the ministries for their respective budgets. Projections of government expenditure, based on the 1984 budget and covering the three years 1984-86, were published in the spring of 1984 as background documents for Parliament. The three-year projections were presented in very broad aggregates while revenue was treated as a one-line entry.

Germany. Since the reform of budgetary law in the late 1960s, the budget plan is embedded in a medium-term financial plan which is presented by the federal government to Parliament each year together with its draft annual budget. Both the plan and the annual budget are developed in light of the fiscal intentions of the *Länder* and local authorities as expressed in the Financial Planning Council, where all tiers of government are represented. Quantitative proposals made by the Council relate to annual nominal growth of total expenditure as well as to net borrowing. These are the basis of the top-down planning system for the annual budget and the plan.

For the plan, estimates of future federal revenues are based on macroeconomic projections and assumptions. The plan also indicates the government's policy for the path of the federal budget balance. Future expenditure is presented in the plan for each year, distributed over about 40 comparatively large blocks. These blocks are aggregated from figures prepared in a bottom-up approach and agreed between the spending ministries and the Ministry of Finance (and approved by the Cabinet) in exactly the same detail as those compiled for the budget year (which are set out in minute detail for parliamentary approval of the budget). By way of developing the individual future cash needs, on the basis of the draft budget's estimates, for the last three years of the planning period, some blocks include allowance for price increases affecting specific existing programmes (*e.g.* indexed social expenditure, interest payments). There is an unallocated planning reserve in each of these three years for further price increases and new programmes. There is also a global provision for increases in wages and salaries.

The most important purpose of the medium-term financial plan is to set priorities in line with the government's policies and to prevent excessive demands being made on the federal budget. In each annual cycle, the previous plan as a whole is brought up-to-date and a new year is added. In the spring (ten months before the budget year begins), there is a general review of prospects and aims. The detailed instructions issued by the finance ministry in December, calling for expenditure bids, generally ask departments to keep them within the upper limits laid down in the current financial plan.

The Ministry of Finance circular calling for departmental bids includes special regulations referring to the increase of current or administrative costs of departments. For several years, in general, an average increase of 2% per annum has been the ceiling, with the further restriction that expenditure for representation and public relations ought to have no increase.

Greece. There is no multi-year budgeting in Greece. However, each annual budget must be consistent with the medium-term qualitative fiscal policy guidelines incorporated in the Five-Year Development Plan. As noted earlier, quantitative targets for total borrowing have been set for 1986 and 1987 as part of a two-year stabilisation programme.

Ireland. While medium-term economic plans are not published regularly, there is a regular cycle of medium-term expenditure planning. Multi-year projections of expenditure in current prices are now sought annually from spending departments. These projections are critical to the overall review of the development of the budgetary aggregates. The Cabinet decides on appropriate targets for the following budget year in the light of medium-term trends. The most recent economic plan, "Building on Reality", covers the period 1985-87. As noted in Section 4 above, the plan specifies broad medium-term targets, expressed as a percentage of GNP for the current budget deficit, the Exchequer borrowing requirement, the public sector borrowing requirement, aggregate non-capital spending and aggregate public capital expenditure. It also specifies cash allocations (capital and non-capital) for departments for each of the years 1985 to 1987.

Italy. The political consensus reached in 1976 on a budget policy to reduce the public sector deficit led to a major reform of budget procedures culminating in Law No. 468 in 1978. This law enabled the government to start making the annual budget a policy instrument to support economic and fiscal/monetary objectives and other policy goals. It recognised the need to transform the budget into an instrument for forecasting and decision making in an economic framework which was internally consistent within the public sector and in which Parliament provided more incisive policy guidance and exercised greater control. It also emphasised the direct involvement of public sector institutions in the task of getting their respective budgets back into balance.

Two versions of the multi-year budget are prepared and published each year. The first, known as the "trend" version, is based on current legislation and shows the expected trend in expenditure and receipts under the financial regulations in force. The second, or "programming", version allows for the effects of potential policy changes. By comparing the two versions of the multi-year budget projections and examining the macroeconomic implications of each set of projections, Parliament is better able to consider and assess the government's proposals for legislative action and the consequent effects on the economy as a whole.

Japan. There is no regular annual cycle of medium-term expenditure planning. Instead, Japan relies on a carefully developed consensus about social and economic goals and problems to assist the preparation of the annual budget. The tenth medium-term social and economic plan, "Outlook and Guidelines for the Economy and Society in the 1980s", published in August 1983, contained a section on broad policy directions, including a chapter on fiscal reform and financial policy which outlined very general aims. In contrast to the ninth plan, no expenditure projections were included.

Against the background of the plan, the Ministry of Finance submitted three reports to the Budget Committees of both Houses of the Diet in February 1984. They developed in more detail the medium-term and longer-term management of public finance and indicated the guidelines within which the Ministry of Finance hoped that spending departments would submit plans each August. They were in effect a declaration of the finance ministry's intent. The first document, "Basic Philosophy Regarding Future Fiscal Reform", included the aim of holding down the annual growth of general expenditure below that of nominal GNP by:

- a thorough review of various expenditure programmes;
- severe restraints on the growth of personnel expenditure;
- increasing user charges for various public service items; and
- the continuation of strict guidelines for government departments' annual budget requests.

The other reports contained scenarios and projections on alternative hypotheses, to help to stimulate widespread appreciation of the issues.

Though there is no comprehensive multi-year expenditure plan, 15 medium-term public investment plans are currently in progress. Nearly all are for five or six years and one extends over ten years. Not all cover the same period. For example, the ninth Road Development Programme covers FY 1983-87 while the third Land Improvement

Programme covers FY 1983-92. These programmes are implemented flexibly taking account of socio-economic change and the fiscal situation.

Netherlands. The government maintains a set of multi-year expenditure projections as well as non-tax revenue projections. At the start of the annual budget cycle, they represent – in constant prices – the outcome of the last budget cycle, adjusted for subsequent policy changes and for changes flowing from recosting existing policies or from new economic assumptions.

The Minister of Finance forms a judgment as to how these projections need to be changed in the new budget, bearing in mind the deficit targets that would be compatible with the Coalition Agreement, the prospects for revenues and the likely scale of irresistible new expenditure pressures.

As the between-budget changes to the projections tend to be additions and there are always policy proposals for new or more spending, the Minister of Finance is almost always seeking cutbacks. Besides, savings from cutbacks achieved in a particular year do not usually increase over future years, even if this is deemed to be necessary from a medium-term point of view. At an early stage, the minister seeks Cabinet endorsement of the total change and the changes he/she proposes for each department. Some candidates are found among the reports flowing from the review procedures described in Section 7 below.

Norway. Multi-year projections for 29 categories of programme spending, covering three years beyond the upcoming fiscal year, are presented to Parliament for information in the annual budget proposal. However, these are not spending plans, but simply forecasts, prepared in the Budget Department, of the possible future cost of existing programmes. Parliament does not approve these projections, nor are they a formal input to formulation of the next annual budget.

Preparation of the annual budget is initiated in January when the Cabinet approves a set of general guidelines and preliminary spending limits for each ministry, based on proposals by the Minister of Finance. In May, the Cabinet meets again to consider budget guidelines in light of detailed budget estimates which have been prepared by ministries and submitted to the Ministry of Finance by April. During the June through August period, the finance ministry holds bilateral meetings with spending ministries to try to arrive at agreed budgets. If necessary, the Cabinet resolves unsettled items during a meeting in August or September, at which time final government proposals on taxation and economic policy are also determined. The government's budget proposals are submitted to Parliament in October, three months before the start of the fiscal year.

Portugal. There is no comprehensive system for medium-term expenditure projections. The budget law imposes an obligation to make clear in the annual budget the multi-year consequences of programmes and projects marked for investment under the *Programas de Investimentos e Despesas de Desenvolvimento de Administração Central* (the capital budget). An updated programme of works has to be submitted each year to enable adjustments to be made to the annual budget and possibly to the programme, depending on its progress.

Spain. There are so far no comprehensive multi-year projections or plans for public expenditure in Spain. The government's rolling four-year medium-term economic programme provides the framework for the general economic and sectoral policies reflected in each annual budget. In addition, a Public Investments Committee, set up in 1980 under the State Secretariat for the Economy and Planning, sets the investment plans, up to four years ahead, of individual ministries. The linking of the annual budget with the multi-year economic plans is one aspect of the major reform of budgetary procedures which began in 1983.

Sweden. Six months before work starts within the administration on the annual budget, the government gives Parliament multi-annual projections of expenditure and revenue and conclusions for budget policy, reflecting the government's fiscal objectives. Parliament only comments on this "*Langtibudget*" (multi-year budget) and thus influences the finance ministry's circular to ministries to start work on the annual budget.

The "*Langtibudget*" covers the current year, the budget year and three forward years. It was originally a mechanical projection of the financial consequences of existing decisions and commitments. It now incorporates more advanced simulations and deeper analysis of the factors behind budget developments drawing on the results of policy reviews and other studies. The scope has been extended to include the local government sector, the social security sector and, to some extent, the financial consequences for the private sector. Through these developments, the "*Langtibudget*" now has a much enhanced role as a foundation for budget policy guidelines for the short and longer term.

Turkey. There is no formal multi-year budgeting system in Turkey. As noted in Section 4 above, multi-year fiscal and expenditure objectives are set for the public sector in each Five-Year Development Plan, and yearly targets are provided via the annual programmes. Multi-year investment programmes are formulated on a bottom-up project basis by agencies in negotiation with the State Planning Organisation.

The annual budget cycle begins in June, six months before the start of the fiscal year, with a budget message issued by the Prime Minister. This message offers a broad statement of principles for the forthcoming budget. On the basis of technical instructions from the Ministry of Finance and Customs in June, spending ministries prepare detailed budget proposals for current expenditure. These are the subject of discussion and negotiation with the Ministry of Finance and Customs over the next two or three months, culminating in decisions by the High Planning Council and Prime Minister. In parallel, ministries prepare and submit investment project budgets for negotiation with the State Planning Organisation and resolution again at the level of the High Planning Council and Prime Minister as required. The draft budget bill is presented to the legislature in October, at least 75 days before the start of the fiscal year.

United Kingdom. The multi-year public expenditure survey (PES), first developed early in the 1960s, continues to cover the whole public sector. This is consistent with the focus in the government's medium-term financial strategy (MTFS) on the borrowing requirement of the whole public sector described in Section 4 above.

Since the expenditure figures are effectively decided in the public expenditure survey, the start of the budget cycle can reasonably be described as the start of the next PES. Within the framework set in the most recently published MTFS, this occurs about a year before the start of the budget year – in fact, close to the budget day that concludes the previous cycle.

The new PES deals with the two years following the financial year that is just starting and a new third year. The baseline for the first two years is taken from the recent public expenditure White Paper that records the result of the previous cycle (adjusted for any changes in the classification of public expenditure), and a baseline for the new final year is generated by the Treasury against the background of the prospects for taxation, expenditure and borrowing which were set out in the MTFS as part of the budget in the previous March or April. Spending ministers are expected to live within their baselines, which represent years settled only a few months before, but if they consider this impossible they submit bids to the Treasury for new or changed programmes and are pressed to make room for them by finding "offsetting reductions" in their existing plans. In the summer, the Cabinet decides the "planning total" for each year of the new PES and the Treasury minister responsible for expenditure then negotiates bilaterally with each spending minister with the aim of achieving a set of programmes that fits into the available total and leaves a sufficiently large unallocated reserve in each year from which the Treasury will be able to accommodate unforeseen developments. In recent years, it has been necessary for a small group of senior ministers to meet to consider unresolved issues arising out of the bilateral discussions and to make recommendations to the Cabinet on how they might be resolved. The total provision for each department is decided in the autumn, and the detailed results are published in the following January in the public expenditure White Paper before the start of the fiscal year in April.

United States. Formulation of a particular fiscal year's budget has usually started in the spring, eight months before it is submitted to the Congress and 18 months before the start of that fiscal year. However, because of the recent intense year-round activity on the budget and increased emphasis on a three-year budget plan, the spring review has been less active during the past two to three years. The starting point for the analysis and the initial target for agency budgets is usually the second year of the three-year budget plan that is then before Congress. The process begins when broad agency programmes are evaluated by the Office of Management and Budget (OMB) and policy issues are identified. Using programme information provided by the agencies and projections of receipts prepared by the Department of the Treasury, the OMB prepares budgetary projections extending over five years. These are presented to the President for consideration, along with projections of the economic outlook, prepared jointly by the Council of Economic Advisers, the OMB and the Treasury, on which the budget projections are based.

During the summer, the President establishes general budget and fiscal guidelines which are essentially policy directions and planned ceilings for the fiscal year that will begin 15 months later and for the four years beyond. These guidelines are promulgated to the spending agencies to guide them in the preparation of their budget requests.

The President's budget is submitted to Congress early in the new calendar year – nine months before the start of the fiscal year. It includes projections based on current policies, as well as projections reflecting the President's proposals. The Congressional Budget Office (CBO) also publishes, soon after the release of the President's budget, multi-year projections of outlays, receipts and the deficit, together with a substantial amount of detail on the economic assumptions which underlie the projections. These baseline projections are similar to the executive's "current services" estimates but are based on economic assumptions which may differ from those of the President. The Budget Committees and the Congress as a whole may use the assumptions, budget estimates and forward projections from the President's budget or from the CBO or some compromise figures.

6. Expenditure control practices

6.1. Introduction

This section reviews some of the ways in which governments seek to make their expenditure control systems both robust and flexible to cope with the turbulence of current events and the uncertainties of the future. Any government wants to have available a range of instruments that allows it some room for deciding how and how far to accommodate new problems and opportunities as they arise. In broad terms, governments want systems and procedures that: continue to be relevant whether aggregate expenditure policy is very restrictive of spending growth or more relaxed; enable the government to achieve its aims for aggregate spending, which may call for sudden action to protect an announced target; and are accepted as reasonable, or as reasonable as prevailing circumstances permit, by those in spending departments whose primary concern is the level and quality of the services provided, directly or ultimately, to the public.

A number of initiatives are, and have been, under way to adapt and develop systems and procedures, so this section is necessarily selective in both the topics reviewed and the examples cited to illustrate them. The aim is to address issues likely to be of wide interest.

The three topics reviewed all address the same fundamental issue: how to keep to the chosen path with the least arbitrary and disruptive interventions in the work of the spending departments. The topics are:

- the use of unallocated reserves in planning and in execution;
- arrangements for in-year monitoring and control of cash flow;
- monitoring and controlling commitments.

6.2. Unallocated reserves

Some countries make provision, within their overall expenditure targets, for an unallocated reserve or contingency funds to provide some room for manoeuvre to deal with unexpected expenditure requirements. Selected country practices are described in this sub-section to illustrate the main general issues.

In some countries – for example, Australia, Canada, Italy and Sweden – some contingency funds are actually appropriated to the budget office at the start of a fiscal year. In Australia, a specific amount (known as the "Advance to the Minister for Finance") is appropriated to be allocated at the discretion of the Minister for Finance. In exceptional circumstances, spending agencies may apply to expend funds from this appropriation. In Canada, this contingency vote is, in effect, only used to adjust departmental salary budgets for wage rate increases not originally provided for, whereas there is in principle no such restriction on the "reserve appropriation" in Sweden. In Italy, reserves totalling about 8-10% of total spending are approved by the legislature to be used to meet the costs of new laws or programmes not yet announced or approved, and to meet unexpected cost overruns on some programmes. In Turkey, a small contingency reserve ("Reserve Fund and Investment Acceleration Fund"), amounting to about 3% of the total consolidated budget, is appropriated to the Ministry of Finance and Customs for use in emergencies.

In the past, prior to the 1982 fiscal year, the United States budget contained a contingency allowance. In fact, the Congressional Budget Act of 1974 requires two explicit contingencies – one for uncontrollable programmes (such as social insurance payments) and the other for programmatic increases. The executive branch has consistently placed the contingency reserve for relatively uncontrollable programmes at zero, and more recently has done the same for the other contingency allowance.

There are alternatives to a formal reserve. For example, in preparing the 1980 budget, Japan adopted the principle of "scrap and build". A new organisation or programme would be "built" only when an existing organisation or programme that had become out of line with the needs of the time was "scrapped" after appropriate review. In the Netherlands, there is no formal reserve. Instead, the government has developed elaborate "rules of stringent budget policy" which apply to in-year control only; these rules specify how both adverse and favourable developments during the course of a fiscal year are to be tackled.

Experience shows that specific multi-year projections and plans tend to underestimate future costs, whether from natural optimism about the ongoing costs of continuing programmes or because, when plans are made, governments are reluctant to incorporate many specific new initiatives in individual departments' plans. In Ireland, the published medium-term profile of capital expenditure for the period 1985-87 incorporates an unallocated contingency provision equivalent to 2.75% of the planning total for 1987, to be allocated in the light of the budgeting outlook for economic and productive infrastructure investments.

Canada and the United Kingdom, which use comprehensive multi-year expenditure plans in the context of a financial plan or strategy, include an unallocated reserve in the total of expenditure shown for each forward year. Germany – which also develops an integrated multi-year plan – includes such reserves only for the last three years covered by its plan – that is, the years beyond the upcoming annual budget.

In these three countries, the contingency margin or reserve is thought of as a buffer or shock absorber protecting the planned total from damage when a particular programme has to be enlarged, or a new programme added, in successive planning cycles to cope with some new need. It may also provide a possible way of protecting individual programmes to some extent if the planned total itself has to be cut; but if there is to be confidence in the usefulness of a reserve, it has to remain at a credible size.

Canada and the United Kingdom use the reserves planned for the upcoming budget year as an operational control during that year. Two practical issues are: first, how the reserve is deployed in the negotiations between the budget department and each spending department to agree how tightly individual departments' programme budgets should be drawn – how far a spending department's plans should include implicit or explicit local reserves; and, second, how best to manage the reserve so as to discourage individual ministers and their departments from regarding it as an easy way out of a new difficulty. The paragraphs below on the use of reserves in Canada, Germany and the United Kingdom illustrate their individual approaches.

Canada. When the multi-year Policy and Expenditure Management System (PEMS) was first developed in 1979, there was an elaborate set of unallocated reserves. The "envelope" for each policy sector (each policy sector contains several programmes that are closely related in terms of broad objectives) contained an operating reserve and a policy reserve. The former was intended as a contingency to meet unforeseen cost increases in the operational planning forecasts based on current policies. The latter was intended to finance new or enriched programmes decided upon by the Cabinet ministers concerned with the use of the money allocated to the envelope. A policy reserve could be zero or negative (i.e. requiring the envelope managers to find savings in existing policies). A policy reserve could be supplemented by savings in existing programmes – other than purely estimating savings – and was intended thus to be an incentive to review priorities and the value for money provided by the several programmes in the envelope. In addition, there was a central reserve, controlled by the Minister of Finance, to meet cost overruns in public debt charges or in major entitlement programmes such as unemployment contributions, where such increases did not arise from policy decisions.

The reserves originally totalled around 6% of planned total outlays, but in recent years they have been significantly reduced to between 3% and 5% of total spending. The Treasury Board Secretariat is responsible for producing a weekly summary of the status of all these reserves in each of the present and three forward years, showing how much is already committed and the remaining balances.

In 1984, the separate operating reserves previously in each envelope were centralised in a single operating reserve controlled by the Treasury Board, which continues to determine which excesses are to be accommodated from this reserve and which must be absorbed by the spending department somewhere in its existing allocation. Envelope-specific policy reserves (those allocated by sectoral policy committees of the Cabinet) were reduced in size, resulting in stronger competition for available funds. Special purpose contingencies began to be provided by the Minister of Finance, however, indicating increased emphasis on centrally managed reserves. The Minister of Finance also continued to control the central reserve, renamed "reserve for statutory overruns" to highlight its specific purpose.

The sum of reserves provided in the 1986/87 fiscal year accounts for 2.6% of total budgetary expenditures (compared to 4.4% in 1985/86), of which 1.6% was not allocated to envelopes but managed centrally. Only 1% was allocated by envelope for new policy initiatives. This orientation toward centrally managed reserves is in conformity with both changes in the roles of Cabinet committees and the increased emphasis on imposing stricter cash limits on spending departments and agencies.

The general effect of the changes is to increase the influence of the Treasury Board over the use of operating reserves and to encourage individual departments to redeploy their own allocations to meet changing priorities, thus protecting the planned total of outlays. The envelope policy reserves continue to be managed by the sectoral policy committees of the Cabinet, although the significant reduction in the size of these reserves has forced greater attention to reallocation of existing resources.

Germany. The multi-year financial plan published each year with the budget implicitly contains a general planning reserve for future years intended to cater for contingencies and extended or new programmes, as well as for some price increases. The size of the global planning reserve included for any future year is not based on any simple formula but rather reflects a judgment as to the expenditure risks inherent in the plan for each year. There is also a special wages and salaries provision for future pay increases for federal civil servants. The size of this wages and salaries provision is based on estimates of the average annual increases in per capita wages. The size of these future-year reserves is not published. As noted earlier, except for the earmarked wages and salaries provision, there is no reserve available for adjustments during the course of implementation of a given budget year, unlike Canada and the United Kingdom.

United Kingdom. The annual public expenditure White Paper shows a reserve within the planning total for each of the three forward years. Recently, the reserve has accounted for 3-4% of the planning total for the first year ahead, rising to 5-6% for the final year.

For the first year, the reserve is managed by the Treasury as an operational control to protect the planning total within the year. All expected overruns that cannot be absorbed by the spending department concerned are debited to it; net savings are credited to it. This means that, for example, excesses of spending by local authorities over the government's plans for them are regarded as a charge on the reserve, as are excesses on demand-led programmes such as social security. Discretionary increases are also charged if they are accepted by the Treasury. The Treasury is therefore very cautious in accepting discretionary claims on the reserve, and also seeks offsetting savings against non-discretionary increases where possible. A spending department faced with the unexpected is always supposed to find savings in its other programmes and to seek access to the reserve only as a last resort. There are standing procedures for submissions to Treasury ministers about claims that are pressed. The Treasury monitors spending closely throughout the year against plans.

If a claim is accepted, and is for a programme financed from money voted by Parliament, a suitable supplementary appropriation has then to be sought and, if the vote is subject to a cash limit, a suitable change in the limit has also to be agreed and announced.

Future-year reserves do not have the same control function as the current-year reserve. The function for future years is to act as a buffer in the planning process. It is typical for the reserves in future years to be wedge-shaped, i.e. larger the further in the future is the year to which they apply. This is to allow for the fact that, as plans firm up for departmental programmes, it is less necessary to allow for such a large measure of uncertainty, so the reserve can be slimmed down somewhat in nearer years.

6.3. In-year monitoring and control of cash flow

All the countries in the study can add to or reduce a year's spending after it has begun, by means of a supplementary budget. In some, the government, without parliamentary approval, can block or delay the use of some previously approved appropriations, over and above any standing arrangements that require a spending department to seek further approval for the use of approved funds on particular items such as capital projects that are above the limits of delegated authority.

An early signal in the mid 1970s of the determination to assert more control over spending was more attention to the actual execution of the annual budget and a greater readiness to cut some spending back during the year. Some of the things that were done were relatively crude and arbitrary in their incidence or effect. As well as needing to contain mounting deficits, there was a wish to convince quickly all concerned that their situation had changed and so speed up changes in their attitudes and behaviour. Countries are now adapting and building on what began as emergency actions: the information needed to monitor how actual spending compares with the budget and to explain divergences provides part of the information needed for better financial management.

The design and operation of in-year control and monitoring systems has to be sensitive to the relationships and balance of responsibilities between spending departments and the budget office. Some of the procedures put in place since the mid 1970s may cause tensions between the budget office and the spending departments in implementing a government's policies as reflected in its expenditure plans. It is helpful to distinguish two main purposes of in-year control and monitoring. The balance between them may affect the chosen form of a country's arrangements.

First, there are the requirements of a central authority responsible for arranging the government's borrowing. When budgetary deficits are significant in a country's economic and monetary conditions, the finance ministry may want very prompt and frequent information about actual spending, and likely spending a few months ahead, to help its forecasting of the government's cash flow and hence to help manage borrowing activities. Some central ability to control, rather than simply monitor, the flow of spending in the very short term may also be required.

Second, and quite separate from such overall cash management requirements, all concerned with the management of individual programmes need to monitor spending compared with the budget, in order both to stay within the available budget and to get best value for money. Countries vary in the extent to which the budget office delegates authority to spending departments to take their own decisions once annual appropriations have been enacted by the legislature and in how actively they monitor departmental management. In some countries, the practices (as described below) are changing as new financial management systems are developed.

Australia. Once Parliament approves the level of programme expenditure, the authority to spend is delegated to spending agencies, with the Department of Finance having only an accounting role. In addition, the Australian government is devolving more responsibility from the centre to spending agencies, by reducing the number of separate line items, especially for administrative expenditure, in the appropriations sought from Parliament. This enables each spending agency to develop devolution of responsibility to its managers. The *quid pro quo* for the consolidated appropriations for administrative expenses was a strict cash limit on these appropriations.

These arrangements are backed by reliable, up-to-date information on actual spending. The Department of Finance provides a computerised bill-paying and accounting service for all departments. Department of Finance officials can access it to a certain level of detail for monitoring information, while each department specifies its requirements from the system for its own monitoring and management purposes. Information can be extracted daily if necessary. The normal arrangement is that the Department of Finance compares monthly spending against profiles prepared by spending departments and reports on significant variations to the finance minister. A tabulation of actual outlays and receipts compared with budget estimates for the whole year is published monthly.

If a department requires supplementation to any of its appropriations to cover unforeseen increases in expenditure, then it is requested to offer, to the maximum extent practicable, savings in other areas.

Belgium. Within the Ministry of Finance, the Budget Department is responsible for expenditure control and participates actively in budget preparation. Some Budget Department staff (finance inspectors) are located in spending ministries and provide judgment, in advance, on the advisability, regularity and legality of spending. The Budget Department also has controllers in each ministry to ensure the availability of appropriation credits and the correct charging of expenditure. These controllers draw attention to all irregular use of appropriations.

Each ministry can commit funds within the limits of its budget approved by Parliament. The government does not have the authority to reduce an appropriation, but it can block access by a ministry to an existing appropriation. In urgent cases, the Council of Ministers can authorise spending where existing appropriations are insufficient or do not exist. These decisions must subsequently be ratified by Parliament. The government can approve modifications and transfers within a budget "article".

During the first quarter of the fiscal year, ministries are required to update budget data and prepare a report on the most important changes.

Canada. The spending departments cannot switch expenditures between parliamentary votes, but have the authority to reallocate expenditure across activities within a vote. These delegated authorities are subject to certain restrictions, such as on the use of funds for salary purposes and essential capital. The former cannot be increased and the latter cannot be decreased by discretionary departmental actions.

The budgetary system prescribes annual reviews of departmental multi-year operational plans which entail input and activity levels of scrutiny. There are no provisions for spending departments to report on actual expenditures to the budget office unless a department submits a request for supplementary appropriations, at which time resource limits and the use of resources are analysed to determine whether the request will be granted.

In certain cases, allotments (i.e. portions of a vote) can be frozen by the Treasury Board, even though appropriations have been voted. Usually, conditions are attached to any subsequent use of these funds.

Denmark. When Parliament votes an appropriation, it delegates the authority to spend to the minister concerned. Recent reforms have increased the managerial responsibility of each spending department and reduced the number of detailed items for which specific finance ministry and parliamentary approval is required. The finance ministry runs a computerised paying and accounting service from which monthly data on payments are drawn. However there is no *ex ante* central control of the payment profile over the course of a year. Most personal benefit payments, such as social security, etc., are made by local governments and reported quarterly for reimbursement. The formal monitoring arrangement introduced in 1984 is that each ministry has to present a comprehensive report to the finance ministry three times a year on how its actual spending is conforming to – or deviating from – its agreed total spending target or "frame". If overruns are envisaged, the responsible minister is required to provide, in these reports, proposals for means to offset such overruns, including possible legislative change proposals. In practice, contacts between the finance ministry and spending departments are continuous, and the need for and scope of remedial action is discussed as necessary.

Finland. A formal system for short-term cash management has been in use since the early 1960s. It is used both in planning cash management operations and for identifying when and where deviations need correcting or offsetting by policy measures. Before the start of the financial year, each ministry provides profiles of the expected monthly pattern of its disbursements. The centralised accounting system provides monthly reports on actual spending which the finance ministry compares with these profiles. There is also a daily cash management system permitting very tight management of short-term cash flow, if necessary.

France. The finance ministry maintains detailed control over spending. When the budget is prepared, each ministry negotiates a detailed breakdown of the "ceiling" allocated to it for new and recurrent operations. A relatively senior member of the finance ministry is located in each spending ministry. While the spending ministry is responsible in an accounting sense for the propriety of its spending, approval of this financial controller is also required before any payment can be made. The finance ministry thus maintains a running control, separate from the subsequent examination by the external auditors, the *Cour des Comptes*.

Prime importance is attached to the problems of financing expenditure. The finance ministry may intervene at any time in the financial year to cancel credits or alter the rate at which they may be spent. This is done under administrative procedures not requiring specific parliamentary authorisation. A supplementary finance act may also be used to delete appropriations (and create new revenues).

Germany. A department's appropriation is specified in great detail in the budget law and, apart from specially marked expenditures, there is no departmental authority to transfer expenditure from one appropriation item to another. All payments connected with the federal budget are made through 16 regional financial offices run by the finance ministry which thus has sole responsibility for maintaining records and preparing the annual accounts for each spending ministry. These offices, whose operations are highly computerised, provide monthly analyses of actual expenditure to the Ministry of Finance, which also obtains reports from spending departments of probable financial needs in the next three months. The execution of the budget is thus under constant monitoring and control and the forward projections are an important input to cash flow forecasts.

When expenditure is likely to exceed the authorised total, the federal finance minister may make commitments or expenditures subject to his/her approval by blocks on expenditure, after having consulted the competent federal ministers (last used as a precautionary measure for the planned 1980 supplementary budget). The Minister of Finance can, under certain conditions (if the need for additional expenditure is unforeseen and unavoidable), authorise excess and/or extrabudgetary expenditure, although this only applies where – owing to the urgency of the additional expenditure – a supplementary budget cannot be enacted in time or where Parliament has already waived the requirement for a supplementary budget in the budget law (namely in cases where the additional expenditure does not exceed DEM 10 million or where it arises from a legally binding commitment). In periods of retrenchment policy with relatively low expenditure ceilings, this happens quite often. Twenty to fifty cases of more than DEM 10 million a year is quite normal.

Not for budgetary control reasons, but for considerations regarding overall economic development, the government may apply the provisions of the Law to Promote Economic Stability and Growth (1967). In the event of a substantial decline in general economic activity, the government may decide to authorise additional expenditure. Additional expenditure to counter an economic recession (*Konjunkturprogramme*) can be authorised by a simplified procedure without the need for a long-drawn-out supplementary budget. The Minister of Finance is authorised by law to raise credits up to DEM 5 billion in excess of the provisions of the budget, as adopted taxation rates can also be decreased. Such economic programmes are prepared by the government and require the consent of the federal Parliament (last used in 1975, as their effectiveness has come under question). In order to avoid an overheating of the economy, the Minister of Finance can block expenditure and the entering into commitment involving expenditure in future years (*Konjunktursperre*) as well as increase personal and corporate income tax rates or reduce depreciation allowances. Apart from this, the government may, with the consent of the federal Cabinet, limit borrowing by the Federation, the *Länder* and the local authorities. It was last used in 1971.

Parliament is informed about all important departures from the budget plan quarterly and about excess and extrabudgetary expenditures.

Greece. The Minister of Finance has the authority to regulate cash outflows by prohibiting ministries from spending more than a certain percentage of total annual appropriations each month. Unspent balances lapse at the end of the year and are not transferred to the next year's budget.

Ireland. Public expenditures may only be undertaken with the authority of Parliament given in either the annual appropriation act or in specific enabling legislation. In addition, they require the sanction of the Minister for Finance which may either be specific (for once-off expenditures) or delegated.

In practice, authority for expenditure on continuing current expenditure programmes, which constitute the vast bulk of expenditure, is delegated to spending ministries subject to approved specific conditions and regulations governing their operation. Spending under delegated authority may not, however, exceed overall cash limits specified for ministries in the annual supply estimates. Similarly, in relation to capital expenditure, authority for expenditure on established programmes such as public housing, hospitals, roads and schools has been delegated to departments within the overall parameters and targets for the programme previously agreed with the Department of Finance. For certain major projects within such programmes, however, and for all major once-off public sector capital projects, specific Department of Finance authority for the expenditure must be secured. Expenditure not having the sanction of the Minister for Finance cannot be charged against money voted by Parliament. If spending departments enter into commitments which do not have this authority, sanction may be withheld if the Department of Finance determines that the commitments ought not to have been incurred.

As noted, the initial cash appropriation for each department is now regarded as a cash limit, though in some cases (such as unemployment costs) the Department of Finance will put a supplementary estimate to Parliament. Each department provides a profile of monthly expenditure (capital and current) at the start of each year and, once agreed, this profile is used, in effect, as a set of monthly cash limits. A department can spend more in a month only with the express approval of the finance minister. Savings in a month cannot normally be carried forward, and a department is required to offset an approved excess in a given month by savings in the remaining months of the year.

Each department has appointed an expenditure control liaison officer to oversee the system and be the focal point of contact with the finance ministry. During the year, each department reports monthly its actual and expected spending with explanations of variations from the profile. From the fourth month of the financial year, a monthly budget trends report (expenditures and revenues) is submitted to the government; by the middle of the year, the government is usually able to assess the need for any remedial action.

Italy. Parliament approves two limits on every expenditure item each year: a limit on commitments and a limit on cash payments. The budget office, and indeed the government, does not have any power to withhold or block the release of funds previously approved by Parliament, unless specific parliamentary approval is first obtained. The Minister of the Treasury presents a statement on actual spending to Parliament every three months. Action is in hand to develop monitoring and "early warning" systems to gather information, throughout the year, about management, cash-flow estimates, interim results, etc. In 1985, Italy implemented a "*trésorerie unique*" which requires that all funds of the enlarged public sector, not simply the state, be held and managed centrally. This system was introduced for a number of reasons, including: to permit the state to finance part of its needs with the liquidity of public organisms; to avoid inopportune demands on financial markets in order to protect the needs of the productive sector; and to avoid having the state budget pay sums destined to be deposited in bank accounts by other elements of the public sector. This system is managed so as to ensure that these other public organisms have full and immediate access to their resources as required.

Japan. To control the flow of spending, each department is required to obtain the approval of the finance minister on its plans for incurring liabilities (contracts, etc.). In addition, detailed profiles of expected disbursements each financial quarter, by each disbursing officer in a department, have to be approved by the finance minister before the beginning of each quarter. Payments can then be made in line with these plans. The approval of the finance minister is needed before a spending department may transfer money during the year from one line item of its detailed budget to another. The finance minister can also call for *ad hoc* reports during the year about actual events and prospects so that he/she can provide any guidance or recommend corrective action that may seem necessary.

Netherlands. The finance ministry delegates a good deal of authority to individual spending ministries but retains the right to specify the budget items for which departments may not enter into liabilities before the budget office of the finance ministry has given its permission. During the year, departments operate under the "rules governing the stringent budget policy", revised in 1979 and 1986. Their main aim is to keep spending within the intended totals and also to protect the multi-year estimates for forward years. The rules prescribe how overspending is to be compensated by savings and how windfall savings may and may not be used.

During the year, monthly discussions are held between the finance ministry and each spending ministry about possible over- and under-spending. In many instances, problems are solved without parliamentary involvement by shifting balances between sub-items, *i.e.* with no effect on the vote; or, under strict conditions and to a limited extent, by shifting from one vote to another. A mid-year "spring memorandum" is presented to Parliament by the government, offering a review of developments and proposing any necessary corrective action.

Norway. The Minister of Finance has been granted authority by Parliament to approve changes to the budget during the fiscal year whether for new items or for cost adjustments to existing programmes. The value of any one change cannot exceed NOK 1 million, but there is no limit on the total value of all changes. Similarly, changes valued at over NOK 1 million each, up to about NOK 3-4 million, may be approved by the government (*i.e.* Cabinet) without prior reference to Parliament. Parliament receives a technical report at the end of the year summarising the value of such changes.

The Budget Department is relatively uninvolved in the implementation stage of budgeting. Each ministry determines the extent to which it will subject its subordinate agencies to some apportionment or blocking of appropriations. Ministries generally require regularly updated forecasts from their agencies regarding total spending for the year. The Ministry of Finance receives bi-monthly reports from agencies on funds actually spent.

Portugal. Staff of the Directorate General of Public Accounts in the Ministry of Finance and the Plan are located in each ministry. They advise in budget preparation and have a key role in ensuring that actual spending conforms precisely to the rules of public accounting. The government has some power to check planned spending during the year. By decree law, it can prohibit the use of one or more twelfths of appropriations previously approved by Parliament for certain purposes. Work is in hand to develop modern cost accounting and monitoring procedures.

In practice, actual spending has tended to exceed the initial budget because, for example, of the need to finance pay increases or higher-than-anticipated interest charges.

Spain. After appropriations have been voted, the spending departments must submit monthly information on current and capital expenditures and projected expenditure. The Ministry of Finance may intervene to control the level of expenditure in order to maintain financial balance or for purposes of economic policy.

Sweden. Agencies, charged with carrying out the policies developed by the ministries, account for virtually all the government's spending other than transfers to other levels of government. In the past, an agency's use of funds has been closely regulated by annual authorisations prepared jointly by the Budget Office of the finance ministry and the relevant ministry and issued by the latter. Two general aims of recent years have been to reduce the degree of detail in this control and to pay grants to organisations only in instalments. Appropriations are now disbursed quarterly in advance or more frequently: previously the whole grant had often been paid out at the beginning of the year. The extent of detailed control may vary amongst agencies, but generally there is substantial scope for an agency to make its own management decisions.

The agencies' use of funds is monitored continuously by external auditing bodies, and their central body, the National Audit Bureau, provides the government with regular assessments of how the budget is developing against plans. This information is used both to assess the government's borrowing needs month by month and to check forecasted budget outcomes against appropriated funds. There are links between this cash-flow monitoring and the extensive work on evaluation also carried out by the National Audit Bureau and other bodies.

Turkey. The Minister of Finance can regulate spending throughout the fiscal year. Shortly after the approval of the budget by Parliament, the finance ministry issues a circular to all agencies stating the main principles governing commitments of funds and the maximum percentage of appropriations to be released within the first six months of the fiscal year. A second circular is usually issued in late June. The principles and percentages of this apportionment of funds depend on: general economic conditions; recent trends in expenditures and revenues; the need to spread current expenditure throughout the year; and the nature of the activities concerned. In addition, there is a separate control on the rate of cash outlays. The Ministry of Finance also exercises a control ("contract visas") on commitments in current and future years. The types of expenditure subject to this control and the limits of commitment are established in the budget act.

If there is a need to achieve savings, the Prime Minister or the Minister of Finance may issue general guidelines regarding spending on specified objects. The annual "Decree about the Implementation, Co-ordination and Surveillance of the Annual Programme" comprises a procedure by which investment programmes can be revised, if necessary, and appropriations can be reallocated accordingly.

United Kingdom. When Parliament votes an appropriation, it delegates to the Treasury the authority to sanction payments from the vote in question. The Treasury in turn delegates authority to the spending departments in respect of most routine expenditures.

Specific Treasury approval is required for significant new proposals and individual projects above agreed financial limits. At the start of the financial year, each department provides profiles of its expected spending in some detail. They report actual spending through the Paymaster General's Office. That office provides reports each month to the Treasury with copies to the spending department. The Treasury's main uses of this monitoring information are for managing funding and as an input to its regular assessments of trends in total public expenditure. Care is taken not to dilute the responsibilities of individual spending departments to stay within the cash limits on most annual appropriations and to give early warning of likely variations in demand-led spending from agreed profiles. Social security expenditure, because of its size and the difficulty of forecasting it even in the short term, is subject to special monitoring arrangements, whether such expenditure is financed from the National Insurance Fund or from annual appropriations. Cuts in-year to approved plans are avoided if at all possible, though departments may be expected to absorb cost overruns in elements of the budget, thus possibly necessitating cutbacks in other elements.

United States. Unlike other countries, the authorities provided in the United States budget are not directly concerned with outlays or cash spending. Instead, the budget provides the authority to enter into obligations that will result in immediate or future-year outlays. Obligations cover: the current liabilities for salaries, wages and interest; agreements to make loans; contracts for the purchases of office space, building and land; and other arrangements requiring the eventual payment of money. Outlays during a fiscal year may be for payment of obligations incurred in prior years or in the same year. Outlays, therefore, flow in part from unexpended balances of prior-year budget authority and in part from budget authority provided for the year in which the money is actually spent.

When the budget is approved by Congress, the director of the Office of Management and Budget (OMB) distributes obligational authority arising from appropriations, and other budgetary resources, to each agency by time periods or by activities to ensure their effective use and minimise the need for additional appropriations. The distribution is called an apportionment.

The basic units for control are the approximately 1 100 budget accounts. The Congress may limit executive discretion in some areas to a much greater level of detail, or expect to be informed if an agency wants to change the particular allocation of funds cited in justifying a proposal to committees of the Congress. Conversely, Congress may allow general or explicit transfers between budget accounts, thus increasing departmental discretion.

Once obligational authority is apportioned, the responsibility for further control rests with the spending agency, and there are severe legal sanctions for any federal officer who over-obligates the amounts available in the account or the apportionment. The primary control is thus over entering into obligations: there is no direct control over cash outlays apart from normal audit controls.

Quarterly reports on obligations and outlays against the apportionment are submitted by spending agencies to the OMB. In addition, detailed reports on the use of funds are prepared monthly by departments for the Treasury and the OMB. The Treasury Department publishes a monthly and an annual report showing monthly and year-to-date information on receipts, outlays, surplus or deficit, debt and other factors affecting the financial condition of the federal government. The OMB uses the monthly reports from spending agencies to track the use of obligational authority against planned use; it also publishes one or more updates each year on total estimated receipts and outlays.

6.4. Monitoring and controlling commitments

This sub-section looks behind the cash budget to examine briefly the nature and extent of monitoring and control exercised over commitments. The use of information about, or controls over, commitments in support of cash spending works in two directions. Making sure that spending stays within a cash limit for a financial year (or shorter accounting period) implies a limit on commitments likely to mature in that period. To the extent that the budget office may have to require cuts in some areas to offset – or help offset – unavoidable overruns in others, it wants spending agencies to have as few commitments, and hence as much short-term cash flexibility, as possible. At the same time, an understanding that a spending manager can count on a minimum level of spending in later years, to the extent of making multi-year commitments or contracts up to such a limit, may be a real help for him/her to make effective use of resources.

Section 3 described how large proportions of government expenditure are based on primary legislation or other commitments that may be difficult to alter. Some other expenditures may be more flexible in principle but in practice can be changed only at the margin in any short period. For example, where it may be possible to reduce or eliminate a function, it is likely to be costly to dismiss the affected civil servants or to retire them prematurely. A ban on recruitment, which is likely to cause problems for personnel management in the longer term, can affect only a small fraction of the pay bill while it continues.

Even with no external controls or reporting requirements to meet, a department that spends a significant part of its budget on procurement is likely to maintain information about its outstanding commitments for its own management purposes. Generally, each spending manager wants freedom to make forward commitments to the extent he/she judges best for his/her programme. More senior managers in a department, who may be faced with the possible need to make savings in one area to offset extra spending in another, will want to limit this freedom. Even more so, central cash managers and budget officials may be loath to see the limited remaining short-term flexibility of spending eroded further.

Arrangements to limit forward commitments and thus retain some flexibility may be informal or formal. Sub-section 6.3 above noted the exceptional practices in the United States and Italy. In the **United States**, the Congress approves the federal budget in terms of the authority to commit or obligate, and does not make cash appropriations. In some cases, notably for some multi-year defence projects, it gives authority for the whole project rather than for each year's work in turn. A change in budget authority in any one year may have an effect on obligations for two or more years, and may affect outlays for an even longer period. Monthly cash outlays are monitored and data published, but no direct control over cash flow is exercised. In **Italy**, the budget used to be based on authorities to undertake commitments. Large outstanding liabilities developed. In consequence, there are now legislative limits on new commitments and on cash outlays in the year covered by the budget.

In 1976, the **Australian** government decided to extend formal commitment processes essentially for reasons of improved budget management. Departments are required to lodge their forward obligation estimates at the time of lodging their budget bids. At the same time as the Cabinet examines budget proposals for the year ahead, it also determines limits on the undischarged obligations which departments may have outstanding at the end of the financial year. Departments must adhere to these limits; however, variations can be approved by the Minister for Finance or his/her delegate. This system of limiting obligations is not an attempt to plan all future expenditure but rather to limit the extent to which future expenditure is pre-empted. The obligation system is nevertheless relatively wide, and includes: legislative undertakings; signing of contracts for buildings, supplies, etc.; and other agreements or undertakings which, while they may not be legally enforceable, will oblige the government to the payment of monies. Certain categories of expenditure, *e.g.* salaries, are generally exempted from the system.

Some other countries control or monitor the rate at which new commitments are made – for example, new contracts are placed. In the **Netherlands**, revenues and expenditures have been budgeted and accounted for on a cash basis since the Government Account Act 1976. The budget bill presented to Parliament thus shows the planned cash outlay for each line item. However, for some line items, a separate column shows a maximum of any new commitments to be entered which will lead to outlays in later years. The indicated maximum amount cannot be exceeded without parliamentary approval. In addition, the Minister of the Budget may determine certain line items for which any new commitments require his/her approval in advance. Commitments generate outlays in later years which are incorporated in the multi-year expenditure projections.

In **Finland**, the traditional in-advance financial control of commitments has gradually been relaxed for routine and financially minor matters. It presently covers only major expenditure commitments, which must be approved by the Finance Committee of Cabinet (or by the Minister of Finance for commitments of intermediate magnitude) even if the necessary funds have been appropriated by Parliament. The same process is also used for discussion of politically or administratively important matters, even in cases not reaching the screening levels for financial reasons. In addition, steps have been taken to gradually diminish the widespread use of "reservations appropriations" under which funds are transferable up to three years following the budget year which provided the appropriation. These are being replaced by a system whereby commitment authorisations in a given year must be financed in accordance with a cash outlays plan, for the current and future years, which must be presented with the request for commitment authority.

In **Germany**, similar to the Australian case, departments are required to lodge their forward obligations estimates together with their budget bids. Action leading to future-year outlays can generally be taken only if specifically authorised in the budget, in which case commitments can be made for future years up to the levels previously shown in the budget plan. Corresponding future cash outlays are included in the medium-term financial plan. A system to monitor the actual use made of authorised future commitments is being developed. Future commitments may be specific as to the future year to which they apply, or may be set out in a block "for future years", in which case they can be used only with the agreement of the Minister of Finance. Specific authorisation is not required for future commitments from entitlement programmes nor current payments (i.e. for wages, salaries and other personnel costs and current expenditures on goods and services including certain rent, leasehold and leasing contracts). Deviations from an authorised future commitment are possible with the consent of the Minister of Finance, who may also act to block the use of previously approved commitments in order to control or limit future spending.

In **Ireland**, capital expenditure commitments for succeeding years are limited to 65% of the budget year's allocation. This figure may, however, be varied with the specific approval of the Minister for Finance. The admissible level of future commitments is determined so as to give programme managers reasonable latitude in entering into multi-year contracts while at the same time leaving adequate flexibility for control purposes. All departments, and state bodies under their aegis, report each month on the level of contractual commitments and other quasi-contractual commitments entered into for the following year.

In **Japan**, as noted above, with regard to those concerned with public works expenditures and other expenditures designated by the Minister of Finance, the heads of the respective ministries and agencies prepare plans for executing the obligations (meaning contracts and other acts which are the causes of the disbursements) of the "Expenditure Budget, Continued Expense and Contract Authorisation" and forward them to the Minister of Finance to obtain approval at the start of the fiscal year.

One obvious application of improved knowledge of commitments already made, or forthcoming, is to improve forecasts of future cash spending incorporated in multi-year plans and projections. A more ambitious use is to control future cash flow by regulating the rate at which commitments are made, as in the Australian and German examples described above. Commitment management can also be used to devise the optimal mix and sequence of projects, for example within a road construction programme, to make best use of cash totals planned for several years ahead.

The spending process for some programmes can be thought of as having four main phases:

- application from the private sector (e.g. in the case of certain grant or loan programmes) or initial design (e.g. in the case of a construction project);
- administrative or ministerial approval;
- entering into commitments (e.g. contracts for construction); and
- actual payment in one sum or by instalments.

Analysis of actual cases can yield the typical intervals between the phases and the variability of individual cases from the average. There may be enough stability in these relationships to warrant the development of formal mathematical models to help managers both to understand and, if necessary, to manipulate cash requirements. The

United Kingdom is an example of a country where such investigations are encouraged. Efforts to improve departmental management, such as the initiatives referred to in the next section, with their emphasis on giving individual managers more responsibility for the good conduct of their programmes, seem bound to promote such investigations.

7. Towards improved productivity and effectiveness

7.1. Introduction

All the countries in the study are seeking how best to promote economy, efficiency and effectiveness in their spending programmes. These goals are not new, of course, but they are particularly important in a climate of continuing expenditure restraint. They are reinforced, in a number of countries, by a reassessment and realignment of the role of the public sector and by examination of the continued relevance or priority of programmes in light of changed circumstances. This section offers a preliminary and selective sketch – both as to countries surveyed and the initiatives addressed – of some of the practices employed to ensure that questions involving the role, relevance, restraint and responsiveness of government programmes are addressed. This section also sketches initiatives in some countries to improve financial management in departments and agencies, and to increase flexibility in programme management by reducing the constraints implicit in an annual budget.

7.2. Efficiency and effectiveness reviews

The main aim of efficiency and effectiveness reviews is to promote a continual search for better value for money and thus make it less painful to constrain spending totals. The task in review procedures is to develop useful information and analysis of how resources are used in particular programmes and, more importantly, what is achieved with these resources. The aim is to develop recommendations, possibly with alternatives, whereby ministers can then clarify and rank their priorities better and whereby public servants are stimulated to be more inventive and constructive in their reactions to demands for economy or cuts. The use of review procedures links with the renewed interest in departmental and programme-level financial management reviewed in the next sub-section. Both developments are part of a search for more feasible, manageable and operationally useful forms of the rational and sophisticated control and management systems elaborated in the 1960s under the rubrics of "planning, programming and budgeting" and "zero-based budgeting".

The focus of a review exercise may be directed at any issue from the basic aim of a policy, or the appropriateness of direct government involvement, to the precise way in which a public sector programme is administered. The nature or objectives of a review may affect the choice of the practices to be followed in conducting the review.

In some countries, use is being made of direct private sector input to reviews, by involving businessmen, management consultants, or others from outside the government domain. Some countries are also promoting more exchanges of staff between the public service and industrial, commercial and financial firms to broaden experience and understanding. By such means, understanding is sought of the extent to which typical private sector management and performance assessment methods can be adapted and applied in the public service.

7.2.1. Efficiency reviews

A review of the efficiency of administration or operations is most likely to be carried out by the spending department concerned, though the need for it may have been suggested by those in the budget office concerned with that department. The budget office may make a specific suggestion of an area for improvement, or it may encourage innovation in the spending department by the means of simply reducing the budget provided to finance operations.

In **Sweden**, for example, for several years the finance ministry assumed an annual gain of 2% in productivity in setting the budgets of executive agencies: their appropriations, having been adjusted for increases in prices and wage rates, were cut by 2% a year. This has been modified to a multi-year target, in which 5% has to be saved by the third year, by such means as the agency itself may propose. These target reductions apply to administrative costs only, which account for about 10-15% of total spending. Most instructions on how to use appropriations for administrative costs have been removed. Only the amount that can be spent on salaries is separately restricted.

In **Canada** since 1984/85, most departments' operating budgets have been increased for wage rate changes, but no adjustment has been made for other increased prices. This denial of inflation adjustments, during a period in which general price increases averaged about 4% or 5% annually, forced departments to find productivity or cost-saving measures if reductions in operations and levels of service were to be avoided.

Most governments now promote administrative efficiency as a matter of policy. In **Japan**, the Second Provisional Commission for Administrative Reform operated in 1981-83 and recommended as follows: "It is particularly necessary to drastically simplify the government administration which has expanded into a huge scale since the times of rapid economic growth. The review and simplification of the areas of administrative responsibility will make it possible for the administration to respond to new demands while keeping down the costs to the people and incrementing the vitality of the private sector. There is also a need to review areas which are essentially in the realm of public administration to make them comprehensive, efficient and effective with the minimum costs to meet the changes of the times."

In **Australia**, it has recently been decided to implement a form of programme budgeting in all Commonwealth departments and budget-dependent agencies over the next two to three years. The primary aim is to enable Parliament, central agencies and spending agencies to focus more attention on the efficiency and effectiveness of government spending. This development is underpinned by the Australian government's Financial Management Improvement Programme which is taken up later in this section.

In 1982, the President of the **United States** established a private commission known as the President's Private Sector Survey on Cost Control led by the head of a major private sector corporation. Its remit was to recommend ways of reducing the cost of government and making it more efficient. In early 1986, the President initiated a programme to improve productivity by 20% by 1992 in selected high-priority functions. Departments and agencies will set their own productivity improvement goals consistent with the overall goal of 20% improvement. They will examine present functions and select those activities which lend themselves to measurement and offer major opportunities for significant improvements. The agencies will determine what changes are best suited to achieving efficiency gains. Finally, they will establish a performance baseline drawn from 1985 data and measure the change in productivity from year to year. Annually each agency will submit its productivity plans to the Office of Management and Budget (OMB), as part of the agency's overall management improvement plan. The plans will include targets and methods for improvement, specific goals, measures to be used, and methods of encouraging employee involvement. The OMB will report to the President and Congress each year on government-wide productivity gains, both accomplished and planned.

In the **United Kingdom**, the new Prime Minister in 1979 appointed a leading businessman as her adviser on efficiency, with a small Efficiency Unit located in the Prime Minister's Office to promote scrutinies of selected areas by individual departments.

Countries have found a need to follow up actively the results of studies to ensure that agreed recommendations are implemented and savings made. Even if not directly involved in the choice of area to be investigated, it seems clear that those concerned in the budget office should be aware of a study and its outcome. They can then follow it up in their annual budget negotiations with the department concerned.

7.2.2. Policy and effectiveness reviews

Policy reviews, whether of the aim of the policy itself or of its form and effectiveness, are likely to involve staff of the budget office as well as those of the responsible department, and perhaps other interested departments.

The time and effort needed to make a useful review varies enormously, depending on the programme area and the questions posed, but there is always a need to make sure a review does not drift into taking longer than it need. Because of this variety, it seems generally the case that review procedures are not tightly tied to the procedures and timetables of multi-year planning or annual budgeting, though the need for a review may often be identified in the course of these exercises. It may also be desirable for the results of the reviews to be considered in the context of budget formulation in order that relative policy and expenditure priorities may be assessed.

An agency active in efficiency and effectiveness reviews in many countries is the government's external auditor. In a number of the countries in this study, there is now a heavy emphasis on value-for-money or "comprehensive" audit alongside certification or compliance audit. In 1983, the **Australian** National Audit Office formally adopted a "comprehensive auditing" approach. This was a further stage in the development of auditing systems with an enhanced emphasis on economy and efficiency. The comprehensive auditing approach involves the planning, programming and conduct of a cycle of audits that examine and assess the legal compliance, administrative compliance, financial regularity, economy and efficiency of the operations of the auditees. Over the cycle, covering a period of years, the range of audits conducted should embrace all those aspects. The efficiency audit element of comprehensive auditing involves an evaluation of the effectiveness of the administrative actions and decisions taken by management in achieving programme objectives within the policy guidelines and legislative framework provided by the government. The emphasis is on auditing of procedures and methods, and on assessing whether the taking, or avoidance, of decisions has followed adequate consideration and been properly documented. The scope of audits embracing efficiency issues extends to examining and reporting on whether the audited entity has administrative machinery in place to enable it to advise the government whether the policy is meeting objectives.

In **Canada**, the Auditor General (the federal Parliament's auditor) conducts compliance audits and also has the power to ascertain whether departments have the systems needed to provide value-for-money evaluations. In the **Netherlands**, the external auditor recently showed a profound interest in value-for-money audit; in addition, private consultants have led to the implementation of policy suggestions in this area. In the **United Kingdom**, the National Audit Office has said that half its work is now value-for-money audit. In the **United States**, and similarly in **Germany**, the General Accounting Office conducts audits and evaluations of programmes, activities and financial operations of federal departments and agencies and their contractors. These reviews address questions as to how resources are managed, controlled and accounted for, how economically programmes are carried out, and whether they are meeting intended objectives.

The following paragraphs briefly describe some aspects of policy or effectiveness reviews in Canada, Ireland, the Netherlands, Sweden and the United Kingdom.

Canada. A Ministerial Task Force on Programme Review, led by the Deputy Prime Minister, was formed in September 1984 to review government programmes on a portfolio-by-portfolio basis. It did not conduct policy reviews *per se*, but was charged to produce a profile of government programmes in each department and across government which could lead to simpler, more understandable programmes and programme delivery more accessible to their clientele, and where decision making is decentralised as far as possible to those in direct contact with client groups. The programme review also was intended to be comprehensive, covering statutory and non-statutory programmes.

Altogether, 19 study teams analysed nearly 1 000 programmes and services of the federal government. Study teams consisted of a mixture of experts drawn from both federal and provincial governments and from the private sector. In addition, a private sector advisory committee, distinct from the ministerial task force, discussed the findings with members of each study team during the review phase.

The analysis and recommendations of the study teams were submitted to task force ministers; those recommendations endorsed by the ministerial task force were then submitted to the Cabinet's Planning and Priorities Committee, chaired by the Prime Minister, for decision as to the further action or programme changes desired.

The government's intention was not to create another centralised bureaucracy, and all study teams were disbanded once their reports had been submitted. A small core, however, remained to track the progress of recommendations through the decision-making process and to ensure that spending departments are aware of implementation requirements.

Ireland. In March 1985, a committee of Cabinet ministers was appointed by the government to review existing expenditure programmes with a view to determining:

- what programmes continued to be useful in terms of serving the objectives for which they were initiated;

- whether the implementation of such programmes could be made more efficient in terms of the cost to the state; and

- whether existing structures made the best use of available resources or whether a more effective structure could be put in place.

The primary objective of the review initiative is to make recommendations that will lead to expenditure savings from the cancellation of outmoded programmes or from the provision of more efficient and effective programmes. The reviews are comprehensive in nature and are carried out by review teams drawn from the Departments of Finance and the Public Service and the department under whose aegis the programme falls. Each programme is reviewed in terms of objectives, priority, means of implementation, benefits, financial implications, etc., and the review team reports within a specified timescale depending on the nature of the programme involved.

Netherlands. The evolution of the Reconsideration Procedure in the Netherlands illustrates some of the practical problems in achieving effective review procedures. The 1980 budget memorandum to Parliament identified the need for a "second circuit which is independent of the budget preparations" to reappraise government responsibilities.

Accordingly, in January 1981, a new and wide-ranging policy review programme was adopted to improve the information base for priority setting at an overall level as well as for decisions about individual policy areas. It was called the "Reconsideration Procedure". The methodology drew on previous experience with programme budgeting and has been described as a zero-base budgeting approach, applied selectively. The choice of subject areas is reported to Parliament (which may suggest others) and the final report of each review is submitted to Parliament before the government decides how to react to its recommendations.

The procedure is steered by a ministerial commission comprising the Prime Minister, the Vice-Prime Ministers (who represent the parties forming the coalition government) and the Minister of Finance. Its counterpart at official level is chaired by the Director-General of the Budget in the finance ministry. Each project is carried out by a working group set up for the purpose and chaired by the department with lead responsibility for the subject. The Prime Minister's Office and the Budget Directorate are represented on all the working parties. The secretariat for all of them and for the commissions is provided by a special unit in the Budget Directorate; this is intended to ensure a common discipline and rigour in the work of all groups.

The main criteria for selecting areas to review, as formulated anew in April 1983, are the following:

- the presence of opportunities for efficient mechanisms of allocation for a publicly provided service – privatisation, decentralisation, deregulation, charging of (higher) prices, etc.;
- time passed since the last general efficiency review in any institutional context, but from a perspective comparable with that of the Reconsideration Procedure;
- decreased priority of a public service or of its level of provision in the light of changed circumstances or the general policy objectives of the incumbent Cabinet;
- balanced distribution over the government departments; and
- size and growth of expenditures.

Guidelines for conducting reviews – including sets of questions to be tackled – have become a crucial part of the discipline that ensures proper fact finding, fundamental rethinking of policies and radical options for change. Each working party has to suggest three or four less-costly policy alternatives, including one leading to savings of at least 20% below the level of expenditure projected for four years hence.

At first, the timing of reviews was *ad hoc*. In April 1983, arrangements were changed to enhance the status of the reviews, partly by linking them to budget processes through a clearly phased timetable. The new arrangements were approved by the Cabinet. Suggestions for areas to be reviewed in the next round were to be made by 1 August and the agreed list included in the budget memorandum sent to Parliament in September. The working groups were to be set up to start work in January. Each had to report finally before 1 November (there was provision for reporting interim findings). In January, the Cabinet was to review the results of the round as a whole and to decide on recommendations best judged outside the budgetary framework. Parliament was to be informed of its conclusions. All other recommendations were to be remitted for decisions in the budget cycle proper for which policy work starts in February when the Minister of Finance proposes budgetary targets to the Council of Ministers (*i.e.* the Cabinet).

This timetable has been found too rigid. Some reviews can sensibly be completed more quickly; others need more time. In July 1985, some additional procedural modifications were approved by the Cabinet. From now on, it will be possible to start reconsideration reviews at any time of the year. This possibility increases the flexibility of the procedure without impairing its efficacy: the rule that all departments have to participate, and that there is an annual check on whether a sufficient number of reviews are being carried out, is maintained. Another modification is that political decision making about completed studies becomes somewhat more flexible as well: both the responsible minister(s) and the Minister of Finance can take the initiative, and decisions need not be submitted to the full Cabinet if no general Cabinet policy is involved and provided the ministers concerned have reached agreement.

The efficacy of the Reconsideration Procedure in relation to its primary aim – the provision of realistic retrenchment proposals – has been fairly satisfactory in the first years after its introduction. In the first two years, retrenchment proposals were developed totalling about NLG 16.5 billion (about 5% NNI). Of these proposals, about NLG 6.5 billion (roughly 2% NNI) has been implemented.

There is an impression that, from 1983 onwards, it is harder to acquire co-operation from departments with respect to particular review projects and that, more in particular, constructive efforts to develop realistic retrenchment proposals become scarcer. The number of studies that contain conflicting points of view are increasing. The modifications of July 1985 were partly aimed at the selection of more politically relevant areas for review. It is hoped that, in this manner, political pressure can be used more adequately in order to stimulate co-operative attitudes inside and outside the government apparatus.

In **Sweden**, the use of parliamentary or expert committees of enquiry to carry out policy reviews is long established. In the past, the terms of reference for such enquiries have sometimes been too general and have led to proposals for costly reforms. Nowadays, they are more constrained: all reports have to include a thorough account of the economic consequences for the central government, the local authorities and the business sector of their proposals. Some recent committees, especially those reviewing the work of government agencies, have been told to include a "tight alternative" in their report, meaning a 15-30% contraction of an activity.

To supplement this type of review, the government set up in 1981 an Expert Group for Studies in Public Finance. The budget director in the Ministry of Finance is one of the members. Most of its members are, or have been, connected with the finance ministry. The group also includes an academic economist and representatives of regional and local governments. The group reports formally to the finance minister, but its reports are widely distributed and used in many quarters. The group meets about six times a year to commission studies and oversee their progress. Topics for research and review may be either policy or its administration; the deadlines may be relatively tight (three or four months); and if new initiatives are proposed, then "financing" must also be proposed via offsets in the same sectoral area.

In Sweden's experience, it is important to create a climate which encourages the participation of ministries and agencies in reviews and a routine that ensures effective links with budget work. Like the Netherlands, the aim is for effective interaction between review practices and the budget cycle, rather than integration in a single process.

United Kingdom. Policy reviews are a well-established practice in the United Kingdom. There is no set procedure for conducting a review; each requires separate decisions on its organisation, objectives, resources and implementation. Policy reviews range from a small scrutiny-type team, through joint Treasury/spending department efforts, to formal interdepartmental committees. In some cases, a review team may be led by a minister, as with the comprehensive review of elements of the social security system conducted in 1984/85. In most cases, Treasury involvement of some kind usually takes place, although there have been reviews with no Treasury participation which have still been successful. In all cases, though, the Treasury will seek at the very least to influence the terms of reference of a review.

The primary aim of policy reviews is to ensure that over a number of years all areas of spending are reviewed, objectives clarified and targets set. Such reviews have an essential role to play in identifying expenditure savings and in allowing a reassessment of priorities both between and within expenditure programmes.

7.3. Campaigns to improve financial management

Some countries in the study have launched specific campaigns or initiatives to promote better financial management in individual ministries and executive agencies. The aim of such campaigns is to set radical changes in motion. As more business-like management styles become the way of life, the campaigns as such tend to merge into the ongoing work of a department.

The key features of these campaigns are the adaptation and use of procedures equivalent to corporate planning in an enterprise and of forms of management to match. In all cases, this is taking the form of more decentralised procedures for making executive decisions and more delegation of such decision making. For this to work effectively, individual managers need clear objectives (and, at lower levels, clear tasks) coupled with responsibility for good use of the resources provided to each in a delegated budget. There is a need for good information, appropriate skills and expert support. Overall control depends on clear accountability for performance within the organisation.

Each budget holder at each level wants certainty in the annual – or longer-term – sum for which he/she agrees to be responsible, and flexibility in how to allocate it between subordinates. This fact affects the extent to which a government aims to provide detailed budgets or a block budget to each main department or main functional area out of what might be thought of as the budget office's block budget of total planned spending. The more autonomy a department or ministerial committee enjoys, in the detailed allocation to its programmes, the less the involvement of the budget minister and his/her staff in how a block is subdivided. With less involvement, their knowledge is likely to be less, and thus their ability to take balanced views across all departments is likely to be diminished. On the other hand, the budget office will have more time to focus on key issues if it is less preoccupied with time-consuming and energy-consuming detailed budgeting.

The following paragraphs summarise initiatives in Australia, Canada, Denmark, Ireland and the United Kingdom.

Australia. This government initiated its Financial Management Improvement Programme (FMIP) in June 1983 in response to recommendations of the "Review of Commonwealth Administration". The programme provides a focus for a range of budgetary and administrative reforms which aim to:

- develop better means of identifying and setting budget priorities;

- focus attention more clearly on the goals and objectives of particular programmes, and the resources they use;

- develop and apply programme management techniques which will improve efficiency and effectiveness in resource use; and

- establish machinery for regular review of programme efficiency and effectiveness.

The FMIP is a two-pronged strategy. The first area of reform is aimed – as with the United Kingdom's initiative – at encouraging departments and statutory authorities to focus more on the management of programmes and achievement of programme objectives, and less on compliance with rules and regulations and the control of inputs. As such, it is complementary to the implementation of programme budgeting referred to earlier in this section. The FMIP is being pursued through:

- encouraging the development of a corporate management style whereby the head of the agency and senior executives, in consultation with the minister, identify agency goals and strategies to achieve them, and set priorities for resource allocation;

- developing a programme approach to management based on a programme structure derived from the agency's goals and embracing all the activities of the agency. The objectives and expected outputs and outcomes of the elements of the programme structure (*e.g.* programmes, sub-programmes, components, sub-components) should be clearly identified, as should the levels and types of resources allocated to them;

- establishing in all portfolios a systematic approach to evaluation of programme efficiency and effectiveness;

- instituting an organisational structure which facilitates management on a programme basis, and where responsibility for achieving agreed objectives within resources allocated is devolved to the line managers as far as possible;

- implementing management information systems which provide relevant and timely information to managers at all levels to enable them to monitor achievement of objectives, control resource use, and set priorities; and

- providing tailored staff development and training for senior executives and staff to improve their resource management and general managerial skills.

The second arm of the FMIP strategy, and seen as essential to the success of the above "voluntary" measures, is the development of an institutional and budgetary decision environment which encourages a much greater emphasis on performance by all those involved in public administration. Steps taken include:

- introduction of portfolio programme budgeting;

- consolidation of departmental administrative appropriations to a single line vote. Previously departments had up to 20 separate items defining amounts for administrative expenditure;

- devolution of authority from central agencies to agency heads in respect of reallocation of funds between notional areas of expenditure in administrative estimates, and establishment control (for other than executive management positions) subject to staff years limits with three broad bands;

- requiring all new expenditure proposals to include a statement of objectives and specification of performance indicators, and a specification of proposed review mechanisms and timetable;

- liaison with parliamentary committees to encourage their focus on agency programme performance with respect to objectives rather than on programme inputs;

- requiring upgrading of information provided to central agencies and to parliamentary committees; and

- upgrading of central agency financial ledger systems and staff monitoring systems, including moves to direct, online access between these and agency management information systems.

The FMIP is controlled by a steering committee comprising senior officers of the Department of Finance, Transport and Defence and the Public Service Board. It is serviced by two small support units, of about ten officers each, in the Department of Finance and the Public Service Board, and has an interdepartmental advisory committee comprising some 12 departments.

Canada. Many basic features of the Policy and Expenditure Management System (PEMS) have their roots in the "Programme Planning and Budgeting System" (PPBS) that was implemented in the late 1960s. The PPBS was introduced in response to two sets of concerns: about factors that affected the ability of the government to control its expenditures; and about those that affected assessment of the effectiveness of these expenditures in meeting their intended policy objectives. Shortcomings with PPBS, as both a control tool and a mechanism for assessment, soon became apparent. The consideration of individual incremental decisions tended to proceed in the absence of an overall expenditure framework. Objectives also proved to be inadequate for evaluation purposes, in part because they stated broad impacts of programmes and, in part, because many programmes had a multiplicity of objectives.

The adoption of an expenditure growth rule in the mid 1970s placed a ceiling on overall expenditure increases. The growing base of spending for ongoing programmes relative to this ceiling, however, eroded the reserves needed for new priorities. Concerns also emerged that the pattern of expenditures, albeit justified by PPBS criteria, was not in accord with changing government priorities. Although based on many fundamentals of PPBS, PEMS provides for a systematic integration of policy .and expenditure management functions, in which incremental bottom-up operational planning is integrated with top-down macro-level controls over budget totals. The budget and annual estimates result from the iterations between the fiscal and operational planning exercises. In its emphasis on results rather than on objectives, moreover, PEMS helps to overcome a major shortcoming of PPBS by permitting a more systematic analysis of linkages between the resource allocation and performance measurement functions – that is, between programme inputs and outputs.

The operational planning framework of each department and agency in the PEM system is based on "planning elements", which are discrete sub-divisions of programmes. Planning elements provide the basis for resource planning in departments and for resource allocation decisions by the Treasury Board. As they conform to the management and control systems of each department, planning elements also identify responsibility centres for purposes of accountability for the efficient utilisation of approved resources.

Operational planning frameworks have formed the basis for meeting long-standing requests from Parliament for more information relating government spending to the achievement of results, thereby ren-dering an improved accountability to Parliament of "value for money" resulting from the expenditure of public funds. The estimates documents now consist of three parts. Part I, *The Government Expenditure Plan*, establishes the basis of the government's accountability to Parliament for the level of government spending and its distribution by policy sector or envelope. The detailed *Main Estimates* (Part II) are intended to support the annual appropriation acts. In addition, a series of "Part IIIs" (*Departmental Expenditure Plans*) describes in detail each programme of a department in terms of its objectives, the manner in which activities contribute to objectives, and the expected results.

Modifications to PEMS since 1984 (see sub-section 6.2 above) have been designed to provide for more effective control over total spending and for greater flexibility and accountability of departments in their utilisation of approved resources. Policy reserves have been reduced and central control strengthened over the remaining provisions for reserves. Moreover, to help realise a stronger expectation that departments live within the budget, line ministers and department managers will receive enhanced discretionary authority to make choices to improve programme effectiveness and efficiency through the reallocation of approved resources. The existing operational planning frameworks, together with improved internal audit and programme evaluation systems, are expected to provide the bases for stricter accountability for the use of approved resources.

Denmark. In the autumn of 1983, the Danish government developed a modernisation programme to reform the public sector. Its main components are a budgetary reform, more reliance on market mechanisms or quasi-market forces, better management methods in departments and agencies, and use of new information technology. The objective is to secure vitality and higher quality of services within a zero-growth framework, and it is intended to do this by giving departments and lower-level managers more discretion and incentives to economise.

Most progress has been made in the area of budgetary reform. In general, this relies on further decentralisation, net expenditure control and even, to some extent, net appropriations.

The control of the post office, the railways and a few other public enterprises (whose transactions are handled gross in the budget) has been relaxed. It now focuses on a predetermined net financial result. Departments and agencies with business-like supplementary activities are allowed to expand these according to simple rules to prevent distortion of competition. All agencies are allowed to use incidental receipts without formal appropriation.

Each department has more scope to move money between its votes, and agencies are free to shift expenditure from one item to another, except that expenditure on pay cannot be increased. The previous facility to carry forward unused money on investment projects is extended to encompass current expenditure as well. Uncommitted balances may be carried forward up to four years, provided that their future use is specified. Finally, most provisions for separate parliamentary approval of minor investment projects, sales of buildings, etc., have been abolished.

In 1986, the former very detailed control on staff is being replaced by a single man-year limit of each agency. Within this, more detailed controls on numbers of senior posts are retained, as an instrument of control over organisational structure.

In 1987, a change from volume to cash budgeting will be implemented. New decentralised financial management systems are being implemented.

As a consequence of the budget reform – and the high priority given to the reduction of the budget deficit – the overall expenditure control has been transferred from gross expenditure to net expenditure. Though the objective still is to limit gross expenditure, the operative expenditure target or "frame" for each minister is fixed as a net figure, which means that increased revenues (except taxes) "count" as savings.

Ireland. A number of measures have been introduced to bring about a substantial improvement in financial systems both at central government level and also at the general public sector level. Major financial initiatives over the past three years include:

● publication of the "Comprehensive Programmes of Public Expenditure";

● prescription of systematic procedures for the appraisal of capital projects;

● expenditure by departments now controlled month by month on the basis of profiles approved at the beginning of each financial year;

● introduction of a formal system of reporting to government on the financial performance of the commercial state bodies based on corporate plans;

● issue to departments of "Guidelines for Financial Management"; and

● publication in September 1985 of a government White Paper on the reform of the public service.

The "Guidelines for Financial Management" which were issued in 1984 require departments to identify, by reference to the "Comprehensive Programmes of Public Expenditure" or otherwise, major expenditure programmes broken down into activities or services, as appropriate, which are suitable for budgeting and accounting on an ongoing basis. This will facilitate greater delegation on an activity basis and so bring the widest range of costs under delegated managerial influence.

The guidelines cover such areas as: planning on the basis of expenditure programmes and activities; identification of individual managers who will have responsibility for programmes and activities; budgeting in accordance with government decisions; the development of adequate financial reporting mechanisms; the adoption of procedures for rolling reviews of the effectiveness of programmes; and the adoption of a programme of internal audit.

This process has received a major impetus with the publication of the government's White Paper on the public service which sets out planned reforms in structures and managerial systems. The guidelines provide a framework for the development of the financial elements of departmental management systems and are an integral part of the new management systems envisaged in the White Paper.

United Kingdom. The government launched its "Financial Management Initiative" (FMI) in May 1982. This called on each of the departments taking part to develop management systems and practices which gave managers at all levels: clear objectives; means of assessing progress towards them; well-defined responsibilities for making best use of the resources in their charge; and the information and expert advice they needed to support these responsibilities.

Each department is developing arrangements tailored to its own functions so that there is a good deal of local variation on essentially common themes. It is too soon for the developments to have had a major impact on the conduct of the government's central budgeting processes, the annual public expenditure survey (PES) or the annual supply estimates. The new emphasis on clarifying aims and objectives and on developing and using output measures and performance indicators to display what is being achieved by individual spending programmes is, however, already resulting in descriptions of achievement (and, in some cases, targets in such terms) in the annual public expenditure White Paper which records the outcome of each annual PES.

The common features of the developing arrangements in departments are:

● An annual process in which the manager of each significant organisational unit describes to the top management of a department what his/her unit has been doing, the objectives, targets and tasks for the coming period, and the resources involved (in terms of staff numbers and cost, other administrative costs and the amount of any "programme" expenditure attributable to the unit). These structured submissions are reviewed by the top management of the department to set priorities and make any necessary changes in the allocation of resources.

● The building up of more decentralised arrangements within each department for budgetary control of administrative expenditure. The heads of individual line commands will thus have a more managerial role than has been customary, with greater responsibility for the efficient and effective use of the resources (in terms of the staff and other administrative resources) allocated to them at the end o each budgetary cycle of bidding and scrutiny. Each senior manager is being encouraged to delegate further within his/her command, wherever it makes managerial sense to do so.

● Growing attempts to tackle the difficult problems inherent in more effective management of expenditure on functional programmes. This involves: putting the responsibility clearly on managers to plan and control the programmes they deal with; more thorough appraisal of policy proposals, to test their likely effectiveness; and more monitoring and evaluation of programmes in operation, to change or weed out those that demonstrate poor value for money.

● Some change of emphasis in the role of a department's principal finance officer, in the direction of servicing the top management and budgeting systems and helping line managers develop the assessment of the spending programmes for which each is responsible and away from direct management of resources for the department as a whole.

● The linking of budgeting for running costs, programme planning and evaluation, and performance measurement from line managers through senior management and into the PES and supply estimates. This issue is one of the key points emerging from the current review of budgeting led by the Treasury's accounting adviser.

7.4. Longer-term assurances to moderate the effects of annuality

The principle of annuality is a prime element of traditional budgeting. The legislature appropriates funds one year at a time, and cash not spent in the year lapses. Much of government is, in fact, continuous and many projects – building a road or training a doctor – take years to complete. In addition, there is a widely held view that, to some extent, the lapsing of funds at the end of the year leads to dysfunctional and inefficient "spending binges" in the final stages of a fiscal year. This leads to an argument that reducing the strictures of annuality would improve the cost effectiveness of the budget. Thus budget departments always face demands for longer-term assurances of funding and have to find the right trade-off between short-term flexibility and longer-term certainty.

One example of multi-year assurances to spending managers is provided by the arrangements in the **United Kingdom** for approval of the investment programmes of individual nationalised industries. Each year the government reviews with each of them their investment and financing plans for the years covered by the annual public expenditure survey. Each industry is then entitled to make firm plans and commitments for investment projects amounting to 100% of its agreed investment programme in the first year ahead, 85% in the second year, and 70% in the third year. These agreements are normally given in the autumn. Specific endorsement is needed from the responsible spending department for particularly large projects.

Currently the **Australian** aid programme is subject to substantial multi-year commitment. A major area of the programme – Australia's assistance to Papua New Guinea – is subject to a five-year aid agreement specifying the amounts of aid allocated to Papua New Guinea each year and the method of disbursement. As well, Australia undertakes biennial commitments of food aid under the Food Aid Convention, enters into specific multi-year commitments for bilateral projects, and may lodge promissory notes with international financial institutions, such as the World Bank, which may be drawn down over several years.

In **Canada**, agreements are possible between the Treasury Board and individual spending departments about multi-year budgets, though still subject to annual appropriation of funds by Parliament. The general elements of such an arrangement include an undertaking by the spending ministry not to seek any supplementation in the years covered by the agreement and an undertaking by the Treasury Board to exempt the programme from further cuts, save in the most extreme circumstances. Multi-year agreements appear to be more useful as a budgeting tool when resourcing the requirements of a small agency with a clearly defined mandate and subject to workload pressures that do not undergo substantial variation. These qualities help to produce a fairly stable environment in which longer-term resourcing agreements can facilitate improved management.

Schemes for "end-year flexibility" are designed to help cope with uncertainties in the timing of spending. In the **United Kingdom**, for example, there is an arrangement covering most departmental capital expenditure (which is also subject to annual cash limits), whereby a department may carry forward up to 5% of its planned capital spending to the next financial year. Technically, the funds are voted again by Parliament and the cash limit is increased in the following year.

As discussed in Section 6 above, the **United States** has an obligations-based budget, under which outlays in a given year may well ensue from obligations of prior years. In addition, in some cases – for example, major defence projects – the obligational authority may cover the entire cost expected to be incurred and may be in the form of multi-year or no-year authority. Also, in the 1987 budget the President announced his intention to consider strengthening the multi-year budgeting process. The Congress also passed legislation requiring that, beginning in fiscal year 1988, the defence budget be prepared and submitted to Congress on a two-year basis.

In **Italy**, the budget documents specify the level of cash outlays arising from previously approved commitment levels. However, these cash outlays must be accommodated with the overall cash limits for a given year which, as noted earlier, are also approved in the dual control system of the Italian budget.

The **German** budget law allows for investment expenditure and expenditure from specifically earmarked revenue to be carried over to subsequent fiscal years. Other expenditure may be declared eligible for carry-over in the annual budget plan, if it is earmarked for a purpose covering several years and if this is in the interest of efficiency and economy. Necessary funds are to be budgeted in order to carry over expenditure (unexpended balances, *Ausgabereste*). These funds are calculated in such a way as to be sufficient to cover the unexpended balances that will have to be spent in the next financial year, unless funds for unexpended balances can be provided from cash savings in the next financial year.

In **Denmark**, the established scheme applying to capital spending by departments and agencies has been extended to also cover current spending. Uncommitted balances can be carried forward for up to four years provided their intended use is specified in the final "supplementary" to the finance bill. If a department's specific use of funds is not detailed in the supplementary, then the funds lapse at the end of the year.

In the **Netherlands**, under certain conditions it is permissible to transfer appropriated funds to the next fiscal year without parliamentary approval. The first condition is that line items eligible for this carry-forward are indicated as such in the budget document. Second, the budget document indicates the maximum amount of transferable funds. Finally, funds must be employed in the next budget year, and the spending department is obliged to show that corresponding commitments were made in the originating fiscal year. However, the Dutch Cabinet has recently decided to abolish this means of carry-forward. In future, unspent balances will be transferred to the next budget year through a supplementary bill requiring parliamentary approval.

A possible further development might be formal multi-year appropriations for certain programmes or agencies to overcome the managerial disadvantages of strict cash annuality while retaining adequate overall control in the short term. In **Sweden**, for example, there is discussion of the possibility of putting the administrative budgets of the agencies that execute many of the government's civil programmes onto a multi-year basis. The aim would be to make it possible to focus budget office effort on thorough reviews of, for example, one-third of the agencies each year. Each agency thus reviewed would then have an agreed programme of changes to make in its performance within three years, and would be assured funding for the whole period so that it could plan how best to meet its obligations.

Notes

1. Countries use different names for the organisation at the centre of government with responsibility for the overall control and management of public expenditure. The Ministry (or Department) of Finance, the Treasury, and the Budget Department are commonly used. In this report, the generic term "budget office" is frequently used along with the terms "budget minister" (the minister primarily responsible for public expenditure) and "budget officials" (those who work in the budget office).

2. The 19 countries that participated in the study are: Australia, Belgium, Canada, Denmark, Finland, France, Germany, Greece, Ireland, Italy, Japan, the Netherlands, Norway, Portugal, Spain, Sweden, Turkey, the United Kingdom and the United States.

3. This section draws extensively on OECD, 1985a.

References

OECD (1984), *Tax Expenditures: A Review of the Issues and Country Practices*, OECD, Paris, ISBN 92-64-12589-2.

OECD (1985a), *The Role of the Public Sector: Causes and Consequences of the Growth of Government*, OECD Economic Studies No. 4, Spring, OECD, Paris, ISSN 0255-0822.

OECD (1985b), *Social Expenditure 1960 to 1990: Problems of Growth and Control*, OECD, Paris, ISBN 92-64-12656-2.

OECD (1985c), *OECD Economic Outlook No. 38*, December, OECD, Paris, ISBN 92-64-12777-1.

ISBN 978-92-64-06087-6
Evolutions in Budgetary Practice
Allen Schick and the OECD Senior Budget Officials
© OECD 2009

Chapter 3

Budgeting for Results: Comparing Country Experiences*

* This text was originally published in 1995 as Chapters 2-10 of the full OECD publication *Budgeting for Results: Perspectives on Public Expenditure Management* (ISBN 92-64-14476-7). At the time of writing, Allen Schick was Professor of Public Policy at George Mason University, Washington DC.

1. The scope of central government budgets

This report deals with budget practices from the perspective of the central government office responsible for the overall control and management of expenditure. What is included in central government spending varies from country to country, but the main issues of scope are much the same. These issues pertain to borderline institutions on the boundaries of the public and private sectors, non-conventional transactions such as loans and guarantees, and incentives that do not entail the direct expenditure of funds but have financial and other effects similar to ordinary expenditures.

These "scope" issues bring into consideration the long-established though often-violated principle that the budget should be comprehensive – that is, it should cover all the financial inflows and outflows of the government regardless of their source or end use. Applied to central governments, this principle would, for example, require the budget to include grants to local governments but not the expenditure by these governments of self-generated funds. It would also require the inclusion of social security, even if it is financed by special funds or trust funds, and state enterprises, even if they have access to capital markets.

The principle of comprehensiveness is not an end in itself but a means of accomplishing vital functions of budgeting. A comprehensive budget facilitates: i) the measurement of the economic consequences of government actions; ii) control of the financial resources of the government; iii) accountability of decision makers and managers in the public sector; and iv) the efficient use of public resources. Despite the vital need for complete information on finances, few if any OECD member countries have perfectly comprehensive budgets that encompass all the financial flows of the government. Conventional expenditures for the operating expenses of government agencies and programmes are almost universally included in the state budget. Exceptions arise only when law or practice treats a particular agency or programme as off budget. More difficult issues arise when the expenditure is unconventional, as is the case when the government makes or guarantees loans or when it provides incentives or preferences through the tax system. This section does not consider social security, which is a growing share of total public expenditures in the OECD area.

1.1. State enterprises

The boundary between public and private enterprises is not always straightforward or well defined. The degree of public control, ownership of the enterprise, and its reliance on public finance are important criteria in defining the boundary. But the lines are blurred when the government owns the enterprise but exercises little control, or conversely when it does not technically own the state enterprise (SE) but nevertheless exercises significant managerial control. Further complications arise with regard to employment, pricing, and procurement policies, as well as the access of SEs to capital markets.

When SEs are included in the budget, the most common practice is to account for them only in terms of the net flows between them and the government, or on a net basis (income minus expenses) rather than on a gross basis. A gross basis would strengthen government control of the enterprise, but it might distort the budget and lead to undue interference and rigid management. Netting income and expenses, on the other hand, shows the contribution of the state enterprise to the government's financial condition and facilitates control of SE borrowing requirements. In the United Kingdom, for example, the operational definition of public expenditure for control purposes includes the net external finance of nationalised industries and most other public corporations. Exceptions to the general practice of net budgeting for SEs is found in Austria where some enterprises (principally the traditional public service monopolies) are presented on a gross basis and in France where budget operations are still performed by departments, not the SEs.

Some countries draw a distinction between enterprises directly owned by the government and those established by it but operated as if they were private firms. In the United States, corporations owned in whole or in part by the federal government are included in the budget, in contrast to those sponsored (but not owned) by it. Financial information on the latter – known as government-sponsored enterprises or GSEs – is annexed to the budget but not included in the revenue and expenditure totals.

Privatisation initiatives in various OECD member countries have reduced the number and financial prominence of SEs. When enterprises are privatised, the funds earned by the government usually are budgeted as receipts or as deductions against expenditure. Either way, the government's short-term budget condition is improved. Despite the emphasis on privatisation, some governments still own major enterprises, especially in public monopolies such as transportation and communications.

Along with privatisation, some governments have moved away from detailed *ex ante* budget (and other managerial) control to managerial discretion and accountability for performance. For SEs operating in competitive markets, the common practice is to give them considerable freedom with respect to standard managerial decisions such as pricing and the choice of inputs. In these SEs, budgetary discussions generally focus on the state's contribution to the enterprise, whether for operating grants or capital financing.

The role of the budget office in overseeing SEs varies among OECD member countries. In Austria, SEs engaged in manufacturing deal with the budget office through an umbrella organisation which submits requests for expenditures and financing. In Canada and France, discussions with the budget office occur under the aegis of the responsible minister. In the United States, the Office of Management and Budget has little involvement in SE operations. In practice, few budget offices exercise ongoing control over SEs. An exception is in France where some older nationalised companies have a resident comptroller who is an employee of the finance ministry and has access to all documents. Over the years, however, this role appears to have evolved from surveillance to maintaining communication between the finance ministry and the SE.

Ex post controls on SEs are largely exercised outside the budget process, typically through periodic audits. In recent years, the trend has been to expand these reviews to performance issues and not only compliance.

Austria. SEs account for 15-20% of the federal budget, even without counting nationalised firms operating in competitive sectors. Two groups of SEs are distinguished for budgetary purposes: public service monopolies such as railways, post and telecommunications, and forests that are wholly owned by the state and generally subject to strict budgetary and non-budgetary controls; and state enterprises operating in competitive sectors which are at least 51% owned by the state and generally autonomous, though the government may exercise some influence through the appointment of directors. All SEs in the first category are budgeted on a gross basis; those in the second category are netted.

The public service monopolies are budgeted in a manner similar to regular departments. Parliament approves their budgets, with separate limits on appropriations for wages, number of employees, investments, and operating expenditures. Rates of pay are also set by Parliament, though not through the budget process. These SEs are not permitted to borrow on their own account, and investments are budgeted on a cash basis as current expenditures. The second type of SEs – nationalised industries – is not subject to these detailed *ex ante* controls. The key channel of government control is the membership of public officials on the boards of these companies. Loans, grants, or capital infusions are processed through regular budgetary procedures. The Audit Bureau prepares yearly reports on public service monopolies and reports on other SEs over a four to five-year cycle.

Canada. As of 1993, the federal government held a 100% interest in 47 corporations with assets of CAD 54 billion and employing more than 117 000 persons. The relationship between the government and SEs was modified by the Financial Administration Act of 1984 which altered the balance between central control and managerial autonomy. Under the rules currently in effect, each parent SE – those wholly owned by the government – must annually submit a five-year corporate plan setting forth its investments and borrowing, its objectives and strategy for achieving them, results for the previous years (compared to objectives) and expected performance for the next year. These plans are presented to Parliament and form the basis for annual appropriations requests. An SE must obtain annual approval (through the yearly corporate plan) to borrow, even when its enabling legislation authorises it to borrow.

Funds advanced by the government to SEs consist of budgetary funds which are not expected to be repaid and are therefore recorded as outlays (which are netted against SE revenues) and non-budgetary funds which are expected to be repaid and are recorded on financial statements as assets. The budgetary funds are generally to provide cash subsidies or cover operating deficits; the non-budgetary funds normally are for capital investment, working capital, and similar purposes.

Finland has reformed the central government budget-linked enterprises into extrabudgetary ones. The reform process started in 1989 and has proceeded to cover a majority of enterprises. The new organisational form allows for wide operational flexibility to enterprises, while preserving the volume of investments and their finance as well as access to major functional choices in parliamentary control. The new operational degrees of freedom are autonomy of operational management, pricing decisions and access to capital markets. Enterprises exposed to competition may be transformed into limited-stock companies and sold to private investors. So far, three enterprises have been transformed into companies and one has been sold. More enterprises will follow: a bill has been submitted to Parliament on the re-organisation of the Posts and Telecommunications as a limited-stock company. The extrabudgetary enterprise may in future be an organisational form for producing compulsory government services.

France. State enterprises play a significant role in the French economy and public sector. Two waves of nationalisation brought French SEs to their current scope and diversity, the first just after World War II, the second in 1981. Since then, the scope of the public sector has been significantly reduced by two privatisation programmes, one carried out from 1986 to 1988, and the other currently under way. In addition to "*entreprises nationales*" in which the state owns more than 50% of the capital and voting shares, there are also various "*sociétés d'économie mixte*" which are partly public, partly private. Only the former are discussed here. The relationship between firms and the Minister of Finance depends on their date of nationalisation and on whether they operate as public service monopolies or in competitive markets. The size of the public sector has been appreciably reduced by the privatisations which came into being between 1986 and 1988 and by those currently under way.

Five main rules govern financial flows from the state to SEs: *i)* capital grants are treated as current expenditures; *ii)* loans are recorded as temporary operations carried out through special treasury accounts; *iii)* dividends from SEs appear as receipts in the general budget while loan repayments are entered as receipts in the relevant special treasury account; *iv)* guarantees are budgeted only to the extent that they lead to outlays; and *v)* subsidies to SEs for the provision of social benefits are budgeted as expenses to the relevant departments when they are remitted to SEs.

Budget control is exercised over payments to SEs, the amounts and conditions under which some may borrow from the private sector, and the wages, prices, etc., of some SEs. Relations between the SE and the budget office are channeled through the ministry responsible for the SE. Contributions from the state to public service monopolies and various other SEs for current operations are decided in the annual budget process. Investment policies of these SEs are reviewed by a special interdepartmental committee to insure that their financial plans are consistent with macroeconomic policy. In the case of SEs operating in competitive markets, discussions with the finance ministry pertain to overall borrowing or to specific requests for an increase in state-provided capital. But other matters are left to the managers of these companies or to government representatives on their boards of directors.

SEs nationalised in the 1940s or earlier have a resident official from the Ministry of Finance who monitors their operations, has access to documents, conveys the policies and preferences of the ministry, and alerts the ministry to developments.

United States. Although the United States appears to have a relatively small state enterprise sector, it has a variety of institutions operating under diverse rules and financial arrangements. These can be classified into four categories.

- Corporations owned (in whole or in part) by the federal government and included in the budget usually on a net basis. Most of these corporations get their capital from the federal government which bears the financial risk and controls their budgets and other operations. Some of these entities have a line of credit at the Treasury, and most are subject to the apportionment of their funds by the Office of Management and Budget. All are subject to audit by the General Accounting Office.

- A few SEs are owned by the government but are off budget. The largest of these is the Postal Service which was removed from the budget in 1981. These are similar to the first category in important regards except for their budgetary status.

● Government-sponsored enterprises (GSEs) are created under federal sponsorship, but are privately owned and managed and are normally intended to be self-financing. Most GSEs serve as financial intermediaries in credit-dependent sectors such as housing and agriculture. Some GSEs draw a portion of their capital from the government which bears financial risk either in the form of explicit guarantees or "moral obligation" – the expectation that the government will come to their aid in case of distress. GSEs are excluded from the budget, but financial information concerning them is annexed to the budget.

● Some private corporations receive federal subsidies either in the form of capital, operating subsidies or guarantees. The government generally exercises little control over these entities, but cash flows to them from the Treasury are budgeted as expenditures.

1.2. Loans and loan guarantees

Loans made to others (including state enterprises) are normally accounted for in the budget and included in any overall expenditure target. This cash basis derives from the fact that loans contribute to the government's deficit or borrowing requirement in the same manner as conventional outlays. Moreover, the general lack of balance sheets and other financial statements inhibits the government from recording loans as assets, as they would be on business statements.

Treating loans as cash outlays has a number of serious shortcomings. One is that loans are made to compete with non-repayable expenditure such as grants in the decision-making process. This treatment makes it appear that loans and grants of equal value entail equal cost to the government when, in fact, the true costs are unequal. Second, when a loan is budgeted as an outlay at the outset, there is no means for the budget to record any cost if the loan is subsequently written off, defaulted, converted to a grant, or forgotten. Third, the cash basis does not recognise that the terms of loans – the interest rate charged and repayment schedule – and the credit-worthiness of borrowers differ and greatly affect the true cost to the government.

Loan guarantees raise some particularly difficult budgetary issues. Inasmuch as cash payment by government occurs only if the borrower defaults, the general practice is not to include loan guarantees in expenditure plans or budget totals. In tendering the guarantee, however, the government does obtain a contingent liability pursuant to which it will have to make payment in the future if, as often happens, default ensues. At the point of default, it is too late for the government to control the cost, though it will have to record any cash payments in the budget.

Understating the cost of loan guarantees makes it difficult to compare them to alternative financial instruments such as grants and direct loans, and also makes it difficult to assess their cost in terms of the risk to the government. Many governments have sought to compensate for the deficient treatment of guarantees by expanding the information on them in the budget and in other documents. In many countries, either the budget or standing legislation limits the total volume of guarantees that may be outstanding or issued during the year.

The budgetary status of loans and loan guarantees has undergone considerable change in recent years. The most far-reaching reforms, introduced in the United States, aim at budgeting for both loans and guarantees on the basis of their estimated cost to the government. Other countries have sought to strengthen financial control by providing realistic assessments of expected cash payments in the budget. Other reforms have included charging borrowers a fee to recoup, or cover a portion of, the cost of the loan or guarantee to the government.

Australia. The volume of direct loans has declined since the late 1980s in consequence of policies that terminated Commonwealth borrowing for states and required government business enterprises (GBEs) to be self-funding. Most guarantees are issued to GBEs as a means of lowering borrowing costs and improving access to capital markets. GBE reforms adopted in 1988 withdrew explicit guarantees on new borrowing, but these enterprises still have implicit guarantees arising from the perception that the government will rescue them from financial difficulties.

Austria. No budgetary comparison is made of the cost of grants, loans, and guarantees. The Ministry of Finance applies a 7% discount rate to measure the value of loans. The resulting estimated values are not entered into the budget. *Ex ante* appraisals of the financial soundness of borrowers minimise credit risks. State enterprises are not financed by direct loans, and it is rare for loans to be converted into grants. To minimise risk, guarantees are made only if they are provided for in laws that impose conditions on their issuance. Apart from export credit insurance, payments under guarantees have been very minimal. Loan guarantees have been issued to state enterprises, but their volume has been diminished by 1986 reforms that removed informal state guarantees on enterprises co-operating under the aegis of OIAG, the government holding company, and a 1991 law, terminating new guarantees to these firms.

Canada. Direct loans are a significant feature of public policy. These may be concessional loans, which are treated as grants and charged to the budget, or non-concessional loans which are at market rates and entail no subsidy. The loans are revalued each year, and mark-downs are taken if the credit risk or interest subsidy is found to be significant. Loan guarantees, which have increased in volume since the late 1980s, can be issued only if authorised by legislation and under terms approved by the Minister of Finance. Reference to loan guarantees must be expressly included in the budget estimates in order to obtain parliamentary authority for the guarantee; however, the expenditure levels cover only cash payments resulting from defaults. When there is an expectation that loans might not be repaid, a reserve (generally equal to 25% of the amount lent) is set up and recorded as a standard expenditure item in the budget. When loans by the private capital markets to state enterprises or the private sector are expected to be fully repaid, they are presented off budget. The government is reviewing existing policies and practices with a view to establishing a new policy to reflect costs of loan guarantees in the government's summary financial statements.

Denmark. Direct loans are not a significant instrument of government policy, and amounted to only 2% of expenditure in 1991. Loan transactions that create financial assets (receivables) are counted in the total budget deficit; repayments are treated as income in the financial transactions account. The subsidy cost of loans is not identified in the budget. No systematic comparison is made of guarantees to other forms of expenditure, but they are generally perceived as having a smaller subsidy than direct loans. Losses on some types of guarantees have been mitigated in recent years by higher premium charges.

Finland. Direct loans play a minor role as a budgetary instrument, amounting to less than 1% of total expenditure. They are budgeted as outlays, while repayments are budgeted as income. Loan defaults, rescheduling, and other irregularities do not appear in the budget. With few exceptions, state guarantees are formally approved by Parliament.

Detailed reports on these transactions appear in the annual closed accounts and the government's report on the management of state finances.

Germany. Direct loans amounted to slightly more than 1% of federal expenditure in 1992. Loans are provided only if repayment is likely. There is no separate budget for financial transactions. Loan disbursements are handled as outlays, payments are counted as revenue. The budget approved by Parliament includes provision for the expected cash requirements arising from defaults on guarantees. Guarantees are issued in many sectors and are monitored by the Ministry of Finance.

New Zealand. Both direct loans and guarantees have diminished in importance as the government has moved – through deregulation, corporatisation, increasing contestability and other innovations – to introduce market principles in the public sector. The budget distinguishes between transactions that create assets and those that do not. Under the new accrual accounting system, write-offs of loans are recognised in financial statements. Guarantees are fully reported in the government's financial statements.

Sweden. The government proposes limits for the use of each loan guarantee programme, and these limits are decided upon by Parliament. A special section of the budget lists changes in loan guarantee limits and cash payments. The budget also provides estimates of expected payments on guarantees during the year.

Switzerland. In 1991, direct loans amounted to less than 2% of government expenditure. When loans are made, a credit scoring system is used to rate the risk. The balance sheet distinguishes between loans that carry normal yields (so that their book value corresponds to their effective value) and those with low yields. The latter are revalued every year. There is a growing use of guarantees, possibly because they have no immediate impact on the deficit and are better suited to many situations. The effective subsidy on loan guarantees is close to zero because they are made only if the financial condition of borrowers is high and payment is probable.

United States. The Credit Reform Act of 1990 (which became effective with the 1992 fiscal year) made fundamental changes in the budgetary treatment of direct and guaranteed loans. Prior to the reform, the budget accounted for loans and guarantees on a cash basis. Direct loans were recorded as outlays when funds were disbursed and were netted in the budget against repayments of principal and interest on old loans. Loan guarantees were budgeted as outlays only when payment was made pursuant to default. In addition to this cash-based system, a separate credit budget, paralleling the regular expenditure budget, was introduced during the 1980s. This separate process provided for the congressional budget resolution to set forth total direct loan obligations and total guaranteed loan commitments for each fiscal year. It also provided for limits on annual loan activity to be set in annual appropriations acts. Some elements of this parallel budget process were continued by the 1990 reform.

The reform shifted the accounting basis for federally provided or guaranteed loans to the estimated subsidy costs of these transactions. The reform was aimed at putting direct and guaranteed loans on a comparable basis (that is, their respective subsidy costs) and to facilitate the comparison of these transactions to grants. The reform entailed complex procedures for estimating subsidy costs for each loan programme and for handling the unsubsidised portion of loans. The new system requires that budget authority and outlays be budgeted and that appropriations be made for subsidy costs. These costs are calculated on a net present value basis using a discount rate equal to the interest rate paid by the government at the time the loan is committed or guaranteed. In making this calculation, all future cash outflows and inflows are estimated, but the administrative costs of processing the loans or guarantees are excluded. In the case of direct loans, the outflows will be the amounts lent, and inflows will be repayments of principal and interest and recovery of assets pursuant to default. In the case of loan guarantees, the outflows are the payments the government will make if the borrower defaults and the inflows will be any recoveries. By discounting these flows to present value, the procedure enables the government to separate the subsidised portion of these transactions from the unsubsidised portion.

2. Global budgetary targets

The growth of the public sector, the changed composition of public expenditure, a less optimistic view in some countries of the government's role in the economy, and concern over the rising debt burden have contributed to significant shifts in the posture of governments toward public spending. In the late 1970s and early 1980s, there emerged a recognition of the need to balance policy objectives against the financial capacity of government, as well as sharpened awareness of the potentially adverse impacts of chronic fiscal imbalances on the overall economy and the future freedom of the government to act.

These concerns led governments to predicate budgetary planning on global targets, typically extending several years ahead, to which annual spending decisions would be accommodated. While the precise links, if any, of these targets to actual budget decisions or outcomes depended on the willingness of political leaders and governments to be bound by preset norms, the targets helped to constrain demand at the start of the annual budget process. The targets put politicians, interest groups, bureaucrats, and other claimants for public funds on notice that there were limits to the responsiveness of government to their demands. The targets were important elements of an education process by means of which expectations were changed from expansion to cutbacks or stabilisation. Thus the targets were "top-down" constraints imposed on the "bottom-up" demands of spenders, their clients and supporters.

A government's global budget norms have to be expressed in simple terms, though they are likely to ensue from complex considerations regarding fiscal and monetary options, the size and role of government, the built-in momentum of revenue and expenditure, and sectoral policies and pressures. Targets that cannot readily be grasped by politicians, civil servants and the general public stand little chance of influencing decisions. To be simple enough to serve their intended purposes, the targets must be summed up in a few numbers representing either future trends or the direction the government wants to go. The study on *The Control and Management of Government Expenditure* (OECD, 1987) found that, in virtually all member countries, budgetary goals were expressed as specific quantitative targets, not as general qualitative statements of intent. Such precision provided a strong message as to the government's financial objectives, and restricted its ability to allow expediency to dictate aggregate revenue and spending levels.

The budget targets used in member countries can be grouped into three categories, as set forth below. Some countries rely on two or more of the practices to influence budgetary developments.

- A **ratio**, usually expressed as a percentage related to GDP or some other indicator of aggregate economic activity. The ratio may relate to the level of public debt, budget balance or government borrowing, revenue or expenditure, or a combination of these factors.

● A **rate of change for expenditure.** A popular guideline has been zero real growth over the stated period, although the target could also allow some rate of increase or call for a reduction in real expenditure. Alternatively, the target may be expressed in nominal terms, and may be published alongside target ratios for the budget balance or revenue burden.

● An **absolute value for the target variable in nominal terms.** Targets in cash terms can be expressed as either the future level of expenditure or the deficit, or as the amount of desired change from some baseline level.

Budget targets are not self-executing nor is it always within the grasp of the government to meet them, no matter how strong its determination. In pursuing stated fiscal norms, the government must be sensitive to the short-term performance of the economy. When recessions occur, fiscal targets will likely yield to the realities of economic conditions. Other shocks – the unification of Germany and the enormous cost of rebuilding and integrating the eastern sector was one of the most prominent in recent times – can force the government to retreat from carefully crafted fiscal objectives. Much also depends on the short-term control exercised by the government over key variables such as interest rates, and the cost of demand-led schemes.

OECD member countries differ substantially in their fiscal performance measured against the targets they set for themselves. Leaving aside the recession which unfolded in the early 1990s, some countries outperformed their targets and some did a lot worse. In both these types of situations – doing better and doing worse – the drumbeat message of hard times and the need for belt tightening lost effectiveness in repetition. By the early 1990s, global targets were institutionalised in the budget practices of many OECD member countries, but they were somewhat less influential as guideposts to budget policy and actions than they had been in the mid 1980s. One should expect, however, that given the toll which the recent recession has taken on the fiscal balances of democratic regimes, the emerging recovery will bring renewed emphasis on stringent targets as a means of fiscal consolidation.

Global targets are likely to be given some impetus among European member countries by the provision of the Maastricht treaty that makes budget deficits below 3% of GDP a condition of joining the European Economic and Monetary Union to be introduced by the end of the 1990s. Those EC countries with budget deficits above the Maastricht target may turn to global targets as a means of bringing their budgets into compliance.

Australia. Beginning in 1985, the federal government adopted a medium-term "trilogy" strategy of not increasing outlays or revenue as a proportion of GDP and of reducing the deficit/GDP ratio. In response to emerging balance-of-payments difficulties, these targets were tightened, with the government committing itself to a real decline in outlays for the 1988/89 and 1989/90 budgets and to a zero net public sector borrowing requirement. After moving to surplus from 1987/88 to 1990/91, the federal budget returned to deficit with the early 1990s recession. In 1992, the government announced a package of measures to provide a short-term boost to the economy, along with a commitment to return the budget to surplus by 1995/96. This target was subsequently deferred a year to 1996/97 and revised in the 1993/94 budget to a deficit of around 1% of GDP by 1996/97.

Austria. In 1987, the coalition government adopted a medium-term programme aimed at reducing the deficit from 5.5% of GDP to 2.5% by 1992. Until the recession, this consolidation proceeded at a much faster pace than had been planned. But the recent deterioration in the economy has compelled a relaxation of fiscal targets, and the current target is to achieve the 2.5% GDP ratio in 1994. In addition to reducing the deficit, fiscal policy aims to reduce the tax burden, holding the growth of public expenditure below that of GDP and stabilising the debt-to-GDP ratio.

Canada. During the 1970s and early 1980s, the government sought to hold the growth of outlays to no more than the trend growth of nominal GDP. This gave way to a strategy that focused more on deficit and debt control. Since 1984, the government has sought to reduce the ratio of expenditures to GDP by holding the nominal growth of programme expenditures (not including debt service) to well below the growth of nominal GDP. In most years, the targets for expenditure have been significantly below inflation, implying real declines in programme spending. The 1991 budget introduced the Spending Control Act which sets legally binding limits on the growth of programme spending (excluding the self-financing unemployment insurance and agricultural insurance funds) of an average of 3% per year over the five years beginning in 1991/92. The 1994 budget indicated that the act would not be extended once it expires in 1995/96. In conjunction with measures to lower the ratio of expenditure to GDP, tax reform has increased the ratio of revenues to GDP. The medium-term strategy to reduce the deficit and debt-to-GDP ratio is based on revenues growing in line with GDP and expenditures growing by significantly less.

Denmark. Expenditure targets have generally been expressed in terms of real growth in public expenditure. The main fiscal objectives adopted in 1983 and pursued through most of the decade were elimination of the central government deficit and zero real growth (exclusive of cyclical changes in expenditure on unemployment benefits) in public expenditure. By the late 1980s, rapid economic recovery had led to balance in central government finances and a substantial surplus in the consolidated public sector. Subsequently, however, rising unemployment expenditure and a slow rate of increase in tax revenue resulted in increasing deficits. The government that took office in 1993 set reduction of this deficit as an explicit objective. The target for expenditure is a growth rate significantly lower than the long-term growth in GDP.

Finland. Beginning in 1977, the government set targets for gross tax rates and limits on state borrowing as part of its medium-term economic policy. The policy announced in 1985 called for stabilisation of the tax burden and the debt-to-GDP ratio through the remainder of the decade. With the breakup of the Soviet Union and developments in Eastern Europe, the Finnish economy was shaken and the previous fiscal targets proved inadequate. In 1990, the government adopted a new scheme of budget ceilings in which the Cabinet decides on expenditure ceilings for each ministry as formal guidance for budget preparation. The targets have thus shifted from overall central government expenditure to the components.

France. Following a brief period of expansion in the early 1980s, the government moved to a more restrictive posture, guided by two fiscal constraints: steadily lower central government deficits and reduced tax burdens, During the 1986-89 period, the actual deficit was consistently less than had been budgeted; in 1990-93, the opposite occurred, and the government faced sharply higher deficit/GDP ratios, despite efforts at expenditure restraint.

Germany. The federal budget has incurred high additional expenditure to promote economic reconstruction in the new *Länder* and to finance social policy measures in support of unification. With one-quarter of the spending budgeted for 1993 related to unification, the federal government has indicated the course to be followed: a 3% limit on expenditure growth in the medium term, a tight rein on public spending, and reductions in annual net borrowing. This consolidation covers regional and local governments as well, with the aim of bringing total public budget deficits down from 5.5% in 1991 to 3% in 1995.

Greece. The operational target for the budget is the ratio of the net public sector borrowing requirement to GDP. The 1991 stabilisation programme aimed at decreasing the central government's borrowing requirement from 13% of GDP to 4% in 1994. Although annual budgets are supposed to meet the targets set by the stabilisation programme, the programme has no binding effect, and the budget has often deviated from the fiscal strategy.

Italy. Policies adopted in the mid 1980s provided for reducing the total borrowing requirement of the extended public sector to about 7-8% of GDP by 1990. The targets implied no real growth in current expenditure and holding real capital spending below the growth in GDP. These targets were not met, and the government presented successive budgets in the late 1980s and early 1990s containing cutback packages. However, chronic deficit slippage has been a prominent feature of budgeting since the 1980s.

Japan. Although the government has not adopted aggregate spending targets for the public sector (or central government) since the early 1980s, it has pursued fiscal reforms aimed at phasing out debt-financing bonds and reducing the ratio of public debt to GNP. The main instrument of fiscal restraint has been strict guidelines which every ministry has to follow in preparing budget requests. Although the guidelines apply principally to operating costs – mandatory expenditure, national defence, and certain other important items are excluded – they have reversed the trend in debt financing.

Netherlands. Budgetary norms are typically enunciated in the coalition agreement negotiated at the start of a government to cover the four years it is scheduled to remain in office. Budgetary targets, expressed as a percentage of net national income (NNI) relate both to the budget deficit and the collective budget (which includes tax and social insurance payments and certain other revenue). The coalition agreement for 1991-94 set the target for the budget deficit at 4.75% of NNI for 1991, declining to 3.25% in 1994. This was the third in a series of coalition agreements, the first covering 1983-86 and the second 1987-90, which substantially reduced the budget deficit. The target for the collective burden during the period 1991-94 provided for it to be stabilised at 1990 levels.

Spain. Since 1983, the medium-term objective has been to control the public sector deficit and curtail public expenditure. With the movement to a single European market, budgeting in the early 1990s emphasised continued fiscal consolidation and a shift from consumption to investment expenditure.

Turkey. The Five-Year Development Plan specifies targets for economic performance and public finance such as total public sector current and capital expenditure, transfers to other sectors, revenues, and fiscal balances. The plan also targets ratios of total public expenditure to GNP. The budget is prepared in the framework of this plan, but the outturn on the deficit has often exceeded planned levels.

United Kingdom. Since 1980, the medium-term financial strategy (MTFS) has provided the framework for monetary and fiscal policy. The MTFS is published with the annual budget and is updated annually. Each MTFS sets forth fiscal projections, usually for four years ahead, covering the public sector borrowing requirement in money (cash) terms and as a percentage of GDP. Under arrangements introduced in 1992, growth in "new control total" is to be constrained to a rate which ensures that general government expenditure (excluding privatisation proceeds) rose more slowly than the economy as a whole over time. On present assumptions, this means that real growth in general government expenditure (excluding privatisation proceeds) should over time be no more than 2% annually.

United States. During the early 1980s, the federal budget deficit soared both in absolute terms and as a percentage of GDP, while the public debt/GDP ratio also escalated. To arrest these trends, the Balanced Budget and Deficit Reduction Act of 1985 (the Gramm-Rudman-Hollings Act) set specific deficit targets for each fiscal year 1986 through 1991. The act contemplated that the deficit would be progressively lowered in each of these years and would be eliminated in 1991. The act also devised semi-automatic procedures (known as sequestration) to reduce expenditures if the estimated deficit at the start of a fiscal year was above target. Congress amended the act in 1987 to adjust the targets and extend the year by which the budget was to be balanced to 1993. Despite some relatively small sequestrations, the actual budget deficit was above the Gramm-Rudman-Hollings target for each of the years from 1986 through 1990. Congress responded to this predicament in 1990 by shifting from deficit targets to controls on legislation affecting receipts and expenditures. These controls, initially effective for the 1991-95 fiscal years, divided spending into "discretionary" and "direct" categories. Discretionary spending is controlled by annual appropriations, which the 1990 reforms limited to preset levels. Direct spending, mainly for mandatory entitlements, was not limited in amount but was subjected to pay-as-you-go (PAYGO) rules which require that legislated increases be offset by spending reductions in other programmes or by revenue increases. Initial experience with the new controls indicated that they somewhat restrained additional expenditure but did not reduce the portion of the deficit due to past legislative decisions on revenue and expenditure. The Congress has now extended the discretionary caps and pay-as-you-go limits through fiscal year 1998. No legislative action was taken to restrain direct spending under current law. However, as part of the agreement, the President transmitted an executive order establishing caps on direct spending. If the caps are exceeded, the President will propose legislation to offset the increases.

3. Expenditure planning: multi-year and annual budgeting

Aggregate budget norms and targets are typically expressed for several years, not only for the year immediately ahead. This multi-year dimension is essential because bringing the budget into conformance with acceptable fiscal objectives usually must be done in stages, with each year's budget progressing toward the stated target. If the annual budget does not subscribe to the global norms, they will not be achieved and the government will risk losing control of its fiscal condition. Yet there often arise tensions between medium-term budget commitments and annual budget pressures, so that rather than moving in the promised direction, the budget reflects the *realpolitik* of the moment.

Multi-year budgeting (MYB) is the bridge between aggregate medium-term targets and annual budgets. MYB has also become an instrument of financial management reform in a number of OECD member countries that have sought greater efficiency and effectiveness in the public sector by restructuring their budget practices. This feature of MYB is considered in subsequent sections of this report.

The origins of MYB are in the perceived need of governments to address the growing size of the public sector and its influence on the economy, as well as the long-term implications of current decisions, such as defence and investment expenditure, which often occur years after the budget makes provision for them. The early MYB systems were introduced during the 1960s and 1970s, a period during which the public sector was expanding rapidly and confidence in the capacity of government to steer the economy on a steady growth path was pervasive. In those years, MYB was a planning device, a means of identifying programme initiatives and setting aside funds for them in future budgets. MYB was itself an engine of expansion, as departments and others saw the plans as entitlements to future increases in budgetary resources. But as the rate of public sector enlargement became unsustainable, MYB was seen as an inappropriate approach. It did not make much sense to plan for expansions that could not be funded or to give rise to expectations that would not be satisfied. There also was concern that economic turbulence and unpredictability had rendered MYB an unreliable guide to future fiscal and programme policy.

In response to these concerns, various governments of OECD countries re-oriented their MYB from plans to projections and from instruments of programme expansion to constraints on future spending. In some, such as the United Kingdom, this re-orientation was signalled by the switch from planning in volume terms to cash planning. In others, it was reflected in rules dictating that the projections be based on unchanged policy – that is, that they merely estimate the future cost of existing programmes and not make room for any initiatives. In a number of countries (the Netherlands, Sweden and the United States), this baseline became the starting point for work on the budget. In most cases, the baseline conveyed a powerful message: that the built-in momentum of existing programmes had already claimed all future resources and that there was no margin for new spending schemes.

Cast as a baseline projection, the multi-year budget functions as a financial constraint to which the annual budget must be accommodated. The constraint is often articulated in terms of the global target embraced by the government. It would thus show the budgetary implications, such as revenue increases or programme cutbacks, of staying on course to achieve the stated targets. To serve as a constraint on current budget policy, the budget must be linked to the annual cycle of expenditure planning. When MYB was part of an expansive planning apparatus, the process was often entrusted to a separate agency that had no direct role in preparing the annual budget. Accordingly, the common practice is to have the organisation responsible for preparing the budget make the multi-year projections. Linkage of the projections and budget has also been facilitated by shortening the time horizon of a multi-year budget to a frame that more closely corresponds to the period for which global budget targets have been established.

Australia. To start work on the budget, the Department of Finance compiles forward estimates of outlays in each of the next three years. These baseline projections include only the estimated costs of approved programmes in the absence of policy changes. The costs of expiring programmes that are likely to be renewed are separately identified. The Department of Finance then assembles the various projections into an overview that is adjusted to a consistent (budget forecast) price basis. Using these projections, the Cabinet indicates broad aggregate targets for the budget and forward years. Decisions made by the government in the budget process are additional to the baseline forward estimates which do not include any allowance for policy changes. Budget decisions focus, therefore, on incremental adjustments – up or down – to this baseline. Although the Cabinet sets broad policy targets, detailed work is left to the Expenditure Review Committee (ERC), a subcommittee of senior ministers. In 1993/94, the Cabinet decided that most policy initiatives were to be fully offset by savings. However, certain high-priority proposals or those too costly to be fully offset were considered outside that constraint. The Cabinet also endorsed a two-stage process in which portfolios were responsible for bringing forward both new policy and savings proposals. The first round called for ministers to submit synopses of their proposals by May 1993. These were then sifted by ministers who nominated items to be further developed in a second round. Detailed ERC consideration commenced at this point, producing expenditure figures for the budget presented in August. However, this timetable will be altered from 1994/95 as the budget will from this date be introduced into both houses of Parliament in May of each year, in order to allow its passage prior to the commencement of the financial year in July.

Austria. The government annually prepares a medium-term budget estimate covering three years beyond the current budget year. This estimate shows the financial implications of measures that have already been decided; it does not reflect other planned initiatives. On the expenditure side, the multi-year budget indicates the financing required to meet approved goals and commitments; on the revenue side, it projects future receipts under unchanged policies. The multi-year budget serves the government's budget preparation, but is not acted on by Parliament.

Budget reform in the early 1990s provided for a multi-year financial programme to integrate the processes of priority setting, policy development and expenditure management. Under this new arrangement, expenditure plans are set for each policy sector and ministry.

Work on the budget, based on directives issued by the Ministry of Finance, starts in May of the previous calendar year. Recently, these directives have laid down strict demands for restraint, with a combined limit covering both discretionary and statutory expenditure. After agencies submit budget requests, negotiations are conducted with the spending ministries at three successively higher levels: in the budget department; by the Minister of Finance; and, if necessary, in the Cabinet Co-ordinating Committee headed by the Chancellor. The outcome of this process is the budget presented to Parliament in October.

Belgium. Budget preparation is launched in February or March by a call-in circular from the Ministry of Finance that has been approved beforehand by the Cabinet. The circular specifies guidelines, norms and assumptions to be applied to budget requests submitted in May. These requests consist of current policy estimates along with separately documented proposals for new measures. The requests for ongoing activities are based on current policy, defined as the legislation and regulations in force at a specified date. Proposals for increased spending are to include offsetting savings. Special attention is given in the requests to about 100 big items which together account for more than 80% of total expenditure. Departments are instructed to provide additional information on these items. The requests are reviewed during June and July in bilateral meetings with the Budget Department after which the Cabinet decides on allocations to each of the big items and authorises expenditure initiatives or cutbacks. Capital projects include three-year estimates and are reviewed by an interministerial commission which recommends an investment programme to the Cabinet.

Canada. The top-down fiscal planning system for establishing fiscal targets is expressed in terms of aggregate budgetary expenditures and net financial requirements. This top-down system interacts with a detailed bottom-up multi-year operational planning system (MYOP). The bottom-up system is initially expressed in constant dollars and deals with each element of spending. The Treasury Board manages the bottom-up operations while the Department of Finance deals with the fiscal planning system in consultation with the Privy Council Office.

Each year the government reviews and rolls forward its fiscal plan covering the current year, the upcoming budget year, and the two following planning years. Projections of revenues, economic conditions, and status quo expenditures are evaluated in the light of governmental priorities – in particular, the medium-term strategy to reduce the ratio of expenditure to GDP. The result is a planned multi-year expenditure path for each year that encompasses. resources for the ongoing operations of government; central held reserves to fund government priorities, public debt charges, and variances from the forecasts for statutory programmes; and spending control measures required to achieve the deficit target. These, in global terms, are set out for the budget year as part of the fiscal plan published in budget documents.

Each spending department develops an MYOP that is subject to review by the Treasury Board, leading to decisions on the resources required to continue existing programmes over a three-year period. At the same time, the Department of Finance updates the forecasts of major statutory payments and public debt charges based on the revised economic outlook. These forecasts, when combined with the results of the MYOP review, constitute the point of departure for the preparation of the expenditure plan, with the first year serving as the basis of the main estimates.

The estimates are presented to the federal Parliament approximately one month before the beginning of the next fiscal year. In the estimates, the government seeks appropriations and reflects financial and authorities requirements for the first year of the approved MYOPs. There is also a recognition of the multi-year costs involved. Of the total estimates, approximately 70% has been previously authorised by existing statutory authority and is presented for information purposes. The balance is the amount for which resources are to be appropriated by Parliament.

Denmark. When the budget is passed by Parliament in December, an appendix to the appropriation bill projects expenditures for each of the next three years at the same price and pay basis as the appropriations, Work on the next budget starts shortly thereafter. The budget department in the Ministry of Finance adjusts the multi-year projections to the pay and price assumptions to be used in preparing the next budget. In February, the Minister of Finance proposes to Cabinet a set of net spending ceilings, one for each minister, and the new aggregate target. These ceilings set the framework for the drafting of budget proposals in the various ministries. In effect, the ceilings delineate an expenditure block for each ministry, allowing it significant flexibility in arranging its budget proposals. Beyond this point, negotiations on the budget focus on accommodating new expenditures and cutback options for ministries that have difficulty keeping within the agreed limits.

Finland. The system of medium-term activity and financial plans adopted in the 1960s remained relatively unchanged until 1990 when a new system of ceilings was introduced, the timetable for medium-term planning was aligned with the timetable for budget preparation, and the time span was shortened to 1+3 years. The ceilings issued by the Cabinet – not the expenditure demands of ministries – now govern the budget process. Budget proposals stress the results to be achieved, not the expenditure items, which was the case in the past. The role of medium-term planning has been redirected to give continuity and background in ministerial and Cabinet decisions. The combined medium-term and budget timetable now has three major milestones: ceilings in February; budget proposals to the Ministry of Finance in May; and the Cabinet budget conference in August.

The new system of expenditure ceilings and the concurrent results-oriented approach to budgeting implies a far-reaching delegation of detailed expenditure decisions to the line ministries and the agencies themselves.

France. No multi-year budgeting process existed until recently, but certain expenditures (for example, defence and overseas provinces) are governed by multi-year legislation that largely determines the amounts to be included in the annual budget. For the first time in France, a five-year orientation law now specifies desired targets for the state budget. This has been an important innovation in efforts to control public finances through the establishment of a medium-term path for deficit reduction.

Formulation of the budget may be divided into four phases:

* Early each year, the Ministry of the Budget prepares a preliminary estimate of next year's expenditures, including both a projection for the current year and an estimate of likely new expenditure. On the basis of this estimate, the Prime Minister, together with the ministers for finance and for the budget, decides on budgetary policy for the upcoming year.

* The Prime Minister then issues "*lettres de cadrage*" to spending ministries in the spring explaining the general policy framework for budget preparation. The main activity during this "*phase de reconduction*" is the rolling forward of the budget for the current year by updating the figures for approved measures ("*mesures acquises*") and for "inescapable new measures" such as the financial consequences of new economic assumptions. The spending ministries submit their "*budget de reconduction*" to the Ministry of the Budget along with proposals for new measures, thereby initiating technical negotiations.

* In June, the Prime Minister issues "*lettres plafonds*" to each ministry, setting ceilings on total current and capital expenditures. These letters go into considerable detail on the measures accepted or required in the next budget. The spending ministries then submit budget proposals, and a second round of negotiations takes place, usually focusing on proposed initiatives and required cutbacks. Ministers are normally given considerable freedom to rearrange their budgets by cutting elsewhere to fund new expenditures.

* The final phase is the technical preparation of the budget to be presented to Parliament.

Germany. Preparation of the annual budget is guided by the medium-term financial plan that is presented to Parliament each year. Both the plan and the budget are developed in the light of the fiscal intentions of the *Länder* and local authorities, as expressed in the Financial Planning Council where all tiers of government are represented. Proposals made by the Council relating to annual nominal growth of total expenditure and net borrowing are the basis for the top-down planning of the budget and financial plan.

Estimates of future federal revenue in the medium-term plan are based on macroeconomic projections and assumptions. The plan also indicates the government's policy for federal budgetary balance, as well as for future expenditure in each of 40 large blocks. These blocks are aggregated from figures prepared in a bottom-up approach and agreed between the spending ministries and the Ministry of Finance (and approved by the Cabinet) in the same detail as those compiled for the budget. In projecting cash needs for the last three years of the planning period, some blocks include allowance for price increases (such as for indexed social expenditures and interest payments). An unallocated planning reserve is set aside in each of these three planning years for further price increases and new programmes, as well as a global provision for pay increases.

The most important purpose of the medium-term financial plan is to set priorities in line with the government's policies and to deter excessive demands on the budget. The detailed budget instructions issued by the finance ministry each year generally call for departments to keep expenditure bids within the upper limits laid down in the current financial plan. The finance ministry also provides special regulations concerning increases in current or administrative costs of departments.

Greece. Although there is no multi-year budget, each annual budget must be consistent with fiscal policy guidelines incorporated in the "Programme for the Convergence of the Economy" which aims at achieving the targets of the Maastricht agreement. Within this framework, preparation of the central government budget takes place in several stages. Early in the summer, the Ministry of Finance issues instructions to all ministries and prefectures for the next year's spending proposals. After approval by the relevant minister and review by the ministry's ordered expense office, the proposals are forwarded to the General Accounting Office which prepares and monitors the budget in collaboration with the general directorates in the Ministry of Finance. The General Accounting Office scrutinises proposals during the August-September period, and adjustments can be made by the Minister of Finance (in consultation with the Prime Minister) to keep expenditure growth within fiscal policy targets. After revenue forecasts are prepared, the Ministry of Finance briefs the government on the budget outlook, and decisions are taken on changes in fiscal policy. Parallel procedures pertain to formulation of the public investment budget but with two important differences. One is that the investment budget is prepared under the aegis of the Ministry of National Economy; the other is that the finance ministry must incorporate, without change, the recommended investment budget in the central government budget.

Ireland. Although there is no formal system of medium-term expenditure allocations, spending departments must forecast resource requirements three to four years ahead. These projections are rolled forward each year and provide input to medium-term economic and budgetary management.

Broad budgetary targets proposed by the Minister for Finance and adopted by the Cabinet provide the framework for negotiations between the Department of Finance and spending ministries and subsequently between ministers. After targets have been adopted, the Department of Finance issues guidelines setting forth the parameters for drawing up the next year's expenditure estimates. The Minister for Finance briefs the government and negotiates with colleagues – individually or in government – regarding the estimates for the next year. When agreed by the government, the detailed estimates are published in advance of the budget, though some final decisions are traditionally made on budget day.

Japan. There is no regular cycle of medium-term expenditure planning, though projections are sometimes used to assist preparation of the annual budget. Guidelines for the budget are decided by the Cabinet at the start of each cycle, in the June-July period. Ministries rely on these guidelines in submitting requests to the Ministry of Finance by the end of August, after which the finance ministry holds hearings and negotiates with spending ministries in hierarchical order, beginning with lower officials and proceeding, if appropriate, to ministerial level. Intensive "revival negotiations" often take place in late December shortly before the presentation of the budget, together with the Fiscal Investment and Loan Plan (FILP), to the Diet. These negotiations do not alter the expenditure totals set in the draft budget. If additional funds are agreed at this stage, they are drawn from unallotted financial resources.

Netherlands. The government maintains updated multi-year projections (MYP) which serve as a financial control for the Ministry of Finance. The MYP reflect expenditure projections for the budget year and the next four years based on policies agreed by the Cabinet, and include estimates sensitive to macroeconomic developments such as interest payments and unemployment benefits. At the start of the budget cycle, they represent the outcome of the last budget, adjusted for subsequent policy changes as well as changes flowing from re-estimates of existing policies and new economic assumptions. The MYP are rolled forward in an ongoing process; each change in budgetary developments results in a corresponding adjustment in the multi-year estimates.

With the MYP as a background, the Minister of Finance submits a "framework letter" to the Council of Ministers in March, thereby initiating formal preparation of the budget. The letter sets forth proposed allocations, including expenditure reductions, to various sectors. The letter may also spell out specific measures to achieve the sought cutbacks. The framework letter is discussed by the Cabinet which takes decisions in March-April. Detailed budgets are then prepared under rules that generally allow departments to substitute other proposals for those made by the Minister of Finance, provided that the budgetary targets are not affected. Intensive negotiations on draft budgets take place in May-June, initially between the Director General of the Budget and senior officials in the spending departments, followed, if issues remain unsettled, by bilateral talks at ministerial level. Expenditure decisions are finalised by the Council of Ministers in July, but further decisions may be made until the budget is submitted to Parliament in September.

New Zealand. The financial management reforms implemented pursuant to the Public Finance Act of 1989 have greatly altered all aspects of government budgeting. Budget decisions are organised around a "baseline" process in which departments are invited to submit draft budgets at two periods, usually October-November and February-March. These baselines are reviewed by ministers who make decisions as purchasers of outputs, on an accrual rather than a cash basis. The government believes that output budgets better inform ministers as to what is being achieved and enable them to judge whether the outputs meet priorities. In recent years, the baselines have been governed by rules which deny departments compensation for increases in input costs, require them to fund policy initiatives from reallocations within existing budgets, and permit extra funding only when it is demand-determined.

Norway. Preparation of the annual budget is initiated in February/March when the Cabinet approves preliminary expenditure ceilings for each ministry, as well as separate frames for policy initiatives. The ministries have the opportunity to propose adjustments. Final limits are decided by the Cabinet in May/June. The ministries then develop proposals within the agreed limits in the beginning of August. The Cabinet resolves unsettled matters in September, at which time final policies on taxes and economic issues are decided.

Portugal. Although the state budget is annual, it may include programmes or projects that entail expenditure over a number of years. The budget presents an indicative schedule of the programmes and projects included in the investment and expenditure plan (PIDDAC), with a time horizon of four years. The state budget also takes into account a reference framework drawn up by the government for the medium term. This framework is given in a finance ministry document known as QUANTUM ("National Adjustment Framework for Transition to Economic and Monetary Union") which sets out no-change and adjustment scenarios for the period 1991-95. The adjustment scenario aims at nominal convergence of the Portuguese economy to the European Community average within this five-year period by means of a fiscal consolidation that produces a sharp and swift reduction in the public sector deficit and sustained reduction in the public debt. The time path of the policy variables set forth in QUANTUM constitute a political guideline and frame of reference for drawing up the annual budget.

Spain. Multi-year planning, which had initially been designed to extend investment planning beyond the budget year, has given rise to multi-year budget instruments that include macroeconomic and budgetary scenarios. These scenarios treat the annual budget as the first step in a four-year process and provide a framework for analysing the objectives of public sector action and possible effects on the economy. Within this framework, the Ministry for Economic Affairs and Finance lays down guidelines for preparation of the budget. The Directorate General of the Budget then draws up corresponding instructions concerning the timetable and procedural requirements of the process. Three ministerial committees play significant roles in budget policy. The Functional Committee for the Budget offers proposals concerning the functional allocation of revenue and expenditure. The Programme Analysis Committee determines the financial requirements of expenditure programmes and ranks objectives according to the priorities laid down by the Functional Committee. The Public Investment Committee co-ordinates investment plans with the multi-year economic framework. After budget proposals have been submitted, the Cabinet may be involved in settling disputes between the Ministry for Economic Affairs and Finance and other ministries, and in approving the draft budget for submission to Parliament.

Sweden. Each spring, the government presents medium-term projections of revenue, expenditure, and the budget balance in the "*Langtidsbudgeten*". The aim of this medium-term budget is to show the financial consequences of existing decisions and commitments for the four-year period ahead. Its scope has been extended to include other levels of government and social security, and to show the financial implications of the public sector for the private sector. This document is neither a programme nor a forecast, but serves as a discussion document for Parliament whose comments influence the finance ministry's instructions at the start of the annual budget cycle.

These instructions are transmitted in a general circular to agencies in February, approximately 17 months before the start of the fiscal year. In addition, individualised circulars, addressing matters of particular concern to the relevant agency, are transmitted to agencies operating under three-year budget frames. The government experimented with a triennial budget system in the mid 1980s and, after several years of pilot testing, decided to implement the new system in all agencies. Each agency must undertake a probing assessment of its activities and performance at the start of its three-year cycle, reviewing what it accomplished in the previous period and setting forth its planned accomplishments for the next three years. This in-depth analysis is guided by a special circular which raises questions and asks for specific information concerning the agency's work and performance. In the intermediate years of the triennial cycle, agencies submit less-detailed budget requests provided that they abide by the spending and performance path laid out for them.

Turkey. Budgeting takes place within the framework of the Five-Year Development Plan submitted by the government to Parliament. The approved plan and annual programmes are binding on the public sector and indicative for the private sector. The sixth plan (for 1990-94) specifies targets for economic, social and cultural development. The plan also specifies ratios of total public expenditure to GDP.

The annual budget cycle begins in June, six months before the start of the fiscal year, with a budget message by the Prime Minister setting forth a broad statement of principles for the forthcoming budget. On the basis of technical instructions from the Ministry of Finance and Customs in June, ministries prepare detailed proposals for current expenditure. These are discussed with the Ministry of Finance and Customs over the next 2-3 months, culminating in decisions by the High Planning Council and the Prime Minister. A parallel process involving negotiations with the State Planning Organisation leads to the preparation of an investment budget.

United Kingdom. The annual public expenditure survey, introduced in the 1960s, sets plans for public spending over the next three years. The government's overall objective for public spending – to reduce it as a share of GDP over time – is set in terms of general government expenditure. But in order to insulate the public expenditure planning process from the effects of variation in the economic cycle, the government also defines a "new control total". This covers around 85% of general government expenditure but excludes cyclically related social security benefits and debt interest. At the start of each survey, the government sets firm ceilings for the new control total, designed to ensure that the government's public expenditure objectives are met. The aim of the survey is to allocate spending across programmes within these ceilings.

The survey begins by establishing the baselines agreed in the previous survey, if necessary incorporating classification changes or transfers of function between departments. Ministers in charge of spending departments then send to the Chief Secretary to the Treasury an assessment of the pressures on their baselines and the scope for offsetting savings. In the light of these submissions, the Chancellor and Chief Secretary report to the Cabinet in June and the Cabinet agrees new ceilings for the control total.

A sub-committee of Cabinet ministers, called the EDX, is then charged with allocating spending between departments within ceilings for the new control total. The EDX is chaired by the Chancellor of the Exchequer. Its decisions are informed by a series of bilateral meetings between the Chief Secretary and spending ministers, and ministers may also be invited to present their views to the EDX. When these discussions are complete, the EDX makes recommendations to the full Cabinet. Following agreement at the full Cabinet, the new plans are presented in the budget in November. The budget on 30 November 1993 was the first to combine the presentation of the new spending plans with proposals for changes in taxation. Soon after the budget, details of the new spending plans are published in greater detail in a series of departmental reports and a statistical supplement to the budget. The plans set for the year ahead are used as firm control totals for the forthcoming financing year.

United States. The President's budget submitted to Congress early each calendar year presents "baseline" projections of receipts, expenditures and the deficit, as well as projections reflecting the President's proposals. The Congressional Budget Office (CBO) issues its own baseline projections, which may differ from those of the administration and are used by Congress in formulating a "framework" budget resolution. Until 1990, this resolution spanned the next three years; since then, however, it has been expanded to five years. Because the multi-year baselines are critical in computing the budgetary impact of legislation, strong efforts have been made for both the President and Congress to rely on common assumptions. For the FY 1994 Budget, the first budget of the incoming Clinton administration, the President announced that his budget would be based on the macroeconomic assumptions of the CBO.

Federal departments begin work on the annual budget 18 or more months before the start of the fiscal year. Each department has internal procedures for assembling its requests, but these must be presented to the President's Office of Management and Budget (OMB) in a standard format. During the summer, the President promulgates general budget guidelines and planned ceilings to guide agencies in the preparation of their budgets. Agencies submit their requests in the fall, following which the OMB prepares "passbacks" which notify agencies of the amounts to be recommended in the President's budget. Agencies have a brief period during which they can appeal these passbacks either to the OMB or to other presidential officers. On occasion, an appeal is made to the President who has the final say on the budget submitted to Congress.

4. Parliamentary control

Legislative control of public expenditure is a fundamental principle of democratic government. There is no exception in the OECD area to the rule that a government may spend public funds only pursuant to legislative authorisation. But the manner in which spending is authorised and the actual role of the legislature in dictating or influencing budget policies varies among OECD member countries.

Annual appropriations are the traditional means of authorising public expenditure. Increasingly, however, parliaments also authorise expenditure in permanent or standing legislation. The changing composition of public expenditure – relatively more on transfer programmes and relatively less on operating expenses – has reduced the importance of annual appropriations (as a proportion of total expenditure) and given added prominence to spending authorised in standing legislation. Despite the decline of annually appropriated funds as a proportion of total expenditure, the vast expansion in the overall size of governments has meant a steady rise in the volume of appropriated funds.

The growth of government and related developments have wrought other changes in parliamentary practices. Democratic legislatures generally take a more independent stance on budgetary matters than they once did, though the degree to which they actually deviate from the government's estimates depends on legal practices, tradition, and the overall relationship between the executive and legislature. Nowadays, it is rarely a question of confidence if parliament exercises some independent judgment and appropriates more or less than the government requested. On the matter of parliamentary independence in the voting of appropriations, practices range from the United States where Congress makes numerous significant changes in the budget presented by the President, to the United Kingdom where supply is voted in the amount requested by the government. Parliamentary independence is frequently expressed in the establishment (or enlargement) of legislative budget staffs and in the strengthening of legislative audit functions.

At the same time that parliaments have become more active on budgetary matters, the growth of government has eroded some of their traditional expenditure controls. At one time, the pervasive practice was for the government to submit estimates in the form of "line items" – long lists of the resource inputs such as personnel, office supplies, utilities, and so on, to be purchased with public funds. Appropriations were often voted in the same detail, giving spending agencies little flexibility in using the resources provided to them. This form of detailed budgeting is still found in some countries (Germany, for example), but the general trend is to reduce the number of items on which expenditure is legislatively controlled and to vote appropriations in broad frames, blocks, or portfolios. In recent years, Australia and Finland have been among the OECD member countries joining this trend. Many countries have also loosened control over "virement", the transfer of funds between votes. The overall result is a shift from parliamentary to bureaucratic control.

The growth of government has also weakened the annuality of legislative control. At one time, parliament decided on the amount to be spent each year through annual appropriations. But annual appropriations are not an effective means of regulating demand-determined expenditure, nor are they effective in controlling expenditure on long-term commitments such as investment projects. Quite a few OECD member countries permit spending agencies to carry forward all or a portion of their appropriations to the next year or beyond. But despite the fact that annual appropriations may determine less than half of government spending in a particular year, parliaments retain annual control as one of their principal instruments for holding government agencies to account. But several countries that have embraced results budgeting have sought to devise means of combining annual appropriations with multi-year control mechanisms.

Belgium. The government budget is highly detailed, totalling about 4 000 pages and organised into four parts: *i)* the appropriation law setting forth aggregate amounts and authorisation of virement between certain items in the budget; *ii)* the appropriation table which is voted by Parliament and specifies the appropriations enacted by it; *iii)* the apportionment table which allocates appropriations to the organisations accountable for them; and *iv)* supporting notes which explain, sometimes in considerable detail, each appropriation contributing to a programme.

All expenditures are appropriated each year on a gross basis either as "split appropriations" which specify separate amounts for commitments and payments, or as "unsplit appropriations" which specify only a single amount. Split appropriations are used for multi-year construction projects and some defence procurement, with the commitments authorised at the start of the project and outlays voted as the commitments come due. When appropriations are voted on an unsplit basis, the unpaid commitments may be carried forward to the next year without further parliamentary authorisation to cover payments on unliquidated obligations.

Canada. The government's plans are presented to Parliament in the *Budget Speech* which specifies revenues, proposed tax changes, and aggregate expenditures, and the *Main Estimates* which detail the proposed expenditures. The *Main Estimates* consist of three parts: an overview of spending plans by policy sectors, economic category and department; the appropriations act and the estimates for each ministry, department and agency; and detailed departmental spending plans presented in a standardised format that describes programmes and their outputs and provides information on resources. The "Part III" expenditure plans take up more than 5 000 pages.

Appropriations are made in two forms: annual appropriations, based on the estimates presented in Parliament and covering about 35% of total expenditure, principally for operating costs and capital investments; and statutory appropriations for non-lapsing obligations such as debt interest charges, transfer payments and certain other special items. The latter are provided in separate acts of Parliament and do not have to be renewed each year. Estimates for annual appropriations must be for services requiring payment during the year. Only statutory appropriations authorise spending in future years. Nevertheless, agencies may enter into contracts involving future payments provided these are conditioned on the availability of future appropriations.

Finland. All expenditure, including entitlements, is voted annually in an appropriations bill divided into ministerial portfolios, subdivided by agency or function, and further subdivided by economic category. Expenditures are appropriated as gross amounts, except in the case of commercial enterprises which receive net appropriations. Parliament makes three types of appropriations: fixed annual amounts; authorisations such as for investment projects, which may be carried forward for up to three years; and appropriation estimates which may be exceeded with the consent of the Cabinet's Finance Committee. The last type is used for pay and most transfers, and accounts for approximately three-quarters of total expenditure. In making appropriations, Parliament may add to expenditure, provided the amount is offset through spending cuts or tax or borrowing increases so as to maintain budgetary balance.

The structure of appropriations has been altered by the introduction of results-oriented budgeting. The formerly separate items for salaries, other consumption, and equipment have been consolidated into a single item. Accordingly, there has been a steep decline in the number of expenditure items voted by Parliament. The number of expenditure items was less than 600 in the 1994 budget proposal, compared with more than 1 200 in 1989.

France. The draft appropriation bill presented to Parliament is accompanied by voluminous annexes (totalling about 10 000 pages) providing details about the particular measure concerned. The blue annexes classify expenditure by title, chapter and article, and provide information appropriate for each category. The titles are standard classifications used by all ministries, and differentiate operating expenditure, public intervention, investments and investment subsidies. The chapters are unique to each ministry – there were approximately 1 400 in a recent year – and are the level at which Parliament binds spending. The government is legally bound to apportion appropriations according to the annexed distribution by chapters, as modified by Parliament. Spending is further divided into articles – mostly organisational units or activities, which are the level at which the Ministry of Finance binds spending. There may also be breakdowns of spending by paragraphs and lines – detailed items of expenditure – but these are only for informational purposes.

All expenditures are voted annually on a gross basis and, unless expressly identified as estimated or provisional, are fixed amounts that cannot, in principle, be exceeded without prior authorisation by Parliament. Estimated appropriations, such as for debt service and social security, account for more than one-quarter of total expenditure and may be exceeded without further parliamentary authorisation as needed to settle legal obligations. Provisional appropriations are used for a small amount of expenditures that are difficult to estimate. These may be supplemented by drawing on a contingency reserve maintained by the Ministry of Finance. Appropriations are voted separately for "approved services" and "new measures"; the former are voted in the aggregate, the latter are divided into ministries and titles. In appropriating funds for capital expenditures, Parliament authorises both "commitments" which remain available for an unlimited period, and "outlays" which are, in principle, only for the budget but in practice may be carried forward almost automatically.

Sweden. The budget proposal submitted to Parliament consists of the draft appropriation bill and supporting material for each ministerial portfolio. Each portfolio is divided into "estimates" – about 800 for the central government – comprising an agency or a distinct investment or transfer programme. Explanatory notes for each estimate summarise what each agency has requested and the minister's response.

Expenditures are voted annually, with most non-tax revenues netted against expenditure. Appropriations may be fixed for a single year, authorisations which may be carried forward 2-3 years (or indefinitely for construction projects), or appropriation estimates which may be exceeded by decision of the Cabinet. The last type of appropriation comprises about 85% of total expenditure and is used for operating costs and most transfers.

United Kingdom. Details of individual departments' spending plans are given in 18 departmental reports and a statistical supplement published in the early spring. Departments have put a lot of effort into the development of useful performance information, which is reflected in the many indicators and targets included in the reports. Shortly before the start of the financial year, "supply estimates" are presented for voted expenditure and for non-public transfer payments. For each departmental portfolio, the supply estimates indicate whether the vote is a cash limit and define the "ambit" of the vote – that is, the purpose to which expenditure will be put, the net amount and the department accountable. This information is reproduced in the appropriation act. The Treasury has (in 1993) put proposals to Parliament which are intended to improve the coherence of the supply estimates and their integration with the information in departmental reports.

Voted expenditures cover about half of total expenditure and are authorised annually. Parliament also authorises expenditure for "standing services", non-lapsing authorisations for debt service and certain other payments. Parliament also enacts two or more supplementary appropriations each year, with any additional spending drawn from the unallocated reserve or offset by reductions in other programmes.

5. Expenditure monitoring and control

As a plan of expenditure for the period ahead, the budget is rarely implemented in exactly the form that it was prepared or approved by the legislature. Changes intrude, whether because of shifting economic or political conditions or because of numerous small adjustments in the details of expenditure. Yet as the authorised plan of expenditure, the budget must be put into effect with due regard to the commitments or expectations established by it and to the rules and limits enacted by parliament. Implementing the budget thus requires a balance between adaptation to changing circumstances on the one hand and adherence to statutory and other strictures on the other. How this balance is struck varies greatly among OECD member countries.

In all countries, there is provision for supplementation of expenditure, whether through additional appropriations or the transfer of voted funds from one use to another. In all, also, funds may be spent only as authorised by law and (with some exceptions) only up to authorised amounts. In most, concern about budget deficits and a sense of fiscal constraint have strengthened emphasis on adjusting to unanticipated needs by drawing on available reserves or by reallocating resources rather than by going to parliament for additional funds. The United Kingdom and some other Commonwealth countries have relied on cash limits as a means of compelling spending institutions to make do with planned resources. The Netherlands has emphasised stringent rules of budget discipline that spell out how spending overruns are to be compensated. The United States has devised sequestration procedures for the automatic cancellation of resources if certain budget targets are breached.

Monitoring procedures have also gained prominence in many countries, propelled by advances in computerisation and in information processing capabilities. Many countries now regularly match the spending outturn against the plan, so that appropriate and timely corrections may be made when variances emerge. In some countries (New Zealand and the United States, for example), there is closer linkage of budgeting and accounting systems, not only to ensure that the two are on a consistent and uniform basis, but also to sensitise managers to the financial implications of their actions.

Somewhat different monitoring arrangements are in place for operating expenditure and transfer payments. The former are likely to be cash-limited or require that offsetting savings be realised to pay for overruns. In these cases, monitoring is an instrument of expenditure control. It gives spending agencies and central authorities early warning as to the steps needed to avert or compensate overruns. The latter, however, tend to be open-ended, and the main purpose of monitoring is informational, to obtain early indication as to whether expenditure plans are on track. If they are not, supplementation will usually be automatic (no parliamentary action is needed) or routine (parliamentary authorisation will come in due course).

This distinction between operating expenditure (variously known as administrative expenditure or running costs) and transfer payments (variously known as entitlements, mandatory expenditure or demand-led expenditure) has recently become more marked in some countries than was previously the case. Denmark is a notable exception to this trend, for it now combines both types of expenditure in the "blocks" used to control spending in ministries. In the United States, by contrast, the Budget Enforcement Act of 1990 established very different rules for controlling discretionary and other expenditure.

In the OECD community, there is a sharp difference in the control of administrative costs between those governments that exercise centralised, *ex ante* control and those that have delegated control to the spending departments. The first camp is headed by France and Germany, joined by other countries (Belgium, Greece, Turkey) that require pre-authorisation of administrative expenditure, such as for personnel and procurement, by inspectors posted in spending ministries but answerable to the Ministry of Finance. This form of control was once the near-universal practice in democratic regimes, and it continues to be used in various countries to ensure that spending is legal and prudent. This form of control is associated with itemised budgets and appropriations as well as relatively large finance ministries.

The second group is headed by the United Kingdom and other Commonwealth countries and several Nordic countries (Denmark, Finland and Sweden). At one time, the governments in these countries exercised centralised control over spending actions. Devolution of control has come in two waves: the first in the 1960s when the growth of government impelled some finance ministries to cede some authority to spending departments, the second in the 1980s (and continuing into the 1990s) when the drive for efficiency and accountability in public expenditure impelled countries to delegate responsibility for spending within agreed budgets to departmental managers. The logic of these devolutions is more fully discussed in Section 8 below on improving managerial accountability and programme effectiveness.

Australia. In line with the medium-term planning strategy and to allow greater flexibility and control of resources for programme managers, significant devolution of administrative costs to spending agencies has occurred. The running costs arrangements give agencies flexibility to move administrative funds from one activity to another and to delay their usage to the following financial period or bring them forward from future appropriations. The *quid pro quo* for enhanced flexibility is that the amounts are cash-limited, an efficiency return is provided to the government and agencies are accountable directly to Parliament for delivering programme outcomes.

These arrangements are backed by reliable, up-to-date information on actual spending. The Department of Finance provides a computerised accounting service for all departments. Department of Finance officials can access it to a certain level of detail, while each department specifies system requirements for its own monitoring and management purposes. The Department of Finance compares actual spending against budget estimates and reports on significant variances to the finance minister.

Supplementation of appropriations for unforeseen expenditure can be provided through a special fund appropriated to the finance minister (if certain conditions are met) or by additional appropriations in the second half of the year. Normally, departments seeking supplementation are required to offer savings in other areas, to the maximum extent practicable.

Austria. The Ministry of Finance has full control of the use of appropriated funds. Pre-authorisation by the ministry is required for significant discretionary expenditures, as well as for subsidies and capital expenditure. The Ministry of Finance also controls commitments and personnel costs. These controls are maintained via monthly allotments and reports. Spending ministries submit their financing needs for finance ministry approval at the start of each month, and they report to the Ministry of Finance on a monthly basis on funds previously spent. Increases or shifts in expenditure require parliamentary approval, but the Ministry of Finance has limited authority to increase or shift authorised expenditures, provided that additional revenues are available.

Belgium. Spending ministries generally have limited discretion in using appropriated funds. Appropriations are divided into about 3 000 allotments, the level at which the Ministry of Finance controls expenditures. Finance ministry approval is required for virement between allotments, but virement is not permitted between allotments for different objects – for example, between pay and other expenditure objects – even in the same programme.

To enforce *ex ante* controls, the Ministry of Finance has inspectors of finance accredited to each spending department. These inspectors closely monitor departmental operations and have access to all files and data. Although they only advise the spending ministries, the inspectors play an influential role in budget implementation. All purchases and subsidies above threshold amounts must be submitted to the inspectors for review. Advice by inspectors may be appealed to the Ministry of Finance. In addition to these controls, all commitments must have a "visa" issued by commitment controllers (who work in the various ministries but are accountable to the Ministry of Finance) certifying that sufficient funds are available.

The government generally has limited scope to reallocate funds. In addition to the constraints imposed by the appropriations and allotment structures, departments are further limited by centralised personnel and procurement procedures.

Canada. Spending departments cannot switch resources between parliamentary votes without seeking Parliament's approval, but may reallocate resources across activities within a vote. These delegated authorities are subject to certain restrictions, such as the use of funds earmarked for essential capital which cannot be decreased by discretionary departmental actions. Commencing with the 1993/94 fiscal year, the federal government has introduced an operating budget (running cost) regime for managing resources dedicated to programme delivery. With the introduction of this regime, central control and monitoring will be significantly reduced. For example, separate controls and reporting on labour consumption (person-years controls) are being eliminated, along with Treasury Board controls on funds earmarked for salary expenditures.

The budgetary system prescribes annual reviews of departmental multi-year operational plans which put under scrutiny input and activity levels. There are no provisions for spending departments to report on actual expenditures to the budget office unless a department submits a request for supplementary funding, in which case resource limits and the use of resources are analysed to determine whether the additional funds should be recommended. In certain cases, frozen allotments (portion of a vote) are established by the Treasury Board, even though the funding has been voted. Such allotments are only released upon satisfaction of conditions established by the Treasury Board.

Denmark. When Parliament votes an appropriation, it delegates authority to spend to the minister concerned. Reforms during the 1980s increased the managerial responsibility of spending departments and reduced the number of items for which specific finance ministry and parliamentary approval is required. The Ministry of Finance runs a computerised paying and accounting service from which monthly data on payments are drawn. However, there is no *ex ante* central control of the payment profile over the course of the year. The formal monitoring arrangement since 1984 is that each ministry reports to the Ministry of Finance three times during the year on how actual spending has conformed to – or deviated from – the agreed spending "frame". If overruns are envisioned, the responsible minister is required to propose means of offsetting the overruns, including possible legislative changes. In practice, contact between the Ministry of Finance and spending departments is continuous, and the two sides discuss the scope of remedial action whenever it is necessary.

Finland. A cash management system in use since the late 1960s was upgraded in 1991 to an online computer system. The new system offers tools for agencies, the Treasury, and the Ministry of Finance to plan their cash transactions more easily and accurately than before.

The traditional *ex ante* financial controls have been reformed, so they are no longer so detailed and input-oriented but cover important legislation, decrees and decisions that affect expenditure in future years, as well as overdrafts of estimated appropriations. The time span of transferable "reservations appropriations" has been shortened to one plus two years, and their volume has decreased since the introduction of a new authorisations system that allows agencies to make commitments whose outlays are disbursed according to a cash outlay plan.

France. The Ministry for the Budget maintains detailed control over spending. It has "*contrôleurs financiers*" accredited to each ministry. All proposed commitments are submitted to the relevant controller who checks them for compliance (authority to commit, accuracy of calculations, correctness of account, accordance with financial management rules) and availability of uncommitted balances. Each spending ministry is responsible in an accounting sense for the propriety of its financial transactions, but approval by its controller is required before payment is made. The controller can refuse to authorise a commitment only for reasons of legality, but can postpone his/her decision if he/she finds the commitment inadvisable, thereby forcing a dialogue with the minister concerned. There is no formal system of appeal of the controller's decisions.

The government has considerable freedom to move funds between different chapters of a ministry's appropriations by means of two procedures: transfer and virement. The Ministry of Finance may transfer funds among chapters as long as the character of the expenditure is not changed. However, transfers are precluded between current and capital expenditures, between personnel and other operating expenditures, and between various types of personnel expenditures. Shifts may also be made between ministries if the character of the expenditure is not altered. Furthermore, the Prime Minister may, by decree, authorise that appropriations be vired between chapters in the same ministry, even if the character of expenditure is changed. The vired amount cannot exceed 10% of the original appropriation. These transfer and virement authorities are exercised centrally. Spending ministries have limited scope to make reallocations without approval of the financial controller.

Germany. A department's appropriation is specified in great detail in the budget law and, apart from specially designated expenditure, there is no departmental authority to transfer funds from one item to another. Payments connected to the federal budget are processed through regional finance offices operated by the Ministry of Finance which has sole responsibility for maintaining records and preparing each agency's annual accounts. These offices provide monthly analyses of actual spending to the Ministry of Finance, which also obtains reports from departments of probable needs over the next three months. The execution of the budget is thus continuously monitored and controlled.

When expenditures are likely to exceed the authorised total, the finance minister may make commitments or expenditures subject to his/her approval by blocks of expenditure, after having consulted the competent ministers. If the need for additional expenditure is deemed to be unforeseen and unavoidable, and supplementary appropriations cannot be enacted in time or Parliament has waived the requirement for supplementary appropriations, the Ministry of Finance can authorise excess and/or extrabudgetary expenditure. Moreover, the government has legal authority to authorise additional expenditure to counter a recession without going through supplementary budget procedures. Conversely, the Ministry of Finance can block expenditures or commitments in order to avoid overheating of the economy. Parliament must be informed of important departures from the budget plan, including excess and extrabudgetary expenditure.

Greece. The Ministry of Finance has quarterly and monthly means of regulating expenditure. It decides on the percentage of certain annual appropriations that are to be spent in each quarter of the year, and determines the amounts that may be spent each month for certain categories of spending. Unspent balances lapse at the end of the year and are not transferred to the next year's budget. However, under certain circumstances, they may be used to cover overruns in expenditure.

Ireland. Public expenditure may only be undertaken with the authority of Parliament given either in the annual appropriation act or in specific enabling legislation. In addition, it requires the sanction of the Minister for Finance which may be specific (for once-off expenditures) or delegated. In practice, authority for expenditure on continuing current programmes, which constitute the vast bulk of expenditure, is delegated to spending ministries subject to conditions and regulations governing their operations. Spending under delegated authority may not exceed overall cash limits specified in the annual supply estimates. Expenditures not having the sanction of the Minister for Finance cannot be charged against money voted by Parliament. If commitments lack this authority, the Department of Finance may withhold sanction if it determines that they should not have been incurred.

Each department prepares a profile of monthly expenditure (capital and current) at the start of the year. Once agreed, this profile is used as a set of monthly cash limits, so that funds underspent in one month cannot be automatically reclaimed in a later month. A department can spend more than planned in a month only with the express approval of the Minister for Finance. Approved overspending in one month must be offset by savings later in the year. Unspent funds cannot be carried forward to the next year, but departments operating under the "Administrative Budget Initiative" launched in 1991 may have some savings in one year reallocated to it in the next year.

Japan. Each department is required to obtain Ministry of Finance approval of its plans for incurring liabilities (contracts and other actions that lead to government expenditure). In addition, detailed profiles of expected disbursements by each departmental disbursing officer must be approved by the Ministry of Finance before the start of each quarter. The approval of the finance minister is needed for a department to transfer funds from one line item to another in its budget. The finance minister can also call for *ad hoc* reports on actual and prospective spending, and can recommend corrective action that is deemed necessary.

Netherlands. The Ministry of Finance delegates substantial authority to spending ministries, but retains the right to specify the items for which liabilities may not be incurred without its advance permission. During the year, departments operate under rules of strict budget policy that aim to keep spending within the intended totals. The rules prescribe how overspending is to be compensated by savings. During the year, also, periodic meetings are held between the Ministry of Finance and each spending ministry about possible deviations from planned expenditure. In most instances, problems are resolved without parliamentary involvement by shifting balances between sub-items or, under strict conditions (and to a limited extent), by shifting from one vote to another.

Norway. The appropriation and budget systems were changed beginning in 1986 to give spending institutions more discretion and flexibility in the use of appropriated funds. These reforms replaced a detailed control system with performance-based incentives to improve cost effectiveness.

Before the start of the year, each ministry issues an allotment letter to its subordinate agencies informing them of the resources at their disposal. Agencies are authorised to spend within their allotments, but they must regularly report on expenditure trends to their respective ministries. The government (and for minor amounts, the Ministry of Finance) has been authorised by Parliament to increase expenditures by up to a preset amount.

Portugal. The Directorate-General for Public Accounts is responsible for monitoring implementation of the budget and, for this purpose, compiles monthly information on expenditures. The Directorate-General calculates safety limits for various categories of expenditure. If these are breached, it informs the Secretary of State for the Budget to ensure that appropriate measures are taken.

Certain changes to the budget, such as transfers between chapters in the organic classification or between functional categories, are within the competence of Parliament. But the budget law allows the Ministry of Finance to transfer funds from the provisional allocation set aside to cover essential expenditure that was not foreseen when the budget was drawn up. Transfers between fiscal years may be undertaken, if provided for in the budget law, for investment expenditures and autonomous funds and departments. These funds and departments may implement budget changes that do not involve increased debt financing or increased transfers from the administrative sector.

Sweden. Virtually all executive activities are entrusted to independent agencies which carry out the policies developed by the ministries. After the budget is approved by Parliament, the government issues allotment letters to the agencies, specifying the conditions under which appropriated funds are to be spent. Each agency's letter spells out the amount and type of appropriation, the purposes or activities for which the funds can be used, a budget specification splitting relevant appropriations into allotments ("*anslagsposter*"), specific limits or conditions – such as those pertaining to pay – and instructions concerning financial management and accounting. The allotment letter may reserve a portion of the appropriation for further Cabinet decision. Agencies have considerable freedom in spending allotted funds. There are no general requirements for pre-authorisation by the Ministry of Finance or Cabinet, but agencies must keep within general guidelines on procurement, personnel and other administrative matters.

Because each agency is normally funded out of a single appropriation, there is limited scope for reallocation among agencies. Within each agency, however, there is substantial scope for shifting among activities, although there are restrictions on shifting between programme and administrative expenditure. Agencies operating under three-year budget frames are permitted to carry over unspent funds to the next year or draw in advance on a limited portion of the next year's appropriation.

Agency use of funds is monitored by external auditing bodies. The National Audit Bureau provides the government with regular assessments of how the budget is developing against plans. This information is used both to manage the government's cash flow and to check budget outcomes against appropriated funds.

Turkey. The Ministry of Finance is empowered to regulate spending throughout the fiscal year. Shortly after the approval of the budget by Parliament, the Ministry of Finance issues a circular to all agencies stating the main principles governing commitments of funds and the maximum percentage of appropriations to be released during the first six months of the year. Another circular, covering the second half of the year, is issued in June. The principles and percentages of the apportionments depend on general economic conditions, recent trends in revenue and expenditure, the need to spread current expenditure throughout the year, and the type of activities concerned. In addition, there is a separate control on the rate of outlays. The Ministry of Finance also controls commitments in current and future years.

Inasmuch as Parliament appropriates funds at the programme level, its approval is required to transfer between programmes. However, transfers among items within the same programme may be authorised by the Ministry of Finance. The transfer of investment expenditure within the same programme requires the consent of both the State Planning Organisation and the Ministry of Finance. Unused funds lapse at the end of the fiscal year.

United Kingdom. When Parliament votes appropriations, it delegates to the Treasury the authority to sanction payments from the vote in question. The Treasury in turn delegates authority to the spending departments in respect of most routine expenditures. This delegation is accompanied by arrangements regarding the information on expenditure that is to be provided by departments.

At the start of the financial year, each department provides profiles of expected spending; as the year progresses, they report actual spending through the Paymaster General's Office, which in turn provides monthly reports to the Treasury. These reports assist the Treasury in managing funds and assessing trends in total public expenditure. Care is taken not to dilute the responsibilities of spending departments to stay within cash limits and to provide early warning of likely variances in demand-led spending from agreed profiles.

Within each department, the principal finance officer (appointed by the permanent secretary with the approval of the Treasury) is responsible for overseeing the management of expenditure. The "Financial Management Initiative" gave departments greater discretion in managing running costs and made them accountable for outputs and results. Building on this initiative, the "Next Steps" initiative launched in 1988 extends the devolution of authority from departments to their constituent agencies. Each "Next Steps" agency has a chief executive who also serves as its accounting officer and is responsible to the competent minister for the performance of the agency.

United States. Appropriations voted by Congress are not directly concerned with outlays or cash spending. Rather, they provide authority to enter into obligations that will result in outlays during either the current or future fiscal year(s). Outlays during a year may therefore be payment for obligations incurred in either prior years or the same years. The budget contains estimates of the outlays expected to ensue during the fiscal year to which it pertains, but these estimates are not cash-limited and may be exceeded by actual payments.

After appropriations have been enacted, the Office of Management and Budget (OMB) apportions budget authority – authority to enter into obligations – to each agency, often by quarters of the year but sometimes for the entire year, or by activities to minimise the need for supplemental appropriations. A single apportionment is made for each of the approximately 1 100 budget accounts and for each of the various funds in the budget. Once budget authority has been apportioned, the responsibility for spending within the budget and for authorised purposes rests with the spending agency. The Chief Financial Officers Act of 1990 established a chief financial officer in the 23 largest federal departments and agencies and assigned this official broad responsibility for integrating budgeting with other accounting and financial management responsibilities.

Congress has established impoundment procedures governing instances in which appropriated funds are withheld from obligation or expenditure. These procedures distinguish between deferrals which delay the use of funds and are only permitted for routine management purposes, and rescissions which cancel previous appropriations. For both rescissions and deferrals, the President must notify Congress of his action. Rescissions take effect only upon the enactment of legislation by Congress.

Congressional approval is required for the transfer of funds between appropriation accounts. Shifts within the same account – known as reprogramming – may be made under procedures spelled out by the relevant congressional committee. Once funds have been obligated, they may be carried over to future years. Unobligated funds may be carried over only if they have been appropriated on a "no-year" basis or for a period beyond the fiscal year.

6. Budgetary reserves

All countries make provision, within their overall expenditure targets, for unexpected requirements during the year. Some require spending departments to return to parliament or the finance ministry to obtain additional funds or re-programme previously provided resources. Others give spending departments considerable latitude in responding to unanticipated needs. One of the more widely used methods is to establish an unallocated reserve that may be drawn upon as needed. Governments, with more or less rigour, embrace the view that it is the responsibility of spending departments to stay within the borders of their allocated budget, and that access to central reserves should be a last resort.

Different country practices indicate that central reserves are much more commonplace than departmental reserves, if only because the former enable the budget office to drive harder bargains. The United Kingdom and Canada have moved away from departmental reserves in favour of a central pool of unallocated resources. The United Kingdom Treasury concluded that departmental reserves weaken the government's ability to assess competing claims across the whole range of programmes. For its part, Canada simplified and centralised its Policy and Expenditure Management System by shifting from envelope-specific to government-wide reserves. Central reserves have one notable drawback: they may tempt departments to spend funds with less care than they might if the reserves were not available. Governments have sought to mitigate their danger through financial management reforms designed to hold managers accountable for actions and results. These reforms give departments more flexibility in the use of funds on condition that they stay within agreed limits.

Where unallocated reserves are centrally maintained, the budget office (or finance ministry) will likely play a role in their distribution. In Australia, an "Advance to the Minister for Finance" is appropriated which may be utilised at the minister's discretion upon application by spending departments meeting the "urgent and unforeseen" or "urgent and in error" criteria. In addition, a provision for running costs borrowings is available for expenditure on running costs as long as funds are subsequently repaid to the budget by the relevant agency. In Canada, the contingency vote is used to adjust the pay bill for unbudgeted increases. In Italy, the legislature votes reserves totalling 8-10% of total spending, to meet the cost of new programmes and/or cost overruns on established programmes. In Turkey, the Ministry of Finance and Customs has custody of funds for use in emergencies.

There are alternatives to a formal reserve. Since 1980, Japan has operated according to the principle of "scrap and build" which requires that new programmes be financed out of savings in old ones. In the United States, the President may propose supplemental appropriations for needs not provided in the regular appropriations. But the current practice is to require agencies to absorb the cost of unbudgeted pay increases, and not to finance them through supplemental funds.

Austria. The annual budget does not provide a general contingency reserve, but token funds may be set aside for a portion of the cost of future pay increases. The budget also provides for carrying forward unspent balances, usually for capital projects. In addition, the budget laws give the government some scope for overspending and permit the Minister of Finance to activate a contingency budget in case of certain economic problems. During implementation of the budget, the finance ministry closely monitors spending rates and freezes a portion of appropriations to serve as a reserve for guarding against over-expenditure. This reserve gives the finance ministry room to manoeuvre to deal with unexpected or unbudgeted costs such as pay increases. Inter-year reserves, most commonly for capital projects, and "earmarked" reserves for expenditures financed by hypothecated revenues are controlled by the Ministry of Finance which regulates withdrawals.

Canada. The Policy and Expenditure Management System (PEMS), established in 1979, involved the preparation of a multi-year fiscal plan which specified annual spending limits or "envelopes" for each of the government policy sectors. Each sector contained a number of programmes linked in terms of their policy objectives. There was a policy reserve within each envelope to fund new or enriched programmes and a centrally managed operating reserve to respond to contingencies associated with the existing policy framework. The reserves initially totalled about 6% of planned outlays, but by 1986/87 this had been reduced to less than 3%.

By the mid 1980s, PEMS had become rule-burdened and bureaucratic. This was largely due to the fact that PEMS with its original policy envelopes fostered incrementalism, while concern was growing over the debt and deficits. In 1984, the government fundamentally changed the PEMS system by abolishing the ministries of state – the secretariats to the sectoral policy committees. This had the effect of strengthening the influence of the Privy Council Office and the Department of Finance.

By the late 1980s, the amount allocated to envelopes for new policy initiatives approximated 1% of planned expenditure. Growing pressures to reduce the reserves, coupled with various expenditure reduction measures, led to frustrations as ministers competed for increasingly limited resources. At the same time, special-purpose contingencies provided centrally by the Minister of Finance became more common as the government restricted its attention to a few key government priority areas. With the approval of the Cabinet Committee on Priorities and Planning, resources would be earmarked in the framework for key policy initiatives. Decision making became more centralised.

In 1989, the government abandoned the policy envelopes and re-organised the Cabinet structure. This re-organisation, while increasing the number of Cabinet committees, did away with the "policy envelopes" and mandated the policy committees to "concentrate on policy" as opposed to getting bound up in transaction issues. Authority to authorise new expenditures was restricted to the Cabinet Committee on Priorities and Planning (P&P) in the case of new policy initiatives. The Treasury Board would have authority in the case of the operating reserve. The reserves that remained were a central policy reserve managed by P&P, an operating reserve and a reserve for statutory overruns. The latter reserve serves as a contingency for incremental requirements arising from changes in the demographic or economic assumptions underlying forecasts in statutory payments.

The centralisation of the expenditure management decision process is consistent with the increasing focus on expenditures as the mechanism for addressing deficit concerns, in particular the mid-term strategy of reducing expenditures as a percentage of GDP.

Netherlands. The annual budget presented to Parliament includes a central allowance for pay and price increases based on inflation forecasts issued by the Central Planning Bureau. The Ministry of Finance allocates sums to departments in compiling the "spring memorandum" early in the new financial year. These distributions are partly automatic and partly discretionary, and spending departments may have to absorb some cost increases within their cash limits. These cash limits are enforced by "rules of stringent budget policy" which govern the manner in which compensating cuts or savings are produced to avoid or minimise net additional expenditure. The basic rule is that offsets are to be sought in the department responsible for the over-expenditure. To assure that this is feasible, some departments withhold a portion of their funds when sub-allocating them to subordinate organisational units. When compensatory cuts are not found, general compensation – on the basis of either *ad hoc* decisions or formula – may be necessary. Although the rules of stringent budget policy have not prevented spending outturns from exceeding the budget, they have comported with the emphasis on collective decisions in the Dutch style of coalition governments.

United Kingdom. The annual public expenditure plans include an unallocated reserve within the planning total for each of three forward years. The purpose of the reserve is to ensure that spending above departmental plans – whether for programme initiatives, policy changes, unforeseen events, or revised estimates – is contained within the planning totals. The level of reserves is normally higher for the later years of the planning cycle than for the year immediately ahead. In the cycle from 1989/90 to 1991/92, the reserves were 2% in the first year, rising to 5-6% in the final year.

For the first year, the planning total becomes a cash limit, and the reserve is the last line of defence in preventing over-expenditure. All additional spending is charged to the reserve, while net savings are credited to it. The reserve is charged for excess spending by departments, excesses in demand-led programmes such as social security, and discretionary increases allowed by the Treasury. There are standing procedures for bids on the reserves which may be made by departments only after considering whether the excess can be offset by reductions in other areas or, if appropriate, by additional receipts. Within the Treasury, claims on the reserve normally are decided at ministerial level. The Treasury monitors the status of the reserve throughout the year, along with the projected outturn for public expenditure. If a claim on reserves is accepted for spending financed by parliamentary vote, the Treasury will present a supplementary estimate and may also have to seek adjustments in cash limits.

Future-year reserves function as a cushion in the planning process, not as an operational control. It is typical for a portion of these reserves to be allocated as the years to which they apply draw near.

7. Budgeting for personnel

Public sector employment has broad economic and budgetary implications. Throughout the period 1960-82, government employment growth in the OECD area exceeded employment growth in the private sector. By the early 1980s, governments in most OECD member countries employed between 15% and 22% of all workers, and their wage bill ranged between 10% and 14% of GDP. The size and cost of public employment inevitably sharpened the interest of budget organisations in personnel policies and personnel expenditures, especially during the 1980s when restrictive fiscal postures were common. Controlling personnel was seen as an opportunity to improve budgetary balance while realising efficiency gains in the public sector.

Most of the instruments for controlling personnel – classification, recruitment, etc. – are not in the hands of the budget office. Among those concerning which budget officials may have a say, wage rates and personnel levels are the most prominent. Many governments have adopted specific targets with respect to aggregate personnel levels, either as a means of downsizing the civil service or constraining its further growth, or as an indirect means of forcing efficiency gains. These global limits are most likely to be applied to central government departments, with state enterprises exempted and certain other categories (such as defence forces) separately controlled. In some countries (Denmark and Iceland), agencies carrying out business activities are budgeted on a net expenditure basis which frees them from personnel controls.

Although personnel controls vary among countries, several patterns emerge. Some countries limit only the total number of positions while others also base controls on salary level or rank. Personnel targets are usually expressed in full-time equivalents or person-years. In general, personnel controls are exercised in the framework of, or parallel to, the annual budget process. Some countries have multi-year targets that aim to steadily reduce staffing levels over a period of years. Germany, Japan, the United Kingdom and the United States are among the countries that have experienced a progressive decline in central government employment over the past decade.

Personnel expenditure is generally monitored and controlled on the same basis as other expenditure, with parliamentary approval required if appropriations are exceeded. Some countries have special personnel monitoring and control systems in place, with periodic reports on staffing, personnel expenditures and related matters. Some flexibility in the use of personnel resources is prevalent in many countries, either by way of shifting among positions during the year, or transferring unused personnel expenditure to purchases of goods and services. Shifts from operating expenditure to personnel tend to be restricted, however, though countries that have undertaken ambitious financial management initiatives (New Zealand and the United Kingdom, for example) may provide more scope for redeploying resources, as deemed appropriate by managers, within approved budget limits. Additional flexibility may be available by drawing on personnel reserves and positions set aside for allocation during the year.

Australia. There are no longer any general personnel controls imposed on departments and agencies. Instead, a cash-limited system has been provided: the running costs arrangements, whereby agency managers have discretion over numbers and levels of staff, subject to service-wide classification standards. Parliament approves changes to running costs budgets, but does not act on the detailed staffing levels. The government does retain some specific controls over the number and level of senior executive staffing.

Canada. Prior to the 1993/94 financial year, person-year controls were applied to full and part-time employment and were imposed on virtually all departments, though military staff and Crown corporations were not covered. Person-year levels are established for each "programme", which generally corresponds to an entire agency in small departments and to a major organisational unit in larger ones. Person-year controls were discontinued as of 1993/94, with the government-wide introduction of operating budgets. The Treasury Board controls the creation and staffing of positions through "target executive count" controls. This system provides each department a base number of approved positions at the senior management and executive levels. Departments are allowed a "flexibility factor" of 1% above this base to accommodate special situations.

Denmark. The personnel is controlled by means of multi-year limits on total pay including pension costs. Commercial enterprises and agencies which perform secondary business activities on a net expenditure basis are not subject to these controls. The Budget Department is responsible for total government personnel and the staffing levels of ministries. Within the Budget Department, the same staff handle personnel controls and the expenditure budget of the respective ministries. During budget formulation, the Budget Department exercises control by means of multi-year limits on total pay. These limits are confirmed by the Cabinet at the same time it sets ministerial spending limits.

Within the limits, ministers are free to set staffing levels of the various agencies and institutions. But more detailed central control is exercised by the Budget Department over changes in management positions. An annex to the finance bill sets forth, for each agency and institution, total person-years for the budget year and the next three years, at each management level.

Finland. According to law reforms enacted in 1992, the agencies required to budget for results were entrusted with the power to establish, change and abolish positions for their personnel. Remuneration for the personnel of these agencies is budgeted under their running costs appropriations. Positions and the necessary funding may be transferred from one agency to another subject to the approval of the line ministry concerned, and between administrative branches of ministries by a Cabinet decision. Details of the 1 300 most senior positions (of which 1 000 constitute judges) are required to be listed in the budget.

The numbers of personnel are regulated by ceilings issued in the annual budget process. On the basis of these ceilings, grand totals for personnel numbers are decided in the annual budget for the administrative branches of all ministries. The ceilings have also been used as an instrument to reduce personnel numbers. The Cabinet decided on 30 April 1991 to cut the number of personnel remunerated from the budget by 5% (6 700 positions) over the period to 1996.

Germany. A single personnel structure covers the entire public service in the Federal Republic, including central, regional and local administration. It also covers research and educational institutions, hospitals, and various state enterprises. A parallel system covers the armed forces. The federal budget approved by Parliament lists authorised posts. It also sets forth personnel allocations to administrative units, but does not assign staff to specific programmes. Changes in the number and grade of staff require the approval of both the federal government and Parliament. New staff cannot be added unless authorised posts are open, even if funds are available. Conversely, the Ministry of Finance may provide funds from a special reserve to enable agencies to fill authorised posts. These rules generally apply to permanent staff, not to temporary employees.

The personnel and expenditure budgets are closely co-ordinated. The same administrative entities are involved in each case and the same procedures are applied. An important feature of the government's policy of consolidation is not to allow personnel levels to increase. When an increase in staffing levels is clearly necessary, attempts are made to find offsetting reductions elsewhere. Other means of restraining staff size are to require proportionate cutbacks in the number of posts by administrative entities or to approve new positions on the condition that they lapse after a specified number of years. Departments are generally free to manage posts as they see fit. The personnel budget is subject to verification by the Federal Audit Office in the same manner as the expenditure budget.

Iceland. Personnel control is the responsibility of the same Bureau of the Budget staff that handle the expenditure budgets of the respective ministries. The Personnel Committee (chaired by the Director of the Budget, with representatives from Parliament and the Ministry of Finance) formally authorises new positions and the transfer of positions between organisations. The budget submitted to Parliament contains information on staffing, but Parliament does not vote on personnel limits or targets. There is relatively little control on personnel usage during the year as long as an organisation's net expenditure stays within the limits set in the budget. Hence, with the exception of positions at the highest policy and management levels, organisations may make in-year adjustments without consulting the Bureau of the Budget. But in filling permanent positions, the responsible department must certify that the necessary funds are available.

Japan. The Total Staff Number Law, which was approved by the Diet, stipulates the maximum number of full-time employees. This law does not cover defence forces, government enterprises, the Diet, or courts – all of which are controlled by other regulations. The staff size of each ministry and agency is determined by Cabinet Order and the budget, within prescribed limits. Staff control is carried out mainly by the Management and Co-ordination Agency which is separate from the budget organisation. However, the Ministry of Finance does get involved in staff control through preparation of the salary budget.

Inasmuch as staff ceilings are set by law, any change in the upper limit can be made only by legislation. Since 1968, the government has adopted a series of personnel reduction plans. The 7th plan, covering the period 1987-91, provided for a 5% reduction in personnel. In adopting this plan, the government also decided to seek comparable reductions in public corporations. The monitoring of staff size is carried out through quarterly reports by each agency and by personnel audits that parallel the spending audits.

Netherlands. Total civil service staff is controlled by ceilings on the number of person-years (or full-time equivalents) and on expenditure for personnel in the various ministries. These ceilings are imposed by the Cabinet and laid down in the annual budget and the multi-year plans. The limits apply only to the central civil service; other parts of the "collective sector" are controlled indirectly through expenditure budgets. Enforcement of the personnel limits has been entrusted to the Directorate General for Management and Personnel Policy (DGMP) in the Ministry of the Interior. Decisions regarding a ministry's financial resources for personnel are made through tripartite discussions between the finance ministry, the DGMP, and the relevant ministry. If not resolved at this level, the matter may be decided by the Council of Ministers. As part of the annual budget, personnel limits are formally approved by Parliament.

During the post-war period, public employment rose while private employment declined. To reverse this trend, the 1983 and 1987 Lubbers governments adopted explicit targets for reducing the size of the civil service over a four-year period. The 1983 policy exempted certain sectors and fell short of its target, but the 1987 drive covered the entire civil service (though not the rest of the collective sector).

No reserves are set aside for adjusting the personnel levels after the financial year has started. The Ministry of Finance monitors the utilisation of agreed expenditure budgets, including personnel spending, on a monthly basis, while the Ministry of the Interior monitors the use of personnel every three months. These central organs may intervene if over-utilisation or other misuse of personnel is suspected.

Norway. Personnel use in the central government is controlled through limits on net new positions and limits on total pay expenditures. The budget specifies net new positions in each organisational unit.

Decisions with respect to net new positions are integrated with formulation of the budget. Personnel ceilings are issued by the Budget Department to each ministry which, in turn, proposes the allotment of personnel resources to agencies. After the budget has been adopted, major changes in personnel have to be formally approved by Parliament, in the same manner as changes in expenditure. Minor changes are under the competence of the Ministry of Finance.

Turkey. Position controls apply to civil servants, contract personnel and permanent workers, but not to temporary employees. Controlled positions are created by the legislature and may be filled with the approval of the General Directorate of Budget and Financial Control. Certain positions within public enterprises are not subject to controls. Personnel expenditures, by programme, are determined by negotiations between agencies and the General Directorate during preparation of the annual budget. Parliament's Plan-Budget Committee considers personnel expenditure as part of its work on the budget bill. During the fiscal year, personnel expenditures and position utilisation are monitored by finance inspectors and budget controllers; after the end of the year, the Court of Accounts (which is responsible to Parliament) audits expenditures and utilisation of unreserved positions.

United Kingdom. Costs of employing civil servants are controlled by running cost limits which cover pay and other recurrent costs of administration. Where pay bargaining has been delegated to an individual department or agency, a control on the civil service paybill component of running costs is also agreed; from April 1994, around half of the civil service will be managed in this way. Provision for civil service pay and other running costs is discussed in the public expenditure survey, where the presumption is that pay and price increases will be offset in whole or large part by improvements in efficiency, with year-on-year changes in the overall paybill where this is required to reflect significant workload changes. Provision for pay in other parts of the public sector is planned on the same basis, though different control arrangements apply.

United States. Total civilian employment in the executive branch is controlled on a full-time equivalent (FTE) basis. Some agencies or programmes are governed by laws establishing minimum employment levels. Permanent law limits the number of positions in the senior executive service. The Office of Personnel Management controls the allocation of these senior posts.

FTE requests are reviewed by the President's Office of Management and Budget along with agency expenditure estimates. The President's budget submitted to Congress includes his recommendations for employment levels, and Congress often specifies FTE levels in committee reports on the various appropriations bills. Inasmuch as most FTE ceilings are administrative rather than statutory, the executive branch has flexibility in shifting personnel resources. Within an agency, FTEs can be adjusted among bureaux or programmes, provided that the agency's total FTE allowance is not exceeded. The President sometimes announces a government-wide limitation on positions, but these targets are not enacted into law. The most recent instance was the promulgation by President Clinton in September 1993 to reduce federal employment levels by 252 000 over a four-year period. The reduction is based on recommendations for government reform included in the six-month national performance review, which was led by the Vice-President and finished its work in September 1993.

8. Managerial accountability and programme effectiveness

The practice of budgeting is evolving in many OECD member countries from a means of ensuring legality and propriety in public expenditure into an instrument for promoting managerial improvement and programme effectiveness in the public sector. This evolution has progressed at different rates in member countries, as the previous discussion of expenditure monitoring and control indicates. It has advanced furthest in those countries that emphasise output or results-oriented budgeting and that have delegated substantial responsibility for expenditure management to programme managers. But it has taken hold to some degree in all member countries and is reflected in the consolidation of expenditure objects into broader categories, the relaxation of central controls, and the increased interest in outputs and performance. In no OECD country is the grip of centralised control as tight and pervasive as it was 30 years ago.

Several characteristics of this development warrant introductory comment. First, legality in public expenditure remains a bedrock requirement of public finance. It is an ubiquitous rule of democratic government that funds may be spent only as supplied or authorised by parliament, and only for allowed purposes. How this *sine qua non* of democratic rule is satisfied varies among countries, but its implementation has been transformed – not uprooted – by the addition of managerial functions to budgeting. Typically, it is accompanied by a shift from *ex ante* controls to internal controls, from pre-audits to post-audits, from auditing individual transactions to auditing systems, and from highly itemised appropriations to block appropriations. Several of these developments are recognisable in the sections above on parliamentary control and on expenditure management.

Second, the evolution has not been steady and relentless; rather, it has occurred in spurts. One of the most prominent of these was the introduction of planning-programming-budgeting systems (PPBS) and similar systems in the 1960s and 1970s. The most recent development has been propelled by financial management initiatives and other reforms launched in the 1980s and continued early in the next decade. This development has not yet run its course; hence a full assessment of its application or accomplishments would be premature.

Third, the devolution of significant budget responsibilities to programme managers inevitably alters the role of the central budget organisation and its relationship to spending agencies. At this stage of development, it is easy to identify what has been yielded up by the budget office, but much more difficult to discern how it fits into the new order of things. Divested of routine controls, the budget office is to be recast into the lead institution for management improvement. Its new niche is to prod and energise, but it may not have the right levels for the job. Moreover, there may be a fundamental contradiction between the notion that spending agencies should (within agreed budgets) take charge of their own financial actions and the expectation that the same budget office which allocates and rations public resources should be the chief instrument of managerial and programme improvement. There will have to be much sorting out of responsibilities before the final verdict is given on this matter.

Finally, the reforms are focused on a vital but (in most countries) relatively narrow slice of the budget: the portion allocated to administrative or running costs. There has been no parallel development with respect to transfer payments, the fastest growing and least controlled part of government expenditure. At first glance, it may appear surprising that the most controlled portion of the budget is the prime target of contemporary management reforms, but there is a certain logic to this emphasis. For one thing, precisely because administrative expenditure is controlled, it may be safe to loosen the reins a bit and give spending agencies greater latitude in using these funds. For another, although it has been controlled, administrative spending has generally crept upwards over the years, and there is evidence that productivity gains in the governments of OECD countries have lagged behind comparable trends in the private sector. The devolution of spending control is typically accompanied by strict restraints on administrative costs, with agencies allowed increases below the rate of inflation. One widely applied formula has been to hold annual increases in these costs 2% below the rate of inflation. The 2% rate has been favoured either because it is sufficiently small to be acceptable or because it mirrors long-term productivity improvement in business firms. But compounded over a period of years, this expenditure squeeze may impel agencies to retrench services or improve performance. Delegated budgeting and related managerial reforms aim at avoiding the first outcome and achieving the second. These innovations depend on a usually implicit (though sometimes explicit) *quid pro quo*: in exchange for giving agencies less real resources, the government gives them more discretion over their money.

While administrative costs may be a declining portion of central government budgets, they loom quite large in the everyday operations of agencies. The rules and procedures governing these expenditures have a lot to do with the behaviour and performance of managers. If the rules bind and constrict, it is argued, managers will operate by the book, giving primacy to the legalities of control and not caring very much about results. They cannot be held accountable for performance because they lack a genuine voice in how funds are to be applied, and they are prevented or discouraged from shifting resources from less productive to more productive uses. Managers cannot manage if they must repeatedly get approval from others before spending appropriated funds, or if their entreaties to shift resources are blocked by external controllers.

There are strong counter-arguments, of course, as evidenced by the governments that have retained centralised control. Some of these positions are rooted in the political and administrative traditions of particular countries and may be difficult to change without remaking basic institutions of government. These considerations notwithstanding, some countries beholden to centralised administration may inch toward a more managerial posture in the years ahead.

Transforming the budget into an instrument of managerial and programme improvement depends on many changes in administrative practice that go far beyond the scope of the present study. But three budget-related reforms are vital, and they are considered in the sections that follow. Managers may be held accountable for performance when they have opportunity and incentives to spend authorised expenditure to achieve agreed programmes; they are held accountable for costs, including costs that under conventional accounting practices may not be charged to their budgets; and they are held accountable for results and performance, especially the results produced by public expenditures. These conditions are interdependent, though far greater attention has been paid to the last than to the other two, and far less progress has been made in accountability for costs than in managerial discretion and performance-based management. The linkage of the three reforms is most boldly recognised in the recent reform of the New Zealand public sector.

8.1. *Managerial discretion*

Recent changes in the budgetary systems of some governments reflect a shift from detailed regulations and managing for compliance to increased incentives and opportunity for managers to use discretion and initiative in achieving expenditure and performance targets. The institutional incentives that have been provided include: allowing spending departments to retain all (or a portion of) savings beyond centrally determined targets; more discretion with respect to the mix of inputs (supplies, equipment, etc.) and the timing of expenditures; greater freedom to reallocate funds between programmes or activities; and wider scope for levying user charges and applying the proceeds to relevant activities. The shift away from strict compliance has been accompanied by renewed emphasis on performance indicators, the negotiation and enforcement of strict spending limits, and new reporting and review requirements.

These managerial incentives have been introduced as a tool for expenditure reduction or restraint on the one hand and enhanced productivity on the other. In the countries that have moved in this direction, there is a shared feeling that a stringent fiscal environment has helped the reforms along. Higher productivity in the public sector is the key stated objective of giving operational flexibility to programme managers. Lower expenditure, decided at the centre, has been the main instrument to force or induce productivity gains. Reductions in resources have driven efficiency, not the other way around.

Assessments of progress in various countries indicate that some success has been achieved in containing or reducing administrative expenditures without major changes in programmes. Managers have been assigned responsibility for achieving planned shrinkage in expenditures; the precise distribution of cutbacks has not been dictated from above. The role of the budget office has been to foster a more performance-oriented managerial climate through the development of new measures and other reforms. But two obstacles have emerged in some countries. One is that the operational constraints on managers are still substantial, with separate controls still common on personnel and salaries, low caps on the resources that can be carried forward to the next year, and barriers to transfers between current and capital expenditure. This problem may cure itself over time as concern that managerial flexibility will weaken the overall control of expenditure abates. The second problem may be more troublesome. It is the propensity of headquarters staff in ministries and departments to replicate the controls divested by budget offices. This tendency has been confirmed by enough experiences to be considered one of the chief obstacles to the realisation of management reforms. To counter it, several governments have moved on to a stage of reform that demarks the relationship between the ministry or department and its constituent agencies.

Australia. The Financial Management Improvement Programme (FMIP) introduced in 1983 has been the Commonwealth's main vehicle for modemising expenditure management and emphasising value for money. A related but later development was the imposition of an "efficiency dividend" – an annual government-wide requirement to achieve efficiency gains by reducing salary and administrative expenditure by 1.25% per annum. Further reform came in 1988 through "programme management and budgeting" which re-oriented the budget and appropriation focus from the level of expenditure on resource inputs to a focus on the objectives of government activity and on the efficient and effective achievement of desired outcomes.

Managerial incentives were provided through a new running costs system which sets cash limits covering all administrative expenditure in each appropriation and allowing for transfers between salaries and other administrative expenditure, as well as the carry-over and borrowings of expenditure between financial years. The efficiency dividend arrangement is currently under review. This system replaced an arrangement which separated staffing controls from financial controls and divided appropriations into up to 20 separate items for administrative expenditure. It therefore represents a substantial expansion in managerial flexibility. It is likely that additional reforms will be undertaken in the years ahead, especially in regard to programme evaluation, performance measurement and accrual accounting. In November 1992, the Australian government decided that departments should move to financial reporting on an accrual basis, as a further step in the government's public sector reform programme. Ten departments produced financial statements on an accrual basis for 1992/93 with the remainder to do so for 1993/94.

In 1992, the government's Management Advisory Board launched an evaluation by an independent task force of the management improvements initiated since 1983. The task force's report was released in July 1993: "The Australian Public Service Reformed: An Evaluation of a Decade of Management Reform". The general conclusions contained in the report are that the management reforms have been well directed, that their benefits have substantially outweighed their costs, and that agencies need to take more active steps to fully integrate the reforms in the public service culture and to make them work more effectively.

Canada. The principal instruments for enlarging managerial discretion have been "Increased Ministerial Authority and Accountability" (IMAA) and running cost budgeting. These arrangements devolve greater authority to departmental management, within an accountability framework, so as to concentrate on results rather than on process. They are a response to the piling up over decades of detailed rules and prescriptions that regulated the implementation of government policy and the expenditure of public funds. IMAA relaxes many central regulations for departments that negotiate contracts specifying what they will spend and accomplish over a three-year period. IMAA involves departments from the start in identifying the room for manoeuvre they need and in getting their judgment on what can be done and on the resources needed to produce agreed results. In exchange for negotiating these performance contracts, departments gain limited carry-forward of capital funds, retention of savings achieved through their managerial initiative, and (in some cases) the use of revenue produced by user fees.

In the 1990s, the IMAA initiative was overtaken by government-wide deregulation and decentralisation of Treasury Board administrative and personnel management practices and the promotion of special operating agencies. The latter extend the IMAA concept by identifying organisational units within departments that may enjoy additional delegated authorities in exchange for establishing a business plan and committing to performance targets. The government is also aggressively promoting the development of service standards and performance reporting across all programmes.

Commencing with the 1993/94 budget, the government introduced a running cost regime for managing operating resources dedicated to programme delivery. This entails a unitary budget encompassing salary expenses, other operating expenses, and minor capital resources, which allows managers to choose the most cost-effective mix of inputs to carry out programmes. With this initiative, separate person-year controls have been eliminated, along with Treasury Board controls on funds earmarked for salaries.

Denmark. Since the mid 1980s, departments have had increasing scope to move money between votes and agencies have had freedom to shift resources between items, except that they cannot increase expenditure on pay. Authority to carry forward unused investment funds has been extended to current expenditure as well. Uncommitted balances may be carried forward up to four years, provided their future use is specified. Most provisions for separate parliamentary approval of minor investment projects, sales of buildings, etc., have been abolished. The formerly detailed control on staff has been replaced by a multi-year limit on total pay, but the number of senior posts is still separately controlled.

In conjunction with budget reform, expenditure control was shifted from a gross to a net basis. The operative expenditure ceiling for each minister is now defined as a net amount, which means that increased revenues count as savings.

Ireland. Recent developments include the introduction of three-year administrative budgets in 1991 which aim at delegating greater authority to line departments (and within departments to line managers) for administrative expenditure and related matters. Each participating department negotiates a three-year agreement with the Minister for Finance stating the total expenditure to be available (in constant terms) in each of the three years, specifies the circumstances (if any) under which these amounts will be changed, allows the transfer of resources between sub-heads (within, not between, votes), allows some carry-forward of resources from one financial year to another, and arranges for monitoring the agreement and resolving any difficulties that arise. To ensure that the devolution extends to operating levels, each department must prepare a plan for internal delegation of authority over administrative expenditure. During the period 1991-93, three-year agreements covered departments employing 80% of the civil service.

New Zealand. The shift from appropriation of inputs to appropriation for outputs has given departments significant flexibility in the use of resources. Chief executives, who are responsible for the performance of their departments, have authority to negotiate wages and conditions and have flexibility to transfer resources between input categories. In managing resources, chief executives are required to produce specified outputs (at specified levels of quality, quantity and timeliness) within the amount agreed by ministers.

Sweden. As previously discussed, Sweden has adopted three-year budget frames for government agencies. Although funds are still appropriated one year at a time, agencies can carry forward savings in one year to the next and, within strict limits, draw in advance on future appropriations. The three-year frames are applied to administrative expenditure which has been subject to extended downward pressure for more than a decade.

United Kingdom. A succession of reforms, beginning with the Financial Management Initiative (FMI) in 1981 and extending through the Next Steps initiative in 1988 and the Citizen's Charter in 1991, have progressively enlarged the scope of managerial flexibility and accountability. The FMI called on each department to develop management systems and practices which give managers: clear objectives and means of assessing progress towards them; well-defined responsibilities for achieving value for money; and the necessary information and expertise. Each participating department was charged to tailor the FMI to its own situation, so there was a great deal of variation in approach and in the pace of reform. The FMI was oriented to budgeting by the multi-departmental review of budgeting undertaken in 1986. This review stressed the need for top management to set priorities, manage resources, and review performance. This was accompanied by running costs limits, also in 1986, giving departments greater control over administrative expenditure, thereby encouraging line commands to take a more managerial role than had been customary in assuring efficient and effective use of the staff and other administrative resources available to them. Senior managers were encouraged to delegate further within their commands so that operational levels were empowered to act as budget holders.

The Next Steps initiative advanced the principles of the FMI and the multi-departmental review through the further enlargement of managerial discretion within a performance and accountability framework. The initiative involves the devolution, to the maximum extent practicable, by departments of executive functions to their constituent agencies. Each agency's chief executive, appointed by the minister, is responsible for resources and results. In 1991, departments and their "Next Steps" agencies were given the opportunity, depending on progress made, to gain greater responsibility for pay bargaining and greater scope to reward performance. The 1991 Citizen's Charter directly links managerial performance to the quality and cost of services provided citizens.

8.2. Accounting for costs

Budget systems generally record expenditures on a cash basis, when payments are made, not when costs are incurred. Cash-based budgeting has two important advantages: it is easy to apply and simple to explain. There is no need for special record keeping or a separate accounting system; needed expenditure data can be derived from payroll records and other readily available sources. Moreover, expenditures represent actual rather than assumed or notional transactions, and there is no need to rely on assumptions. But cash-based budgeting misstates the true cost of carrying out government programmes and activities. It often assigns costs to the wrong activity or the wrong time period, such as when managers consume centrally provided maintenance, printing or automotive services at no cost to their budgets. These "free goods" distort the allocation of public resources and drain managers of incentives to be efficient.

Costs also are misstated when they are recorded as bills are paid rather than when goods and services are consumed. This problem occurs in current budgets that do not charge for withdrawals from inventory and in capital budgets that do not charge for depreciation of assets or use of capital. Cash-based budgeting also misstates the cost of loans made by the government, as has been noted in sub-section 1.2 above: it overstates the cost of loans when they are issued and understates the cost if they are defaulted or forgiven.

Accurate information on costs is crucial from a number of vantage points:

● in promoting freedom of managerial action in a decentralised budgetary environment, and holding managers accountable for results;

● in optimising resource allocation decisions, and assessing the cost effectiveness of programmes;

● in facilitating comparison between public and private sector activities, so as to assess contracting-out arrangements, user charges, and other market-type mechanisms;

● in evaluating the effects of government activity on the public sector's net worth.

Cash and cost accounting serve fundamentally different objectives. The former is concerned with allocating inputs to organisational units in such a manner that the legal control of expenditure is assured; the latter is concerned with efficiency in the allocation of public resources. The proper attribution of costs can be used in a number of budget-related tasks:

● in programme evaluation, to assess the optimal mix of government programmes and activities;

● in levying user charges according to the principle that beneficiaries should bear the full cost of the services they receive;

● in making budget decisions to determine how much to spend for a wanted volume of goods and services;

● in managerial reform to encourage managers to take responsibility for their actions.

The last of these is especially pertinent for governments bent on modernising the public sector. The emphasis on productivity, performance and effectiveness depends on means of allocating cost fully and accurately to specific programmes and activities. Performance has little meaning independent of the cost of producing it. Traditionally, however, input-oriented budgeting has not paid much attention to cost allocation. Intra-governmental services have often been provided centrally and at no cost to customers. Programme managers have been free to use these at no cost to their programmes; and they could not substitute their "share" of the consumption of these goods or services for consumption of alternatives. The accountability requirements on which recent reforms have been conditioned call managers to account for the resources they consume in the process of producing outputs. The sought-after enhancement in accountability will be lost or diluted if managers do not have full responsibility for costs.

Full attribution of costs requires far-reaching modifications in accounting systems, including the breakdown of the budget into cost/responsibility centres – discrete activities that can be held accountable for the work they perform and the resources they spend, as well as distinctions between fixed and variable costs and the development of other cost measures that allow units of input to be directly linked to units of output. It may also require new relationships between intra-governmental suppliers and their customers, and new methods for budgeting capital expenditures.

Canada. The government does not have a full cost allocation system, but it does attribute three types of costs to the programme or agency responsible for them: certain personnel-related expenses; rentals and accommodations; and centrally provided financial accounting services. Some personnel costs, such as the government's contribution to supplementary health services for its employees, are appropriated in one sum for the entire government. This single appropriation is then "spread out" among departments and agencies in proportion to their share of total person-years in the government sector. This cost allocation is shown "below the line" in departmental budgets and is not included in their appropriations. Moreover, the amount charged to each department is estimated at the start of the year and is not adjusted for actual spending on supplementary health services. It should be mentioned, however, that certain personnel-related costs, such as the government's payment to pension and unemployment benefit schemes for its employees, are included in departmental budgets.

Rental and accommodation charges are allocated by the Public Works Department, the main operator of government office space, on the basis of equivalent market rates in the area where the building is located. In allocating costs, Public Works makes no distinction between government-owned or leased buildings, nor does it base charges on its actual costs. Finally, the Department of Supply and Services apportions the cost of financial services among users on the basis of the number of cheques issued by each department.

In sum, the government allocates costs on the basis of mechanical "rules of thumb" that do not reflect actual costs and do not allow spending agencies discretion in the use of the resources charged to them.

New Zealand. Reform of the public sector has been reliant on a shift from cash-based to accrual accounting. The accrual basis provides for the full attribution of costs to the programmes or accounts incurring them and for costs to be charged to the outputs they purchase through a new accounting structure. The new system specifies four types of appropriations: i) for capital contributions – that is, for public funds invested in a department; ii) for payments, such as grants, where no output is purchased; iii) for expenses of outputs purchased; and iv) for "payments on behalf of the Crown" – that is, transfers to other entities. Appropriations for "payments on behalf of the Crown" must in turn be identified as being for capital investments in other organisations, payments for outputs or unrequited payments.

The precise method used for attributing costs to output classes is left to individual departments. The department must demonstrate that it has a financial management system that is capable of providing timely and materially accurate financial information on an accrual basis and that identifies the full cost of resources consumed, including, where appropriate, the cost of funds employed and the allocation of overhead costs.

Managers have considerable flexibility in determining the mix of inputs in producing outputs, as well as freedom to manage balance sheets by buying and selling assets, provided that no unauthorised infusion of capital is required. As purchaser, the government has the opportunity to assess the quality, timeliness and full cost of the outputs produced and to compare with the outputs available from alternative suppliers.

Cost attribution thus puts pressure on managers to produce outputs as efficiently as those available from other sources.

Sweden. A cost attribution system was introduced in 1973 to facilitate the comparison of government ownership and leasing of buildings. The system focused principally on appraising investment decisions, not on controlling the amounts charged to agencies for rentals and accommodations. The system was applied to cost control in the late 1970s and 1980s as part of the government's imposition of a 2% reduction in administrative costs. The identification and apportionment of rental and other accommodation costs was an important aspect for computing the productivity gains each agency was required to achieve. The three-year budget frames tested in the 1980s and implemented government-wide in the 1990s have further enlarged the scope for cost allocation by giving managers greater discretion with respect to the resources at their disposal, including rental costs.

United States. Although federal law enacted in the 1950s provides for cost-based budgets, the prevailing practice is to budget for cash and commitments. Two developments, however, point to more serious attention to costs in the future: one is credit reform which requires that direct and guaranteed loans be budgeted on the basis of estimated subsidy cost; the other is the establishment of the Federal Accounting Standards Advisory Board and the assignment to it of responsibility for recommending new accounting rules and practices. In the case of loans, the subsidy cost includes all estimated costs, except the administrative expenses of processing the loans. The concept of subsidy cost may be used as a model for other transactions where the cash basis provides an inadequate measure of the government's financial risk.

Although cash budgets constrained by spending limits are expected to continue to be the primary budget structure, the Office of Management and Budget will be developing a recommendation for a capital budget presentation working with the Federal Accounting Standards Advisory Board. The presentation will be incorporated in the FY 1996 budget.

9. Budgeting for results

The link between public sector performance and the overall performance of the economy is now widely recognised by the governments of OECD member countries. The view that economic efficiency depends on the effectiveness of public programmes and policies has led to reappraisals of how public tasks are carried out and how performance and results are measured. This reappraisal has pointed in three closely related directions: the measurement of performance, the freeing up of managerial discretion and initiative, and the use of the budget as a means of improving results. The second of these has already been discussed; hence, this section deals primarily with the two other developments.

Performance measurement in the public sector is not new. Many OECD member countries have had experience with some form of planning, programming and budgeting system (PPBS) or with similar systems that tried to link budgets and performance. One of the principal lessons is that information obtained from performance measurement is only one of many elements in a policy decision. Another lesson is that it does not suffice to focus solely on the upper policy-making echelons. Care must also be taken to instil managerial responsibility and attention to results at all levels of management. In Australia, "programme management and budgeting" (PMB) has linked the aggregate control framework to the achievement of value for money by individual departments and managers. PMB has focused attention on planning objectives, budgeting, implementing strategies, and assessing programme outcomes. Evaluation has been the linchpin of the management cycle, providing a tool for managers to continuously improve the quality of decision making about achieving value for money.

While considerable work is under way on devising and sharpening quantifiable measures, the main emphasis is on overcoming obstacles to their use in managing organisations and allocating resources. As has been noted, considerable progress has been made in some countries in re-orienting financial management from compliance to performance by freeing budget holders from most *ex ante* controls while demanding more accountability for what they accomplish and spend. The ultimate objective is, in some countries, to fashion the budget into a "contract for performance". In exchange for obtaining control of agreed resources, managers would commit themselves to specific outputs (or other performance targets) and (in some cases) to the results or outcomes ensuing from these outputs. In most countries, however, the drive for performance is less closely linked to budgeting but has a broader scope: to strengthen the capacity of managers to take initiative and responsibility for providing public services in a productive and effective manner.

In measuring performance, a distinction is often drawn between measures and indicators. Performance measures are quantified statements of outputs and results related to the objectives sought. Performance indicators, by contrast, are proxies for outputs and results that cannot be measured or are difficult to directly measure. Some countries also draw a fundamental distinction between outputs, which are the direct results of government actions, and outcomes, which are the changes in social conditions that result from a combination of outputs. In an education programme, for example, the outputs may be measured by test scores and the percentage of students advancing to a certain level of proficiency in mathematics. The outcomes may be measured in terms of the percentage of students completing schooling or advancing to higher education. In drawing this distinction, governments typically assign responsibility for outputs to programme managers and responsibility for outcomes to senior officials or ministers.

The governments of OECD countries have identified a core of ideal characteristics for performance measures and indicators. These should be consistent over time and between units, and comparisons should be made only with similar programmes. They should be simple, well defined and easily understood, and should emphasise those aspects that are important to decision making. Ideally, emphasis should be given to a limited number of key measures or indicators which reflect the programme's purpose or objective, or which signal whether the programme is worth continuing. It is fundamentally important that managers' performance should only be measured for those areas for which they have control. It also is a good idea to inform managers of the use to which the data will be put, and to avoid situations where considerable effort is expended in measuring performance but the collected data are then stored away without being used.

Increased effort is now being made to measure the quality of services, especially from the standpoint of taxpayers or consumers. This emphasis reflects rising concern about the quality and cost of public services. The quality of services has several measurable dimensions: timeliness, responsiveness to consumer needs, the manner in which they are delivered, etc. Quality may be measured by means of consumer (or citizen) surveys, as well as by more objective techniques. For example, the quality of garbage collection is gauged in some American cities through a photographic rating system in which the cleanliness of randomly selected streets is periodically evaluated. In the United Kingdom, the Department of Social Security has developed a quality assessment package to measure the performance of its local offices. Some of the key features of the package are a postal survey of client attitudes and assessment of service by type of contact, such as office, telephone, correspondence and home visits.

It is rare that performance measurement is an end in itself. Five gradations of managing for results can be identified, ranging from the publication of performance measures to budgeting for results.

Performance reporting is the systematic publication of data on results to citizens or clients. Being systematic means that key measures are selected in advance and reports on them are issued on a regular basis. Performance reporting goes beyond the descriptive information often found in the annual reports of governments or agencies. It examines results from the perspective of those who pay for or are impacted by public services, and assesses how well their interests are being served. Performance reports sometimes concentrate on a specific policy area, such as school performance as measured by standard test scores, or hospital performance as measured by adjusted mortality rates (that is, rates adjusted for the age, sex, health, and other relevant conditions of patients). When concentrated in a single policy area, performance reports open the possibility for comparisons among institutions, such as schools or hospitals, providing similar services. Where consumers have choice in selecting the institution to provide the service, performance reports aim to turn them into informed "shoppers". Performance reports are also used to assess a broad range of government services at one period in time. In these instances, the reports become means of rating the overall quality of governmental performance.

Performance objectives take the process a big step further by specifying in advance the results expected or promised. The objectives can either be short-term targets tied to current actions or long-term visions of where the government or agency should be heading. Performance objectives are intended to mould behaviour – that is, to mobilise the resources and attention of the government in the preferred direction. To affect behaviour, it is necessary that the objectives be carefully selected, that they pertain to matters of high concern to the agency or citizens, that they be as few as is reasonably possible, and that they be quantified. Publication adds weight to the objectives and conveys the sense that the government is committed to their attainment.

One type of approach applied in private sector firms to enhance performance against key objectives, which is gaining increasing recognition but does not appear to have made much headway to date in the public sector, is benchmarking. Benchmarking involves an organisation in mapping its key operational processes, identifying crucial processes and key performance indicators, and then searching for best practice in terms of those indicators wherever it may occur. Benchmarks are performance objectives that represent the best practices (or results) found in organisations facing similar situations. Benchmarking may be useful when many institutions provide the same service – for example, in motivating under-performing laggard hospitals to bring their practices up to the level of better-performing institutions. However, it is not necessary for an organisation to limit itself to benchmarking against similar organisations; for instance, a hospital might enhance its performance through benchmarking its admission processes against those of a hotel. In the public sector, benchmarking may be a means of spurring agencies to identify "role models" whose performance they would then seek to match or surpass.

Performance auditing subjects the statements by governments or agencies concerning their performance to review by auditors. This form of auditing is still in its infancy, and the precise role and scope of auditors in reviewing results is not well defined, but one may anticipate that financial auditing will be the model used in performance auditing. The specification of performance objectives and reporting on results will be a management responsibility. The task of auditors will be to review these statements to determine their reliability and accuracy. In order for auditors to carry out this role, it will be necessary to develop performance principles and standards similar to those applied in financial management.

Performance contracts specify the output or results that an agency or a manager is committed to produce with agreed resources. The signed contract is hammered out in negotiations between a spending agency and a central organ (such as the budget office) or between an agency and its managers. In some countries, the contract spells out the relationship between the ministry and its constituent agencies. The contract usually runs for three years or longer, during which performance is monitored to ensure that the terms are being met. A full review at the end of the contract period sets the stage for a new round of negotiations.

Performance contracts may be preconditions for easing *ex ante* controls on agencies, or they may be used as employment contracts for senior managers or executives. While performance contracts are a relatively new development, their use is likely to spread in the years ahead as governments devise means of linking operating conditions and results.

Performance budgeting is an implied contract that links resources provided to outputs promised. The linkage can range from a "lockstep" relationship in which a marginal unit of resources produces a marginal unit of output, to one in which the budget merely lists the expected results associated with the budgeted volume of resources.

No OECD country currently practises a form of budgeting in which quantified performance is the sole basis for resource allocation. New Zealand probably comes closest to this model in its system of output-based appropriations. The experiences of Australia, Canada and the United States are more typical. In these countries, the prevailing view is that performance measurement is more useful in determining how to make best use of available resources than in determining what the allocation should be. A number of practical considerations have induced governments to shy away from a strict link between resources and performance. One is that there often is substantial uncertainty as to whether spending agencies can deliver promised improvements in performance even if they get the requested funds. The more explicit the link, the more visible will be the failure, and the consequent demoralisation or discrediting of performance budgeting, if departments fall short of meeting their targets. More importantly, the performance orientation is aimed at changing management style and behaviour, not just at improving the budget process.

In most OECD member countries, programme managers – not budget officials – are the prime users of performance measures. There is concern that excessive reliance on performance measures to allocate resources might generate controversy over the reliability of the data and deter managers from co-operating. If this were to occur, the supply of data might dry up or the quality might be impaired.

Budget staff have an important role in performance management, though one that generally stops short of a tight link between results and resources. The budget office typically has a strong role in designing performance systems and in prodding departments to adapt to the new managerial culture. It also has a voice in deciding which measures are appropriate and an opportunity to use performance data as one of the factors in making budget allocations.

Australia. The development of performance indicators has proceeded under the aegis of two related reforms: the Financial Management Improvement Programme (FMIP) and "programme management and budgeting" (PMB). As has been discussed, these reforms focus government budgeting and parliamentary scrutiny on objectives and outcomes, and encourage departments to assess and improve performance. PMB is the instrument for identifying objectives and placing them into an agreed framework that makes it possible to set performance targets for managers at all levels. The programme structure (programmes, sub-programmes, components, and sub-components) arrays objectives in hierarchical order, with those at lower levels more capable of being quantified than those at higher levels.

The Department of Finance has issued a series of guidelines for the formulation of performance measures. Some address conceptual questions, such as the definition of various types of measures; others provide guidance on the use of measures in budgeting and other managerial activities. Use of performance measures is mandatory in the portfolio documentation presented to Parliament justifying departmental estimates. The portfolio documentation, known in 1993/94 as the "programme performance statements", was refocused as part of Australia's decision to bring down its budget in May 1994, prior to the commencement of the financial year on 1 July 1994 (previous budgets were generally brought down in August). New policy proposals accepted by the government are highlighted in a new document, known as *Portfolio Budget Measures*. Reporting of the contribution of those measures to the achievement of programme objectives will also occur within agency annual reports after the conclusion of each financial year. The government requires new policy proposals to be accompanied by statements of objectives, performance measures, and plans for future evaluations. Department of Finance guidelines suggest that the measures be as specific as possible so that they can contribute to decisions on programmes and priorities. The guidelines also suggest that the previous year's performance be reviewed in terms of the achievement of plans, targets or initiatives set for it. The "programme performance statements" are linked intimately with "programme management and budgeting" and have become the primary vehicle for the presentation of programme performance information to Parliament; they are thus an important element of ministerial accountability to Parliament. The early budget will mean a substantial change in budget documentation, including the programme performance statements, but there will be a continuing emphasis in the new documentation on outcome-focused performance reporting.

Canada. Departments have been required to measure and report on performance since the early 1970s, but this requirement has been given greater impetus by the "Increased Ministerial Authority and Accountability" reforms discussed earlier. Other relevant developments include publication of performance information in the estimates submitted to Parliament and efforts to improve financial management. Each department participating in IMAA prepares an annual management report that triggers an assessment of performance based on targets set forth in the memorandum of understanding negotiated by it and the Treasury Board. Every third year, an accountability review is conducted, pursuant to which specific directives may be issued to spur the efficient and effective use of resources.

Since 1982, Part III of the estimates set forth planned and actual results as well as other performance data relevant to resource requirements. Treasury Board instructions advise departments to furnish information that assists Members of Parliament in understanding and assessing performance. The Comptroller General (in the Treasury Board) monitors preparation of the "Part IIIs" to see that significant evaluation findings are reported accurately. The "Part IIIs" contain a great deal of information on work activity and costs, but they vary considerably in content and quality. The Auditor General (who reports to Parliament) has conducted periodic assessments of the "Part IIIs" and has prodded departments to improve their performance measures. The 1977 legislation establishing this office empowers the Auditor General to report on whether funds have been spent with due regard to economy and efficiency, and whether satisfactory procedures are in place for monitoring effectiveness.

Denmark. Productivity improvement has been a key component of the fiscal constraint maintained since 1983. Greater efficiency has been sought by adjusting budget allocations for expected productivity gains, re-organising work to improve performance, and providing agencies with positive incentives to be more productive. Budget allocations for personnel expenditures are made in reference to productivity targets. Each agency's target is derived by examining its mix of personnel and computing the productivity gain that each type is expected to achieve, based on trends for comparable work in the private sector. Agencies may retain savings achieved by increasing their productivity above the budgeted target.

Since 1987, the trend data included in the supplementary material that accompanies the finance bill have been presented in a standard format. Quantitative data are reported, for all major accounts, for: service, production and activity; resources and capacity; and productivity.

An improved format was introduced in the 1994 budget. It establishes a consistent link between accounting data and performance data, and a separate identification of general management and auxiliary functions of each agency. However, the coverage of performance indicators is still far from complete.

Finland. The new "budgeting for results" approach applied as of 1990 requires that the results to be achieved are described in the budget proposal with work, efficiency and effectiveness measures, if possible. The line ministries agree with the agencies on detailed, and possibly adjusted, results targets and supervise their achievement. Results-oriented budgeting, which in the 1994 budget covers more than 80% of the running costs of agencies, gives agencies much more flexibility to select the means of achieving their objectives than the former line-item budget did. This flexibility has allowed numerous agencies to apply management by results and other business management methods to improve their efficiency and effectiveness.

Starting from 1993, an amendment to the Constitution and the budget law allow the application of net budgeting to activities financed by user charges.

Sweden. Some efforts to measure performance are directly linked to budget decisions; others are independent of budgeting but have the potential to influence the allocation of resources. The main formal link is through the three-year budget frames described in previous sections above. The triennial budget system calls for agencies to furnish trend data on performance during the previous five years, along with projections for the next three years. As has been noted, agencies entering the three-year cycle go through a more elaborate process in formulating their budgets. At the outset, each agency receives specific directives from its competent ministry, in addition to the general directives issued by the Ministry of Finance. The general directives require agencies to report on past performance, assess current objectives and arrangements, and develop measurable targets for the work to be done and results to be obtained over the next three years. The special directives are tailored to each agency's circumstances and pertain to the evaluations to be undertaken, priorities and alternatives, and policy options. Although the three-year frames cover only administrative expenses, the review process extends to programme objectives and expenditures as well. Agencies are called upon to assess their total performance across their full range of activities. In effect, increased flexibility in administrative matters is offered as an inducement for agencies to make a broad, probing assessment of overall performance. The Agency for Administrative Development (SAFAD) and the National Audit Bureau have been assigned responsibility for devising procedures to be used by agencies in reviewing their performance.

United Kingdom. The development and application of performance measures are a central feature of the Financial Management Initiative (FMI) and subsequent reforms. The reforms encourage quantification wherever feasible so as to facilitate assessment of the extent to which programmes have achieved their objectives and provided value for money. As the reforms have unfolded, spending departments have been given substantial responsibility for selecting the appropriate measures, collecting data on results, and publishing them in departmental reports. Inasmuch as the FMI and the other initiatives discussed earlier are intended to spur managers to take responsibility for their actions and performance, they do not prescribe a uniform approach for all departments. Within the broad objectives and guidelines of the FMI, each department is free to develop the management style and system best suited to its circumstances. But as executive operations "graduate" to agency status under the "Next Steps" initiative, they are expected to operate within an accountability framework that specifies resources and performance targets. The most recent initiative is the Citizen's Charter published in 1991. It emphasises qualitative aspects of performance and the responsiveness of public services to the preferences of their users. The Charter insists on published standards of service, such as guaranteed maximum waiting times for certain National Health Service procedures.

The FMI and the initiatives following it conceive of the budget as a contract for performance in which departments commit themselves to concrete targets in exchange for agreed resources. The linkage of budgets and outputs is promoted by giving prominence to performance measures and targets in annual departmental reports. Though progress is somewhat uneven across departments, three trends can be discerned: i) a shift from simple workload or output measures to more advanced performance measures; ii) emphasis on measures of service quality; and iii) greater emphasis on operational measures at agency level.

United States. Performance measurement has a long history and is highly developed, but its application in budgeting and other decision processes has been quite limited. However, a spate of recent developments is likely to give significantly greater weight to matters of performance in the years ahead.

A 1992 survey of more than 100 federal agencies conducted by the General Accounting Office found widespread use of performance measures. All of the surveyed agencies claim to measure final outputs or products, 93% say they have work or activity measures, 91% claim to measure the timeliness of services, 83% profess to have internal measures of quality, 71% collect data on outcomes, and 63% aver that they assess customer satisfaction. Few of these measures find their way into the federal budget, though some may play a role in influencing budget allocations. Performance measures are also collected in many American cities and state governments. It is now common for municipalities to publish standard test scores on school performance. An emerging emphasis is in issuing a comprehensive report on the quality of government. In 1992, for example, the City of Portland, Oregon, issued its first annual performance report on six vital public services. The report also presented the results of a citizen survey and compared Portland's results to those of other cities. The State of Oregon has established a progress board that has set measurable objectives for the state at fixed periods: 1990 (the baseline year), 1995, 2000 and 2010.

Interest in performance-based government has been stimulated by some recent developments, including the following:

● Legislation enacted by Congress during 1993, the Government Performance and Results Act (GPRA), requires federal agencies to prepare annual performance reports comparing actual *versus* planned results, explaining why particular goals (if any) have not been met, and reporting on programme evaluations. The legislation also provides for pilot tests of performance budgeting and of new forms of managerial flexibility and accountability.

● The Chief Financial Officers Act of 1990 provides for the systematic measurement of performance, and annual reports on progress in improving financial management. Pursuant to this legislation, the Office of Management and Budget has issued guidelines for the development of performance measures to be appended to financial statements.

● The Governmental Accounting Standards Board, which has cognizance of state and local – but not federal – accounting practices, has recommended the development of reporting and audit procedures for "service efforts and accomplishments" indicators of various governmental functions.

● The report of the national performance review strongly supports the GPRA, and includes numerous recommendations for implementing the act as quickly as possible.

These and other recent developments lend support to the spreading belief that performance-type budget systems will come to be more widely used in the years ahead.

Effective systems for the allocation, management and control of public sector resources are fundamental elements of good governance. The juxtaposition of the need for continuing fiscal restraint with demands for more and better public services is changing budgetary practices in OECD member countries. The budget is increasingly being used as an instrument for promoting managerial improvement and programme effectiveness in addition to its control and allocation functions.

ISBN 978-92-64-06087-6
Evolutions in Budgetary Practice
Allen Schick and the OECD Senior Budget Officials
© OECD 2009

Chapter 4

Modern Budgeting: Overview*

---

* This text was originally published in 1997 as the overview of the full OECD publication *Modern Budgeting* (ISBN 92-64-16216-7). The overview provides an interpretation by Allen Schick of the Brookings Institution, Washington DC, of budgeting reforms in 1994-96 in five member countries: Australia, France, New Zealand, Sweden and the United Kingdom.

The management revolution that is restructuring the public sector in many OECD member countries has been under way for more than a decade in some countries and is only starting in others. The duration of this revolution attests to the difficulty of uprooting old rules and habits, as well as to the staying power and determination of reformers. The task has not been completed in any of the countries that have sought to transform public administration, but in none is there serious risk of abandoning reform and reverting to the traditional command-and-control relationship between the centre of government and public agencies and between the centre of departments and operating units. The traditional governing structure concentrated control of human and financial resources at the centre and operational responsibility for delivering services at the bottom of organisations. At one end of government were the controllers, at the other end the controlled. The centre issued rules, monitored compliance with the rules, and intervened as it thought appropriate; the operating echelons complied, or at least pretended to. With control in one place and responsibility for producing in another, public sector managers often were managers in name only. Some of the more venturesome became skilled in outwitting the controllers; others merely complied. Many undoubtedly sought to do as much public good as they could within the constraints they faced.

This arrangement governed not only the management of expenditure but other administrative operations as well, especially those pertaining to the recruitment and remuneration of staff. As outmoded as it may appear to some today, command-and-control public administration grew out of two widely shared values: a determination by governments to restrain the growth in public employment and expenditure, and a commitment to assure uniformity and consistency in the provision of public services. Whatever these virtues, the first objective has been overtaken by the vast expansion in the scope of government, particularly in transfers and grants; the second has been largely accomplished. With the growth of government, the centre became increasingly cluttered by detail, diverting policy and managerial attention from larger programme and financial matters.

Many national governments eased central control in the decades after World War II by consolidating items of expenditure into broader categories and giving agencies somewhat greater flexibility in using resources. Some attempted to strengthen budgeting as a policy process through innovations such as planning-programming-budgeting (PPB) systems, but these top-down reforms generally were unsuccessful and did little or nothing to improve managerial capacity at operating levels. The current spate of reforms, by contrast, does aim to improve public sector management. They are centred around accountability frameworks in which the government entrusts spending agencies with flexibility in using resources, in exchange for holding them responsible for results. The repertoire of devices for enforcing managerial accountability includes strategic and operational plans, performance measures and targets, contracts for personal and organisational performance, decoupling service delivery from policy making, new accounting rules and annual reports, more active use of evaluation and auditing, and financial inducements and sanctions. The mix of new instruments varies among the countries that have ventured along these lines, but in all there has been marked devolution of financial and overall managerial control and the introduction of novel arrangements for holding agencies and managers to account.

In the five countries examined here – Australia, France, New Zealand, Sweden and the United Kingdom – there is professed consensus within government that the centralised model no longer suits the needs and conditions of public management. What is needed is less rigidity in the provision of services and more responsiveness to local conditions and customer preferences. Rigid rules, it is widely agreed, have impeded adoption of the best available practices and have forced managers to settle instead for middling uniformity. It is important to acknowledge, however, that traditional public administration still is favoured in some prominent OECD member countries where centralised financial and personnel control is regarded as a virtue. Germany and Japan may fit this model, as do some smaller member countries.

Although the sample discussed is small, the five countries span three of the main political-administrative cultures found in the OECD community: the Westminster system, the French administrative tradition and the Scandinavian model. The American separation-of-powers form of government is not included because its administrative "reinvention" was in its early stages when the research was conducted in 1994 and 1995. The German bureaucratic model is excluded because that country has taken few steps to decentralise management in the Federal Republic, perhaps because its attention to the complex task of unification has crowded out some other governmental matters.

Not only do the five countries reviewed here have different governing traditions, they also had different administrative arrangements before restructuring commenced. France has a long tradition of detailed supervision by financial controllers stationed in the Ministry of Finance, and it has moved cautiously to enlarge the operational discretion of local managers. It lags behind the other countries because it started somewhat later and has had much further to go. But there is substantial evidence of progress as the reforms move from the experimental stage to implementation across the public sector. Sweden is at the other end of the spectrum, for it has a long history of small ministries and relatively autonomous agencies. Sweden gives managers more latitude than is found in some other countries, so that although the innovations have been less dramatic than elsewhere, they have been effective. The three Commonwealth countries are sufficiently differentiated in administrative practices and in their reforms to justify a separate look each. At the eve of reform more than a dozen years ago, the United Kingdom had already retreated from the doctrine of Treasury control that it had practised for more than a century. The "Financial Management Initiative" launched in 1982, the "Next Steps" initiative commenced half a dozen years later and the recent "fundamental expenditure reviews" have all been spurred by political support at the top of the government for reshaping the public sector. Australia entered the reform era with highly centralised controls, but in the past dozen years it has discarded many personnel and financial restrictions and adopted a variety of political and administrative arrangements to stimulate management improvement. As a small country with an open economy, New Zealand felt its future well-being threatened by powerful international forces, and it responded by creatively adapting commercial practices to public management.

1. The task of reform

The five countries have faced similar problems in restructuring their national administration. All must redefine relationships between the centre, which is politically accountable for governmental performance, and operating units where services are provided and most resources are spent. Defining this new relationship has been difficult because new management procedures must be devised in place of the discredited *ex ante* controls. The new controls must safeguard the government's interest in total expenditure and programme priorities, and they must also promote efficiency in public management and quality in service delivery. In visits to the five countries, this writer sometimes encountered the view that once central intervention in administrative details has ended, spending agencies should be free to chart their own course without substantial direction from the top. This is a naive and wrong-minded view which, if not challenged, may undermine or discredit reform. The point must be made that reform does not open the door to an "anything goes" attitude to public money. But the fact that complaints about central interference persist in the face of a truly massive withdrawal of central organs from the details of expenditure highlights the difficulty of defining new roles and relationships. With the exception of Sweden, which has a long-standing and established division of labour between ministries and agencies, every country has had difficulty drawing a clear line between the responsibilities of central and operating institutions.

Each country faces considerable pressure on its operating budget. In fact, running costs (adjusted for inflation) and staffing levels have declined over the past decade. The trend has given spending agencies mixed messages. On the one hand, it has spurred them to actively search for efficiencies; but on the other, it has generated some apprehension that the reforms have more to do with cutting resources than with improving management. The concern emerges in conflicts over efficiency dividends (Australia), the adequacy of spending levels (New Zealand), mandated spending cuts (Sweden), and cash limits (United Kingdom).

All of the countries must motivate managers to take initiative and responsibility for what they spend and produce and to accept that the performance of their organisation depends on their personal performance. There has been an enormous turnover of senior and middle managers in New Zealand and the United Kingdom, as many officials discomfited by the new managerialism have left on their own accord or have been encouraged to depart. Many of the new managers have had substantial work experience in the private sector and are more at home in the new regime than they would have been in the old administrative structures. The importation of new managers appears to be inconsequential in Australia and France. These two countries, along with Sweden, seem to have confidence that "letting managers manage" suffices; New Zealand and the United Kingdom have acted on the presumption that it is necessary to "make managers manage". Each government must determine what is acceptable risk, as operating agencies are given discretion to spend resources and take other actions that may have important political or financial ramifications. This issue is least troublesome in Sweden, where the line between ministries and agencies is well marked, and most pressing in the United Kingdom, where the new independence of agencies has called into question the Westminster doctrine of ministerial accountability.

In all of the countries, restructuring is seen as a long-term effort to change managerial behaviour and organisational culture. The initial steps, entailing procedural changes such as the divestiture of *ex ante* controls, were relatively easy. With the exception of France, this stage has been largely completed. France is lagging because it started later than the others and must overcome the strong tradition of running the country from the centre. The second part of the bargain – getting civil servants to manage for results and transforming state agencies into performance-driven producers of public services – has taken much more time. One may wonder whether, in the absence of market discipline, this objective will ever be fully attained. Even when a management ethic has taken hold, as it has in several of the countries reviewed here, one cannot be sure that it has been institutionalised. A change in leadership or in the circumstances facing an agency, a budget crisis or other factors may swiftly undo years of progress. Perhaps it will only be when the reform era has closed and the innovations have become routines of public management that the commitment to performance will be truly tested.

Each government has devised an instrument of choice to ensure that performance information influences organisational behaviour. Australia relies on a heavy dose of programme evaluation, both before policies have been initiated and after they have been funded. France is emphasising responsibility centres as a means of imbuing civil servants with awareness that their actions can make a difference in the quality of service. Sweden has placed increasing reliance on annual reports that are audited for reliability of financial and performance statements. The United Kingdom looks to framework documents and performance targets to concentrate managerial attention on key objectives and results. New Zealand invests considerable resources in negotiating performance agreements for chief executives and purchase agreements for agencies. In the four countries that have had extended experience, today's favoured instrument was not yesterday's. There is much evidence of trial and error and of willingness to try out new approaches in the hope that they will prove more effective than previous ones. The search for new methods arises out of a fundamental gap between producing performance information and acting on the basis of performance. Every country faces the problem that no matter how much it generates by way of performance information, decisions may be taken and resources allocated in disregard of objectives and results. Australia is trying to narrow this gap by closely linking programme evaluation to policy work in the Cabinet. Sweden has enhanced the role of auditors (who are responsible to the Ministry of Finance) in examining agency performance. The United Kingdom has placed increasing weight on the selection of both "Next Steps" and "Citizen's Charter" targets and on comparing results to targets. New Zealand reviews departmental key result areas (KRAs) in the light of government-wide strategic result areas (SRAs).

The introduction of new methods has also aimed at invigorating the reform effort. To restructure management, the government must demonstrate its continuing commitment to the task and sustain interest among senior and middle managers. Precisely because implanting a performance ethic takes more than a decade, it does not suffice for the government to announce an initiative and then let matters run their course. At frequent intervals – the experience thus far suggests no more than four to five years apart – the last steps must be renewed by new steps. If business management is a guide, performance-driven agencies may be in a continuing state of flux with only a few years between one wave of reforms and the next.

New Zealand also fits this pattern, even though it legislated a full menu of changes at the start. The reforms enacted in 1988 and 1989 were comprehensive in scope, but they were established in law, not merely in government guidance or exhortation. Nevertheless,

New Zealand also has fine-tuned its reforms in the light of experience. In fact, most of the procedures now used by New Zealand departments were initiated after the legislated reforms had been enacted.

Because of the difficulty of implanting a performance culture, every country has had a spate of disappointments; none has accomplished everything it set out to do. The United Kingdom learned that the "Financial Management Initiative" (FMI) had produced better information, but had done little to liberate managers at operating levels; it subsequently learned that "Next Steps" had energised the newly established agencies but had not yet transformed the central departments. Australia has been vexed by the problem of packaging performance information into a useful format, and it has also been disappointed by the apparent uselessness of the programme structure. New Zealand has made relatively little headway in measuring outcomes, and the relationship between ministers purchasing services and agencies supplying them has not been sufficiently clarified. Sweden has been disappointed by the failure of the multi-year budget frames to deepen the quality of budget work. France has found that, despite government guidelines, some important ministries have dragged their feet in devolving responsibility to local agencies. In each country there is ample scope for complaint and criticism, but the disappointments do not hide the fact that enormous progress has been made. Because the reforms have been so ambitious, they are bound to fall somewhat short of the mark.

To this observer, one of the most encouraging characteristics of the reforms is that they have not been treated by public managers as just the latest in a long series of managerial fads. Managers have welcomed the reforms and have related them to the quality of their work and the satisfaction they get from the job. Support for reform has persisted at ministerial level and in senior official ranks. It would be unrealistic to expect ministers to regard management innovation as uppermost on their political agenda, but they have accorded it moderately high priority in several of the countries and have demonstrated interest in all.

Beyond the impressionistic evidence, there is strong reason to believe that restructuring public management has brought sizeable efficiency gains that are reflected in lower staffing levels and reductions in real operating expenditures. Many agencies are doing more with less. While hidden reductions in service levels or quality have certainly occurred, few agencies have compensated for lost resources by cutting services. The growing practice of publishing performance targets and results discourages agencies from degrading services in the face of resource constraints, but an even more important influence has been the spread of managerial responsibility in service agencies. It is hard to form a judgment on how the managerial changes have affected programme outcomes. While there is no reason to suspect that outcomes have been adversely affected by the reform, neither is there a strong basis for claiming that they have been improved.

2. Markets and managers

The five countries have taken two broad approaches to improving public sector performance. One has been to apply or stimulate market behaviour in government agencies; the other has been to empower and motivate managers to improve performance. The market-type mechanisms include privatisation and contracting out, accrual accounting and cost recovery, and contracts for individual or group performance. The array of management tools include planning and evaluation, devolution and flexibility in using resources, targeting and measuring performance, and corporate planning and programme evaluation. Every country has its feet in both camps, but the mix of approaches varies. New Zealand has embraced market principles more rigorously than any other country, and it has sought to stimulate market discipline by distinguishing between the government as owner and the government as purchaser, by levying a capital charge for the government's financial investment, by contracting for the services of chief executives, and by negotiating purchase agreements for the "sale" of outputs from agencies to ministries. France hews most closely to a managerial model, empowering responsibility centres to operate as quasi-autonomous units. The government in the United Kingdom has espoused a market ethic, but it also places great reliance on managers accepting responsibility for their work and performance. Australia and Sweden tilt to the management end of the spectrum, yet both have given scope to user charges, commercialisation and other market-type mechanisms.

The differences between the two approaches should not be overstated for, after all, governments do not operate in genuine markets. Yet the two approaches pull in different directions. A managerial posture puts great confidence in "letting managers manage"; a market approach insists on "making managers manage". The first approach relies on empowering managers to take initiative and responsibility; the second relies on prices and contracts to compel efficiency and accountability. The extent to which market-type behaviour can be induced in the public sector is being tested by the New Zealand reforms. Simulated markets are not real markets, and contracts between government entities (such as purchase agreements in New Zealand and framework documents in the United Kingdom) are not the same as truly arm's-length agreements between unrelated parties. The internal contracts negotiated in these countries lack strict enforcement; indeed, failure of one party to perform may leave the other party with no remedy but to honour the contract nonetheless.

The difference between a market ethic and a managerial ethic is reflected in treatment of the savings that accrue from increased efficiency. Each country has to decide whether agencies should retain a portion or all of the savings or should remit them to the government by lowering their resource base. Considering the issue from a managerial perspective would probably lead to the conclusion that there would be significant advantage in allowing the agency to benefit from the savings. Taking away the dividend would penalise managers for being efficient, while allowing them to keep it would provide an incentive to seek further efficiencies. Inspired by its market orientation, New Zealand has come to a different conclusion. Allowing agencies to keep the saved resources would enable them to spend on services that were not contracted for in the budget. It would almost be equivalent to paying more for goods even though the price has dropped.

This example points to a critical difference between private and simulated markets. Private markets charge prices; government-induced markets pay costs. When prices are set by markets, suppliers have a strong incentive to improve efficiency; when prices are set at cost, the incentive is weak or non-existent. This inherent difference between markets and governments strongly suggests the desirability of supplementing market discipline with managerial incentives in the public sector.

Marketising public management tests the boundaries of the public sector. If government services can be fairly and efficiently supplied by commercial vendors, then one may question whether these services are so distinctive that they must remain in the public sector. Three of the countries (Australia, France and Sweden) prefer the public delivery of government services. Except for state enterprises that already operate on a commercial basis, these countries generally prefer that public services be the responsibility of civil servants working in government agencies. The British government has primed various services for privatisation or contracting out, but it has not carried this development as far as some fear it might and others believe it should. New Zealand is an unusual case, for it has high regard for public institutions but has gone further than any other country in adapting market practices to public management. Thus far, its unique amalgam of public and market behaviour has worked rather well, but tensions may emerge in the future.

Market principles have influenced management reform in many countries. This influence is reflected in the emphasis on considering recipients of public services as customers, not as clients. Customers have power, clients do not; customers can take their business elsewhere, clients cannot. Being a customer is also different from being a citizen. Customers are more efficacious than citizens, for though the latter have rights, their interests may be ignored. The recourse provided by the voting booth pales by comparison with the recourse available in the marketplace. The difference between citizens and customers is not only metaphorical; it is the difference between classical public administration that values uniformity and fairness in the provision of services and the new managerialism that values responsiveness to the demands of customers. It is also the difference between regarding government as a provider of services and regarding it as the architect or guardian of a good society. These differences lead to others, between a concern for outputs (the volume of goods and services provided) and a concern for outcomes (the social conditions resulting from government action). It is of some interest that, although the United Kingdom's Citizen's Charter refers to citizens, the principles it enunciates value them as customers. A customer-oriented government is a service state. Its performance can be objectively measured in terms of the efficiency with which it produces outputs, and subjectively in terms of the extent to which customers express satisfaction with the services they receive. None of the governments has narrowed its interest to customer concerns alone; all have taken a much broader view of the public interest, as reflected in efforts to measure outcomes, improve policies and programmes, evaluate results, and place their budgets on a sounder financial footing. All, however, have learned that it is much easier to improve services to customers than to address the larger role of the state in society.

3. Decoupled *versus* consolidated government

The different perspectives of the role and performance of government clash on one of the important planks in the reform agenda – the organisation of government. For generations, it was a settled principle of public administration that common activities (those serving similar objectives of clients) should be consolidated in a single organisation. Departmentalisation was seen as having many benefits, not the least of which were a narrower span of control and the synergy made possible by grouping complementary programmes together. The establishment of consolidated departments was long regarded as one of the triumphs of modern public administration. (Sweden was different, for it favoured a multiplicity of separated agencies.) Departmentalisation was associated with other administrative reforms, such as the establishment of a comprehensive budget process, a national civil service, and the capacity to set priorities within each sector. The costs of consolidation included a vast apparatus at the centre of departments and the layering of bureaucratic organisations, but these were deemed acceptable because they strengthened the ability of the government to co-ordinate and control the making and implementation of public policy.

Australia still endorses this administrative model, as reflected in its move to mega-departments and portfolio budgeting. In the Australian view, large, encompassing departments facilitate the establishment of objectives and priorities within portfolios. Commingling policy making and service delivery in the same organisation permits ideas and insights derived from one of these activities to enrich the other. For example, the experiences of line managers in providing services may enable policy makers to better understand the impacts of their programmes. In the course of doing their job, these managers may gain insight into why some approaches produce the desired outcomes while others do not. In the Australian view, quarantining service providers in a separate organisation, while preoccupying them with outputs and disregarding what they may know about outcomes, would rob the government of vital performance information that can feed back into policy evaluation. It should be noted, however, that the 1996 National Commission of Audit urges the separation of service delivery from policy making.

The integrated model has been challenged by a concept emerging out of a branch of economics known as principal-agent theory. This contemporary theory argues that principals (for example, those making policy at the centre of government) may not be able to effectively control or monitor the performance of agents (for example, those who implement the policies in operating units) because the latter have their own interests and the costs of ensuring compliance are likely to be quite high. Those who argue this position believe it likely that government policy will be captured by service providers who have informational advantages – they know more about the services than do those who make the policies. The solution devised by reformers attuned to this theory is to decouple agents from principals and to narrowly define the task assigned to service agencies so as to facilitate the monitoring of the policies that providers are mandated to carry out. Application of this line of reasoning has led to the proliferation of single-purpose agencies, such as those established pursuant to the "Next Steps" initiative in the United Kingdom.

Theory aside, there is a strong basis for concluding that decoupling agencies from departments has boosted the awareness of service managers that they are indeed in charge, that they are not just one link in a long chain of command, and that they have the means and opportunity to shape their agency to be a productive, performance-driven organisation. In visits to decoupled agencies in New Zealand and the United Kingdom, this writer sensed a new excitement that was not present in other well-run organisations. It was as if these agencies were given a fresh lease on life and empowered to make their own way with the resources and policy directives given to them.

Decoupled agencies are animated by a fresh sense of purpose – an awareness that they are not quite the same entities they were prior to being separated from their parent departments. They produce their own business plans and annual reports, they keep their own books and publish financial statements, they set performance targets and establish service standards. Each has its own chief executive and organisational identity. Quite a few have used their new authority to re-examine missions and working methods, and some have re-engineered the way they operate. Much of this vigour undoubtedly is due to the newness and fanfare of being launched as a distinct agency. At some time, the newness and excitement will fade away, and each agency will simply be a production unit in a vast state apparatus. It will be at that point that the efficiency, morale and advantages of separateness will be open to examination.

In addition to liberating and energising agencies, decoupling aims at shaking up departments and streamlining their operations. When agencies are split off, the argument runs, the parent departments should concentrate on policy guidance rather than service delivery. Their staff should be pruned and delayered, and operating responsibility should devolve to the agencies. Perhaps because it is a small country, New Zealand has had greater success in refocusing departments than has the United Kingdom. In both countries, however, the expectation that the two entities will have an arm's-length relationship, in which the department will bargain hard to get more outputs at lower cost from its agencies, has proven to be somewhat unrealistic. When an agency is the only (or preponderant) supplier of the department's outputs, the two sides tend to develop an accommodating rather than a contestable relationship. The volume and price of the goods or services contracted for will be significantly influenced by what the agency believes is achievable and by what the department has to spend. Typically, it will not be a case of one side dictating terms to the other under the threat of purchasing the goods and services from an alternative source. The two entities also are likely to be interdependent as regards policy advice. Agencies have an interest in the direction that policy is taking, and departments have a need for the information and insights gleaned by their agencies in the course of providing services.

Several issues have been raised concerning the reliance on decoupled agencies for services and resources. These issues are set forth below in the form of questions because they cannot be resolved with the evidence and experience accumulated thus far.

- Does the agency format narrowly emphasise efficiency and outputs at the expense of effectiveness and outcomes?

- Do agencies ignore the collective interest and thereby pose political risk to the government?

- Is the provision of public services unduly fragmented among disconnected or competitive agencies, each doing its own thing without strong co-ordination from the centre?

- Do ministries or departments have a sufficient capacity for making informed policy and monitoring performance?

- Does the establishment of independent agencies undermine traditional public service values and impede mobility of civil servants within government?

- Does the operational independence of departments threaten the doctrine of ministerial accountability?

Australia and France have opted for devolution as an alternative to decoupling. The operating units observed in Australia appear to enjoy much of the independence found in decoupled agencies, and they have taken active responsibility for developing and carrying out a work programme and for spending and reporting on financial resources. These units are responsible for social security and taxation, two governmental functions that have well-established field offices and highly valued uniformity and consistency in performing assigned tasks. These characteristics may allow more successful devolution than in organisations that have more diversified responsibilities. The French situation varies among ministries, with substantial progress on devolution in some but hardly any progress in others. But as additional ministries move in this direction, it may be possible to gain the benefits of agency status without incurring some of the risks.

4. Flexibility and performance

Regardless of the form of organisation, the key issue is the extent to which operating units apply the new flexibility given to them to improve the efficiency and effectiveness of services. The basic flexibility pertains to shifting funds among items of expenditure and between fiscal years. Each country (except for France) allows almost complete discretion in spending within cash limits on running costs. The main restrictions pertain to the number and remuneration of senior officials. France still maintains separate controls on personnel, but these may be eased as reform progresses. This writer has not heard any complaints of abuse of spending discretion by departments or agencies. Some concern has been expressed that funds would be wasted if each administrative unit (such as a branch or division of a local agency) were given control of its own budget. In some cases, the finance ministry has urged fuller devolution while headquarters staff in spending departments have taken a more cautious approach, pointing to the lack of management skills and experience in individual units and to the inefficiencies of scale that might result from allowing each unit to spend as it wishes.

Shifts between fiscal years have been liberalised by permitting agencies to carry over unused funds and to pre-spend a portion of the next year's budget. Typically, the amount that may be carried forward or pre-spent is limited to a certain percentage of appropriated funds. These limits guard against hoarding of funds at a rate that would jeopardise the capacity of central agencies to control future spending. The new arrangements combine annual appropriations control and multi-year flexibility in implementing the budget. In several countries, spending flexibility is regulated by allowing agencies to earn interest on funds carried forward and by charging interest on pre-spent funds.

Entrusting managers with responsibility for their operating resources has not compromised spending control. It has proven easier to maintain cash limits when managers are given a fixed budget within which to operate than when spending details are controlled by outsiders. Managers have demonstrated that they can maintain timely and accurate financial records and that they can compile financial statements that comply with accounting standards. Some countries (New Zealand and Sweden) are confident that spending units can responsibly manage their cash, and they are moving to increase the role of these units in disbursing funds and maintaining their own bank accounts. Some problems have been encountered at lower managerial levels, where experience and technical skills are more limited. The French solution has been to devolve managerial responsibility at the pace that responsibility centres (or other devolved units) demonstrate capacity to follow the rules and prudently use their resources. The budget ministry has devised a formal rating system for measuring the readiness of a local unit to assume responsibility for its resources.

In every country, flexibility in using resources is linked to increased accountability for financial and operating results. Each country has introduced new instruments for compiling performance information and reporting on results. New Zealand relies on contracts between agencies and ministries. France builds performance measures into contracts between responsibility centres and ministries. In Australia and Sweden, departments and agencies compare planned and actual performance in annual reports. The United Kingdom requires "Next Steps" agencies to negotiate key performance targets with their departments, with results succinctly displayed in the government's annual "Next Steps" report.

Although there has been a significant upsurge in the volume of performance indicators, the impact of this information on managerial behaviour is less certain. The British government has had substantial success because it deliberately targets a small number of measures and publicises them in prominent reports. Australia has taken a different tack, encouraging departments to measure or describe the full array of outputs and outcomes that pertain to their programmes. But although Commonwealth departments generate and produce vast quantities of performance information every year, the impact of this material on programme and management decisions is limited. New Zealand specifies output targets in purchase agreements, but it has made less progress in measuring and monitoring outcomes.

In theory, the budget should be one of the principal means by which performance measures affect public policy. It should not be difficult to devise a performance-based budget system in which each increment of resources is directly linked to a planned increment in outputs. (It is not practicable, however, to directly link resources and outcomes.) Yet the governments examined here have not closely linked performance and budgeted resources, preferring instead an arrangement in which data on actual or expected results are just one of several influences on the budget. New Zealand has forged the closest link: it budgets and appropriates by object class rather than by items of expenditure, and it provides for planned outputs to be specified in purchase agreements between agencies and ministries. However, each output class typically consists of multiple performance measures, so that it is not easy to determine the portion of an appropriation allocated for the production of particular outputs. Australia and Sweden have shifted the bulk of performance information from budget documents to annual reports, thereby concentrating attention on actual rather than planned performance. The expectation is that past results will feed into future budget decisions, but neither government formally allocates resources on the basis of performance. In the United Kingdom, each department now publishes its own public expenditure report; these documents contain a considerable amount of performance information, but the direct impact on the budget may be more apparent than real.

The current wave of reforms is aimed at changing managerial behaviour, not just at rationalising budget choice. Managers – not budget makers – are intended to be the prime users of performance information. There is some apprehension that if resources were allocated on the basis of performance, the quality of the information might degrade because managers would be reluctant to produce data that would be used against them at budget time. Budget officials want performance measures, along with other information, to be available when they allocate resources. They also want a strong role in prodding departments and agencies to improve performance and to implement new accountability methods. But budget officials do not believe that the state-of-the-art performance measurement is sufficiently advanced to justify an explicit cause-effect linkage of resources and results.

5. Accounting and auditing

If the relationship of budgets and results is relatively loose, though somewhat closer than it once was, the measurement of performance is taking on increased prominence in financial management through the overhaul of accounting systems and the extension of audit requirements to agency financial statements and annual reports. This development is proceeding in several stages. One is a shift from cash-based to accrual accounting; a second is the requirement that departments and agencies maintain their own financial accounts and publish annual financial statements and reports; a third is the comparison of planned and actual performance; and a final stage is the audit of financial and performance statements. In some countries (New Zealand and the United Kingdom) the accounting reforms have been extended to the budget; in others (Australia and Sweden) they have not. However, recent developments indicate that Australia will also apply accounting standards to the budget.

Accrual accounting has been implemented in New Zealand and is being introduced in Australia and the United Kingdom. The governments moving in this direction have accepted the principle that commercial standards should be applied except when they do not suit the operations of public entities. The accounting reforms are seen as an important part of the process of transforming spenders into managers. Those who manage public money must be accountable for costs. They must know the full resources expended and they must control those costs. The logic of accrual accounting requires that operating units be charged for the cost of the accommodations they occupy, the assets they use, and (in some cases) the indirect costs of operations. Two conditions must prevail for accrual accounting to be more than a bookkeeping exercise: managers must have genuine choice in deciding whether to bear the costs; and the costs they are charged must have an impact on the financial resources available to them.

- If, for example, managers were charged for government-supplied accommodations, they should have the option of relocating to other premises. If they lack real choice, and must use assigned space and pay whatever is charged, full-cost accounting would be counterproductive. Rather than empowering managers to take responsibility for costs, it would tell them that they are powerless to run their own operations.

- The second condition is that costs affect the resources available to the agency. If an agency were charged for depreciation, this cost should reduce the resources otherwise available for operations. In New Zealand, for example, the capital charge levied on the net assets of departments is part of each agency's operating costs; the higher this charge, the less money is available for other expenditures. Controlling costs in this manner suggests that the accrual basis be extended to budgeting and not be limited to financial reporting. New Zealand has already moved in this direction, and the United Kingdom has announced its intention to do so. It is worth noting that when the budget is placed on an accrual basis, expenditure is still controlled on a cash basis. Thus, the United Kingdom intends to maintain cash limits on running costs after accrual methods are introduced.

Although accrual accounting and budgeting require some start-up investment in training and information systems, the agencies studied here indicate that they have had little difficulty making the switch. But in many cases, agencies see this merely as a technical requirement rather than as a management tool. Some agencies are using accrual accounting to facilitate full-cost recovery through user charges or efficiency improvements through the measurement of unit costs. In the future, one can envision the use of the new accounting systems to budget on the basis of marginal (rather than average) costs, to distinguish between fixed and variable costs in resource allocation, to compare lease or buy options, to establish the actual cost of loans or guarantees issued by the government, to measure the incremental cost of outputs, to determine benchmark or standard costs, to analyse the variance between planned and actual costs or performance, and so on. To do these things, governments will have to greatly improve their competence in cost allocation and analysis, which is a different way of looking at budgets than standard expenditure computations.

Financial statements, prepared according to accepted accounting principles, are rapidly becoming standard features in department and agency annual reports. The array of financial statements is similar to that found in commercial organisations. Agencies indicate that they have had relatively little difficulty in compiling the data, but they do not generally make much use of these statements in internal management. As in the business sector, these statements satisfy external reporting requirements. It may be that the greatest value of these financial reports is the process of preparing them. To compile financial statements, agencies must maintain timely and accurate accounts, and they must be informed on the condition of their assets and liabilities. In every country, there has been a marked increase in the accounting responsibility placed on departments and agencies. In several countries, it no longer suffices for the Treasury to publish a combined statement for the government; spending units have to keep their own books.

Annual reports also contain an increasing amount of performance information. This portion of the reports is not as standardised as the financial statements, and probably never will be. At present, much of the performance information is descriptive; agencies use the annual report to enumerate many of the things they did during the year. As annual reports take on more importance – as is the case in Australia, New Zealand and Sweden – agencies will be required to present a more systematic comparison of actual against planned performance. This requirement may be enforced by subjecting both the financial statements and the performance information to audit. Sweden has already taken this step: it has given the National Audit Office broad scope to review the annual reports of all agencies and to qualify those reports that have material shortcomings. This role fits easily into the Swedish system because the audit office is under the jurisdiction of the Ministry of Finance. In other countries, however, the audit office is accountable to parliament, so that aggressive review of annual reports or of other documents sometimes generates tension between parliament and the finance ministry. In Australia, Department of Finance officials have been wary that an active role by the audit office in reviewing programme evaluations and performance information might dampen the willingness of managers to take a hard look at their operations. Nevertheless, the trend is unmistakably in the direction of broadening the role of auditors in reviewing statements made by government agencies concerning their performance.

6. Policies and programmes

In the OECD community, running costs typically account for less than 20% of central government expenditure. A much larger share of the budget is spent on programmes: transfers to households, subsidies to businesses, grants to other governments and other programme expenditures. These expenditures have been rising much more rapidly than running costs and are much more rigid. It would be wasted opportunity if administrative operations were modernised, but the methods by which programmes were selected, implemented and carried out were unchanged. In fact, most of the governments reviewed here regard enhanced programme effectiveness as a key objective of reform. Yet few of the innovations discussed thus far would have much impact on the mix or effectiveness of government programmes, or on the amount spent on them. The logic of restructuring assumes that well-run organisations will re-examine programme cost and performance, but there is little evidence that this expectation has been realised.

In a fundamental sense, what government does – its objectives and policies, and the priorities and programmes on which it spends money – are political issues, not management issues. Performance information and the other instruments discussed above can influence policy and programme decisions, but they are rarely the only or most important influences. Moreover, these decisions cannot be routinised in ways that administrative operations often are. Political and policy actions tend to be opportunistic, taken according to no fixed schedule but on the impulse of political leaders when conditions are deemed right. For this reason, the episodic activities of Swedish study committees may have greater impact on public policy than does the scheduled evaluation of programmes such as occurs in Australia. For generations, the British government has issued major policy pronouncements in White Papers that are published when the government sees fit to do so. These papers are not published according to any fixed schedule, but they often influence ensuing policies.

Several countries have sought to rationalise government programmes and policies through strategic planning, outcome measures and programme evaluation. Strategic planning is the most ambitious of these instruments. It differs from conventional planning in that the object is not merely to change programmes but to transform the organisation itself. The key questions raised in a strategic review pertain to what the organisation should be, not simply to what it should do. This type of question is most likely to elicit a strategic review when new agencies are launched, as in New Zealand and the United Kingdom. The process of defining what the new organisation should be helps build group identification and enables the agency to project itself as a transformed entity. Once the agency is an ongoing operation, its annual business or operating plan might be more relevant for management decisions than the longer-range strategic outlook would be.

Strategic planning has much fuller application in business than in government. The most important strategic decision for a business is whether to enter or exit a particular market – whether, for example, to remain a typewriter company or to abandon that line of business and become an information processing company instead. In government, fundamental decisions on whether an agency should operate a particular programme are made through the political process, not by public agencies. Yet strategic planning can facilitate change by an agency when conditions are supportive. In New Zealand, for example, the Customs Department has been largely transformed from an organisation that interdicted illegal goods and enforced tariffs to one that facilitates international trade. In this case, department leaders suggested that the change was expedited and legitimised by strategic planning, but would have occurred in due course without the strategic exercise. This transformation, which has occurred in the customs operations of other countries as well, points to strategic planning as an opportunistic rather than a routinised activity.

The reform agenda has two principal means of changing programmes: outcome measures that feed back to programme decisions, and periodic evaluations. The former typically are compiled annually; the latter require a longer time frame. In every country, the government has encountered considerably more difficulty measuring outcomes than outputs. Measuring outcomes is not a temporary or transitional problem; it will not be solved by installing better performance information systems. It has not been solved in New Zealand by making ministers responsible for outcomes, or in Australia by investing heavily in programme evaluation, or in the United Kingdom by targeting a few key measures, or in Sweden by investing in effectiveness audits. It certainly will not be solved by incorporating these measures in annual budget exercises. Outcomes are difficult to measure and apply because they relate to matters beyond the direct control of the responsible agency. Outcomes measure social conditions, not only organisational performance.

Although governments may not cause outcomes, they must be aware of them. Outcome measures are directional signals that tell an agency whether it is getting closer to or further away from vital social objectives, not because the agency is to be blamed or credited for the results but because it should know whether its programmes are accomplishing what is intended. Outcomes are strategic measures that spur an agency to question what it is doing and where it is heading. An agency should have only a few strategic measures; too many would dim the signal and might have a paralysing impact. It should not be hard to define a few such measures. They relate to the essence of the agency – the reason(s) why it exists and carries out particular programmes. In selecting such measures, an agency would do well to be guided by its answer to the following questions: why do we exist at all, and how do we know whether we are succeeding or not?

These are strategic questions; like strategic planning, they focus on the organisation itself rather than on the things it does. Yet there also is ample room for assessing programmes in the light of the objectives set for them. Australia has gone further than any country in injecting evaluation into the stream of policy and budget decisions, but it has discovered how much easier it is to conduct evaluations than to use them in making decisions. Efforts to increase the use of evaluations run up against two problems. One is the anomaly that the influence of evaluations on government actions rises when they are integrated into decisional cycles, such as annual budget formulation, but that routinised evaluations tend to lack depth and are therefore less likely to disturb the prevailing allocation of resources and programmes. Second, the culture of evaluation is one that looks for means of improving programmes by finding shortcomings in existing operations. Evaluation is not likely to be long supported by government if it habitually finds failure in government. Programme evaluation operates at the intersection of politics and management. It challenges both the objectives of government and the assumptions of programmes. For this reason alone, it is more difficult to institutionalise than most other items on the reform agenda. The stakes are higher and the political risks greater.

7. Pathways to reform

There are many roads to reform of the public sector. When a country embarks on restructuring public management, it must take a path that is compatible with its political and governmental conditions. What works or is acceptable in one country might not succeed in another. The threshold question for the many OECD member countries that have not sought to fundamentally change management practices is whether they should start down this path at all. Why, in the light of the problems encountered by the countries examined here, should any other country make the enormous investment in reforming public management? Why should political leaders try to change the managing culture of government departments when the task will take a decade or more to complete, and when the payoffs in better public services will take some time to materialise?

Contemporary management reform has been driven less by political logic than by budget pressures and a sense that public institutions have become outmoded and inefficient. Undoubtedly, management reform in the public sector has been influenced by parallel developments in business management, but the greatest influence has come from awareness of the need to do more with less. Politicians can curry some voter approval by projecting a modern, reformist image. But the search for votes has not been the main motivating force, nor is it likely to be in the future. In fact, politicians risk being punished by voters if reform is perceived as dismantling the modern state or weakening its capacity to perform. The Labour Party paid a price at the polls in New Zealand in national elections following its bold reform of the public sector. Reformist governments also have been replaced in France and Sweden, though the management changes probably had little to do with the election results in these countries.

In each of the countries surveyed here, public sector restructuring has survived a change in government. In every case, the successor government has built on the reforms already under way and has deepened or extended them. In the United Kingdom, the "Financial Management Initiative" was broadened by "Next Steps". In France, the Rocard initiative was reinforced by Prime Minister Juppé's circular which converted the responsibility centres from pilot tests to national policy. In Sweden, the triennial budget frames introduced by the Social Democratic government were implemented by the centre-right coalition that succeeded it. In New Zealand, a Labour government enacted pioneering reforms that were subsequently endorsed and broadened by the National government. And in Australia, the 1996 change of government was followed by a National Commission of Audit that applauded previous initiatives such as the forward estimates, evaluation strategy and running costs regime and proposed some additional innovations. In all of the countries studied, formal assessments sponsored by the government came to the conclusion that the reforms have had a positive impact on public management. In none of the countries did the assessment call for a return to the old ways.

The analysis offered here says more about changes in procedure than about changes in behaviour. Yet the true payoff in government restructuring comes from the latter. Because the analysis was done while restructuring was under way – it has not yet been completed in any of the countries – it does not provide a final judgment of the sustainability of the reforms. There is reason to expect that, sooner or later, reform runs out of steam, perhaps because the government's interest or agenda turns to other matters, perhaps because the core ideas and standards of public management change. Some aspects of reform are likely to be subject to political controversy, particularly the fragmentation of the civil service and the contracting out of core government functions. Nevertheless, judging from the length of time that the governments in the five countries have persisted with efforts to modernise public management, we can expect important changes to endure. If they do, contemporary governments should have more efficient public sectors, though not necessarily more positive programme outcomes. There is considerable evidence of efficiency gains resulting from decreases in staffing levels and forced reductions in operating expenditures, but none of the countries has yet undertaken a systematic examination of programme results to determine whether and how they have been affected by the changes under way. The countries are laboratories of new management practices. They provide the OECD community with a rich menu of possibilities for coping with fiscal stress, upgrading public sector efficiency, improving the quality of services and responsiveness to customers, and changing the operating culture of government departments and agencies. There is much to be learned from their experiences, and many new possibilities for organising work and delivering services have been opened. Now is one of the truly exciting periods in the evolution of public management. But there are also many questions to be asked. Governments bent on reforming management practices must seek their own answers.

8. The process of reform

One of the first choices for restructuring governments is whether to proceed on an across-the-board basis or in a more piecemeal and gradual manner. Should prospective innovations be pilot-tested first, as they were in Sweden, or imposed in advance, as they were in New Zealand? Pilot tests have the obvious advantage of enabling the government to build support for the reform, garner some experience and make adjustments before the changes are fully launched. But there is also the risk that pilot-testing will dissipate interest and support before the reforms have been institutionalised. Moreover, because it is conducted under experimental conditions, a pilot may not be a true test of how a reform will operate when it is fully implemented. Despite extensive advance testing, Sweden found that a fixed three-year cycle was unduly rigid and was not appropriate for all agencies. On the other hand, implementing the reforms through political (or management) blitzkrieg might bring quick results but increase the need for major adjustments as experience accumulates. This has been the case in New Zealand, which has been compelled to add many features that were not contemplated when the reforms were initiated. In view of the far-reaching nature of the reforms, it is likely that adjustments will have to be made along the way, regardless of the manner in which they are introduced.

With the five models examined here, governments might experiment with more than one type of reform. They might try to "mix and match" elements from different countries – for example, Australia's evaluation strategy with New Zealand's output measures and purchase agreements, or France's responsibility centres with Sweden's multi-year budget frames. The problem, however, is that the more varied and complex a management system is, the more costly it is to manage. The new managerial regime imposes substantial informational demands on departments; governments must guard against overburdening their administrative organs by melding together requirements from different management systems.

Management reform generally has been an amalgam of top-down guidance and bottom-up implementation. Without impetus from the top, reform is not likely to get off the ground, and even if it does, implementation will be uneven. France decentralised reform by enabling ministries to innovate as they saw fit. Some ministries enthusiastically embraced reform, while others only went through the motions and made few genuine changes. New Zealand, by contrast, took a highly centralised approach that blanketed the entire state sector with uniform rules and requirements. Its approach might not be easily transplanted to larger, more diverse political systems. At some point, managers must be brought into the process; they must feel that the reforms are workable and that their concerns are being addressed. If they are not, managers may subvert the reforms – usually not by opposing change but by being indifferent to it. Changing the culture of management cannot happen without changing the behaviour of managers.

Regardless of the approach taken, reform will not be quick or easy. A country considering an overhaul of public management faces a decade or more of innovation and experimentation and is likely to move in directions that were not foreseen when the reforms were initiated.

9. Governmental organisation

In each of the countries, restructuring has been targeted at the processes by which decisions are taken, resources are managed, information is gathered and reported, and ministers and officials are held to account for what they have done and accomplished. In Australia and Sweden, these changes have taken place within pre-existing organisational structures; in the other countries, the creation of new organisations has been an important "driver" of reform. Australia has not established new organisations, though it did re-organise departments within broad ministerial portfolios. As noted earlier, the government that took office in 1996 may decide to separate service-delivery agencies from policy-making departments. Sweden has found no need to re-organise because its governmental structure defines the roles of ministries and agencies.

Can management be reformed within conventional or pre-existing organisations? The answer depends on the objectives of re-organisation. If, as often was the case in the past, organisational responsibilities are shifted among departments to shake things up by disturbing existing arrangements, then re-organisation is not likely to have much impact on performance. This type of re-organisation is no longer in vogue; it is generally recognised that the unintended effects may outweigh the intended ones. If, however, administrative responsibilities are re-arranged to make agents (service providers) accountable to principals (ministers or top managers), then the re-organisation can fundamentally alter organisational performance.

In many of the countries, there is a formal demarcation between policy and service. Is this distinction tenable? Does it clarify roles and responsibilities, or does it muddle accountability by ignoring the interdependence of policy and administration? There is no doubt that the roles can be formally differentiated; the question is whether the formal distinctions hold up in practice. In several decoupled countries, three layers of government have emerged: the ministerial level at which political responsibility is lodged; the department which exercises managerial responsibility on behalf of the government; and the delivery agencies which are responsible for providing the services. Inevitably, problems have emerged in relations among the entities. When there is a breakdown in services or a failure to perform, is it a political or managerial responsibility? Are the policy makers at fault, or those managers who have failed to perform as expected?

When several entities share responsibility, difficulties may emerge in their relationships and in enforcing accountability. Some matters will fall between the cracks of the accountability system. In the United Kingdom, for example, the relationship between agency chief executives and departmental permanent secretaries requires clarification. New Zealand has experienced some difficulty in sorting out the respective responsibilities of ministers and chief executives. In these and other countries, a period of adjustment may be needed before the new roles are fully institutionalised, devolution takes root, and understandings are forged. But more than settling in may be required to work out differences in perspectives. Do the new relationships invite protracted tension and misunderstanding? Can contractual arrangements, such as framework documents and performance or purchase agreements, establish trust between policy makers and managers or compensate for the lack of trust? Is there an inherent contradiction between the doctrine and expectations of devolution on the one hand and the responsibilities of elected politicians and senior managers on the other? What is the appropriate distribution of risk among the various entities and levels? Is it feasible in democratic regimes to wall off political risk from managerial discretion? The urgency of these questions is largely a function of the organisational changes under way. The issue is less troubling in Sweden, where the separation of ministries and agencies is well established, than in New Zealand and the United Kingdom, where long-standing doctrines of ministerial accountability have been challenged.

In all of the countries, restructuring has strained relations between central agencies and line departments. The expectation of managers that they will be free to spend as they will and to operate their agencies without central interference clashes with the ongoing responsibility of central agencies for legality, efficiency and effectiveness in public expenditure. In reforming public management, it is much easier to specify what central agencies should stop doing than to decide what they should continue (or start) to do. Questions that must be resolved in sorting out the respective roles include: What is the proper division of responsibility between the finance ministry (or similar organisation) and spending departments? How are disputes between the two to be resolved when the spenders feel that central intervention infringes on their managerial discretion and the central agencies feel that failure to intervene would weaken financial control? When is central guidance appropriate, or even essential, and when is it meddlesome? What should the central agency do when it detects inadequate capacity (or will) in newly independent departments to manage their own operations? What should be the balance between advising and prodding, between encouraging agencies to get on with the task of managing their affairs and intervening when they are not up to the task? The answers will differ from country to country, but in none can post-reform public management abandon central oversight and guidance.

Management reform has uncluttered budgeting from many of the details of expenditure. The expectation was that budget offices would thereby be freed up to work on larger strategic and policy issues: the control of total expenditure and programme innovation. In some models, the budget was to become the central organ for strategic management in government, prodding departments and agencies to adopt the reforms and change their operating methods. This model portends a fundamental transformation in the role of the finance ministry (or similar organ) from a controlling organisation into a leader of management reform. This transformation clearly is under way in Australia, New Zealand and the United Kingdom, though the affected agencies do not always acknowledge the extent to which their relationship with the budget organisation has been altered. Change is less pronounced in Sweden, but only because the Ministry of Finance has always been relatively small. There is evidence of change in the French budget ministry, but it will probably be another few years before the full impact of modernisation is felt.

What would a transformed budget organisation be? During the "reform" period, budget officials do not have to face this question because they are busy with transitional work, getting rid of old rules and prodding agencies to adopt new methods. But once reform has been normalised, the budget office will have to reflect on how it fits into the operations of government, which controls it is to maintain, and what levers it must have to induce recalcitrant agencies to produce. In a culture of management that professes to value devolution, defining a useful role for central departments is not an easy task. The British Treasury has tackled this question in a fundamental review that has produced a smaller, delayered organisation. Other governments can be expected to consider the issue in the years ahead.

In much of the reform literature, the relationship between central organs (such as finance ministries) and the operating departments is portrayed in confusing terms. The role of the centre, it is said, is to assist but not intervene, to make strategic decisions but not the everyday ones, to control total spending but not the particulars, to devise new management methods but not to impose them, to encourage the measurement of results but not to allocate on the basis of results, to push for efficiencies but not to capture (for the government) the financial benefits of efficiency, to speak for devolution but to allow each department to devolve in its own way. Other mixed messages can be added to this list, but the point is obvious to any budget official who has wondered why the finance ministry is not applauded for the strides it has already taken. Budgeting in the future will be a difficult balancing act, for it will have to reconcile the conflicting roles and responsibilities ascribed to the budget office.

In sorting out its future niche, the budget organisation will be pulled in two directions. One is for budgeting to become integrated into financial management through closer links with accounting and auditing, cost and output measurement, management information systems, and other management routines. The other direction is to become the policy-making centre of government, to be at the frontier of programme development and strategic thinking. On paper, the two roles can be harmonised. In fact, Australia has vigorously sought to integrate both roles: to build budgeting into the routines of financial management as well as into the opportunities for policy innovation. This combined role is the ideal, for the regularities of budgeting make an excellent instrument of financial management while the decision-impelling characteristics of budgeting make it an excellent instrument of strategic choice. Packaging the two roles in the same organisation will not be an easy task, however.

10. Means of accountability

Although accountability is a key element of reform in all of the countries, the means of securing it differ. The United Kingdom has taken the position that true accountability lies in turning over as much as possible to the market, either by privatisation or by contracting out. This determination to extend the boundaries of the market to the public sector implies little confidence in the conventional means sought in Australia. New Zealand also seeks to inject market discipline into the public sector, but does so by recasting the budget into a contract for specified outputs. France takes a different approach, relying on the commitment of public managers to perform well, while Sweden seeks to enhance accountability by relying on the division of labour between ministries and agencies. The selection of instruments depends on the objectives sought by the government. If the aim is to significantly slow the growth rate of public expenditure, then restructuring is likely to rely on market-type mechanisms. If, however, the principal objective is to improve efficiency in public expenditure, then decentralised management combined with an emphasis on performance measurement might be preferred.

In one way or another, all the countries place some weight on the measurement of performance. They do so either because it is a vital feature of the accountability framework or because these measures substitute (if only weakly) for markets. Reliance on performance measurement opens the door to practical questions which reform-minded governments must face. Who should have the last word in selecting the appropriate measures? Is it preferable to devise a large number of measures that cover the range of activities or outputs, or would it be better to concentrate on a few, even if this entails neglecting certain aspects of performance? How does one wean agencies away from process and efficiency measures and toward those that address outcomes and results? What should be the link between output and outcome measures? What, if anything, should governments do to avert distortions in behaviour resulting from the use of measures as official targets?

The foregoing questions pertain to the development of measures. Additional questions arise concerning their use. By itself, measuring performance changes little or nothing. What matters are the steps taken after the data are gathered. To what extent should performance data be audited to assure accuracy? What interventions should be made if performance falls short of the target? What should be the role of parliament in reviewing performance and initiating corrective actions? How should the measures be enforced through performance agreements or other procedures?

11. Linkage of performance measures to budget allocations

New Zealand and France may be at opposite poles in relating performance data and other management changes to budget policy. New Zealand expressly links budgets and performance; it makes appropriations by output classes. The French seem wary of coupling budget policy and performance, preferring instead to have budget allocations reflect the government's policies and priorities. The tighter the relationship between budgets and performance, the greater the need for cost accounting methods that allocate the full cost of services to outputs. Given the primitive state of cost accounting in many countries, full-cost attribution is not currently feasible.

The progressive introduction of business accounting practices – such as accrual accounting – into the public sector should make it feasible to base budget decisions on performance information. Nevertheless, questions may be raised concerning the implications of this trend. Should managers be charged for costs over which they lack effective control? For example, does it serve managerial accountability to charge managers for space occupied in government-owned buildings when they must use the assigned accommodations? What gain is there in allocating overhead or other costs that are outside the manager's discretion? Ideally, the use of commercial-type accounting should keep pace with the expansion of managerial discretion, but this ideal may be difficult to translate into concrete practice.

Finally, in considering the linkage of budgets and performance, one should not lose sight of the fact that restructuring directly touches only on operating (or running) costs, not on programme expenditures, which are much more prominent in government budgets. The logic of restructuring assumes that well-run organisations will also examine the cost and performance of the money spent on transfer payments, grants and subsidies. But the analysis provides little evidence that this expectation has been realised. When all is done, if restructuring reaches only to the internal operations of agencies, industrial democracies will enter the next century more efficiently managed but with budget crises at least as severe as those many have faced in the past two decades.

ISBN 978-92-64-06087-6
Evolutions in Budgetary Practice
Allen Schick and the OECD Senior Budget Officials
© OECD 2009

Chapter 5

The Changing Role of the Central Budget Office*

---

* This article was originally published in the *OECD Journal on Budgeting*, Vol. 1, No. 1, 2001. At the time of writing, Allen Schick was a Visiting Fellow, Governmental Studies, Brookings Institution, Washington DC, and Professor, School of Public Affairs, University of Maryland, United States. Boxed comments were made in 2009.

1. Introduction

The traditional role of the central budget office is incompatible with the management reforms unfolding in various OECD member countries. These reforms are grounded on the principle that managers must be permitted to run their operations without undue outside interference. The logic of reform is that only when managers are free to use money and other organisational resources within agreed budgets can they be responsible for the organisation's successes or failures. In countries where a culture of reform has taken hold, there is consensus that halfway measures do not suffice, that managers either are free to act or are not. It is not a matter of relaxing one or another restriction, but of reshaping the operations of public institutions and the behaviour of those who work in them. The budget process is one of the main arenas in which the machinery of government is undergoing fundamental transformation.

This article examines the central budget office as an agency of government; it does not consider the budget office's relationship with the national legislature. This relationship has undergone significant change in countries where the legislature has become more independent in budget matters and has established its own budget staff. In the past, it was common for national legislatures to rely on the government's budget office for advice and information. The government's near-monopoly on budget information and options rendered the legislature subservient to its will. This situation has been changed by the legislatures demanding a more active role and by arming themselves with staff that produce their own economic forecasts and policy analyses. In some countries, the central budget office has been cast into an adversarial relationship with the legislature, which has become more active in amending the budget presented by the government.

The traditional role of the budget office has been to function as a central command-and-control post, specifying the items of expenditure, monitoring compliance with regulations, ensuring that the inputs are those agreed in the budget, and intervening as deemed appropriate. This role cannot coexist with the discretion accorded managers in the new public administration. Either managers decide on the items of expenditure (personnel costs, supplies, rental fees, and so on) or others do it for them. If the latter, managers do not have genuine freedom to operate according to their best judgment.

Defining a new role for the central budget office that is compatible with contemporary managerial concepts is a difficult task, for it entails balancing the critical need of the government for financial discipline against the need of managers for freedom to act. Simple divestiture of control is not a viable option, for doing so would destroy the discipline on which all budgeting rests. This article explores the role and behaviour of the central budget office in a devolved environment that shifts decision-making authority with respect to the particulars of public expenditure from central institutions to line agencies, and from headquarters in these agencies to subordinate units and field offices. The article discusses changes in the three basic roles of the budget office – controlling the totals, establishing priorities, and seeking efficiency – that might be conducted in the new environment of devolved management.

Not all OECD member countries have embraced a culture of reform. By "culture of reform" we have in mind innovations that uproot established practices of public administration and radiate through the public sector. Where this culture thrives, reform is comprehensive rather than piecemeal, at the core of government rather than at the periphery, institutionalised rather than pilot tested. This culture does not pertain only to budgeting, but to other managerial actions as well. In countries animated by a culture of reform, managerial discretion is not an alternative form of public administration; it is the way the government operates. The countries in the vanguard of this movement include Australia, New Zealand, Sweden and the United Kingdom.

France is an important and innovative addition to this list. For centuries, France operated one of the most centralised financial control systems in the world, with staff posted in the Ministry of Finance deciding whether particular expenditures should be made. Central control was meant to assure uniformity in the public service, but it also bureaucratised public administration. Early in the current century, the French Parliament devised and enacted legislation that loosens control and shifts the focus of the central budget to promoting performance. The new mode of budgeting has impelled a cultural change in the French Ministry of Finance but, half a dozen years after the reform was launched, the central budget role has not been fully determined.

What about the many OECD member countries that have not reformed public management or have taken only halting steps in this direction? Is the managerial revolution of such limited scope that it should interest only those countries that have already introduced major reforms or are contemplating doing so? I think not. Most OECD member countries are affected by the conditions that have impelled the transformation of public institutions.

Regardless of their posture on managerial reform, central budget offices cannot ignore the powerful tensions stressing contemporary government: pressure to curtail or eliminate chronic deficits, but not by raising taxes or taking away benefits that citizens have come to expect; consensus that the era of expanding government is over, but demographic trends that harbinger major spending increases in the decades ahead; demands for devolution and decentralisation, coupled with the spreading internationalisation of economic policy; a loss of confidence in the capacity of democratic governments to perform what is expected of them, but pressure to entrust government with even more responsibility for the public welfare; and a rising portion of the budget allocated by statutory formula amid efforts by governments to achieve greater flexibility in allocating resources.

Governments facing these tensions cannot effectively control the budget by operating the detailed controls that served them so well in the past. Trying to do so may weaken their control of the totals, hobble efforts to reprioritise the budget and degrade the efficiency of public expenditure. This is the paradox of contemporary budgeting: central control of the items of expenditure may not give the centre effective control of the budget.

Contemporary pressures on public finance have weakened the efficacy of two of the traditional tools used by the central budget office to control expenditures: *ex ante* specification of the items of expenditure and allocation of the increment. In the past, itemised budgeting protected the totals, while decisions on the increments secured the government's priorities. Itemised control has been attenuated by the growth in total spending – especially in entitlements – incremental priority setting by the inadequacy of increments to finance the built-in growth in expenditures. Controlling the items of expenditure no longer secures control of the totals because: i) the totals are so large and the individual items are so small; and ii) most spending is for entitlements that are not subject to itemised control. All that *ex ante* control accomplishes is to take away from managers their discretion over running costs. In fact, over the years, most OECD member countries have relaxed *ex ante* controls by consolidating the line items into broader frames, increasing the threshold for expenditures that agencies may make without prior approval, and giving managers more flexibility in implementing the budget.

The inadequacy of spending increments also has eroded central budget control. During much of the post-war era, central budget offices influenced government priorities by concentrating on the increment – the additional amounts to be spent in the next or subsequent budgets. Although the increment may have been small relative to the totals, it was the portion that politicians and spending agencies cared about the most. By allocating the increment, the budget office determined which programmes would grow and which initiatives would be undertaken. But incremental budgeting requires increments to allocate. Whether because of weaker economic growth, the built-in rise in entitlement spending, or the reluctance of politicians to raise taxes, spending increments are not currently available in some countries and are not as robust as they once were in others.

If its old role no longer suffices, a budget office has to reconsider what it does and how it fits into the machinery of government. In the course of examining itself, the budget office may have to assess the efficacy of the controls it operates. What levers does it pull to assure compliance with government policy? How does it assure that the bits and pieces of public expenditure do not add up to more than the government wants to spend? How does it make room in constrained budgets for new priorities? How does its voice for fiscal discipline get heard above the din of multiple, often conflicting, demands on government? The countries that have embraced reform have been compelled to address these questions; others are likely to follow suit.

In countries that have decided to transform public administration, the incompatibility of central control of operations and managerial freedom has forced the budget office to revamp its operations. In the typical case, the budget office has divested most (or all) *ex ante* control of running costs and now leads the effort for management improvement. It has a major role in devising new institutional arrangements, integrating budgeting with other management processes, prodding departments and other public entities to measure performance and evaluate results, developing new guidelines and methods for holding managers accountable, and installing new information and reporting systems. As they have withdrawn from the old roles, reformed budget offices have been busy with the new ones.

The full extent of this behavioural revolution is often not recognised by the newly freed managers. Despite the transformation, one still encounters the view that control is as centralised and the budget office as interventionist as before. Managers in spending departments frequently complain that the budget office substitutes its judgment for theirs and is unwilling to entrust them with full discretion to manage their own operations. These perceptions are reinforced by instances in which spending agencies are constrained or overruled by the budget office on particular issues. For example, when the budget office imposes across-the-board cuts on running costs (as has happened in Australia, New Zealand and Sweden), managers take that action as evidence that nothing has changed and that the budget office's grip is as tight as ever. There appears to be a naive view among some line managers that reform means *carte blanche* to spend as they want, as if they were not part of a larger government. Evidently, some managers do not understand that devolution of operations must be accompanied by centralisation of policy making. Reform cannot mean that spending agencies get their way regardless of the budgetary consequences of their actions. If it did, budget offices would soon reimpose the old controls.

In withdrawing from operational control and focusing on strategic policy issues, some central budget offices have gone through an institutional identity crisis. They know what they are no longer to do, but are much less certain as to what they should do. Adjustment has been especially difficult for budget offices embedded in large, powerful finance ministries; in these cases, restructuring the budget function cannot be divorced from consideration of the ministry's overall role. In the United Kingdom, for example, Treasury control has been a bulwark of government for generations. Some of the initiatives impacting on its operations were launched outside the Treasury. Once the reforms were implemented, the Treasury conducted a fundamental review of its operations and reorganised its budget (and other) work. Other countries, however, have refocused the budget office as part of the process of giving managers operational discretion.

It was noted above that some reformed budget offices have become the central outposts for managerial innovation, to the extent that this is now seen as one of the organisation's most salient roles. In my view, this may be a transitional phenomenon. During the early reform period, there is need for central guidance and for a clearinghouse on new ideas and practices. The budget office can advance the cause of reform by producing handbooks and other materials that explain the new processes and advise managers on best (or improved) practices. It also can busy itself revising budgetary forms and procedures and evaluating the progress of reform. The transitional period is likely to be quite extended, for every country that has made the effort has found it necessary to adjust the reforms on the basis of early experience. The Australian, Swedish and British reforms have stretched well over a decade.

Once the reform processes stabilise, efforts to direct managerial improvement from the centre will coexist uneasily with the commitment to managerial discretion. There is a limit to how much the budget office can do in prodding agencies to upgrade their operations, and there is substantial risk that if it pushes too hard, managerial initiative will dry up and a compliance mentality will return. In the long run, managerial innovation must be entrusted to the managers, not to central policy makers.

There is another reason why managerial reform is not likely to be a permanent niche. Managerial leadership is an inadequate basis for budgetary power. What has made the central budget office the powerhouse of government is not that it advises agencies on good practices, but that it allocates resources.

Managerial advice can be ignored; budget decisions cannot. Budget offices often leverage their power over resources to induce agencies to change management practices. But a budget office whose budgetary role is enfeebled will be weak in other matters as well. After reform, no less than before, the core role of the budget office must revolve around the allocation of resources and the routines of preparing and reviewing budgets.

Although budgeting must be the core budget office responsibility, this work may be conducted differently in the future than it was in the past. The basic routines of requesting and making appropriations continue, though they may require somewhat different skills, techniques and information than once were common in budgeting. For example, reformed budget offices are likely to spend less time on implementing the budget than once was the case, but more time monitoring what agencies accomplish with available funds. This change follows from the principle that managers should have broad latitude in spending appropriated funds, but should be closely held to performance objectives.

All budget systems – reformed and traditional – have three basic budget tasks: to maintain aggregate fiscal discipline, to allocate resources in accord with government priorities, and to promote the efficient delivery of services. Fiscal discipline pertains to effective control of the budget totals. An effective budget system is one that has disciplined totals (in contrast to accommodating totals). Allocative efficiency is the capacity to establish priorities within the budget, including the capacity to shift resources from old priorities to new ones, or from less productive to more productive uses, in correspondence with the government's objectives. Operational efficiency is the capacity to progressively reduce the cost of producing the goods and services for which resources are provided. Although the terminology may be unfamiliar, every central budget office is involved with maintaining aggregate fiscal discipline, striving for allocative efficiency, and promoting operational efficiency. How they go about these tasks distinguishes traditional and reformed budget offices.

Budgetary capacity can be assessed in terms of performance in each of the three dimensions. Strong fiscal discipline means that the totals do not merely rise to meet demands. Aggregate fiscal discipline refers not only to the decisions taken in formulating the budget, but also to pressures that arise during the year when the budget is being implemented. Allocative efficiency means not only that the government channels incremental resources to new priorities, but that it has the will and the procedures to transfer funds from lower to higher valued uses. Operational efficiency implies that the budget impels agencies to raise productivity and thereby reduce the cost of goods and services purchased by government.

These essential functions of budgeting are examined in the sections that follow in terms of the role of the central budget office, sanctions and incentives, and informational requirements. In the course of discussing each of these functions, I will explain how a reformed budget system differs from a traditional process.

2. Aggregate fiscal discipline

Control of the totals is the first purpose of every budget system. There would be no need for budgeting if the totals were permitted to float upward to satisfy all demands. Spenders would spend what they wanted without central review or constraint. But if aggregate control is fundamental to budgeting, the form it has taken has changed over the years, and along with it the role of the budget office. In most OECD member countries, budget development was guided by a balanced budget norm. The operative rule was that in any fiscal period spending should not exceed current revenue. Countries differed in their application of this rule; some applied it only to current expenditures, others to capital investments as well. Some included funds carried over from previous periods in calculating current revenue; others did not. Inasmuch as this was a time of relatively limited government, the burden for assuring balance generally fell on expenditures. Balance was enforced through strict constraints on spending; the logic was that if the parts of the budget were effectively controlled, so, too, would the total.

Strict budgetary balance was superseded after World War II by a more flexible rule that allowed the totals to accommodate cyclical changes in economic conditions and secular changes in budgetary demand. The impact of the new norm on aggregate fiscal discipline was remarkable. Government outlays in OECD member countries averaged 28% of GDP in 1960 and about 40% two decades later, a growth rate in excess of 0.5% a year. These spending trends indicate laxity in fiscal discipline that was justified in terms of the economic and social gains achieved through higher government expenditures. The weakening of fiscal discipline also was reflected in the rise of budget deficits, especially after the first oil shock in 1974.

The persistence of high deficits and political resistance to tax increases induced many OECD member countries to reassert fiscal discipline by stabilising the share of public expenditure in GDP. Some countries moved in this direction in the late 1970s, others in the 1980s; most introduced global fiscal norms that targeted medium-term reductions in deficits, spending or taxes. In most cases, these norms were political statements of intent that were loosely related to the budget and lacked strong enforcement mechanisms. As a result, many of the norms were ineffective. Even countries which achieved temporary success in disciplining the totals when the economy was robust were compelled to relax aggregate fiscal discipline when the economy weakened. According to a report by the United States General Accounting Office (1994), four countries (Australia, Germany, Japan and Mexico) that had extraordinary success in restoring fiscal balance during the 1980s experienced a new bout of surging deficits during the early 1990s, demonstrating that although "significant structural improvement in fiscal policy is possible in modern democracies... such progress is difficult to sustain".

This difficulty has led some countries to experiment with new forms of fiscal control that lessen cyclical gyrations and make it easier to restore fiscal discipline when the economy recovers. The main difference between this and the earlier stage is that countries are linking the aggregate controls more closely to the process of budgeting. This does not ensure, however, that they will be any more successful than in the past in avoiding cyclical shocks to the budget.

The global recession which began in the United States in 2008 and then spread to many other countries provides strong evidence of how fiscal discipline is undermined by economic shocks. Not only did built-in stabilisers generate sizeable deficits, but national leaders felt compelled to add further stimulus by cutting taxes and boosting expenditures. Short-term pressures crowded out consideration of long-term fiscal implications.

The central budget office cannot impose or enforce a fiscal norm by fiat; a fiscal rule that truly constrains government spending or the deficit must be accepted by the government, and strong enforcement mechanisms must be in place. But the budget office does have the lead role in maintaining aggregate discipline, and it must be strong enough to withstand pressures to evade the norm by removing some transactions from the budget and to override the rule when politicians or sectoral interests regard it as too constrictive. Several comparative studies of democratic regimes have found that success in maintaining fiscal discipline depends on the strength of the finance ministry and the cohesion of the government. In most OECD member countries, the position of the budget office is enhanced when it is housed in a large finance ministry that has broad governmental powers. But even when this occurs, economic or political circumstances may weaken the ministry's resolve to maintain fiscal discipline. Germany and Japan, for example, have powerful, encompassing finance ministries. The German Minister of Finance may be overruled by Cabinet only when the Chancellor sides against him/her; Japan's Ministry of Finance has had extensive regulatory powers extending to banking, securities and other sectors, in addition to a powerful role in revenue and spending policy. But even in these countries, fiscal discipline was undermined: in Germany, by spending pressures following unification; in Japan, by the deepest recession since World War II.

In both Germany and Japan, the Ministry of Finance no longer occupies as commanding a position as it once did. In Germany, weakening of the finance ministry was propelled by unification; in Japan, the principal factor was prolonged economic stagnation. Unification induced German politicians to circumvent financial controls in order to pay the enormous cost of integrating the eastern *Länder* into the country. In Japan, stagnation and other factors led to stripping away substantial portions of the finance ministry's jurisdiction. The lesson from both countries is that political leaders no longer want an overly dominant finance ministry at the centre of government.

Various studies have shown a strong correlation between the stability and cohesiveness of the government and the size of the deficit and the ratio of debt to GDP. The key finding is that the more fragmented the government, the less able it is to assemble a majority in support of the tough measures required to maintain fiscal discipline. The most cohesive governments are majoritarian systems in which a single party constitutes the government (in the case of parliamentary regimes) or controls both the executive and legislative branches (in the case of presidential regimes); the weakest are those in which the governing party or coalition lacks a majority in parliament. In general, the more parties comprising the coalition, the less capacitated the government will be to establish and enforce fiscal rules. Fiscal discipline may be problematic when (as often happens in coalition governments) one party controls the finance ministry and another controls the social welfare portfolio.

The changed composition of public expenditure – much more spent on entitlements and relatively less on consumption and investment – has affected the manner in which the budget office maintains fiscal discipline. In the past, the budget office reviewed the items of expenditure and recommended the amount that should be made available for each. It also policed implementation of the budget to ensure that money was spent only for approved items and that the amounts spent did not exceed authorised levels. It took the position that total spending could not be controlled unless the individual items were. Contemporary fiscal control is moving in the opposite direction, however. In some countries, the budget office has disengaged from the items of expenditure and has taken the position that it can control total spending only by constraining the sub-aggregates, such as the total running costs allowed each department or the total programme spending resources allocated to each portfolio. The budget office is willing to concede discretion over the items of expenditure to spending agencies in exchange for firm agreement as to the amounts they will have. For example, as a *quid pro quo* for gaining flexibility with respect to running costs, agencies must operate within firm limits. Often, as will be explained in the section below on operational efficiency, these limits are tightly constrained by across-the-board cuts and other rules that impel agencies to make choices among spending items.

Several versions of these limits have been tried in OECD member countries. Since the 1991 fiscal year, the United States has imposed a statutory limit on total discretionary appropriations, along with procedures for allocating this total among the various parts of the budget. It has not, however, made much progress in divesting *ex ante* control of spending items. Australia, New Zealand and the United Kingdom limit running costs and give managers considerable discretion in operating within these limits. Sweden curtailed central surveillance of spending items while imposing steep across-the-board cuts on operating expenditures.

In a few countries, there has been a parallel development with respect to programme expenditure. Australia has given ministers considerable leeway in reallocating resources within portfolios, though it also assigns a major role to the budget office in operating the portfolio budgeting system. But it is much more difficult to apply the new form of budget control – central withdrawal from the items, but tougher constraints on the subtotals – to entitlements. Entitlements typically are open-ended; spending is driven by exogenous factors such as demographic trends and changes in economic or social conditions rather than by explicit budget choices. Budget decisions may play an important role when an entitlement is established, as well as when marginal adjustments are made in an existing programme, but most year-to-year changes in entitlement spending are automatic. The budget records the amount spent; it does not decide the amount. Not only are entitlements open-ended, but spending on them is likely to deviate from budget projections during periods of economic weakness, when other changes (such as a fall in revenues) may unbalance the budget. The problem, many governments have learned, is that fiscal balance is not easily or quickly restored when the economy recovers. The structural impact on the budget lingers for as many as five to ten years after a bout of economic weakness.

Establishing fiscal discipline in the entitlement budget may require limiting or disabling the built-in stabilisers by placing global limits on all entitlements or on particular categories, or by capping some programmes. A few countries have had some success in capping particular entitlements, such as health care, and others are likely to experiment with new controls in the years ahead. These controls are controversial and can be introduced only with a high degree of political support. Health is the sector where efforts have been most pronounced, because this has been among the most volatile and fastest-growing parts of the budget. The typical limits on health spending constrain payments to providers or raise fees on beneficiaries, but they usually avoid curtailing services. It is highly probable that in the very near future, a substantial number of budget offices will be involved in efforts to restrain the growth in transfer payments and other mandated expenditures through rules that are triggered if these programmes exceed budgeted thresholds. These efforts will be highly political; they will require legislative actions that go beyond normal budget decisions.

Central budget offices have had few enduring success stories in maintaining aggregate fiscal discipline when spending has been driven by entitlements. Nevertheless, the elements of a control system have been introduced in various countries. The main elements include the following:

- A medium-term framework for stabilising the budget aggregates. The medium term is essential because it is easy to evade budget controls when they pertain only to the current or the next fiscal year. The typical framework includes projections of future budget aggregates, budget norms (see next paragraph) and means of enforcing the norms. Developing and operating this framework is likely to be a major preoccupation of the budget office in the 21st century, perhaps superseding work on the annual budget. In the future, annual budgets will be even more driven by multi-year constraints than they have heretofore.

- Medium-term norms must be realistic – that is, they must be achievable through politically acceptable actions. Yet they also must be constrictive, for if they merely accommodate prospective demands on the budgets, there would be no gain in having them. Developing the norms must engage key political actors: Cabinet, the head of government, perhaps the political parties and, in the case of coalition governments, a formal agreement among the governing parties. The norms must also have some built-in enforcement – that is, some budgetary action occurs if the norms have been breached.

- Aggregate norms are not likely to be effective if they pertain only to the totals; there must be a means as well of controlling the main subtotals. These may include limits on operating costs and other discretionary spending. These limits constrain the portion of the budget that is most amenable to cutbacks; they demonstrate that the government is willing to retrench its own operations in the quest for fiscal discipline. If the government cannot constrain the growth in discretionary spending, it is not likely to have much success in controlling other, more politically sensitive expenditures.

- As noted previously, limits on mandatory spending are likely to be part of the toolkit of future budget offices. It is unlikely that democratic governments will go so far as to disable built-in stabilisers – doing so would disadvantage dependent persons in times of economic adversity – but they may be willing to take steps that slow the growth of these expenditures and reduce their volatility.

To enforce fiscal discipline, the budget office may need an enriched supply of information. Most central budget offices are skilled in macroeconomic analysis; most also work with models that relate demographic trends and economic changes (such as changes in prices and employment rates) to demands on the budget. Many budget offices have experience in constructing baselines and estimating the impacts of policy changes on projected revenues and spending. Some already use these data in medium-term frameworks; more will do so in the future.

Budget offices are evolving into entities that deal more with assumptions than with hard data. In the future, the actualisation of the revenue and spending levels set in the budget will depend on whether the underlying assumptions are realised. Accordingly, budget offices will have to monitor the economy and society even more closely to detect changes that may have major budgetary impacts. In other words, the budget office of the future will devote more of its resources to looking at what is happening outside government and less to what is happening inside. In looking outward, some budget organisations may investigate the feasibility of developing leading indicators of budgetary change to assist their early identification and assessment of cyclical changes in the economy and in other conditions affecting revenues and expenditures.

Fiscal norms are not self-enforcing; the government must have the capability to enforce fiscal norms and to correct any breaches that have occurred. Absolute prohibition against violating the norms may be too rigid to withstand political pressure for spending initiatives or tax cuts, or the *force majeure* of economic circumstances, but governments may have more success with flexible norms that permit trade-offs within budget constraints – for example, rules requiring that any additional spending causing the deficit to rise be offset by cuts in other expenditures or by revenue increases. A version of this rule has been applied by the United States since 1991 to revenue and spending legislation. The rule only covers deficit increases resulting from legislative action; it does not apply to automatic spending or deficit increases resulting from changes in economic conditions.

> This rule, known as PAYGO (pay-as-you-go) led to protracted dispute between President George W. Bush and congressional leaders. The original rule provided that both revenue reductions and mandatory spending increases would have to be offset. When the rule expired in 2002, President Bush urged Congress to adopt a revised version that would be applied only to spending increases. The resulting impasse led to a hiatus during which no restriction was in effect.

Flexible rules have two main advantages: they furnish a safety valve for political pressures to expand programmes or provide tax relief, and they enable the government to change budget priorities. But flexible rules require a vigilant and powerful budget office that can estimate the impact of proposed policy changes on future budgets and can intervene when the changes breach fiscal norms. Whether rigid (like the Treaty of Maastricht) or flexible (like those currently applied in the United States), fiscal norms set the stage for an ongoing battle between claimants on public resources and guardians of the purse. The central budget office will not win every battle against wily and politically potent claimants whose arsenal of tricks include proposals that hide the full cost of policy initiatives, efforts to take programmes off budget, and bookkeeping arrangements that underestimate budgetary impacts. In the future, no less than in the past, the budget office will be engaged in a struggle to guard the budget against these and other gimmicks. The irony is that the more effective fiscal norms are, the more claimants will seek to evade them. Over the long run, one cannot be certain that central budget offices will be able to uphold fiscal discipline unless they have steadfast political support.

3. Allocative efficiency

Aggregate fiscal discipline can be a mixed blessing. While it stabilises the totals and makes them congruent with government policy, a fiscal norm that constrains spending below the total that would otherwise occur tends to freeze old programmes and priorities into the budget and new ones out. The more austere the norms and the longer they are maintained, the greater the risk that budget priorities will be rigidified. The risk is greatest when fiscal increments are lacking and the only way for the government to accommodate programme initiatives is to take resources away from current budget holders. How does the budget remain fresh and supple when there is little or no money for emerging priorities? How can the government think strategically and allocate resources to fulfil its vision? These and similar questions point to the importance of allocative efficiency in formulating the budget.

Allocative efficiency refers to the capacity of the budget system to distribute resources on the basis of the government's priorities and the programme's effectiveness. Allocating resources is the stock-in-trade of the central budget office; this is what the office does when it reviews agency bids for resources and recommends how much each should receive. In traditional budget arrangements, the process is open-ended; agencies can ask for as much as they want. Invariably, the total demanded is in excess of available resources, thereby giving the central budget office the lead role in deciding where increments should be allocated and whether any reallocations should be made. In fact, the greater the excess of bids over resources, the greater the role of the central budget office in operationalising the government's priorities.

There are a number of strong reasons for centralising reallocations in the budget office:

● The budget office can reallocate more broadly among sectors than can a line department or ministry.

● The budget office has a more comprehensive and possibly more objective view of the government's strategic interests and programme priorities than a single department that is likely to be beholden to sectoral interests.

● The budget office can promote reallocations based on evidence of programme effectiveness rather than subjective criteria.

● The budget office can establish rules and procedures to guard against evasion of fiscal discipline by underestimating the future cost of programmes to which resources are to be reallocated.

● Without strong pressure from the centre, departments may protect existing programmes rather than reallocate resources to new ones.

● Departments have incentives to launch programmes at low cost while building spending increases into future budgets. If permitted, this behaviour would undermine both aggregate control and the government's capacity to establish programme priorities.

Despite these justifications of centralised resource allocation, the current conditions of budgeting – fiscal constraints, inadequate increments, and pressure to make room in the budget for new priorities – may argue for a new approach in which spending departments are encouraged to generate policy changes. This would entail a fundamental reorientation of the central budget office; it would act more as the referee of the reallocation system than as the reviewer of departmental budgets. The reasons for reorienting the budget office in this direction need to be carefully considered. A useful starting point is the observation made above that traditional budget formulation was organised around allocation of incremental resources. Incremental budgeting enabled the government to respond to fresh demands while maintaining a relatively low level of intra-governmental conflict. Conflict was low because explicit trade-offs generally were avoided: winners gained by claiming incremental resources, not by taking from those who already had shares in the budget.

Priorities were rearranged by awarding different growth rates to the various parts of the budget. As noted above, the budget office was at the hub of this incremental process; by allocating the increments, it influenced the future direction of the budget.

Although policy makers concentrated on the additional resources to be allocated, the budget process was structured to facilitate comprehensive review of expenditures. Spending departments submitted detailed justifications of all items of expenditure, not just of the increment. The budget office had a licence to review and challenge the items and to seek the cutback or elimination of those it considered unproductive or of lesser value. Formally, the process was highly adversarial; in outcome, however, the process was relatively calm. Conflict was mitigated by the availability of incremental resources and by the tendency to continue almost all ongoing programmes. Although all of the budget was nominally reviewed, almost all escaped serious review. Few changes were made, except for those financed by additional resources.

Incremental budgeting suited the times, but it was a flawed means of allocating scarce public resources. It tolerated allocative inefficiency, and it contributed to the creeping enlargement in the relative size of the public sector. It weakened aggregate fiscal discipline by making the totals accommodate the parts. Aggregate spending was the sum of approved demands on the budget; it was not fixed independently of those demands. Spending agencies proposed numerous programme initiatives, but these generally were means of bidding for more money, not means of trading off within fixed budgets.

The perceived need for fiscal discipline may tempt the central budget office to tighten its grip by forcing reallocations from old to new programmes. This would seem to be a logical response to the contemporary budget predicament, for if the spenders will not make the trade-offs, the budget office can do the job for them. Nevertheless, the end result may be much conflict and little reallocation. The threat of losing resources and coveted programmes may impel spending departments to resist the trade-offs and savings demanded of them. These departments have formidable weapons at their disposal. They can withhold the information needed to make rational trade-offs; they can enter into log-rolling coalitions with other claimants to protect their respective budgets against cutbacks and reallocations; they can mobilise support among affected interests and within government. Judging from the past, it is by no means certain that the budget office will win the battle for reallocation. It may end up instead with *status quo* budgets.

The budget office operates at a disadvantage *vis-à-vis* the spending departments when it aggressively seeks to reallocate resources. It may lack sufficient programme information and political support to do the job. Departments know a lot more about their programmes – what works and what does not – than does the budget office. Departments also know a lot more about the political risks of changing programmes and policies. This asymmetry is due to the high cost of obtaining programme and political information, as well as to the understandable reluctance of departments to cast their preferred programmes in an unfavourable light. In other words, the budget office is beholden to the spending departments for much of the information it needs on how well programmes are working. The budget office can ease this dependency by establishing its own evaluation capacity or by installing a performance measurement system, but if it wants reliable performance data to inform budget choice, it will have to give departments a prominent voice in the process. If it does not, the budget office may face a familiar predicament. Although many evaluations are completed, few are used in allocating resources.

How does the budget office give spending departments a prominent voice in the reallocation process without jeopardising the government's fiscal and programme priorities? Australia provides an interesting example in this regard. In Australia, reallocation is promoted by shifting the initiative for proposing policy changes from the centre of government to the spending departments and by encouraging these departments to initiate trade-offs among their programmes within prescribed budget constraints. In this model, the focus of budgeting shifts from the items of expenditure to policy changes, and from nominal review of the entire budget to concentration on proposed additions and subtractions. The trade-off becomes the main unit of decision in budgeting. Trade-offs are made explicitly – that is, by having departments nominate the programmes to be cut or expanded and by having the government decide which of the proposed savings and additions are to be incorporated into the budget. Departments are free to propose trade-offs within their area of responsibility; the broader their portfolio, the more robust the programme changes can be. It probably would be a good idea to allow departments to implement minor changes unilaterally so that the government can focus on those policy initiatives that have major programme and financial impacts.

> In Australia, the incentive to make trade-offs has been weakened by 17 consecutive years of economic expansion. The consequent surge in revenues made it possible for the government to finance costly policy initiatives (including reductions in tax rates) without curtailing existing programmes. In this case, the machinery for trading off remained in place, but the behaviour of budget makers was altered.

In such a reallocation scheme, the role of the central budget office is different but still quite important. It has a lead role in operating the trade-off system and in ensuring that the policy changes are consistent with the government's fiscal norms and programme objectives. The budget office establishes guidelines and procedures for proposing and reviewing policy changes, maintains baselines and data bases for measuring the budgetary impacts of policy changes, advises ministers and the Cabinet on policy proposals, and either operates or promotes the ongoing evaluation of programmes and measurement of performance. As it undertakes these vital tasks, the budget office reduces its involvement in (or withdraws from) some traditional budgetary activities. It no longer reviews detailed items of expenditure; rather the items (those pertaining to running costs as well as those concerning programme operations) are handled by the affected departments within guidelines set by the government or the budget office. This devolution of traditional budgetary tasks promotes managerial efficiency (discussed in the next section) and frees the budget process for programme decisions and policy changes.

A budget system oriented to reallocation is likely to have most of the following elements:

- The government establishes medium-term fiscal objectives and, assisted by the budget office, determines the margin (if any) available for programme initiatives or the net savings required to meet its fiscal target. The margin is calculated on a net basis: new spending minus savings from programme cutbacks.

- The margin is allocated among ministries, in accord with the government's strategic priorities. Within its target, a ministry can increase the resources available for programme enhancements by proposing cutbacks in other parts of its portfolio.

- The budget office maintains a baseline for projecting future budget conditions if current policies are continued and for measuring the budgetary impact of policy changes. The baseline is projected for three or more years beyond the year for which budget decisions are being made, so that the medium-term impacts of policy changes can be assessed.

- The budget office demands that policy changes be advanced in terms of their expected programme effectiveness. Ministries should propose changes in the light of evaluation findings, and they should specify in advance how programme initiatives are to be assessed. Ministries also should systematically relate data on programme outcomes and effectiveness to their budget proposals.

- Cabinet actions on the budget concentrate on policy changes, not on the items of expenditure. Policy changes (subtractions and additions) are incorporated into the baseline, which is then rolled forward one year and becomes the starting point for the next annual budget cycle.

These elements have been the central features of the Australian budget system since the mid 1980s. Annual budget decisions are made in reference to forward estimates, the baseline of authorised spending for the budget year and the three following years. The forward estimates are not just projections of future spending; they are the spending levels that will be approved in future budgets unless revisions are made as a result of policy changes or changes in underlying economic or programme conditions (such as changes in price levels or in programme participation rates). By definition, therefore, a policy change is a revision to the forward estimates. Proposed policy changes in Australia are considered in a prescribed sequence that includes identification of policy options, the costing of policy changes in discussions between the affected department and the Department of Finance and Administration, trilateral negotiations between the Treasurer, the Minister for Finance and the portfolio minister, consideration of policy proposals by a Cabinet committee, and final Cabinet decision. As noted, the budgetary impacts of these decisions are entered into the forward estimates.

> The orderly process outlined here has been undermined during the past decade by *ad hoc* budget decisions that are made year round, outside the structured budget process. In Australia, *ad hoc* decisions have been accommodated within the budget framework by a sustained surge in revenues. Nevertheless, the Department of Finance and Administration has been greatly weakened by the tendency to make policy changes whenever it is politically expedient to do so. In fact, *ad hoc* decisions have become common in many countries, including those that lack a medium-term fiscal framework or the resources to finance the new claims made on the budget. The impact of *ad hoc* policy initiatives warrants much more study than it has received thus far.

It would be beyond the scope of this article to provide a full description or assessment of Australia's reformed budget system. A recent evaluation concluded that the reforms greatly increased the likelihood of savings options being adopted by ministers. Moreover, savings measures in a particular ministry are much more likely to be adopted when the ministry itself is arguing for them rather than when they are presented by the central budget office, with the knowledge and skills of the programme agency being devoted to criticism and obfuscation.

4. Operational efficiency

The distinction between programme costs and operating costs is often made in budgeting for government programmes, with different decision rules applied to each of these expenditure categories. During periods of budgetary constraint, for example, the government may approve modest increases in programme expenditures while freezing or imposing across-the-board cuts on operating expenditures. This "double standard" may ease the budgetary predicament of cross-pressured politicians, who often face voter demands for reduced government spending (or taxes) and for enriched programme benefits. But what makes sense for harried politicians may complicate the work of programme managers who must maintain a high level of programme output while making do with less resources.

Tight operating budgets have become the norm in OECD member countries. Retrenchment in this portion of the budget has become a recurring phenomenon, as financially stressed governments have sought savings in their most controllable and least politically sensitive expenditures. Cutbacks in operating expenses rarely suffice to close the budget gap, but they convey the appearance that the government is doing something to correct its fiscal imbalances. In budgeting, there are two easy ways for the government to obtain these savings. One is for it (via the central budget office) to closely control the items of expenditure and to restrict the authority of departments to spend on personnel, supplies and other operating inputs; the other is for the government to give departments greater operating discretion within fixed budgets. The two approaches point in opposite directions. The first gives the budget office greater involvement in the details of expenditure; the second requires it to withdraw from most of the details. The first approach emphasises legality and propriety in public expenditure; the second seeks efficiency in the use of public resources.

Over the years, central budget offices have differed in the extent to which they have intervened in operating decisions. Some have required that operating expenditures be approved in advance by central controllers; others have given substantial discretion to operating managers. In many countries, the squeeze on operating expenses has spurred the budget office to relax the controls and to seek means of improving managerial efficiency. Where this has occurred, the budget office has been compelled to re-examine its role and operations. It is no exaggeration to say that, in the past, involvement with operating details was the main preoccupation of the budget office, especially during implementation of the budget. In a growing number of OECD member countries, most operating matters are now in the hands of departmental managers. What is the appropriate role of the budget office in this new environment? How does it translate managerial discretion into managerial efficiency? Where does it fit in now that it no longer dictates the terms of expenditure?

The new role of the central budget office revolves around maintaining a system of accountability for the government. This entails prescribing information systems and reports, sharpening the capacity of spending departments to measure productivity and output, comparing results against expectations, and (as previously discussed) managing the process of change. This is a different role than the one budget offices became accustomed to play during the century-long evolution of government budgeting, but it is an important role and one that can keep them both busy and in the thick of resource allocation.

The problem with this role is that accountability for results may be difficult to enforce in public institutions, and trying to do so may impel the budget office to recapture some of the controls it surrendered in the name of managerial freedom. In every country that has moved in this direction, devolution of managerial control has advanced much further than has the assimilation of new accountability methods. The *quid pro quo* of giving managers more freedom in exchange for making them accountable for results is asymmetrical: the former is much easier to accomplish than the latter. Even in New Zealand, where extraordinary progress has been made in installing new accountability measures, the budget office is in a relatively weak position to demand improvement when results fall short of the mark.

If the main purpose of managerial freedom is to improve efficiency in the delivery of public services, it is essential that productivity gains be measured and not just assumed. Governments need objective, systematic and reliable means of measuring the volume and cost of outputs across a range of public services. It does not suffice that just a handful of selected performance targets be measured. What will be required is sufficient information on trends in public sector productivity that the government can report with confidence.

One can expect, therefore, that reformed budget offices will devote considerable resources in the years ahead to strengthening the accountability of spending entities. This may entail an overhaul of the accounting and information systems, stronger sanctions and incentives to perform, tougher demands on managers to act as change agents in their organisations, new contractual means of specifying and monitoring outputs, greater use of net appropriations and market-type mechanisms to drive productivity improvement, more extensive application to the public sector of the logic and techniques of managerial and cost accounting, ongoing redesign of the budget documents and appropriations measures, and more. This is a full agenda, more than many budget offices will be able to handle.

Although it is possible that some reformed budget offices will reverse course and recapture previously surrendered controls, the greater likelihood is that additional budget offices will join the bandwagon for reform. Unless there is widespread discrediting of the managerial revolution, today's reforms will become tomorrow's norms. There may be a few holdouts – countries which for cultural or political reasons retain command-and-control management – but these will be outnumbered by the countries which embrace devolution. Some will do so wholeheartedly, others with a degree of reluctance; some will decentralise as little as they can get away with; others will drive devolution as far as it can go.

5. Conclusion

Aggregate fiscal discipline, allocative efficiency and operational efficiency are complementary tasks in budgeting. A well-developed budget process should serve all three objectives. Moreover, accomplishing one of these tasks advances the others as well. Nevertheless, in the practice of budgeting, the three roles may get in one another's way. They require different types of information, work orientations and skills. Getting all three to work in tandem may entail enormous transaction costs – more than a government may be willing to bear. The more typical approach may be to emphasise aggregate fiscal discipline because it is vital to the political interests and financial stability of the government and operational efficiency because it comports with the contemporary value orientation of private and public management, but to go slow on change in the allocation system because it entails a fundamental reconsideration of the role of the central budget office. As appealing as this approach may be, it should be recognised that, over the long run, the greatest payoff of reform is likely to be in improved programme allocations.

Reference

United States General Accounting Office (1994), *Deficit Reduction: Experiences of Other Nations*, GAO/AIMD-95-30, General Accounting Office, Washington DC.

ISBN 978-92-64-06087-6
Evolutions in Budgetary Practice
Allen Schick and the OECD Senior Budget Officials
© OECD 2009

Chapter 6

Can National Legislatures Regain an Effective Voice in Budget Policy?*

* This article was originally published in the *OECD Journal on Budgeting*, Vol. 1, No. 3, 2002. At the time of writing, Allen Schick was Visiting Fellow, Governmental Studies, Brookings Institution, Washington DC, and Professor, School of Public Affairs, University of Maryland, United States. An afterword was written in 2009.

Two contemporary developments are buffeting legislative work on the budget. One is the drive to discipline public finance by constraining the fiscal aggregates; the other is the effort to enlarge the legislature's role in revenue and spending policy. Whether these trends turn out to be complementary or contradictory will shape the budgetary role of national legislatures in the years ahead. One scenario is for the legislature to reinforce fiscal discipline by taking responsibility for the budget's totals; another is for it to undermine discipline by bombarding the budget submitted by the government with legislative amendments that trim revenues or boost expenditures.

The early signs point to the former course, but the history of budgeting and some contemporary research assume the latter. In a number of countries, the national legislature now votes the budget totals, in addition to its traditional work on revenue and spending measures. While this role still is exceptional, there is good reason to believe that it will spread to many countries during the next decade. Maastricht-type rules and other efforts to stabilise public finance may spur national governments and their legislatures to frame budgetary decisions within preset totals. Where this occurs, legislative work on the budget will parallel the government's and may result either in greater co-operation or greater rivalry between the two branches. In some countries, the legislature's new responsibility for the overall budget will buy it greater independence in fiscal policy; in others, the legislature will behave more as a partner than as an adversary. The probability is that adversarial relationships will predominate in presidential systems and co-operative relationships in parliamentary regimes. But other variables, such as voting rules or the party system, may intervene to induce co-operation in governments where power is formally divided and to generate friction in countries where power is formally shared.

Legislative activism may lead in an entirely different direction, however – not to greater fiscal discipline but to budgets in which pressure to spend more and to tax less generate chronic deficits and a progressive rise in the share of national income spent by the government. As unlikely as this may appear to contemporary promoters of legislative activism, it was the predominant view of legislatures throughout the 20th century. In many countries, the legislature voluntarily yielded budgetary power to the executive because it accepted the view that parliamentarians cannot constrain their political inclination to tax less and spend more. Legislatures entrusted budgetary authority to the government because they could not trust themselves to make responsible financial decisions. This attitude is endorsed by prominent scholars who correlate the legislature's capacity to amend the budget with fiscal outcomes. For example, in an influential paper published by the European Commission, Jörgen von Hagen found strong empirical support for the hypothesis that limits on the amendment power of parliament, and other rules, strengthen fiscal discipline and result in relatively small deficits and public debt (Hagen, 1992). There is good reason to challenge this finding, but its validity is less important than its widespread acceptance.

Although there are some notable exceptions, national legislatures generally are now more active in budgetary matters than they were in the post World War II era. An OECD study reported that legislatures in more than half the countries surveyed had a larger budgetary role than they had a decade earlier (OECD, 1998). The evidence of legislative activism is plentiful: new committees charged with legislative or oversight responsibilities; enlarged budget staffs; a vast increase in the flow of budget-related information from the government to legislators; and increased vigilance by independent or legislative auditors in reviewing the propriety and efficiency of expenditures. But adding institutional capacity does not itself ensure that legislators will stake out an independent position on the budget. To do so, they also need the political capacity to reject salient elements of the government's budget.

In dealing with budgets and other matters, legislatures face tension between the self-interest of members to promote their careers or to do good for constituents and the collective interest of the institution to produce sound, coherent legislation. As individuals, members tend to favour increased spending on particular items; as institutionalists, they have an imperative to adopt prudent revenue and spending totals. Numerous variables influence the manner in which legislators resolve these cross pressures, including party discipline, the electoral system, budget rules, and relations between the government and the legislature. As these variables differ among countries, so too does legislative treatment of the budget. Westminister-style legislatures characteristically resolve tensions between the budget's parts and totals by severely restricting the power of legislators to amend the government's budget; congressional-style legislatures typically allow members broad scope to revise the budget and make their own revenue and spending decisions. European parliaments generally fall between these extremes; they permit legislators to modify the budget, but restrict changes to the totals.

Although legislatures differ in their budget roles, three stages can be discerned in their evolution:

- emergence of the legislature's power to tax and spend;
- development of government capacity and processes to formulate and implement the budget; and
- introduction of a legislative budget process.

The first two stages coincide in countries that embraced democracy only recently; they are separated by generations or centuries in countries that have a long history of democracy. In these countries, the first stage evolved in the course of efforts to build an independent national legislature; the second emerged in the course of developing administrative institutions. The third stage is under way in some countries, but has not yet started in many others. It may never emerge in countries which assign a passive role to the legislature on budget matters.

Each stage is described in the sections that follow. The aim is not to conduct an historical tour of budgeting, but to shed light on the contemporary fiscal role of democratic legislatures and to explain why taking a more active and independent posture may be beyond the reach of some. Parliaments are tradition-steeped institutions; getting them to change is not simply a matter of grafting new practices onto the old, but of rethinking their place. This certainly is the case with respect to legislative budgeting, for new responsibilities must be accommodated both to long-standing appropriations processes and to political relations with the government.

The legislature's new role in budgeting cannot come from the government's weakness. If the government is incapacitated in managing the nation's finances, the legislature also will be unable to do so. This interdependence distinguishes contemporary reform from past efforts to build legislative fiscal capacity. It means that the legislature's role must be defined more in terms of policy, accountability and performance and less in terms of control and restriction. It remains to be seen whether contemporary legislatures and their election-oriented members are willing and able to fulfil this very different role.

Section 1 surveys the first two stages and explains why national legislatures which rose to power on the principle that they should control the purse ceded budget initiative to the government, thereby giving ministers and officials much of the financial prerogative that had once been wrested from the Crown. Section 2 analyses the factors that have enfeebled many contemporary legislatures in tax legislation and appropriations. Section 3 discusses recent efforts in a number of countries to establish legislative budget processes. This development has not yet run its course, and its spread to countries which currently restrict legislative budget initiative is problematic. The concluding section presents alternative scenarios regarding the future budget role of national legislatures.

1. Legislative appropriations and executive budgets

Some national legislatures which trace their lineage back hundreds of years had more effective financial powers centuries ago than they have today. This anomaly lies at the heart of debate over the budgetary role of contemporary legislatures. Explaining it is facilitated by distinguishing between appropriations and budgets. Before governments prepared budgets, democratic legislatures made appropriations. This historical sequence is important for two reasons: first, it indicates that legislatures had fiscal power before governments had budgets; second, it suggests that budgetary practices emerged because legislative action was deemed to be an inadequate means of fiscal control. The details may differ from one country to another, but the pattern is near-universal: legislatures appropriate, governments budget. This section outlines the story of appropriations and budgets as it unfolded in England and France, two of the earliest countries to impose legislative control of the purse. These countries faced similar struggles in reining in the Crown's appetite to tax and spend, but they resolved the issue differently. England proscribed legislative initiative, France did not. Each country has served as a role model for many others, even for countries which have never been ruled by monarchs.

England's struggle for legislative pre-eminence dates back to the Magna Carta in 1215 when King John covenanted with the barons not to levy any tax without their assent. But far from settling the issue, this great event set the stage for almost five centuries of conflict between the Crown and the people's representatives. The King had several advantages in this contest: his own income which was commingled with tax revenue, authority to decide when Parliament met, and the asserted right to spend as he wanted. But when his resources were depleted or inadequate, as in time of war, the King had to call upon Parliament to replenish his treasury. Over time, Parliament extracted concessions in exchange for supplying the needed money. One was to separate the Crown's own money from the public's; another was to insist that money be spent only on authorised purposes. To enforce its will, the House of Commons devised the tactic of voting appropriations near the end of the session, after the King had already spent some of his own money. Inasmuch as he could not be certain that the appropriations would be forthcoming, he had an incentive to be prudent in managing expenditure and in complying with the dictates of the

House of Commons. However, this means of controlling public spending contributed to the decline of legislative power. With appropriations voted after the fiscal year was under way, Parliament came to merely endorse spending that had already been incurred. When the government replaced the Crown as the spender, *ex post* appropriations became mechanical exercises rather than a means of financial control.

The House of Commons curtailed its power in yet another way by adopting a standing order in 1706 that, with some changes in language, persists to this day:[1]

> This House shall not accept any petition for any sum of money relating to the public service, nor shall it pass upon a motion which would bring about a vote on a subsidy or on a charge against public revenues... unless upon recommendation of the Crown (Erskine May, 1976, p. 707).

According to Erskine May, the pre-eminent parliamentary authority, this rule codified "constitutional practice which had become established long before the passing of that order ... it was the natural result of the constitutional relations between the Crown and Parliament at the time when the practice was established" (Erskine May, 1976, p. 706). Inasmuch as the purpose of tax legislation and appropriations was to restrain the Crown, it made no sense for the House of Commons to vote money that had not been requested. With the transfer of financial authority from the Crown to the government, the House of Commons found itself barred by its standing orders from initiating expenditures and by political *realpolitik* from denying requested funds. Its vaunted power of the purse was reduced to hollow ritual.

The legislature's acquisition of financial power followed approximately the same path in France as in England, but there were some notable differences between the two countries. The French monarch insisted on unfettered power to tax and spend, while legislative bodies, initially composed of the privileged classes but broadened over centuries to represent the people, asserted authority to control the purse. During long periods in the 15th to 18th centuries, the King had the upper hand because he rarely convened the *États Généraux*, which was the legislative assembly. In fact, this body did not meet at all in the 175 years from 1614 to 1789. Another complicating problem was the practice of the King to commingle public funds with his own. He felt no compunction in doing this, because the King claimed an absolute right to use all money as he wanted.[2]

In contrast to England, where legislative authority emerged in a gradual, largely peaceful manner, in France it required a revolution to establish the principle that no tax could be levied without the consent of the National Assembly. In contrast to the House of Commons, which limited its fiscal power, the National Assembly did not restrict its power to initiate taxes or appropriations. Moreover, it asserted a more direct role in reviewing how appropriated funds were spent. A 1791 decree proclaimed that "the Assembly shall itself definitely examine and audit the accounts of the Nation". An accounting bureau, under the direction of the Assembly, was charged with reviewing expenditures.

In the more than two centuries since its Revolution, France has experienced a number of political upheavals which have affected financial relations between the government and the legislature. A recurring issue has been the competence of the National Assembly to take an independent position on appropriations. The country has gone through alternations in legislature-government relations, with periods of legislative dominance followed by changes which have constricted legislative independence. Thus, in response to the independent – some would say irresponsible – exercise of financial power by the

National Assembly during the pre-war Third Republic, the Constitution of the Fifth Republic constrains legislative independence.

1.1. *The budget: aiding and constraining legislative action*

Thus far, the word "budget" has been avoided because, during the formative period of legislative control of the purse, official budgets did not exist. It is generally agreed that this word was first used to describe government financial practices in England during the 18th century, more than 100 years after Parliament's authority in taxation and expenditure was finally secured. The word budget was first used in official French documents early in the 19th century; it then spread rapidly to other developed countries. One of the earliest formal definitions appeared in an 1862 French law which described the budget as "a document which forecasts and authorises the annual receipts and expenditures of the State..." (Stourm, 1917, p. 2). This definition contains the seeds of two rival conceptions of budgetary practice. One views the budget as a plan for a future period, normally the upcoming fiscal year; the other regards it as an authoritative decision on future receipts and expenditures. As a plan, the budget is a set of proposals that carry no special weight other than the influence the government has to sway legislative actions; as an authoritative decision, the government may tax and spend, subject to routine legislative approval, on the basis of the revenues and expenditures set forth in the budget. As a proposal, the budget does not expressly infringe on the legislature's primacy in financial matters; as an authoritative decision, it dictates or overrides legislative preferences.

Governments budgeted their revenues and expenditures before they had formal budget systems – that is, they compiled revenue and spending in a single document that was transmitted to the legislature at regular intervals. But as governments expanded during the 19th century, it became increasingly desirable to co-ordinate the claims on their finances by preparing comprehensive budgets. Rather than propose or decide revenues and expenditures in bits and pieces, the budget enabled the government to present a complete picture of public finance to the legislature. The formalisation of budgeting coincided with other major reforms in public administration, such as professionalisation of the civil service, standardisation of accounts and bureaucratisation of government operations.

The formalisation of budgeting did more than rationalise public administration; it also altered the balance of financial power between governments and legislatures. With government decisions on the budget preceding legislative action, tax legislation and appropriations were either constrained or strongly influenced by the government's preferences. Even those parliaments which retained legal authority to deviate from the government's budget were politically subordinated to its dictates. It became common in developed countries to assess legislative revenue and spending decisions in the light of the executive's budget recommendations. The budget became the authoritative metric for measuring legislative action. The budget impelled a Copernican revolution in public finance. The legislative supremacy which had been hard earned in centuries of struggle was surrendered on the battlefield of executive budgets.

It was taken for granted in all countries that budgeting is an executive function carried out by the executive, not by the legislature. Only the executive had the organisation and capacity to co-ordinate the spending bids of its various departments and agencies; only it could implement actual spending by these entities. In fact, efforts by some legislatures to bolster their capacity to review the government's spending plans met with strong opposition in some countries on the ground that they were trespassing on executive responsibilities. Stourm reports that the eminent French economist Léon Say opposed efforts by the National Assembly to establish a permanent committee to review the government's budget:

> The Committee on Budget wants to put itself in the place of the administration and to prepare the budget itself instead of being satisfied with receiving it for the purpose of control. The Chairman of the Committee on Budget has become to some extent the First Lord of the Treasury... The opponents of ministerial power see at once the benefits they could derive from this new institution (Stourm, 1917, p. 289).

Say's view, which expressed the sentiments of the times, was that the legislature's job is to control public finance – that is, to vote appropriations that limit the amount to be spent. Its job is not to plan and co-ordinate public finance.

In most developed countries, legislators welcomed the new budget practices, for they brought order and coherence to tax legislation and appropriations. Legislators now had a fairly comprehensive view of how the parts fitted together and of total revenue and expenditure. Moreover, standards of good budget practice were codified in a set of principles which gained acceptance in most countries. These principles included annuality in budget decisions, comprehensiveness of budget accounts, and specification of the objects of expenditure. Only a few national legislatures resisted the rapid spread of the budget idea. The strongest objections came from the United States Congress, which sensed that entrusting the executive with budgetary power would weaken its authority on taxes and appropriations. Congress acceded to an executive budget process in 1921, later than all major European countries and only after the costs of world war had demonstrated the need to discipline public finance. When Congress acted, some political experts predicted that the President's new budget power would spell the end of legislative supremacy.[3]

Why did budgeting, which was seen as strengthening legislative fiscal control, turn into a means of subordinating the legislature? The answers lie less in the realm of legal authority and more in politics. The budget submitted to the legislature is the end product of a lengthy process of organising, monitoring and controlling public finances. Putting together the budget and overseeing its implementation engages a vast enterprise of specialists centred in the finance ministry or a similar organisation at the top of government. This ministry's reach extends to all government departments and agencies, and entails sifting through vast amounts of financial and operational data. To do its job well, the finance ministry must also assess political demands and interests, as well as the efficiency of expenditure. When the budget is submitted, the finance ministry knows a great deal about public finance, and the legislature knows very little other than what the government wants of it. This information asymmetry places the legislature at an enormous disadvantage. Even with standing committees and modest staff resources of its own, the legislature is no match for the government. While they can compensate somewhat through the hard work of sifting through the estimates, legislators rarely acquire a deep understanding of how public money is spent or of the implications of appropriating more or less than was budgeted by the government.

The vast growth of government, beginning in the last decades of the 19th century and accelerating through most of the 20th, further diminished the legislature's influence. With growth, the budget's line items were consolidated into broader categories. For example, rather than specifying each position in the public service, the budget estimates the amounts to be spent in each job classification or in a group of classifications. In some countries, consolidation was taken further, so that a single sum was entered for all personnel expenditures. Consolidation made the budget less unwieldy, but also reduced legislative control over individual line items. Another by-product of government expansion was that the budget came to be seen more as a statement of public programmes and objectives and less as an instrument of financial control. The budget also matured into a means of guiding and stabilising the economy, and its totals acquired a fiscal salience that transcended the individual items of expenditure. In some countries, the budget also gained status as the means by which the government managed its administrative entities and operations and prodded them to improve efficiency. As laudable as these transformations were, they subordinated financial control to larger budget purposes. In a legal sense, little had changed; politically, hardly anything was the same.

2. The decline of national legislatures

Contemporary scholars speak routinely of the decline of national legislatures, not only in budgetary matters but in the full range of legislative responsibilities. Decline has occurred, they agree, despite the fact the modern legislatures are better organised and resourced than before. In their view, the decline has little to do with internal legislative operations, but to three external developments that have stripped parliaments of independence and control:

- the rise of disciplined political parties which set the legislative agenda and compel legislators to vote the party line;
- the enormous escalation in public spending, and the concomitant shift away from spending on housekeeping and security functions to spending on entitlements and income support; and
- the rise in interest groups and corporatist political arrangements.

In combination, these trends reduced many parliaments to debating clubs which have ample freedom to deliberate but not to decide. Although it is a sweeping generalisation which brushes aside important differences in political culture and structure, the "decline of parliaments" hypothesis appears to fit most OECD member countries.[4]

During the past 100-150 years, party lines have stabilised in many countries, and solidaristic parties – organised to enforce political discipline – have become the norm. In quite a few parliaments, the only scope members have to express independence is on private bills in which the government takes little interest. Budget deals are made outside parliament, within government or by party functionaries, and then ratified within it. Extra-parliamentary budgetary arrangements prevail in majoritarian regimes where the budget is imposed on parliament by government *diktat*, and in coalition regimes where the parties to the coalition hammer out agreements that frame parliament's work for the life of the government. In some countries, the budget is negotiated through formal party channels which parallel the government's budget process. In Japan, the dominant Liberal Democratic Party has standing committees which review the Ministry of Finance's budget and make final decisions which are then transmitted to the Diet. The role of parties is especially prominent when the government takes significant policy initiatives or prepares a budget package which is adopted in a single vote. One insightful observer of Nordic parliaments concludes that:

... the penetration of the internal machinery of assemblies by solidaristic political parties has significantly limited the efficacy of parliamentary activity. Briefly stated, party control has tended to mean that the legislative function of assemblies, *i.e.* the successful initiation of proposals, has been subordinated ... (Arter, 1984, p. 32).

A second driver of parliamentary decline has been the vast expansion in the scale of government. In the OECD community, the growth in public spending during the period 1960-80 averaged more than one-half of a percentage point relative to GDP each year. At the start of this period, government spending in OECD member countries totalled 29% of GDP. Two decades later it was 40% (OECD, 1985, Table 6.5). Most of the rise was in spending on entitlements, which must be paid regardless of the government's financial condition or other demands on the budget. Social security transfers were 6.8% of GDP in 1960 and 16.2% in 1980. As government expanded beyond its watchman responsibility of maintaining domestic order and protecting citizens against external threats to one whose main financial effort is to sustain the economic well-being of its people, the traditional role of legislatures in restraining the exercise of power no longer fitted well. Expansionary government needs empowerment, not restraint, and empowerment depends on a stable supply of money to the government. An expanded state needs secure financing which is not impeded by legislative whim or impasse. While expanded entitlements weaken executives, who also are beholden to commitments made by their predecessors, they do even more damage to legislative capacity, for parliaments typically finance income transfer schemes in permanent legislation which, unlike conventional budget expenditures, do not require periodic legislative approval.

Expansion of the state strains legislative capacity to oversee the executive, not only because there is so much more to review but also because effective power shifts from elected ministers to non-elected officials who work in massive bureaucracies that are shielded from public view and are difficult to penetrate. Despite innovations such as the ombudsman and enlargement of legislative staffs, it is not an easy task for legislators to control a state that has grown so large and active. More importantly, enlargement of the state has stirred interest in performance and results rather than with legality and propriety in public expenditure. Citizens want governments to do more for them, not to be held back by stingy legislators.

Growth of the state has affected legislative power in yet another way. Although it is conventionally assumed that legislators add to the budget, government executives have been the prime movers in stretching the programmatic boundaries. For decades, the budget presented by governments regularly proposed programme initiatives and spending increases in excess of the rate of increase in prices or in economic activity. Governments also regularly proposed, and parliaments adopted, tax increases to finance incessant programme expansions. As noted earlier, the legislative contribution to spending increases was typically marginal. Thus expansion itself connoted a shift in the balance of power between parliament and the government.

The third blow to legislative capacity has been delivered by the multiplication and activism of interest groups. All democratic countries have many more politically active groups than they had a generation ago, but a vital distinction must be drawn between pluralist and corporatist versions of the relationship between such groups and the government. The pluralist model, which is most evident in the United States, narrows group interests; the corporatist model broadens these interests. In pluralist societies, the sheer number of groups impels them to take a narrow view of their interests; consequently, the demands they make on legislators (and other political actors) typically deal with marginal matters which can be satisfied with a little more or less taxing or spending. The budget impact of pluralism is to discourage legislators from focusing on the big picture. The marginalised legislature is busy with a large number of amendments that may attract much political notice but barely make a dent in the government's budget plans. In corporatist societies, major government policies are made in consultation with conglomerations of groups which represent a broad swath of interests. There may be one such conglomeration speaking for industry, another for workers, another for municipalities, etc. In some cases, the government maintains formal, continuing relations with these "social partners" and acts only after it has discussed policy initiatives with them. But once the government and corporatist interests have reached agreement, the legislature either has no role or must go along.

2.1. Decline in the legislature's budget role

The foregoing paragraphs deal with the overall place of modern legislatures and governing institutions; they do not single out their budget powers. But a legislature cannot be influential in financial policy if it has been marginalised as a policy institution. The 1998 OECD survey confirms that contemporary legislatures are perceived to have a weak budget role. Tables 6.1 and 6.2 summarise country responses in that survey to the following set of questions:

● Does the legislature typically enact the budget as proposed by the government?

● Are there any restrictions on the ability of the legislature to modify the budget proposed by the government? If so, what form do these take?

● How many amendments to the budget (in number and amount) are typically proposed by the government and opposition members of the legislature respectively? How many of these are typically approved?

Most countries responded that they make no changes or only minor adjustments in the budget proposed by the government. Among the countries that have numerous legislative amendments, most reported that these do not significantly change the government's budget.

In some countries, the bulk of the adopted amendments come from the government itself or from legislators affiliated with it. This pattern indicates that working with the government rather than against it may be the most productive route to legislative influence. After it submits the budget, the government may accept or offer amendments, either to thwart opposition or to reward loyal members by embracing their proposals. In some countries, robust, behind-the-scenes negotiations between the government and legislative leaders give parliament some opportunity to influence the budget at the margins.

The OECD survey indicates that constraints on legislative influence arise more out of political considerations than from formal restrictions on parliament's power to amend the budget. Table 6.2 drawn from the survey compiles country self-assessments on the restrictions faced by their legislatures. In pointing to political rather than legal factors, the data suggest that even if budget rules were changed to accommodate a broader legislative role, underlying political conditions may preclude significant change in legislative behaviour. A corollary of this conclusion is that the impact of efforts to empower the

Table 6.1. **The legislature's authority to amend the government's budget**

Australia	The House of Representatives may modify the budget, but it rarely does so because the government holds a majority in the House.
	The Senate may not initiate taxation or appropriations bills, nor may it amend such measures. It can, however, refuse to pass revenue or appropriations bills until they are amended to its liking by the House.
Austria	The National Council may amend the draft budget submitted by the government, but it usually only makes slight corrections.
Belgium	The ability of the Chamber of Deputies to modify the budget is not limited by law, but the legislature faces at least two constraints in practice. First, Belgium has committed to some unrestricted and recurring expenses that are not subject to debate. Second, a major modification to a budget proposal by the Chamber of Deputies would be the equivalent of calling for a "vote of confidence" regarding the government.
Brazil	The National Congress may amend the budget, but it cannot increase total spending or modify payroll expenditure, debt service, or constitutional transfers. Amendments must be within the parameters of the annual Budget Guidelines Law and quadrennial Multi-Year Plan.
Canada	Although there are no formal restrictions, it is difficult to adopt changes once the budget has been introduced in Parliament. Legislators often consult with the government before the budget is formally submitted.
	Defeat of the budget in the House of Commons implies a defeat of the government and leads to new elections.
Chile	The Constitution severely curtails the budget role of the National Congress; Congress discusses the budget but may not revise revenue estimates or increase expenditures. It may cut variable expenditure.
	Adopted amendments have only a marginal impact and are usually presented by the government pursuant to negotiations with Congress.
Czech Republic	Parliament may modify the budget but must not contravene the various laws that circumscribe its ability to do so.
Denmark	In principle, legislators may present budget proposals; in practice, they lack the administrative capacity to prepare such proposals.
	Parliament may make changes to any part of the government's budget proposal before adopting it.
Finland	Parliament's right to make changes to the budget is not restricted, but it is constrained by certain procedural rules.
France	Current law dictates that Parliament may not raise spending above a pre-established ceiling or lower revenues below a pre-established floor. If some legislators wish to change either or both of these numbers, Parliament must first vote to approve their proposal.
Germany	In theory, various budget regulations provide the only constraint on Parliament's ability to change the budget. In practice, however, legislators face additional constraints, since about 80 to 85% of budget expenditures are required by various laws and treaties.
Hungary	The Constitution does not restrict the National Assembly's ability to modify the budget. The Public Finance Act dictates that the legislature must decide the amount of the budget deficit, as well as budget expenditures and revenues for each chapter. After those amounts have been voted, legislators may only reallocate amounts within the chapters.
Iceland	Parliament is not formally constrained in its ability to change the budget.
	The government almost always has a majority in the legislature, and that majority usually consults with the government prior to modifying the budget.
Ireland	The *Dáil* may only vote appropriations requested by the government.
	The legislature may not amend expenditures, but it may, and does, make changes to revenues.
Italy	Parliament may modify the budget. It is restricted by the financial covering principle that applies to proposed increases in spending or decreases in revenue.
Japan	The administration develops and proposes the budget; the Diet may modify the budget as long as the modifications are consistent with the Constitution.
Korea	The National Assembly may reduce the budget as it sees fit, but the government must approve proposed budget increases.
New Zealand	The Standing Orders of the House of Representatives dictate that it will not pass a measure that will have a significant impact on the government's fiscal aggregates.
	The government may veto a spending proposal if it will affect the Crown's overall financial position. This veto cannot be overturned by the House.
	Members of the House may propose changes that would affect votes, and the government may veto such proposed changes.
Norway	Parliamentary parties may introduce any budget measures they wish, but the legislature is constrained by financial obligations to the beneficiaries of the National Insurance Scheme and state employees, and by the statutory rights of Norwegians to health care, education, and law and order.
Portugal	The Assembly of the Republic has no restrictions on its ability to make changes.
Spain	The Constitution specifies that the government must approve proposed increases in expenditure or decreases in revenue before these may be discussed in Parliament.
Sweden	Parliament has no restrictions on its ability to make changes.
Switzerland	Around 80% of expenditures cannot be reduced, because they are the product of legal prescriptions or contractual commitments.
	The Constitution specifies the maximum tax rates that may be imposed.
Turkey	The budget is reviewed first by the Plan and Budget Committee and then by Parliament. During the first step, members of the Plan and Budget Committee may propose whatever changes they wish; during the second step, legislators may not propose changes that would increase expenditures or decrease revenues.
United Kingdom	The House of Commons may amend tax proposals.
	The House of Commons cannot increase the government's spending proposals, and in practice its ability to do anything other than accept them is very limited.
	The House of Lords is not significantly involved in the budget process.
United States	Congress faces no specific restrictions on its power to change the President's budget. However, revenue and spending legislation are controlled by budget enforcement rules that have been in effect since 1990.

Source: OECD (1998), "The Role of the Legislature".

legislature will vary among countries. Depending on political variables, changes that induce the legislature to take a more active role in the budget in some countries may induce continuing passivity in others.

The OECD survey invited each country to offer a brief response, without supporting analysis or explanation. Some of the details can be filled in by revisiting an insightful study published a quarter of a century ago on the budget role of six European parliaments. David Coombes and his colleagues (Coombes, 1975) generally concluded that parliament had become marginalised on budget policy. The following paragraphs, adopted from this study, assess the legislature's budget role in four of the countries.

In Germany, K.H. Friauf notes, the government and its parliamentary majority are not regarded as politically identical. There is some separation of power between the two which allows the *Bundestag* to express its own will. The *Bundestag* can amend the government's budget without raising a question of confidence. But Friauf concludes that although the government frequently accepts additions to the budget offered by the *Bundestag*, "the total amounts involved in additional expenditures voted by Parliament are usually insignificant when set against the total volume of the budget" (Friauf, 1975, p. 81). Inasmuch as Friauf's conclusions were drawn mostly from the Adenauer years, it may be appropriate to reconsider them in the light of more recent developments, especially those since the unification of Germany – a period during which the *Bundestag* was called upon to vote tax increases and cuts in some social programmes. The distaste of these actions and the weakening of the government's ruling coalition may have enlarged legislative budgetary influence.

Alain Dupas begins his article on parliamentary control of the budget in France by noting that in "France, as in many other representative democracies, the decline of Parliament has become a favourite theme for political theorists ... The belief that Parliament's examination of the budget must now be considered an unimportant ritual is one which many experts and politicians of all shades will support ... Today, all real power has passed to the executive; the debate on the budget is no more than conversational and the parliamentary role is limited to the registration of governmental decisions" (Dupas, 1975, p. 104). Later in his analysis, Dupas softens this harsh conclusion by arguing that the National Assembly can modify the budget. He describes the Assembly's distinction between *crédits votés*, which are the expenditures authorised for the current year, *services votés*, which are the costs of carrying out approved activities in the next year, and *mesures nouvelles*, which are proposed initiatives for the next year. This arrangement institutionalises a form of incrementalism, for it invites the legislature to concentrate on changes to the base of authorised expenditures. Incrementalism is a fact of budgetary life, whether or not it is formalised in procedural rules. The relevant question is whether in behaving incrementally, Parliament "rubber stamps" or revises the proposed budget. One feature of the French system suggests a limited parliamentary influence: the *services votés* in the general budget are approved *en bloc* rather than by individual item or budget chapter. Despite this practice, Dupas concludes "it would be the opposite of the truth to maintain that the French Parliament is no more than a register for budgetary decisions. Constructively or otherwise, voting on the budget gives Parliament an opportunity to make its mark" (Dupas, 1975, p. 129).

Table 6.2. **Legislative modification of the government's budget**

Australia	The legislature typically enacts the government's budget.
	The House of Representatives does not usually offer amendments, as the government always holds a majority. Most amendments are proposed by opposition senators, and most of these amendments fail.
Austria	Although the National Council can in principle amend the budget during the time allotted for that purpose, it usually only makes slight changes.
Belgium	The Chamber of Deputies typically adopts the proposed budget, with the majority coalition voting in favour of the budget and the opposition voting against it.
	During the first trimester of the budget year, departments have the opportunity to propose changes in their budgets. In general, the legislature rarely makes significant mid-year adjustments.
Brazil	During a recent three-year period, the National Congress made a large number of amendments to the budgets proposed.
Canada	Parliament typically enacts the government's budget; during a recent three-year period, the legislature offered few, if any, significant budget amendments.
	The opposition may make minor amendments to the budget if the government assents.
Chile	Most of the budget is not significantly modified by the National Congress. When changes occur, they are usually the result of negotiations between the legislature and the government.
Czech Republic	Parliament enacts the government's budgets with minor changes only.
Denmark	Parliament typically enacts the government's budget, including the numerous amendments the government proposes.
	Amendments proposed by the opposition usually fail.
Finland	Parliament usually approves the government's budget bill.
	The most important approved amendments come from the government.
	Few amendments proposed by individual legislators pass.
France	The government's budget is always adopted by Parliament, but the legislature might make changes prior to approving it. These do not significantly affect the balance of the budget and do not modify the bulk of the budget's revenues and expenditures.
Germany	Parliament reviews the budget before passing it. The review process includes consultations between legislators and ministry officials.
Hungary	The National Assembly has made numerous amendments to each of the government's budget proposals.
	A large portion of proposed amendments aim to secure funds for minor development projects or other purposes; these do not significantly influence the financial commitments or internal structure of the budget.
Iceland	Parliament usually passes the government's budget.
	During a recent two-year period, the legislature made numerous amendments to the budget. All of the amendments were offered by the government or by its supporters.
Ireland	The *Dáil* usually offers a significant number of amendments to the budget. Typically, only government amendments are approved.
	Legislators cannot propose amendments to the expenditure side of the budget.
Italy	Many minor amendments are proposed each year, and Parliament typically passes a number of them.
Japan	When the ruling party dominates the legislative majority (as usually has been the case), the government's proposed budget is normally approved without alteration.
Korea	The National Assembly typically modifies the government's budget. Government and opposition parties conduct talks to determine the changes to be made. They usually only make small modifications.
New Zealand	The House of Representatives usually enacts the budget proposed by the government. Few, if any, amendments are proposed, and usually no amendments are enacted.
Norway	Typically, Parliament enacts the government's budget after making a number of small changes, but its behaviour depends on the political situation. During the 1990s, minority governments negotiated with opposition parties.
Portugal	The Assembly of the Republic typically makes relatively minor changes to the government's budget.
	The government does not propose amendments; the number of amendments proposed by parliamentary groups varies.
Spain	All political groups represented in Parliament submit amendments to the budget.
Sweden	Parliament typically enacts the budget proposed by the government.
	Opposition parties can propose changes to the budget during a two-week period.
Switzerland	The Federal Assembly adopts the budget after making changes to the government's draft.
	Most changes proposed by members of the governing coalition are approved, while most of the changes proposed by opposition members are rejected.
Turkey	Parliament does offer amendments to the government's budget. During a recent three-year period, these amendments only had a small impact on the budget as a whole.
United Kingdom	The House of Commons enacts the government's proposals. A number of amendments are usually made to the budget bill, but the government is almost always the proposer of these changes.
United States	Congress does not vote on the President's budget, but in acting on revenue and spending measures it often deviates from the President's proposals.

Source: OECD (1998), "The Role of the Legislature".

This surprising conclusion is openly challenged by P. Lalumière, who notes that the 1958 Constitution of the Fifth Republic "reaffirms Parliament's power of decision in budgetary matters while multiplying the legal restrictions on exercising this power… In fact, the actual working of the budgetary institutions betrays an important decline in parliamentary influence" (Lalumière, 1975, p. 125). According to Lalumière, "budgetary debates no longer provide the parliamentary assemblies with an opportunity to exercise real influence over the choices proposed and thereby over government activity. The majority of observers now admit that the institution of Parliament has been effaced in this way" (Lalumière, 1975, p. 129).

Nowhere is the budgetary decline of parliament more noticeable than in Britain. J. Molinier sums up the process by which the House of Commons – the cradle of budgetary democracy – lost all formal influence over revenues and expenditures:

> The emergence of two large mass, coherent and disciplined parties with national support and alternating in power, led in effect to a transfer to the Cabinet of what was essential in the financial and other powers exercised previously by the House of Commons. Having stripped the monarchy of its financial prerogatives, Parliament was in turn stripped of its financial competencies by the Cabinet … Today the House of Commons is hardly able to participate effectively in the determination of the budget (Molinier, 1975, p. 168).

The British Parliament is distinguished from other national legislatures in that both its budgetary success and decline occurred much earlier than in other countries, and its loss of budgetary role has been greater. As an outlier, it is a model that few legislatures have emulated but most have rejected. Nevertheless, there are elements of the British experience in the many countries which have sought to avoid the fate that has befallen the House of Commons.

In Italy, the frequent turnover in government and the constant bargaining and bickering among coalition partners gives the legislature abundant opportunity to shape budgetary outcomes. But in Italy the problem is not that Parliament is weak *vis-à-vis* government, but that both have been undermined by political instability and financial rigidity. Valerio Onida describes the reality of Italian budgeting in these words:

> The budgetary system is dominated by the concept of strict parliamentary control. It is designed to place tight restrictions on government expenditure and to ensure that these are respected. In reality, however, parliamentary control is emptied of all significance. The root of this apparent contradiction is most likely to be found in the fact that the type of parliamentary control for which this system is designed … is quite different from the control which the assemblies really want (Onida, 1975, p. 220).

Onida points to a significant change in legislative practice that has been under way in many OECD member countries: "the increasing tendency for the locus of decisions regarding both the overall amount and the particular use of expenditure to move out of the annual budget altogether into the procedure for passing ordinary laws which require and provide expenditure in particular sectors for a fixed number of years, often for many years" (Onida, 1975, p. 228). This observation is endorsed by other participants in the symposium who find that a large part of the national budget, consolidated in fixed expenditures or flowing from laws passed many years earlier, for practical purposes evades all control. While not mentioned, most of these laws are entitlements which weaken not only legislative control of

Table 6.3. **Changes in the legislature's budget role during the period 1988-98**

Australia	The role of the legislature has not changed substantively in recent years, although Senate committees now have access to more information when considering the estimates.
Austria	The role of the National Council has not changed over the past ten years.
Brazil	There have been no substantial changes in the role of the National Congress over the past ten years.
Canada	Parliament's role in the budget preparation process has expanded. The government now produces an economic and fiscal statement each fall; this statement has enhanced the legislature's pre-budget consultations. The budget has emerged as a major policy statement.
Chile	In recent years, the National Congress has debated budget ceilings and limits on budgetary flexibility within those ceilings.
Czech Republic	The legislature's role has changed dramatically since the transition from socialism.
Finland	The role of Parliament has become smaller because the budget bill has become less itemised, and there has been an increase in extrabudgetary funds and organisations.
Germany	The role of Parliament has not changed much over the past ten years, although legislators must now offset any proposed spending increase with a cut in spending elsewhere in the budget.
Hungary	Since the transition from socialism, the legislature has been much more involved in the creation of budget laws and in the process of making budget decisions.
Ireland	The number and scope of *Dáil* committees has increased significantly in recent years. This development has meant that the annual estimates receive greater scrutiny by the *Dáil*.
Italy	In 1997, Parliament changed the budget process in ways that have allowed it to evaluate available resources and their utilisation more easily.
Japan	The institutional framework for the role of the Diet has not changed since World War II. Lately, though, some individuals have argued that the legislature should deliberate the contents of the budget more fully.
Korea	There have been no significant changes in the role played by the National Assembly in the budget process.
New Zealand	The Fiscal Responsibility Act of 1992 has increased the amount of information put before Parliament during the budgeting process. The government must now provide Parliament with a statement indicating its broad strategic priorities for the upcoming budget, its fiscal intentions for the next three years, and its long-term fiscal policy objectives.
Norway	The role of Parliament varies with the political situation. The proportion of seats held by the government in the legislature has an impact. In 1998, the government held only 42 of the 165 seats in the legislature; this situation probably increased the role of the legislature.
Portugal	The Assembly of the Republic has become more active over the past ten years. Possible reasons for this change include the recent expansion of its budgetary responsibilities and the fact that the present government is not represented by a majority in the legislature.
Spain	Parliament currently has the same pre-eminent role in the budgetary process that it had ten years ago.
Sweden	Sweden recently instituted a new budget process. It has yet to be determined if Parliament's role has changed as a result.
Switzerland	In response to the sharp deterioration of the Swiss government's finances in recent years, the Federal Assembly has come to play a more active role in budget discussions.
United Kingdom	In recent years, legislators have added a greater number of pages to the Finance Bill between its publication and Royal Assent. This change suggests that either the number or length of amendments, or both, has increased.

Source: OECD (1998), "The Role of the Legislature".

the purse but the government's capacity to regulate short-term fiscal outcomes. Arguably, legislatures cannot regain financial control if the budget itself is out of control.

3. Restoring legislative budget capacity

In the distant past, legislatures leveraged their power of the purse to gain independence as governing institutions. The competence of legislatures to decide taxes and spending and to enforce their dictates on monarchs and executives opened the door to an active role in establishing government programmes and policies. Can the budget once again be the wedge that enables resurgent legislatures to reclaim the budget powers yielded in the past century? An expectation exists that parliamentary bodies are tooling up to once again take centre stage in budgeting. But recapturing legislative hegemony in public finance cannot be achieved by reverting to the control posture that served legislatures so well in the past. While citizens may welcome more control of government, they also want more programmes and benefits from government. They want the schools to be well staffed and the social security cheques and other payments to arrive on time. If fiscal control gets in the way of these widely shared objectives, it will be brushed aside by legislators and executives alike bent on giving citizens what they want.

The problem for contemporary legislatures is that in the past they fought for a foothold in budgeting in order to represent the people. Today, the people do not want them to serve as controllers, for doing so would limit the flow of money and programmes. Accordingly, legislators have to define a new role, that of promoting fiscal discipline, improving allocation of public money, and stimulating administrative entities to manage their operations more efficiently. Fulfilling these new roles requires:

- enhancement of legislative capacity and resources to deal with budget issues;
- changes in both executive and legislative budgeting to promote fiscal discipline, allocative efficiency and operational efficiency;
- new tools for reconciling long-term commitments such as entitlements and other "sticky" expenditures with short- and medium-term budget objectives; and
- redefinition of relationships with the government that recognises the strong influence of political parties and interest groups on legislative behaviour.

Resourcing the legislature for a renewed budget role is the easiest of the required changes, though it may stir up conflict both within parliament and between it and the government. One move has been to expand the role of standing committees to deal with the budget. These committees are authorised to review the estimates, take evidence, demand information on the budget, and recommend legislative action. In countries where the legislature may amend the budget, its committees also recommend changes in the fiscal plans submitted by the government. There are, however, significant differences in the way committees are structured to deal with the budget. One pattern is to assign full responsibility to a finance or budget committee; another is to disperse jurisdiction among sectoral committees. The first eases the task of co-ordination and promotes consistency in legislative budget action; the second allows wider scope for sectoral interests to influence the budget. The first encourages examining the budget in fiscal terms; the second encourages a programme orientation. The centralised model facilitates fiscal discipline; the dispersed model may complicate the task of maintaining discipline.

A well-balanced legislature needs both a programme outlook and a fiscal outlook; both considerations must be welded together in producing a legislative position on the budget. Accordingly, a third version has gained popularity in recent years: it empowers sectoral committees to review relevant portions of the budget and recommend legislative action within an overall fiscal framework maintained by the finance committee. As will be discussed below, some countries have formalised this arrangement in a two-step process, in which the legislature first votes budget totals and then sectoral committees make recommendations consistent with the agreed totals.

Responsible and effective legislative action on the budget depends on adequate information concerning the activities financed with public funds and the results ensuing from government programmes. It also requires information on how changes to the budget submitted by the government may affect activities and programme results. Getting these types of information has not always been easy because budgeting in many countries is still wedded to inputs, with detailed estimates of the amounts allocated for personnel, equipment, supplies, travel and other items. In the past, efforts to shift budgeting to a more programmatic orientation have not been successful. The well-known failures include public expenditure management (Canada), *rationalisation des choix budgétaires* (France), programme budgeting (Sweden), programme analysis and review (United Kingdom) and planning-programming-budgeting systems (United States). It is highly unlikely that the legislature will take a programmatic orientation if the government does not.

The failed reforms all involved efforts to rationalise budget practices within government. The legislature was not directly affected, though advocates of the reforms typically argued that it too would benefit from an enriched supply of budget information. Contemporary reforms concentrate explicitly on the information given to legislatures, and even more importantly on the form and content of estimates and appropriations. Led by New Zealand, which has shifted both estimates and appropriations from inputs to outputs, a number of countries have drawn the conclusion that successful implementation of budget reform within government is contingent on changing the way the legislature makes fiscal decisions. While this thesis appears sound, it opens up a critical question: will the legislature be better able to influence the budget and maintain accountability for expenditures and results if it is supplied programme and output information, along with a flow of analytic and evaluative reports? On the surface, the answer appears obvious: the legislature is always better off with this type of information than with line-item data. But the verdict is not in yet, for legislators inured by generations of practice to review input detail may be disadvantaged by the complexities of a programme-oriented budget and overwhelmed by the volume of information given them. In this regard, it bears mentioning that most developed countries have not joined the performance budgeting bandwagon. Most have settled for injecting more data on performance into their budgets, but have stopped short of removing the input data and fundamentally restructuring the estimates and appropriations.

One of the frontiers of changes in budgetary information and structure entails a shift from cash-based accounting and budgeting to an accrual basis. More than half a dozen countries are in the vanguard of this movement, including Australia, Iceland, the Netherlands, New Zealand, Sweden and the United Kingdom. The shift to an accrual basis has been given momentum by the Maastricht accords whose enforcement depends on application of internationally accepted accounting standards and on conversion by the IMF of its government finance statistics to an accrual basis. In terms of prospective impact on legislative behaviour, a distinction must be drawn between accrual accounting and accrual budgeting. If only the accounting basis were changed, the effect on legislative action would be modest. The legislature would have cost-based information to supplement the conventional cash-based estimates. But if a government were to budget on an accrual basis, the impact might be truly significant, for the form and content of the estimates and appropriations would also be changed.

The supply of information has also been enriched in some countries by building the capacity of audit offices to assist the legislature. While the relationship of the audit office to the legislature varies among countries – in some the audit office is directly responsible to the legislature, in others it is an entirely independent entity, and in a few it is responsible to the government – these organisations have become more active over the past decade in reviewing the financial and programme performance of government departments and agencies. The list of countries requiring audited financial statements is growing from year to year and, though lagging behind, so too is the list of countries expanding the audit function to cover substantive results.

To make effective use of the avalanche of information, modern legislatures have added staff, invested in information technology and professionalised their operations. There is a marked trend to expand the staffs of standing committees, so that they can sift through the voluminous information and assist legislators in examining executive proposals, devising alternatives and amendments, and reviewing performance. The up-staffing of legislatures is not limited to budget work, but it is in this area that some of the most dramatic changes are likely to occur. While still few in number, more and more legislatures are inching to the view that they cannot truly exercise independent judgment on the budget if they do not have expert staff to help them do the job. The question for these legislatures is not whether to add a position here or there, but whether to establish a separate legislative budget organisation. Although it rarely is a model for other legislatures, the United States Congress may be a good example in this area. The Congressional Budget Office established in 1974 has garnered considerable acclaim for its objective analysis and forthright budget projections. Staffed by more than 200 professionals selected on a non-partisan basis, this office has exerted considerable influence on United States budget policy. Other national legislatures may follow its lead, but their budget organisations are likely to be more modestly sized.

Resourcing the legislature does not itself ensure that it will assume a larger or more effective role. The legislature must also define how it fits into overall governance. The three trends identified in the previous section that account for the decline of legislatures are not going to be reversed. Public spending is not likely to decline as a proportion of GDP, nor will the fraction of the budget allocated to entitlements shrink. Political parties will not disappear, though their ability to enforce discipline may be weakened; and the number of interest groups is likely to climb in the years ahead, though corporatist arrangements may give way to more pluralistic patterns. How, then, can a legislature stake out a truly independent position when it is beholden to entitlements, whipped into line by party leaders, and pressured by groups bent on protecting their interests? The answer is: not easily. But perhaps the best way to address this question is by considering the specific budget tasks in which legislatures may participate. Three of these tasks – fiscal discipline, allocative improvement, and operational efficiency – were briefly mentioned earlier. Discussing each in turn sheds light on the niche that contemporary legislatures may carve for themselves.

Before doing so, it would be appropriate to discuss the traditional role of the legislature as a restraint on the exercise of government power. Clearly, this role survives in most countries, though not as robustly as before. In a legal sense, the doctrine of control has not been impaired. Stripped to its essentials, it means that government may not spend more than authorised in law or for other than authorised purposes. *De facto*, however, control does not mean the same today as it once did. Nowadays, appropriations tend to be "lump sum" and are intended as much to authorise as to limit spending. Moreover, entitlements generally are established in permanent legislation which does not specify or limit the amount to be spent.

Currently, legislative budget work has as much to do with making policy as with controlling executive action. This entails a more integrated examination of the budget than many legislatures are prepared to undertake, as well as capacity to specify in law or by other means the performance required of those who spend public funds. Some legislatures have sought to hold on to a control orientation by shifting from *ex ante* control of expenditure to *ex post* accountability for expenditures and results. But in view of the fact that reporting and auditing of performance are still underdeveloped in most countries, one cannot be certain that legislatures are prepared for this new assignment.

To maintain fiscal discipline, a responsible legislature must give precedence in its decisions to budget totals before it takes up the various parts. The Czech Republic, Sweden and a few other countries have introduced a two-stage budget process involving both governmental and legislative decisions. In the first stage, decisions are taken on the aggregates as well as on the amounts allocated to major sectors. The aggregates are prepared by the government and transmitted to the legislature for review and, in a few countries, approval. Some months after the first stage has been completed, the government presents estimates, and these are voted under the rule that the sum of all the voted amounts may not exceed the aggregates agreed in the first stage. Enforcing the totals is dependent on adequate information concerning the cost of programmes and the prospective impact of policy changes. It also requires controllers in both the executive and the legislature to maintain discipline in the face of spending pressures. In legislatures which parcel the budget among sectoral committees, this watchman role falls to the budget committee which monitors what each of the other committees is doing. The price of enforcing discipline in this matter is to generate friction among legislative committees as they fight for budget shares.

Contributing to improved allocation of public money requires that the legislature take a programme perspective and that it be prepared to shift money from lower priority and less effective activities to higher priorities and more productive uses. Realistically, however, this is a momentous task, especially for legislators schooled in the politics of distribution. Redistribution does not come easily to legislatures, if at all. But in light of the determination of many countries to reduce or stabilise public expenditure, the only way to find resources for new priorities will be to take them from older ones. Redistribution may be most difficult in the case of entitlements, where citizens have been programmed to expect benefits from the government as a legal right. Nevertheless, quite a few OECD member countries have been compelled by budgetary *force majeure* to trim these payments, though typically only at the margins. As ageing populations add to budget pressures, one may see even more vigorous efforts to curtail entitlements in the future.

Efforts to reduce the budgetary burdens imposed by permanent law may be difficult for yet another reason. Quite a few countries draw a distinction between legislation and the budget (or appropriations). The former establishes law and policy, the latter provides money. Changing the amounts spent on entitlements means that, in addition to budgeting fewer resources for these programmes, underlying laws must be modified. There is a need to link legislative action on the budget with actions affecting such laws. Some governments have begun producing budget packages which combine revenues, spending and changes in standing law. The United States has had a reconciliation process since 1980 which enables Congress to use its budget to initiate changes in revenue and entitlement legislation. Reconciliation is not used every year, only in those where major changes in budget policy are undertaken.

Finally, legislatures may participate in the contemporary movement to improve the quality and efficiency of public services by appropriating funds on the basis of expected or actual performance. A legislature which rewards or ignores poor results will get poor results. Legislatures should be in the vanguard of demanding better information on performance, relying on performance measures in appropriating money, and specifying in advance the performance expected of government agencies.

4. Legislative budget futures: alternative scenarios

Future legislatures will have more resources to carry out budget responsibilities. They will have staff, committees and information. But will they have an effective role? The answer will differ in each country which tools up for budget work. But for ease of analysis, let us draw four different scenarios and the implications of each. The four scenarios are arrayed from the least to the most effective budget role.

The first scenario leaves the legislature better informed but with no real power to alter the budget, either because it is barred by law or its own rules or because political realities foreclose significant alteration to the budget. Such legislatures may persist with the habits of the past and tinker with minor adjustments, while taking credit for helping constituents and promoting their political careers. This role is similar to that played by many legislatures in the recent past. Perhaps having staff and budget responsibility will broaden legislative perspective and ambition and thereby generate bigger changes to the budget. But the more likely outcome is that the legislature will be all dressed up with additional capacity, but with little opportunity to shape budget policy.

The second scenario has the legislature transforming itself to challenge the government's policies and priorities by preparing a full-fledged budget. Rather than adjusting revenue and spending plans at the margins, the newly empowered legislature deploys added resources to act independently of the government. This scenario leaves several important questions: Will an independent legislature have the requisite political support to sustain its ambitions? Will the political system be able to bear the elevated conflict and tension that will certainly arise when the legislature charts its own course on the budget? Which will give way first, party discipline or the legislature's drive to forge ahead?

The third scenario has elements of the first two. The legislature has more resources and is more active but, rather than using its resources to act independently, it holds the government to account for its financial and substantive results. In playing this role, the legislature may target performance *ex ante* and review results *ex post*. To succeed in this role, the legislature's attentiveness to performance cannot be sporadic: it must be sustained and it must be informed. The best model for this role is the Public Accounts Committee in the United Kingdom House of Commons. But there is one important difference: rather than focusing only on how public money was spent, a modern legislature would have to expand accountability to what was accomplished with the money.

The final scenario has the legislature participating with the government in developing budget policy. It would still vote estimates, but its larger role would be to work with the government in setting out a medium-term framework along with sectoral policies and statements of policy. Partnering with government can proceed through the party system, through coalition agreements and through other instruments of budget policy. It is hard to quite define this emerging role because no contemporary legislature fulfils it, though a few come close, such as Sweden. The task in budgetary partnership, as in other co-operative relationships, is for each party to have its own say, but for both to work together toward a resolution of differences. This may be a difficult undertaking, both in governmental systems where separation of powers pulls the executive and the legislature apart and in parliamentary regimes where party discipline welds them together.

Throughout this article, we have considered how modern legislatures can change budgeting. It may be appropriate to conclude by reversing the question and considering how modern budgeting may change parliaments. One undertone of the article has been that budgeting would empower parliaments. But perhaps the opposite is closer to reality: under the pretext of empowering legislatures, might it be that budget responsibility would weaken them? This possibility arises out of three characteristics of legislative budgeting:

- Budgets limit what the legislature may do with public money.

- Budgets intrude on other legislative functions, such as law making.

- Budgets have the potential to turn legislative work into a technocratic exercise.

Each of these possibilities warrants reflection.

Budgeting introduces limits into legislative work: some of these may be imposed externally, others are market-driven, and still others are self-imposed. External constraints come from many sources: convergence criteria (such as those introduced via Maastricht), accounting standards and transparency codes. The market also constrains by exacting penalties (such as lower growth or higher interest rates) from countries which manage their finances imprudently. But the constraints which provoke the most concern are those imposed on itself by a legislature when it shifts from just making appropriations to also adopting budgets. Some of these limitations are procedural: they govern when and how the budget is to be considered or amended, how the budgetary effects of policy changes are to be measured, whether or how multi-year decisions taken one year may be reconsidered in a future year, and so on. There are also formidable substantive rules, the most important of which is that legislative actions must be consistent with the budget framework.

In promoting an enlarged role for legislatures in budget policy, it must be recognised that budgeting is inherently a confining process. To budget is to routinise financial choice in accord with a set of rules and procedures, to bar action outside the boundaries of the budget, to rule out certain actions and to rule in others. Budgets bring discipline to legislatures, just as they do to governments. In the absence of budget rules and procedures, decisions can be taken whenever there is the will to do so; with budgets, decisions must be orderly and consistent, and framed in both time and amount within preset boundaries. A legislature behaves in a more disciplined manner when it budgets than when it does not.

The second concern about enlarging the scope of budgeting is that decisions on revenues and spending may sprawl to other legislative work as well. Rather than legislation being walled off from the budget, it is defined in budgetary terms, and the fate of substantive law often depends on budgetary decisions. In countries where the legislature has been most active on the budget front, much of the session is devoted to financial matters. This has happened both in the United States Congress and in the Italian Chamber of Deputies. In some congressional sessions, two-thirds or more of the recorded votes have been budget-related. In Italy, efforts to have separate budget and legislative sessions have broken down under pressure to consider substantive laws under the expedited rules provided for budget actions.

To some parliamentarians, the greatest risk of expanded responsibility for the budget is that their work will become more technocratic and therefore will be based less on political judgment and more on technical expertise. Where legislative budgeting flourishes, legislative budget staffs grow, as does the business of measuring fiscal impacts, the use of accrual rather than cash methods, and reliance on assumptions rather than actual numbers. In some countries, one can detect the emergence of a pattern in which elected parliamentarians do the bidding of permanent staff.

How should one respond to these legitimate concerns? Not by denying them but by suggesting that the spreading influence of budgeting occurs even if legislatures are beholden to their old ways and unprepared for enlarged responsibilities. A capacity to budget does not transform politicians into managers; it enables them to exercise political power in a disciplined manner. In this writer's view, only legislative Luddites will oppose this new role.

Afterword

In the brief period since this article was published, national legislatures have continued to expand their budget role. However, this generalisation must be qualified by recognition of the wide differences among legislative bodies. The role that befits the constitutionally independent United States Congress does not suit Westminster systems which weld the legislature into a dependent relationship with government budget matters.

Nevertheless, several trends are discernable in most national legislatures. One is the bolstering of legislative budget staff, a second is the legislature's engagement in fiscal policy issues, and a third is heightened attention to audit findings. Increased budget staff reflects both greater independence by the legislature and pressure for the legislature to stake out its own position on tax-spending issues. Having their own staff enables parliaments to deviate from the government's economic and revenue forecasts and to make major changes in budget proposals. The extent to which enlarged staff change executive-legislative relations depends on whether staff are assigned to existing committees or are placed in a separate legislative budget office. The legislature is more likely to carve out an independent role when it has its own budget office.

National legislatures generally are more attentive to fiscal matters than they were in the past. This is a natural outgrowth of the spread of fiscal rules and of pressure to constrain budget aggregates. It bears noting, however, that in times of economic crisis, the government reclaims leadership and the legislature's role diminishes. In these situations, the legislature is bypassed altogether or quickly does the government's bidding, without considering alternatives.

Finally, the growing prominence of audited financial statements has emboldened some legislatures to shift the office responsible for this task from the government to itself. Once this shift occurs, the audit function may be broadened by the legislature to include monitoring of performance and evaluation of programmes.

Notes

1. This was initially passed as a resolution in 1706 and made a standing order in 1713. For the current text of this order, see Erskine May (1976), p. 707.

2. The historical evolution of the legislature's financial power is chronicled in Stourm (1917), pp. 24-29.

3. See Fitzpatrick (1918) who characterised the executive budget concept as a fatal step toward autocracy.

4. The decline of parliaments is discussed in Arter (1984), especially pp. 31-41.

References

Arter, David (1984), *The Nordic Parliaments: A Comparative Analysis*, St. Martin's Press, New York, United States.

Coombes, David (ed.) (1975), *The Power of the Purse: A Symposium on the Role of European Parliaments in Budgetary Decisions*, Praeger Publishers, New York, United States.

Dupas, Alain (1975), "Parliamentary Control of the Budget in France: A View from Inside the National Assembly" in David Coombes (ed.), *The Power of the Purse: A Symposium on the Role of European Parliaments in Budgetary Decisions*, Praeger Publishers, New York, United States.

Erskine May (1976), *Treatise on the Law, Privileges, Proceedings and Usage of Parliament*, 19th edition (Sir David Lidderdale, editor), Butterworths, London.

Fitzpatrick, Edward (1918), *Budget Making in a Democracy*, The Macmillan Company, New York, United States.

Friauf, Karl Heinrich (1975), "Parliamentary Control of the Budget in the Federal Republic of Germany" in David Coombes (ed.), *The Power of the Purse: A Symposium on the Role of European Parliaments in Budgetary Decisions*, Praeger Publishers, New York, United States.

Hagen, Jörgen von (1992), *Budgeting Procedures and Fiscal Performance in the European Communities*, Economic Paper No. 96, Directorate-General for Economic and Financial Affairs, Commission of the European Communities, Brussels.

IMF (2001), *Government Finance Statistics Manual 2001*, Statistics Department, International Monetary Fund, Washington DC.

Lalumière, Pierre (1975), "Parliamentary Control of the Budget in France" in David Coombes (ed.), *The Power of the Purse: A Symposium on the Role of European Parliaments in Budgetary Decisions*, Praeger Publishers, New York, United States.

Molinier, Joel (1975), "Parliament's Financial Powers: A Comparison of France and Britain", in David Coombes (ed.), *The Power of the Purse: A Symposium on the Role of European Parliaments in Budgetary Decisions*, Praeger Publishers, New York, United States.

OECD (1985), *Historical Statistics 1960-1983*, OECD Publishing, Paris.

OECD (1998), "The Role of the Legislature", PUMA/SBO(98)4, OECD, Paris.

Onida, Valerio (1975), "The Historical and Constitutional Foundations of the Budgetary Systems in Italy" in David Coombes (ed.), *The Power of the Purse: A Symposium on the Role of European Parliaments in Budgetary Decisions*, Praeger Publishers, New York, United States.

Stourm, René (1917), *The Budget*, D. Appleton and Company, New York, United States.

ISBN 978-92-64-06087-6
Evolutions in Budgetary Practice
Allen Schick and the OECD Senior Budget Officials
© OECD 2009

Chapter 7

Agencies in Search of Principles*

* This article was originally published in the *OECD Journal on Budgeting*, Vol. 2, No. 1, 2002. At the time of writing, Allen Schick was Professor, School of Public Affairs, University of Maryland, United States, and Visiting Fellow, Brookings Institution, Washington DC. An afterword was written in 2009.

Why agencies, and why now? The proliferation of agencies is not accidental; it entails much more than merely rearranging the organisational map of government. There is a logic to the popularity of agencies that sheds light on the current state of democratic governance. Every government that embraces agencies does so for its own reasons but, as diverse as they may appear to be, all the reasons are the same. Some governments set up agencies to empower managers, others to emphasise service delivery, still others to evade personnel controls or other administrative constraints. As different as these motives may be, all attest to the belief that the inherited department-centred model no longer satisfies the organisational needs of government.

Why not? One set of explanations is rooted in the theory and practice of management. A body of literature that first emerged in economics, then influenced business management and later migrated to public administration, challenges the once-dominant view that tightly integrated and controlled organisations are more efficient than fragmented, self-operated units. The argument against integrated organisations can be summarised as follows: hierarchical, centrally controlled organisations lack initiative, are slow to adapt to changing conditions and are not adequately responsive to the interests of those they serve. Giving agencies operating autonomy spurs them to innovate and improve performance. Because they are freed from departmental fetters, agencies are inherently more adaptive and responsive.

From this "new" managerial perspective, the rise of agencies is simply the latest stage in the never-ending process of organisational change and experimentation. Every generation has its favourite managerial style, and as concepts of good practice evolve, so too does the organisational structure of government. The current fascination with agencies will not be the last instalment. In fact, one should not be surprised if integrated departments return to favour in the not too distant future.

Managerial developments are not the whole explanation, however. They tell us why the few countries that have adopted the tenets of "new public management" (NPM) have created agencies; they do not explain why other countries that still have old-fashioned public administrations have also established quasi-autonomous agencies. This article hypothesises that the agency movement has profound implications that affect the role and capacity of the state. Creating agencies may be part of a process of breaking up the state into political enclaves, each with its own interests, power base and financial resources. Departments were the building blocks of the 20th century state; the disestablishment of departments may be a hallmark of the post-modern 21st century state. The 20th century state was predicated on the concentration of power; the emerging 21st century state may be built on confederate lines, with agencies, sub-national governments and NGOs vying with the nation-state for legitimacy, resources and authority. If this argument is valid – and it will require more than creation of some agencies to confirm it – then much more is at stake than the configuration of organisational units.

Defining agencies as instruments of management skews the discussion to questions of efficiency, such as: Is the civil service more or less productive when it is employed under an agency model than in centralised departments? Are agencies more willing to innovate than entities housed in departments? Broadening the issue to governance gives rise to questions concerning the changing role of the state, its control over devolved entities, and relationships with citizens. At this stage of analysis, one can only suggest a few of the many questions that may warrant consideration. These include: Does the government have the capacity and will to effectively oversee the actions of its agencies (and other devolved entities) and to intervene when appropriate? How should policy making be linked to service provision, and what should be done when those who command the two sets of processes clash?

A number of writers have grappled with the difficulty of labelling agencies. Because they are diverse in structure and function, agencies do not fit under a single rubric. Some are within departments, but have operational freedom; some are free-standing units that have no formal links to departments. Some are new units established when the government took on new responsibilities; some are old units that have been restructured. The roster of agency functions includes regulation, policy advice, service delivery, tax collection, police work, technical assistance, research, and just about every activity found within government. The only common element is that agencies are not departments – that is, they are not conglomerations of multiple activities. The typical agency has a single or relatively narrow purpose, and each has substantial operating independence, even if it is still housed within a department.

Every agency has its own story, but all the stories are the same. To be an agency is to be an alternative to organisational integration. This facet of agency proliferation is captured in the Canadian concept of agencies as "alternative service delivery" units. Inasmuch as many agencies are not service providers, the label is unduly constrictive. Nevertheless, the word "alternative" conveys a sense of where agencies fit on the organisational map. They are not just free-standing entities; they challenge long-accepted practice. (The word "alternative" is often used to connote anti-establishment behaviour. Thus "alternative medicine" refers to treatment that does not conform to conventional practice, and "alternative dispute resolution" refers to mediation and other non-adversarial means of resolving legal disputes.) The "service delivery" part of the label also is revealing, for it suggests that this has become the defining role of the state. If it is, what special status, if any, is conferred on the state as a service provider? Does it have a superior claim in performing this role compared to other providers? How is the character of the state transformed by depicting service as its principal responsibility? Does the "service delivery" label mean that the big questions on the scope and boundary of the state have been settled, at least for the time being, and politics revolves around lesser issues of how its job should be performed?

In suggesting that agencies are alternatives to centralised government, no claim is made that promoters of this model purposely seek to weaken the state. On the contrary, many proponents argue that the state will be strengthened by freeing up central organs, such as the cabinet and the finance ministry, to shape policy and monitor performance. Rather than being captured by service providers, policy makers would keep their distance from them, thereby preserving their capacity to set objectives, communicate expectations and assure that their instructions are carried out. Cordoning off service provision in agencies would clarify the responsibilities of politicians and managers, and would give ministers incentives and tools to hold providers accountable.

In assessing the agency model, one should pay less attention to motive and more to effect. The motive might well be to strengthen those at the top, but the reality might be a lot different. Once service providers gain operational independence, the state's monopoly in the authoritative exercise of governmental power is undermined. Nominally, agencies are (as the word denotes) agents of the state; in fact, however, they often act in their own interest, and empowering them with administrative independence gives them license to pursue self-interest. It is for this reason that the rise of agencies has the potential to challenge the state.

In light of the foregoing discussion, it is appropriate to consider both the managerial and governmental roots and implications of agencification. Section 1 views agencies as instruments of management, and as means of enhancing efficiency in public administration. Section 2 reviews some of the conceptual roots of agencification. Section 3 deals with the implications for governance, especially as regards legitimacy in the exercise of power. The concluding section suggests that agencies may generate a counter-reaction to preserve the state's cohesion and special status. Such a counter-reaction is already under way in some countries that have most fully embraced the agency model.

1. Agencies as instruments of management

Agencies are an old idea that has been invigorated by contemporary management reform. The typical government had agencies before it had departments. When it added a new activity that could not be accommodated within an existing organisation, a government created a new agency – not because it had a grand design but because it needed to have an organisation responsible for the work. The expansion of government inevitably led to the proliferation of agencies and to an over-extended span of control, weak co-ordination of related activities, and an unruly public administration. Most governments responded to this predicament by consolidating the separate agencies into functionally integrated departments. Thus, just as agencies are now valued in some countries as antidotes to over-confining departments, departments were once the favoured solution to the excessive fragmentation of agencies. Historically, departments and agencies have been rival forms of organisation: departments have multiple subdivisions and responsibilities; agencies have a single responsibility and a simple organisational structure. Departments promote integration, uniformity, rule-driven behaviour; agencies promote diversity, adaptability and self-governance.

The form of organisation makes a difference. One cannot argue that the contemporary flight to agencies is significant without also recognising the importance of the departmental form. Organisational structure makes a difference because it influences who has power and how services are provided. One should think of organisational structure as a boundary that influences behaviour just as the geographic boundaries of countries do. In particular, organisations matter because they determine whether related activities are integrated or separated, and whether policy and services are conjoined or decoupled. The linkage of related activities and of policy and services has managerial and political implications.

Every national government has a portfolio of activities, some of which have no salient connection to one another, but some of which do. National defence and lower education are examples of the first situation; providing job training and unemployment benefits may be examples of the second case. There is no basis for placing defence and education within the same organisation; job training and unemployment services, however, may either be placed in separate agencies or integrated in a department that is responsible for other income-support schemes. Having separate agencies encourages managers to give singular attention to their assigned responsibilities; integrating related activities in a department encourages managers to co-ordinate their work. Inasmuch as a sharp focus on both services and co-ordination are desirable, there is no permanent solution to this organisational issue.

A similar problem vexes the connection of policy work and service delivery. Every democratic government must both connect and separate its political and administrative organs. It must connect them so that managers and other service providers comply with the policies and rules laid down by political leaders. But it must also disconnect administrative matters from direct political involvement so that managers are free to act in a fair and efficient manner, without regard to political considerations. No democracy can abide governing arrangements which free managers to disregard the policies made by duly selected leaders, and no democracy can allow politicians to intrude in administrative matters without regard to the rights of interested parties. The first criterion justifies the placement of operating units within departments headed by ministers or by senior managers appointed by them; the second dictates the operational independence of administrative units. Striking the right balance between co-ordination and subordination on the one hand and independence and flexibility on the other requires that politicians and managers be both empowered and restrained. Each must have authority and resources to carry out basic responsibilities, and each must be deterred from acting in ways that encroach on the other's domain. The result is an organisational map that is repeatedly restructured through legislation and practice to promote one vision or the other.

In drawing organisational boundaries, a key issue is whether the greater concern should be to promote policy coherence or to protect administrative due process. Where the former predominates, government agencies are likely to be consolidated into functionally integrated ministries or departments corresponding to the main sectors of public policy – transport, education, health, etc. But when administrative independence and responsive services are the paramount considerations, activities tend to be dispersed among free-standing agencies, many with their own boards. The former results in a small number of large organisations; the latter typically ends up with a large number of small organisations.

Through most of the 20th century, the functionally integrated model predominated in democratic countries. But this was not the prevailing arrangement during the 19th century. In the early years of the administrative state, the preferred practice was to separate politics and policy from administration by establishing independent entities to handle new governmental responsibilities. It was widely accepted at the time that government is more efficient when administration is walled off from political influence. Independent agencies were associated with other administrative reforms, such as standardised accounting systems and a meritocratic civil service. But as national governments expanded their activities and added free-standing agencies, many were troubled by an overextended span of control, inadequate co-ordination and lack of uniformity in administrative procedures. These concerns spawned an administrative counter-movement to merge the previously separated entities into departments.

Sweden was one of the few countries to abjure functionally integrated departments. It elevated agencies to constitutional status by barring ministers from intervening in particular administrative cases. This "ministerial rule" doctrine does not prevent the government from providing policy guidance to agencies, but it has been applied in ways that give agencies substantial operating freedom. The Swedish model is said to have influenced a number of countries to establish independent agencies.

In contrast to Sweden, during the 20th century most countries departmentalised their public administrations. Functional integration in government paralleled, and was strongly influenced by, vertical integration in business organisations. The latter internalises within the firm production and assembly of the various components that go into final products; the former internalises within the department the various activities contributing to the same objective. Vertical integration enables the firm to more fluidly co-ordinate production. During the heyday, vertical multi-national firms (such as General Motors) dominated their markets and reaped huge profits. The evidence appeared compelling that this form of organisation was more efficient than firms beholden to outside suppliers.

Functional integration in government led to a relatively small number of departments, typically no more than 15, each of which contained related activities which may have previously been assigned to separate agencies. Once functional integration became the norm, governments habitually placed new activities within pre-existing departments. Exceptions were common, however, and it was a rare national government that had no agencies outside its departmental structure. Moreover, specialised bureaux within departments carried out particular tasks, so that the traces of agencies were not entirely erased by functional integration. But the bureaux operated within bureaucracies – that is, within large organisations that imposed uniform rules and procedures on their constituent units. Some bureaux had *de facto* independence; most, however, were truly subordinated by their departments.

Functional integration joins policy making and service delivery in the same organisation. It assumes that a close linkage of the two is beneficial because operational results can feed back to policy. Although integration makes for an elongated, hierarchical chain of command, in its heyday it was thought to reduce administrative costs and friction, facilitate oversight by headquarters staff, reduce the number of officials reporting to political leaders, encourage co-ordination of related activities, and promote uniformity in the provision of public services. Of course, governments that have recently established independent agencies reject this classical view of public administration. They see functional integration as inefficient because it values compliance over performance and uniformity over initiative.

Functional integration does not itself resolve the question of how policy advice and service delivery should be linked. Although they coexist in the same department, there is still a need to distinguish one from the other. Several devices have been introduced over the years to maintain separation within an integrated framework. One is to reserve top positions for political appointees, but to require that the remainder be set aside for career civil servants. Another is to impose procedural rules that assure administrative due process free of undue political influence. Such rules specify how civil service positions are to be filled and purchases made, the form of accounts, and other administrative procedures. The effectiveness of rules within integrated organisations often depends as much on behavioural norms as on legal constraints. Within a country's political administrative culture, there are informal understandings of where the boundaries are drawn and how they are enforced, when and how politicians may intervene in administrative matters, how contact between political and official levels is to be maintained, and so on.

To obtain the benefits of functional integration, it does not suffice that policy and operations be separated; it is also necessary that they be linked. In blueprint, the relationship is supposed to work fluidly by having policy guidance and procedural rules flow downward, and information on activities and services flow upward. Policy makers would tell administrators what to do (and not to do) and would provide the financial and organisational resources to carry out assigned tasks, while managers would report on their work and on compliance with the policies and rules handed to them. Audits would verify the reliability of reported information and evaluations would assess the effectiveness of policies. Of course, the relationship between policy makers and advisors rarely conforms to this blueprint. In practice, it is apt to be more interdependent and less hierarchical. Managers make policy and policy makers often dictate how activities are to be managed.

Functional integration generates both co-operation and conflict. Sometimes, policy makers and managers work side by side, without regard to status or formal roles. They fight on some matters and agree on others, and there are zones of indifference – matters on which some have a strong interest but others do not – which enable them to coexist in the same organisation in relative harmony. Formally, policy makers have the upper hand when interests collide; in fact, however, subordinates may have the advantage because they can withhold or manipulate information on what they are doing to subvert their departmental masters. Agents can opportunistically protect their self-interest because they know more about what is happening within their areas of responsibility than principals do.

2. Agencies as instruments of new public management

The principal-agent problem – which arises out of the differentiation of interests among those who work in hierarchical organisations (and in other settings) and asymmetric information on organisational activities and performance (principals are dependent on subordinates for much of what they know about services and results) – is one of the main conceptual drivers in discrediting vertically integrated firms and functionally integrated departments. While they once were seen as business superpowers that dominated their markets, many vertically integrated firms such as General Motors now are regarded as organisational dinosaurs that are inefficient, captured by their internal suppliers, and slow to change. Nowadays, many successful firms outsource production and rely on external suppliers for various administrative services such as payroll, product design and marketing. The "virtual" firm, which is divested of all functions other than its strategic core and contracting activities, is rare, but so is the fully integrated firm.

Disintegration has not advanced as far in public institutions, for most national governments still house major activities in big departments. Although all national governments have some agencies, only a few have reorganised their public administrations on this basis. Stray agencies tend to be creatures of expedience; they are often established because it seems the sensible thing to do in the particular case, not to fulfil some grand design. But when a country purposely decouples agencies from departments, it is likely to be motivated by the argument that independent, single-focus entities are more efficient than departmentalised ones. For some governments, the logic of agencies is rooted in the innovative concepts and practices of new public management (NPM). Stripped to its essentials, NPM asserts that the performance of public organisations is enhanced when managers are given operating discretion and are held accountable for their actions and results. The operational independence of agencies is only one of the innovations of NPM; others such as performance targets and contracts may be dependent on the agency model.

Successful innovations have many parents, and NPM is no exception. It has roots in classical public administration where the argument has long been made that civil servants cannot be held accountable for performance if they lack freedom to manage, and in business management where the capacity to mobilise organisational resources defines effective leadership. One of the main conceptual roots is in "new institutional economics", a field that focuses on principal-agent relationships, transaction costs, incomplete contracts and other notions to explain why integrated organisations may be less efficient. It would take this article too far afield to analyse these and other concepts, but it is worth stressing that the form of public organisations is strongly influenced by the form of business organisations. The influence may not be direct or immediate, but over time it is the most powerful explanation of change in the structure of public administration.

NPM has two core principles: one is to "let managers manage" by deregulating the use of operating resources; the other is to "make managers manage" by specifying what is expected of them and measuring their performance against these expectations. This *quid pro quo* – giving managers discretion in exchange for strict accountability – is promoted by carving out a specific area of responsibility for each agency and empowering its managers to operate as they deem appropriate. But having been given discretion, managers must openly account for what they have done and accomplished. The two sides of the bargain are supposed to be interdependent: it is not reasonable to make managers accountable for performance if they are not free to manage; and it is not prudent to give them operating freedom if their performance does not matter. In practice, it often is much easier to fulfil the first part of the bargain than the second. It is much easier to divest administrative controls than to enforce strong accountability. This is certainly likely when expedience is the justification for agency independence. In these situations, it is easy to forget about the accountability part of the bargain.

Properly organised, agencies contribute to both operational efficiency and managerial accountability. Even though it has operational independence, each agency should be clearly responsible to its minister or parent department. Having been separated from its department, an agency remains tethered to it by means of performance targets that give advance notice of what is expected, contracts or framework documents that spell out its responsibilities, and reviews and reports that assess results. Performance is the shared concern of departments and agencies; it should foster an ongoing dialogue between the two sides to the relationship. It should link policy and operations, politicians and managers, money and programmes, plans and results. It depends on a steady flow of data on what is expected and has been accomplished, as well as on key persons who maintain watchful vigilance over actions and results. If those in authority do not pay attention to performance, measurements and other information will be of little value.

The NPM template for implementing the agency model is best exemplified by the United Kingdom's "Next Steps" initiative which was launched in 1988 and has been characterised by a parliamentary committee as the most ambitious management reform of the century. The core idea of Next Steps is summed up in a government report that recommended agencies "should be established to carry out the executive functions of government within a policy and resource framework set by a department" (United Kingdom, 1988). Although the first part of this recommendation has received most attention from countries that have sought to imitate Next Steps, the second part, which refers to the parent departments' role, warrants equal emphasis. Next Steps freed agencies to operate under the tutelage of their departments. Whitehall, the phalanx of British departments, was not dismantled; it plays a critical role at every stage of agency existence – from initial consideration of whether a particular activity should be entrusted to an agency, to thorough review of the candidate agency's resources and mission, launch of the agency, ongoing review of performance and periodic assessment of whether it should be continued.

Although few governments have fully adopted the British model, many have been influenced by it. Agencies would not be in the vanguard of organisational change if Next Steps or a similar innovation had not become an international success story. In view of Next Steps' salience in the contemporary agency movement, it is important to comprehend its underlying rationale and mode of implementation. Derek Lewis, the former head of the Prison Service who was removed from his post by a minister dissatisfied with his performance, provides a splendid explanation of Next Steps:

> It was a myth that ministers ran major government services such as the Benefits Agency or the Passport Office; they had neither the knowledge nor the skills to do so. But as long as the myth persisted, the civil servants, who were really in charge of the day-to-day operations, were not being given the authority to get on with the job, nor were they being held responsible for the performance of the agencies. The intention of Next Steps was to describe more precisely the respective jobs of ministers and civil servants, and to get away from the confusion that had persisted hitherto. Ministers would be responsible for setting policy, approving the agencies' plans, setting targets and monitoring performance; the civil servants in charge would be given the autonomy to get on and make it all happen. The performance of the agency and its chief executive would be closely monitored by key performance indicator … Agency status also brought with it many tools that were commonplace in the private sector. The essential were: Clarity of roles, operational autonomy, the delegation of decision making and holding agencies and their chief executives responsible for results (Lewis, 1999).

Measured against these aspirations, many contemporary agencies in other countries fall short of the mark. Governments have granted independence without either clarifying roles and responsibilities, or putting the machinery of accountability into place. In many countries, agencies have been misbegotten at their creation, and it is highly unlikely that they will be set aright after that, for they have acquired independence without paying for it in the currency of performance. So little has been demanded of them at the outset that it is hard to ask more from them later on. One of the neglected lessons of Next Steps is that what happens before an agency is launched has a direct bearing on how it performs afterwards. Few countries have replicated the care with which the United Kingdom examined each candidate for Next Steps status before deciding whether and how to proceed.

In the Next Steps process, agencies go through a life cycle that typically consists of eight stages:

● "Candidate status" is the stage in which an entity (or activity) is designated as a candidate to become an agency. This stage lasts three to nine months, during which an assessment is made of the appropriateness of this form of organisation.

● "Prior options" is a formal review which considers the entity's mission and alternative ways of performing it.

● Ministry-agency relationships are clarified, including matters on which the agency will be authorised to govern itself.

● A framework document formally spells out the agency's objectives and operating conditions, the responsibilities of the chief executive, relationships with the parent department, and various financial and personnel arrangements.

● A chief executive is recruited in open competition and employed under a term contract that specifies working conditions and performance expectations.

● Performance targets are published each year, giving the agency explicit notice of how its performance will be assessed.

● Annual reports compare actual and targeted performance and include audited financial statements.

● Periodic reviews are conducted at least once every five years to evaluate how the agency has performed and to consider changes in its operating charter.

Every country that sets up agencies does so in its own way. Some, like the United Kingdom, proceed via administrative processes; some do so via legislation. Some act in a piecemeal manner, establishing an agency when it deems it ripe to do so; some introduce a comprehensive process for conversion to agencies. Regardless of the approach, however, all governments have to grapple with the questions considered in the Next Steps process. Doing so before an agency is established enhances the government's capacity to balance independence and accountability.

3. Agencies as instruments of governance

Judging from the reasons provided by various governments, agencification has been driven by managerial considerations. But conditions of agency creation suggest that political factors are also at play. In most cases, decisions on agencies are made by political leaders who see something in this format that makes sense to them. Moreover, where it is implemented, the agency model has important, sometimes profound, implications for the role and authority of ministers and the capacity of government to make and enforce policy. Countries that create agencies are not merely importing a new administrative structure; they are making big changes in the operations of government. Inevitably, therefore, political factors weigh heavily in decisions to establish agencies.

To probe the political logic of agencies, one might inquire: What has happened in the role or conduct of government that makes it receptive to this form of organisation? Agencies have arrived at a particular time in the evolution of democratic governance. What is distinctive about this time that renders integrated departments less politically appealing and single-focus agencies more so? One clue in addressing this issue is to focus not on what has changed, but on what has not. During approximately the past two decades, the size and scope of government in developed countries has been remarkably stable. National governments have neither rolled back the boundaries of the modern state, nor have they expanded it. Few have seriously tried to do either. Of course, within the state there has been ongoing realignment of programmes and some substitution of new activities for older ones. Although one should be cautious in generalising across countries that are at different stages of political or policy development, it appears that many of the big governance questions have been settled or put aside, at least for the time being. This was the theme sounded by United States President Bill Clinton in his second (1997) inaugural address: "… we have resolved for our time a great debate over the role of government. Today, we can declare government is not the problem, and government is not the solution." A similar sentiment has been expressed by Jonathan Rauch, an American political journalist, in his book, *Government's End*: "… it is possible that the government has reached its end… its overall scope and shape is no longer negotiable. They have evolved to a state from which they cannot, if you will, unevolve" (Rauch, 1999, p. 193). If Rauch intends this conclusion to be an immutable statement on the future of government, he is certainly wrong, for the current equilibrium might turn out to be only a pause. But as a statement of democratic politics in our times, his conclusion appears to be valid, not only for the United States, but also for the many other advanced democracies where, despite the political rhetoric, there is little programmatic difference between left-of-centre and right-of-centre governments.

The boundaries of the contemporary state are well demarked in the developed world. They include traditional watchman functions, such as the maintenance of law and order, protection against external threat, and basic health and safety measures. As vital as these are, in most national governments these traditional roles account for a declining proportion of public employment and expenditure. The bulk of public human and financial resources is allocated to the direct provision of services or to financial support. Ours is an age when the definitive role of the state is as a service provider or financier. This is a leading factor in the emergence of agencies, which in Canada and other countries are predominately service-providing organisations.

A service-providing role portends a fundamental transformation in the relationship between governors and governed. Where this relationship was once defined in terms of the rights and obligations of citizens, it is now often characterised in terms of the entitlement of customers to public services. This difference goes beyond labels, for it connotes not only that the language of business has penetrated the public sector, but that government performance is defined through terms and concepts more befitting a commercial than a political relationship. At first consideration, it may appear shocking that people may have greater leverage *vis-à-vis* government as customers than as citizens. But citizenship invests people with a limited voice and virtually no power of exit; customership arms them with both voice and exit. In today's world, it is the customer who is sovereign, because contemporary governments have been socialised to give primacy to services; this is why the state has grown so large and why efforts to cut it down are so feeble. And this is what the demand for performance is about.

With its boundaries marked out and the big questions resolved, at least for the time being, the policy functions of government have become somewhat attenuated. Can anyone claim that today's governments in the OECD community make policy with a reach comparable to that made by predecessor governments a generation or more ago? True, there is much more formal policy analysis than was previously available, but a lot of it is tinkering at the margins of the relatively fixed boundaries of the state. Much of what parades as policy analysis these days deals with efficiency in the provision of services. Policy analysts compare the costs and benefits of alternative delivery systems; they do not have an influential role in setting the boundaries.

The agency model is a congenial form of government for the provision of services. In contrast to the departmental structure, it purports to separate policy from operations and to give each agency a clearly defined focus on the service for which it exists. A department has a portfolio of responsibilities; an agency has a specialised responsibility. It is noteworthy that Australia has been one of the few countries to counter the agency trend, preferring to group programmes in broad portfolios rather than separate them into individual agencies. Australia has been an outlier in yet another way, making much larger policy and programme adjustments than have been tried in other OECD member countries. Departments made sense for Australia; agencies were the preferred way for other countries.

Without stretching the analogy too far, one can think of agencies as the "boutiquing" of government. In the same way that modern department stores often are organised into specialised boutiques, each with its particular market niche, the modern government department is divided into boutique-like agencies, each with its particular line of work. And as each boutique is a profit centre in the department store, each agency is a service centre in government.

This perspective drives governments to have more rather than fewer agencies. The logic of departments is that they should be few in number, so that cognate activities are grouped together; the logic of agencies is that each service should have its own unit so that none is neglected. An agency that has multiple tasks can be expected to perform one or more of them poorly. An agency with a singular task has an incentive to perform its sole responsibility well.

The service-providing state is a state whose performance is measured, targeted, reported, audited, analysed, budgeted, and so on, in contemporary life. After all, performance is what service is all about, whether it is defined in terms of access, efficiency, volume, courtesy, or other qualitative or quantitative dimensions. The word performance tells us that the boundaries have been set, now perform – that is, get on with the job. There would be little service to measure if government were not in the business of providing services. Performance, like services, de-politicises government. It is the common interest of liberals and conservatives, and parties of most political stripes. In the 2000 American presidential election campaign, Vice-President Al Gore noted that while he and his opponent George W. Bush disagreed on various educational issues, "we both are in favour of having new accountability on schools, new performance measurements." Consensus on performance crosses party lines because all sides are assessed by citizens *qua* customers in terms of the quality of public services.

But where there are services, there are alternative means of delivery. As policy maker, the government has unrivalled authority organs of state power. As service provider, the government is only one option, for it has no monopoly on how services are provided or by whom. The United Kingdom's National Health Service, for example, was built to provide universal, uniform care for all citizens. Over the years, however, it has faced growing competition from private providers who charge for their services.

As service providers, national governments have at least three competitors: sub-national governments, non-governmental organisations (NGOs) and business firms. Each is reputed to have advantages which have led some countries to take some direct service responsibilities from the national government, leaving it with a financing role. Sub-national governments are closer to the customer and can adjust their services to local needs and interests. The rationale for fiscal decentralisation is similar to that used in making the case for agencies: a government should be responsive and flexible, and should not insist on one-size-fits-all services. National governments and big departments are too remote from those they serve, too wedded to uniformity and procedural rules to give adequate attention to their customers. In some countries, decentralisation may be a prerequisite for reaping the benefits of agencification.

The same logic explains the contemporary fascination with NGOs. In poor countries, NGOs often are promoted or financed by international organisations in the expectation that they will be more honest, caring and efficient in bringing services to the truly needy; in developed countries, they may be financed by the government as a means of enhancing efficiency in public services. In some developing countries, NGOs have acquired informal recognition as substitutes for the government. They are seen as having a legitimacy that the government itself lacks. This broader concept of NGOs opens up troubling questions about democratic legitimacy which have been conveniently shoved aside by caring more about the rights of customers than of citizens. If government habitually fails to perform, why not bypass it altogether and rely on NGOs instead?

Business organisations are the third type of substitute. In almost every democratic country, public services are still overwhelmingly provided by public organisations, but the definition of "core" has shrunk in some countries. Some consider air traffic control as an appropriate candidate for privatisation; some have contracted out policy advice; many rely on commercial firms to audit their financial statements. Some view agencies as a springboard for privatisation; others see them as a means of retaining service delivery in public hands. These distinctions aside, it is increasingly accepted that government and business are alternative service providers, and that choosing between the two should turn on which does a better job. Furthermore, it is now widely accepted that for government to be an efficient service provider, it must be organised along business lines, with managers given latitude to use resources as they deem appropriate.

Herein lies the fundamental challenge of agencification: not that it parcels out responsibility among quasi-autonomous enclaves, but that it is a key part of rethinking the role of the state. In an historical perspective, the state is special as the national repository of public authority. This specialness is being eroded, for while the state may have a monopoly in exercising governmental authority, it does not have a monopoly in providing services. Services do not depend on legitimacy and authority, but on getting the job done, satisfying customers and efficiently producing outputs. Once the state is cast as a supplier, it is prudent to select the form of organisation and mode of delivery that are best suited to the particular task, even if the upshot is a weakened state. In the service-oriented state, performance matters; in designing organisations, it may be the thing that matters most.

4. Restoring departmental capacity

Is it possible to reconcile a service-providing, agency-structured government with a strong, effective state? The answer is "yes", but doing so requires a shift in focus from agencies to departments and ministries. The key question should be not whether agencies have freedom to operate efficiently, but whether departments have incentives and opportunity to effectively guide the agencies responsible to them and to oversee their performance.

In some countries, government weakness is regarded as a virtue. This may be the case in those transitional countries which have embraced various reforms that dismantle the command-and-control structures erected during their communist past. Agencies, privatisation, fiscal decentralisation and devolution of administrative responsibility are means of constraining state power. In these countries, the rationale for agencies has more to do with political ideology than with managerial performance. These countries will not move forcefully to reinvigorate the state until they stop being more concerned with over-centralisation than with performance.

In contrast to these countries, most countries that have converted to the agency structure have been swayed by the argument that this move will strengthen the state by clarifying missions and objectives, enabling central authorities to set performance targets and monitor results, and giving agents (those who provide services) incentives to perform according to the dictates of their principals (those in parent departments and central organs). This theme is echoed in the popular management literature which urges governments to steer, not to row. After all, this is the way successful businesses are managed; it should also be the way effective business is run.

Improperly applied, the steering rather than rowing prescription may lead to government that does neither well. Two problems come into play: the freedom that agencies exploit when they gain operational independence; and the capacity of ministries and departments to provide policy guidance and oversee results. It is naive to assume that agents who opportunistically pursue their self-interest when they are formally controlled by principals will be more compliant when they are organisationally independent. It may be equally naive to assume that departments which give inadequate attention to service performance when operations are run by their own administrative subdivisions will be more attentive when services are hived off to independent entities. Principal-agent problems are more likely to arise out of asymmetries in salience and attention than in information. To put the matter bluntly, agencies care more about their services and performance than departments do. The government of the United Kingdom was able to implement Next Steps without encountering opposition from Whitehall because the big departments did not care much about services and felt little loss when they were relocated to independent agencies. Why should they care more about services now that agencies have operational independence?

In the agency model, too much emphasis is placed on the operational independence of service providers and not enough on the behaviour of departmental overseers. For the relationship to work – that is, for agencies to comply with the policies and targets set out by those to whom they are formally responsible – it is not enough for managers to be free; their departments must actively guide and vigorously monitor what they do. To assess how well the agency model is working, one must examine whether the parent department is living up to its responsibilities.

Sweden is a case study of how difficult it may be for ministries to guide and oversee agencies. With as many as 300 agencies which employ upwards of 98% of state employees, the 12 ministries are not up to the task. Not only are agencies protected by the doctrine of ministerial rule against outside interference, the meagrely staffed ministries devote most of their resources to Cabinet and legislative work and other policy or political matters. If they assign anyone to watch over agencies it is likely to be a junior person, not someone with real authority. Since the mid 1980s, the Swedish government has taken a number of initiatives to enhance its ability to guide agencies and monitor their performance, but none have been particularly successful. These initiatives have expanded the operational discretion of agencies, established a multi-year framework for specifying policies and performance targets, required agencies to report on results, and strengthened the audit process. The government has also overhauled the budget process to focus on results, and it has used the annual "letters of instruction" from ministries to inform agencies of the performance expected of them in the next year. Despite these moves, the government appears to be only marginally more effective in steering agencies than it was when the reforms were first launched more than a decade ago. The mismatch in agency-ministry staff is so great that the government has limited capacity to pay attention to agency performance. In Sweden, there is an ongoing dialogue between ministry and agency staff, formal and informal discussions throughout the year which partly compensate for imbalances in the relationship. Nevertheless, the fact that the government has felt impelled to introduce a series of reforms attests to the perception that it lacks means to steer its many agencies.

New Zealand's managerial system is centred around chief executives who have full responsibility for their departments. However, departments account for less than half of the money that is financed by the state budget. Most funds and many key services, such as health care and education, are provided by Crown entities, non-departmental bodies that have broad operational autonomy. There are approximately 70 Crown entities, plus 2 600 school boards. Most Crown entities have a policy-making board which appoints the chief executive. Each Crown entity has its own accountability framework which typically includes a statement of intent negotiated with the responsible minister and an annual report. Despite these arrangements, studies by the Treasury and the State Services Commission have found serious deficiencies in the relationship between the government and its Crown entities. These include: uneven and inadequate monitoring by departments and inattention by ministers to the Crown entities for which they are responsible; unresponsiveness or disregard by Crown entities of government policies; incomplete and inconsistent accountability requirements; and inadequate governance arrangements, along with confusion over the legal status of some Crown entities. The government has drafted legislation to clarify the status of Crown entities, but the heterogeneity of agencies has complicated the task of resolving this matter.

The United Kingdom experience is most instructive, not only because the reputed success of Next Steps has spurred other countries to adopt the agency model, but because the Blair government that came to office in 1997 has distanced itself from agency-centred public management. Without disowning Next Steps, it has shifted the focus from agencies to departments and the centre of government. A clue to this reorientation is contained in the *2000 Next Steps Review* (relabelled the *Executive Agencies Review*). In contrast to the previous editions of this annual publication which listed agencies in alphabetical order, the table of contents of the 2000 edition only lists the departments; it has no entries whatsoever for agencies. This may seem a small matter; it is not. The rationale for focusing on agencies is that citizens should have easy access to those who serve them. Restructuring the report is one of a number of signals given by the Blair government that agencies are to be subordinated to departments and that the latter are to be the instruments by which the government formulates policy and sees to its implementation.

While the Blair government still says positive things about Next Steps, it has a modernisation agenda that depends on strong policy direction from the centre of government. Modernisation aims to make services more responsive and to improve their quality, but in contrast to Next Steps, which pursues this objective through fragmentation, it does so through policy and organisational integration. Moreover, instead of separating policy from operations, modernisation wants them joined. The government issued a White Paper, *Modernising Government*, near the end of Blair's first year which did not even mention the Next Steps initiative. Instead of removing services from departmental custody, it made them central to departmental performance, and rather than relying on agencies for service performance, it placed responsibility on departments. In a sharp break with the logic of agencies, the White Paper relied on departments to take the initiative in promoting change. "Within Whitehall," the White Paper insisted, there should be "a new focus on delivery – asking every permanent secretary to ensure that their department has the capacity to drive through achievement of the key government targets and to take personal responsibility for ensuring that this happens".

Where does this department-centred strategy leave agencies? Agencies have survived, but with somewhat less autonomy than the initial design promised. Excessive independence, the modernisation logic dictates, gets in the way of policy cohesion and service integration. This theme is sounded in *Wiring It Up*, a manifesto on integrated service delivery published by the Cabinet Office in 2000. Revealingly subtitled "Whitehall's Management of Cross-Cutting Policies and Services", this report demands stronger leadership from ministers and senior civil servants and it urges "using the centre (Number 10 [Prime Minister's Office], the Cabinet Office and the Treasury) to lead the drive to more effective cross-cutting approaches whenever they are needed". The report extols the Whitehall vertical management structure because it is "highly effective in delivering many of the government's key policies". The model favoured by the Blair government is hierarchical, with rules and guidance flowing down and information flowing up. *Modernising Government* has a different view of public management than the one on which Next Steps is based. The agency model promotes the break-up of the civil service into administrative enclaves, each with its own salary and working arrangements. *Wiring It Up* insists, as its title suggests, that civil servants should become accustomed to working across organisational boundaries. The report envisions the central government working to co-ordinate and improve the delivery of services. The critical relationship would be between government departments and local authorities; agencies would participate as departmental subdivisions, not as independent entities.

The Blair government has expanded the annual expenditure review process into a means by which departments negotiate formal public service agreements (PSAs) which specify the outcomes and results they will accomplish in the next three years. Recent PSAs for the 2001-04 fiscal years set out approximately 160 "commitments which the government can be held accountable for, and which departments will report on every year in departmental reports". The role of agencies in the PSA process is to contribute to achieving departmental objectives. The approach is top-down: "high-level performance targets," the 1999 Next Steps review stated, "will be cascaded to agencies to assist their attainment".

The government requires that each Next Steps agency be reviewed at least once every five years. The latest instructions for these reviews stress that "agencies do not exist in isolation from the rest of government, and so greater emphasis will be placed on considering the performance of agencies in the context of their contribution to wider departmental and governmental objectives". From a strictly legal perspective, the new emphasis does not change agency-department relations. Departments are formally accountable for policy guidance, programme co-ordination and service results, just as they always have been; and agencies still are accountable within their respective spheres of operations for costs and outputs. However, the new attention to departmental responsibility for services inevitably eats into agency autonomy. Agencies are to do their department's bidding, even if it means doing things the department's way rather than their own.

Much more is at stake in this realignment than operational relationships between departments and agencies. The Blair government has taken charge of the instruments of management to promote its policy ambitions. Aided by a refocused Treasury and a large, active Cabinet Office, Blair runs the government from the centre, with the public service agreements representing commitments by which the government itself will be measured. Blair's interests lie in policy and results, but he knows that services connect the two. If the modern state is perceived to be a service provider, as was argued earlier in this article, then it would be untoward for the government to stand aside and allow agencies a free hand in providing services. In bringing agencies within the ambit of Whitehall, the Blair government does not want to intervene in operating detail, except when its strategic aims are at risk. It does, however, want to ensure that agencies operate in accord with government dictates to produce the intended results.

Next Steps was a harbinger of the agency movement; it exerted a strong pull on governments that were seeking to modernise the public sector. Does the new stress on departments presage a rethinking of the agency model? Part of the answer lies in distinctive features of Next Steps. It was implemented by administrative action, without any change in the legal relation between agencies and departments. Ministers and permanent secretaries are as accountable for the use of resources and service results after Next Steps as they were before. Next Steps gave rise to some knotty questions concerning the responsibility of agency chief executives, and occasional confusion as to who should answer to Parliament on particular matters. Nevertheless, because of the manner in which Next Steps was implemented, there is nothing to undo restoring departmental leadership. The Blair government has been able to reassert departmental authority without formally retreating from Next Steps. Countries which have legally separated agencies from departments may have a tougher job if they want to reunite the two.

But even countries that have granted agencies statutory independence may be impelled to pull back a bit. As in the United Kingdom, the issue is not whether to have agencies – this form of organisation will thrive for some time – but whether agencies should be decoupled from departments or subordinated to them. To the extent that all governments have a need to co-ordinate policies and services and to join up their many fragments of organisation, the British experience is instructive. Governments will connect agencies and departments; they will have both, and neither will be independent of the other.

On this basis, one can foresee a pattern of government management that is different from what has been tried heretofore. Initially there were agencies, then they were swallowed into departments, and recently agencies gained substantive autonomy. Until now, agencies and departments have been rivals. The ascendancy of one has spelled subordination of the other. In the future, departments and agencies will coexist, in close alignment, but with each having its own zone of responsibility. When things are going well, the two will stay out of each other's way. When things are not going well, each may blame the other, and the challenge for government will be to make sure that accountability does not fall between the cracks.

Afterword

The "agency movement" has slowed considerably during the half dozen years since this article was published. Nowadays, national governments seem more intent on building up the capacity of conglomerated departments than in investing decoupled agencies with operating authority. Moreover, theoretical claims of advantages of agency-centred government are rarely heard these days. Although agencies still operate, there no longer are purposeful efforts to shift responsibility for service delivery from departments to agencies.

Agencies have waned because they fragment government and thereby make policies less coherent and public services less efficient. The proliferation of agencies impairs the capacity of government to deal with issues that cross organisational boundaries. A government that has more than one hundred organisational enclaves faces more difficult challenges than one which has fewer than two hundred departments. Many contemporary tasks of national governments require the co-ordinated efforts of service providers in order to produce the benefits promised to citizens. Whether the objective is to assist single parents to raise their children or elderly persons to cope with infirmity, to be effective the government must draw on the skills and resources of multiple organisational units.

Paradoxically, therefore, the decline of agencies has been motivated by the same service orientation that once gave rise to them. In the heyday of the agency movement, some governments were convinced that multi-purpose agencies preferred policy making over service delivery. Now, single-purpose agencies are disfavoured because each can provide only a portion of the services required by the recipients. The sharp contrast between the original aim of agencies and current sentiments suggests that there is no perfect or permanent solution to the service-delivery problem.

The lack of an ideal organisational arrangement also suggests that agencies were not just a fad. They addressed a significant need of government and may well be revived when large, clumsy departments prove inadequate for the tasks assigned them.

References

Lewis, Derek (1999), *Hidden Agendas: Politics, Law and Disorder*, Hamish Hamilton, London.

Rauch, Jonathan (1999), *Government's End: Why Washington Stopped Working*, PublicAffairs Books, New York, United States.

United Kingdom (1988), *Improving Management in Government: The Next Steps*, Her Majesty's Stationery Office, London.

United Kingdom (1999), *Modernising Government*, Presented to Parliament by the Prime Minister and the Minister for the Cabinet Office by Command of Her Majesty, March, CM 4310, The Stationery Office, London.

United Kingdom (2000), *Wiring It Up: Whitehall's Management of Cross-Cutting Policies and Services*, Performance and Innovation Unit, January, The Stationery Office, London.

ISBN 978-92-64-06087-6
Evolutions in Budgetary Practice
Allen Schick and the OECD Senior Budget Officials
© OECD 2009

Chapter 8

Does Budgeting Have a Future?*

---

* This article was originally published in the *OECD Journal on Budgeting*, Vol. 2, No. 2, 2002. At the time of writing, Allen Schick was Visiting Fellow, Governmental Studies, Brookings Institution, Washington DC, and Professor, School of Public Affairs, University of Maryland, United States. Boxed comments were made in 2009.

Budgeting is a work in progress. The process is never quite settled because those who manage it are never fully satisfied. To budget is to decide on the basis of inadequate information, often without secure knowledge of how past appropriations were used or of what was accomplished, or of the results that new allocations may produce. Most people involved in budgeting have experienced the frustration of having their preferences crowded out by the built-in cost of past actions. Budgeting is a deadline-driven process, in which sub-optimal decisions often are the norm because a government does not have the option of making no decisions. When one cycle ends, the next begins, usually with little respite and along the same path that was trod the year before. The routines of budgeting dull conflict, but they also are a breeding ground for frustration.

Within this pressured world, those who make budgets or are affected by them yearn for a more rational and orderly process. Reform is the Holy Grail of budget people, their unending quest for a better way to parcel out money and plan the work of government. Sometimes they embrace "big bang" reforms, such as planning-programming-budgeting systems (PPBS) and zero-base budgeting; usually, however, they strive for incremental adjustments in one or another element of the process. Tinkering is ongoing because the adopted changes rarely produce the promised improvements. In budgeting, the failure of one reform begets another reform.

If budgeting is a work in progress, does it have much progress to show? Have procedural reforms changed the way budgets are compiled or implemented? The clear evidence is that there has been significant change both in the budget practices of most OECD member countries and in their budget policies. In most countries, items of expenditure have receded in prominence and now are consolidated into broad categories. Nowadays, the budget has more information on programmes and performance, and its time horizon has been extended beyond a single fiscal year to the medium term. Over the past two decades, budgeting has been more closely integrated with other financial management processes including accounting systems and financial statements. On the policy front, spending growth is slower than it was during the post-war period, but entitlements claim a larger share of central government financial resources. Nevertheless, revenues and expenditures are closer to balance in most countries, though few have managed to sustain a balanced budget through an entire economic cycle. Reform has made a difference, but not a very big one.

My task in this article is to imagine how the practice of budgeting might evolve in the years ahead. As someone trained in data and detail, I find it difficult to contemplate the future without connecting it to the present and past. Budgeting is incurably incremental, not only in the amounts allocated for particular purposes, but also in the adjustments made from time to time in its operating rules and procedures. To comprehend where budgeting is heading, one must know where it is now and how it got there. To facilitate discussion, the launch of the OECD Working Party of Senior Budget Officials (SBO) in 1980 is used as a break point in the evolution of budget systems. The establishment of the SBO not only provided a forum for the exchange of ideas, but was itself part of the movement to reconsider budget practices. If budgeting has changed, it is not because the SBO exists; rather, the SBO exists because of the impulse to change budgeting.

In considering how budgeting has changed, it is useful to distinguish between three types of innovation: macro-budgetary, distributive and micro-budgetary reform. Macro-budgeting deals with the budget aggregates and with the maintenance of fiscal discipline; distributional issues pertain to the allocation of costs and benefits through budget decisions; micro-budgeting is concerned with the operation of government programmes and agencies. This classification is similar to the three-level structure of budgeting devised by the World Bank that identifies the core functions as aggregate fiscal discipline, allocative efficiency and operational efficiency (Campos and Pradhan, 1996). With respect to each of these functions, this article first describes and assesses recent innovations and then contemplates how budgeting might evolve in the decades ahead.

My sense is that the next two decades may bring more fundamental change than occurred in the two previous decades, possibly through broad political and trans-national developments rather than through frontal efforts to alter budgetary procedures. Some changes will be the natural progression of developments already under way; others will emanate from changes in relations among governments. While discussion of the future is inherently speculative, evidence for most of the possibilities discussed here can be found in *avant-garde* ideas germinating in the fertile minds of budget scholars and practitioners.

The concluding section turns to the question in the title of this article: does budgeting have a future? The question may appear trite and the answer obvious, for unless governments fade away, government budgeting is here to stay. There is little reason to believe that government may be markedly smaller in the future; it is more likely to be somewhat bigger. Yet the question wells out of the analysis in this article. The trends and possibilities discerned in this article suggest a future in which budgets may be bigger but budgeting weaker. This is a prospect that should concern those to whom the processes of budgeting have been entrusted.

1. Macro-budgeting: from stimulus to constraint

When the first SBO met in 1980, it was animated by a sense that one era in public finance had ended and another had just begun. During the previous half dozen years, OECD member countries experienced oil shocks, stagflation (low growth and high inflation), rising unemployment and escalating fiscal deficits. These adverse conditions were a marked departure from the buoyant conditions that characterised the post-war boom, during which economic growth propelled government expansion.

The post-war expansion is summed up in a few statistics. In 1960, the first year of the OECD, total government outlays of OECD member countries averaged 29% of GDP; two decades later, these outlays averaged 40% of GDP, an increase of more than one-half percentage point per year. Most of the growth was in social security transfers which doubled from 7% of GDP to 14%. The huge expansion of government was not happenstance; it was promoted by governments which re-engineered their budget practices to boost spending. Some national governments discarded or revised long-standing balanced budget rules, and many embraced the Keynesian doctrine that fiscal policy should aim to stabilise the economy, even if the short-run effect was to destabilise the budget. Many governments eased the line-item controls they had imposed to constrain spending and permitted or encouraged spending departments to actively bid for additional resources in the annual budget process. Virtually all developed countries weakened budget discipline by enacting legislation mandating the expenditure of funds on various entitlement programmes. Not only did governments expand programmes and spend more each year, but political leaders were expected to submit expansive budgets. In fact, the vigour of their leadership was often assessed in terms of the new and expanded programmes included in their budgets.

Economic expansion fuelled significant increases in government revenues, but these often did not suffice to cover expenditures. When revenues were insufficient, many governments either raised taxes or ran small deficits. Neither course of action entailed much political risk, and neither was seen as fiscally irresponsible.

When economic conditions deteriorated in the 1970s, public budgets were still on an expansionary course. There was an unsustainable imbalance between the momentum of the budget and the capacity of governments to maintain a prudent fiscal course. This writer commented on the predicament in a paper presented at the 1981 meeting of the SBO: "*force majeure* rules public finance" (see Chapter 15).

At the early SBO meetings, the most urgent task facing budget officials was to curtail runaway spending growth. Many governments sought to constrain public spending by imposing fiscal targets in advance of the annual budget preparation cycle. Some expressed these targets in nominal terms; others did so as a share of GDP. Some targeted outlays; others focused on total revenue or the fiscal deficit. The early targets were set independently of the budget process without careful consideration of revenue capacity or spending pressure, or of the steps needed to implement them. Few were accompanied by enforcement mechanisms or other changes in budget rules. The targets were political statements whose primary purpose was to signal that the era of unconstrained growth was over. A few had the intended effect and led to smaller deficits or lower spending growth. However, many were set at unrealistic levels and had to be abandoned far short of their stated goal. In some countries, the absence of effective enforcement mechanisms spurred wily politicians, often with the assistance of budget experts, to devise creative means of subverting the targets by hiding the true volume of public spending or of the deficit.

Second-generation targets that emerged in the late 1980s and the early 1990s have been somewhat more effective to the extent they are linked to budget decisions and are enforced through procedural or substantive constraints on government action. The most important recent innovations have included fiscal targets encased in medium-term expenditure frameworks, targets imposed by international treaties or organisations, accrual accounting and budgeting, baseline projections used to estimate budget impacts of current actions, codes of fiscal responsibility that require transparency in government fiscal policy and pronouncements, and a two-step budget process that separates decisions on the aggregates from those on particular items or programmes. Each of these is briefly described in the paragraphs that follow.

1.1. Medium-term expenditure framework (MTEF)

An MTEF is an arrangement in which annual budget decisions are made in terms of aggregate or sectoral limits on expenditures for each of the next three to five years. Australia led the way in the MTEF movement during the 1980s by expanding its forward estimates into multi-year targets that rapidly gained standing as the basis on which spending departments bid for resources and the annual budget is compiled. In the Australian model, the MTEF was not grafted onto the pre-existing budget process; it became the budget process – that is, the means by which the government parcels out money to spending portfolios. Most of the expenditure details compiled in the annual estimates were devolved to departments, thereby freeing up the Cabinet for policy work on the aggregates, allocations to the main budget sectors and policy changes.

In Australia, the forward estimates (which are medium-term projections of the revenue or spending that will ensue from approved policies) are rolled ahead each year and are updated for price changes, re-estimates of revenue and of programme expenditure and policy initiatives. Without the direct involvement of political leaders, the MTEF would be little more than a technical exercise, more a matter of projections than of policy decisions. Moreover, without a firm commitment to constrain future spending, the forward estimates would be regarded by the government as an entitlement to more money in future years and as a weapon to wrest bigger allocations from the budget.

The reputed success of Australia's reforms has spurred interest in the MTEF. But although many countries claim to be applying a medium-term expenditure framework, few use it in the manner intended by its architects. In some countries, it is little more than a multi-year projection; in others, it is a technocratic exercise that does not involve strategic decisions by political leaders.

1.2. *The internationalisation of fiscal targets*

The conventional wisdom that targets are effective only when they are imposed by governments on themselves has been challenged by the emerging role of international organisations in devising and enforcing fiscal constraints. The leading development has been the application of the Maastricht convergence criteria to the fiscal aggregates of the member countries of the European Economic and Monetary Union. Although the targets were agreed in 1992, they did not become fully effective until the end of the decade when the euro was introduced. At launch, proper enforcement mechanisms were not fully in place, and opportunistic politicians manoeuvred, with some success, to outwit the new rules. But with each year that the criteria have been in place, EMU gives evidence of a stronger, more vigilant monitoring capacity. Nevertheless, the long-term effectiveness of externally imposed rules cannot be gauged until the affected countries have gone through a full fiscal cycle. The rules took effect during an upturn in Europe's economic fortunes, thereby easing the political burden of meeting them. The true test of externally imposed targets will come during periods of economic weakness.

> Although the EC has strengthened its monitoring capacity, it has been compelled to relax the rules. As originally codified, the rules did not distinguish between cyclical and structural imbalances. They therefore were more stringent during periods of economic weakness than during buoyant times. The revised rules permit fiscal targets to be temporarily breached when justified by economic conditions.

A parallel though less structured development has been the imposition of fiscal conditionalities on financially troubled countries drawing assistance from the

International Monetary Fund (IMF). Typically, the IMF insists that aided countries meet specified fiscal targets, and it enforces compliance by releasing each *tranche* only if it is satisfied with the affected country's performance. The targets usually demand fiscal contraction, as measured by the size of the budget deficit or by the growth of public spending. IMF conditionalities have come under strong criticism from those who believe that its fiscal demands have made matters worse for countries whose economies are already contracting. With a growing chorus of critics, it remains to be seen whether the IMF will continue to obtain fiscal constraint from countries drawing assistance from it.

> The IMF has acknowledged that pressuring governments to adopt austere fiscal policies when the economy is contracting may adversely affect households at the very time that personal incomes are declining. The IMF has moved toward a more flexible posture that distinguishes between countries that maintain prudent fiscal policies and those that do not. The former may receive short-term adjustment assistance that enables them to weather economic difficulty without trimming social programmes or raising taxes.

1.3. *Accrual accounting and budgeting*

The point has already been made that fiscal targets are meaningless if they are not effectively enforced. An essential feature of enforcement is that financial flows and conditions be accurately recorded. To satisfy this requirement, a government must convert from cash accounting to the accrual basis. Ideally, it should also put its budget on the accrual basis.

> In a subsequent article in the *OECD Journal on Budgeting* ("Performance Budgeting and Accrual Budgeting: Decision Rules or Analytic Tools?" – see Chapter 14 here), I reconsidered the efficacy of applying accrual rules and concluded that they should be required for audited financial statements but not for budgets. It is feasible to enforce fiscal rules when a government budgets on the cash basis. Moreover, it is practical to measure a government's compliance with fiscal constraints by examining year-over-year changes in its assets and liabilities, as reported on the balance sheet

Cash accounting and budgeting provide abundant opportunity to misreport the government's true financial actions. Payments or receipts can be pushed back to the previous year or forward to the next; future costs, such as pension benefits, can be removed from the budget; the government can sell assets and book the income as current revenue; it can hive off certain expenses into off-budget accounts; and so on. Left to their own wills, budget-pressured politicians tend to engage in as much budgetary legerdemain as they can get away with. They issue guarantees and take on other contingent liabilities which do not appear in conventional financial reports or budgets; they sweep idle cash from state enterprises into their own accounts; they shorten the fiscal year to 11 months or expand it to 13; they use unrealistic assumptions in making appropriations or in projecting future budget conditions. The opportunities are as boundless as are the imaginations of budget evaders.

The accrual basis inhibits these opportunities by requiring that revenue be recorded when it is earned (rather than when it is received) and expenditures when the liability is incurred (rather than when payment is made). A growing number of countries have adopted the accrual basis for financial statements, but barely a handful have done so for the budget. As a consequence, some governments now report budget results that differ materially from those reported in financial statements.

1.4. Baseline projections

One of the objectives of the MTEF is to extend the budget's horizon beyond a single fiscal year. Doing so depends on reliable projections of macro-economic conditions, future revenue and spending if current policies were continued, and the impact of policy changes on future budgets. The conventional method for making these projections is to construct a baseline budget and to measure policy changes against the baseline. Budget organisations have been making these estimates for decades, but what is now different is that the projections are published and have become the authoritative metric for assessing the future budget effects of proposed or approved policy changes.

In the MTEF, the baseline is used both to establish the fiscal framework and to determine whether expenditure changes are consistent with the framework. Inasmuch as future conditions are not yet known, the baseline and estimates of policy change are grounded on assumptions concerning economic performance, the behavioural responses of persons affected by policy changes and other variables. Countries which use baselines to establish and enforce expenditure frameworks must have rules for how the projections are made and how policy changes are measured as well as procedures for dealing with deviations from the baseline. They must also assign responsibility for maintaining the baseline and assuring that policy changes are accurately measured against it. In a few countries, managing the baseline and related controls has become the finance ministry's most important budget responsibility.

1.5. Two-stage budget processes

In conventional budgeting, fiscal targets are perennially at risk of being overridden by spending pressures during preparation of the budget. In all budget systems, there is a tension between the budget's totals and its parts. During expansionary periods, the parts (programmes, departments, accounts, etc.) usually win out, with the result that by the end of the process the government agrees to spend more than it intended at the start. One objective of the MTEF is to prevent breach of the fiscal aggregates by insulating them from upward spending pressure from particular programmes. But when the budget totals are decided together with the parts, it is highly likely that total spending will be more than the government initially wanted.

To counter this tendency, a few governments, such as Sweden, have split budget preparation into two distinct phases that are several months apart. In the first stage, the government updates baseline projections, reviews current macro-economic forecasts and the budget outlook, and establishes a medium-term expenditure framework. This framework may deal only with the aggregates or (as is the case in Sweden) with major spending sectors as well. At this point in the process, no formal consideration is given to particular claims on the budget. The macro-budget is submitted to the legislature which votes the spending totals. Several months later, the government compiles the estimates for the next fiscal year. These spending amounts must be within the aggregates previously set by the government or the legislature. Rules similar to those used in maintaining the MTEF are applied to estimate the consistency of particular spending decisions with the budget aggregates.

1.6. Have the targets made a difference?

Have the fiscal targets and related innovations disciplined public finance, or are they the latest in a long list of budget reforms that have made little difference? The OECD has addressed this question by comparing spending as a proportion of GDP in countries that were members of the Organisation before the first SBO convened. The study shows marked deceleration in spending growth and more modest fiscal imbalances than in previous periods. But the rise in public spending has not been reversed; virtually every country reports that such spending is now a higher share of GDP than was the case one or two decades ago. The era of big increases is over, but government budgeting still is incremental, building the next budget on the results of the last one. As a consequence, government spending accounts for a higher proportion of GDP than when the SBO was established. To meet targets, governments have trimmed some entitlement programmes at the edges and have made deep cuts in subsidies to enterprises. Most have trimmed operating costs by imposing across-the-board cuts or by seeking to boost efficiency. They also have made greater use of fees and other charges to finance particular programmes. From the vantage point of voter-pleasing politicians, many of the cutbacks have entailed difficult choices, but their chore may have been eased somewhat by the new rules and procedures discussed in this section. Yet a fair assessment of two decades of tinkering with the machinery of budgeting is that the process is not all that different than it was before the launch of the SBO, and that the underlying pressures and imbalances of public finance have not been eliminated.

2. Macro-budgetary futures: neutralising the political pressure to spend

There is a strong probability that public spending will continue to rise as a percentage of GDP in developed countries as their populations age. The pace of increase will depend principally on the cost of social insurance and related programmes, as well as on overall economic trends. Will the rate of increase be similar to that experienced during the pre-SBO decades, or will it resemble the smaller rise of the 1980-2000 period? Of course, even a modest increase would be atop spending which already exceeds 50% of GDP in many European countries. This means that if OECD member countries do about as well in the next two decades as they did in the previous two, they will be doing worse. Moreover, the risk that they will do much worse is far greater than the probability that they might do a little better.

The vulnerability of OECD member countries pertains not only to total expenditure but also to their fiscal balance. To finance the escalating costs of social schemes and the still-rising expectations of citizens, governments of OECD countries will have to extract more revenue from enterprises and households than they have done heretofore. As high as the tax burden already is, it may have to be considerably higher in the decades ahead.

Governments may manage to escape fiscal meltdown by reversing long-standing social policy privatising social insurance schemes or stringently targeting benefits to their neediest citizens. These moves would roll back the boundaries of the welfare state to a far greater degree than has been attempted by any democratic leader in recent times. Pushed to the wall by the reality or prospect of rising tax burdens or huge budget deficits, the next generation's politicians may accede to such Draconian measures as their only recourse.

My sense, however, is that we are in for another long spell of muddling through chronic fiscal pressure that, like chronic back pain, gets attention but not so much as to compel a marked change in life-style. In muddling through, governments will struggle to constrain the fiscal aggregates within some acceptable, though expanding, envelope. Their task will be facilitated by changes in both the information content and procedures of budgeting, some of which are described in the paragraphs that follow. But even with rule changes that arm guardians of the public purse with new authority, fiscal discipline will be a difficult political and economic chore. Politicians will have their fingerprints on the controls, and they will garner blame for matters over which they have little genuine control.

2.1. The time frame of budgeting

Rutted in a fiscal quagmire that seems unending, future budget makers will regard the medium term as inadequate for their work, just as contemporary MTEF architects regard the single fiscal year as inadequate for theirs. From tomorrow's vantage point, the two to three years tacked on to the end of the annual budget cycle by the MTEF will be seen as a too-modest venture that obscures the longer-term outlook. The conventional MTEF is a couple of years shorter than the standard five-year planning horizon.

This time frame was selected to assure that medium-term decisions are realistic and relevant to annual budget actions. Governments opting for an MTEF have been justifiably concerned that the longer their budget projections are extended, the greater the uncertainty they will encounter. They also are concerned that it is impractical to make longer-term decisions because, as each year is rolled forward, seemingly resolved issues can be reopened.

Despite these sound arguments for a medium-term perspective, my sense is that, as governments face increased pressure to regulate public finance, they will lengthen the budget's time horizon to five or more years. The United States has moved to a ten-year baseline for estimating the impact of current policy changes on future budgets. The longer frame makes it somewhat more difficult for politicians to evade fiscal discipline by delaying the effective date of policy changes. In most developed countries, the longer horizon portrays deteriorating fiscal conditions, as the proportion of the population drawing pensions and other state-financed benefits rises. There is some risk, however, that lengthening the perspective might introduce greater unrealism into budget projections. If this were to occur, a ten-year term or longer horizon would undermine fiscal discipline.

2.2. Fiscal sustainability and vulnerability

The time frame is not only a matter of years but of perspective as well. Extending the perspective from one year to several and from several to a decade transforms the central fiscal issue from the current balance to future sustainability and to the vulnerability of the budget to surprises and shocks. Sustainability refers to the capacity of government to continue on its present fiscal course in the light of prospective economic conditions and its revenue/expenditure position. Sustainability is always for the long haul; interest in it derives from the realisation that, although a country may appear to be in good fiscal health, future claims or conditions may adversely affect its budget capacity. For example, most EMU countries improved their budget positions during the run-up to the euro, but they nevertheless face the question of whether the financial commitments they have undertaken will be sustainable when the percentage of the population dependent on pensions rises.

To take sustainability seriously requires that governments devise measures of their capacity to continue on the present budget course. These measures would have to gauge built-in expenditure pressure, revenue trends, sensitivity of the budget to demographic and economic changes, and (if feasible) the influence of political conditions on the budget. Economists are more skilled at analysing trends than in predicting changes, especially those that occur with little advance notice. Looking back at the Asian financial crisis of the late 1990s, however, economists have concluded that there was advance evidence that several countries were headed into trouble. They believe it possible to convert hindsight into foresight through bold development and measurement of risk.

Even if the early measures are crude and unreliable, they may influence the fiscal posture of national governments. Medium-term projections also are often wide of the mark, but they still frame the budget debate. In budgeting, questionable data are preferable to no data, because the government must act. In most policy areas, the government may defer action until it is satisfied with the information at hand; it does not have this option in budgeting.

Vulnerability analysis and other types of risk assessment will play an increasingly prominent role in budgeting. One can anticipate that governments with a budget horizon beyond a single fiscal year will be the most likely users of such analyses. International organisations may also become involved by assessing fiscal performance in the light of vulnerability criteria. For example, the EU might assess the budgets of member countries in terms of sustainability or risk factors rather than in terms of annual or medium-term outlooks. One can foresee circumstances in which the EU will demand that a member country revise its budget even though short-term criteria have been met.

2.3. Using the balance sheet to measure fiscal condition

Barely a decade ago, a far-fetched idea was proposed: that a country's fiscal outcomes be measured in reference to its balance sheet rather than to the budget. What seemed a novel approach some years ago may become commonplace in the future, as national governments shift from budget-based assessments to ones drawn from conventional financial statements. If this were to occur, it would be a Copernican revolution in financial management, transforming the traditional relationship between budgeting and other financial processes.

Since its emergence more than a century ago, modern budgeting has operated within a largely self-contained process. Decisions have been made, recorded and carried out almost exclusively in reference to the documentation produced by the budget process. Financial condition and performance have been measured in terms of the entries in the budget, without regard to other sources of financial information. Self-containment has walled off the budget from financial statements such as balance sheets, and the results shown in the budget have often differed materially from those reported elsewhere. In many countries, financial statements have adhered to prevailing accounting standards, while the budget has been prepared in accord with its own conventions. Financial statements have been subject to audit; budgets have not.

Several factors are pressing to break down the distinction between budgets and financial statements. One is the application of new accounting standards, including the accrual basis in government finance; another is the previously noted effort by independent authorities to assess country budget policies; and a third is the effort to strengthen financial management in government by integrating budgeting and accounting activities and standards. The natural evolution of these changes is to rely on financial statements in lieu of the budget.

In their 1993 article urging this approach, Bléjer and Cheasty argued that the balance sheet is the best available measure of the fiscal surplus or deficit. They noted that the budget is not a comprehensive statement of financial flows; it is by definition limited to those transactions included in the budget, and it counts these transactions in ways that are peculiar to budgeting. Budgets do not include off-budget or extrabudgetary funds, nor do they accurately value assets, liabilities and risks. The balance sheet is a broader statement that includes all of an entity's transactions, whether or not they are included in the budget. The balance sheet recognises depreciation, deferred costs and reserves for defaults and other risks. When the government obtains revenue from the sale of assets, the budget reports a gain in revenue whereas the balance sheet shows no change in net assets.

In applying the balance sheet to fiscal outcomes, a decline in net worth (assets minus liabilities) would be recorded as a deficit; an increase would mean a surplus. But to use balance sheets as measures of fiscal outcomes, the government would have to publish timely financial statements. Few governments now do, but many more can be expected to do so as accounting practices become standardised across countries.

The potential displacement of budgets by financial statements has several important implications. First, it will give impetus to efforts to impose accounting standards on government budgets. If this movement succeeds, it will make little difference whether financial condition and performance are measured in reference to the budget or to financial statements. Second, it threatens displacement of the central budget agency by other financial management experts in government. To retain authority, budget specialists will have to become more knowledgeable about accounting practices and will have to pay attention to balance sheets and other statements. Third, various budget decisions are likely to be made in terms of their impact on the balance sheet rather than in terms of how they are recorded in the budget.

> The probability that budgets will be displaced by financial statements appears to have receded, although it is likely that there will be greater harmonisation of accounting and budgeting standards in the future. The budget's pre-eminent status as a statement of government ambitions requires that it not be confined to the accounting straitjacket of financial statements.

2.4. Budgeting for contingent liabilities

Whether from the vantage point of the budget or of the balance sheet, future governments will deal more forthrightly with contingent liabilities such as guaranteed loans and insurance programmes. Conventional cash-based budgets do not properly record government exposure to various contingencies because no payment is made until a default or other event occurs. The budget does record these payments, but at that point the expenditure is beyond effective control. The failure to properly budget for contingent liabilities induces governments to substitute guarantees for conventional expenditures and to take risks that may imbalance future budgets. This temptation is especially strong when the government seeks to impose fiscal discipline by curtailing expenditure or reducing the reported deficit. Various studies have shown that fiscal adjustment invites evasion, with the result that the reported savings often are illusory. Although trend data are not available, there is reason to believe that national governments have increased their exposure to risk through various guarantee and insurance programmes. Even though risk taking by governments may be appropriate, the lack of adequate information may induce them to underestimate or ignore future costs.

As with other shortcomings in fiscal discipline, an early step must be to obtain information on the problem, following which appropriate controls may be devised. This is not a simple task, because risks come in many forms and pervade modern economies. Moreover, contingent liabilities are outside the boundaries of conventional accounting. The definition and recognition criteria applied to government financial accounts pertain to direct liabilities, not to those dependent on uncertain events such as defaults on loans or the collapse of banking institutions. There is no agreement among the countries that have sought to regulate fiscal risks on the appropriate approach, or even on whether the budget is the best instrument for this purpose. The following paragraphs describe the methods applied by New Zealand, Hungary, Canada and the United States.

As part of its reform of the public sector, New Zealand requires all departments to prepare audited financial statements. The government then produces consolidated financial statements, to which it appends statements of quantifiable and non-quantifiable contingent liabilities. The former are contingencies whose costs can be estimated. These costs are not recorded in the budget or on the balance sheet, but the information does alert government to prospective payments arising out of contingent liabilities.

In Hungary, the Public Finance Act limits state guarantees to a certain percentage of budgeted expenditures, but most guarantees – including those issued by state institutions such as the Hungarian Development Bank or for various strategic purposes – are exempted from the limit. The annual budget appropriates an amount for expected calls on guarantees, and it also limits the volume of guarantees that each state institution may have outstanding during the year. When guarantees are issued, the government publishes information on estimated risk, the reasons for tendering the guarantees and other relevant matters. Although the system appears to be effective for the guarantees covered by it, some major contingent liabilities have been excluded, with the result that payments often exceed the amount set aside in the budget for guarantees.

Canada subjects loan guarantees to a budget review that is similar to the scrutiny given to direct expenditure. Each department proposing guarantees must provide an economic analysis of projected benefits and risks, including projections of cash flows and debt service. Funds must be reserved in the budget for possible losses; sponsoring departments finance these reserves from fee income or annual appropriations. New loan guarantee programmes must be approved by the finance minister and authorised by parliament. Finally, departments and Crown corporations must report on their contingent liabilities; these are published as notes to the government's annual financial statement.

Since the early 1990s, the United States has applied special budget rules to loans and loan guarantees. It replaced the previous practice of budgeting for these transactions on a cash basis with one in which the estimated subsidy cost of loans and guarantees is budgeted as an outlay. Subsidy cost is defined as all projected cash inflows and outflows discounted to present value. In the case of loan guarantees, the inflows may consist of origination fees and recoveries on defaults; the outflows are the payments made by the government pursuant to default. Thus, guarantees generate budget outlays, even though no funds may actually be disbursed until later fiscal years.

Although it may take some time, the budgetary treatment of guarantees and other contingent liabilities is likely to become increasingly standardised. Once audited financial statements become prevalent, they may evolve into instruments for reporting on the cost of contingent liabilities. Perhaps the most sensible option would be to provision for estimated losses from guarantees on the government's balance sheet. If actual losses diverge from the estimate, the amount provisioned would be adjusted to reflect this experience. Corresponding entries would be made on the government's budget, which would show estimated or actual losses as expenditures.

2.5. *Fiscal policy and economic management*

Steering the economy by means of the budget is one of the premier responsibilities of modern governments. Political leaders pay attention to fiscal matters because their performance often is measured in terms of the performance of the economy. In governments of the future, however, major fiscal responsibilities may be entrusted to an independent authority which would be empowered to adjust tax rates and certain expenditures in response to projected or actual changes in economic conditions. As outlandish as this idea may seem, it was the subject of extended discussion at the 2000 meeting of the SBO (OECD, 2000). Drawing upon recommendations by the Business Council of Australia, a paper presented at that meeting argued that an independent fiscal institution be empowered to make across-the-board adjustments in tax rates without prior legislative approval. The case for fiscal independence rests principally on two observations:

- fiscal policy is biased in favour of expansion – it favours increases in current expenditure, leading to future increases in taxation; and
- governments are prone to fiscal drift, with serious lags in implementing policy changes.

Both defects, proponents of fiscal independence argue, are due to the influence of politics on government action. The proposed solution would curtail fiscal expansion and facilitate adjustment by transferring fiscal control from politicians to independent experts.

The proposal aims to reconstruct fiscal policy so that it is conducted in a way that is analogous to monetary policy. Just as the latter is managed by an independent central bank, the former would be conducted by an independent institution that is free of direct political influence. One may argue that the parallel is not justified – that enabling independent authorities to adjust tax rates has greater political consequence than empowering them to manipulate interest rates. One also may argue that independence in tax policy would strip democratic governments of their generic power and would call into question the responsiveness of governments to voter preferences. These and other objections aside, however, it is apparent that a line has been crossed in thinking about the future conduct of fiscal policy. An idea that was hardly discussed a few years ago may foreshadow the future world of fiscal discipline.

In reflecting on the establishment of an independent fiscal authority, it is necessary to distinguish between advice and policy. It is one thing for a government to seek independent advice on economic conditions and fiscal options but quite another to entrust the making of fiscal policy to an independent body that can adjust revenues or expenditures in accord with its own views. Germany comes to mind as a country that has long relied on independent advice, but places full authority to make policy in the hands of elected political leaders. Although it is near-universal to vest authority over monetary policy in an independent central bank, at present I see little prospect for extending this arrangement to fiscal matters.

2.6. Fiscal discipline without power

This section began by considering how future governments might bolster fiscal discipline; it ends with a proposal that concedes the lack of government discipline and looks for relief outside the political process. Governments of the future may be compelled to account to outside authorities, to maintain their budgets in a form dictated by others, to have their budgets audited as to content and process, and to have the authority over key aspects of budget policy transferred to others.

In a globalised future, national governments may have bigger budgets but less effective influence over them. If they budget in a fiscally disciplined manner, it may be because they have been weakened, not because they have been empowered. To the extent that their budgets impose external costs on other countries or on the international community, they may be required to submit their policies to external review. Even the biggest countries may be compelled to formulate budget policy in open economies, in which events outside their borders impinge on their fiscal capacity. National governments will be increasingly sandwiched between meta-national and sub-national governments, in which fiscal decentralisation coexists with fiscal internationalism. Pulled in opposite directions, their budgets may be beholden to decisions taken by others.

This conclusion is highly speculative, for it would mark a retreat from an age in which legal sovereignty and political power are concentrated in the nation-state. This form of governance may prove to be more durable and adaptive than the bad-case scenario in the previous paragraph indicates. It may be that the determination to maintain fiscal discipline will impel countries to recentralise control of public money, or that international authorities limit their role to specifying accounting rules and aggregate policy but do not play a role in substantive policy. Another possibility is that, in the globalised future, national governments will become the functional equivalent of contemporary sub-national governments, articulating local interests and demanding a share of international budgets for their own use. With so many plausible scenarios, the only thing that is certain is that the fiscal future will be different from today's fiscal arrangements.

3. Distributive budgeting: from allocation to reallocation

The second set of budget issues identified at the start of this article pertains to the allocation of government funds to sectors or programmes. This concern is omnipresent because budgeting is inherently an allocative process. Whether it is structured in terms of expenditure items, accounts, organisations, activities or some other classification, the main issue in budgeting is how much should each entry get. This question has two dimensions: the efficiency of public expenditure and the priorities of government. The first criterion dictates that money should be allocated so as to optimise efficiency across and within programmes and sectors; the second dictates that government should allocate money in accord with its objectives. There has been a tacit belief in budgeting that the two criteria can and should be reconciled – that the government should frame its priorities in the light of analysis or evidence on the effectiveness of different programmes. In fact, major reforms such as PPBS assume that both political priorities and allocative efficiency will coexist if the budget is prepared on a rational basis.

Efficiency in allocation has been pursued principally through investment in programme evaluation and outcome measures. In recent decades, relatively little weight has been given in developed countries to restructuring the budget along programme lines. This approach is still tried in some developing and transitional countries, sometimes as a means of consolidating the detailed items of expenditure into broader categories. But there is consensus these days that changing budget classifications does not itself change budget allocations; the only difference is in the manner in which expenditures are reported, not in the activities to which they are allocated. Moreover, it also is generally recognised that pure programme classifications which ignore or supersede organisational boundaries complicate the task of holding managers responsible for results.

3.1. Evaluation

Evaluation is an oft-tried strategy with spotty results. It has proved easier to conduct programme evaluations than to use them in allocating resources, and easier to ignore or explain away adverse findings than to take tough measures to improve programme performance. Evaluation gives the government information; it does not require that the government apply the information in budgeting. Many OECD member countries have had occasional success in conducting and applying evaluations, but (to this writer's knowledge) only two have had a comprehensive evaluation strategy. Canada organised a vast effort around the Comptroller General in the 1970s; Australia adopted an ambitious evaluation strategy in the late 1980s. Canada's effort bore little fruit; Australia's produced significant reallocation of budget resources. Canada is thought to have failed because it centralised evaluation, thereby dampening co-operation by spending departments which may have been adversely affected by the findings. Australia is thought to have succeeded because it gave affected departments a big stake in designing and using evaluations.

> Australia maintained an active evaluation strategy for approximately one decade – from the late 1980s until near the end of the next decade, when the strategy was abandoned with little public notice as part of an ill-designed effort to devolve budget work from the Department of Finance and Administration to sectoral ministries. Arguably, intensive evaluation diminishes in effectiveness over time or as it becomes merely another routine that must be completed each year.

Australia's evaluation strategy called for each portfolio (which consists of one or more departments) to prepare a comprehensive plan scheduling the evaluations to be conducted over each of the next several years. When a minister proposes a new programme (within the forward estimates process described earlier), the proposal has to include a description of how the initiative will be evaluated. The evaluations are carried out by the affected departments but the Department of Finance oversees the process, including methodology and design and publication of results. The Department has made a sustained effort to feed evaluations into the budget process and has published an annual report estimating the percentage of that year's decisions influenced by evaluative findings.

3.2. Outcome measurement

A related development has been the systematic definition and measurement of outcomes. These indicators, which generally measure the impact of policies on social conditions, are distinguishable from output measures which are discussed later in this article. There is a burgeoning literature on the measurement of outcomes, but entrenched difficulty in applying the results to budget decisions. Outcomes usually lie beyond the direct control of the government department carrying out the programme, and usually derive from a confluence of factors, not just policy intervention by the government. It is questionable whether a cause-effect relationship can be attributed to changes in policies and in social conditions.

Governments that seek to measure outcomes spend an inordinate amount of time arguing over whether a particular measure is an intermediate or end outcome, whether it is an output or an outcome, the difference between impacts and outcomes, and so on. These sterile debates have impeded the application of useful measures by government. In my view, the most productive way to think about outcomes is as directional signals, not as causal statements. They should provoke a government to assess whether social conditions are moving in the expected directions and whether policy changes should be considered. For example, regardless of whether it is responsible for the trend, a government should be aware of whether infant mortality rates are rising or declining and should take appropriate actions in response to the data. Even if it is not responsible for the results, the government should be cognisant of them.

> Regretfully, sterile debate over the definition of outcomes has not abated in the years since this article was published. Decades of disappointment have reinforced my view that outcomes should be regarded as strategic rather than budgetary measures. They should inform the government about critical trends and issues, but should not be directly linked to budget allocations. The closer their connection to the budget, the greater the problems in linking changes in expenditure to changes in outcomes.

In view of the weak cause-effect relationship, it generally would not be useful to base performance budgeting systems on an explicit linkage of the amounts spent and the outcomes experienced. It may be useful, however, to publish outcome measures as supporting information in the budget.

3.3. Strategic planning

The second path taken by reform of budget allocation has been to make the budget more responsive to government priorities. It may seem obvious that a government cannot budget on the basis of its priorities if it does not have them. But the long-standing tendency in budgeting has been for a government to be inexplicit about its priorities – to have priorities imputed from the allocations actually made rather than to state them in advance. According to this line of reasoning, explicating priorities generates undue conflict and complicates the task of producing the budget. It is better, therefore, for a government to prepare the budget without an explicit statement of objectives or priorities. If a particular programme is allocated more money than another, one can infer that it is deemed to be of higher priority.

The counter-argument is that if a government does not know its priorities, the budget will not reflect them. In view of the entrenched claims of past decisions and the active role of spending departments and interest groups, the budget will not have much money for new priorities unless the government makes a determined effort to set aside funds for them.

Strategic planning has emerged in recent times as the main innovation in enabling a government to structure its budget on the basis of missions and objectives. In contrast to earlier reforms, such as programme budgeting and PPBS which sought to integrate policy planning into the budget process, strategic planning stands apart from budgeting. It is not constrained by the time or funding pressures of budgeting, but neither is it assured direct input into budget decisions. Also in contrast to past planning efforts, strategic planning focuses on government organisations rather than on programmes or activities. The key question is not what a government should do but what its departments and agencies should be. For example, a strategic plan might consider whether the mission of the customs agency should be to encourage trade or to interdict illegal imports. On the basis of a strategic decision on missions, the agency might restructure operations and realign its budget priorities, although budget issues are not foremost during formulation of the strategic plan. Once the plan is approved, the agency or government would be expected to allocate resources in accord with it.

Its separation from budgeting enables the strategic plan to take a deeper look at purposes and objectives, but it potentially diminishes the probability that the plan will influence the budget. Agencies generally like strategic planning because it portrays them in a favourable light and bolsters their claim for more resources. But the more a strategic plan tries to influence the budget, the less strategic it is likely to be.

3.4. Redistributive budgeting

As with the fiscal aggregates, the SBO marked a change in budgeting as a distributive process. One of the early SBO meetings considered a paper on budgeting as a decremental process; other meetings focused on cutback budgeting. The change in orientation has been due to the reorientation of budgeting from a process which annually allocates increments to favoured programmes to one which has little margin (and sometimes none) for spending initiatives. This change in fortune has been due to the built-in claims of entitlements and other mandatory expenditure, the less robust economic growth of the past two decades, and efforts to strengthen fiscal discipline. The last of these factors is especially important because the more successful a government is in constraining the totals, the greater the risk it runs that old priorities will be frozen into the budget and new priorities will be frozen out.

When incremental resources are available, budgeting is a distributive process in which the government responds to fresh demands by allocating additional resources to them. Incremental budgeting has been lauded by some observers on the ground that it stabilises the process and reduces conflict, and has been criticised by others on the argument that it biases spending upward and rewards inefficiency. These arguments aside, there is little doubt that, in the pre-SBO period, incrementalism was the norm. However, incrementalism requires increments – additional resources that can be spent on some purposes without taking money away from other purposes. In the two decades since the launch of the SBO, budget increments often have fallen short of the expected growth in expenditure. To make matters more difficult for governments, they can no longer tax their way out of budget problems.

As a consequence, budgeting has been moulded into a somewhat redistributive process, in which funds are recycled from old programmes to new ones. The word "somewhat" reflects the reality that redistribution fuels conflict, and budgeting is a process that must dampen conflict. Redistribution is not wholesale change; it is tinkering here and there to free up money for current needs. Redistribution is always difficult, but it has been made more so by the heightened activism of interest groups on the periphery of government who lobby to protect their budget stakes. As budgets have got tighter, groups have become more assertive, and many now have informal roles in budgeting.

> Despite occasional cutbacks and reallocations, explicit redistribution still is rare. Budgeting remains a distributive process, in which the key question is how additional resources should be allocated. It should be noted, however, that to the extent that they have less capacity to debt finance current expenditure, sub-national governments do practise cutback budgeting from time to time.

Redistribution does not depend on turning budgeting into a zero-based process. Wherever it has been tried, zero-based budgeting has failed. It fails because budget makers cannot ignore past decisions and commitments, nor can they uproot programmes without regard to the impacts on the government agencies carrying them out. No matter what budget process is used, the current year's expenditure will always be the best indicator of the next year's spending. When it occurs, redistribution is only at the margins of the budget, not the wholesale termination of ongoing programmes.

3.5. Using the medium-term expenditure framework to promote reallocation

In addition to promoting fiscal discipline, a medium-term expenditure framework facilitates reallocations in accord with the government's strategic priorities. The MTEF determines the margin (if any) available for spending initiatives or the net savings required to meet the fiscal targets. Proposed reallocations are measured against the preset margin or savings to assure that policy changes are consistent with the government's fiscal objectives. Because policy changes typically have a greater impact on future budgets than on the one immediately ahead, it is important to assure that claimed savings in next year's budget do not end up as net increases in future budgets.

Medium-term spending constraints are not self-enforcing. The drive to reallocate can open the door to ploys by spending departments to substitute more costly programmes for the ones they are currently operating. Without vigilant monitoring by the finance ministry, spending departments may overstate the savings from programme cutbacks and underestimate the cost of new programmes. To thwart these tactics, it is essential that the MTEF include baseline projections of authorised spending in each of the next several years.

Measuring proposed policy changes against the baseline has become one of the most important tasks of the central budget offices in MTEF countries.

Reallocation is facilitated when the government specifies a resource envelope for each sector or major spending department. In the course of setting these envelopes, the government may reallocate across sectors by deciding that some sectors should be permitted increases above the baseline and others should be required to produce decreases. These inter-sectoral reallocations should be made at the highest level of government. In parliamentary regimes, they typically involve the prime minister and the cabinet. Much reallocation is likely to be within sectors, and this may be encouraged by devolving responsibility to line ministers. Arguably, more reallocation will occur if spending ministers and managers have a role in generating policy changes. Doing the job centrally at the top of government may result in much conflict and little reallocation. The threat of losing resources and programmes may provoke departments to block the trade-offs demanded of them. Although they are not at the centre of power, spending departments have formidable weapons at their disposal. They can withhold information needed to make cost-effective trade-offs; they can enter into log-rolling coalitions with other spenders to protect their budgets; they can rally affected interest groups to oppose reallocation.

To gain the co-operation of spending departments, it is sensible to give them a prominent voice in reallocation. A devolved arrangement would free up the cabinet to focus on major policy changes rather than on spending details. It would give sectoral ministers the lead role in developing programme changes within their portfolios, provided that the proposed changes are within the MTEF sectoral resource envelope and are consistent with overall governmental priorities. In Australia, the birthplace of MTEF, the forward estimates may be set at a level which accommodates spending increases or mandates cutbacks. Within the forward estimates, a minister may propose spending increases for some activities to be financed by savings in other activities. In this devolved arrangement, ministers have unilateral authority to approve changes below a certain amount; changes above the threshold require Cabinet approval. This system puts the finance minister in the role of refereeing the reallocation process, managing the trade-off system, and ensuring that programme changes and budget reallocations are consistent with the government's fiscal norms and policy objectives.

4. Distributive budget futures: who will get what?

Despite the attention paid it, redistribution is a side-show in budgeting; the main event is still distributing money, usually on an incremental basis to powerful claimants. Notwithstanding the bleak scenarios which show budgets and demographics on a collision course early in the 21st century, budgeting will continue as a process for distributing spending increases to agencies, households and other beneficiaries of the government's largess. On the basis of political trends, one can expect budgeting to become more open and sensitive to demands by claimants mobilised to protect or enlarge their shares. Voters, interest groups, NGOs and others will become more assertive and the budget will become more transparent about who is benefiting and who is losing from the government's financial decisions. Thus, even as budgeting becomes more technocratic, it will be more politicised. The upshot will be more conflict in budgeting, as rival interests vie for advantage. Yet because of the compelling need to resolve each year's budget, new methods will be devised to regulate friction over resource allocations.

4.1. E-budgeting

Information technology will open the budget to greater pressure from affected interests. It will give interest groups – which have multiplied in all democratic countries – information and access, more timely data on past or pending budget action, and greater opportunity to influence outcomes.

Many governments now prepare the budget in electronic form and make key documents available via the Internet. Most of this information has long been public; what is new is the ease with which it can be accessed and manipulated. Through browsers and search engines, interest groups will keep informed on budget options, the line-up of those favouring or opposing particular courses of action, the persons or offices responsible for making the decision, and other details that enable them to intervene more effectively in the budget process. Moreover, as Internet use becomes commonplace, matters which once were held in confidence will be posted on the web. Governments will be impelled to relax their secrecy and the budget will become more permeable.

A key issue is whether any information should be posted before the budget has been decided. It would require only a few keystrokes to make agency requests, baseline projections, proposed policy changes, spending options, budget assumptions and other relevant information available on the Internet, and only a few more to enable viewers to submit comments on a message board.

4.2. Plebiscitary budgeting

Once budget information and options are widely available, the government will be able to use new communication technologies to poll citizens on pending issues. The types of polls are as varied as are the forms in which governments make budget decisions. One possibility would be to survey public opinion on broad questions, such as whether the government should seek to reduce the deficit by raising taxes or cutting expenditures; another would be to present citizens with specific questions, such as whether transport spending should be increased by 3% or 5%. Other options would be to ask voters to rank various programmes or sectors in order of priority or to indicate whether spending in each programme or sector should be increased, decreased or maintained at the current level. A government can try to replicate actual budget decisions by asking voters how they would allocate a fixed amount of money among various claims on the budget. Polling can be interactive, with successive rounds of questioning beginning with broad issues and then narrowing to the specific issues faced by budget makers.

Depending on how it is conducted, a plebiscite can be either advisory or a means of making budget decisions. In the former situation, the government would have timely data on voter preferences, but it would be free to take whatever budget decisions it wants; in the latter case, the government would be bound to implement voter preferences in the budget. Turning budget decisions over to a plebiscite would have profound implications for democracy. Voters would have a direct channel to express their preferences, but they would also have to be more consistent on budget matters. If the ballot were properly worded, they would not be able to vote for both smaller programmes and bigger government. Plebiscitary budgeting would provoke interest groups to be more active and to lobby voters for support on budget matters. The activities of government would come to resemble a permanent campaign, in which the period between elections is filled with government-sponsored public opinion polls, year-round advertising blitzes and other efforts to sway voter sentiment and budget decisions. In some countries, the extensive use of polls by government leaders has already blurred the distinction between campaigning and governing. Plebiscitary budgeting may be nearer than we think.

4.3. Formal group participation

On most issues, voters interact with the government through the intermediation of interest groups. In all democratic countries, many more such groups now exist than did a generation ago, and the number interested in the budget is vastly greater than it once was. The proliferation of groups has been accompanied by a breakdown in corporatist institutions, in which a government regularly consults with social partners (such as representatives from labour unions and business) before adopting major policy changes. Rather than negotiating with a handful of leaders, the government is now exposed to a phalanx of groups which have conflicting agendas and demand more from the budget than it can bear.

Budgeting would break down if government gave too many groups a seat at the table. Nevertheless, one can envision a future in which political leaders formally discuss budget issues with interested groups before they act. While it is unlikely that groups will be given a formal veto over government action, an informal veto may be just as good for them.

As the number of groups multiplies, their span of interest narrows. Rather than being interested in whole sectors, groups pay attention to particular projects or activities. Accordingly, one can see a future in which more groups get something from the budget, but for most the slice will be quite thin. Slicing the budget can be done by earmarking funds to particular geographic areas or projects. With thinner slices, more groups come away with something, but the total claim on budget resources is modest.

4.4. Class-based budgeting

Buying off interests by giving them small amounts of money may be a sensible accommodation to the hyper-pluralism of contemporary democracy. But there still will be powerful broad-based groups more interested in overall allocation policy than in getting a little extra money for a few projects. In the past, these groups concentrated on the amounts allocated to particular sectors; in the future, they may be more concerned about whether particular socio-economic classes are getting a fair share of the budget. This interest is reflected in the compilation of a "women's budget" or a "children's budget" by NGOs in various countries. These types of budgets are not analytic exercises; they are advocacy statements which marshal data on the allocation of budget resources to argue that particular classes in society have been disadvantaged.

Class-based budgets will be prepared in the future covering major fissures in society: men *versus* women, rich *versus* poor, young *versus* old, one ethnic or racial group *versus* others, one region against another, and so on. What will be new about them in the future is that, rather than being issued by outsiders, they will be published under the imprimatur of the government, first as supplementary schedules to the regular budget documents, but over time as authoritative statements. Once this occurs, class-based budgets will become decisional classifications; in the course of producing its budget, the government will decide how much to spend on rich or poor, men or women, young or old, etc.

When this situation comes to pass, national budgets will become flash points for social conflict, sharpening the adversarial trade-off characteristics inherent in budgeting with scarce resources. As part of this combat, the protagonists will fight over classifications and analysis of expenditure. For example, one can anticipate protracted arguments over who are the end-beneficiaries of government expenditure on higher education, and over whether this expenditure benefits the rich because a higher proportion of them attend universities or the poor because university education gives them opportunity to improve their economic position. These debates will be truly divisive if public money is allocated on a class basis.

Implementing class-based budgets will require new accounting rules and procedures, possibly similar to those devised in recent years for generational accounting. As has been the case with respect to efforts to account for the incidence of spending and taxes by age cohorts, class-based budgeting will stir up interminable conflict over the assumptions used in estimating budget allocations. It remains to be seen, however, whether this form of budget warfare will lead to more redistribution or to higher spending. The first possibility will materialise if the various classes compete for budget allocations; the latter will occur if the classes collude to get more for each.

4.5. Allocating national income

Whether by sector or class, the budget battles of the future will be over how much should be allocated to each set of claimants. The shares can be expressed as percentages of total expenditure or as the proportion of incremental resources allocated to each. These types of calculations are pervasive in budgeting; the main difference is that, in the future, the trade-offs may be more explicit.

But there is another possibility that is anything but conventional. Rather than allocating budget shares, the budget will allocate shares in the national income. This novel idea is rooted in a 1989 proposal by the late American economist Herbert Stein who urged that the United States should budget "not the $1 trillion in the government's budget but the nearly $5 trillion in the national income. And what has to be compared is the value of alternative uses of the national income, not of the budget. The problem is usually discussed in terms of a trade-off between defense expenditures and other government expenditures. In fact, the relevant and realistic trade-off is between defense expenditures and all other uses of the national output" (Stein, 1989).

Stein's proposal illustrates the inclination of economists to turn analytical tools into decisional rules. It is analytically useful to examine the shares of GDP spent on health, defence, education and other purposes. But does this mean that the budget should be decided on this basis? Operationalising the notion that both public and private uses of national income should be budgeted would likely require a central planning apparatus that would generate the rigidities and inefficiencies rife in planned economies. It is possible, however, to envision the allocation of the government's expenditure of budget resources rather than the all-national output along the lines suggested by Stein.

One argument in favour of the Stein model is that it would force explicit trade-offs among competing claims on national income or budget resources. In contrast to conventional budgeting in which bids for resources are decided serially, often in isolation from one another, this approach would compel a government to weigh the relative merits of requests. Inasmuch as the total spent cannot exceed 100% when (as is likely) budget requests exceed that amount, some will have to be cut for others to get their shares.

Arguably, making budget trade-offs more explicit and transparent will do more to politicise allocations than to improve their efficiency. Looking to an uncertain budget future, one can foresee political pressure to allocate portions of the budget in percentage terms. For example, parliament may decree that not less than a specified percentage of GDP or of total expenditure must be allocated to health, education or some other programme. Quite likely, claims entitled to a fixed share would have a preferred position in the budget, while those not receiving such allocations would have to compete for any remaining resources. Obviously, this double standard will motivate strong groups to seek legal entitlement to fixed budget shares. If they succeed, budget allocations will be both politicised and rigidified.

4.6. *International norms*

Entitling certain sectors to shares in the budget or in national income would be consistent with the trend to base allocations on normative rules rather than on the discretion of political leaders. At present, most normative allocations are concentrated in mandatory transfers to households and grants to regional or local governments. These two categories now account for well over 50% of national government outlays in industrialised democracies. They will account for an even higher percentage in the future.

Nowadays, national governments operate two parallel budget systems. One is organised around recurring (typically annual) budget decisions, the other is driven by normative rules which specify eligibility standards and payment formulas. The former is legally discretionary; the latter is mandated by standing law. Although annually appropriated funds garner most of the attention during preparation of the budget, they cover a shrinking portion of total expenditure. Rule-driven spending usually is prescribed in permanent law that continues in effect unless it is modified by new legislation. These expenditures are controllable, but most carry over from one year to the next without substantive change. One may confidently predict that many governments will be impelled by fiscal and demographic pressures to cut back mandatory expenditures in the decades ahead. If they succeed, they will merely slow, not reverse, the growth of these expenditures.

Most current normative allocations are country-specific; each government adopts its own rules. In the future, however, many will be determined by norms that cross national boundaries. International and regional organisations will prescribe minimum standards of expenditures for various social programmes such as health, education and environmental protection. These organisations will promulgate convergence criteria in either money or programme terms. For example, they may dictate student/teacher ratios or require that a minimum percentage of GDP be allocated to public education. They may establish standards which compel governments to allocate certain amounts to particular programmes. For example, they may decree that a government must have at least 500 childcare places for each 1 000 children between the ages of one to five, or that all schools offer certain courses. The variety of norms is as boundless as the interests of affected groups.

At the outset, many criteria will be advisory or indicative; over time they will become binding, and governments will be required to account for expenditures in ways that enable international monitors to audit compliance.

One particularly burdensome set of norms will pertain to revenue sharing between the national and local or regional governments. The former will have responsibility for extracting taxes from citizens; the latter will be the real spenders. Under the banner of fiscal decentralisation, national governments will be put in the politically difficult position of being blamed when things go wrong, but will have inadequate authority to put them right.

4.7. Budgeting without allocating

Since its inception, budgeting has been depicted as a process for allocating funds among alternative uses. Many of the decisions have pertained to the allocation of incremental resources, but the increments normally have been of sufficient consequence to invest budgeting with political and financial importance. Budget decisions have mattered because they have determined how these resources were spent.

Over time, however, the decisional capacity of budgeting has been chipped away by statutory requirements, international treaties and obligations, changing fiscal relations between the central government and sub-national governments, the shift in fiscal risk from enterprises and households to governments, and the demands of interest groups. The cumulative effect of these developments has been to transform much of budgeting into a means of accounting for past decisions. The scenario drawn in this section indicates that an even greater portion of expenditures will be budgeted in this manner in the future. As unsettling as this conclusion may be, it may be an appropriate condition for mature democracies whose voters want neither big expansion nor big retrenchment of government and where the most important issues have been settled (at least for the time being) by decades of policy adjustment and programme accretion. In these countries, most voters are clustered near the centre, and the political parties fight loudly but over small matters. Democratic stability is no minor accomplishment, and it is due in part to the dulling of political conflict by budgetary stasis.

The loss of budgetary flexibility was a recurring concern of the early SBO meetings and has appeared on the agenda in various forms over the past two decades. Entitlements are a growing part of national budgets, and they are here to stay. The damage they do to the budget is compensated by the security they bring to households. Anyone who bemoans the spread of the entitlement state must marvel at the economic well-being it has brought to its citizens. The two developments are interlinked, making the budget the dependent variable in the political relationship between citizen and state. But what is new and somewhat alarming, if the future envisioned here is credible, is the rigidification of heretofore discretionary expenditures. The big allocative questions still in the hands of national governments – how much to spend on services – will be decided by norms and formulas in future budgets. The last preserve of budgeting is threatened by the same logic that has made entitlements so popular and pervasive. Ensure interests and groups their share in the budget by making allocation a matter of legal right rather than of discretion. Give cities and communities their shares, the old and the young, the schools and the health clinics. Budgetary choice may be weakened, but all for the good of society.

Perhaps this scenario will turn out to be another false alarm and budgeting will persist as a robust allocative process. But if normative budgeting materialises, it will be necessary to stop thinking of it as an allocative process and to recognise that it has metamorphosed into something that appears to be the same, but is not.

5. Operational budgeting: from control to performance

Fiscal discipline and financial allocation are principal concerns during preparation of the budget. The third objective of budgeting – promoting efficiency in the provision of public services – focuses largely on the implementation of the budget. While the first two objectives get most of the attention in "big bang" reforms, operational matters consume most of the work time of budget staff. The flow of communications during budget execution and the sheer number of actions that are reported and controlled dwarf other work demands of budgeting.

Despite its sometimes lowly status, operational budgeting is important because it affects the cost and quality of services, the volume of government expenditure, the size of the civil service, and relations between citizens and the government. Citizens know their government through the services they receive from it.

Operational issues were not prominent at the early SBO meetings because the agenda was dominated by the big issues discussed above. But operational issues gained attention in the second half of the 1980s, as innovative governments in Australia, New Zealand, Sweden, the United Kingdom and elsewhere sought to improve public performance. Each of these countries moved boldly to shift budgeting from compliance to performance by giving managers freedom to run their operations as they deemed appropriate. Several forces stimulated this transformation, including the importation of novel managerial practices from the business sector, recognition that the persistent rise in operating costs was compelling the government to spend a higher share of national output, the ability of politicians to take credit for cutting expenditures without drawing blame for cutting programmes, and realisation by budget officials that they were over-controlling the most controlled portion of the budget.

The operational budget agenda parades under a number of monikers: "new public management", managerialism, performance-based budgeting and marketisation. The names reflect different approaches to the same issue. Some use market-type mechanisms, others rely on managerial skills and judgment, others on strong accountability arrangements. All recognise that transforming operational budgeting requires major changes in the managerial systems within which budgeting is embedded. In contrast to past reforms which sought to change budgeting without regard to public management, recent innovations have been grounded on the presumption that budgeting is a subset of management and cannot be reshaped in isolation from other processes to which it is linked.

Most OECD member countries have made little progress in dismantling managerial control mechanisms, though most appear interested in improving operational performance by easing budget controls. There is no single model for moving in this direction, nor a single innovation that will accomplish all the sought changes in government operations. The handful of innovations discussed below have been selected because of their breadth and wide application.

5.1. Managerial discretion

An essential step in shifting operational budgeting to performance has been to dismantle many of the operational controls that have been applied for generations. The typical controls pertain to inputs and operate through the detailed itemisation of different objects of expenditure such as travel, supplies, utilities and personnel. Each type of control has its own rules and procedures which are enforced by controllers at the centre of the government or in departmental headquarters.

In response to the vast expansion of government, many countries have partly decontrolled public spending by consolidating the items into broad categories and by giving spending units some discretion in shifting funds among the items. Many also have placed greater reliance on internal controls, in which the spending agency is responsible for assuring the legality and propriety of expenditure, in contrast to external control which vests this responsibility in central agencies. A few have gone much further and have eliminated virtually all centrally maintained controls over operating expenditure. Instead of splitting the operating budget into numerous pockets of money, they now give agencies a lump sum for all running costs. Within this operating budget, managers decide how much to spend on travel, salaries and other items. The operating budget is cash-limited, barring agencies from spending or requesting more than was provided, even if inflation outruns the estimates on which the budget is based. Moreover, some countries subtract an "efficiency dividend" from the operating budget to reflect expected gains in productivity. This dividend is typically in the range of 1-2% a year, and it pressures agencies to be more efficient in using operating resources.

Where decontrol is taken seriously, it is not confined to the centre of government but is devolved down to operating and field units. Each field unit or local office gets its operating budget and, within certain restrictions, has freedom in spending these resources. Thus, managerial flexibility redefines both the relationship between central agencies and departments, and between department headquarters and field units. The logic of this strong commitment to decontrol is that managerial improvement can occur only if managers are free to use their skills and professional judgment in running their operations. They are either free to manage or not. If they are, services are likely to be more efficient and delivered in a more flexible, responsive manner; if they are not free, managers will stress compliance, even if some controls have been eased.

But this logic has not triumphed everywhere. In some influential OECD member countries, a premium is still placed on uniformity in services and central control still predominates, though not to the full extent it did a generation or two ago. In some, there is concern that managerial discretion will undermine the civil service system and lead to the replacement of career officials with short-term appointees, as has occurred in New Zealand and the United Kingdom. In fact, attitudes toward the civil service sum up key differences between the reform-minded and status quo countries. The latter countries sense the loss of a civil service ethic; the former see rigidities in the traditional public service. This is an issue for which there can be no final resolution, nor any single best way.

Central agencies have been deeply affected by the march of managerialism. As recently as a generation ago, their main function was to maintain administrative controls, especially those regulating personnel and finance. In some countries, various control agencies have been abolished – for example, the personnel agency in Australia and the Accommodation Board in New Zealand. But governments do not have the option of doing away with their finance ministries or their budget departments. Some finance ministries have led the drive for managerial reform; others have gone along reluctantly. All have to go through a period of adjustment, unlearning old roles and relationships and defining new ones. They must decide how to draw the line between letting operating managers manage and intervening with advice or restrictions. They must decide how much control should be thrown overboard and exactly what should be retained. And they must figure out how to retain power at the centre of government when much of their power base has been surrendered.

5.2. *Performance targets and reports*

There are two sides to the new managerialism. One is summed up in the phrase "let managers manage" and revolves around the divestiture of input controls; the other is implied by the phrase "make managers manage" and has to do with the imposition of strong accountability measures to assure that managers are not abusing their discretion and are producing the intended results. In every reformist country, it has proven easier to move ahead on the first agenda than on the second. But the countries which have progressed the most in freeing up managers have also been the most creative and demanding in introducing new accountability regimes.

Accountability deals with both money and performance, and in the guise of performance budgeting tries to mould the two together. On the spending side, accountability entails the accrual basis which purports to hold managers accountable for the full cost of operations and audited financial statements. A few countries have broken new ground in the costing of services. New Zealand has been the most venturesome, charging operating budgets both for depreciation and for the use of capital (computed as net worth on an entity's balance sheet). Managerial-minded countries also require departments or agencies to publish annual reports discussing their operations and comparing planned and actual results. On the performance side of the ledger, managerialist governments generally require that performance targets be specified in advance and that actual results be measured against the targets. These countries have invested heavily in developing performance measures and compiling relevant data, though some of the effort has been wasted in sterile debates on the differences between outputs and outcomes or between intermediate outcomes and end outcomes and so on. The approaches taken by various countries appear to differ, but all emphasise comparison.

The United Kingdom favours a small number of targets for each agency; these are compiled in an annual report issued by the government in a single document that compares targets and results for the past year and provides new targets for the year ahead. The advantage of targets is that they are tightly focused; the disadvantage is that they may exclude important elements of performance. The United States requires each department and each major agency to produce an annual performance plan discussing what it hopes to accomplish in the year ahead and an annual performance report discussing what was actually accomplished in light of its plans. New Zealand and Sweden generally rely on annual reports to assess results.

As performance measures and reports become more common, these will likely be subject to review by auditors who may comment on the accuracy of the data or on the interpretations drawn from them. It is also probable that some standards will emerge on compiling and analysing performance information. It is unlikely, however, that these standards will be as authoritative as those which govern the reporting of financial results. The future evolution of performance measures will depend as much on how the data are used as on how they are collected and presented. Performance measurement rests on the questionable assumption that measuring and publishing results will make a difference in the results. The managerial movement rests, however, on a different proposition: that unless managers have strong incentives to be efficient and productive, generating data will make little difference. This is why performance measurement is seen as a subset of managerial reform rather than as the main event.

5.3. *Performance contracts*

One way to increase the use of performance information is to incorporate it into contracts which specify the results to be achieved. While the term "performance contract" is sometimes applied to relations between the government as a purchaser of services and outside vendors, recent developments in contracting pertain to relationships within government. Contracts are now formalised in some countries to specify the pay and responsibilities of senior and middle managers. The chief executives of New Zealand departments are employed under term contracts (for up to five years) which specify the key results expected of them. Similar employment contracts are negotiated between senior and middle managers and on down the administrative chain of command. These contracts enable managers to negotiate their own pay and terms of employment without regard to standard civil service rules. A similar arrangement prevails in the United Kingdom for the chief executives of government agencies.

Performance contracts have also been introduced to specify the outputs or services to be provided by government entities. In the United States, department heads (who are political appointees) negotiate performance agreements which indicate the steps they will take to improve operations, introduce services or make other changes. Rather than being comprehensive statements of all the results to be achieved, these agreements concentrate on matters that the government and department heads deem to be of particular importance. In New Zealand, ministers negotiate annual performance agreements with the chief executives of their departments, specifying the services and other outputs to be provided during the fiscal year and the resources that will be made available for these purposes.

> Formal performance agreements have made little headway, and they probably are less used now than a decade ago. In the United States, formal performance agreements between the President and department heads were ignored shortly after they were negotiated. In the United Kingdom, public service agreements have usually been performance targets set by the Treasury with little input from sectoral ministries. In New Zealand, employment contracts are still widely used, but formal purchase agreements have been replaced by more general statements of intent.

These and similar contract-like documents are not genuine contracts. For one thing, the relationship between the parties to the agreement is not truly arm's-length; for another, the government does not normally have effective redress if managers fail to perform. If the school principal does a poor job, she or he can be dismissed, but the government rarely has the option of closing the school or cutting its budget. Moreover, the contracts rarely specify all the services or outputs to be provided; rather, they identify those matters of particular interest to one or both parties. It may be fruitful to think of the contracts as establishing an ongoing relationship and a basis for discussion between the respective parties. They can use the terms of the agreement as checklists to review progress in achieving particular milestones or as talking points in periodic meetings between the two sides. They are signalling devices which spur managers to focus on certain aspects of performance and put them on notice as to what is expected of them.

5.4. Autonomous agencies

For decades, efforts to improve public management involved the integration of activities and services into broad departments, each with a broad swath of responsibilities. There was a department for transport, another for education, another for health, and so on down the standard list of government responsibilities. In creating functionally integrated departments, governments strove to eliminate free-standing agencies and to place those that survived within the departmental structure.

Managerialism has given rise, however, to the dismantling of cohesive departments by removing operating units and giving them broad independence to carry out their assigned responsibilities. While this development has occurred in only a few countries, others may join the agency bandwagon in the years ahead. Typically, when an agency is established, the government (sometimes through the parent department or ministry) defines the matters over which it has operating discretion, its duties and functions, and the manner in which it will be accountable for financial and substantive performance. The government appoints a chief executive who has full authority to run the agency.

> As discussed in Chapter 7 ("Agencies in Search of Principles"), there appears to have been a reversion to sectoral departments as the managers of the government's policy aspirations. In various countries, agencies are still entrusted with service responsibilities, but strategic policy making is lodged in departments and central organs.

New Zealand and the United Kingdom provide alternative models of agencification. The United Kingdom created independent agencies to free service providers from central control; New Zealand created agencies to free policy makers from undue influence by service providers. In the United Kingdom, approximately 75% of the civil servants employed by the central government work in the 130 Next Steps agencies which have been formed during the past decade. These agencies were established pursuant to a government study which found that previous budget and management reforms, such as the financial management initiative launched by the Thatcher government in 1982, had failed to improve the provision of services. The report recommending independence for service agencies was titled *Next Steps*; hence the entities created pursuant to its recommendations are commonly referred to as Next Steps agencies.

Before it launches an agency, the government defines its responsibilities and assesses its capacity for self-management. It then recruits a chief executive and draws up a framework document which spells out what the agency is to do, its relations with the parent department and the discretion it will have. The government publishes annual performance targets for each agency and, as noted earlier, compares results to the targets. Approximately every five years, the government commissions an independent review of the agency's operations and performance and decides whether it should be continued, terminated or restructured. The Next Steps process is widely regarded as having brought significant improvement in the efficiency and quality of services. It has both reduced compliance costs and enabled agencies to be more flexible and responsive in delivering services. Despite the origin of Next Steps in the Conservative Thatcher-Major government, it has been continued by the Labour government headed by Tony Blair.

In contrast to the United Kingdom which was motivated to free service providers from the clutches of Whitehall, New Zealand separated service provision from policy advice to give ministers freedom in defining policies and in purchasing services. In New Zealand, appropriations are made by classes of outputs and are voted to ministers who may purchase services from their own departments or from alternative providers. This formal distance between them enables ministers and departmental chief executives to negotiate the purchase agreements mentioned earlier. Each department's chief executive has discretion in hiring staff, using available resources, organising work and producing the required services. Accountability is maintained through annual reports and audits, output measures, and evaluation of the chief executive's performance.

The reputed successes of the British and New Zealand models have spurred other countries to create independent agencies. But as agencies have become entrenched, both New Zealand and the United Kingdom have become concerned that the number and independence of these entities impedes efforts to co-ordinate policies and programmes that cross organisational lines. Both countries have sought to develop a "whole-of-government" perspective which may diminish the operating independence previously granted to agencies.

5.5. *Market-type arrangements*

Manageralism relies on the skill, judgment and professionalism of those who produce government services to improve operating results. Without this premise, it would make no sense to decontrol public management and empower civil servants to act as they see fit. But not all reformers agree that entrusting managers with operating discretion will improve results. Some hold that nothing short of customer sovereignty through competition and choice will make governments responsive to citizens in designing and providing services. In contrast to managerialism where choice is vested in service providers, a market-type approach gives choice through vouchers, price mechanisms, user charges and other devices to those who receive services. And in contrast to managerialism which introduces contracts within the government, the market approach uses privatisation and contracting out to promote genuine competition.

At its core, the market approach is predicated on the argument that, as long as a government has monopoly power in the provision of services, it will be wasteful and indifferent to the interests of those it serves. Accordingly, a government should either privatise services or open them up to competition.

The market strategy has little appeal to those who believe that there is inherent advantage in having public services provided directly by the government. Arguments and evidence that citizens can get a better deal if they are free to purchase services are irrelevant to those who believe it wrong to privatise public responsibilities, such as schools, or to subject them to market-type competition. It is likely, therefore, that marketisation will be confined in most countries to commercial activities, such as telecommunications and other trading activities, and will not significantly penetrate core public services.

6. Operational futures: government as a producer

In view of the clashing position on public *versus* market provision of services, it is difficult to envision how government operations may be carried out in the future. But on the assumption that efforts to privatise or contract out basic services will continue to be resisted and that market penetration will be marginal, this section considers a number of innovations that may extend the boundaries of managerialism and bolster market-type arrangements within government. In other words, governments will continue to budget for and provide services, but will do so in ways that heighten sensitivity to the cost and quality of services.

6.1. *Performance budgeting*

Allocating resources on the basis of services to be provided is an old, appealing and elementary idea that has made surprisingly little headway. Many governments include performance information in their budgets, but doing so does not mean that they systematically make spending decisions on this basis. The concept of performance budgeting intended here is one in which each increment in expenditure is expressly linked with an increment in output or performance. Implementing this concept requires that a government has reliable data on the unit cost of services and that bids for resources are structured in a manner that facilitates the marginal analysis of costs and outputs. Few governments currently have this capability, though many compile performance information.

In conventional budgeting, a sum of money is exchanged for the total output or work of a spending unit; in performance budgeting, the outputs are disaggregated into units, cost factors are attached to each unit, and the total exchanged depends on the volume of units and the amounts paid for them. Implementing this strict version of performance budgeting requires governments to have cost accounting systems which distinguish between fixed and variable costs of government services and measure the marginal cost of changes in the volume or quality of services. While this technical feat is currently beyond the capacity of most governments, the main impediments to performance budgeting are bureau-political. Spending agencies are uncomfortable with breaking down their work into standard units, and also uncomfortable with the notion that the amount they get should depend expressly on the amount they produce. This, more than the technical problems, is the reason why performance budgeting – which was a leading budget reform half a century ago – has made so little headway.

> Progress in implementing a true performance budget that explicitly links resources and results has been slow. On the other hand, progress in providing performance-related information in the budget has been quite rapid. In surveys of budget practices, a majority of governments respond that they have performance budgets, by which they generally mean that decisions are informed by performance data and that much less attention is paid than in the past to detailed expenditure inputs.

Nevertheless, performance budgeting is an idea whose time will come. Progress in measuring and costing outputs, and demands for both efficiency and quality in the provision of services, will impel governments to allocate on this basis. Of course, once budgets explicitly link increments in resources and services, it will be a simple task to outsource government work and to exchange resources and outputs on a commercial basis through market mechanisms. Thus, performance budgeting, which seeks to implant managerialism in government, has the potential to uproot it.

6.2. Price-based budgeting

Once a government has the cost and output data needed to formulate a performance budget, it may take bolder steps to improve public management by budgeting on the basis of price rather than cost. A price-based budget is one in which a government authorises expenditure in terms of the amount agreed to be paid rather than on the basis of the cost of producing the services.

For generations, governments have prepared budgets by adding up the cost of the inputs purchased by agencies. But if a government appropriates more, agencies have more to spend on inputs; if it gives them less, they must spend less. If civil servants win pay increases, or if more staff are added to an agency's payroll, the government votes more money, regardless of the volume of output produced. This behaviour means that, in budgeting, the cost of inputs always equals the price of outputs. If the cost of inputs rises, so too does the price of outputs; if the government reduces the price of outputs, it thereby also reduces what agencies spend on inputs.

As conventional as this pattern is in government budgeting, it is alien to most economic exchange. A customer typically is indifferent to the cost borne by the supplier. As a consequence, an efficient supplier may profit by economising on inputs; an inefficient supplier may lose money because the cost of inputs exceeds the price charged for outputs. Significant gains in operating efficiency can be reaped in government by severing the relationship between cost and price. A government would negotiate a price without regard to the cost borne by affected agencies in producing the agreed services. Assuming, however, that services are supplied in house by government agencies and are not outsourced to commercial vendors, there would have to be strong assurance that the price is right, that it is reasonable and that an efficiently run agency can supply the services for the amount that it will be paid. Without this assurance, there is substantial risk that the price will be too low, resulting in hidden reductions in output (or in quality) or inability of the agency to pay its bills. It would be quite different for a commercial vendor to close its doors because it undercharges for services than for a government agency to be insolvent because it cannot operate at the agreed price. It is the difference between firms going bankrupt and schools shutting down. One is a common occurrence, the other is truly rare.

Except in areas where output is contracted out, governments do not currently have the know-how to budget on the basis of price. Governments lack cost accounting systems to measure what particular services should cost, nor are most of their basic services subject to competitive tenders. Yet, significant progress has been made in separating price from cost. When a government allocates a running cost budget to an agency without tallying up the cost of inputs, it moves in the direction of the price basis. Similarly, when it cash-limits this budget or subtracts an efficiency dividend from the amount provided, the government weakens the link between price and cost. Price-based budgeting will be a difficult feat, but it is feasible.

6.3. Variable budgets

Performance-based and price-based budgeting are associated with another practical innovation: a shift from fixed budgets in which total spending does not depend on the amount produced to variable budgets in which the amount paid by the government is determined by the volume and quality of output. As alien as it may seem to government budgeters, variable budgeting is standard business practice. Although some portions of their budgets may be fixed, firms allocate production costs on the basis of the volume produced, and many tie expenditures on research and development or other variables. Governments do not, however, because they regard appropriations as fixed limits on the amounts that may be spent. In effect, a government buys all the output of its spending agencies at a fixed price; it does not spend more or less if the amount produced deviates from the budgeted level.

Arguably, the amount paid should depend on volume; if it does not, the government will overspend when output falls short of the budget, and it will risk hidden cuts in services when output exceeds the budget.

A critical difference between fixed and variable budgets is that the latter are inherently performance budgets and the former are non-performance budgets. After all, in a variable budget, spending varies because performance varies. But when expenditures are fixed, the budget is indifferent to performance even if the government professes to have a performance budget. Devising a variable performance budget entails three adjustments in budgeting. First, expenditures have to be based on price rather than cost. Ideally, a price should be set for each unit of output rather than for total output. Second, the concepts and methods of cost accounting have to be utilised to distinguish between fixed and variable costs as well as between marginal and average costs. Without adequate cost accounting, the government will not have sufficient information to set a fair price for services. Third, it is necessary to distinguish between expenditures which should vary with volume and those which should not. As a general rule, variable budgeting should be applied only to those services when the demand for services is exogenous; it is not directly influenced by the entity providing the services. The passport agency should have a variable budget because it has little immediate control over the number of applications. But the police agency should have a fixed budget because it decides how many patrols to undertake. If its budget varied with volume, it would be able to boost its budget by providing more services. Variable budgeting would require a case-by-case determination of funding arrangements. Within an agency, some services may have fixed appropriations while others may warrant variable expenditures.

6.4. Citizen (customer) rights

In the future, government performance will be a right of citizens. In the same way that citizens are entitled to health care or income support, they will be entitled to performing schools, on-time transport, courteous civil servants, prompt handling of applications, and other public services. When this occurs, performance will have been transformed from a means of measuring and assessing services into assurance that services will be provided as set forth in the budget.

Services as rights of citizenship will not happen all at once. These rights will be tried in some areas and then extended to others. At first, the rights may be poorly defined, with inadequate specification of qualitative features; over time, the rights will be elaborated, as they have been in so many areas of social conduct. The early rights may have weak redress or none; they will be rights without remedy. But remedies will be introduced gradually, including compensation for sub-par services. One practical remedy would be to empower citizens to obtain services from alternative providers when the government fails to meet the standards. Another would be to give citizens vouchers enabling them to purchase services from any eligible provider. If this were to occur, citizens would be empowered as customers, with the right to take their business elsewhere when they are dissatisfied.

Prototype citizen's rights models are emergent in the Citizen's Charter idea pioneered in the United Kingdom and imitated elsewhere. Although the Citizen's Charter was alleged to have started as a political stunt, it matured into a serious effort to spur qualitative improvements in services. Entitling citizens to certain services may be an effective, attractive option for those who believe that public services should not be privatised or contracted out. Of course, entitling citizens will be efficacious only to the extent that they receive the promised services. As in other entitlements, the objective is not to compensate failure but to assure performance. If performance is not forthcoming, defining services as entitlements will be a hollow gesture.

6.5. Receivership

Under the best of circumstances, not all agencies will provide citizens with the services to which they are entitled. Shortfalls in performance may be due to improper management of agency finances, lack of skills needed to carry out assigned responsibilities, an uncaring attitude, or citizens who are indifferent to the quality of services or do not know how to obtain improvement. In these circumstances, the most appropriate remedy may be to place operations in the custody of a receiver who is authorised to replace staff, manage the budget and take other actions needed to raise performance to acceptable levels. An alternative would be to give citizens the option of obtaining services from other providers, but this may be of little value for citizens trapped in poor communities.

Receivership is not a new idea, though it is rarely applied to public programmes. It typically refers to situations where the entity is insolvent and unable to pay its expenses. But the concept can be readily adapted to governmental programmes where money is ample but performance is below minimum levels.

The future shape of government operations is highly uncertain, more so than for the two other budgetary functions discussed in this article. With equal plausibility, one can envision governments yielding to markets or governments digging in and protecting their traditional ways. The probability is that governments will move in different directions, with some making broad use of contracts and others relying on rules and controls. Almost all will pursue improved performance, but they will take different paths.

Doing nothing will not be an option, however, because citizen expectations will continue to rise. Governments will be confronted with a choice: improve performance, spend more on operations, or degrade services. Most will opt for performance, but they will succeed only if they are willing to dismantle many of the control and compliance systems which shape the structure of government and the provision of services.

7. Does budgeting have a future?

Of course, the answer is "yes" if the question refers to procedures for preparing and implementing budgets. No less than now, future governments will compile budgets that account for revenue and expenditure. National legislatures will appropriate funds, spending agencies will file reports and carry out authorised programmes, auditors will review financial reports, and on and on. Procedurally, budgeting will be in robust health.

The answer may be "no", however, if what is implied is that budgeting will be less capacitated to decide the finances and direction of government. Many of the developments already under way as well as those that may lie in the future will remake budgeting into the dependent variable in government finance and policy. Rather than driving decisions on money and programmes, budgeting will be swept along by powerful tides. The budget will duly register what has been decided already or elsewhere, whether by formula or by others, but it will not be the forum for making many of the decisions.

The following paragraphs sum up major developments under way in budgeting's fiscal, allocative and operational roles. The list is not complete, but it nevertheless adds up to a strong case that budgeting will be displaced from its favoured position.

- Sandwiched budgeting: national budgets will be influenced by international rules and requirements which prescribe how they manage their finances and what they spend money on, as well as by local or regional governments which will have claim to much of the nation's tax revenue.

- Normative budgeting: an increasing portion of national budgets will be allocated by fixed norms which will govern transfers to households, grants to sub-national governments and programme allocations.

- Exogenous budgeting: revenues and expenditures will be increasingly dependent on outside influences – economic and social conditions, capital flows, exchange rates, the age and income structure of the population, medical technology, child-rearing practices and service levels. Changes in these factors will compel automatic adjustments in national budgets.

- Government as financier: the national government's main budget responsibility will be to levy taxes that finance spending by others – international organisations, households and sub-national governments. The services it directly provides will account for a declining share of the budget. The separation of taxing authority and spending authority will generate both political and budgetary stress.

- Balkanised government: national governments will be fractured into numerous independent agencies, each with its own budget and each empowered to operate and manage its resources as it deems fit. Ministries or departments will still be responsible for developing policies and co-ordinating programmes, but they will have weak leverage vis-à-vis the independent agencies.

- Higher expectation, less trust: budgets will be made in a political environment in which citizens demand much more from the government but have low confidence that it will perform well. High expectations will pressure the government to spend more and improve services; low trust will make it difficult for the government to extract more revenue from its citizens.

Budgeting has a future, but it will be determined by what government becomes. Budgets and governments are intertwined; it is not possible to envision robust budgeting unless the government is strong and capacitated, and it is not possible to have strong government if its budget lacks the capacity to regulate public finance. The key question therefore is how government will evolve in the decade ahead. Answer that question and the question in the title of this article also will be answered.

References

Bléjer, Mario and Adrienne Cheasty (eds.) (1993), *How to Measure the Fiscal Deficit: Analytical and Methodological Issues*, International Monetary Fund, Washington DC.

Campos, Ed and Sanjay Pradhan (1996), "Budgetary Institutions and Expenditure Outcomes: Binding Governments to Fiscal Performance", Policy Research Working Paper No. 1646, The World Bank, Washington DC.

OECD (2000), "Greater Independence for Fiscal Institutions", PUMA/SBO(2000)4, OECD, Paris.

Schick, Allen (2007), "Off-Budget Expenditure: An Economic and Political Framework", *OECD Journal on Budgeting* 7:3.

Stein, Herbert (1989), *Governing the $5 Trillion Economy*, Twentieth Century Fund, New York, United States.

ISBN 978-92-64-06087-6
Evolutions in Budgetary Practice
Allen Schick and the OECD Senior Budget Officials
© OECD 2009

Chapter 9

Opportunity, Strategy and Tactics in Reforming Public Management*

* This article was originally published in the OECD Journal on Budgeting, Vol. 2, No. 3, 2002. It draws upon material provided by 11 OECD member countries participating in a project on modernising public management (Australia, Canada, Finland, Germany, Ireland, Netherlands, New Zealand, Norway, Sweden, United Kingdom, United States). At the time of writing, Allen Schick was Visiting Fellow, Governmental Studies, Brookings Institution, Washington DC, and Professor, School of Public Affairs, University of Maryland, United States. Boxed comments were made in 2009.

Every successful public management reform is an amalgam of opportunity, strategy and tactics. Opportunities are country-specific conditions that facilitate some reforms and delay others; strategies are policies and actions that set goals for government and for the tasks to be undertaken in implementing wanted change; tactics are the methods used to mobilise support for reform and to overcome obstacles to it.

Although opportunity is rooted in local conditions, when similar reforms occur in many countries it is likely that common change-generating conditions also spill over national boundaries. Management reform may become ripe because of elections and changes in government, shifts in public sentiment, a budget crisis or programme failure, the drive of politicians or managers to be innovators, and the seepage of new ideas into the conventional wisdom on how public organisations should be run. Reforms that appear in many countries may flow from a world-wide slowdown in economic growth or from broad, cross-national attrition in confidence in government. Opportunity both facilitates and constrains; it opens up some possibilities and shuts off others. But opportunity is not just there for the plucking; it must be detected and exploited. And constraints are not ironclad bars to innovation; they can be surmounted or evaded by wilful politicians and managers.

Strategy is the deliberate effort to create a future that is materially different from what would ensue if prevailing conditions were allowed to run their course. Strategy requires verve and vision – the will to set into motion change-driven processes, to establish objectives and priorities, to tear down old institutions and practices and to make way for new ones, to take the risks that accompany change, and to have confidence in what government should become and the steps required to achieve that vision. Strategy does not necessarily mean making big plans, for it can also entail embedding a culture of ongoing, incremental change in public institutions. In fact, strategy often involves choices between these two approaches or some variant of them. Strategy also entails implementing actions and the commitment to give the change process essential support and resources.

There is sometimes tension between opportunity and strategy, for the more one is beholden to the former, the less attention one might give to the latter. Often opportunistic reformers, by contrast, have a tendency to leap to the untried and risky. Despite the current affectation of labelling just about every government plan or reform as strategic, genuine strategic change is rare because it is difficult to pull off. The temper of much contemporary management reform is reflected in Ireland's case. Referring to the government's "Strategic Management Initiative" (SMI), Ireland observes that the focus is essentially on management issues and challenges rather than on the role and function of government and whether these should be radically changed. As a result, the primary thrust remains on service delivery and better management of all aspects of administration; in short on delivering better government. But it is also acknowledged that a reform of the magnitude being pursued may be expected to lead to a process of questioning the role and functions of government.

Does Ireland's SMI rise to the level of being regarded as truly strategic? Is its strategic management initiative an effort to transform public administration or to make spotty improvements? Is it animated by an overriding conviction that big changes are imperative – that even if the task is hard and must be pursued piecemeal rather than all at once, it should be undertaken? Similar questions can be asked of the German, Dutch and Norwegian reforms, and perhaps of initiatives in other countries as well. Does it matter whether reform is purposely strategic or merely opportunistic? Perhaps not, for some strategies fail and some opportunities blossom into much bolder innovations than were contemplated at the outset. The United Kingdom's management reform started modestly, with efficiency reviews and a financial management initiative, but they grew into a fundamental restructuring of public institutions and the opening up of public services to market competition and greater citizen/customer influence.

While it is likely that a well-developed strategy will produce different outcomes than would a reform born solely of opportunism, confining strategic thinking to the launch stage may condemn the enterprise to failure. It is a mistake to define goals and paths at the outset and to then follow the script regardless of what ensues. On the basis of almost 40 years of observing government reforms in many venues, this writer would argue that the failure to systematically evaluate what has been accomplished is one of the greatest threats to durable innovation in public management. Over the years, in many countries management reforms have tended to live an unexamined life. They typically begin with much fanfare but, after a decent interval, most just fade away or are displaced by the next wave of reform. There are notable exceptions to this generalisation, however. In countries that have advanced the farthest in rebuilding public management, the early innovations have been rigorously assessed and recalibrated. New Zealand is a case in point. It is often said of that country's far-reaching reforms that they were propelled by a coherent, integrated set of principles. True enough, but a large number of the practices that now distinguish New Zealand's public management were not in the first tranche of state sector reforms. Purchase agreements came later, as did strategic result areas, key result areas, departmental forecast reports, strategic plans and efforts to assess the government's interest as owner of state entities. The constant in New Zealand's reform has been the purpose of change, not the toolkit of management practices. In New Zealand and elsewhere, the best strategy may be to set a course at the start, forthrightly monitor progress, be honest about what has worked and what has not, and make numerous mid-course corrections.

> This observation pertains to all innovative countries. In all current public management, practices differ significantly from those introduced during the first wave of reform two decades ago. Change is continuous as governments learn from past successes and failures, and as concepts of good management practice evolve. Change also is driven by realisation that, once innovative practices become routines, they become hardened into rules and procedures that must be complied with and lose the capacity to improve performance.

Doing all this requires effective leadership. Successful reform does not just happen by itself; it depends on leaders who exploit openings and give impetus and direction to change. Strong leaders do not just "read" opportunities; they make them – by moulding public opinion, bringing new blood with new ideas and initiative into government, reaching beyond safe and traditional constituencies to build coalitions in support of change, and taking political and managerial risks that broaden the possibility of change. Strategic reform requires this and more: leaders who venture beyond today's opportunities and constraints and boldly envision a different future, who then mobilise the political and institutional resources of government to produce transformative improvement in the structure and performance of public organisations, and who bolster support for their strategy by elevating public expectations concerning the results that government delivers.

Strategy without opportunity cannot advance the cause of reform very far. Without favourable conditions, strategy becomes visionary, lofty ideas that have little prospect of being implemented. Indeed, without the right opportunity, strategy can end up as a substitute for action, fostering the impression that big changes are under way even though no implementing steps have been taken. On the other hand, opportunity without strategy is likely to exhaust itself in faddism, drifting from one fashionable innovation to the next, without leaving a lasting imprint.

Tactics blend together opportunity and strategy to enhance the odds that intended changes will be successfully implemented. Tactics entail judgments on the pace and sequence of innovation, the organs that should be entrusted with the task, the sectors on which reform is to be concentrated, the political cast given the reforms, the extent to which the government associates or distances itself from the changes, decisions on whether to proceed by administrative fiat or through legislative authorisation, and many other implementation decisions. A good tactician considers how strategy can best be executed in the light of available opportunities. Tactical skill requires institutional memory, a keen sense of timing, and hard-nosed decisions on the approach to be taken.

Although management reform must be a blend of opportunity and strategy, the proportions matter. During the post-war period, management reform was predominantly opportunistic; during the past two decades it has become increasingly strategic. There is a synoptic ambition in contemporary reform that was absent in earlier waves of innovation. Today's reforms are bolder, more uprooting, more goal-driven and more animated by the conviction that management has to be transformed and improved in order to strengthen democratic governance. The shift in orientation has been due to many factors, the most prominent including: declining confidence in government, upheavals in management theory and business practices, revolutionary developments in information technology, pressure to devolve resources and responsibility from central organs to local governments and field units, efforts to slow or reverse the enlargement of government, and – most important of all, in an age in which citizens expect more from government but think less of it – a realisation that business-as-usual management is not good enough.

1. The roads not taken

Whether opportunistic or strategic, there are significant differences between today's reforms and those tried in earlier times. The generalisations set forth in this and other sections do not fit all countries. Some countries have been more opportunistic, others more strategic. Nevertheless, the paths they have taken are different from the ones favoured in previous reforms.

1.1. *Contemporary reform is more likely to be comprehensive than piecemeal*

Contemporary reform is not confined to a few institutions or a single process. The aim is to uproot entrenched management practices and behaviour, not just to upgrade the civil service system or budget procedures. Even when implementation is spread over an extended period, as has been the case with the United Kingdom's "Next Steps" initiative, the comprehensive reach of the reform agenda is manifest at the outset.

In striving to restructure public management, some governments have resolved to reform all major sectors and administrative units. Others, however, have opted to pilot test their reforms before deciding on full implementation. Germany, for example, tested flexible budgetary management arrangements before it enacted legislation that authorised the new practices. Similarly, Sweden conducted a closely monitored test of three-year budgetary procedures before launching comprehensive management reform.

Often, however, pilot testing slams the door on further innovation, for it conveys the message that the government is not really committed to reform or is uncertain about the direction it should take. The key to successful pilot tests that promote innovation is for the government to establish a strong commitment to reform in advance by specifying the steps it will take, when the tests have been completed, to revamp management systems and practices.

1.2. *Contemporary reform is not confined to particular administrative processes*

For generations, management reform has been compartmentalised along the main lines of public administration. One set of reforms has sought to rationalise budget decision making, another has targeted civil service practices, still others have sought to improve public procurement, cash management, accounting systems or other parts of the machinery of government. In this way, activities that should have been linked were cordoned off into separate specialisations. Accounting reform proceeded on one track, budget innovation on a second, advances in auditing on a third. One group of reforms aimed at raising productivity, a second experimented with performance budgeting, a third introduced performance audits. The obvious interdependence of these isolated reforms was neglected because the principal aim was to improve a particular process, not to lift managerial capacity.

Not surprisingly, reforms that concentrate on particular tasks rather than on managerial systems and behaviour rarely make much headway. Budget reform is a case in point, for it has been premised on the mistaken notion that the process by which funds are allocated can be revamped without taking account of the information generated by the accounting system, the demands made by auditors, the incentives provided by civil service rules and other administrative procedures, the embedded habits and norms of budget makers, the interface between managers and politicians, and numerous other managerial considerations. In much contemporary reform, by contrast, budgeting is regarded as part of a grid of interconnected practices and processes. Budgeting cannot be reshaped without also restructuring the management framework within which financial resources are spent and activities carried out. The same can be said for reforming the civil service and other basic management systems.

1.3. *Contemporary reform seeks to devolve rather than concentrate managerial authority*

Reforming public management impels governments to assess and modify existing organisational structures. The assessment might lead to the establishment of new entities, a redefinition of organisational boundaries and responsibilities, or the elimination of some units. But there is a marked difference between the restructuring favoured in the not-so-distant past and some contemporary realignments. Once, reformers sought functional integration by consolidating related programmes and activities in the same department. All educational activities were grouped in a Department of Education, transportation services in another department, the provision of health care in a third, and so on. This made for a small number of big departments, as well as for the concentration of managerial resources and authority at the centre of each department. Inasmuch as there is no perfect functional alignment, the quest for integration led to frequent reorganisation.

This type of reorganisation still occurs, as in Australia's consolidation of its departments into broad portfolios during the 1980s. But the main thrust these days is in the opposite direction – breaking up functionally integrated, multi-purpose departments into a number of service delivery entities, each with a clearly defined mission, operating independence and performance targets. There are two main reasons for decoupling services and operations. On the one hand, large departments that are structured as holding companies for loosely related activities tend to be top-heavy, slow-moving and inefficient entities that have high operating costs, quash innovation and give managers muddled messages as to the performance expected of them. On the other hand, in functionally integrated departments, service providers "capture" policy makers, feeding them advice that blunts innovation and weakens accountability.

In the decoupled model, core departments retain important functions in policy making and advice, setting standards and targets, and overseeing the performance of operating agencies. This form of organisation is still quite new, and not enough experience has accumulated to assess its long-term effectiveness. Already, however, concern has been voiced that departments may have been weakened to the extent that they cannot carry out essential co-ordinating functions. It may be that in the enthusiasm to liberate operating managers, inadequate attention has been given to the resources and authority needed at the centre of government and in departmental headquarters to rationalise programmes and policies that cut across agencies and to maintain strict accountability.

The United Kingdom, which pioneered the decoupled model with its Next Steps initiative, moved to restore departmental capacity shortly after the launch of the Blair government in 1997. Although it retained agencies, the government ceased publication of the annual *Next Steps Review* which set performance targets and reported results for each agency. Instead, the government emphasised public service agreements, which linked budget allocations and strategic objectives for each department. In effect, the Blair government strengthened departmental accountability for the results achieved by agencies.

1.4. Contemporary reform relies on incentives, not just formal rules, to change behaviour

In traditional administrative reform, it is often assumed that changing the formal rules suffices to alter the actions and performance of managers. This presumption is rooted in the command-and-control model of public administration, in which central authorities promulgate and enforce rules, and subordinates comply. But a succession of failed reforms and new theories and evidence in business management, institutional economics, organisational theory and related fields have driven home the message that informal rules and managerial incentives must be changed in order for a high-performance managerial ethic to take hold. Changing the formalities does not make much of a difference if the self-interested behaviour of managers sabotages organisational objectives.

Many governments have concluded that the best way to motivate managers to improve performance is to set clear and reachable performance targets, give managers sufficient flexibility so that they can improve operations, and hold them personally and organisationally responsible. This orientation dominates the strategic reform agenda.

1.5. Contemporary reform is concentrated on operations and service delivery

In line with the emphasis on modifying incentives and behaviour, the focus has shifted in many countries from strengthening policy making to upgrading line operations, the delivery of services, the productivity of the public service and the responsiveness of government to the interests of citizens/customers. Top-down reform inevitably leads to "one size fits all" rules which circumscribe operating discretion and deter field managers from tailoring their services to suit local conditions. In top-down reform, the relationship between the centre and operating units is hierarchical: the former make policy, set the rules, issue orders and demand compliance; the latter are supposed to carry into effect the policies handed down to them and to produce the information demanded by superiors.

> But, as noted later in this article, a top-down perspective is essential to give reform a strategic orientation. Even when reform aims to devolve managerial responsibility, central agencies have a critical role in designing and promoting change. Moreover, when the main focus is on policy and objectives rather than implementation and service delivery, it is essential that political leaders and senior managers be actively engaged in demanding managerial improvement.

Top-down administrative structures have serious shortcomings: they demand compliance and uniformity when flexibility and diversity are called for; they stress inputs and neglect results; and they spur managers, who have a job to get done, to evade or subvert the rules. Beneath the veneer of rule-based public administration, an informal managerial ethic flourishes, softening the rules and loosening the rigidities. Entrepreneurial managers devise means of outwitting the controls while paying lip service to them. They manage to travel even when the travel budget is depleted, fill positions when a hiring freeze is in place, procure IT without going through central procurement, and so on. The problem with this behaviour is that many managers spend more time evading onerous controls than driving their organisations to higher performance.

2. Opportunity

The fact that many countries have similar reform objectives suggests that the opportunities are not entirely dependent on local situations. Some opportunistic conditions cross country boundaries; others do not. This section considers both types of opportunity.

2.1. *Timing*

Opportunities come and go. For some reforms, the right time has arrived; for others it has already passed. During the 1990s, Canada appears to have had significant success in rigorously reviewing its programmes, but it made little headway when it undertook to rationalise its programmes through the "Policy and Expenditure Management System" (PEMS) during the 1980s. Of course, there are material differences between the current and the previous approach, but they do not fully explain why one innovation has promoted the realignment of government programme expenditures while the other one had little to show for the substantial investment made in it.

Innovations yield different outcomes, depending on when they are tried. The saying "an idea whose time has come" applies as much to government reform as to other innovations. Two decades ago, Canada invested heavily in building evaluation capacity in the Comptroller General's Office. It is generally thought that the impact on programme and budget decisions was modest. About a decade later, Australia launched an ambitious evaluation strategy that has made a measurable difference in the reallocation of resources.

> The optimistic tone about reallocation has not been justified by experience during the past decade. Explicit reallocation – shifting money from one programme or spending unit to another – remains difficult, even when governments provide incentives through medium-term expenditure frameworks or other approaches. Holders of budget resources do not readily yield in the face of evidence that the funds could be more productively spent elsewhere. It may be that the most fruitful path to reallocation is the one taken recently by Singapore. It cuts a fixed percentage of each agency's budget and puts the savings into a pool that is allocated through the budget process. In contrast to across-the-board cuts which aim to reduce government spending, the Singapore approach aims to free up significant amounts of money for reallocation.

Arguably, Canada learned from its earlier PEMS experience and has undertaken programme review in a more effective manner, and Australia learned from Canada's failure to implant an evaluation culture. But this cannot be the sole explanation of the earlier failures and later successes. In the period 1960-90, just about every country that tried to build a formal programme analysis and review system failed. The Netherlands made little progress with a reconsideration procedure that involved the Cabinet in selecting programmes for re-examination; Sweden had little results from programme budgeting; the United Kingdom installed and then discarded a programme analysis and review system; the United States adopted an ambitious planning-programming-budgeting system (PPBS); and other countries also introduced similar innovations. In this writer's view, the earlier reforms may have been premature: voters and politicians were not yet convinced of the compelling need to halt the growth in government spending and to reallocate resources from lower to higher priorities. Although programme reallocation still is difficult, the political mood of today has been much more hospitable to efforts to rearrange government programmes and expenditures than it was during the post-war growth spurt.

2.2. Government

Elections and changes in government open or narrow opportunities for management reform. In fact, major changes in government organisation or programmes often are launched by new governments shortly after taking office. The British reforms were initiated shortly after Margaret Thatcher became Prime Minister in 1979; they were extended (by means of the Citizen's Charter) a decade later by John Major shortly after he became Prime Minister, and redirected by Tony Blair after his election in 1997. Australia, Canada and New Zealand also adopted reform agendas shortly after new governments were inaugurated. Several factors explain the impulse to innovate at this stage in the political cycle:

- A new government is more inclined to change course than one which has held power for an extended period; it also has the energy and fresh ideas to break new ground.

- When the old government is defeated at the polls, the election may be regarded by the successor government as a mandate for change.

- In coalition governments (such as the Netherlands), the process of forming the government often entails negotiations among the coalition partners as to the policy changes and reforms to be undertaken. There definitely has been a trend towards more detailed coalition agreements which spell out what the government will do during its tenure.

- An incoming government may confront a crisis that requires immediate attention and makes big changes politically attractive.

One election does not make for lasting reform. Basic reforms that uproot established practice must have staying power beyond a single election, and preferably beyond a single government. The countries that have made the most headway in restructuring public management are those in which the reform process has been carried forward and deepened by successive governments. Moreover, reforms are most likely to endure when they survive a change in government from one party (or coalition) to another.

In many countries, basic reforms started by one government have been continued by the next. A shift in political orientation from left to right, or in the opposite direction, has not interrupted the reform process. Perhaps the most interesting case of reform surviving political change has occurred in the United Kingdom, but the same pattern is found in other countries as well. The Thatcher-Major management reforms would be of little current interest if they had not been continued and extended by the Blair government.

> The British approach to management innovation differs from that of most OECD countries. Major innovations are introduced simply by changing practice, without new legislation and with no announced termination of an existing practice. The government merely stops doing one thing and starts another. For example, there was no official announcement of the change from agency-centred to department-centred management. This seamless method allows for experimentation and adjustment, and enables the government to claim both continuity and progress in public management.

Political orientation has not been a reliable indicator of the pace or direction of reform. New Zealand's Labour government introduced market-oriented reforms following its election victory in 1984. In some countries, a centre-right government has promoted management change; in others, a social democratic government has taken the initiative. Regardless of their political affiliation, ministers and senior civil servants have supported the drive for management improvement. Their leadership has spelled the difference between reform that is stillborn and reform that transforms the public sector.

2.3. Ideas

When leaders innovate, they often are propelled by powerful ideas that give them confidence that what they are doing is the right thing. Significantly, however, ideology does not play a role in contemporary reform. Today's political leaders are looking for ideas and practices that promise to improve the services government is providing, not to redefine the role and purpose of government. They do not have to be *avant-garde* to innovate; they can draw from a body of developing and accepted ideas concerning the organisation and operation of the public sector, including the following:

- Performance improves when managers are told what is expected of them and results are measured against these expectations.
- Performance improves when managers are given flexibility in using resources to carry out assigned responsibilities.
- Performance improves when operational authority is devolved from central agencies and departmental headquarters to operating levels and units.
- Performance improves when government decisions and controls focus on outputs and outcomes rather than on inputs and procedures.
- Performance improves when managers are held accountable for their use of resources and the results they produce.

Not all reform ideas are as widely accepted as those listed above. Some still are contested or untested. These include propositions that performance improves when: i) citizens/customers have choice in selecting the supplier; ii) government services are outsourced; iii) public organisations are run along business lines; or iv) service delivery is separated from policy making. Although not all contemporary management ideas have been widely applied, this writer agrees with the observation of B. Guy Peters that "contemporary reforms are driven by ideas. ... This characteristic distinguishes the current round of reform from some of the tireless tinkering that has tended to characterize administrative reforms" (Peters, 2001, p. x). As we shall see, ideas in currency have provided the strategic underpinning for transforming public management in industrial democracies.

2.4. Innovators

Ideas rarely sell themselves; they need promoters with sufficient authority to persuade leaders to risk new approaches. In the past, the reform agenda in many countries was set by special commissions or task forces that were established to study particular issues or problems. Typically, the commission would produce a well-publicised report containing a number of recommendations and then turn the implementing job to existing government organs. Some countries still draw innovative guidance from *ad hoc* entities, but the more likely source these days is from within government itself. The senior civil service has been a fertile source of reform ideas. Ireland describes the role of the senior civil service in the reform process.

In every country, the innovators have come from political echelons or the top ranks of the public service, not from operating levels. Strategic reform has not bubbled up from below, nor should it be expected to. The broad scope of reform requires perspectives and power that are held either in central agencies or departmental headquarters. However, top-down reform runs into problems if it is perceived by subordinate units as just the latest exercise in administrative centralisation.

2.5. Crisis

In public management, as in other endeavours, crisis can be a spur for change. When leaders become convinced that the course the country is on is unsustainable, they may embrace remedies that would not be tried in normal times. At least two countries (Finland and New Zealand) went through a serious economic crisis that called into question established policies and practices; at least one (Norway) has not experienced any significant crisis. Most of the countries have been impelled by a progressive erosion in confidence that the course they were on – progressive enlargement in the relative size of government, steadily rising tax burdens, stagnant or declining productivity in public institutions, and (in a few countries) a perceived decline in the public service performance – could be sustained. In other words, decline rather than crisis has been the primary motivating factor.

3. Strategy

There are many paths to management reform, and different governments have pursued similar objectives in different ways. This is not surprising, for management reform must comport with a country's political administrative values and traditions. In fact, one can discern as many strategies as there are countries, for even countries proceeding along the same general path combine elements of various strategies in different ways. Without claiming to be comprehensive, this section discusses four strategies: market-driven reforms that rely on competition, prices and contracts; managerial reforms that rely on the professionalism, skill and public service ethic of managers; programme review which relies on policy analysis and evaluation to reallocate resources and redesign programmes; and incremental deregulation that relies on ongoing review of rules and practices to streamline management and remove wasteful controls.

The four approaches have some important common elements. All strive to make public services more efficient and responsive; all seek to strengthen accountability for results and resources; all encourage greater variety and flexibility in the provision of services. But even when they share objectives, the four strategies proceed differently. A market strategy would lead a government to divest certain tasks or activities; it would favour the most efficient (or least expensive) supplier, even if the outcome was a truncated, weakened civil service. A managerial strategy, by contrast, would seek to strengthen public service norms by giving "rank and file" civil servants a greater voice in running operations and in accommodating variations in local conditions. A programme strategy seeks to optimise social outcomes by shifting resources from lower priority to higher priority programmes. An incremental strategy looks for opportunities to deregulate and ease management rules.

Underlying the various strategies are different conceptions of the future role of the state. The market strategy draws a sharp distinction between the state as policy maker and the state as service provider. It has a strong preference for hiving off the delivery of services to non-governmental entities or to operationally independent agencies. The managerial model allows a broader role for the government in providing public services but wants these activities to be less hobbled by bureaucratic rules and more sensitive to the wants of recipients. The programme strategy envisions a state whose primary responsibility is to produce desired social outcomes within severe resource constraints. The incremental model seeks a state which continues to function along familiar lines, but is less burdened by old rules and requirements.

Each country can be slotted into one or more of these categories. Some classifications are straightforward. The main thrust of New Zealand's reforms has been to establish market-like arrangements and incentives within government. Ireland and several other countries have emphasised managerial reforms. Canada has pursued a programme-oriented strategy and has made considerable progress in aligning public expenditures and programme results. Germany has maintained an incremental approach for an extended period, making frequent adjustments in rules and operations to improve management.

These classifications conceal an important feature of reform: most countries pursue more than one strategy. Each country's hybrid is distinctive. The United Kingdom, for example, has both market and managerial innovations; Canada uses both programme and managerial strategies. In every country, however, one strategy usually is paramount. A country seeking to enhance public performance may turn to markets for some purposes and to public managers for others; it may also review programme commitments in the light of political demands and resource constraints.

If the applications are hybrids, why be concerned with defining and classifying strategies? Why not consider each country's bundle of innovations on its own terms without fitting it into preset categories? The answer is that each strategy raises particular questions which should be addressed in assessing the prospects for success. In the market strategy, one must ascertain whether true conditions for competition have been established. Just labelling something a market or a contract, or assuming that the means of providing a service is contestable, does not make it so. In the managerial strategy, the key issue is whether adequate accountability mechanisms are established. In the programme strategy, the key issue is whether the government has the political will and strength to allocate resources and take other actions on the basis of a fundamental review of programmes. And, finally, in the incremental approach, the overriding question is whether the government can sustain interest and support for reform over an extended period. If these key questions are not addressed in a forthright manner, reforms that showed much promise at launch may fade away, leaving few traces that they were ever tried. This was the fate of many past management reforms; thinking strategically can help avert a similar fate for current and future reforms.

3.1. *The market strategy*

"If there is a single alternative to the traditional model of public administration favoured by contemporary politicians, academics and probably the public," Peters writes with some overstatement, "it must be the market model" (Peters, 2001, p. 23). Market-type arrangements have penetrated core public services in some OECD member countries, but not in most, and not everywhere in the same manner. The political culture has a role in shaping both receptivity to market-oriented solutions and the type of solution adopted. A fair assessment of management reform would conclude that marketisation has been much more widely applied in state enterprises and business-type activities than in basic public functions. For example, education still is publicly financed and provided in virtually all countries, and the use of market-type devices such as vouchers or alternative schools still is quite limited though more extensive than a decade ago. In the core public sector, it has proven exceedingly difficult to establish true markets in contrast to simulated ones.

In this writer's view, the main contemporary influence of business practices on government management innovation has not been in generating competition but in changing the concept of public organisations. For decades, the vertical integration of firms (internalising the production of components) was paralleled in the public sector by the functional integration of departments (combining in the same entity the various programmes contributing to the same objective). Vertically integrated firms were as layered, hierarchical and bureaucratised as big government departments. In both, command-and-control systems ran from the top to the bottom, and uniformity and compliance were enforced by central controllers who wrote the rules and monitored the actions of subordinates. Nowadays, however, vertical integration is widely regarded as rigid and inefficient, and many large firms have been reorganised into semi-autonomous business units which outsource much of their production. A number of governments have followed suit, breaking up integrated departments into small units and contracting out some functions.

Although the market strategy affects the form of government organisations, its principal objective is to create markets within government. This model is predicated on the expectation that consumer choice and competition will drive service providers to be more efficient and responsive. But competition and choice operate in two distinct domains: one is in the relationship between customers and suppliers, the other is in the relationship between government entities purchasing and providing services. The two types of markets – one external, the other internal – give rise to different issues. External markets – such as are created when government operations are privatised or contracted out, or when citizens are given the option of selecting their providers – raise questions concerning the adequacy of information available to consumers, the differential impact of choice on the affluent and the poor, and the transaction costs of empowering consumers to select providers. Deeper concerns pertain to whether marketising public responsibilities might crowd out important social values such as equality and uniformity in the provision of services, a public service ethic, and the sense of citizenship that one develops through government-provided education and other basic services.

Internal markets raise more complex questions, though ones not likely to receive as much attention because they involve transactions within government. These internal transactions may include the purchase of services by the government or ministers from departments, purchases by departments from line or field units, and purchases by departments from autonomous agencies. Even when the trappings of markets, such as contracts and prices, are introduced, the fact remains that relationships within the government are not truly arm's-length. And because they are not, the gains from competition may be illusory rather than real.

New Zealand, which has advanced much further than any other country in establishing internal markets, relies on a network of contracts to formalise relations between in-house purchasers and providers. It has performance agreements for department heads, fixed-term contracts for senior and middle managers, purchase agreements for ministers to contract for services at agreed prices from departments, and contracts by which departments purchase services from other government entities. A number of structural and operational changes have been made to institutionalise the contractual relationship, including: *i)* ministers have a free choice to purchase services from departmental or other sources; *ii)* the outputs to be produced are specified in advance; and *iii)* fulfilment of the terms of the contracts is monitored through reports and audits.

> New Zealand relies much less on contracts now than it did 20 years ago when it redesigned the public sector. Performance contracts still establish terms and conditions for employment of senior and middle managers, but purchase agreements and similar contract-like arrangements that set the outputs to be delivered have been downgraded. One reason is that New Zealand now gives more weight to outcomes than to outputs; another may be recognition that contracts between one arm of the government and another lack genuine attributes of contracts. They serve more to encourage dialogue than to enforce performance.

There is no doubt that New Zealand has been extraordinarily creative in building contracts into government. No other country has extended contractual relationships into so many areas of public management and programme operations. But as creative as New Zealand's internal markets are, they may be weak substitutes for genuine markets. Real markets have actual rather than just potential contestability; real markets specify the unit cost of outputs, not just total costs; real markets allow redress if the contract has been breached. Several questions need to be considered in appraising the robustness of internal markets. To what extent do ministers actually purchase services from the outside sources rather than from government entities? Have ministers cancelled contracts because they were dissatisfied with internal suppliers? Is the amount paid by the government adjusted if the volume or quality of outputs varies from the contracted terms? What recourse does the government have if internal suppliers fail to fulfil the terms of their agreements? Do government departments have the requisite skills to negotiate contracts and monitor compliance? What are the transaction costs of maintaining an extensive network of contracts? What evidence is there that organisational performance has been improved? The answers to these questions should shed light on the suitability of a market strategy in other countries.

3.2. *Managerial strategy*

The managerial strategy is predicated on the presumption that "letting managers manage" by liberating them from *ex ante* controls on inputs and operating procedures maintained by central controllers (especially with regard to human and financial resources) boosts organisational performance. The driving assumptions are that public managers want to do a good job, that they are committed to the prudent and efficient use of public money, that they care about the quality of services and whether recipients are benefiting, and that they have a strong public service ethic. But, the argument runs, they have been held back from doing their best by rigid rules which enforce uniformity and hamper managerial initiative. Take away these assumptions and "letting managers manage" injects a dangerous permissiveness, an "anything goes" mindset into the conduct of public business. Worse yet, it gives opportunistic managers licence to pursue their self-interest at the expense of the government or citizens.

The management strategy sweeps away practices that once were regarded as bulwarks of rule-based public administration. At one time, standardising rules and procedures was regarded as a signal advance in government. All agencies were required to budget the same way; all had to abide by the same rules in hiring and paying civil servants; and all were subject to the same procedures for buying goods and services, arranging accommodations and travel, and so on. The bulging rule books were regarded as *prima facie* evidence of sound administrative practices; line-item budgets dictated the number and cost of the myriad things purchased by spending units. Just about everything that cost money had its own rules and enforcement procedures. The fact that the rules circumscribed administrative discretion was regarded as a virtue, for civil servants could not be trusted to do the right thing on their own. They had to be monitored and controlled. Upholding the legality and propriety of administrative actions through central control was the foremost objective of public administration.

The managerial ethic argues, however, that whatever laudable purposes the control regime may have served in the past, it has become counter-productive. The controls impel managers to care more about inputs than outputs, more about procedures than results, more about complying with the rules than on improving performance. A managerial strategy strips away most centrally enforced controls. One approach is to selectively discard rules and procedures that appear to be the least useful or the most onerous; another is to broad-band various administrative rules (for example, reducing the number of civil service or budget classifications). The fullest expression of managerialism is to give managers global budgets, with discretion to use the resources as they deem appropriate. In this arrangement, managers have a fixed budget for operating (or running) costs and must keep within that budget, but they have freedom to decide how much to spend on salaries, travel and other expenses. They may still be required to comply with some residual rules concerning, for example, fair employment practices and competitive tendering of contracts. But most operating decisions are left to the discretion of managers. They no longer need advance approval from central controllers.

Many countries have elements of a managerial strategy in their administrative reforms; these countries include Finland, Germany, Ireland, the Netherlands and the United Kingdom. Some of these countries have taken bold steps to devolve managerial discretion to the operating levels which provide direct service to the public; others still retain significant managerial authority in departmental headquarters.

In explaining the broad appeal of managerialism, one is struck by a seeming anomaly. The present age is one in which trust and confidence in government is at a low level in many OECD member countries. Yet the managerial strategy depends on entrusting managers with greater discretion and on trusting them to be prudent, efficient and responsive in carrying out their responsibilities. What is the rationale for broadening managerial freedom at a time when there appears to be little confidence that managers will act in the public interest? Some governments feel that declining (or stagnant) operating budgets and a sense that the old controls do not work give them no choice but to loosen constraints on managerial discretion. Others believe that improved performance will come with managerial freedom and will boost confidence in the government. Whether because of the first motive or the second, today's governments take the position that the easing of controls must be accompanied by a strengthened accountability framework for managers. Vital elements of the managerial strategy are the *ex ante* specification of performance targets or expectations and the *ex post* review of actual performance. "Letting managers manage" must be linked to "making managers manage".

The jury is out on whether investing in managerial performance will be repaid with higher trust and confidence in government. This writer is of the view that the low esteem of government has less to do with actual performance than with rising demands on government. It may be that when citizens want and get more from government, they nevertheless remain dissatisfied that they are not getting enough.

Like the other strategies discussed in this article, the managerial strategy opens the door to difficult questions as to whether the reforms have yielded, or are likely to yield, the expected results. One area of concern is the link between "letting" and "making" managers manage. It is much easier to fulfil the first part of the bargain than the second. It is much easier to remove controls than to enforce accountability. In fact, accountability frameworks – the specification of targets, reporting on results and auditing of performance – still are relatively undeveloped in a number of the countries pursuing a managerial strategy.

The managerial strategy relies extensively on performance measurement. While considerable advances have been made in defining various types of measures, there is at best sketchy evidence that the behaviour and performance of managers have been significantly influenced by the new information. It is one thing to measure performance, quite another to manage on that basis. Moreover, most governments relying on a management strategy have had more success in measuring outputs than outcomes, and they have tended to devise measures that put their performance in a favourable light. They generally have shied away from measures that challenge them to overhaul operations or to significantly raise their level of performance.

> Over-emphasis on performance measurement is a formidable obstacle to results-based public management. In many countries – especially those that are newly come to the performance movement – measurement is a substitute for management. Governments cram copious amounts of performance data into their budgets, but do not allocate resources on that basis. Rather than quantifying outputs, embedding a performance culture in public administration will do more to improve results.

The managerial strategy relies on the assumption that civil servants are committed to the public's interest rather than their own. But are they always? What safeguards are there when self-interest takes over or when government employees behave opportunistically, exploiting their discretion to do as they please?

These concerns do not call the managerial strategy into question. Rather, they indicate the need for careful assessment of what has been accomplished under the new regime, how managers have actually behaved, and the effectiveness of the accountability mechanisms put in place.

3.3. Programme strategy

The programme strategy is built on the idea that the most urgent task in reforming the modern state is ensuring that public resources are effectively allocated to achieve the fundamental objectives of government. From this perspective, the two previously discussed strategies – turning various tasks and responsibilities over to market-like institutions, and entrusting managers with operating discretion and holding them accountable for results – apply mostly to the operational work of government. The programme strategy urges that defining objectives and establishing policy should be accorded higher priority.

This is an old issue that will not be settled in the current round of reform. The issue is contested on many fronts: outputs *versus* outcomes, efficiency *versus* effectiveness, doing the right thing *versus* doing things right, centralisation *versus* devolution, top-down *versus* bottom-up reform, and so on. In the past, the emphasis was on strengthening policy capacity at the centre of government or in headquarters; today, most countries are focusing on operational matters.

> Perhaps a more balanced view is that innovative governments are proceeding on both fronts: strengthening strategic capacity at the centre, and improving the quality and efficiency of public services. It is likely that management innovation will falter if only one of the approaches were taken. A strong policy capacity is essential to define objectives but, without attention to services, new policies end up as empty promises. Conversely, aiming to improve access to, or the quality of, public services will account to little if government does not link services to objectives.

Can the two approaches be melded together? Yes, but they rarely are. For most governments it is hard enough pursuing the limited reforms that one or another of the strategies dictates. Canada is one of the few, however, that has taken an eclectic approach, combining a substantial commitment to programme review along with a wide range of management initiatives affecting service delivery, citizen participation, deregulation, the civil service, financial management and a number of other administrative practices. But programme review has been the centrepiece of the Canadian reforms. It was launched in 1994, at a time when the country faced serious financial and budgetary pressures. As one Canadian colleague observed, programme review addressed not only pragmatic questions of programme design and delivery, but more fundamentally, fundamental questions of the role of the federal government, which anchored the ensuing changes to programmes. Although programme review has not formally covered transfers to individuals or other levels of government, these have been separately reviewed in a parallel exercise.

Canada's programme reviews assessed each ongoing programme in terms of six questions: Does it serve the public interest? Is there a necessary and legitimate role for government? Is the current role of the federal government appropriate? Should the programme be carried out, in whole or in part, by the private or voluntary sector? If the programme is continued, in what ways can it be improved? And is the programme affordable within the fiscal parameters of the government?

Canadian officials strongly believe that the reviews have made a significant contribution to the country's successful fiscal consolidation. When the reviews were initiated, the federal government seemed hopelessly mired in oversized budget deficits; barely four years later, the government reported that it had balanced the budget. Although the bulk of the reviews were concentrated in the first years, the government has taken steps to institutionalise the process and link it to expenditure decisions. Toward this end, it has established an expenditure management system to feed the results of reviews into budget actions. Learning from the unsuccessful Policy and Expenditure Management System tried more than a decade earlier, the government has built strong reallocation requirements into the new system: with few exceptions, programme initiatives have to be funded through savings in existing programmes.

Some reform-minded countries initially focused on service delivery and operational efficiency, and over time broadened their perspective to review programme effectiveness and outcomes. Thus, a decade after launching the Next Steps initiative, the United Kingdom undertook a series of fundamental reviews. Canada, however, has moved in the opposite direction. After consolidating its fiscal position through programme reviews and other policy changes, it set into motion more than half a dozen initiatives aimed at strengthening managerial capacity.

In considering the programme strategy, one must be mindful of past efforts to link strategic objectives to budget allocations. These efforts include Canada's PEMS system mentioned earlier, the PPBS in the United States, and the reconsideration procedure in the Netherlands. None was successful, though each had a temporary impact on budgetary procedures and decisions. Truly fundamental programme review requires an enormous amount of time and information, fuels conflict and often produces relatively modest reallocation. It has been difficult to integrate in-depth reviews with the ongoing routines and procedures of budgeting.

> The United States has had considerable success with its "Program Assessment Rating Tool" (PART) that is managed by the Office of Management and Budget (OMB) in tandem with annual review of departmental spending bids. Under PART, approximately 20% of federal programmes are reviewed each year in terms of four criteria, and the results are compiled into a numerical score. Although there is no direct link between the PART score and programme allocation, the OMB used the score to pressure departments to remedy deficiencies in their programmes. As PART has evolved, its main purpose has been to promote programme improvement, not to threaten departments with a loss of resources.

Why should the results be more favourable this time? Perhaps because countries have learned from past failures and perhaps because there is now a stronger commitment to contain the cost of government by weeding out ineffective and low priority programmes. In looking back at the PEMS failure, the Canadian government perceived that, while the allocations to envelopes (sectors) were supposed to be ceilings, they often were regarded as floors, adding to pressure on public expenditure. This time, therefore, the programme review progress is much more explicit in demanding reallocations within fixed budgets. Moreover, contemporary programme review does wrestle with fundamental questions that were slighted in earlier periods. These pertain to the role and functions of government, its relationship with the private and voluntary sectors, and the future affordability of commitments undertaken when public resources seemed to be more abundant and confidence in public institutions was higher. The times may be ripe for a strategic realignment of government objectives and programmes. If they are not, the programme strategy will not make much of a difference; if they are, the results will be different this time.

3.4. Incremental strategy

Mounting any of the strategies discussed thus far entails a substantial commitment of political and organisational resources and (in some cases) a leap of faith that the innovations will bring promised improvements. Understandably, therefore, some countries have taken a cautious approach, moving incrementally as opportunities become available. The obvious advantage of this approach is that particular reforms can be adopted when they seem the right thing to do, and the reform process can be fine-tuned as circumstances and opportunities change.

German reform seems to fit this model. Whether because its federal make-up inhibits leap-frogging innovation or because the government has been preoccupied with unification, the country has adopted a series of measures aiming to streamline the state and reduce costs. There have been doses of privatisation and deregulation, new requirements that proposed legislation show projected costs, reductions in the number of federal ministries and other federal entities, new management instruments focused on measuring costs and performance, and some efforts to decentralise responsibility for resources. These and other initiatives have been packaged into an "action programme" to increase the effectiveness and economic viability of the federal administration. The aim of the reforms is to reduce the size of the state by identifying tasks which can be transferred to subordinate authorities or the private sector, or abolished altogether.

Germany notes that comprehensive reform of the administrative apparatus was attempted in the 1970s, but many of the proposals made at the time were not implemented. The current modernisation programme, by contrast, emphasises constant improvement. It is carried forward in small steps (mosaic theory) and is not based on a holistic approach. Accordingly the ministries follow different concepts for their modernisation measures. If one tried to reform all elements of public administration which require change, it would be too time-consuming and demanding. A step-by-step approach is therefore necessary.

Incremental reform has several potential drawbacks. One is that the many small steps might not add up to significant change; another is that reform will be directionless, propelled by expediency rather than by strategy; a third is that the government may lose interest in the endeavour along the way. Incremental reformers who take one step at a time, and allow the previous step to determine the direction of the next one, can produce a lot of motion that signifies little. It is important, therefore, that incrementalists clarify at the outset the aims of their reforms. It is also important that the reforms show sufficient progress to sustain an interest within government, and that they build on one another. The fact that Germany had the same government for an extended period may explain the staying power of its reforms. In some countries, the government of the day has lurched from one reform agenda to the next, without integrating the various initiatives into a coherent strategy.

4. Tactics

No strategy is self-implementing. As it embarks on a course to transform public management, a government faces myriad decisions on how the reforms should be carried out, by whom and when. It also must take steps to build support for, and interest in, the reforms. These and related tactical considerations often dominate the reform agenda; in some cases, they spell the difference between robust and tepid progress. This section briefly discusses a few of the many tactical issues that a government faces in implementing a reform strategy.

The pace and scope of reform are common tactical issues. One option mentioned earlier is to test pilot all or some elements and defer decisions on full implementation until the results have been evaluated. At the other extreme, the government may mandate comprehensive implementation by all departments and agencies. Still other options are to implement reforms according to a staggered schedule (some agencies or elements the first years, others the second, etc.) or to allow each department to decide the extent and timing of its participation.

There appears to be less test piloting in the strategic reforms than in past waves of reform. However, some governments have given departments discretion on restructuring their management practices. The rationale for this permissiveness is that management reform cannot succeed unless operating departments welcome the changes and have a say in how they are implemented. If reforms are forced on departments, or if they are committed to the prescribed changes, or if they feel that the changes do not meet their needs, only meagre improvement will be forthcoming.

Even when departments are entrusted with wide discretion in implementing recommended reforms, the government may consider assigning oversight responsibility to an existing central agency or an *ad hoc* entity established for that purpose. The finance department is the obvious candidate for this role, but not always the most appropriate. Its control of the purse strings can get in the way of encouraging managers to improve performance. But if the role is entrusted to a rival unit, the finance department may try to undermine the reforms.

In developing a reform programme, the government may proceed by administrative fiat or it may seek legislative authorisation. Most governments have taken the first course, preferring the flexibility that administrative action gives them. A few, most notably New Zealand, have embedded their main reforms in law. But even countries that have taken the second course have found it necessary to make adjustments outside the ambit of the legislation. They have had to experiment and adapt in order for the reforms to be sustained.

Many tactics are country-specific, and generalisations about the most effective approach are questionable. What works in one country might not in another. Perhaps the best advice one can offer on tactics is for the government to invest reform with sufficient institutional resources and political support, to have a firm idea of where it is heading, and to keep an open mind on how it should get there. If the current wave of reforms has stayed around much longer than previous ones, it is because governments have been adaptable and tactics have been moulded to needs.

5. The path ahead

Strategic reform takes time. Most of the countries participating in the project have been at it for a decade; the British government is completing its second decade, and much additional work and innovation lie ahead. In fact, there is no real end to the task of improving public management. As new problems arise and as novel ideas displace old ones, governments redefine their expectations. Successful reforms open up fresh opportunities; failed reforms impel governments to go back to their drawing boards and try again.

Regardless of the progress made thus far, all reforming countries face the task of institutionalising the changes they have made and preparing for the next generation of management innovations. All have to guard against lapsing back to their old ways, while building in capacity for continuing improvement. Most still have to work out an acceptable balance among the various strategies. All have to reconsider the role of central agencies and their relationship with operating units, and all have to strengthen the means of maintaining managerial accountability.

> To emphasise what was said earlier, reform that is not revitalised becomes just another routine that must be complied with. This may be true of all management innovations, but is especially applicable to those that focus on performance.

Beyond the current agenda lies a melange of issues and possibilities pertaining to the future configuration of public management. The leading questions here deal with the impact of emerging information technology on the delivery of public services, the potential for changing relations between citizens and the state, the future make-up and role of the civil service, the boundaries of the market and public organisations, and the extension of the logic and instruments of performance management into core areas of governmental service. Although the distinction between current issues and the future agenda is somewhat arbitrary, it is useful to distinguish between those reforms that lie within the current interests of national government and those that might emerge in the future. There is a high probability that just about all reformist governments will tackle the current issues, but a significantly lower probability that they will deal with potential future issues.

5.1. Reversion to control-and-compliance public management

No matter how much progress a government has made in dismantling traditional control mechanisms, it must be vigilant against retrograde reforms that restore the old order. The main risk is not that governments will throw their management innovations overboard and reinstall discarded practices, but that they will impose rules and procedures in piecemeal fashion in response to particular problems. Relapse might be due to an actual or perceived abuse of managerial discretion, parliamentary demands for information and controls, or the unease of risk-averse public managers with performance-based systems. Each reinstalled rule or requirement may be justified in its own right, but the cumulative impact may be to reintroduce compliance-centred management.

It is not easy to guard against a return to the old ways. There are two main approaches for dealing with this tendency. One is to concede that there is a natural inclination to add controls, and to periodically review the rules and purge those which are deemed redundant or inapt; the other is to institutionalise the precepts of managerial discretion and accountability in law and behaviour so as to discourage inroads. The first path bows to the inevitability of recentralisation, the second seeks to thwart it.

5.2. Continuous improvement

Improving public management should not be a one-shot affair, done once and for all. Lasting and sustainable progress requires that each reform build on the last, that governments learn from experience, and that they search for opportunities to raise expectations and performance. But it is not easy to build this capacity into public institutions, many of which go through bursts of innovation and change followed by pause and consolidation. This cyclical pattern enables the government to transmit new rules and expectations down the ranks, instruct employees in innovative practices, acquire needed information, and test new procedures and requirements. Governments which rush from one partially implemented innovation to the next suffer from "reform fatigue" and confusion. In some such countries, this writer has encountered senior managers pleading for breathing space to assimilate the last reform before the next one is urgently thrust upon them. Matters are made worse when each round of reform promises the same things but has distinctive nomenclature and procedures.

In markets, competition forces change. In governments, the prod is often a performance measurement system that periodically raises the targets to impel monitored organisations to do better. Using performance measures as an engine of change requires that the targets:

- be few in number, so that they send strong signals as to what is expected and provide a clear basis for assessing progress;
- challenge agencies to make changes in programmes or operations that will enable them to meet targets;
- are jointly selected by each agency and the central authority responsible for overall government performance;
- are monitored and audited to ascertain whether the targets have been met; and
- are part of a larger managerial framework that encourages agencies to improve performance.

This is not a full itemisation of the characteristics of a performance measurement system, but each item above is especially relevant to the task of driving organisations to continuous improvement.

Few governments that claim to have performance management systems fulfill these criteria. The characteristics listed here are essential conditions for governments that want performance data to transform their policies or operations.

5.3. Balancing the reform strategies

This article has noted that some countries have focused on operational management and others on programme effectiveness. Ideally, the two strategies should go hand in hand, for programmes depend on well-run organisations to achieve their objectives, and operations produce public good only to the extent that they serve governmental objectives. The longer a country stays at the task of reforming public institutions, the greater the likelihood that, having started with one of these strategies, it will gravitate to the other. Combining the two is not simple, because they require different types of information, have different uses and perspectives, and engage different parts and levels of government. Assuming that a government intends to proceed on both fronts, it has to decide whether to combine the two strategies in a unified reform or to separate them. To this writer's knowledge, Australia is the country that has grappled most with this question. Beginning in the 1980s and continuing into the present decade, it has sought to integrate a financial management improvement programme with programme budgeting. The combined FMIP/PB initiative has made significant headway in realigning programmes and in improving management, but the relationship between the two parts of the reform package has not always been easy.

5.4. *The role of central agencies*

One of the tensions between programme and managerial strategies has to do with the changing role of central agencies, particularly those dealing with financial and human resources. These agencies once served as the central command-and-control posts of government, but this role is not compatible with the new managerial ethic. Some central agencies have retooled themselves to the drive for devolution and flexible management. But driving reform from the centre in the name of decentralisation sometimes gives the wrong message to departments on the receiving end. Rather than hearing that they are to be freed up to run their own operations, they fear that the new performance regime is a ploy to get them to supply information to be used against them by central controllers.

Central agencies are in a quandary. If they allow each department or agency to pursue reform its own way, they risk getting very different managerial arrangements than the ones they wanted. If they intervene to dictate how departments and agencies should run their affairs, they risk being accused of violating the precepts of managerialism. Moreover, having divested many of the controls that were, for generations, the source of their power over operating departments, central agencies may be too weak to compel compliance with their views as to how government should be managed.

The evolving role of central agencies differs from country to country. In some, the finance ministry (or a similar organisation) has unrivalled authority over management matters; in others, the government has established a separate agency to oversee the reform drive. In some, the finance ministry has a firm sense of its role and relationship to operating units; in others, the finance ministry is going through an identity crisis, seeking to carve out a niche that enables it to retain considerable administrative authority within the managerial framework. In all, the finance ministry (and other central agencies) faces the task of prodding agencies to get on with the business of reform.

5.5. *Strengthening managerial accountability*

It was noted earlier that more progress has been made in devolving managerial authority than in enforcing managerial accountability. Dismantling old controls has proved easier than establishing new performance-based accountability. There is significant risk, therefore, that managerial flexibility will be discredited by misbehaving officials who take the new freedom as licence to breach the public trust. Some abuses may be real, others only perceived; either way, they may impel governments to rein in public managers by reinserting centrally enforced rules and standards. The indiscretions need not be major to spur this reversal; even minor lapses can impel ministers and parliamentarians to demand more control.

What should be done? Some, or all, of the following, depending on the quality of accountability systems already in place:

- Train managers and civil servants in their responsibilities under newly devolved arrangements. Do not take for granted that they know what is permitted and what is not.

- Review rules pertaining to employment, finance, contracting and other managerial actions to determine whether there are gaps that have to be closed.

- Indoctrinate managers in the principle that they are personally and professionally responsible for good conduct in their organisations.

- Assess financial reporting systems, the quality of financial statements and audit practices, and take appropriate steps to elevate standards to acceptable levels.

- In countries which rely extensively on outsourcing, develop a corps of public servants who are skilled negotiators of contracts with private parties and overseers of compliance. These skills are much more highly developed in business firms than in government departments.

- Improve performance reporting systems, including the audit of reported results.

6. The next generation

The current wave of management reforms will not be the last. Developments, already under way, will expand the envelope for novel, as yet untried management arrangements. These include: the diffusion of information technology that facilitates interactive communication within government and between the government and citizens; rising expectations concerning the volume and quality of public services; the weakening of civil service norms and increased reliance on temporary, part-time and non-public employees; further encroachment of markets and competition onto the provision of public services; and adoption of practices that make performance measurement more a reality than a slogan.

These changes are both independent of one another and interconnected. Establishing remote, interactive communication between governments and citizens covering a wide array of services and relationships may proceed on its own but, once it is in place, it opens the door to reconfiguring the civil service, bringing the market-type mechanisms into core public services and taking performance-based management seriously. Alternately, while the development of new technologies might speed up communication and enable remote interaction with citizens, it may do little to change the way governments might retain a career-based civil service system or might rely on the overall labour market to obtain workers as needed.

In a leap of vision, one can foresee government of the future organised along very different lines than it is currently. A futuristic public service would work out of homes or out of communications hubs; it would consist of workers hired by business firms under contract with government; citizens would have broad choices in the public services they purchase; government departments would shrink to core political-policy functions;

governments would adopt variable budgets, in which the volume of resources is linked to the volume of outputs and other measures of performance.

In the medium to long term, the direction taken by a government will closely track the direction taken by business organisations. If the "virtual" firm becomes the model of business organisations, it will also become – with some lag – the model of government organisation.

In other words, if one were able to foresee how the market sector will evolve, one would be able to foretell how the public sector will change. Lacking such foresight, this writer urges governments to attend to the near-term agenda and defer visionary plans until the future has arrived.

Reference

Peters, B. Guy (2001), *The Future of Governing*, University Press of Kansas, Lawrence, Kansas, United States.

ISBN 978-92-64-06087-6
Evolutions in Budgetary Practice
Allen Schick and the OECD Senior Budget Officials
© OECD 2009

Chapter 10

The Performing State: Reflection on an Idea Whose Time Has Come but Whose Implementation Has Not*

* This article was originally published in the *OECD Journal on Budgeting*, Vol. 3, No. 2, 2003. At the time of writing, Allen Schick was Visiting Fellow, Governmental Studies, Brookings Institution, Washington DC, and Professor, School of Public Affairs, University of Maryland, United States. Boxed comments were made in 2009.

The contemporary nation-state exists to perform – to provide financial assistance, public services and other benefits to its people. How well the government performs influences the economic and social well-being of citizens, the mindset that voters take into the election booth, the programmes and behaviour of politicians and bureaucrats, and the relationship between government and the governed. Delivering services and writing cheques are not the sole functions of the modern state, for it still has traditional watchman responsibilities such as defending the country against external threat and maintaining domestic health, safety and order. Although the old tasks are essential, in most nation-states they have been surpassed in the sentiments of citizens and in the fiscal accounts of government by a vastly broader array of public services than were provided generations ago.

Government not only does more than it once did, it carries out many tasks differently. One of the themes of this article is that a performing state is inherently a state in transition, adapting to changing conditions and opportunities. Performance is not a static measure, but one that requires ongoing feedback from situations and results to policies and action. Among the many transformations that the performing state has experienced is in its role as unifier of the people through symbols and actions that forge a common national identity. As the provision of services has gained prominence, diversity has gained ground over uniformity because citizens differ in the services they want or need. The performing state must serve the people, even if doing so requires that it serve them differently.

This logic has led some modernisers of the nation-state to devise more supple forms of public administration that aim to enhance performance by giving public managers broad discretion in operating programmes and using public resources. Once it is accepted that one size does not fit all, it is easy to conclude that uniform rules and procedures impede good performance by blocking managers from doing their best to produce planned results. This reasoning has impelled some national governments to deregulate public administration, but many others have sought to improve performance within the framework of established administrative controls. Thus, while performance is the common objective of nation-states, governments have chosen different paths to this end. The differences are typically labelled old *versus* new public administration, but an even more critical difference is in the status of the state itself. In some countries, performance has led to reliance on alternatives to the state for delivering public services while, in others, the state still has a monopoly on the provision of most public services. The most prominent alternatives include devolution of resources and authority from the national government to local or regional bodies, reliance on NGOs (non-governmental organisations) to design and deliver public services, use of international organisations to establish and carry out public policies, and recourse to various market-type arrangements. The anomaly of the performing state is that innovations that begin as efforts to strengthen governmental performance sometimes culminate in arrangements that bypass or undermine the state.

Performance is a demanding test. When the state fails to meet the test, its legitimacy and competence may be called into question, and policy makers and interest groups may seek substitutes that promise the results they want. To put the matter bluntly: in the performing state, performance is more important than the state. The modern state has primacy only to the extent that it performs. Inasmuch as the state still has first claim on national loyalty and tax revenues, the initial *tranche* of performance-enhancing reforms strives to empower the state. But when this fails to produce results, alternatives to the states may be favoured.

The foregoing paragraph summarises a key conclusion of this article. The process by which this conclusion is reached takes the article through three stages. Stage one, in the next section, explores the idea of performance, what it means and why it has so much currency. The second stage examines various pathways to performance and indicates that, even when the idea is accepted, there are multiple – sometimes conflicting – routes for bolstering public services. The third stage returns the discussion to the state and the alternatives to it that have gained popularity in recent times. The article concludes with a discussion of implications of the performing state for national governments and their budget practices.

1. The idea of performance

Performance is a deceptively simple idea: simple because it is easy to express key concepts and objectives; deceptive because it is hard to apply these ideas in government. The basic idea is that government should deliver efficient services and operate efficient programmes. In the burgeoning literature on performance, efficiency generally is associated with outputs (the goods and services produced by government) and effectiveness with outcomes (the impacts of government programmes on society). Efficiency has both quantitative and qualitative characteristics that include the volume and cost of services, response times and error rates, the accessibility of services and the courtesy with which they are provided, and citizen/customer satisfaction with services. Effectiveness means that programmes are in accord with the priorities and objectives of government, and produce the expected or desired impacts.

It is widely accepted that outcomes are the most important dimension of performance, but it is also recognised that outcome data are often unavailable or costly to obtain, and that even when data are available, the causal relationship between government policy and social conditions may be problematic. In countries that take performance seriously, reforms that aim to improve outcomes tend to end up focusing on outputs instead. This "second best" situation certainly is more productive than spending years in the quest for ideal outcome measures. Outputs are a useful indicator of performance because citizens know government by observing the condition of school classrooms and the number of students per class, the distance from home to health clinic and the waiting time once they get there, the treatment given them by police officers, and the countless other contacts that ordinary citizens have with government agencies and public employees. Outputs are the face presented by government to its people. If citizens deem services inadequate, they will not regard government as performing well.

Outputs and outcomes, however, are not sufficient measures of government performance. They are snapshots of what government is doing or accomplishing at a particular point in time; they do not uncover the factors that contribute to or delay the results, nor do they indicate whether government will have the capacity to perform in the future. A full measure of performance must recognise that outputs and outcomes are the end results of government at work, and that there are both antecedent factors that drive the results and future indicators of government's prospective performance. It is the task of performance measurement to comprehend the past and indicate the future, and to dig beneath the surface results to explain why government performs as it does.

Performance does not just happen. Government – political leaders, public managers, civil servants, and the agencies they control or work in – must care about results and actively search out means of doing better. They must continually scan the world outside the four walls of their bureaucracies to discern changes under way that call old policies and methods into question and open fresh opportunities to do better. Caring about results must ripple through the ranks; it must define government and shape what it does and how it operates.

Performance is not a measure frozen in time. For government to perform well, it is not sufficient that its internal operations be efficiently managed; it is also essential that government adapt to changing circumstances. A community health clinic that excels when the women it serves are of child-bearing age would not be effective if it continues to offer obstetrical services when residents have aged and no longer bear children. True performance requires that the focus shifts from inside government to outside. This shift entails a redefinition of the role played by outcome measures. The prevailing concept is that these measures inform government on whether its programmes are having the intended effects. In a performing state, however, much of the utility of outcome measures lies in informing government of how social conditions have changed so that it can adapt accordingly. The key question is not whether government has caused a particular outcome, but whether a particular outcome should spur government to examine its programmes and policies and take corrective action.

A performing state thus is one that continuously reads its environment and adjusts how and what it does in response to new information. In the same way that a successful firm thrives by monitoring its market and changing its product mix, prices and other policies in response to changes in consumer preferences, technological developments and the entrance (or exit) of competitors, an effective government transforms itself in response to changes in family patterns, income distribution, technological advances and other opportunities. Of course, government has a more difficult time adapting because it lacks the pressure provided by markets and the signals supplied by prices. Yet, performing governments do change, even when they profess to be staying the same.

In the performing state, every measure of performance can be constructed as a measure of change. Change can be benchmarked against other governments, compared to past times or measured against targets or objectives. In fact, as will briefly be discussed in the next section, performance targets have become popular because they enable government to assess change against a preset standard. A performing state is not satisfied with the results it gets just by staying the course, but proactively seeks improvement by canvassing the world around it and changing both its objectives and its programmes.

By this standard, few states are good performers, which is one reason why the drive for performance pervades all types of countries – developed, developing, transitional and emerging market. In all types, there is the sense that actual performance is not good enough and that, by performing better, the state will become a more efficient producer of public services and more effective in operating programmes. But the idea of performance goes beyond these tangible gains to the belief that a performing state has more buoyant economic prospects, sturdier democratic institutions, a more just society and greater political stability. To the extent that these conditions are lacking, the argument runs, it is because nation-states have been sub-par performers.

A cursory survey of the four types of countries suggests that these larger political benefits may be elusive. Developed countries regularly score high on cross-country governance scales and anti-corruption measures. Almost all provide high quality public services, and most have sophisticated information and evaluation systems to assess performance and take corrective action when results fall below expectations. Despite their positive ratings, most developed countries have been beset in recent decades by a decline in trust and confidence in government and political leaders. A recent study found a loss of confidence in all but two of the 13 trilateral countries surveyed (Pharr and Putnam, 2000). One popular interpretation of this trend is that citizens think less of government because they take its benefits for granted. The fall in public esteem occurred during a period in which the welfare state stretched its boundaries. In every developed country, there has been a significant rise in the share of government expenditure transferred to households through social security and other entitlements. Looking at the loss of trust, one is tempted to conclude that citizens are biting the hand that is feeding them. In view of this pattern, it is unlikely that emphasising performance will be reciprocated by more positive attitudes. Arguably, a performance-oriented government may furnish voters with more grist for discontent by shedding light on shortfalls in results and organisational failures. In the same way that no person is a hero to his/her valet, no state is fully successful in the eyes of its citizens when its performance is fully revealed to them.

The drive for enhanced performance has been pioneered in some Commonwealth and Scandinavian countries that some regard as among the best-managed regimes in the world.[1] Why should these countries care more about improving themselves than countries that are deficient in providing public services? Part of the answer may be that well-run governments are better positioned to take performance seriously than are countries that have pervasive management shortcomings. Another part of the answer is that performance is to government what self-actualisation is in Maslow's hierarchy of needs. Only when basic requirements have been met is the state ripe to manage for results.

Even the best developed countries can improve by focusing on results. The performance drive implies (and sometimes avers) that nation-states have a natural tendency to underperform. They are held back by lack of competition in the delivery of public services, by rigidities of bureaucratic rules and procedures, and by political pressures and constraints. Moreover, if they do not strive to do better, they will surely do worse, because they will not adapt to the opportunities opened up by technological innovation, changes in socio-economic conditions, and other developments. In developed countries, the focus on results aims to narrow the gap between actual and potential performance.

In developing countries, where many or most people live in wretched circumstances, reformers hope – and it may be little more than a hope – that making government more effective will stimulate development and improve the well-being of citizens by creating favourable conditions for investment and entrepreneurship. But half a century of failure should teach us that the path to development is not assured. Performance may prove to be the latest fad that frustrated reformers have grasped in a desperate effort to break out of the path-dependent pathologies that have condemned a sizeable fraction of the world's population to abject living conditions. Some poor countries lack resources to implement significant gains in performance; some are too corrupt to put donor aid to productive use. A strong case can be made that the least-developed countries may benefit more from old-fashioned administrative controls than from new-fangled performance-based procedures (see Schick, 1998). The shifts from compliance to results and from inputs to outputs and outcomes may be premature in countries that still lack basic accountability systems.

> The passage of time has made this conclusion more compelling. Developing countries have not thrived by leaping to advanced practices that strain administrative capacity, put the soundness of the financial system at risk, and (in some cases) open the door wide to corruption and misuse of public resources. Governments that lack reliable data on inputs cannot manage on the basis of outputs. It would be appropriate for international organisations to pay greater attention to the sequencing of reforms and to avoid the temptation to promote *avant-garde* practices.

It is imperative that poor countries improve public performance; if they do not, they will be no better off a generation from now, regardless of the inflow of donor assistance and the emphasis on millennium development goals. Paradoxically, however, they may progress more by building sturdy administrative processes than by embracing the cult of performance. Rather than introducing pay-for-performance schemes, they would do better to hire and promote civil servants on the basis of merit, pay them fair wages, demand a day's work for a day's pay, and teach them to be accessible and courteous to citizens. Having a budget that corresponds to actual expenditure is more valuable than having a budget that purports to show the outputs or outcomes purchased with public money. Across the gamut of administrative processes, basic skills and capacities should be emphasised; if they are, better performance will ensue, even if there is no explicit attention to results.

The performance orientation may hold more promise for emerging market countries that have already improved their economic capacity.

> Emerging market countries have been among the most active in modernising public management. Korea is a case in point. After the East Asia financial crisis, the government recognised that public performance had lagged behind development of the economy. During the decade since the crisis, it shifted from an input-based to a programme-based budget system, integrated the budget and planning processes through a medium-term framework, and focused budget decisions on policy changes. Brazil, China, Mexico and Russia have also moved to upgrade their budget and management capacities.

In countries undergoing rapid development, there is a tendency for modernisation of the state to lag behind development of the economy. This can be a drag on development, for the government is likely to have weak accountability and widespread corruption, and to experience a lack of professionalism in the public service as well as other pathologies carried over from less favourable times. Moreover, as the economy matures and personal income rises, citizens tend to become more attentive to governmental matters and demand improved public services. The schools that once were deemed good enough, no longer are. Poor sanitation, disregard of environmental damage, inadequate health services, primitive transport and other deficiencies are no longer acceptable when the economy surges. In emerging market countries, economic improvement elevates expectations of what government can or should do for its people. Performance-based government would seem to be the right prescription to boost public services in these countries.

Yet, even in these countries, a performance orientation should be embraced cautiously if it entails the dismantling of established administrative controls. Divesting financial and civil service rules before a performance mindset has been effectively introduced is a risky strategy that may open the door more to misdeeds than to results. A cautious approach developed in Thailand may be worth adopting in other countries. The Thai government has specified a number of hurdles or standards that public agencies must surmount before they are permitted to operate with broad discretion. The hurdles cover the main administrative processes including budgeting, human resources, procurement and information systems (World Bank, 2002). Although it has not been applied rigorously in Thailand, the "hurdles" approach enables government to strengthen accountability as a precondition for giving managers operating freedom.

> In retrospect, the "hurdles" approach was not successful, and within a few years after it was introduced, the Thai government abandoned it. To my knowledge, there has not been a systematic assessment of this failure. Like many other managerial innovations that have arrived over the years with so much promise, it just disappeared. In my view, the approach failed because the hurdles were set too high. Rather than dealing with the basic capacity, they assessed the readiness of government agencies for self-management in terms of seven sets of advanced practices. More realistic hurdles might have been more effective in inducing managerial improvement.

Perhaps more than any other type, transitional countries have come under the spell of performance – especially the European countries that covet accession to the European Community. Transitional countries have had to rapidly transform their economic and governing institutions while raising public services to internationally acceptable levels. Performance has appealed to these countries as an alternative to the centralised public administration carried over from their socialist past. Focusing on performance enables transitional governments to set reasonably challenging targets for improving public services and operations. Nevertheless, there is considerable risk that these countries will be more successful in ridding themselves of old rules and controls than in promoting a performance ethic in the public service.

In all countries, the difficult part of performance is applying it in the ongoing work of government. The idea is inherently appealing and self-justifying, but getting government to operate on the basis of performance requires major changes in managerial culture, in the interface between politics and administration, in the expectations of civil servants, in the allocation of financial resources, and much more. The performing state is a different species than the nation-states that reigned in the 20th century. Nowhere is it fully implemented, though some countries have made much more progress than others.

2. Pathways to performance

There are many paths to performance, but none is sufficiently well marked to assure success. Some rely on administrative procedure, others on political or professional commitment. Some are grounded in "new public management", others fit comfortably within traditional public administration. It is useful to operationalise performance in sequential terms, arraying various innovations in a logical sequence so that one builds on others. The approach taken in this section emphasises the sequence and conditions under which performance can thrive. It begins with attitudes and moves to managerial actions, and then from management to politics.

All performance has both formal and informal dimensions, but the balance between the two varies with the type of tool used. Internalised norms lie at the informal end of the spectrum, contracts and legal entitlements at the formal end. In the march to performance, governments have increasingly looked to formal remedies, but unless these are underpinned by informal commitment, the forms may prove to be meaningless. One of the shortcomings of the contemporary performance movement is the neglect or undervaluation of the political and normative bases of good government.

Performance also has both managerial and political dimensions. Without political encouragement, managers may have difficulty focusing on what their work is supposed to accomplish; without committed managers, politicians cannot progress in implementing their visions. Because politicians and managers often speak different languages and have variant interests, it is hard to get the interface between them right. When breakdowns in performance occur, the culprit often is confusion or misunderstanding over the respective roles and responsibilities of elected leaders and senior managers. Getting the relationship right is a necessary condition for the performing state.

2.1. Performance as ethic

The performance movement is new, but nation building through effective state programmes is not. The rise of the nation-state in the 19th and 20th centuries was due in substantial part to truly breathtaking governmental accomplishments. The long list of successes includes universal education, pensions and other income supports, amelioration of poverty, construction of efficient transport systems, prudential regulation of business activity, and promotion of science and technology. Because governments in developed countries performed well, life expectancy was extended, urban squalor was diminished, infant mortality plummeted and many contagious diseases were eliminated. How did governments manage to perform well before performance was explicitly on their agenda? Part of the answer has to do with advances in the machinery of government – in particular, the introduction of merit-based civil service systems and modern budget systems. The nation-state came of age along with advances in public administration. But this is not the whole of the answer, and possibly the less important part. Government excelled in nation building because it attracted many of the best and brightest to public service. Careers in government were esteemed, not merely by those whose meagre skills left them with few employment opportunities, but also by graduates of elite schools who saw public service as a calling. The yearning to do good through government work led many public employees to care about performance, even though the word was not yet in vogue and even though results were not formally measured. Truth be told, the public service ethic coexisted with the spoils system in many countries, but in the managerial ranks, the notion of doing good while serving the state often predominated.

A public service ethic is the bedrock of governmental performance which depends at least as much on people as on machinery and process. This view clashes sharply with the principal-agent model popularised by "new institutional economics" (NIE) and imported into the public sector by "new public management" (NPM). NIE and some versions of NPM teach that public employees are self-interested, opportunistic agents, slackers who feather their own nest at the expense of the public interest.[2] In this view, public agents can be made to perform only if they are actively monitored and given clear instructions as to what is expected of them and strong incentives to do the job right. The notion that agents might do more than is formally expected of them because they have internalised public service values may be alien to NIE/NPM, but it is familiar to generations of students who overcame educational handicaps because of teachers who stayed after class to help them, the police officer who coached the community sports team and never asked for pay, the visiting nurse who stopped to see shut-ins after her daily rounds were done, and countless other examples. Of course, this was never the whole story of public employment, or even the larger part, but it was the stuff out of which governments performed and earned the trust of their people, and communities and states were built.

In most developed countries, the ethic of public service still exists, but not as robustly as in the past. It has been eroded by powerful socio-economic forces including the widened gap between public pay and private opportunity, increased reliance on private markets and contractors to provide public services, and decline in the esteem with which public employees are held. When public service is just a job, no special value attaches to having the work performed by government employees. With tasks specified in contracts, it would seem to make little difference whether the work is performed by persons on the government's payroll or by firms which get the contract through competitive tenders. As long as the work process or output can be specified, public service and private employment are interchangeable. The job goes to the better performer, as measured by price or other variables.

Arguably, a public service ethic is most needed when private means are used to provide public goods. In these cases, there is heightened risk that public values will be degraded by firms which live up to the letter of the contract but do no more than what is specifically required of them or cut whatever corners they can get away with. Contemporary governments face a difficult predicament: attrition in the ethic of public service makes outsourcing and competition attractive, but without such an ethic, entrusting the task to private hands may drive out what remains of the value of serving the public. Some countries distinguish between "core" public responsibilities which they do not contract out and "standardised" services which are subject to commercial tender. Regardless of where they draw the line, all governments face a need to rebuild a public service ethic. Doing so entails much more than recruiting and training qualified, committed public employees. Public service will not be valued in government unless it is valued outside.

2.2. Performance as focus

An internalised performance ethic is no longer sufficiently widespread to sustain the public service. External pressure and reinforcement is needed in most situations to keep public agencies and personnel focused on the purpose of work rather than on the procedures they have been programmed to follow. Focus is the bridge between internalised behaviour and external enforcement, and the basis for formal means of enhancing performance. Focus means paying attention to results, keeping them in mind, and using performance as a reference point for contemplating how well one has done or how one should go about future tasks. As insipid as it may appear, focus has the potential to be a powerful tool, for it calls attention to the purposes that underlie ongoing work and organisational routines. When politicians and managers are focused on results, they behave differently than when their attention is taken by process.

True focus is ongoing and sustained, not a once-in-a-while reflection on objectives or missions. The latter is tried often enough, but rarely with lasting results. To make a difference, an organisation must be obsessed with purpose, so that the critical actions it takes in allocating staff and resources, designing and delivering services, assessing results and feeding back the findings to new decisions are all done through the lenses of performance. Having explicit objectives contributes to focus, but is rarely enough. It is not uncommon for organisations to specify objectives but to forget them when critical decisions are made. European Community accession is an excellent contemporary example of focus at work, for the candidate countries took many actions, which might otherwise have been beyond reach, with that end in mind. Focus was reinforced by the recurring visits of European Community officials who repeatedly cautioned that accession would depend on progress in fulfilling the Community's requirements.

Mission statements and vision statements have become popular means of focusing organisations on missions and objectives. Typically, a participatory process is used to draft and refine the statement, and once it is finalised it is prominently displayed in the organisation's offices and publications. There is little basis for expecting these statements to have much impact on the organisation, for once their novelty wears off, they become part of the background clutter that is screened out by employees. They see the statement but rarely reflect on what it means or on its implications for how they carry out their work. These statements begin as a display of public regard and end up as public relations. Focus demands sustained attention; it must be renewed and reinforced. If it is not, work routines will drive it out.

Strategic planning is another popular tool for focusing on organisational missions and purposes. It too is often developed through a participatory process that aims to examine how the entity should transform itself in response to changing circumstances or opportunities. In government, however, these plans tend to be more descriptive than strategic, and serve more to justify expanded budgets and programmes than to re-examine purposes and operations. When confronted with plans that have done little to reposition the organisation, managers often explain that the process by which they were prepared is more important than the document. In other words, the focus attained during formulation of the strategic plan is lost once the agency reverts to business as usual.

Mission statements, strategic plans and numerous other contemporary management innovations that purport to spur organisational change tend to have a short-lived Hawthorne effect. For a time, they energise staff to focus on what they are doing and why, but without reinforcement the effect fades away. In both business and government, this has been the fate of most training programmes, retreats and similar activities. When the message of the retreat clashes with the realities of work, the latter prevails. Maintaining focus has much in common with dieting to lose weight. One has to be obsessive to stay on course. Since most dieters lose focus, the weight-loss industry booms with business from repeat customers; much the same occurs in the quest for government performance, as the failure of one reform begets another.

2.3. Performance as measurement

The effort to focus government on results has given rise to a vast performance-measurement industry. Measurement is the most conspicuous means of orienting government to performance; it is often the first step, and sometimes the only one as well. Measurement is not a new tool, however. It was central to the scientific management movement early in the 20th century and to the emergence of public administration as a discrete field of study and practice. One of the first systematic treatments was by Clarence Ridley and Herbert Simon who, in 1938, proposed specific measures for education, transport, libraries, public works, health and other public responsibilities. Their measurement scheme was based on the notion that "the result of an effort or performance indicates the effect of that effort or performance in accomplishing its objective" (Ridley and Simon, 1938, p. 2). They proposed, for example, that educational performance be measured in terms of truancy and delinquency rates of students and the cultural level of the community.

By contemporary standards, the early measures were unsophisticated. The vast recent literature on performance measurement has undoubtedly added to the methodological stockpile, but it is questionable whether government performance has advanced much as a consequence of having more or better measures. One of the curious features of this literature is the endless arguing over what is an output and what is an outcome, whether a particular measure is an end outcome or an intermediate outcome, and whether goals, objectives and targets mean the same things or are different. Surely there is something amiss when, after decades of work, so many discussions of this subject contain basic definitions, as if words such as inputs and outputs are beyond ordinary comprehension. The interminable arguments over words make it appear that measurement is an end in itself, that measuring performance fulfils its purpose by generating definitions. Perhaps this is why Donald Kettl, a leading American public administration expert, has suggested that "measuring government performance is like the weather. Everybody talks about it ... but there is no consensus on how to do it" (Kettl, quoted in Osborne and Plastrik, 2000, p. 249).

Performance measurement has a problem, but not the one noted by Kettl. The big problem is not in measurement but in application. Much attention has been paid to the former, but not enough to the latter. With some notable exceptions, governments that invest in measuring performance rarely use the results in managing programmes. They do not base civil service salaries on performance, nor do they hold managers accountable for performance or allocate resources on this basis. Efforts to budget on the basis of performance almost always fail, as do reforms that aim to link pay and performance. It is common these days for governments to present performance information in budgets, annual reports and other official documents. But publication is a poor substitute for genuine use.

One of the misconceptions of the performance movement is the notion that organisations are transformed by having information on how well they are doing. This optimism is rarely justified, for organisations – both public and private – have enormous capacity to assimilate or deflect data on results without changing their policies or operations. It requires sustained political and managerial will to reorient an organisation in response to information on what it is doing or hopes to accomplish. In fact, genuine organisational change may be a precondition for effective use of performance information. It is not that information transforms organisations, but that transformed organisations are primed to apply information on their performance.

This lesson emerges from the "Next Steps" initiative in the United Kingdom, which is widely regarded as one of the most successful machinery-of-government reforms of recent decades. Next Steps transformed the government of the United Kingdom by separating service delivery from the policy functions of ministries. Services were entrusted to more than 100 quasi-autonomous agencies, each of which had an operating charter (called a framework document) that spelled out its responsibilities and the manner in which it would be held accountable. Each agency negotiated annual performance targets with its parent ministry, and each reported results against its targets.[3] To the extent that Next Steps succeeded, it was because newly independent agencies and empowered managers were able to apply performance measures in designing and delivering services. Without transformed agencies, performance measures would have had little impact.

As explained in Chapter 7 ("Agencies in Search of Principles"), when the Blair government was formed in 1997, it de-emphasised the Next Steps initiative and gave priority to rebuilding the policy-making and strategic capacity of ministries. In seeking improved performance, Blair adopted a "whole-of-government" perspective that assessed agencies in terms of their contribution to broad social objectives, in contrast to Next Steps which focused on each agency's particular outputs.

It is exceedingly difficult to measure organisational capacity. Not only do multiple variables come into play, but capacity has more to do with future potential than with past performance. The "balanced scorecard" – one of the most widely applied contemporary innovations in performance measurement – has been applied by both business and government to measure this capacity. It is based on the notion that good performance depends on strong organisations. The balanced scorecard considers outputs to be only one of four essential sets of performance measures. The other measures pertain to internal organisation processes, staff morale and quality, and customer needs and satisfaction. The word "balanced" in this system means that organisation and internal processes have parity with outputs and outcomes in measuring performance. As explained by the architects of this approach, the scorecard balances "outcome measures – the results from past efforts – and the measures that drive future performance" (Kaplan and Norton, 1996, p. 10).

Some designers of performance measurement systems regard the balanced scorecard as a retreat from the basic output-outcome orientation. Harry Hatry, the leading American performance measurement expert, is concerned that the balanced scorecard "implies that all these areas are of equal value. But we've been trying to get public officials to focus on outcomes … there's a danger of a return to an over-emphasis on internal process" (Hatry, quoted in Walters, 2000, p. 60). The balanced scorecard may turn out to be just another fad in the never-ending parade of management reforms. But even if it does not have lasting influence, the scorecard drives home the message that organisation matters; results do not just happen. Performance is not manna that falls from heaven to be harvested without organised effort. For government to be effective, its departments and agencies must perform. Public organisations and the people who work in them must be mobilised and motivated, funded and empowered, and able to carry out activities that generate intended results. If organisations fail to perform, government will also fail.

2.4. Performance as management

Getting government organisations to manage for results is the central aim of the performance movement. This is a difficult task, for it requires changes in both the culture of government organisations and the ways they are managed. To perform effectively, organisations must question inherited purposes and objectives, redefine what they are and how they operate, discard embedded habits and routines, and redistribute authority and responsibility among managers and between them and political leaders. These are much harder tasks than those promised by popularisers of NPM in best-selling books with upbeat titles such as *Reinventing Government* and *Banishing Bureaucracy* (Osborne and Gaebler, 1992; Osborne and Plastrik, 1997). NPM is only a small part of the performance movement, albeit an influential one; but it would be a mistake to conclude that countries that are still tethered to traditional modes of public administration are uninterested in results and have not acted to modernise public services. Performance is not the exclusive property or interest of one movement; it is the Holy Grail of most contemporary public management innovation.

Regardless of the path taken, performing organisations require adjustments both in their operating culture and in managerial capacity. It is necessary to "let managers manage" by giving them appropriate operating discretion. But liberated managers cannot be expected to behave much differently if the organisations they lead are hostage to a mindset that blocks them from changing the way they operate.

Performance depends on organisation – that is, the combination of human, financial and other resources to produce a collective result. Yet if organisation is the enabler of performance, it often is an inhibitor as well, for it values internal needs and norms above outside demands and conditions. This tendency occurs in business when firms disappear because they are unwilling to adjust to changes in market conditions, and in government when civil servants remain wedded to old missions even though newer ones are more pressing. Organisations have a culture, a "shared system of beliefs, mores, values, attitudes, practices, roles, artefacts, symbols and language. It represents a group's collective wisdom and aspiration … [and] guides how a group solves problems, how they approach mundane tasks … Culture is reflected in the structure of social relationships – within and outside the group – and defines obligations and rights among a group of people who possess a common identity" (Ewing Marion Kauffman Foundation, 2002, p. 51). Culture-bound government agencies have a distinctive personality and characteristic ways of operating that are passed on from one generation of employees to the next. They have a self-image – a shared sense of their fundamental mission or purpose, the things they do, how they respond to outside demands or resolve internal conflicts – that is not easily uprooted by changing circumstances. They may want to perform better but, trapped in their cultural warp, they may not know how. Change is too high a price to pay. Countless firms disappear because they are unwilling to transform themselves; government agencies have a much lower mortality rate, but not necessarily better performance.

Hundreds of books are published each year advising firms and governments on how to lead and transform organisations. But despite the surfeit of advice, governments have a limited array of tools for getting culture-bound organisations to perform. One is to reorganise existing entities; another is to create new ones. Reorganisation was once a favoured gambit; it no longer is because the cost of reshuffling the organisational chart is high and the gains are uncertain.[4] Creating new agencies is expedient when government is expanding and adding employees, but not when austerity is the order of the day. Some tools mentioned earlier may spur organisations to adjust objectives or operations. These include strategic planning and performance measurement and reports. Organisations committed to self-transformation may change their leadership, retrain staff, cultivate support from interest groups and politicians, and take other steps that evade or weaken roadblocks to change.

NPM aims to transform government organisations. It is predicated on the argument that traditional means of regenerating organisations are inadequate. It favours "shock therapy", stripping away operations and service delivery from integrated departments and entrusting them to free-standing agencies that have broad operating freedom, and privatising government activities or introducing market-type arrangements within governments such as competition, prices and internal contracts. In some countries, NPM has gone even further, empowering the recipients of public services to select their providers. These moves have often generated more controversy than change, for in most countries the provision of public goods through private markets is still rare. The public service ethic may have waned, but the presumption that public services should be delivered by public employees persists.

The second pathway to organising for performance is to enlarge managerial capacity and discretion. In organisations, compliance is usually the enemy of performance. To the extent that managers define their responsibilities and accomplishments in terms of following prescribed rules and procedures, their attentiveness to results diminishes. Alternatively, if they are driven to perform and define their work and that of their organisations in terms of outputs or outcomes, they may seek to evade or outwit rules which get in the way of results. Of course, well-functioning organisations must have rules and should produce results. But it is the accretion of rules and procedures over time that penalises performance, and it is the compliance mindset engendered by excessively restrictive rules and procedures that the performance movement aims to counter.

Boosting performance thus requires fewer controls and less emphasis on compliance. Governments that are committed to performance within the framework of traditional public administration generally have sought to reduce compliance costs by stripping away redundant or outmoded rules and procedures. NPM-oriented governments have gone much further, removing virtually all restrictions on managerial discretion, dismantling established command-and-control systems and the agencies that run them, and putting managers on notice that they will be held accountable for results. NPM advocates believe that weeding out some controls does not suffice, because new controls grow up in their place, and that managers cannot be truly wedded to performance as long as they are tethered to procedural requirements.

NPM is conflicted, however, on the behaviour of public managers. On the one hand, it liberates managers on the expectation that, once free to exercise discretion, they will apply their experience and knowledge to bolster organisational performance. On the other hand, NPM tends to view managers as opportunistic agents who exploit inherent asymmetries in information – they know more about what they are doing and accomplishing than their bosses do – to put self-interest above the public interest. The principal-agent problem is not window dressing for NPM; it underlies the critical NPM argument that it is hopeless to try to improve public performance by restoring a public service ethic. In dealing with the principal-agent predicament, NPM has branched in two directions. One is "managerialism" – relying on the verve and initiative of managers, plus a large dose of accountability, to get them to perform; the other is "marketisation" through privatisation, competition, customer choice, internal markets, pricing schemes and other market-like arrangements.[5] NPM countries typically blend the two together, but managerialism remains the dominant form.

Even in NPM countries, managerialism is an unfinished reform. Much more progress has been made in freeing up managers than in enforcing accountability for results. It is rare for governments to base pay on performance or to fire managers for failing to reach performance targets. Few governments have performance budgets that link allocations to expected or achieved results, and few systematically give feedback on performance to policy makers. Though performance auditing has made some headway, it is much less developed than conventional financial auditing.

There is little doubt that organisations perform better when attention is paid to performance. Effective leadership also adds to an organisation's performance, as do systems for measuring and reporting on results. Successful organisations learn and adapt, changing what they do and how they work in response to both internal and external signals. But performance is only one of the drivers of change, and not always the most important one.

2.5. Performance as contract

The fundamental difficulty of transforming government organisations into performing units has induced some countries to devise stronger measures for assuring that promised results are achieved. In the market sector, contracts – and the powers, rights and obligations conferred by them – are essential institutions for holding parties to voluntary transactions accountable for performance. Accountability is enforced through a web of actions and relationships involving: the negotiation and implementation of agreements requiring specific performance by each party; monitoring compliance through oversight, reports and audits; and recourse for failure to perform. Although formal contracts are incomplete – for they cannot specify all relevant terms and conditions or anticipate all the circumstances and issues which may arise during implementation – they are a vital means of communicating expectations and getting results. Without formal contracts, the business sector would be significantly smaller and poorer, with less-developed economic institutions and fewer transactions.

Governments make extensive use of contracts in purchasing goods and services from outside suppliers, but internal performance contracts within government are still rare – though a few countries (most notably New Zealand) rely on contracts to define relations and obligations of ministers and managers. Internal contracts, like those with outside parties, typically specify the resources to be provided and the goods or services to be produced. For example, New Zealand uses performance agreements to specify the key results to be produced by chief executives and purchase agreements between ministers and chief executives to specify the outputs that departments are to provide.

In contrast to formal performance contracts, informal contracts based on expectations and relationships are quite common. An implicit contract exists when the parties to a relationship know what to expect from one another, even though their mutual obligations have not been formally specified. Government budgets are blends of formal and informal contracts – formal because they legally limit the amounts and purposes of expenditure, implicit because much of what will be done with the money is unstated. Although he was referring to practice in the United States, Aaron Wildavsky's description of the budget as a contract can be applied, with appropriate changes in terminology, to virtually all national governments: "Congress and the President promise to supply funds under specified conditions, and the agencies agree to spend them in ways that have been agreed upon … [The budget] imposes a set of mutual obligations and controls upon the contracting parties. The word 'mutual' should be stressed because it is easy to assume that control is exercised in a unilateral direction by superiors … A budget thus becomes a web of social as well as legal relationships in which commitments are made by all the parties, and where sanctions may be invoked (though not necessarily) equally by all" (Wildavsky, 1964, p. 2).

Yet the budget is not a full-fledged contract, for it carries out other functions in addition to expressing agreements on public funds. It is a political appeal to voters, a statement of government ambitions, a guide to economic policy, a basis for organising the work and activities of government agencies, a process for extending past decisions and understandings into the future, a means of financing agencies and activities. Wildavsky concludes "that the purposes of budgets are as varied as the purposes of men … Nothing is gained, therefore, by insisting that it is only one of those things when it may be all of them or many other things as well" (Wildavsky, 1964, p. 4). By being more than a contract, the budget becomes less of a contract. Its commitments carry weight, but not always or everywhere to the same degree.

Contract-like characteristics pertain to other internal government processes as well. Like the budget, the civil service system is an amalgam of formal requirements and informal understandings. The formal elements specify the manner in which public employees are to be recruited, promoted, reviewed, paid, and so on; the informal elements define how people actually get jobs and the work they actually do. In the drive to performance, governments have to rebalance these processes so as to give greater prominence to formal elements. Thus, a true pay-for-performance system bases remuneration on the extent to which *ex ante* targets are met or exceeded, or on the comparative outputs of workers. A true performance-based budgeting system would explicitly link increments in resources to increments in results.

There are few technical impediments to formal contracts such as these. The fact that they are rarely applied in government indicates that there are behavioural barriers to contracting for performance. A full account of these impediments would be too far-reaching, but it should be possible to identify those that bear most directly on the efficacy of contracts as an instrument for enhancing performance.

Contracts narrow accountability to the matters expressly agreed to, in contrast to a normative sense of responsibility for serving the public. When contracts are used to formalise responsibilities and relationships, the specified items often become a checklist that informs the performing party of what it must do to fulfil its obligations. But just as a party to a private agreement is not bound to perform tasks not specified in the agreement, a party to an internal government contract cannot be called to account for failing to provide unspecified services. Managing by contract thus leads to managing by checklist, as managers take care to assure that itemised tasks are completed. One of the arguments against outsourcing government responsibilities is that, in contrast to public employees who have a broad range of unspecified responsibilities to serve the public, private suppliers are bound only by the terms of the contract.

Contracts bias management to emphasise outputs rather than outcomes. The former can be specified in contracts because they are within the control of those providing services; the latter cannot be specified because they often lie beyond the effective control of service providers. New Zealand's contractual model expressly holds managers accountable for outputs, but despite the lip service given to outcomes, the impacts of government policy are often slighted (see Schick, 1996). Governments that define performance in terms of social outcomes tend to eschew the use of contracts in the public sector.

Contracts between politicians (such as ministers) and managers are intended to strengthen political leaders so that managers perform according to their dictates. But contracts within government rarely have the same effect as those between private parties. For one thing, within government, politicians and managers rarely have an arm's-length relationship; for another, politicians often have little or no effective recourse when managers fail to perform. New Zealand's purchase agreements which specify the services to be purchased by ministers from departments typically have been drawn up by the chief executives and agreed by the minister who makes only minor changes. More importantly, politicians often have to turn the other cheek if managers fail to perform according to expectations. They cannot close down the department of education or sack thousands of teachers. In some cases, they are pressured to reward poor performance by increasing the resources provided.

> During the past decade, New Zealand has sought to shift public management from an output basis to an outcome basis. In lieu of purchase agreements, entities now prepare "statements of intent" that set out objectives for the year ahead or beyond and indicate how available resources will be deployed. Whereas purchase agreements spelled out the services that entities would supply to ministers, statements of intent establish expectations with regard to performance.

Clearly, contracts within government are not real contracts. Nevertheless, these formal agreements may enhance performance by spurring the parties to the contract to focus on results. In fact, when this writer questioned senior managers in New Zealand and other countries, almost all referred to the relationships facilitated by the contract rather than to its formal terms. In other words, despite their formality, agreements within government are actually relational contracts. In contrast to formal contracts, which are discrete agreements bounded by fixed terms, relational contracts are ongoing; they extend as long as the parties to the relationship continue to interact. These contracts derive their force from the incentives of the parties to behave in a co-operative, trustworthy manner because they are interdependent. Ministers need managers to produce public services; managers need ministers to get them resources and political support. Writing and implementing a formal contract may strengthen rather than displace this relationship by giving the two sides periodic opportunities to discuss progress and problems. Managers gain access to ministers; ministers gain opportunity to obtain better information on results. When the relationship works well, the parties may review progress under the contract, but they certainly may discuss other matters affecting the relationship as well. They are not confined to the matters formally specified in the agreement.

Thinking about contracts in relational terms has certain advantages as well as drawbacks. The gains include compensating for the incompleteness of formal contracts, establishing expectations and obligations that are recognised by the parties to the relationship even though they may not be recognised in law, building trust and co-operation among persons whose interests are interdependent and who must work with one another on a continuing basis, and achieving lower transaction costs. But widespread reliance on relational rather than formal aspects of contracts may have serious drawbacks. To the extent that the parties to the contract are not at arm's-length, they have weaker capacity to enforce its terms. A cosy relationship may encourage collusion and log-rolling at the expense of the public interest; and by making contracts and transactions less transparent, the door may be opened to corruption. In low-income countries, informality impedes development by making it difficult to mobilise and efficiently use capital. The formalisation of contracts has undoubtedly been one of the critical enablers of development in western countries. Yet even in these countries, performance under formal contracts often depends on the quality of the relationship.

2.6. Performance as right

If legal form does not suffice to assure good performance, the ultimate remedy may be to define public goods and services as rights to which eligible beneficiaries are entitled, and to provide for administrative or judicial recourse when government fails to perform. Actually, performance as a right is quite advanced in the developed world and, in the form of entitlements, underpins much of the welfare state. Social security, health care, unemployment benefits and numerous other entitlements give eligible persons a right to payment from the government. Because these payments are defined as rights, the government has little or no discretion and must provide them regardless of its financial condition or other claims on its budget. In the future, performance as a right will spread beyond payments to services. In the same way that citizens are entitled to pensions and unemployment aid, in the performing state they will be entitled to schools that educate all children, transport that is safe and accessible, civil servants who promptly and courteously process public business, and other services. This rights development is under way in the most advanced democracies; it is likely to spread in the decades ahead. When the right to good service is universalised, the performing state will be a reality – provided, of course, that the state survives as the provider of public services and guarantor of rights.

Services as rights will not happen at once; they will initially be defined in sectors which directly involve citizens, such as education and health care, and will spread over time to other areas. At first, the rights may be poorly defined, with insufficient specification of the quantitative and qualitative dimensions of performance. But under pressure from interest groups, NGOs, the courts and others, the rights will be more precisely specified. In most cases, making service rights more precise will expand their scope, so that the net effect will be to enlarge the responsibilities of government. Many of the early service rights will be symbolic and lack effective redress. They will be rights without remedies, but these will set the stage for enforceable rights, including compensation for sub-services or the opportunity to obtain services from alternative providers.

The "performance as rights" movement will branch off in two directions corresponding to the divergent paths taken in "new public management". One will be to define rights as entitlements of citizenship; the other will be to vest power in customers. The first sees performance through the work of public organisations, the latter through market competition. The two versions will coexist, but the balance between them will vary significantly among countries. Within the same country, certain services will flow through the public sector while others will be purchased through market-type transactions. It is not an exaggeration to say that much of the future character of the nation-state will depend on how the clash between the two models of service rights is resolved. The future state will look and perform differently if its people are treated as customers rather than as citizens.

Forerunners of both the citizen and customer models have emerged in some advanced countries. Citizen's charters express the rights of citizens to satisfactory public services; contracting out and vouchers manifest reliance on markets for public services. The Citizen's Charter was pioneered in the United Kingdom more than a decade ago and has been partly imitated in a number of countries since then. Although there is reason to suspect that the Citizen's Charter was launched as a political stunt, it rapidly matured into a legitimate effort to spur improvement in public services. The typical Citizen's Charter has three basic elements: service targets, such as the timeliness of public transport; recognition of superior services through awards and other means; and compensation when services are below a certain standard. This process has obvious appeal to governments that want to demonstrate fidelity to performance; over time, however, the Citizen's Charter is likely to become another set of procedures that has little impact on performance.

In the end, the effectiveness of statements ascribing rights to citizens depends on the role of the courts. It is probable that defining services as rights of citizenship will lead to greater judicial involvement in setting service standards, measuring results and allocating public resources. One should not be surprised if courts prescribe minimum service levels, eligibility rules and corrective action. The portion of national budgets that is effectively controlled by current political decisions is small in most developed countries; it will shrink further as performance is defined as a right. One can foresee future budget battles over whether particular services should be designated as rights and over the measures that should be used in assessing public services.

The alternative path would turn citizens into customers by empowering them to select the providers of the services they receive. One option would be for government to distribute vouchers that enable recipients to purchase services from approved providers; another would be for government to allow private vendors to compete in providing public services. Once a government decides that it will not be the exclusive provider of public services or that citizens are entitled to choose the services they want, it has an enormous range of possibilities in designing and delivering services. Some of these will be discussed in the next section, which argues that the special role of government is undermined by the strong pursuit of performance.

Favouring markets over government implies that citizens are in a weaker position than customers to demand good performance. One reason is that political democracy gives citizens a limited, usually indirect, voice through the ballot box. They may vote "yes" or "no" on each candidate or each issue, but they lack opportunity to express views on particular services or to demand improvements. Once elected, political leaders sift through the cacophony of citizen demands and balance them against pressures from interest groups, public bureaucracies and other political functionaries. A government rarely gives citizens better housing or more accessible health care merely because they voted it into power, and certainly does not change the way services are delivered because of election results. In contrast, the connection between customer and supplier is much more direct, even when the supplier is a government entity. What turns citizens into customers is their capacity to choose suppliers. This characteristic empowers them in ways that citizenship cannot.

This is not the place for considering the full ramifications of transforming citizens into customers, but it should be noted that the contemporary disengagement of citizens in many democratic countries from political activity – whether because the benefits received from government are taken for granted or because the benefits are inadequate or undervalued – feeds into this transformation. The decline of the nation-state begins here – with transforming citizens into customers. Clearly, this step is not lightly taken, and most democratic regimes have not yet advanced significantly down this path. But if performance persists as the driver of public policy and the measure of public services, it is likely that additional steps will be taken in this direction in the decades ahead. And if they are, basic roles and attributes of the nation-state may be called into question.

One likely consequence of the financial crisis that spread across continents in 2008 is to diminish the ardour of governments for market-type financing and provision of public services. With governments taking the lead role to revitalise national economies, the notion of turning citizens into customers will lose appeal. It remains to be seen, however, whether the vital role of governments in stimulating economic activity and providing a financial safety net will restore trust and confidence in political leaders and institutions.

3. Governance: governing without (national) government

The previous section argued that the drive for performance has impelled governments to devise ever-stronger means of assuring good service. At one time, a strong public service ethic was deemed sufficient, then means of maintaining a performance focus were added, followed by an array of measurement tools, management changes, contractual obligations and legal rights. Each device was found somewhat wanting, leading to the next step in the chain of performance, with the possible exception of the last one which confers on citizens a legally enforceable right to good service. Anything that gets in the way of the effective exercise of these rights is suspect, even if it is government itself. In effect, government conveys rights, but if it cannot live up to its promises, other institutions may take its place.

The nation-state played a critical role in the rise of political democracy and markets. The world would be poorer and less democratic, and individuals would have less freedom and fewer public services, if the nation-state had not flourished during the past century. It is not happenstance that the nation-state grew in size and prominence at the same time that markets boomed and individuals gained in affluence and personal liberty. But like other hoary institutions, the nation-state is fraying at the edges, and the demand for good performance has focused attention on its real or imagined inadequacies. The bill of particulars against the nation-state *qua* performer is formidable: it is alleged to be too distant from citizens, too uniformist in the design and delivery of public services, encumbered by rigid, aloof bureaucracies and by cumbersome, performance-draining procedures, insensitive to the diverse needs and interests of citizens, more beholden to compliance and control than to performance and results, more responsive to the powerful and affluent who have less need for their services than to the poor and weak who are utterly dependent on the state, and unable to cope with global forces that spill beyond national boundaries. These allegations notwithstanding, the nation-state has not withered away, nor will it in the decades immediately ahead. It still is the main financial engine and rule maker for public services.

Nevertheless, the demand for performance is nibbling at the special status of the state. Fiscal and programme decentralisation have transferred resources and authority from the centre to local governments; free-standing agencies have gained operational autonomy from the state to which they are nominally subservient; global institutions have made inroads in some of the most vital functions of the state, including criminal justice, national defence and economic policy; and NGOs have become purveyors of public services and often have quasi-governmental status at international fora. Finally, as already discussed, markets are increasingly used to provide public services.

These alternatives are encompassed in the word "governance" which has supplanted "government" in many discussions of political institutions and public policy. While some see governance merely as a broader term, others view it as a substitute for the nation-state. Governance connotes that tinkering with the machinery of government through civil service reform, budget practices and administrative reorganisation – the stuff of public management during the past century – does not offer sufficient improvement in performance. The alternatives legitimised by the governance label imply that the trappings of political democracy do not suffice; having free, contested elections does not assure good public services. What is needed instead is a redistribution of political power. Every alternative to the nation-state takes power from some and gives it to others.

The case against the nation-state as a performer rests on two distinct grounds: one is managerial, the other political. The former leads to new means of service delivery, the latter to new arrangements of political power. Every alternative to the state presents a "democracy deficit", a euphemism invented by proponents of new forms of governance to camouflage serious political deficiencies. For the new governance crowd, sacrificing a little (or maybe a lot) of political democracy on the altar of performance is a reasonable price for getting the results they want.

This posture is evident in the push for new global institutions. International organisations have become self-appointed legitimisers of new forms of governance that lack the most basic elements of political democracy. These organisations have been justified on the ground that there exist "international public goods" that countries cannot adequately supply because of their geographical limits. Such public goods are most apparent in environmental policy, for the quality of air and other ecological values do not respect national boundaries. Environmental protection is only one of the public goods that have been internationalised. Maintaining peaceful relations among countries and prosecuting persons accused of crimes against humanity are well on the way to becoming international public goods. Economic stabilisation and income redistribution remain critical national responsibilities, but it is not much of a stretch to accept the argument that the world would be a better place if economic policies were co-ordinated and income disparities among countries were reduced. These examples suggest that the internationalisation of public goods is still in its infancy. Deep inroads in the functions of the nation-state are likely to emerge in this century.

At the same time as being pressured to cede policy responsibility to international authorities, the nation-state has faced demands to localise public services by entrusting operational control to municipal or regional governments. The case for decentralisation rests principally on the argument that national governments are too distant and too wedded to "one size fits all" management to accommodate variations in local needs and preferences. The traditional means of bringing government services to the people – for example, regional and field offices – do not go far enough because these entities lack political and managerial independence. They are arms of the national government and do not answer to local authorities. To make a genuine difference, the decentralisation argument runs, it is necessary to transfer services – particularly in vital sectors such as health and education – to local governments, along with the money to pay for them. The state may continue to play a role in prescribing basic or minimum requirements, but operational details, including the manner in which services are delivered, should be decided locally.

Fiscal and service decentralisation usually widen the democracy deficit. In most countries, voter turnout is lower in local elections than in national ones, government activity is less transparent, and the risk of corruption is higher. However, these deficiencies are often brushed aside by the claim that services improve when responsibility is localised. Decentralisation is part of a broader strategy to divest national governments of direct responsibility for delivering services. The main roots of this strategy can be traced to an influential article ("The Sickness of Government") by management guru Peter Drucker a generation ago. Arguing that national governments are inherently inept providers of services, Drucker urged that they should focus on policy rather than services – they should steer and leave the rowing to others (Drucker, 1978, p. 233). The notion that steering should be separated from rowing has led not only to decentralisation but also to the creation of autonomous agencies responsible for providing public services. Although agencification has not made as much headway as decentralisation, it too leads to the hollowing out of the state.

Can a state efficiently steer, but not row? What leverage does it have when the rowers – local governments or autonomous agencies – want to go in a different direction? Perhaps not enough, for once they have operational independence and resources, local governments and agencies have political weapons of their own to blunt pressure from the national government. They certainly are not passive, compliant implementors of the national will. Shorn of operational control, the state may become the tax collector that pays for services provided by others but has little say in how they perform. This is not a politically attractive position, but it may be the one that characterises the future nation-state.

Decentralisation and agencification keep public services within the ambit of government, but there are those who argue that performance will not improve unless there is genuine competition and unless recipients have choice in selecting their providers. As long as government has a monopoly, the argument runs, it has weak incentives to respond to the differentiated wants of citizens. The claim that the state is an uncaring, inefficient provider is strongest in poor countries where government is often absent or corrupt. In some poor countries, international organisations and others have disinvested in the nation-state by channelling resources to NGOs – organisations whose self-proclaimed legitimacy does not depend on adherence to the tenets of political democracy. NGOs are a mixed bag, and many do not have significant service responsibilities. But those that do often combine services with lobbying and various quasi-governmental responsibilities. NGO is a strange appellation: it indicates what these entities are not, but does not say what they are. It conveys a powerful anti-state message. As varied as they may be, NGOs have one common, overriding characteristic: they are not governments. They are alternatives to the state because, in the eyes of the proponents of this new form, the state has failed.

Most NGOs violate basic principles of political democracy. They are self-appointed, not elected; they claim to represent the people, but the people do not pick them. They usually are not accountable to anyone else, with the exception (in some cases) of their funders; they sit alongside elected government leaders at international fora, but are not governments; they have few of the checks and balances that characterise most democracies, but instead often combine lobbying, policy-making and service-delivery functions. Yet NGOs are justified on the grounds that governments elected to serve the people do not serve them well. Governments do not perform. And in a world where performance matters, this is justification enough for legitimising NGOs.

While they disown the state, NGOs have a strong interest in public policy, defined as policy that affects society. This distinguishes them from markets, another non-governmental challenger to the nation-state. As private mechanisms for providing public goods, markets differ from NGOs in that choice resides with consumers rather than leaders. On this ground, therefore, markets come closer to fulfilling democratic requirements than NGOs. Markets, however, have other characteristics that may impair their capacity to fairly provide public services. They deny services to those unwilling or unable to pay the going price. To ease this problem, countries that rely on markets typically provide financial assistance such as vouchers to low-income persons and require private vendors to serve all eligible customers.

In one sense, markets are the most radical alternative to the state, for they take the provision of public services out of public hands. But in another sense, they are far less radical, for they have long coexisted with government in providing social goods. The new instruments – global institutions and NGOs – have entered a world long dominated by big government and big markets. Like for government, the language and methodology of performance is familiar to markets, though the latter typically define performance more narrowly than public institutions do. Global institutions and NGOs, however, have generally thrived on promises and potentials, and they have not been put under the microscope of performance as intensely as governments and markets. But as global institutions and NGOs grow in prominence, they too will be reviewed and challenged in terms of the results they produce.

4. The performing state: from idea to practice

Where do the inroads made by local authorities, autonomous agencies, global institutions, NGOs and markets leave the state? To stress what was said at the outset, the state still is the provider or financier of most public services. The state has not withered away, nor is it likely to do so in the foreseeable future. Yet the disinvestments in the state should not be ignored – certainly not the erosion in public support and trust. But, as argued early in this article, the nation-state may find that better performance does not absolve it of the charge that it is an inadequate performer, either because expectations rise faster than results or because results are rarely good enough. One failure of the state can outweigh hundreds or even thousands of successes. The fate of the contemporary state is to fail even when it performs.

Of course, this generalisation does not apply to all countries. It fits the best-managed countries best, and poor countries hardly at all. In between are the many states that do a reasonable job of serving the public but can (and should) do much better. Some of these countries may be abetted by the performance-enhancing instruments discussed earlier, such as measurement, management and contracts. But there is considerable risk that these devices will be introduced as substitutes for performance, as ends in themselves rather than as means of revitalising or re-engineering public service. In many countries, management reform has been a substitute for genuine reform of management. This has been especially true with respect to performance measurement. At the end of the day, improving performance is essentially a matter of getting organisations and the people who work in them to behave differently. Caring about results, as part of a public-regarding ethic or imposed changes which impel politicians and managers to focus on what they are accomplishing and how well they are serving the public, remains a necessary element of a true striving to perform.

It is in poor countries where the call for performance is most urgent that the case for alternatives to the state is most persuasive. Decades of development work have had little impact on states mired in corruption and inefficiency. Good intentions have gone awry, and waves of managerial and government reforms have yielded a meagre harvest. These are countries in which the gulf between the idea of performance and the practice is so wide and the outlook so hopeless that it is necessary to design new modes of governance based on the alternatives discussed in the preceding section. Transitional countries face a different prospect. Their need is to rebuild the nation-state on the foundations of political democracy and markets. Most already have a performing state, albeit not as effective or efficient as it can be. They should be wary of alternatives to the state. The same generalisation fits emerging market countries, which have strong states but inadequate political accountability. They, too, should rehabilitate the state and not unduly rely on substitutes.

It is characteristic of reform movements that they sweep aside differences in the conditions of countries. If a few countries claim success with agencies or decentralisation, others climb onto the bandwagon or are pushed on board. This reformist zeal leads to much imitation and little replication, as countries mindlessly turn good ideas introduced elsewhere into technical exercises. In the march to performance, every country must be mindful of where it is now; if it is not, it will not reach the promised land of performance.

5. Getting the budget to perform

Government cannot perform if its budget does not. No matter how determined government is to orient management and service delivery to results, if budget allocations disregard performance, politicians and managers will too. But getting the budget to be an instrument of performance has proven exceedingly difficult to implement. The history of budget reform is laden with many failures and few successes. Yet it is also true that budgeting can contribute to performance even when the government lacks a formal performance budget. This concluding section explores why performance budgeting is an elusive goal and what can be done within the framework of conventional budgeting to bolster government's commitment to results.

Budgeting combines several of the performance-enhancing characteristics discussed in Section 2. First, it brings extraordinary focus to government, marshalling managerial and political resources to produce an annual statement of revenue and expenditure. There are few things that government does that are so focused, and certainly few that recur each year. Although evidence is lacking, participants in the budget dialogue inevitably touch on matters of performance when they negotiate spending levels: how well programmes are working, what can be done to improve them, is government getting value for money, and so on.

Second, budgeting is ready-made for robust use of measurement. The quantitative character of budgeting makes it an ideal instrument for linking the amounts spent with the results produced. Yet few governments link money and results quite this way, which is one reason why performance budgeting lacks success.

Third, budgeting is a critical element of public management. No public organisation can operate without money, and control of the money would seem to be an expedient means of driving it to perform. But, to anticipate one of the arguments made later in this section, the connection between performance budgeting and management may be the reverse of what reformers have expected. Rather than the budget leveraging and defining management, it is management that sets the conditions under which budgets are made and implemented. If managerial conditions discourage performance, the budget will not be oriented to performance. One important implication of this hypothesis is that it is futile to reform budgeting without first reforming the overall managerial framework.

Fourth, a budget can be conceived of as a contract, both in the sense that it stipulates the resources that will be made available and the activities to be carried out and also in the sense that it links politicians and managers in an understanding of how organisations are run and what they do. Performance budgeting can be thought of as an effort to formalise these contracts by explicitly stating the results that will be produced. But budgeting may be an example of relationships in which informal contracts are superior to formal ones, at least to the extent that the latter are difficult to negotiate and enforce.

Finally, budgeting operationalises the concept of performance as a right by entitling citizens to certain payments from government. Performance budgeting seeks to extend the reach of entitlements to services as well – that is, to vest citizens with a right to accessible, high-quality services. This is performance budgeting's most difficult challenge, for it goes to the core of what it means to be a performing state. In a performing state, performance budgeting will be assured and superfluous. It will be assured because government will be driven to perform, and it will be unnecessary because government will perform even if the budget is not formally structured to do so.

Performance budgeting is an old idea with a disappointing past and an uncertain future. Its American debut took place in 1949 when the Hoover Commission on the Organisation of the Executive Branch of the Government recommended that "the whole budgetary concept of the federal government should be refashioned by the adoption of a budget based upon functions, activities, and projects; this we designate a 'performance budget'" (Commission *Report*, p. 8). The fact that this concept re-emerged half a century later (but relabelled by some as performance-based budgeting) suggests the lack of progress in the intervening years. Despite repeated efforts, the budgets of almost all countries are centred around inputs – the items that go into running government organisations, such as personnel, supplies, travel and accommodation. These line items dominate budgetary discourse; they are rarely purged by performance budgeting. When performance budgeting was launched in the United States, a prominent scholar wrote that its simplicity is a delusion. "In fact, it is extremely difficult budgeting … it is easier to budget and control funds simply on the basis of organisation and object. For the performance budget does not replace these; it is in addition to them. Accounts still have to be kept, payments still have to be made, and accountability still must be maintained in terms of organisation and object" (Mosher, 1954, p. 81). In other words, when a manager has to choose between alternative budget formats – one that provides information on the amounts needed to cover the wages of employees and other expenses, the other providing information on the cost of producing goods and services – the former is likely to be preferred.

Performance budgeting is complex in yet another way: it comes in numerous varieties. Just about every government that puts information in its budget regarding workload, activities or services claims to have a performance budget. To clarify what the term means, it may be useful to distinguish two polar versions of performance budgeting, a broad definition that accommodates virtually any application and a strict definition that is limited to budgets that meet certain criteria. Broadly defined, a performance budget is any budget that presents information on what agencies have done or expect to do with the money provided to them. Strictly defined, a performance budget is only a budget that explicitly links each increment in resources to an increment in outputs or other results. The broad concept views budgeting in presentational terms; the strict version views it in terms of allocations. Many governments satisfy the broad definition; few satisfy the strict definition.

The difference between the two approaches goes to the heart of the performing state. Supplementing the usual budget schedules with information on activities cannot inspire government to take performance seriously; allocating money on the basis of the volume of goods and services delivered has a chance. But for this version of performance budgeting to work, it must be supported by cost measurement that enables government to link increments in resources to increments in results. Few governments have this capability. Cost accounting is a prerequisite for this version of performance budgeting, and few governments have invested in it because they have little incentive to do so. In contrast to business, they do not have to recover costs and they rarely charge for services on the basis of the volume supplied. Moreover, government budgets are fixed; the amount allocated does not vary with the volume. Agencies do not typically obtain more money during the year if volume rises above budgeted levels, nor do they have to return money if volume falls below. Most firms by contrast have variable budgets in which the resources available vary with the volume produced.

> Perhaps because of its fixation on results, performance budgeting has neglected the cost side of the ledger. To develop a true performance budget system, it is necessary to distinguish between fixed and variable costs, as well as between average and marginal costs. Doing so requires governments to have reliable cost allocation systems that attribute costs to the activities that incur them. Budgeting on the accrual basis is not a precondition for performance budgeting, but allocating overhead and indirect costs is.

If performance budgeting is so difficult, is the performing state beyond reach? Not necessarily, for it is erroneous to assume that governments which have conventional input-based budgets ignore performance. Some do care about results and strive to allocate resources on the basis of actual or expected performance. Nevertheless, performance is not the only consideration, nor often the most influential one. Whether they have a results-focused or an input-based budget, governments are impelled to take account of political pressures and past commitments in deciding how to spend public funds. Performance has a seat at the budget table, but it must interact with those who have different orientations.

How much influence performance has depends on who else is at the table – that is, the orientation of the politicians and managers who make the budget. As mentioned earlier, performance budgeting can thrive only when it is embedded in managerial arrangements that make results paramount. This writer is not aware of a single sustained implementation of performance budgeting that was not accompanied and reinforced by transformations in public management that enhanced performance. Governments that do not manage for results do not budget for results, even if they install the outward trappings in performance budgeting. The same interdependence pertains to all major budget innovations, not only those that deal with performance. Budgeting cannot be significantly changed in isolation from the management context in which it operates. This linkage makes budget reform harder and easier – harder because the reform agenda must be broadened to encompass public management, easier because performance budgeting can be successfully implemented when management drives for results.

Performance budgeting has a prominent niche in the performing state, perhaps more as the end result of being attuned to performance than as the enabler of performance. This entails a sort of Copernican revolution in budgeting. Rather than being the locomotive that drives government to change, performance budgeting is the caboose that confirms the transformations that have been made. To achieve true reform, it may be better to follow the parade than to lead it.

Notes

1. Managerial reform in Australia, France, New Zealand, Sweden and the United Kingdom is discussed in OECD (1997).

2. This view of public service was expressed in New Zealand Treasury (1987). This brief prepared by the Treasury for the newly elected government exerted a strong influence on subsequent reform of the public sector in New Zealand.

3. A favourable assessment of the Next Steps initiative is presented in Osborne and Plastrik, 1997.

4. There are exceptions to this generalisation. In the late 1980s, Australia consolidated its departments into large "portfolio ministries", and in 2002, the United States consolidated various units which had previously been in separate departments into a new homeland security department.

5. See B. Guy Peters (2001) for a discussion of these and alternative models of governance.

References

Commission on the Organisation of the Executive Branch of the Government (1949), *Report*, Government Printing Office, Washington DC.

Drucker, Peter F. (1978), *The Age of Discontinuity*, Harper Torchbooks, New York, United States.

Ewing Marion Kauffman Foundation (2002), *Set For Success*, The Ewing Marion Kauffman Foundation, Kansas City, Missouri, United States.

Kaplan, Robert and David Norton (1996), *The Balanced Scorecard: Translating Strategy Into Action*, Harvard Business School Press, Boston, Massachusetts, United States.

Mosher, Frederick C. (1954), *Program Budgeting: Theory and Practice*, Public Administration Service, Washington DC.

New Zealand Treasury (1987), *Government Management*, The Treasury, Wellington.

OECD (1997), *Modern Budgeting*, OECD Publications, Paris.

Osborne, David and Ted Gaebler (1992), *Reinventing Government*, Addison-Wesley Publishing Company, New York, United States.

Osborne, David and Peter Plastrik (1997), *Banishing Bureaucracy*, Addison-Wesley Publishing Company, New York, United States.

Osborne, David and Peter Plastrik (2000), *The Reinventor's Fieldbook*, Jossey-Bass, San Francisco, California, United States.

Peters, B. Guy (2001), *The Future of Governing*, University Press of Kansas, Lawrence, Kansas, United States.

Pharr, Susan and Robert D. Putnam (eds.) (2000), *Disaffected Democracies: What's Troubling the Trilateral Countries*, Princeton University Press, Princeton, New Jersey, United States.

Ridley, Clarence E. and Herbert A. Simon (1938), *Measuring Municipal Activities: A Survey of Suggested Criteria for Appraising Administration*, The International City Managers Association, Chicago, Illinois, United States.

Schick, Allen (1996), *The Spirit of Reform: Managing the New Zealand State Sector in a Time of Change*, State Services Commission, Wellington.

Schick, Allen (1998), "Why Most Developing Countries Should Not Adopt the New Zealand Model", *World Bank Research Observer*.

Walters, Jonathan (2000), "Buzz over Balances", *Governing*, May.

Wildavsky, Aaron (1964), *The Politics of the Budgetary Process*, Little, Brown and Company, New York, United States.

World Bank (2002), "Thailand's hurdle approach to budget reform", *PREMnotes No. 73*, Poverty Reduction and Economic Management Network, The World Bank, Washington DC.

ISBN 978-92-64-06087-6
Evolutions in Budgetary Practice
Allen Schick and the OECD Senior Budget Officials
© OECD 2009

Chapter 11

The Role of Fiscal Rules in Budgeting*

* This article was originally published in the OECD *Journal on Budgeting*, Vol. 3, No. 3, 2003. At the time of writing, Allen Schick was Visiting Fellow, Governmental Studies, Brookings Institution, Washington DC, and Professor, School of Public Affairs, University of Maryland, United States. An afterword was written in 2009.

Budgeting is a rule-driven process that regulates the raising and spending of public money. Detailed rules govern the submission of bids for resources by spending units, review of these bids by the finance ministry or another central organ, compilation of the annual budget, legislative action including the voting of appropriations, expenditure of funds during the financial year, and reporting on financial stocks and flows. Why have many national governments adopted new budget rules when they have a plethora of old ones? The new rules do not replace existing rules – although they may modify them – thereby adding to the complexity of established budget processes, and often adding as well to the time it takes to complete the main steps in the annual budget cycle. Why add to the complications of an already difficult process? If it is because the old rules do not work, why is it expected that new ones will make much of a difference?

Furthermore, the old rules generally empower budget makers by enabling them to allocate resources according to the preferences of government. Fiscal rules, by contrast, constrain budget makers, taking away much of their authority to decide aggregate revenue and spending policy. These rules typically prescribe the balance between revenue and spending policy. Every fiscal rule is a limit on the exercise of political will. Why have democracies accepted or imposed fiscal limits on themselves, and why should we expect these limits to be effective when they run counter to the preferences of voters and politicians?

Some fiscal rules have been adopted by national governments on their own initiative; some have been imposed by international agreements such as the European Union Stability and Growth Pact or by conditionalities dictated by the International Monetary Fund (IMF) and other international financial institutions. Some are embedded in fiscal responsibility laws that require the national government to establish fiscal targets in advance of annual budget work; others arise out of the process of preparing and approving the budget. Although most national governments still operate without preset fiscal constraints, the number of countries employing them is likely to increase in the years ahead. Compared to past budget reforms that had little success, the fiscal rules movement has altered budget practices in the countries that have taken the rules seriously.

Fiscal rules are effective only when they are supported by other changes in budgeting including:

- lengthening the time frame from a single year to the medium term;
- baseline projections (or forward estimates) of future budget conditions;
- estimates of the impact of policy changes on future budgets;
- procedures for monitoring budget out-turns and for taking corrective action when necessary; and
- enforcement mechanisms to assure that opportunistic politicians do not breach the rules.

Fiscal rules will not make much of a difference if the budget horizon is limited to a single year, if monitoring and enforcement are weak, and if future impacts are ignored when budget decisions are made.

Fiscal rules also depend on political leaders who are willing to operate within the constraints, even when they are thereby compelled to take unpleasant actions such as reducing services or boosting taxes. When political will is lacking, as is often the case, compliance will be weak. But if political rules work only when politicians want them to, why have them at all? If political support is forthcoming, rules are unnecessary; if it is not, rules will not work. I will return to this issue later in the article. For the present, however, it suffices to aver that rules serve to fortify politicians who want to make hard budget choices.

This article offers a preliminary assessment of fiscal rules. Section 1 addresses a key question: why have fiscal rules emerged as an attractive budget innovation? What is it about contemporary public finance that has prepared the ground for this reform? Section 2 inquires whether the type of fiscal rule makes a difference. Some rules are stated in absolute terms, others are indexed to GDP or another measure. Does the type of constraint influence budget outcomes, or is the manner in which it is applied paramount? Section 3 considers the budgetary arrangements that facilitate or impede compliance with fiscal rules. The concluding section assesses fiscal rules in the light of the economic and political conditions under which they operate.

This article does not address the staying power of fiscal rules. Do they gain legitimacy and strength the longer they are in place, or do rules weaken as claimants for public resources learn how to beat the system? My sense is that fiscal rules have a limited effective life and must be reinvigorated or replaced from time to time. However, because these rules have been applied for barely a decade, more experience is needed before their long-term effects can be evaluated.

1. The age of fiscal rules

Fiscal rules are a response to alleged shortcomings in budgeting that produce outcomes that politicians and voters do not want and would reject if they had a fair opportunity to do so. The shortcomings lead to expansionary government that consumes a rising share of national wealth, elevates tax and debt burdens, and produces large, chronic budget deficits. Proponents of fiscal rules argue that the fundamental problem is that conventional budgeting is an open-ended process that permits government to accommodate demands by spending more than it has. Fiscal rules aim to counter this tendency by compelling budget makers to tax and spend within fixed constraints that do not waver with shifts in political sentiment or economic conditions.

Four interlocking lines of reasoning feed into the fiscal rules movement. One is the argument that sound budget procedures often produce unsound budget outcomes. The second is the burgeoning evidence that budgeting in democratic countries is inherently biased to produce expansionary outcomes. The third is the realisation that abandonment of strict balanced budget rules has left budget makers without firm guidance on appropriate fiscal aggregates. The final strand is a body of research which argues that differences in budget outcomes among countries are due to differences in the rules under which governments make tax and spending decisions. These strands have fused together to build a strong case for fiscal constraints to offset the perceived defects of conventional budgeting.

1.1. *Good procedures do not assure good budget outcomes*

Fiscal rules deal with substantive budget outcomes, in contrast to procedural rules which deal with how the tasks of budgeting are carried out. Every national government prescribes budget procedures that cover the many steps in the annual cycle. Over time, the procedures have been hardened into routines that are repeated year after year with little or no change. Budget procedures define the roles and relationships of participants in the process, how the various tasks are done, the information required, and deadlines for action. The routines of budgeting ease the tensions and conflicts that are inherent in the competition for scarce resources.

As a set of routines, budgeting differs in some particulars from one venue to another. Each government has distinctive terminology and rules, but the differences tend to be small. Early in the development of budgeting, the basic routines were codified into principles that were recognised as good practice. The most important principles were:

- comprehensiveness (the budget should include all revenue and expenditure);
- accuracy (the budget should accurately record transactions);
- annularity (each budget should span a single fiscal year);
- authoritativeness (public funds should be spent as authorised in law); and
- transparency (the government should publish timely information on receipts and expenditures).

The procedures and the principles that underlie them constitute due process in budgeting. The term "due process" connotes that if the procedures are proper, the outcomes that ensue from them are right. In the same way that the judgment of a court is governed by due process, the legitimacy and soundness of budget decisions are measured by the procedures used, not by substantive objectives or criteria. Whatever results from a budget process that applies proper procedure is correct. If, for example, the budget is comprehensive and all bids for resources are submitted in proper order and are reviewed by the appropriate budget authority, the allocations made to spending units and the budget totals should be deemed correct.

Due process is indifferent to outcomes. It has no preference for more or less spending, balanced or unbalanced budgets, rising or stable public debt burdens, higher or lower taxes, or other budget outcomes. What matters is that the procedures are followed. In this regard, due process in budgeting is analogous to due process in litigation. If proper judicial procedure is applied, the ensuing verdict must be accepted. Due process in budgeting is based on the same premise.

Due process in budgeting is politically neutral. It can accommodate both left and right-of-centre governments, as well as politicians who want to contract or expand government. It is quite common for an incoming government that has a markedly different political agenda than the government it has replaced to retain the inherited budget procedures. Because due process is neutral, actual budget outcomes vary with shifts in political or economic conditions. As these conditions differ from one country or time to another, so, too, do spending decisions and fiscal outcomes. Due process gives politicians free rein to mould budgets according to their preferences. Political will is unconstrained, provided it is exercised through prescribed procedures.

Due process has made budgeting into a self-contained activity, with its peculiar language, rituals and forms. In most countries, budgeting has its own ways of counting money which differ from the accounting principles used for financial statements. In all but very small governments, due process is in the custody of central staff who make the procedural rules, oversee compliance, and have sufficient institutional memory and administrative authority to maintain due process. Over time, the procedural requirements have accreted, giving budget controllers more things to do and orienting the process more to compliance than to outcomes.

No government can effectively manage its finances if due process is materially impaired. Nevertheless, due process is an inadequate basis for regulating public finance because it generates or permits unwanted, adverse outcomes. The unsatisfactory fiscal performance of many developed and developing countries impels the conclusion that sound budget procedures often produce results at variance with those sought by the government or deemed appropriate by outside experts. For decades, international organisations have assisted developing countries in installing sound budget systems, but in most cases fiscal outcomes have persistently been sub-par. Most developing countries now have formal budget systems that meet basic standards. What they do not have are disciplined budgets, effective programmes or efficient operations. Improving budget procedures will not suffice to alleviate the deeply rooted problems these countries face.

Budget results generally appear to be more favourable in affluent countries, but the differences may owe more to the abundance of resources than to the quality of budget practices. A fair reading of fiscal trends over the past half-century supports the conclusion that fiscal discipline has often been lax in the developed world. In OECD member countries, public spending now averages 20 percentage points higher relative to GDP than it did in the early 1960s. During this extended period, developed countries have had many more deficits than surpluses, despite the surge in revenues due to economic growth and tax increases. Fiscal imbalances have been more pronounced during periods of economic weakness, but they have regularly occurred during expansionary times as well. Because developed countries generally do not face the capital flight and economic destabilisation that periodically beset poor and emerging market countries, they have been able to finance budget imbalances without much difficulty. Rich countries like to credit their good fortune to fiscal discipline, but the truer explanation may lie in economic plenitude, not in budget rules and procedures.

1.2. Biases and rigidities in budget decisions

Why is it that generally accepted budget practices do not assure disciplined fiscal results? Part of the explanation may lie in biases embedded in budgeting that spur higher spending in excess of available resources. Although budgeting is a process for rationing resources, it invites spending units to demand more money each year. Some governments have rules that limit the amount spenders may request, but most permit them to ask for as much as they want. It is a rare spending unit that requests only as much or less than it obtained for the previous year. The common pattern is for spenders to seek increases, to have a portion of the requested increase denied by the finance ministry (or the budget agency), and to get more than it had last year. This arrangement tranquilises the budget process by giving major participants much of what they want. Central budget officials get power and spenders get money. Budget officials get credit for cutting the budget and spending units get money to continue or expand programmes.

It is not only that spenders want more; government leaders and a phalanx of interest groups want to give them more. Little opprobrium attaches to a government that presents a budget with spending increases; this is a normal occurrence, built into the expectations of budgeting and the behaviour of participants. Government leaders often point to spending increases as evidence of the good they are doing. It is the budget that cuts which stirs political unrest and analytical curiosity, not the one that adds this year's increases to last year's and to those of the years before that. In this situation, the budget totals become pliable, accommodating constraints that can be adjusted as needed to fit the spending pressures facing government.

These pressures are unbalanced, and they unbalance the budget. One of the well-known biases of budgeting is that the benefits of expenditure are concentrated while the costs of taxes are dispersed. The more concentrated the benefits, the greater the share that beneficiaries gain, giving them strong incentive to campaign for even more from government. On the other hand, taxes are dispersed among the paying population and each taxpayer's share is miniscule, leaving each with only a weak incentive to oppose spending demands. Add to this the proliferation and activism of interest groups, and government is exposed to near-irresistible demands for public money.

Everywhere, budgeting is an incremental process that extends the past into the future by focusing on marginal adjustments. Almost all governments format the budget to concentrate on changes from the previous year's base. The budget and the supporting documents typically show spending for one or more past fiscal years, the year in progress, and the next fiscal year. This structure formalises incrementalism by concentrating budget decisions on the amount by which each programme or account varies from the previous year. Incrementalism undermines fiscal discipline by impelling governments to accommodate fresh demands by spending more, not by substituting new priorities for old ones. Incremental budgeting is a process of allocating increases, not of reallocating money from less effective to more effective uses. Arguably, if budgeting were less incremental and more open to a review of "base" expenditures, governments and deficits would be smaller.

Attempts to uproot incrementalism through zero-base budgeting and other innovations have been unsuccessful. Incrementalism thrives because it simplifies the process by significantly reducing the number and scope of decisions that have to be made within the constricted time frame available for compiling the budget, and because it reduces conflict by protecting spenders and groups against deep cuts in existing programmes. When the budget is incremental, conflict is normally confined to small deviations from previous spending levels. But the price of budgetary peace is elevated spending levels.

Budget outcomes are also biased in many countries by the stickiness of public expenditure. In most developed countries, more than half of central government expenditure is mandated by permanent laws that entitle citizens to ongoing payments from the government. These entitlements must be paid regardless of the condition of the budget or of other demands for public funds. In some years, statutory increases in expenditure consume all of the incremental resources available for allocation. Typically, spending on entitlements is driven by demographic and economic trends, such as the age structure of the population and unemployment rates, rather than by annual budget decisions. In countries where benefits are linked to price changes, the government may have no margin for policy initiatives unless it spends more than it takes in.

The spread of entitlements has weakened fiscal discipline and budgetary due process. Typically, entitlements have been enacted without due consideration of downstream budget impacts and without adequate information on their prospective cost. In contrast to standard budget estimates and appropriations that are for fixed amounts, entitlements tend to be open-ended, with expenditure determined by exogenous factors. Much of the procedure of budgeting is irrelevant to statutory entitlements; as they grow in prominence, these pre-determined expenditures transform budgeting from a means of deciding future expenditures to one of accounting for past decisions.

Despite the damage they do to budgetary due process, entitlements can be regulated through the budget. It is not uncommon for financially stressed governments to trim entitlements at the margins in order to generate savings that would reduce the deficit or free up money for other purposes. Less frequently, they make fundamental changes that reduce the long-term impact of entitlements on future budgets. However, the usual course of action at budget time is to leave entitlements in place and to provision resources in the budget for mandated payments.

To sum up this discussion, upward spending biases are grounded in the political imbalance between concentrated benefits and dispersed costs, the sway of interest groups, incrementalism in budget decisions, and sticky expenditure. Unless governments constrain the fiscal aggregates, the budget's totals will stretch to accommodate spending demands. Good procedures are not an adequate defence against these pressures.

1.3. Changes in fiscal policy

Even where due process reigns, substantive policies often influence budget outcomes. Many governments have formal rules or political understandings that define the acceptable budget balance or constrain either the tax burden or spending levels. International organisations often impose fiscal conditionalities on countries receiving assistance. Political expectations and imposed conditions may be reinforced by substantive budget rules that are not policy neutral but predispose budget outcomes in certain directions. Indeed, the fiscal posture of many developed countries has gone through three distinct stages: the balanced budget norm, dynamic fiscal management and, currently, fiscal targets. These stages are discussed in the paragraphs that follow.

Prior to World War II, virtually all democratic countries embraced the balanced budget rule, including some that often breached the rule or did not have any legal constraint on unbalanced budgets. The operative norm was that spending during a fiscal year should not exceed that year's revenue. Governments differed in applying this rule: some applied it only to current revenue and expenditure, others to investment income and expense as well. Some counted money carried over from previous fiscal years, others included cash received during the year. The balanced budget norm did not distinguish between periods of economic growth and stagnation, nor did its time horizon extend beyond a single year to a full economic cycle. Because it was rigid, the balanced budget rule was often breached. Few national governments kept total spending within revenue during wartime or recession; some even had difficulty during good times. But although the norm was often dishonoured in practice, most governments paid homage to it as the right thing to do. Moreover, even when the budget was unbalanced, governments used the norm to constrain spending demands and the size of the deficit.

The balanced budget norm was superseded after World War II by a flexible rule that allowed the totals to accommodate cyclical changes in economic conditions and secular changes in government policy. The new rule came in several versions. One was that government should maintain balance over the course of the economic cycle rather than in each year; another was that government spending should not exceed the revenue that government would take in if the economy were at full (or high) employment. In other words, governments that have cyclical deficit should still have structural surpluses. Governments differed in the extent to which dynamic fiscal response should result from built-in stabilisers (such as the automatic fall in revenue or rise in unemployment payments when the economy weakens) or from discretionary policy changes. Over time, dynamic fiscal policy was applied in various countries to mean that government should act to reduce the gap between actual and potential output.

Even when the economy was strong, however, deficit spending was common in many democratic countries, as was a steady up-drift in the ratio of public expenditure to GDP. With aggregate constraints loosened, claimants had the upper hand in demanding more from government. It was deemed more important to balance the economy than to balance the budget, and it was not difficult to make a strong case for additional spending on the grounds that it would have beneficial stimulative effects. But whatever its virtues, an accommodating fiscal posture was called into question by the deterioration in economic performance of many industrial countries after the oil shocks in the mid 1970s and early 1980s. High, persistent deficits came to be seen as a structural problem that does not disappear when the economy recovers. But high tax burdens and weaker economic growth led governments to conclude that they could not restore fiscal balance simply by raising taxes, as they had often done during the post-war years. Instead, they had to exert stronger discipline over the budget aggregates, especially over total expenditure.

In striving to reassert fiscal discipline, governments had to devise new approaches that differ from the balanced budget norm and accommodating fiscal policy. A strict, unyielding balanced budget rule is unworkable because the budget is highly sensitive to economic fluctuations and cannot be kept in balance when output falls and unemployment rises. A zero deficit rule would be violated during most years of an economic cycle, not only during recession but also in its aftermath when the country is struggling to regain its economic strength. But if the balanced budget norm is an unworkable policy guide, so too is an accommodating fiscal stance. Some governments have come to the conclusion that active demand management is not a viable option and that policy should be oriented to the long-term prospect instead. Many now regard chronic fiscal imbalance as a drag on the future economic capacity. Almost all perceive that the once-accepted distinction between structural and cyclical deficits is misguided because one year's cyclical deficit worsens future structural imbalances.

1.4. The impact of fiscal institutions on budget outcomes

Faced with the impracticality of a strict balanced budget rule and the adverse outcomes of accommodating budgets, some countries, international financial institutions, and the European Union have gravitated to fiscal targets which permit constrained deficits but are set in advance of budget decisions by the affected government or outside authorities. Like the balanced budget rule, the targets are fixed rather than elastic but, unlike this norm, they permit outcomes that deviate from strict balance. When they work as intended, the targets constrain the fiscal options available to budget makers.

Fiscal targets have been propelled by a body of research showing that institutions – the term used by economists in referring to fiscal rules – affect budget results. One of the most influential studies was conducted by Jörgen von Hagen for the European Commission in the early 1990s, but his findings have been replicated in other regions. Von Hagen classified each EU country in terms of whether it has centralised or fragmented institutions at each of the three main stages of budgeting: compilation of the government's budget, legislative spending actions, and implementation of the budget. He defined budgeting as centralised if the finance minister has a strong role in setting and enforcing fiscal targets and in resolving conflicts over spending, if the legislature is barred from amending the budget or increasing aggregate expenditure, and if the finance minister has authority to block expenditure and to assure that actual spending does not exceed authorised levels. Applying this scheme to EU countries, von Hagen found that budgetary arrangements that give the prime minister or finance minister strategic dominance over sectoral ministers, that limit the amending powers of parliament, and that allow little opportunity for modification during implementation are "strongly conducive to fiscal discipline, i.e. relatively small deficits and public debt" (Hagen, 1992, p. 53). Similar conclusions have been drawn in subsequent studies that used somewhat different variables. Reviewing the findings that emerged from a decade of research, Poterba and von Hagen argued:

> Large deficits may be avoided by strategic design of the budget process, that is, by institutions that distribute authority and facilitate agreement on the efficient outcome. Effective institutional design of the budget process to reduce the spending and deficit bias of government promotes a comprehensive view of the costs and benefits of public policies. If centralisation of the budget process relies on delegating power to an individual decision maker, the key is that this individual be driven by particular spending interests than by the spending ministers. If centralisation relies on common agreements on fiscal targets, the key is that these targets be agreed upon early in the budget process, that the agreement is negotiated by all parties involved, and that the agreement is backed by strong enough punishments to make it binding throughout the budget process (Poterba and von Hagen, 1999, p. 10).

These conclusions suggest that the type of fiscal rule and the manner in which it is developed and enforced determine its effectiveness. All fiscal rules are not created equally, and all are not equally effective. Determining why some rules work and others do not is a difficult but necessary task.

Research on fiscal rules has had a definite impact on budget practice. It has influenced both the Maastricht Treaty and the Stability and Growth Pact. And it was cited by Sweden when the government reformed its budget machinery in the mid 1990s. The notion of fiscal constraints has obvious appeal at a time when national economies are linked to regional and global forces, and when economic growth and budget increments are less robust than they once were. With or without fiscal rules, contemporary governments are operating in a more constrained environment than was the case during the post-war boom. Arming them with rules may make the task of regulating public finance somewhat easier. But having rules is not the same as living with rules. The test of all rules is not whether they are adopted but whether they produce the expected behaviour. In the case of fiscal rules, having a constraint and enforcing it involves different actors and different politico-economic considerations.

2. Variations in fiscal rules

All fiscal rules share a key characteristic: they must be set before the budget is decided. If they are not, the rules cannot constrain revenue and spending actions. Beyond this common feature, fiscal rules branch off in many different directions. This section considers four sets of issues in formulating and operating fiscal rules:

● Are they hard or soft constraints?

● Who sets and enforces them?

● Which fiscal aggregates do they regulate?

● What should be the accounting basis applied in making and enforcing rules?

2.1. *Hard* versus *soft constraints*

A constraint is hard when it cannot be modified by the government in response to changing economic conditions or political preferences; a soft constraint is one that the government may adjust when it prefers to change fiscal course. There are varying degrees of hardness or softness, but these polar definitions point to basic choices that a government must make in entering a fiscal regime. A parallel issue is whether fiscal rules should be permanent and continue from year to year without having to be readopted, or should be decided anew each year before the budget is adopted. Hard constraints tend to be permanent; soft constraints usually are recalibrated annually or after a change in government. Both types of rules may be prescribed by constitution, statute, international agreement, or some other binding decision. Temporary rules may be set in coalition agreements, medium-term frameworks, fiscal responsibility laws, or the annual budget law.

The Maastricht criteria and the Stability and Growth Pact are leading examples of hard, ongoing constraints. Although they have escape clauses, these rules continue in effect from year to year and are intended to be firm constraints on the budget policies of the affected governments. A somewhat more flexible approach is to decide the rules each year (or every few years) and to budget within the newly agreed constraints. Countries that budget within a medium-term expenditure framework (MTEF) generally take the more permissive approach. In Australia, which pioneered the MTEF model, multi-year forward estimates are the starting point for considering departmental bids for resources. These bids must be within the resource framework set by the government. In Sweden's reformed budget process, the totals are decided by the government and parliament each year before work commences on the annual budget. The fiscal responsibility model developed by New Zealand and adopted by a number of developed and developing countries also relies on a soft constraint. Each year, the government presents a policy statement setting forth its medium- and long-term fiscal objectives several months before it presents the annual budget. The fiscal responsibility model does not dictate a particular outcome, but it does require that government be accountable for changes in fiscal course. The central idea is that political leaders should be free to make fiscal choices, but they should do so in an open manner.

Seen in this light, the key issue is not the hardness of the constraint but the extent to which fiscal rules restrict political action. One view is that the very purpose of the rules should be to counter the bias of politicians to act in a fiscally undisciplined manner; another view is that rules are sturdier when they are made and enforced through the working of democratic politics. In practice, the differences between the two approaches may be narrower than the labels suggest. Fixed constraints are rarely as hard as they purport to be, as the Eurocrats monitoring compliance with the Maastricht Treaty and the Stability and Growth Pact have come to learn; and politically set targets can be strong constraints on government, as New Zealand experienced near the end of the 20th century when the coalition government maintained a disciplined fiscal posture despite economic weakness. It may be that politically set targets are effective only when democratic institutions are robust and government is held to account by voters. In countries where accountability is weak, the government may find it expedient to abandon the targets set through fiscal responsibility mechanisms.

At first consideration, it may appear that permanent constraints – which do not bend with shifts in political or economic winds – are more effective than annually set ones which may be moulded to suit the preferences of the government of the day. Yet there may be circumstances where annual constraints have greater impact than permanent ones, as well as instances in which indicative policies carry greater weight than constrictive rules. This argument rests on two premises: first, annually reset policies tend to be more realistic and achievable than permanent rules; second, annually (or periodically) established constraints may have more political support than permanent rules which have not been endorsed by current office holders. No matter how hard they are, constraints cannot work if they are fundamentally at variance with current economic or budgetary realities, or if they lack political support. When constraints are political orphans, opportunistic politicians may conspire to evade them by delaying payments, devising extrabudgetary arrangements, building up contingent liabilities, or using other bookkeeping tactics.

The choice between constrictive and indicative rules depends on institutions, which differ from country to country. Indicative constraints may suffice to control budget aggregates when institutional arrangements promote fiscal prudence. On the other hand, hard rules may be appropriate in countries that have experienced fiscal laxity. If this generalisation is valid, the designers of fiscal rules must come to grips with an anomaly: when hard constraints are most needed, they may be least workable; and where conditions are most hospitable to fiscal constraints, they may be least needed.

2.2. How are fiscal rules set and enforced?

Ideally, democratic governments should establish and enforce their own fiscal rules, but in at least two prominent situations, they are now set and monitored externally. One is in the European Union, where fiscal rules have been set by treaty and are overseen by Commission staff; the other is in countries that are subject to conditionalities imposed by the IMF or other international organisations. Although a handful of European countries have been found in violation of the Maastricht Treaty and the Stability and Growth Pact, it is fair to conclude that the fiscal posture of most EU countries was more disciplined both prior to and since the launch of the euro than it would likely have been in the absence of external constraints. However, it is an open question whether EU enforcement will be as effective when member countries are pulled by political or economic conditions to go their own way. In the case of developing and emerging market countries, the impact of external conditions may vary with the extent to which they are dependent on external aid or face the risk of capital outflows.

Externally imposed rules change the balance of political power within affected countries and enable politicians to shift the blame to outsiders for taking unpleasant measures. Nevertheless, external pressure may be a weak substitute for self-discipline. It is the affected government that must act to uphold the rules; if it does not, outside enforcers will not be able to make the rules work. Opportunism and deception are rife when politicians are pressured to act against their self-interest. They have numerous opportunities to conceal the government's true financial condition. As fiscal rules have become more widespread and stringent, outside enforcement has intensified. EU experts review budget submissions by member countries to assess compliance with the EU accounting rules; IMF staff closely oversee financial actions by countries subject to IMF conditionalities. Nevertheless, even when outside monitors detect budgetary legerdemain, their only viable option may be to let the affected country breach the rules.

Self-imposed rules also are only as effective as permitted by the political arrangements which generate them. The early literature on fiscal rules concluded that majoritarian regimes (in which one party controls the government) are more disciplined than coalition governments (which divide power among two or more parties). But contrary to this expectation, coalition regimes sometimes are more disciplined than those run by a single party. For example, the Netherlands, which has never had a single-party government throughout its democratic history, had extraordinary success in the 1990s in fulfilling self-imposed fiscal rules. To explain why coalition governments may be more successful, researchers have distinguished between rules adopted through delegation of power and those developed through political commitment. Governments that rely on delegation typically empower the finance minister to set the fiscal targets and assure that budget estimates and spending results are consistent with them. This arrangement is not suitable for coalition governments where the finance minister may come from one party and sectoral ministers from other parties. When, as is likely, the coalition partners have conflicting views on government policies and finances, they will not entrust final budget authority to the finance minister. Instead, if they are determined to act in a disciplined manner, they may negotiate a coalition agreement that sets out the boundaries of the budget, including fiscal aggregates, for the life of the government. It is the commitment of the coalition parties to stay within this framework that gives discipline to fiscal rules. During the 1990s, coalition agreements became more detailed in some countries and contributed to their success in regulating the budget. Coalition agreements are effective only when they are credible commitments – that is, the parties to the agreement have a strong incentive to abide by the terms because, if they do not, the government will collapse. Some governments have introduced new budget procedures to assure compliance with the coalition agreement during formulation and execution of the budget. New Zealand, which is a newcomer to coalition government, has established a "fiscal provisions" system for calculating the budgetary impact of policy initiatives and assessing whether they are consistent with the agreement.

A fiscal commitment is worth no more than the willingness of those who make it to comply with its terms. Although the parties to an agreement may pay a political price for violating it – new elections and a potential backlash from voters – politicians may judge it better to break the constraints than to live with them even when they are predisposed to abide by the agreements. One year's understanding may turn into a future year's misunderstanding. All budget commitments are at risk of being overtaken by changing conditions such as a weakening economy, shifts in public sentiment, an international crisis, and so on. Arguably, therefore, commitments (like coalition agreements) covering only the three or four years of a government may have a better chance of being honoured than those that span a longer time frame.

2.3. Which fiscal aggregates are regulated?

In managing public finance, a government produces at least four fiscal results: total revenue, total spending, the deficit (or borrowing requirement), and the public debt.

Governments that budget on an obligation basis also report on the total obligations issued or outstanding. Additional aggregates may be calculated for contingent liabilities and annual changes in total revenue or outlays. Governments that publish consolidated financial statements also report on total assets, liabilities and net worth. The various aggregates may pertain only to the central government or may cover other portions of the public sector as well – social security, public enterprises, sub-national governments, and extrabudgetary funds. Each aggregate has the potential to be limited in a fiscal rule, but the most common rules pertain to the balance between revenue and expenditure.

The various fiscal aggregates can be targeted in different ways: in absolute terms, as a percentage of the gross domestic product or of another index; in real (inflation-adjusted) terms; or as a rate (or amount) of change over a previous fiscal period. Expressing public expenditure or other aggregates as a proportion of GDP facilitates trend analysis and comparison among countries, and recognises that the sustainability of a government's fiscal position depends on the volume of national output. Nevertheless, focusing only on the deficit (or revenue or expenditure) as a percentage of GDP may bias fiscal outcomes. If a government seeks to stabilise revenue or spending as a share of GDP, it may accept real spending increases when the economy is expanding but find it difficult to contract spending when the economy is weak. Over the course of an economic cycle, this pattern may lead to a progressive rise in the fiscal aggregates relative to GDP.

Constraining only a single fiscal aggregate may distort budgetary behaviour. If the deficit were the aggregate targeted, the government might contrive to meet the constraint by selling assets, deferring expenditure, or relying on non-recurring revenue. A broad set of fiscal rules may discourage this type of response, especially if the targets include the government's net worth, a measure that is not affected by asset sales or by the shift in receipts or payments from one fiscal period to another. Few governments, however, now produce comprehensive financial statements that are sufficiently timely and reliable to provide a basis for fiscal control.

In devising fiscal rules, the key consideration should be the sustainability of the government's financial position – that is, whether its policies can be continued in the future, especially if economic conditions become adverse. Sustainability has led developed countries to concentrate on the debt-to-GDP ratio and developing/emerging market countries to focus on the primary balance. In contrast to the deficit that measures financial balance within a single year, the debt ratio signals changes in financial strength over an extended period. A rise in the ratio may indicate that this trend cannot be sustained indefinitely because the debt burden is increasing faster than national output. Maintenance of a minimum primary balance has become a popular fiscal rule for developing and emerging market countries because they need a large surplus to finance external debt and to discourage capital flight.

The specific form the fiscal rule takes may be of less consequence than the manner in which it is adopted and enforced, and the number of years it covers. There is currently no basis for concluding that a rule limiting the deficit is more or less effective than one limiting the debt or total expenditure. A fiscal rule is effective if it is realistic and enforced and covers several years. A rule that lacks these characteristics will be weak regardless of whether it pertains to one or another of the budget aggregates.

2.4. *What should be the accounting basis?*

Although the form may not matter, the accounting basis used in applying the rule certainly does. Fiscal rules are vacuous if they are not undergirded by clear accounting standards that determine how the aggregates and the actions that feed into them are calculated. Not surprisingly, the fiscal rules movement has been accompanied by the elaboration of accounting standards for budget documents. While the cash *versus* accruals issue has received most of the attention, other issues also arise in defining and enforcing fiscal rules. Fiscal rule makers generally prefer the accrual basis, because cash transactions are subject to manipulation. Key differences between cash and accruals – such as the timing of transactions, asset sales and contingent liabilities – affect the aggregates reported in budgets. The cash basis gives politicians wide opportunity to defer or accelerate the recognition of receipts and payment, to sell assets and book the income as current receipts, and to shift from direct to contingent liabilities. To avert these ruses, the EU and the IMF have shifted to a modified accrual basis that purportedly enables stricter enforcement of fiscal rules. It should be noted, however, that the accrual basis is not a fail-safe mechanism against deception. Accounting scandals in the business sector, where the accrual basis prevails, teach us that all accounting rules are subject to manipulation and evasion. Moreover, the accrual basis may be particularly vulnerable to distortion because it relies on complex, often hidden, assumptions for calculating financial stocks and flows. The most prudent course may be to rely on both cash and accrual measures in devising fiscal rules and monitoring compliance.

Cash *versus* accruals is related to a second accounting question: should budget aggregates be reported on a gross or net basis? In the gross basis, inflows and outflows are accounted for separately; in the net basis, certain inflows may offset outflows. The debt-to-GDP basis is usually computed on a gross basis; it measures the total owed by the government. This ratio is not reduced by the amount owed to the government or by other assets held by it. In contrast to the balance sheet, which reports net worth (assets minus liabilities), the gross debt measures only liabilities – and only those liabilities that are in the form of debt. Arguably, the net basis is superior because the aggregates would not be affected by the sale of financial assets. A government can lower the gross debt by selling assets, but this transaction would not change the government's net worth, though it would alter the volume of assets and liabilities.

Grossing *versus* netting also pertains to rules that constrain total expenditure. Most national governments obtain revenue from user charges, state-owned enterprises, and other commercial-type activities. If it accounts for finances on a gross basis, this money would be booked as revenue. If it uses the net basis, some or all of this income might be budgeted as an offset to expenditure. Netting *versus* grossing does not affect the reported size of the deficit, but it does affect total revenue and spending; hence, the issue is important when the fiscal rules limit these totals. The net basis is popular in some countries because it gives spending units an incentive to charge users for services. Sweden, however, opted for the gross basis in the 1990s when it established a system to regulate total and sectoral spending. In Sweden's current system, total spending limits are disaggregated into 27 sectors, each with its own sub-limit. In this arrangement, amounts paid by Sweden to the European Union are budgeted as expenditures and amounts received from the EU appear as revenue. The two flows are not netted out. Sweden selected the net basis because it provides stricter limits on total spending. In the net basis, the limits are elastic because the total spent can be increased by generating offsets.

3. Adjusting budget practices to enforce fiscal rules

Fiscal rules are only as good as their enforcement. Inasmuch as the rules are not self-enforcing, spenders can be expected to stretch or evade them when opportunities are at hand. A key element of enforcement is to empower independent overseers to review budget actions and to point out actual or potential violations. This model is used by both the EU and the IMF, as well as by governments that subject fiscal policies and outcomes to independent audit. Enforcement that relies on intervention after the breach has occurred is inherently less effective than arrangements that deter violations before they occur. For this reason, some governments that take fiscal discipline seriously have restructured their budget processes to promote fidelity to the rules.

One of the most prominent adjustments has been to extend the time frame of budgeting from one year to three or four years. An annual budget process is an invitation to evasion, for it encourages opportunists to defer expenditure until the next year or to accelerate receipts to the current year. It is not difficult for creative budget makers to dress up one year's accounts so that they appear more favourable than they really are. When pressured to abide by fiscal constraints, some governments have shortened the fiscal year to 11 months or lengthened it to 13; some have made spending or revenue provisions temporary in order that the current budget fit into the constraints; some have used one-off revenue gains or spending cuts to defer the bad news to the future. These ploys are somewhat more difficult and less attractive when fidelity to the rules is measured over the medium term rather than for a single year. The medium-term expenditure framework (MTEF) or some similar arrangement has been introduced in various countries to assure that the budget's path is consistent with the rules.

Along with an MTEF, governments have introduced means of measuring the budget impact of policy changes. This capacity is essential because of the tendency to underestimate future impacts when policy initiatives are taken. Measuring impact is itself a two-step procedure. First, it is necessary to estimate future budget conditions if policies were continued without change; this step entails the use of baselines or forward estimates that project the revenue or spending that will ensue in future years from current policy. Second, the government must have technical skills and procedures to estimate the changes in spending or revenue that may flow from policy changes. This is an exceedingly difficult task, for the estimates must consider behavioural responses in addition to the direct consequences of policy shifts.

Compliance with fiscal rules may be strengthened when the government splits the budget process into two separate phases: a framework stage during which the aggregates (and possibly major sectoral allocations) are decided, and an estimates stage when detailed budgets are prepared. When the two tasks are combined, the budget's totals may be hostage to its parts – that is, pressure to accommodate spending demands impels the government to set the totals higher than it prefers or the rules allow. By separating the two actions, the government sets the aggregates first without adding up expenditures for each account or spending unit. The totals are decided in a framework that focuses on fiscal rules and conditions rather than on the amounts needed for each activity financed in the budget. Once the aggregates have been set, detailed estimates are prepared under rules that limit them to the amount provided in the framework.

Fiscal rules have arrived at a time when national legislatures are increasingly independent and active in budget matters. Legislative amendment of the budget submitted by the government is now common, except for countries still operating within the

Westminster framework. As legislative changes become more frequent, the risk increases that the totals will be breached. To counter this, a few countries now provide for the legislature to vote the fiscal aggregates, either in tandem with its consideration of the budget or in a separate framework stage. Countries that permit legislative amendment are introducing means of providing parliamentarians with timely information on the future budget impact of these changes. As legislatures enhance their budget role, one of the challenges facing budget architects will be to balance the impulse for independence with the need to be fiscally responsible. The future of legislative-governmental relations will be strongly influenced by the manner in which this balance is maintained.

Strictly enforced fiscal rules may constrict government's capacity to respond to new needs and priorities, especially when the economy is sluggish and ample increments are not available for allocation. To counter this tendency, some governments operating under fiscal rules have introduced means of encouraging spending units to reallocate resources from lower to higher priorities. An MTEF is well suited for this purpose, for the framework gives each sector a resource envelope for each of the next several years. Within this envelope, sectoral ministers have scope for shifting resources, with low risk that their budgets will be cut. Of course, if proposed reallocations expose spending ministers to cutbacks, they will adjust to this reality by freezing old priorities into the budget.

When they are realistic and anchored in political commitments and budget procedures, fiscal rules constrain a government's capacity to respond to spending demands. Two prominent types of contemporary spending, however, may be resistant to these constraints. One is entitlements mandated by law, the other is contingent liabilities. Entitlements are essentially a political problem and are discussed in the next section in the context of the political and economic conditions under which fiscal rules are made and implemented. The contingent liabilities problem arises out of the fact that conventional budgets cover only direct liabilities; contingencies enter budget accounts at the point that payment must be made (such as pursuant to default on a guarantee), when it is too late for the budget to effectively control the amount spent. In some cases, governments that appear to have behaved in a fiscally prudent manner face enormous pressure on their budgets because of previously unrecognised contingent liabilities. Apparently, this has recently been the case in Argentina and some other developing and emerging market countries.

Contingent liabilities come in many forms, and every national government has them. Some contingent liabilities are explicit (they are established in law or contract) while others are implicit (they are grounded on expectations of government behaviour). Obviously, government knows less about these implicit risks than about explicit liabilities, but the budget impact may be greater. To maintain fiscal discipline, governments must regulate contingent liabilities. Doing so is difficult because practices have not been standardised and contingent liabilities are usually incurred outside the budget process. Several approaches have emerged over the past two decades including:

- setting aside money in the budget for estimated calls on guarantees;
- limiting the volume of guarantees outstanding or issued during the year;
- reporting on contingent liabilities in the budget or financial statements;
- sharing risk with recipients of guarantees by charging fees or other payments;
- reviewing guarantees in tandem with bids for direct expenditure; and
- budgeting for estimated future cost when the guarantee is authorised.

It is likely that, as fiscal rules are applied more extensively, new tools will be devised for regulating guarantees and bringing them within the ambit of budget control.

Fiscal rules are not simply a matter of adding aggregate targets to the stockpile of budget procedures. Where they work, the rules transform both the formal practices of budgeting and the behaviour of participants in the process. The changes discussed in this section were introduced in the early years of fiscal rules. For these rules to become fully embedded in budgeting, additional changes will be introduced in the future. While the details of future budget innovations are currently unknown, their direction is clear. Budgeting will adapt to protect the aggregates from pressure to spend or borrow more, to assure that, in both preparing and implementing the budget, governments operate within preset constraints, and to require legislatures to be more disciplined at the same time that their budget role is augmented.

4. The impact of politics and economics on fiscal rules

Fiscal rules operate at the crossroads of politics and economics. The relationship between rules and political and economic conditions is bilateral. Every rule has the potential to redistribute political power, alter budget outcomes and other policies, and influence economic conditions. But the reverse also holds: political and economic conditions influence the effectiveness of budget rules. This concluding section explores a neglected issue in the fiscal rules debate. Can rules be effective when politicians do not want them or when economic conditions are unfavourable? If the answer to this question is "no", then why have rules at all? The short answer is that, although rules cannot ignore political and economic pressures, they may affect the way these pressures are processed in budget decisions. Fiscal rules have effect, even when they are not effective.

Budget rules are political rules; they are made by political leaders and are enforced or breached by them. The effectiveness of fiscal constraints depends on the willingness of politicians to abide by them. When the rules work, it may be because voters and politicians have a preference to be fiscally disciplined; when they do not, it may be because they prefer more spending or lower taxes. Poterba and von Hagen recognise this pattern in noting "that budget rules are not randomly assigned to nations … but rather are the product of deliberate choice by voters or their elected representatives. This makes it difficult to evaluate observed correlations between budget rules and budget outcomes; perhaps the observed relationships are simply due to a correlation between a third factor, voter preferences, and the observed manifestations of voter preferences" (Poterba and von Hagen, 1999, p. 11).

Recent work by von Hagen and others recognises the importance of political commitment in regulating budget outcomes, but they define commitment as a key element of fiscal rules rather than as an enabling condition that gives the rules effect. In so doing, their reasoning comes close to being tautological: commitments are budget rules that constrain spending or deficits; when these are not constrained, it is because commitment is lacking. This circular reasoning leads to the conclusion that rules are always effective. A more balanced view is that rules matter when politicians are predisposed to act in a fiscally disciplined manner by making it easier for them to resist spending or borrowing pressures. The rules fortify politicians who want to be fiscally prudent, but they do not stand in the way of those who are determined to spend more or tax less than the rules allow.

A fiscal commitment is worth no more than the willingness of those who make it to comply with its terms. When commitment wavers, fiscal discipline erodes. It may be the natural fate of such commitments to degrade over time as pent-up pressure for money overwhelms the rules. In the end, all budget rules may be inherently weak and made to be broken, either explicitly or through accounting tricks, and governments therefore have difficulty maintaining a disciplined fiscal posture for an extended period. If this is so, sooner or later every country faces a need to reinvigorate its fiscal rules.

Case studies of fluctuating budget results indicate the fragility of fiscal rules. In the early 1990s, the United States General Accounting Office examined the experiences of five countries reputed to have moved from large deficits to budgetary balance. The five countries (Australia, Germany, Japan, Mexico and the United Kingdom) restructured their budget rules, established top-down, multi-year limits on aggregate spending, and took steps to curtail the public sector wage bill and some social benefits. A few also reduced payments to sub-national governments or trimmed capital spending. In all of the countries, political leaders actively promoted fiscal discipline by defining the acceptable parameters of fiscal policy, and persuaded politicians and voters to accept budgetary austerity. The GAO concluded that the experiences of these countries "indicate that eliminating deficit is possible in modern democracies and that leaders can succeed in mounting the case for prompt action before crisis ensues" (United States General Accounting Office, 1994, p. 12). But it also found that sustaining the sense of urgency and the fiscal balance over the longer term is difficult. In fact, by the time the GAO published its study, four of the five countries had reverted to budget deficits. Recent experience in the United States tracks that of other countries. It moved swiftly from a large budget deficit in the early 1990s to a large surplus at the end of the decade, and back to an even larger deficit a few years later. The shift from deficit to surplus was abetted by fiscal rules that constrained spending increases and tax reductions. But once the surplus arrived, politicians contrived to spend more and tax less than the rules permitted. The rules remained the same but political behaviour did not. In the American case, political will to live by the rules was broken by surpluses; in other countries it has been broken by deficits. This has been Germany's fate over the past decade. In the run-up to the euro, it insisted on tough fiscal rules, but it was the first country to be castigated by the European Commission for breaching the rules. The financial burden of unification and protracted economic weakness broke Germany's traditional adherence to fiscal discipline.

Sometimes the sequence is reversed, and a country that once lacked the political capacity to discipline its finances acquires the will to do so. The Netherlands once was deemed to be hopelessly mired in deficits; it was the nesting ground of the "Dutch disease", a term that referred to an affluent country that lives well beyond its means. Over the past decade, however, the country has maintained one of the strongest fiscal positions in Europe and it is now celebrated for the "Dutch model": structural reforms that corrected many of the imbalances in the economy and stabilised the government's finances. For the most part, the Netherlands acted on its own initiative, not because it was pressured by the Maastricht Treaty or Stability and Growth Pact rules. As mentioned earlier, the Netherlands perfected the coalition agreement as a powerful means of staying on course during the full term of each government. What mattered was not that each incoming government negotiated a coalition agreement, but that it took the terms seriously and produced annual budgets consistent with the agreed fiscal targets. The government of the day did not relax fiscal discipline during good economic times. It did not use the surge in tax collections to finance programme expansions that would burden future budgets. One can explain the success story of the Netherlands as due to either new fiscal institutions or to political resolve. But the Dutch experience makes it clear that without sustained political commitment, renewed by five consecutive governments over a span of two decades, coalition agreements would have been mere scraps of paper, stringent budget rules would have been violated, and fiscal outcomes would have been much less favourable than they actually were.

Political commitment is especially important in today's budgetary environment, which differs in at least two critical ways from past conditions. One difference is the prominence of mandatory accounts in national finance; the other is the activism and influence of interest groups. These developments have combined to make it much more difficult to maintain fiscal discipline, regardless of the political orientation of the party (or parties) in power. In the past, politicians had an easier job acting in a disciplined manner because almost all spending was discretionary and budgeting was a closed process in which interest groups had relatively little influence. Politicians did not need explicit fiscal rules to be disciplined; nowadays, they need rules, but the rules may not suffice.

When spending is dominated by entitlements, increases automatically result from demographic and economic trends; they do not require an explicit budget decision. In contrast to traditional budgeting, therefore, in which the normal role of politicians is to allocate increases, a budget of entitlements may require politicians to allocate cutbacks by disentitling beneficiaries to payments prescribed in law. This is a much more onerous budgetary chore, for which few politicians are temperamentally suited. Fiscal rules might not ease their plight. However, with entitlement spending rising automatically, it does not suffice for a government to resist demands for more money; it must also roll back these increases.

Entitlements make fiscal rules necessary; they may also make the rules ineffective. The ultimate test of fiscal rules may be their impact on entitlements. If these rules are implemented by political leaders with determination to curtail entitlements, they will be effective. If, however, governments prove unable or unwilling to challenge entitlements, fiscal rules will not make much of a difference.

The political task of bringing entitlements within the ambit of budget control has been greatly complicated by the vigilance of organised groups in protecting their interests. Not only do contemporary democracies have many more active groups than was the case one or two generations ago, but many groups have greater access to budget makers than they once did. While most national budgets are not yet fully open, they are much more transparent than before, and the process is more exposed to outside influence. Contemporary politicians often are cross-pressured by budget guardians who want them to take the steps necessary to uphold fiscal rules and by interest groups that oppose the curtailment of benefits. When the rule enforcers are outside the political system, as is the case in the EU and the IMF, they may be insensitive to the political difficulties facing the government. In some countries, the only way for the fiscal rules to survive is for the government to put its own continuation on the line.

4.1. *Economic cycles*

The political cost of adhering to fiscal rules is largely a function of economic conditions. The task is reasonably easy when the economy co-operates but challenging when it does not. Can governments maintain fiscal discipline under adverse economic conditions? Judging from experience in developed countries, the answer is "yes" and "no" – yes, in terms of discretionary fiscal stimulus; no, in terms of the impact of built-in stabilisers on key budget aggregates. During the post-war period, it was common for governments in developed countries to counter economic weakness by cutting taxes or raising expenditures. The enlarged budget deficit was justified on the grounds that it would stimulate economic recovery. Developed countries generally do not actively manage the economy this way any more. Many have found that the added costs (such as higher interest payments), approved when the economy is weak, continue to burden the budget when the economy recovers. Fiscal rules offer additional deterrence against undertaking stimulative budget action when the deficit is rising because of economic weakness.

But if governments' enthusiasm for discretionary policy has been dampened, built-in stabilisers still register on budget outcomes. An automatic drop in revenue or rise in social benefits can produce large, unplanned deficits in excess of the levels permitted by fiscal rules. A government can try to stay on fiscal course by raising taxes or trimming payments, but it generally is inopportune to do so when the economy is stagnant. Governments that stick to fiscal rules in these circumstances may unwittingly deepen or prolong the recession and still fall short of what is demanded by the rules. Developing and transitional countries also face unstable budgets during economic difficulty, but it is during these times that they are most dependent on external aid and may therefore be subject to conditionalities imposed by international organisations. These countries also risk capital flight, illiquid financial institutions and political instability. To the extent that they are dependent on capital inflows to stabilise or develop their economies, these countries may be compelled to constrain public spending or raise taxes in the hope that fiscal discipline will be rewarded by long-term improvement in economic conditions.

The status of fiscal rules when the economy is weak has roiled the European Union. Several countries have been cautioned by Brussels that their budget path violates the Maastricht criteria and the Stability and Growth Pact and that corrective policy changes are necessary to bring the deficit within acceptable limits. At one point, the President of the European Commission was quoted as characterising the rigid rules of the EU as "stupid" because they do not adequately allow for slippage when the economy is weak. Some member countries have suggested that a review of the EU fiscal rules would be appropriate. The issue has not yet been resolved, and member countries may have difficulty devising a substitute rule that is both disciplined and accommodating. Moreover, the problem of what to do during unfavourable economic times will not go away even if the rules are relaxed. The only fiscal rules that do not generate economic problems are those that have no teeth. But rules that do constrain government action – which, after all, is the purpose of having rules – can neither be ignored nor fulfilled during bad times.

4.2. Economic shocks

Shocks are far more destabilising than cyclical downturns, for they jar a government off its fiscal course and the after-effects linger for an extended period. When the shock is truly severe, the government may never have the option of restoring the *status quo*, and it may face pressure for fundamental political or economic change. Although the line between shocks and cyclical disturbances is difficult to draw, the distinction between the two is useful, for there is no prospect of a country upholding fiscal norms when the underpinnings of the economy have been uprooted. Shocks may be due to war or the collapse of political order, or to any other event that causes profound, lasting transformation in a country's economic structure. Arguably, the drive to unify the country has been a shock for Germany for, though it began as a bold decision to fully integrate the eastern *Länder* into national economic and political systems, the effort has been far more difficult, costly and time-consuming than had been expected at the outset. Large deficits, mountains of public debt, and the uprooting of Germany's fiscal prudence have been legacies of unification.

Shocks are much more prevalent in developing and emerging market countries that have inadequate slack to counter economic adversity. In developing countries, a steep drop in commodity prices or exchange rates or sudden capital flight can unhinge the government's fiscal plans. Yet, it is when budget deficits are spiralling out of control that these countries are most in need of the discipline that fiscal rules bring. It is when things are falling apart that a disciplined approach to public finance is most urgent. In these circumstances, constraining expenditures and generating more tax revenue will not produce fiscal balance, nor will these moves assure that the government achieves pre-shock targets. But they may moderate and shorten the after-effects on political and economic order.

In dealing with shocks or cyclical problems, it is essential to distinguish between fiscal balance and fiscal discipline. Losing the former may be unavoidable, but holding on to the latter is feasible, even under stressful conditions. It is in this predicament that well-developed fiscal rules that focus on sustainability of the country's fiscal position may be most valuable. But while the feasibility of rules usually is raised in periods of economic weakness, this writer is persuaded that the true test of rules occurs in good times when economic plenitude spurs voters and interest groups to demand more of government and politicians respond with tax cuts or spending increases. The seeds of most fiscal collapses are sown during good times when the possibility that resources will not be as plentiful in the future and that the government's fiscal path is not sustainable is crowded out by the exuberant expectation that economic growth, buoyant tax collections and other favourable conditions will continue endlessly. When they do not, the revenue forgone and the spending commitments made during spurts of growth generate fiscal turmoil when the government's coffers are empty and it lacks the means to fulfil its promises.

Some governments try to assure that they will be able to make it through periods of weakness by setting aside money in stabilisation or "rainy day" funds when their economy is strong. These funds rarely accumulate sufficient resources to cover shortfalls due to recession or shock. The reason for this is that a government decides how much to set aside in these funds in terms of what is left over after taxes have been cut or programmes expanded. The amount is inadequate because it is determined in the context of today's politics, not tomorrow's need. In other words, stabilisation funds are not sufficiently counter-cyclical, nor do they take account of the sustainability of the government's financial policy.

Counter-cyclical policy is an old concept that has not been heard much in recent times. This concept is worth reviving, if only because fiscal rules may strongly encourage pro-cyclical behaviour. The Maastricht criteria and the Stability and Growth Pact rules open the door for government to tax less and spend more in good times and to do the reverse when the economy weakens. Even though the rules permit the fiscal imbalance to widen when the economy is weak, the adjustment is too small to accommodate the fiscal swings resulting from cyclical changes in economic performance. To put the matter bluntly, a government that is permitted to run a 1-3% deficit when the economy is strong will not be able to hold the line at 3% when the economy weakens. A government that wants to live by the rules through all the ups and downs of an economic cycle must have rules that produce surpluses when the economy is strong.

How big should the surplus be? Or to put the question differently, how much of a projected surplus should be surrendered through tax cuts or spending increases that will persist when the surplus vanishes? Here's where the concept of sustainability can contribute to counter-cyclical policy. A government should not increase spending or reduce revenue in good times that it will not be able to afford in bad times. In measuring sustainability, a government should engage in sensitivity or risk analysis by estimating whether it would be able to afford the loss of revenue or the higher expenditures under adverse economic scenarios. In my view, fiscal rules should be set with this counter-cyclical, sustainable objective in mind.

This approach would counter the pro-cyclical, expansionary bias in fiscal rules and put public finance on a prudent, sustainable course. Fiscal rules should have most of their bite when the economy is strong; if they do not, they may do much harm and little good when the economy is weak.

Afterword

Fiscal rules are here to stay. They have become a permanent fixture of budgeting in well-managed countries because they provide a basis for regulating key fiscal aggregates. Establishing firm constraints on deficits or debt does lead to more prudent fiscal outcomes, but only when politicians are willing to abide by preset limits or when enforcement mechanisms are sufficiently effective to block violation or evasion of the rules.

There remains much unfinished business with respect to the design and operation of fiscal rules. The jury is still out on whether fixed rules, such as those established by the Stability and Growth Pact, are superior to those set by government each year through its own fiscal responsibility process. The latter can be more easily adjusted for changes in economic or political conditions, but they can also be more easily bent by opportunistic politicians. Nevertheless, as the article argues, all fiscal rules are dependent on political will.

They are also dependent on the economy. Fiscal rules that appear to work well during buoyant times often are bypassed or eviscerated when the economy is weak. Of course, this pattern suggests that favourable fiscal outcomes may be due more to the economy than to budgetary discipline. On the other hand, adverse outcomes may derive more from economic contraction than from lax fiscal policies. This conclusion argues for next-generation fiscal rules that formally distinguish between structural and cyclical outcomes. It should also lead to significant change in the policies of international financial institutions when developing or emerging countries encounter fiscal stress due to adverse economic circumstances.

If mild economic downturns unravel fiscal rules, economic shocks – such as those experienced near the end of this century's first decade – uproot them entirely. In no country was the rush to bail out financial institutions or to provide tax relief to distressed households or firms impeded by aggregate limits on government debt or deficits. When the economic crisis subsides and fiscal conditions stabilise, it will be the task of national governments to devise new rules to cope with elevated debt burdens and projections of future imbalances as ageing populations claim more public funds. This will not be an easy task, but the necessary step must be to establish rules that constrain during good times, when governments are flush with money and everything seems to be going right. It is only when governments discipline themselves during times of plentiful budget resources that they will be able to act responsibly when the economy is in difficulty and resources are scarce.

References

Hagen, Jörgen von (1992), *Budgeting Procedures and Fiscal Performance in the European Communities*, Economic Paper No. 96, Commission of the European Communities, Brussels.

Hallerberg, M. and J. von Hagen (1999), "Electoral Institutions, Cabinet Negotiations and Budget Deficits in the European Union" in James M. Poterba and Jörgen von Hagen (eds.), *Fiscal Institutions and Fiscal Performance*, The University of Chicago Press, Chicago, Illinois, United States.

Poterba, James M. and Jörgen von Hagen (eds.) (1999), *Fiscal Institutions and Fiscal Performance*, The University of Chicago Press, Chicago, Illinois, United States.

United States General Accounting Office (1994), *Deficit Reduction: Experiences of Other Nations*, GAO/AIMD-95-30, General Accounting Office, Washington DC.

ISBN 978-92-64-06087-6
Evolutions in Budgetary Practice
Allen Schick and the OECD Senior Budget Officials
© OECD 2009

Chapter 12

Twenty-Five Years of Budgeting Reform*

* This article was originally published in the OECD *Journal on Budgeting*, Vol. 4, No. 1, 2004. At the time of writing, Allen Schick was Visiting Fellow, Governmental Studies, Brookings Institution, Washington DC, and Professor, School of Public Affairs, University of Maryland, United States. Boxed comments were made in 2009.

The network of senior budget officials (the SBO) was launched in 1980 as an *ad hoc* response to the budget stress that beset most developed countries in the aftermath of oil price shocks, high inflation, and economic stagnation. The long post-war expansion had come to a halt, but spending pressures did not abate, leaving national governments with large structural budget deficits. Voter sentiment and fiscal realities precluded political leaders from easing their country's budget plight by boosting taxes. Their only recourse was to take a stricter line on spending, and they needed budget tools that could do the job for them. Meeting for the first time under OECD auspices, senior budget officials perceived that they faced similar predicaments and could learn from the experiences of member countries.

When they met, budget officials brought a distinctive perspective to the SBO, for they bridge the political and administrative domains of government. Every budget is a statement of policy by elected leaders and an administrative plan for the ongoing operations of public programmes and agencies. Senior budget officials are brokers between these realms. They deal on a continuing basis with politicians and administrators, and they must be sufficiently agile to satisfy both constituencies. Most budget directors are drawn from the ranks of senior civil servants, but to succeed they must be alert to political demands and perspectives. This quality – managerial capacity and political astuteness – has characterised both the SBO delegations and discussions at the annual meetings.

The mystery of the SBO is not that the meeting became a regular event but that it took so long for budget officials to convene. Before the SBO, budget officials lacked an international forum for exchanging views and discussing recent developments. They probably were among the few governmental professionals who did not meet periodically. This lack was due, I believe, to an inherent characteristic of budgeting that has had an impact on the content and conduct of SBO meetings. Budgeting is an inward-looking process in which officials and politicians communicate within the confines of the government. Each bureaucratic echelon talks about spending matters to the levels immediately above and below it; ministers and department officials converse throughout the year with their own budget staffs and during the budget season with the central budget office; senior budget officials discuss financial and programme issues with cabinet members and parliamentarians. For the most part, budgeting is government talking to itself, with outside interests eavesdropping and occasionally joining in. Budgeting has the village quality so well described a generation ago by Heclo and Wildavsky in their splendid 1974 study of the United Kingdom's budget practices. Each government has its particular language for these conversations, embedded in forms, classifications, and rules of the budget process, as well as in the behaviour, roles and relationships of those who make and implement budgets. There are universal elements in the language of budgeting, but every country has its peculiar ways and terminology, and these reinforce the insularity of budgeting.

Having met for the first time a quarter of a century ago, budget officials discovered that they share common interests and concerns. Breaking down the insular perspective of budgeters has not been easy, however, and did not occur immediately upon the convening of the SBO. In its first decade, the SBO typically began each meeting with descriptions by delegates of practices and innovations in their country. Although the presentations rarely generated substantive discussion, they encouraged budget officials to be more open in discussing budget practices. A generation later, some delegates are still guarded in sharing experiences and appear more willing to describe new reforms than to explain how past innovations have actually worked. Others, however, come to SBO meetings eager to discuss successes and failures and to trace the evolution of budget practices from one generation of reform to the next.

Over time, the SBO meeting has secured a niche on the calendars of most OECD member countries and has become an annual routine, like the preparation of the budget. As routine, there is risk of the discussions going stale, of repeating that which was taken up in the past. There is a need, therefore, to freshen the discussion, both by pointing to future issues that budget officials may face and by broadening the scope to consider matters that have generally been outside the SBO agenda. I hope this article contributes to invigorating future SBO meetings.

The 25th annual meeting is an appropriate occasion for assessing the practice of budgeting and for reflecting on the challenges and opportunities that may impact budgeting in the decades ahead. I am honoured to have been invited to provide a forthright assessment of the SBO, and hope that my somewhat critical observations do not detract from due consideration of the important issues facing budgeting. In preparing this article, I have benefited from attendance at more than half the SBO meetings, review of almost all the agendas, and perusal of many SBO documents accumulated by me over the years. This article is one observer's musings on the evolution of budgeting, as viewed through the SBO framework. Other observers would undoubtedly draw different lessons from the same material.

In viewing contemporary budgeting through the SBO, I am mindful that the picture which emerges is incomplete. Over the years, the SBO has evolved from an annual meeting into a platform for year-round activities on the functioning of budget systems. In fact, the SBO has nurtured four sub-networks, each focusing on a particular facet of budget practice. One network deals with accounting issues and links budgeting with other financial management tasks. Another addresses the challenges of orienting budgeting (and public management generally) to performance and results. A third recognises the growing role of national parliaments in budget policy, and the fourth frames budgeting within the organisational structure of government. From time to time each network feeds into the SBO, but each has its own network of practitioners and scholars. The SBO has also encouraged and sponsored a compilation of a comprehensive database on budgeting practices, as well as in-depth holistic reviews of budgeting in particular countries.

> As the SBO approaches its 30th year, its activities have continued to expand. It sponsors active networks in all major regions of the world and conducts periodic surveys of budget practices that have become an authoritative database for scholars and practitioners. It has deepened involvement in two ongoing issues: using the budget as an instrument of improved government performance; and the evolution of accounting rules, especially those pertaining to the accrual basis.

Paradoxically, the greatest accomplishment of the SBO has been to launch these networks while keeping the high-level meeting for themselves. They meet once a year, but research and dissemination continues throughout the year.

Section 1 of this article provides the context for the SBO by comparing the budget performance of OECD member countries before and after the convening of these annual meetings. The contrast between the two periods is striking, for there has been a fundamental reorientation of budgeting from expansion to constraint. While this shift has been spurred by the SBO, changes in political and economic conditions have been more important factors than the machinery of budgeting. Budgeting has been the dependent variable; it has been remoulded from time to time to fit changing political preferences and economic circumstances.

Section 2 considers budgeting from the vantage point of the SBO agenda. It examines the main topics discussed at the meetings and also reflects on why some important issues have been outside the SBO purview. My not-surprising conclusion is that when they meet, budget officials converse on the matters that preoccupy them on the job – the techniques and processes of budgeting. These are their daily concerns, and these are what they want to learn about from counterparts in other countries. This confined agenda comes at a cost, however, for it pulls them away from the political, economic and social conditions that influence both the behaviour of budget makers and the outcomes of the process.

The SBO shows evidence of breaking out of this confined agenda, though at a slower pace than this writer would like. The comprehensive country reviews are especially noteworthy, for they provide a template for taking a broad view of the forces that shape budgeting in each country.

> Recent SBO meetings have focused on issues that broaden its interests beyond the ongoing routines of budgeting. Two such interests are tax expenditures and public-private partnerships (PPPs). In considering tax expenditures, budget officials have explored the principles of a sound, fair and efficient tax system; and they have delved into the economic rationale of PPPs as well as the manner in which they are accounted for in the budget.

Section 3 turns to the basic functions of budgeting and questions whether governments are adequately suited to perform essential tasks. The key functions considered here are:

- establishing a fiscal framework that is sustainable over the medium term and beyond;
- allocating resources to programmes on the basis of government priorities and programme effectiveness;
- operating government and delivering public services efficiently;
- assuring that the budget reflects citizen preferences; and
- assuring that spending units are accountable for their actions.

Some of the conclusions presented here are drawn from previous SBO (and other) work, but the focus is on overall budget capacity, not on specific reforms.

The questioning tone of this article's perspective has been influenced by the "beyond budgeting" movement that has spread from the business sector to government. This movement regards budgeting as an impediment to strategic decision making and argues that firms and governments are impeded by the routines of budgeting from managing themselves effectively. Although this movement has not significantly influenced budget theory or practice, it has raised important questions that should not be ignored in thinking about the future of budgeting. Interest in the "beyond budgeting" concept has been sparked by a sense that, although the process has undergone numerous reforms, fundamental limitations persist. Despite repeated efforts to uproot incrementalist tendencies, budgeting serves better as a means of continuing the past into the future than as a means of shaping the future directions of government or society. It may be that the agenda of budget reform will have to be bolder and broader if it is to significantly alter the way the process is used or the results produced.

> The "beyond budgeting" concept appears to be much less promising than was the case when this article was written. Few governments have taken it seriously, perhaps because the notion of putting expenditures on automatic pilot would undermine democratic governance and fiscal discipline. In retrospect, "beyond budgeting" was more an expression of frustration with the routines and frictions of budgeting than a practical method of managing public finances.

1. Budget trends: 1960-2000

In 1930, during the bleak years of the Great Depression, John Maynard Keynes, the 20th century's pre-eminent economist, predicted in a mass circulation magazine that our grandchildren will enjoy economic affluence that far surpasses anything previous generations had experienced. Keynes' prediction was based solely on the arithmetic of compounding: if developed economies were to grow at a rate of about 2% per year, output would double every generation or so. Keynes' prescience was not fulfilled until the post-war period, but actual economic growth in OECD member countries turned out to be vastly higher than he had foreseen. Real GDP averaged almost 5% annual growth during the period 1960-73, the earliest years for which the OECD publishes such data. With this growth rate, economic output in 1973 was double what it had been in 1960. Inasmuch as growth was even more buoyant in the immediate post-war period, it is likely that economic output in OECD member countries was at least four times greater in the mid 1970s than it had been a quarter of a century earlier.

The economic boom fuelled and financed a vast expansion of government. Total government outlays in the OECD community rose from an average of 28% of GDP in 1960 to almost 39% in 1980, the first year of the SBO. This one-half percentage point increase per year in spending as a share of GDP is truly extraordinary in view of the post-war economic boom. Government spending in OECD member countries averaged at least six times more in 1980 than it had done 30 years earlier. Although part of the spending increase was due to the rise in the prices of goods and services produced by government relative to the overall price level, most of the spending increase was due to a real rise in public spending. The post-war era offers strong validation of Wagner's Law – the proposition that, as it becomes more affluent, a society spends a rising share of its wealth on public goods and services. With affluence, citizens demanded better roads, more teachers, additional educational services, expanded health care, stronger environmental protection, and other services. With the exception of national defence, virtually all sectors gained resources.

In the aftermath of depression and war, citizens in OECD member countries coveted economic security, and national governments responded by establishing or enlarging various income-support schemes. More than half of the total rise in relative public spending was in social security transfers, which soared from 7% of GDP in 1969 to almost 13% two decades later. The resulting change in the composition of public expenditure greatly complicated the task of managing public finances. With a rising portion of the budget spent on entitlements, OECD member countries could not as easily adjust spending levels to changes in their fiscal position.

The advance in public spending was broad and relentless; in most countries, it rose almost every year. Spending increased in good times when resources were plentiful and often also increased when the economy weakened and the budget was tight. It increased in good times because governments could afford to spend more, and in less favourable circumstances because governments felt obliged to counter the shortfall in economic performance. Spending grew because governments took on new commitments and because of the momentum of old commitments.

Although an expanding economy fed more money into government coffers each year, revenue increases often did not keep pace with escalating demands for public goods and services. Governments frequently boosted tax rates to finance additional spending. Taxpayer resistance was low as long as disposable (after-tax) income was also rising. Consumers had more money to spend on their individual wants; governments had more to spend on collective wants.

Budget processes were contoured to serve the new political and economic realities. Some changes were formal, but the most important ones were behavioural. Budget officials relaxed the input controls they had maintained for decades and consolidated line items into broader categories that gave spending units greater flexibility in using appropriated funds. The central budget office still cast a critical eye on spending demands, but it also joined the search for ways to enhance public services. In a few countries, efforts were made to reorient budgeting to the objectives and performance of government. Programme budgeting, planning-programming-budgeting systems and other reforms were attempts to adapt budgeting to the active, enlarged role of government. They failed for a variety of reasons, one of which was that budget offices were ill prepared to change their own behaviour. Yet, even though they fell short of their lofty ambitions, the reforms encouraged budget offices to move away from a control role and to explore means of using the machinery of budgeting to improve government performance.

A more successful transformation occurred in the fiscal posture of government. At the start of the post-war boom, most OECD countries gave lip service to the balanced budget rule; by the end (in the mid 1970s), most had an accommodating posture that allowed the government to spend more than it took in when justified by economic conditions. Balancing the economy through fiscal policies that promoted growth, stable prices and low unemployment was regarded as more urgent than balancing the budget. The budget became a pliable instrument of fiscal policy, with built-in stabilisers and discretionary tax and spending decisions shaping each year's outcome. At first, deficit spending was deemed to be justified when the economy was weak; over time, deficits came to be regarded as appropriate whenever actual or projected output was below the economy's potential. Many OECD member countries devised new fiscal tools to determine the appropriate size of the deficit. These typically distinguished between structural deficits that occur when governments spend more than a fully-employed economy would yield in revenue, and cyclical deficits which result from the economy operating below potential. As long as the economy continued on an upward course, public debt was a stable or declining share of GDP. The fact that economic growth persisted was evidence enough that modest deficits do not damage the economy. Quite the opposite, spending in excess of revenue enabled society to make fuller use of economic capacity, gave governments additional resources to finance programme improvements, and enhanced the well-being of citizens.

The expansion in government did not crowd out private enterprise. Business boomed alongside government, and the notion took hold that each owed a good part of its success to the other. Markets supply governments with money, and governments establish favourable conditions, such as an educated workforce and a fair distribution of income, for business to flourish. Government employment in OECD member countries rose 2.7% a year during the period 1960-73, but industrial employment also advanced, though at a slower pace of 1.4% a year. Unemployment was low, averaging only 3.2% during the entire period, and productivity gains were high, with real GDP per worker rising 3.8% a year. Consumer prices advanced 4% a year, but real interest rates were very low: less than 2% in most of the countries for which data are available.

The halcyon years came to an abrupt end with the oil shocks of the 1970s. Economists conventionally mark 1973 as the close of the post-war boom. Real GDP growth slipped to 2.8% a year during the period 1973-79, and other vital economic signs also deteriorated. Unemployment averaged 5% a year, and inflation (as measured by changes in consumer prices) exceeded 10% a year. Budget deficits climbed to 2.5% of GDP – still a manageable level, but a harbinger of worse fiscal outcomes in subsequent decades. Governments could justify deficit spending to spur their sluggish economies, but they could not muster sufficient financial resources or political support to do so. As stagnation set in, many questioned the standard prescriptions for combating economic weakness. The post-war Keynesian hegemony showed deep fissures, with dissidents challenging the efficacy of demand management and arguing that fixed rather than elastic fiscal targets and smaller tax burdens were needed to restore economic vigour. Changing course was difficult, however, for the budget model they used was asymmetrical. It was far easier to increase spending than to cut it, and easier to incur a deficit than to curtail it.

These adverse conditions were the backdrop for establishing the SBO. In step with the times, early SBO meetings grappled with managing cutbacks and shifting the budget from an incremental to a decremental path. Delegates shared experiences, such as Japan's scrap-and-build policy that required spending initiatives to be offset by cutbacks, the "reconsideration" procedures introduced in the Netherlands to review existing programmes, Sweden's "cheese slicer" that pared 2% a year from operating budgets, and the United Kingdom's experience with cash limits that set hard constraints on spending. The new mood was summed up in a Canadian government report that introduced an "envelope" system for managing public expenditures and urged that budgeting be reoriented from a process that uses programme analysis to rationally expand government into a rationing system that constrains the size of government.

Viewed in the light of its original emphasis, the SBO has had modest success. It has not curtailed deficits, which were higher in the 1980s than in the previous decade and, as Europe's difficulty in enforcing the Stability and Growth Pact demonstrates, still persist at an elevated level in quite a few countries. Government spending has stabilised, however, and is now only slightly higher as a share of GDP than it was two decades ago. Trend data suggest that many countries practise "*status quo*" budgeting. Government commitments and public expectations rule out significant shrinkage in the boundaries of the welfare state, while persistent deficits and opposition to tax increases rule out major expansions in public spending. In many OECD member countries, budgeting has settled into a process of snipping existing programmes at the margins to make room for targeted enhancements. With spending neither growing nor shrinking significantly as a portion of GDP, budgeting has been oriented to extracting greater efficiency and performance from government agencies.

> Recent SBO meetings have examined fiscal rules and the sustainability of governmental fiscal positions. These subjects are an important part of the everyday world of budgeting. Yet it would be unreasonable to expect the SBO to break the pattern of deficit spending. A sound budget process will produce deficits when political and economic conditions drive governments to spend more than they take in. It is the task of budgeting to inform politicians of the implications of the choices they make; in democracies, it is not the job of budgeting to tie the hands of elected leaders so that they are barred from existing choice.

There are two main exceptions to *status quo* budgeting. One occurs when a government has a surge in revenue that exceeds normal incremental demands on the budget; the other occurs when a financial crisis makes it difficult to sustain incremental budget policies. The quality of budget institutions is particularly important in these circumstances, and the true test of the budget office's effectiveness may come when faced with these opportunities. When windfall revenues open the door to expansion, a government needs a budget process that can sift through the options and select cost-effective policies; when crisis knocks at the gates, a government needs the capacity to make hard choices and to scale back government commitments in a politically acceptable way. Leadership is essential in both situations, but so too is the machinery of budgeting. A robust process enables a government to put expansionary funds to good use and to pare spending to acceptable dimensions.

2. The SBO agenda

There have been few surprises on the SBO agenda; most of the topics have been matters that budget officials deal with year after year. As might be expected, they have given repeated attention to the entitlements and transfer payments that now dominate the budgets of many countries, but they have not made much headway in establishing effective control of these expenditures. Every few years, the SBO reflects on the time frame of the process, yearning for a medium – or longer – term consideration of programmes and spending commitments, but unable to abandon the annual framework that drives the budget cycle. From time to time, they have grappled with off-budget accounts, state-owned enterprises, and other practices that are weakly regulated, if at all, through budget decisions. They occasionally are introspective and review changes in the role and operation of the central budget office and its relation to other governmental organs. Periodically, they get updates on developments in programme evaluation, performance measurement, and other innovations. One recent innovation has attracted considerable interest. Each year the OECD selects a member country's budget system for in-depth, critical review and discusses its findings at the SBO meeting in tandem with publication of a report on the country.

These reports have consistently been of very high quality and have covered legislative authority, financial management and the overall performance of public management in assessing country practices. Interest in these assessments is reflected in the fact that countries now invite the OECD Secretariat to undertake a critical assessment.

Some topics have gained prominence in recent years. The SBO now shows greater interest in the budget role and resources of the national legislature, and in linking budget work to accounting and other financial management operations. As already noted, the SBO has established networks in these and two other areas. The networks reflect not only a broader perspective but, more importantly, strong efforts to connect budgeting to other government activities that pertain to managing public money, such as legislative work and accounting practices. When the SBO started, each country had its own budget conventions and rules; over the years, the differences have narrowed, largely because of pressure to standardise accounting practices. Although the cash basis still predominates, budget officials have studied accrual methods as well as the relationship between budget statements and financial reports. The SBO has given repeated attention in recent years to the performance management movement, especially the use of the budget to allocate resources on the basis of results. The performance and results network launched by the SBO reflects the budget community's awareness that the management of public expenditure is an integral part of public management. This represents a fundamental reorientation in budgeting. When the SBO was started, the prevailing view was that budget systems can be modernised independently of the management culture within which budgets are made and implemented. This perspective has been displaced by one that recognises the dependence of budgeting on overall managerial capacity.

The recurrence of certain issues lends support to the notion that there are no permanent solutions in budgeting. Entitlements will be a problem as long as budgeting is practised, as will efforts by spending units to evade budget control. Deficits are a perennial issue, as are the time frame of budgeting and linking resources and results. These will still be on the SBO agenda 25 years from now, as might some issues that do not currently engage the interest of budget officials.

The SBO is reform-minded, focusing on recent innovations in OECD member countries. Budget officials are genuinely interested in what counterparts in other countries are doing and why. There is usually an ample stockpile of recent innovations, and reformers are eager to display their new methods for others. Many budget officials aspire to make big, transformative changes, even though they usually settle for marginal ones. Their aspirations speak to an enduring characteristic of budgeting. Those who make and implement government budgets yearn for better ways to handle these chores. There is too much friction and not enough of the right kinds of information. Muddling through one year, budget officials know the next year will likely be as abrasive and difficult as the cycle just completed. They know that decisions are made with inadequate evidence on how money is spent or how much is needed. They strive to focus on the future, but are driven to short-term expedients that enable them to meet deadlines and patch up differences. They are powerful, but they also are aware of the limits on their power imposed by political realities and financial commitments or expectations.

Who in budgeting has not thought from time to time, "There must be a better way"? This sentiment is the wellspring of the endless, frustrating quest for innovation. Reform is the better way, or at least promises to be. It is the quest to transform budgeting into a more rational, less incremental process. And though it may lead to some new methods, most reform falls far short of the mark. The unending parade of reforms is strong evidence that budgeting is still wedded to incremental norms, that short-termism crowds out the longer run, that it is more important to get the work done on time than to get it right.

There are many reasons why budget reforms come up short, the most important of which may have to do with an overriding need to complete budget work on schedule, no matter how inadequate the data are. Budgeting would be a more rational process if it were less essential, if politicians and officials had the option of gathering all the information they need to optimise public spending. Budgeting would pay more attention to results if it had sufficient time to measure results and feed the data into decisions; it would have a longer perspective if it were not bound by the 12 months of the fiscal year; and it might be less incremental if the decisions were taken by experts rather than politicians.

Budget reform must manœuvre within boundaries that are largely fixed. The most limiting boundaries are political, temporal and informational. As formidable as these limits are, reform might make more headway if past reforms were systematically examined. Budget officials should strive to learn as much from the many past failures as they do from the relatively few successes. The SBO gives much more play to the promise of new reforms than to the results of old ones. The old reforms just fade away, to be replaced by the next generation of innovations – which in many cases has the same objective as previous generations. Reforms come and go, but the quest to make budgeting a more rational process goes on.

The SBO gives reform-minded countries a platform for presenting their new ideas; it should also encourage them to explain what they learned from past disappointments. The SBO has an enormous stockpile of experience to draw from. Every area of reform is a fertile opportunity for critical analysis. The following are just a few of the many possibilities that may interest budget officials:

- Why has programme evaluation been useful at some times and in some places, but not in others? Why, for example, did Australia have more to show for its investment in evaluation than Canada?

- Under what conditions do fiscal rules, such as those promulgated by Europe's Stability and Growth Pact and by fiscal responsibility laws, regulate the size of the deficit? Can these rules operate under adverse economic conditions?

- What is the experience of the countries that have introduced the accrual basis into budgeting? How has it affected the way resources are allocated and used?

- How do countries reconcile a multi-year framework with the annual budget process? Do they keep to the multi-year plan or remake the budget each year?

The rapid spread of medium-term expenditure frameworks (MTEFs) to more than 100 countries adds weight to the argument that this device warrants closer scrutiny than it has obtained. Do MTEF governments truly integrate the annual budget into medium-term decisions? Does the baseline (or forward estimate) bias budget decisions and complicate the task of regulating future expenditure? Is the medium term (3-5 years) far enough ahead to change the behaviour of politicians and officials? These are but a few of the questions worth exploring.

Addressing these types of questions would provide governments a firmer basis for deciding whether and how to restructure their budget practices.

2.1. *The SBO non agenda*

Budget reform is typically framed within the boundaries of the process: how will particular procedures or requirements be altered if one or another change is introduced? Budget reform is rarely considered within the broader context of government economic and social policy. Because of this confined perspective, much that has happened during the SBO years has been absent from its agenda. The effect has been to treat reform as a technocratic exercise rather than as a means of repositioning the process to better serve contemporary socio-political ends. Nevertheless, many reforms on the SBO agenda have been driven by the political and economic contexts of budgeting. When governments seek to impose fiscal rules, for example, they almost always have been influenced by concern over economic conditions. Similarly, when governments strive for better performance, they are responding to citizen concerns over the efficiency and results of government programmes.

> Rereading this paragraph, especially the lines pertaining to the technocratic orientation of reform, I sense that it ignores a fundamental point about budgeting: to budget is to engage in a bundle of routines that are repeated year after year, sometimes with modification, but often without material change. These routines make budgeting a process. Perforce, therefore, attempts to change the process require adjustment in the routines of budgeting. Yet just because budget officials focus on routines does not mean they are oblivious to larger political and socio-economic issues.

During the past quarter of a century, commerce and culture have been increasingly globalised, making countries more interdependent and less in control of their own budget fate. Interdependence has not yet run its full course; by the time it does, matters that now are domestic will have been internationalised. Agricultural policy and social expenditure are two such issues, but certainly not the only ones. New transnational structures, such as the European Economic and Monetary Union, have been established and more are likely to emerge in the decades ahead. It is not far-fetched to foresee income redistribution defined as a regional or global issue, and for international courts to prescribe or proscribe particular expenditures. The Cold War has ended, allowing defence's overall share of national budgets to decline, but the scourge of terrorism has spread, putting future budgets and underlying socio-economic conditions at grave risk. The revolution in information technology has boosted efficiency in both business and government, and has taken much of the rote work out of compiling and implementing the budget. It also has opened the door to much greater transparency in budgeting, giving citizens access to data that were previously unavailable or withheld. In almost all member countries, the population is ageing and, along with it, the national budget as well. There will be less money in future budgets for programme initiatives. Budgeting risks becoming an accounting of past decisions rather than a means of making new ones.

Less dramatic trends – but certainly important ones – in the conduct of politics have affected budgeting. In most OECD member countries, citizens now have less trust and less confidence in government and its political leaders, and are less attentive to political matters.

The ideal that the best and the brightest seek careers in the public service has faded, and making a career in government is less attractive to young people. Citizen disengagement has been accompanied by a vast increase in the number, activism and influence of interest groups and NGOs, which operate across all sectors and (in most countries) pay considerable attention to budget matters. Interest groups and NGOs vigilantly guard their interests, demand more from government, and campaign against cutbacks. Contemporary national governments also are pressured by global and local entities, and have less space for independent action than before. Under the banner of fiscal decentralisation, quite a few national governments have transferred money and power to regional and local authorities.

In most developed countries, the state has become the risk holder for society, sheltering citizens against the financial wounds of illness, old age, unemployment, disability, and other conditions that reduce personal incomes below a legally defined level. The pooling of risk via government has brought many advantages, including greater economic stability and a fairer distribution of income, but it has taken a bite out of budget control. As risk holder, the government's budget is swayed by social and economic developments that are largely beyond its control, especially within the frame of a single fiscal year. The transfer of risk to government has fed citizen expectations that public benefits are a matter of entitlement. High expectations and low trust in government create budget pressures with which political leaders have difficulty coping.

Although budgeting has been greatly impacted by changes that have unfolded over the past 25 years, the SBO has not offered a window onto these developments. With few exceptions, it has tended to its own business, centred on the machinery of budgeting. This confined perspective may be due to the insularity of budgeting discussed earlier. The budget has, however, assumed the status of the pre-eminent policy document of governments. In the days of expanding government, substantive policy decisions could be made outside of the context of the budget, as the necessary resources would be readily available. Nowadays, all substantive policy decisions must be made in the context of the budget. It is therefore high time for the SBO to take a wider perspective on budgeting.

There is nothing awry with the SBO focusing on internal budget processes, but the discussion would be enriched by framing it within the larger movements that drive public spending. It is understandable that the revenue side of the budget has received scant attention because tax policy and administration are in the jurisdiction of other government units. It would be useful to discuss revenue projection methods, tax expenditures, and other features of revenue that have a direct bearing on expenditure management. In a similar vein, it would be useful to have fuller discussion of intergovernmental fiscal relations, which affect both the revenue and spending sides of the budget.

3. Budgeting's future agenda

Future SBO meetings will concentrate on matters that budget officials deal with year after year. But it also behoves them to view issues in terms of the overriding purposes that contemporary budgeting serves. While practitioners and observers may disagree on the particular end of budgeting, there is agreement that a sound budget system serves multiple, coexisting purposes. I find it useful to define good budgeting in terms of the following criteria:

- The budget should establish a stable, sustainable fiscal position for the medium term and beyond.

- The budget should facilitate the shift of resources to more effective, higher priority uses.
- The budget should encourage spending units to operate efficiently.
- The budget should be accessible to citizens and responsive to their interests.
- The budget (in tandem with other financial management practices) should assure accountability in the expenditure of public money.

This is an ambitious agenda that cannot be fulfilled, for standards are continually being adjusted upward. The paragraphs that follow set out issues in each of these areas that may be grist for future SBO meetings.

3.1. Sustainable fiscal policy

The fiscal posture of government will be at issue as long as budgeting is practised. The contemporary role of government and its entanglement in economic matters rule out application of a strict balanced budget norm. But open-ended, unconstrained deficits that result because politicians have incentive to tax less and spend more, or from swings in economic conditions, are likely to be unsustainable and to diminish a country's future economic prospect. It is now widely accepted that political incentives bias budgets toward higher deficits, as politicians favour current voters over future taxpayers. When political leaders behave this way in less developed countries, they may destabilise the economy and provoke a run on capital markets. The adverse effects are likely to be less apparent in affluent countries and may not emerge for some time. In fact, there may be short-term benefits, as deficit spending stimulates demand and thereby veils the long-term costs. The political bias to spend in excess of current revenue may be reinforced by short-term economic gains.

These conditions greatly complicate the task of stabilising fiscal policy in OECD member countries. The favoured contemporary solution has been to set fixed fiscal rules, such as those prescribed by the Stability and Growth Pact, and to entrust enforcement to an outside or independent entity that is not swayed by domestic political pressures. But recent difficulties in enforcement of the Stability and Growth Pact call into question the staying power of fixed fiscal rules, even those that allow a modest deficit. These rules may be effective in the short run, as they were in the run-up to the European Economic and Monetary Union. But the longer they are in place, the weaker the rules become, especially when the economy swings from growth to stagnation. Fixed rules which permit modest deficits may be as unworkable as fixed rules which prescribe balanced budgets. The only alternatives, within the framework of fiscal rules, are pliable rules that are adjusted in response to changes in actual or projected economic conditions. Of course, this would return OECD member countries to the situation that prevailed during the post-war "Keynesian" period, but with two big differences. One is that the economies of most OECD member countries are not booming; the other is that enforcement of the rules may be in outside hands. It remains to be seen whether fiscal limits are more stringent when compliance is monitored and enforced by a regional or international body.

Establishing and maintaining a workable fiscal regime should preoccupy the SBO in the years ahead. While fiscal rules have received some attention at recent SBO meetings, economists have colonised these issues as their own. The vast literature on fiscal institutions produced over the past decade attests to the confidence economists have in their capacity to explain why some countries incur deficits and others do not, and to design rules that would constrain deficits. I am not sure that economists have a comparative advantage on this issue. Their models tend to be simplistic and self-fulfilling, and they know less than budget officials about the political and bureaucratic pressures that drive public spending. Budget officials certainly have a deeper understanding of how procedural rules affect spending outcomes. They have a lot to contribute to the design of effective fiscal rules.

3.2. Effective allocation

At its core, budgeting is a process for allocating resources among competing demands for public money. Anyone who has worked in budgeting knows that this is not a fair competition and that old claims on the budget have an advantage over new ones. No matter how it is structured, budgeting decisions are anchored in the past, varying usually only in small increments from one year to the next. It is time to call a halt to the reformist war against incrementalism and to acknowledge that this is one feature of budgeting that will not and (according to some) should not be abandoned.

If budgeting is inherently incremental, can governments keep spending fresh and responsive to changing priorities? This question is urgent because an ageing society will make national budgets even more rigid, while a changing society will require that budgets be more adaptive. Contemporary budget developments address this problem in quite different ways. One approach arises out of the "beyond budgeting" argument referred to earlier in this article. It considers budgeting in both business and government to be rigid and confining, and urges strategic policy makers and programme managers to devise alternative processes such as strategic plans and operational goals for steering large organisations. The "beyond budgeting" advocates claim that these methods have been applied in some business firms but that the applicability to government is questionable. Budget reformers, by contrast, have not given up on the process, but are continually searching for means to inject a capacity for change into resource decisions. Contemporary change-oriented reforms include a longer time frame, more programme evaluation, and fuller use of performance targets and outcome measures. A third approach seeks to transform budgeting by coupling it to other change-driving processes – such as strategic and programme planning – that facilitate policy adjustments. The three paths differ fundamentally in their assessment of budgeting's capacity for effective allocation. The first gives up on budgeting, the second has confidence that conventional reforms will suffice, the third makes budgeting dependent on other processes. In my view, none has sufficient promise to materially enlarge governments' scope for change.

To finance emerging financial demands, future governments may be impelled to increase taxes if economic growth does not provide sufficient new money. Governments will be able to spend more on new priorities only if they have more to spend. Alternatively, they may continue to make incremental policy adjustments to finance marginal reallocations from lower to higher priorities. One likely tactic will be to tinker with entitlement formulas and user charges in order to save some money on pensions or health care. While such savings will not derigidify budgeting, they will enable pressured governments to muddle through from one year to the next. This is a common way of pacifying the budget. Dealing with budget pressures one year at a time, the future will take care of its problems.

3.3. Efficient operations

Over the years, the SBO has devoted more attention to the operational performance of government than to the other core functions of budgeting. This is not surprising, because budget officials are involved on a continuing basis with the operations of government. Although transfer payments may claim the largest share of the budget, operational issues claim the largest share of budget officials' time. Expenditures for running operations and delivering services are the portions of the budget decided each year and the areas that budget makers look to for short-term savings to align revenues and expenditures.

Performance budgeting has long been the favourite instrument for getting governments to operate more efficiently and to improve public services. As one whose Ph.D. dissertation some 40 years ago was on performance budgeting, I expect this subject to absorb the attention of budget officials for a very long time. Budgeting on the basis of actual or expected results is a simple but elusive objective. It is simple because the idea has universal appeal; it appeals to common sense and should be what budgeting is about. It is elusive because linking resources and results is difficult and complicates the task of producing the budget.

The impediments to budgeting on the basis of results are numerous; the ones outlined briefly here pertain to the budget's role in managing government programmes and agencies. To begin with, performance-based budgeting comes in so many varieties that the term does not offer much guidance on how budgeting is to be structured. At one end of the spectrum, it may connote only that the budget contains supporting information on the outputs and activities of spending units; at the other end, it may indicate that each increment of resources buys an increment of results. The former is so undemanding that just about any government that has workload or output data can claim to budget on this basis; the latter is so challenging that few governments can meet its standards. For governments that want to take credit for aligning resources and results, it is tempting to settle for the least demanding version. When they do, just about the only thing changed is the appearance of the budget. Resources and results continue to go their separate ways.

Although it is beyond the current reach of most governments, the demanding version offers useful clues about what it takes to budget on the basis of results. To budget for results, governments must also manage for results – that is, they must organise administrative operations and deliver services to optimise the outputs that agencies produce. It is naïve to think that a government can manage on one basis and budget on an entirely different one. If management is regimented – with administrative actions centrally controlled and managers evaluated on the basis of compliance with procedural rules – it will be futile to try to budget for results. If managers do not care about results when they go about daily tasks, the budget will not care about results either. The practice of budgeting is encased in public management, and it is only when spending units are mobilised to perform well that a government will be able to budget for performance. A government's dependence on transforming management vastly increases the difficulty of orienting the budget process to results.

Linking resources and results is also a technical challenge, for it requires data on the cost of producing outputs that are currently unavailable in all but a few countries. Getting cost data requires managerial accounting systems that break down output into standard units and distinguish between fixed and variable costs and between average and marginal costs, and thereby enable governments to estimate the cost of producing each increment of output. Linking resources and results may also require two more fundamental changes: a shift from budgeting on the basis of the cost (or expenditure) of operations to budgeting on the basis of the price paid for services; and a shift from fixed operating budgets (in which the volume of resources does not vary with the volume of output) to a variable budget. Inasmuch as neither of these transformations is under way, most governments that seek to link resources and results end up with performance budgets that resemble conventional budgets.

A government can manage for results without having a full-blown performance budget, either by introducing market-type arrangements that enable recipients of public services to select their suppliers or by enabling providers of these services to operate efficiently. If performance improves through either of these ways (or, more likely, through a combination of both), the government will be better primed to budget for results.

3.4. Democratising the budget

The history of budgeting is the history of democratic institutions. From the Magna Carta hundreds of years ago, through the emergence of legislative assemblies in the Middle Ages to the development of modern budgeting, the aim has been to limit the power of those in elected or appointed office to spend public money. This is the main reason why budgeting has for so long been grounded on rules and procedures that control the actions of spenders.

This model of budgetary democracy no longer serves the people sufficiently well. In fact, critical features of budgeting may hamper democracy and thwart the capacity of the public to decide how public money is spent. The insularity of budgeting, noted at the outset of this article, veils most spending discussions from public view. At best, budgeting practises a form of *ex post* democracy, with the public informed only after decisions have been taken. Genuine public participation has been impeded by the growth of government and the elaboration of complex budget rules as well as by the emergence of strong political parties and the enforcement of party discipline in national legislatures. On the periphery of budgeting, interest groups and others sometimes join in the discussions, especially in countries with corporatist or pluralistic tendencies, but their influence is uneven and may come at the expense of under-represented interests.

Redemocratising the budget will have higher rank on the SBO agenda in the decades ahead than it has had thus far. It is highly probable that the standards of "democratic adequacy" will continue to rise, opening the process more, giving a more diverse array of interests the opportunities to influence budget decisions. One channel of discussion might be the legislature's role and capacity in modifying the budget submitted by the government; another might be the opportunities opened up by the information revolution for e-budgeting and other new forms of dissemination and decision. Greater attention might be given to: the distributive effects of national budgets; which groups or sectors get benefits and which do not; and the means by which certain stakeholders might participate more actively in allocating public funds. One should not be surprised if budget officials debate the lack of transparency in compiling the budget and question whether the veil of secrecy ought to be lifted from the process.

At the dawn of the information revolution, there were predictions of how budgeting would be opened up to citizen participation through interactive voting schemes that enable citizens to express their preferences on various budget options. In many countries, the Internet is used as a passive instrument – to inform citizens of decisions already taken – not as a means of enabling voters to register their preferences in advance.

At future SBO meetings, voices will be heard arguing that opening the process to outside scrutiny or participation will greatly complicate the task of making ends meet. It is hard enough to reject claims behind closed doors; it may be impossible to do so in the open. The more constrained future budgets are, the greater will be the insistence of affected interests that they have a seat at the table. A strong dose of budgetary democracy will hobble the always difficult task of reallocating money from some uses to others. It may be that the only prudent way to redemocratise the budget is to combine it with measures that safeguard fiscal discipline.

3.5. *Genuine accountability*

It is an article of faith and practice in OECD member countries that spenders must account for their use of public funds. Toward this end, financial reporting and auditing systems have been established in each country. These generally are regarded as reliable and in compliance with standards prescribed by accountancy and audit groups. In recent years, the SBO has examined the spread of accrual standards and has considered whether these are suitable for the budget, which traditionally has been on a cash basis.

Accruals *versus* cash opens the door to a larger question: the operation of the budget process within the government's financial management framework. To my knowledge, the SBO has not examined integrated financial information systems which use advanced information technology to connect the myriad financial operations of government. Although the main selling point of integrated systems is that they improve efficiency and reduce error, tying the budget into them is likely to change both its content and the manner in which it is prepared. Rather than having its own way of counting and compiling the numbers, budgeting will be beholden to accounting rules.

4. SBO 2029

The mood was sombre as delegates from the 107 member countries gathered in Qatar for the 50th annual meeting of the SBO. Fewer than a handful of countries were absent, and those represented at the meeting came in delegations of 5-10 political leaders and experts. Some years earlier, the SBO was formally disbanded and a meeting of senior budget ministers took its place. But out of habit or nostalgia, the meeting was still universally referred to as the SBO. Budget directors were members of the country delegations but, with few exceptions, each country sent a minister to speak on its behalf and vote on the matters before the body. The switch from officials to ministers was due to the transformation of the SBO into the legislative body of the OECD for establishing standards of good budget practice. Inasmuch as each country's financial condition was implicated in these decisions, first a handful and over time almost all countries entrusted the work to political leaders who were authorised to speak and vote for their government.

As a standards-setting body, the SBO had a full agenda that no longer accommodated abstract papers by academics. The agenda was congested, with barely enough time during the two days to handle the weighty questions that had to be resolved. Some countries urged that the SBO meeting be lengthened to as much as a week, but ministers protested that two days were all they could spare. To assure that these days were efficiently organised, the SBO had restructured itself around a handful of formal committees, each with a defined jurisdiction and each empowered to make authoritative recommendations to the plenary. In each country, executives and parliamentarians had already been briefed on the agenda, and instructions were issued as to how delegates should vote. The main committees treated accounting rules, fiscal integration, budget procedure, social rights, and legal matters. The Legal Committee was the only one that did not make formal recommendations. Rather, it was responsible for advising the SBO on the budgetary consequences of recent rulings by the International Court of Social and Economic Justice.

The report of the Accounting Rules Committee had been presented months earlier in a disclosure document that evoked widespread criticism. It recommended that the standards applied to country budgets be revised to cover new types of financial instruments and downstream liabilities. The existence of these standards was no longer controversial, though it had been about 15 years earlier when budget directors fought a losing battle to allow each country to set its own budget standards. The majority, however, determined that national economies were so interdependent that it was essential to prescribe budgetary accounting rules. The issue before the SBO in 2029, as in most previous meetings, was whether to prescribe additional standards in response to the invention of new financing arrangements. On the basis of statements issued by the leaders of many countries, it was expected that the proposed standards would occasion robust discussion at the SBO meeting but that they would be approved by an overwhelming majority. After all, no political leader wants to be exposed to accusations that the official budget reports are false or misleading.

The Fiscal Integration Committee is making yet another effort to fine-tune deficit and debt rules in response to cyclical changes in economic conditions. This is a perennial issue, for which there is no permanent solution. This year's report deals with a particularly troublesome issue: the fiscal destabilisation arising from shocks and other major disturbances. At one time, it was thought that shocks were problems only in less developed countries, but the globalisation of terrorism and other factors have brought this risk to some of the most developed countries. The initial draft called for a waiver of fiscal rules in case of fundamental shocks, but some countries objected that this was too permissive and would open the door to wholesale evasion. A compromise was reached to suspend fiscal rules for affected countries for as many as three years, but it is certain that this question will be on future SBO agendas.

The Budget Procedure Committee is grappling with a question that has vexed democratic governments for the better part of a decade. Pursuant to an international court ruling, the SBO decided years earlier that representatives of key groups should have the right to attend all budget negotiations, including bilaterals between the finance minister and each sectoral minister. The SBO has dragged its feet on opening the process, but the courts have given it a deadline by which it must designate eligible groups. If it fails to act in time, the courts will impose their own decision. The Budget Procedure Committee has proposed that each government be authorised to make its own selection. This artful compromise may buy time, but it is likely that the courts will revisit the issue.

The Social Rights Committee is the only committee with members from non-OECD countries. Its charter is to prod developed countries to redistribute resources to citizens of less developed countries. The first such redistribution was done under the auspices of the Millennium Development Goals for the year 2020. The second occurred during the past decade, pursuant to the second-generation goals, and the Social Rights Committee has devised a formula for the latest set of goals which run to the year 2040. A close vote is expected on a motion to defer consideration of this issue for at least a year.

The Legal Committee produced an annual compilation of court decisions that have a material impact on government revenue or expenditure. During the past year, 853 such rulings were issued by courts in member countries and another 17 by international panels. The net impact is estimated to exceed 2% of GDP in the OECD area.

During the delegates' lunch, the OECD Secretariat arranged for a retired budget director to reflect on the 50 years of the SBO. She delighted the assembled delegates by recalling the long-forgotten debates about performance budgeting, multi-year targets, and the like. "We took it all so seriously, then," she concluded.

The archives of the SBO contain a variant set of minutes on the 2029 meeting. According to this version, in 2029 the SBO discussed budgeting for results, getting a longer-term perspective, and the legislature's growing role. No votes were taken, and no conclusions were reached.

Reference

Heclo, Hugh and Aaron Wildavsky (1974), *The Private Government of Public Money*, University of California Press, Berkeley and Los Angeles.

ISBN 978-92-64-06087-6
Evolutions in Budgetary Practice
Allen Schick and the OECD Senior Budget Officials
© OECD 2009

Chapter 13

Sustainable Budget Policy: Concepts and Approaches*

Concern about fiscal sustainability has been fuelled by the projected ageing of populations in OECD countries and the likely surge in government spending on pensions and health care. For the most part, it has not been driven by worries about the current fiscal position of countries. Multiple dimensions of sustainability are discussed: solvency, growth, stability, fairness. Modes of sustainability analysis are related to existing budget practices, including baseline projections, balance sheet analysis, fiscal gap analysis, and generational accounting. The article concludes with a discussion of how to build sustainability analysis into the budget process and how to manage the sustainability process.

* This article was originally published in the OECD Journal on Budgeting, Vol. 5, No. 1, 2005. At the time of writing, Allen Schick was Visiting Fellow, Governmental Studies, Brookings Institution, Washington DC, and Professor, School of Public Affairs, University of Maryland, United States. An afterword was written in 2009.

It was not long ago that fiscal sustainability was an issue only for underdeveloped and emerging market economies that have fragile capital markets, rising debt and an expanding public sector, and are vulnerable to cyclical disturbances or financial contagion. Recently, however, concern about fiscal sustainability has spread to advanced countries, some of which have established ongoing processes for assessing their capacity to maintain their fiscal position for an extended period. Australia, New Zealand and the United Kingdom review fiscal sustainability as part of their new fiscal responsibility regimes introduced during the past decade. Member countries of the European Union comment on sustainability in their medium-term budget frameworks submitted to the European Commission (EC) pursuant to the Stability and Growth Pact, and the EC reviews the long-term outlook in its annual report on fiscal policy. The United States annually reviews the long-term sustainability of Social Security and Medicare, the two largest claimants on future budgets.

Concern about sustainability has been fueled by the projected ageing of populations in OECD countries and the likely surge in government spending on pensions and health care. For the most part, it has not been driven by worries about the current fiscal position of countries. In fact, countries with sound positions (such as Australia and New Zealand) have been in the forefront of this movement. Interest in sustainability has been stirred by innovations in accounting and economic analysis such as accrual accounting and budgeting, the application of present-value analysis to government budgets, intergenerational accounting, and fiscal gap analysis. None of these is standard budget practice, but some are likely to be built into the routines of budgeting in the future. It is also likely that countries will experiment with different techniques and that some will build sustainability analysis into the annual budget process, while others will conduct such studies as a free-standing exercise.

In migrating from underdeveloped to highly developed countries, fiscal sustainability has shifted in focus from the near term to the distant future. In less developed countries, the immediate concern is whether the government will be able to service its debt if capital flees, the currency depreciates, and interest rates surge. This is the principal focus of sustainability work carried out by the International Monetary Fund. Its "assessments have two main dimensions: indicators of public debt and deficits, and medium-term fiscal projections" (IMF, 2002, p. 12). In OECD countries, the focus is on the long term, typically 30-50 years ahead. Even countries that have had persistent budget deficits and elevated debt loads do not sense impending fiscal crisis; in fact, they have little difficulty financing current budget shortfalls. But many OECD countries are concerned that, although their current fiscal posture is sound or manageable, it might not be a generation or two from now as future governments become encumbered with the costs of past policies and commitments. Inherently, fiscal sustainability in the OECD area has a long-term perspective that aims to prepare for the future by sensitising governments to the need for prudent action to sustain economic well-being for future generations.

Fiscal sustainability is more than projecting the future; it is about the urgency of policy changes as well as the need for new budget tools to assess governments' fiscal position because conventional instruments are not up to the task. A medium-term expenditure framework (MTEF) and fiscal rules, two of the most prominent contemporary innovations, extend the time frame of budgeting 3-5 years ahead, but they are not attuned to long-term issues. An MTEF does not look far enough ahead and, coupled with hard constraints, may spur some stressed governments to engage in budgetary legerdemain which improves the medium-term outlook at the expense of the country's long-term fiscal health. This is not mere speculation, for a number of EU countries have used one-off savings to meet requirements of the Stability and Growth Pact (European Commission, 2004).

Although their time horizon is too short for sustainability work, the MTEF and fiscal rules introduce techniques, such as baseline projections, which can be extended to analyse a country's future fiscal position. Fiscal rules also have relevance because they sensitise governments to the downstream implications of budget policy. But the fact that governments and academics are working to devise new accounting and reporting tools to gauge sustainability indicates that existing techniques do not suffice.

This article is based on the expectation that sustainability will be an essential element of future budget work. Section 1 makes the case that sustainability has multiple dimensions arising out of the diverse perspectives of those urging attention to the issue. Some of the main approaches to analysing sustainability are described in Section 2, which discusses their application to the budget process. The concluding section focuses on means of feeding sustainability results into the formulation of budget policy.

1. The multiple dimensions of sustainability

The shift to a long-term horizon has expanded the ways governments and international organisations think about sustainability. The term has retained its original meaning as a measure of the solvency of government, but it has acquired several dimensions that pertain to governments that have no difficulty meeting current obligations. Contemporary sustainability analysis focuses on fiscal conditions that may retard economic growth, cause tax burdens to rise, or transfer significant costs to future taxpayers. The added dimensions reflect concern that governments have accumulated long-term liabilities that do not appear in current budgets or balance sheets but that may disadvantage future generations when they come due. The expanded concept of sustainability is grounded on the norm that responsible governments should not do harm that will appear decades after the relevant policies were adopted.

Four dimensions of sustainability may be delineated. Although they are separated here for analysis, in practice they tend to appear in tandem:

- Solvency: the ability of government to pay its financial obligations.
- Growth: fiscal policy that sustains economic growth.
- Stability: the capacity of government to meet future obligations with existing tax burdens.
- Fairness: the capacity of government to pay current obligations without shifting the cost to future generations.

The four dimensions overlap, but it is useful to draw their implications by examining each separately.

1.1. Solvency

Solvency is usually thought to be a problem in some underdeveloped or emerging market countries, particularly those that have boosted public spending, taken on additional debt, and have an inadequate tax base. When misfortune arrives – often brought by a cyclical downturn or financial contagion – capital flees, currency plummets in value, and the government must roll over debt at very high interest rates while borrowing more to stay afloat. These are countries to which the IMF rushes with emergency assistance, in exchange for which it demands that they restore solvency by correcting unsustainable fiscal imbalances. A typical IMF demand is that the government run a primary surplus in order to finance its debt.

Solvency can be an issue in any country that takes on excessive debt. Although they may not face capital flight in the foreseeable future, affluent countries are sometimes tempted to debt finance current obligations, whether in response to political pressure or out of confidence that they can afford to do so. Some observers believe that this is the current fiscal predicament of the United States and that its current course is unsustainable. In budget projections that run to 2050, the Congressional Budget Office concluded that, under certain plausible budget scenarios:

> …the growth of debt would accelerate as the government attempted to finance its interest payments by issuing more debt – leading to a vicious circle in which ever-larger amounts of debt were issued to pay ever-higher interest charges. Eventually, the costs of servicing the debt would outstrip the government's ability to pay for them, thus becoming unsustainable (CBO, 2003, p. 14).

The CBO warning relates to the long-term outlook. The 50 years covered by its projections are a long way off, but the CBO argues that it is appropriate to take action now to abate long-term imbalances. It provides specific examples of how timely action can avert projected insolvency.

Solvency is typically measured in business in reference to the firm's net worth. Applying this method to government is difficult because few have comprehensive balance sheets that cover all liabilities and assets. Moreover, net worth is a misleading measure in government because it does not include the power to generate additional revenue by raising taxes. Nor does it include the value of future pension liabilities. At best, the balance sheets now produced in national governments provide an incomplete but nevertheless useful statement of financial condition.

1.2. Growth

Sustained growth is one of the twin objectives of the European Union's Stability and Growth Pact (SGP) which commits euro zone countries to budget imbalances below 3% of GDP and gross debt below 60%. The case for these limits rests on the argument that growth will not be sustainable if deficits and debt breach these parameters. Thus, the broadened concept of fiscal sustainability encompasses the notion that governments should manage their finances prudently so as to assure future growth. In line with this reasoning, the United Kingdom's long-term fiscal objective is to ensure "that the public finances are sustainable, contributing to a stable environment that promotes economic growth" (HM Treasury, 2004, p. 4). In this light, fiscal policy is adjudged to be unsustainable if it would cause potential output to be lower at some future time than it would otherwise be. The logic of this argument runs as follows: the best way for the government to meet future obligations, which certainly will be greater than today's, is by having a robust economy which supplies the government with additional revenue from the dividends of economic growth. If, however, fiscal imbalances diminish future growth, the dividends will be smaller or vanish altogether, and the government will be hard pressed to cover its obligations.

This reasoning led the European Commission to argue, in its 2004 review of public finance in EMU countries, that "the risk of unsustainable public finances increases considerably if the Member States do not achieve the SGP goal of budget position of 'close to balance or in surplus'". The report concluded that this position "is in the economic self-interest of Member States both individually and collectively … it creates room for budgetary manoeuvre to either cut taxes or to increase growth-enhancing expenditures on items such as investment and R&D" (European Commission, 2004, p. 59).

Sustaining growth by running balanced budgets represents a sharp break with post-war economic doctrine which typically regarded deficits as appropriate in bad times and manageable in good times. This reversal in economic reasoning has been due to several transformations: from viewing the budget as an instrument of short-term cyclical adjustment to seeing it as a means of undergirding structural soundness over an extended period; from looking at the budget as a policy statement for a year (or few years) immediately ahead to treating it as a strategic plan of future government financial capacity; and from formulating the budget as an instrument of government expansion to constraining it to be a stabiliser of government size. These shifts correspond to changes in contemporary political sentiment. Confidence in the capacity of government to sustain growth by taxing and spending more has waned. Moreover, recognition that the bulge in government spending will be in the form of transfer payments that subsidise consumption has weakened analytical support for the expansionary policies that once were popular.

1.3. Stability (stable taxes)

Maintaining the tax burden at or near current levels has become a dominant objective of fiscal policy in many OECD countries. This objective is highlighted in Australia's *Intergenerational Report* which views "a balanced budget over the medium term, given a reasonable degree of stability in the overall tax burden" as "one of the key requirements for sustainable financial arrangements" (Commonwealth of Australia, 2002, p. 2). In running 40-year projections, the report assumes that Commonwealth revenues will remain a constant proportion of GDP. A key aim of the report is to assess the risk that tax burdens will rise in the future to accommodate spending pressures. It concludes that the Commonwealth's fiscal position may be unsustainable because the projected trajectory of spending would compel higher taxes (or a larger debt) in the future.

The underlying premise of this sustainability argument is that tax burdens are already very high and that governments should adopt prudent fiscal positions that obviate pressure for future increases. In this version, the objective is to sustain tax burdens at their current level or lower. This dimension of sustainability is congruent with contemporary sentiment in most OECD countries and is reflected in the leveling off of tax burdens after decades of steep increases. Of course, sustainability recognises that taxes cannot be constrained if downstream spending demands are not. The notion that spending pressures must be abated to lower the probability of higher taxes in the future is as prevalent in countries with relatively low tax burdens as in high-tax countries. Even countries that have current budget deficits have joined the tax-cutting parade. At times, such behaviour would have been viewed as undermining sustainability; nowadays, it is often seen as diminishing the risk that taxes will be higher in the future.

During much of the 20th century, the tax burden and economic output expanded throughout the OECD area. In many (certainly not all) countries, it came to be accepted that by producing an educated workforce, efficient transport, income security, and other social goods, expansionary government establishes favourable conditions for economic growth. Taxes were the price paid by households and firms for purchasing government-supplied goods that elevated living standards. Governments (and most voters) were not troubled by the rise in taxes because disposable incomes were also rising and governments were supplying more benefits. Sustainability strongly indicates that times have changed, partly because tax burdens are hovering around 50% in some countries, partly because of diminished trust and confidence in government performance. It matters little that popular images of government may be wrong; it does matter that voters look to governments for lower taxes.

Here is where sustainability enters the picture, for spending trends embedded in government commitments and political expectations point to sizeable tax hikes in the future. Arguably, the surest way to maintain solvent government in the decades ahead is to generate sufficient additional tax revenue to cover the looming rise in public spending. The sustainability norm seeks to deter this option by defining tax stability as a core fiscal objective.

1.4. Fairness

The final version views fiscal policy as sustainable when tax burdens and expenditure benefits are equitable across generations. In this perspective, it is not fair to provide benefits to one age cohort that will have to be paid for by taxes levied on younger cohorts. This concept of sustainability is embedded in Australia's *Intergenerational Report* which asserts: "Fiscal sustainability ... ensures future generations of taxpayers do not face an unmanageable bill for government services provided to the current generation." Further, a sustainable fiscal stance "promotes fairness in distributing resources between generations of Australians" (Commonwealth of Australia, 2002, p. 2). The United Kingdom's *Long-Term Public Finance Report* declares a primary objective of fiscal policy to ensure "that spending and taxation impact fairly both within and between generations" (HM Treasury, 2004, p. 4).

Operationalising fairness may be more difficult than measuring budget balances for, as Peter Heller has observed, "there is no single definition or universally accepted measure of fairness ... Should future generations be expected to bear a higher tax burden than current generations would be willing to accept for themselves, because they will be richer? What obligations should future generations have toward current working generations?" (Heller, 2003, p. 130). Budget makers have enormous difficulty assessing fairness among current beneficiaries and taxpayers; it is even more difficult to reason through equity issues across generations, from those who are newly born to those who are nearing the end of long lives. Not only do layers of assumptions have to be made about distant tax burdens and expenditures, but normative questions demand attention. Would a fairness norm rule out any difference across generations or only those (in the words of Australia's report) that are truly "unmanageable"? Perhaps it is the sharp divide across generations that gives rise to fairness concerns: today's citizens are (by a wide margin) net gainers; tomorrow's generations are projected (also by a wide margin) to be net losers. However, there is another way of defining this issue. Government policies that distribute costs and benefits may be regarded as a social contract across generations. In the same way that today's citizens pay higher taxes and enjoy elevated material well-being compared to their forebears, future taxpayers should be expected to pay for and enjoy the greater affluence and enriched public services bequeathed to them. The counter-argument is that the social contract has been broken by the prospective huge shift of costs and benefits across generations. Today's older citizens have negative effective tax rates (taxes minus benefits) in excess of 25%; tomorrow's will have positive effective net tax rates in excess of 50%. This breaches any social contract that may have been accepted in the past.

Here is where sustainability joins up with fairness. Grossly unfair distributions are not sustainable in either political or economic terms – politically, because future payers are likely to rebel against confiscatory tax rates; economically, because the well-being of the country will be retarded by the overriding need for tax rates that are strong disincentives for work, saving and investment.

The four definitions of sustainability focus as much on the tax burden as on the public debt, though (of course) elevated debt can be expected to exert upward pressure on tax rates. In contrast to developing and emerging market countries where sustainability is a concern that arises out of inadequate tax mobilisation, in industrial countries the problem is that tax rates are already very high. But in all types of countries, sustainability analyses project that the ratio of tax revenue to GDP will have to rise to finance commitments that will come due in the future.

2. Modes of sustainability analysis

Because it is a new area of analysis and because making assumptions about the future can be done with a variety of techniques, there is no standard way of projecting taxes and burdens 30-50 years ahead. One approach is to examine the future from the vantage point of the country as a whole; another is to look at it from the position of an individual taxpayer who will receive a flow of costs and benefits from the government; still another is to consider a similarly situated age cohort. Some techniques build on standard budget methods to project the future; others are grounded in accounting rules and analyse the future by means of a balance sheet. Some take a whole-of-government perspective; others focus on major programmes (such as social security) that have long-term implications. All require heroic assumptions about economic and social trends such as rates of growth, price changes and life expectancy. Rather than discuss methodological differences, this section relates various techniques to existing budget practices. If sustainability becomes an ongoing issue, it is highly likely that budget practices will evolve to incorporate an elongated time frame into analyses of revenue and spending proposals.

2.1. Baseline projections

Governments that have moved to a medium-term expenditure framework (or have otherwise lengthened their time horizon) typically use baseline projections to connect current budget policy to medium-term fiscal outcomes. Sustainability analysis often uses similar techniques, but extends the time frame 30 or more years ahead. Baseline projections begin with the government's current budget position (including policy changes that have already been approved but will not take effect until some future date). In constructing baseline projections, the overriding assumption is that existing revenue and spending will be continued as far ahead into the future as projections extend, without any substantive change. Of course, these projections are based on critical assumptions about GDP, wage and productivity trends, interest rates, and much more. In constructing a baseline, a government has to reckon with revenue or spending provisions that are time-limited – that is, under current law, they will not remain in effect for the entire period covered by the baseline. In many such cases, there is strong probability that expiring provisions will be extended. Therefore, dropping time-limited items from the baseline may provide a misleading picture of future budget conditions. New Zealand's practice is to systematically report on such provisions, thereby allowing citizens and others to exercise judgment on whether it is realistic to assume that they will not be continued. This provides a fuller view of fiscal trends, but it is not the practice in other countries that rely on baselines.

Baseline projections are inherently unrealistic because it is highly unlikely that budget policy will be frozen as the number of pensioners receiving public money escalates. It is also unrealistic because (in most governments) the baseline projection does not assume significant changes in economic performance as a consequence of tax and spending policies.[1] Despite these limitations, baselines serve two valuable purposes in budgeting that can be applied to sustainability projections. First, they provide insights into future budget conditions if a government stays on its fiscal course. This is especially useful in contemplating a distant future in which demographic and other conditions may be quite different from what they are today. Second, baselines provide a basis for estimating the impact of proposed or adopted policy changes on future budgets. In these projections, any variance between the baseline projection and revised estimates is defined as the future budget impact of policy change. In this way, baseline projections enable policy makers to assess the impact of changes in revenue or spending policies on the government's fiscal position.

Although baseline projections usually provide point estimates, in anticipating the future it would be preferable to present a range of plausible fiscal outcomes. Within the range, estimates would be differentiated by the assumptions on which they are grounded. It also would be feasible to base projections on alternative scenarios of key variables such as life expectancy, health costs, economic growth and interest rates. A surfeit of scenarios might drown the projections in confusion, but it would be sensible to construct 3-5 scenarios. Finally, it would be prudent to "stress test" long-term baseline projections to assess how they might be affected by significant changes in underlying assumptions.

In sum, while long-term forecasting is not yet common in budgeting, it almost certainly will become standard practice in many countries in the years ahead. Because baseline projections can be lengthened from the medium term to the distant future, they are likely to become the most frequently applied technique of government in assessing long-term sustainability. However, budgets will automatically have as dominant a position in exploring sustainability as they have had in estimating annual or medium-term budget conditions. Economists and other policy analysts will vie to construct novel means of relating current budget postures to long-term sustainability.

2.2. Balance sheet analysis

During the past decade, some analysts have viewed the balance sheet as a fuller and more reliable statement of financial condition than the budget. In contrast to budgets which include only those flows that are within its ambit, the balance sheet includes all (explicit) assets and liabilities, regardless of their budget status. Moreover, it includes all liabilities, not only those that are sovereign debt. The structure and content of the balance sheet are regulated by national or international accounting norms and are independently audited. Although national budgets usually are on a cash basis, the balance sheet accrues income and expense, thereby enabling a government to recognise certain downstream liabilities long before they become due. Properly constructed, a balance sheet would provide a comprehensive account of the government's net worth and of future payments likely to arise out of existing liabilities. For these reasons, various scholars have urged that the government's fiscal position be assessed in reference to the balance sheet rather than the budget (Bléjer and Cheasty, 1993).

But the balance sheet has inherent limitations that greatly diminish its utility as a measure of long-term sustainability. One problem is that the balance sheet recognises only explicit liabilities, but many obligations of government are embedded in expectations about how it will behave in the future; another is that the balance sheet recognises liabilities arising out of past actions, not future obligations arising out of current policy. In assessing long-term sustainability, however, implicit commitments and future obligations weigh far more heavily than those that are explicit or have already been incurred. In fact, no government records future pension obligations on its balance sheet, though some append notes in which various matters that do not meet recognition standards are discussed. This is an area where accounting norms are likely to evolve in the future, but it would be imprudent for the balance sheet to show implicit liabilities or prospective payments for liabilities that have not yet been incurred. Doing so would make implicit obligations explicit, worsening the government's financial predicament and loading it with future payments that it might otherwise avoid.

The balance sheet is a snapshot of financial condition at a point in time; it is not a projection of what might occur in the future. It does not include revenue or obligations that have not yet accrued, nor does it differentiate between liabilities that may come due within the next year and those payable in the distant future. It does not assign a present value to the taxing capacity of government or to future revenue flows from the existing tax structure. In fact, pursuant to established accounting rules, the balance sheet completely ignores the capacity to generate revenue in the future. It does, however, account for certain unfunded liabilities – that is, for incurred liabilities that are not financed by accrued revenue. Some finance experts have argued that the balance sheet presents a misleading picture of future financial condition and that net worth is not a useful measure of a government's solvency; others have noted that the balance sheet applies identical recognition rules to liabilities and assets, that net worth is a relevant measure of a government's capacity to finance incurred liabilities, and that the balance sheet is not designed to be a prognosis of future financial condition. What the balance sheet can do is to provide a starting point (other than the baseline) for projecting future sustainability, but doing so requires consideration of matters that are not recorded on the balance sheet.

The balance sheet and related financial statements are likely to have greater prominence in assessing current and prospective fiscal conditions. One reason is the expansion of accounting and reporting standards to cover matters that were not previously recorded; another is the prospect of linking (or integrating) financial statements and the budget. At present, few national governments pay attention to the financial statements they are required to prepare; they see these statements as a technical chore that has little to do with the decisions they make or the financial issues they confront. This situation is likely to change as accounting standards are elaborated and monitored by national and international organisations. Recent developments in the United Kingdom may be a harbinger of a broader scope for these statements. The British government has announced that, beginning with the 2006/07 financial year, it will publish whole-of-government accounts (covering national and local governments and public corporations) based on generally accepted accounting principles. In addition to accounting for incurred obligations, these new accounts will provision for certain future liabilities and will contain notes on contingent liabilities. This approach expands the balance sheet to include or provide information on various liabilities that have not yet accrued. The United Kingdom's approach is not likely to be an isolated move, for the International Public Sector Accounting Standards Board and other authorities are devising new rules that will expand the information that must be reported. As accounting practices are expanded, leading-edge governments will apply the same standards to budgets and will conform or reconcile them to financial statements. The integration of budgets and financial statements will unfold in stages, probably over an extended period, but it will provide a fuller basis for assessing fiscal sustainability.

2.3. Fiscal gap analysis

Fiscal sustainability is a problem when there is a gap between a targeted debt level and the debt that would ensue if tax and spending policies were continued without change. In measuring this gap, the government (or analysts) selects a target year as well as a target for the debt/GDP ratio. In other words, gap analysis focuses on a fixed point in time, not on a stream of years. This method enables a government to calculate the primary balances it will have to run to assure that the projected deficit does not exceed the targeted level. A fiscal gap of zero would indicate that current fiscal policy is sustainable – that is, the debt target can be met without increasing the tax burden or cutting future expenditures. A fiscal gap above zero would indicate that the projected debt exceeds the target and that the government will have to boost revenue or curtail spending to sustain its fiscal objective.

Fiscal gap measures can be developed for a number of target years (for example, 2030, 2040 and 2050) as well as for a range of debt burdens (40% of GDP, 50% or 60%). By adjusting the debt target and year, a government can construct alternative scenarios and policy paths for the future. Thus, in contrast to baseline projections which often highlight the unsustainability of fiscal trends, gap analysis emphasises the policy response required to maintain (or restore) sustainability. Projections focus on the fiscal problems that lie ahead; fiscal gap studies indicate the scale of change in revenue and spending policy needed to stabilise public finance. Of course, gap analysis itself is grounded on long-term projections and is therefore sensitive to the time frame and underlying assumptions.

One variant of fiscal gap analysis, generally referred to as the intertemporal budget constraint (IBC), calculates the primary balance (the surplus or deficit exclusive of interest payment) required to stabilise the debt burden (or eliminate it, in some versions). This calculation is done by discounting to present value all projected future revenue and spending flows plus the current debt burden. An intertemporal budget gap exists when the present discounted value of projected primary balances does not cover the current debt burden. This method extends gap analysis in several ways: it calculates the prospective gap for an indefinite period rather than for a target year; it recognises that the present value of fiscal gaps depends on the timing of future financial flows; and it establishes a fiscal constraint – the debt burden – to guide policy. But like all long-term projections, the IBC is sensitive to the starting year of the projection and the discount rate.

2.4. Generational accounting

The approaches discussed thus far define sustainability in terms of the aggregate fiscal position of government. They do not focus on the fairness of fiscal policy across generations – that is, on the benefits that each age cohort will receive (mostly in transfer payments) and the taxes it will pay. Age cohorts may be defined by year of birth or may be grouped into broader categories such as five-year intervals or decades. Net transfers (taxes paid minus transfers received) are calculated for each cohort. Generational balance (or fairness) exists when future generations have the same net transfers as current generations. Country studies typically show that while current generations have negative tax rates (they receive more from government than they pay), future generations face extremely high tax rates (in some cases, confiscatory).

Generational accounting is a controversial instrument (OECD, 1997). Its advocates propose to replace the traditional method of accounting for the government's revenues and expenditures, and to thereby shift the accounting basis from the present stock of assets and liabilities to long-term flows to and from citizens. Generational accounting is a relatively new technique and is still undergoing development. Its key value may well lie in bringing together disparate information on the future implications of public finances in a single number that is comprehensible by the public at large. It can also be a useful tool in assessing changes in tax or expenditure policy which affect the distribution of costs and benefits across generations. But the apparent simplicity of generational accounting masks the many assumptions underlying it, including the assignment of revenues and expenditures to specific generations. It can be reasonably concluded that, rather than replacing traditional measures of government revenues and expenditures, generational accounting will provide useful supplementary information along with a variety of other methods that shed light on long-term financial trends.

3. Budgeting for sustainable public finance

Fiscal sustainability is (or should be) a vital issue for all national governments in the OECD area because spending pressures will escalate as populations age and as prior commitments or expectations for income transfers and health services come due. In some OECD countries, demands on the budget will not peak for another 30-50 years; in others, they will mature much earlier. Almost all face a fiscal future in which a larger share of the budget is allocated to age-sensitive programmes. Many, possibly most, will trim commitments/ expectations in order to avoid significantly higher debt or tax burdens. It may be politically expedient to defer action until problems are imminent, but it would not be fiscally prudent to do so.

Some countries (such as Australia, Sweden and the United Kingdom) have acted decisively to ameliorate future budget pressures by restructuring their pension systems or pre-funding future payments; most have made no adjustments or only marginal ones that will not significantly ease demands on future budgets. A few (such as New Zealand) have moved to accommodate future fiscal pressures by reducing the current debt burden. Norway has locked away much of the revenue from oil and gas exploration to assure that these monies are available to future generations. However, setting up reserves is not a viable option for countries struggling with current budget imbalances. Nor is it feasible, for countries that have annual budgets or medium-term frameworks, to extend the time boundaries of the budget process to the next 30-50 years. Many countries are still developing techniques to assess the impact of current revenue and spending decisions on the next 3-5 years; they do not yet have the capability to budget for a much longer horizon.

Yet the distant future cannot be ignored, for it will creep up on fiscally stressed governments one year at a time. As far off as it may be, the future can be foreseen – not with perfect certainty, but with a sense of the magnitude of the trends that await coming generations. By modelling future trends and calculating the present value of future revenue flows and spending demands, governments can sensitise themselves and voters to the fiscal path that lies ahead. Some may be spurred to revise tax or spending policies on the basis of the new information, while others may lack sufficient political strength or will to change course. All would have a fuller picture of how future fiscal prospects might be affected by current budget actions. Many will become more vigilant in considering options that would worsen future budget conditions.

Significantly, countries that have systematically examined the long-term fiscal outlook tend to have taken the strongest measures to assure sustainability by restructuring pension systems or setting aside funds for future needs. In fact, efforts to ease long-term budget pressures have preceded the publication of long-term sustainability reports. Perhaps governments that have already acted to reduce long-term fiscal pressures are more inclined to be transparent about their future so as to deflect political pressure to reverse their reforms. But all countries can benefit from boldly facing up to their future budget predicament.

3.1. *Building sustainability analysis into the budget process*

One option for facing the future would be to formally include long-term projections in the annual budget or medium-term framework. These projections would be updated each year, the same way that medium-term estimates are rolled forward. The projections would be baselines; they would assume that current (or approved) revenue and spending policies will be continued and that no significant changes will be made. The budget would set out the key social and economic assumptions that underlie the long-term projections, including the estimated impact of fiscal trends on national output, prices and interest rates.

Although it may be feasible to attach long-term baselines to the budget, it would not be prudent to do so. One should distinguish between a budget, which is inherently a plan for one or more financial years, and a projection, which is an assumption about how the future might unfold. The budget presents the government's revenue and spending proposals, including policy changes; baseline projections assume that existing policies will not be changed. The budget recommends a specific amount for each revenue or spending item voted by the legislature; the projections often provide a range of estimates or alternative scenarios. The projections will be revised frequently before the target year arrives, as policies change, new methodologies are used and fresh information or insights impel changes in basic assumptions. Some revisions will be exceedingly large, opening the projections to misinterpretation when the distant outlook improves or deteriorates. If sustainability projections were to be published in the core budget, they might be mistaken as government recommendations rather than as forecasts.

Although these projections should not be integrated into the budget, neither should they be entirely separate from it. The risk that long-term projections will be ignored is no less a problem than the risk that they will be misused. The best course would be to report on the long-term prospect in a separate document, but to summarise key findings in a supporting schedule that is included in the budget. This is the tactic used by the United Kingdom. Australia publishes an intergenerational report every five years as one of a series of papers that accompanies the annual budget. No country has established a long-term budget framework comparable to the medium-term frameworks that are now in vogue. While a medium-term framework constrains the budget actions that a government takes in the light of their impacts on revenue and spending levels for each of the next 3-5 years, the long-term projections have not yet been hardened into budget constraints.

It is highly probable that some governments will move to regulate the long-term budget impacts of current decisions. The budget resolution adopted by the United States Congress in 2005 contains a new provision (effective only in the Senate) that bars consideration of any measure that would cause mandatory spending to increase by more than USD 5 billion in any of the four ten-year periods between 2016 and 2055. This provision may be waived by supermajority vote and does not pertain to the House of Representatives. Nevertheless, it indicates the direction that budget rules might take as governments strive to constrain politicians from shifting costs to future generations.

Expansion of the time horizon will take different paths, but governments moving in this direction are likely to take (or consider) the following steps:

- First, they will develop baseline projections of future revenues and expenditures under current law. Without these baselines, it will be difficult to gauge the impact of current decisions on future budgets.

- Second, governments will develop capacities to estimate the changes that will occur in future revenues or spending as a consequence of policy change. These estimates will be made at the time the policy change is considered or adopted. They often will be wide of the mark, but they will sensitise governments to the reality that today's actions alter future budget conditions.

- Third, the methods for estimating these impacts will vary among governments. Some will estimate the present value of changes in future revenues or expenditures; others will estimate these impacts in current or constant amounts, and some will calculate the changes as a proportion of GDP.

- Fourth, some governments will establish rules restricting the government's authority to take actions that would increase future deficits (or debt) or reduce projected surpluses.

The procedures outlined here would regulate policy changes that affect future budgets. They are generally similar to those used by governments that have medium-term expenditure frameworks but, rather than working with a 3-5 year horizon, they have a 30-50 year perspective. There is no significant methodological difference between a medium-term framework and a distant one, but it must be recognised that the further ahead one looks into the future, the shakier the assumptions are. The problem is not only that long-term estimates are unreliable and will likely prove to be wrong; there is also a risk that opportunistic politicians will manipulate the process in ways that would adversely affect future budget conditions. For example, suppose a government were to adopt a "deficit neutral" rule barring any revenue or spending change that would increase future deficits. It would be possible for a government to "pay for" spending increases in one programme by proposing offsetting cuts in other programmes. The trade-off would not be an equal exchange, however, if the savings were canceled (or trimmed) before they took effect.

Regulating policy changes in reference to baseline projections would not deal with imbalances that are already embedded in the budget. This approach might deter governments from making matters worse; it will not, however, restore sustainability in countries where governments are on a fiscal course that would compel significant future increases in the tax or debt burden. It would be appropriate, therefore, for such governments to introduce policy changes that ease future budget pressures. It is not within the scope of this article to recommend substantive changes in tax or spending policy, but a generalisation can be offered that pertains to a broad swath of national policy. During the past half century, national governments in industrial countries have become the holders of risk for society. They have taken on a broad array of direct and contingent liabilities that typically come due decades after critical policy decisions were made. Most of these liabilities pertain to income support in the form of pensions, health care, disability insurance, unemployment benefits, and other transfers. The countries which have a more favourable long-term outlook tend to be those that have shifted some of the risks back to households. Doing so is, of course, highly controversial and may have some adverse political or social side effects. But no matter what means they employ to measure sustainability, governments will not be able to sustain their fiscal course if they continue to be the holders for all major financial risks in society.

It behoves national governments to take an inventory of the risks they are holding and to report on them in supplemental notes appended to annual financial statements. Some direct, certain liabilities should be recognised on the balance sheet, but those that are contingent, implicit or remote should not. Governments should also explore arrangements for contingent liabilities that reduce moral hazard and their exposure to future adverse events.

3.2. *Managing the sustainability process*

As envisioned in this article, governments should consider four complementary approaches for bolstering sustainability:

- One would be to construct long-term fiscal scenarios using cutting-edge socio/ econometric techniques such as generational accounting and present-value accounting.

- Second, governments should extend baseline projections beyond the medium term using methods that have been applied in medium-term frameworks.

- Third, governments should estimate the impact of current policy changes on the long-term fiscal outlook.

- Finally, governments should reconfigure fiscal risks, so that a greater portion is shared by households and current generations.

Some have suggested that sustainability work requires a greater degree of independence than conventional budget tasks and should therefore be conducted outside government. While a government should not have an exclusive claim in assessing future fiscal conditions, it should have a prominent role. All four responsibilities outlined in the preceding paragraph should be assigned to the government. In countries that assign a broad swath of fiscal and economic responsibilities to the finance ministry, it would be the appropriate institution to lead sustainability work. In those countries that have separate budget and economic management institutions, it would be appropriate for both to co-operate in carrying out these responsibilities. Because of the specialised skills and experience required for constructing baselines, it would be unwise to exclude the budget office from this work. When a government reports on sustainability, its findings are likely to be regarded as more authoritative than those produced by outside analysts. The attention that sustainability reports have earned in Australia, New Zealand, the United Kingdom and a few other countries is a strong indicator of the advantage of conducting this work in house. Moreover, when the government takes responsibility for the findings, there is a greater probability that it will act to ameliorate downstream problems.

Although long-term sustainability does not normally vary significantly from one year to the next, there is considerable gain in routinising the process by reporting each year. The annuality of these reports fosters an expectation that the government will take the problem seriously and that its findings will be fed into the budget and other decisions. The "OECD Best Practices for Budget Transparency" (OECD, 2002) call for a report assessing the long-term sustainability of current budget policies to be issued every five years, or when major changes are made in revenue or spending programmes. The OECD stresses that all key assumptions underlying the projections contained in the report should be made explicit and a range of plausible scenarios presented. Reporting at five-year intervals would be a considerable gain for governments that do not currently produce any long-term forecast but, as sustainability becomes more embedded in budget work, best practice may be to shorten the interval and to report annually or every other year.

The manner in which key findings are presented will strongly influence the consideration they receive. Sustainability analysis is complex, open to a variety of methodological approaches, and often produces a range of estimates and an array of scenarios. For the results to filter to the media and the public, it is important that they be presented in ways that non-experts can comprehend, even if doing so requires that some of the findings be simplified. One example of effective communication is the annual report of the trustees of the Social Security system in the United States. Each year the report captures front-page attention because it specifies the year in which the Social Security fund will be depleted if current policy continues without change. The trustees are appointed by the government but exercise independent judgment in their report, which is regarded as an objective and authoritative forecast. The most recent report, issued in March 2005, projected that the main medical insurance fund will be exhausted in 2020 and that the Social Security fund will be exhausted in 2041. The report also contains 75-year actual forecasts that show Social Security expenditures rising from 4% to 6% of GDP and Medicare expenses soaring from 3% to almost 14%. Layers of assumptions undergird this single statistic, and these are appropriately discussed in the body of the report. It should be feasible to devise simple measures for the various types of sustainability analyses that national governments and outside experts have used to portray the fiscal future.

This article began by noting that sustainability concerns have migrated from underdeveloped to developed countries and have shifted from medium- to long-term concerns. The long term may appear distant, but in re-engineering fiscal policy, it is already here. Most persons who will receive public pensions and health benefits 40 or 50 years from now are already in the country's workforce, contributing social insurance taxes and building expectations of what they will receive from the government. Sooner or later all countries will have to confront the reality of expectations outracing means. Those that take on the task earlier will find it somewhat less onerous than those that tarry.

Afterword

As these lines are being written, the long-term fiscal perspective required for sustainability analysis has been crowded out in many OECD member countries by the severe economic contraction and financial sector crisis that unfolded in 2008. Almost all governments have acted to stabilise financial institutions and to stimulate demand for goods and services. The immediate result has been to unbalance budgets and to add to the debt burden that will be borne by future generations.

Despite the vast sums allocated to financial bailouts, it is too early to assess the impact on long-run sustainability. For one thing, a number of governments have strived to structure relief in ways that do not damage their long-term fiscal position; for another, if fiscal relief – including government purchase of distressed assets – averts a deep or prolonged economic downturn, the fiscal future will be more favourable than if economic events were permitted to run their course without strong government intervention.

It is likely that the outsized cost of financial rescues will prod governments to take measures that assure future sustainability. One possible approach would be to build sustainability projections into audited financial statements issued annually by national governments. During 2008, the United States Federal Accounting Standards Advisory Board (FASAB) proposed to require annual publication and audit of sustainability projections. Another approach would be to strengthen enforcement of fiscal rules, especially during favourable economic times when budgetary balance or low deficits mask future trouble. A third approach might be to impel national governments to boost tax burdens or to trim future transfer payments. Regardless of the approach taken, sustainability projections and analyses are certain to be prominent features of future budget work.

Note

1. See Crippen (2003) for useful advice on dealing with the inherent uncertainty of long-term budget scenarios.

References

Bléjer, Mario and Adrienne Cheasty (eds.) (1993), *How to Measure the Fiscal Deficit: Analytical and Methodological Issues*, International Monetary Fund, Washington DC, *www.imf.org*.

Commonwealth of Australia (2002), *Intergenerational Report 2002-03*, Budget Paper No. 5, The Treasury, Parkes ACT, *www.treasury.gov.au*.

CBO (Congressional Budget Office) (2003), *The Long-Term Budget Outlook*, December, CBO, Washington DC, *www.cbo.gov*.

Crippen, D. (2003), "Countering Uncertainty in Budget Forecasts", *OECD Journal on Budgeting*, Vol. 3, No. 2, OECD, Paris, pp. 139-151.

European Commission (2004), *Public Finances in EMU*, Office for Official Publications of the European Communities, Luxembourg, *http://europa.eu.int*.

Heller, P.S. (2003), *Who Will Pay? Coping with Aging Societies, Climate Change, and Other Long-Term Fiscal Challenges*, International Monetary Fund, Washington DC, *www.imf.org*.

HM Treasury (2004), *Long-Term Public Finance Report: An Analysis of Fiscal Sustainability*, HM Treasury, London, December, *www.hm-treasury.gov.uk*.

IMF (International Monetary Fund) (2002), *Assessing Sustainability*, IMF, Washington DC, *www.imf.org*.

OECD (1997), "Budgeting for the Future", OCDE/GD(97)178, OECD, Paris, *www.oecd.org/gov*.

OECD (2002), "OECD Best Practices for Budget Transparency", *OECD Journal on Budgeting*, Vol. 1, No. 3, OECD, Paris, pp. 7-14.

ISBN 978-92-64-06087-6
Evolutions in Budgetary Practice
Allen Schick and the OECD Senior Budget Officials
© OECD 2009

Chapter 14

Performance Budgeting and Accrual Budgeting: Decision Rules or Analytic Tools?*

Performance budgeting and accrual budgeting are analytic tools that provide information and insights which are not available through conventional approaches. But neither innovation is ready for widespread application as a decision rule in the budget process. This article urges fuller understanding of these innovations and their implications, and more systematic use of performance and accrual information for policy makers.

* This article was originally published in the *OECD Journal on Budgeting*, Vol. 7, No. 2, 2007. At the time of writing, Allen Schick was Visiting Fellow, Governance Studies, The Brookings Institution, Washington DC, and Professor, School of Public Affairs, University of Maryland, United States. An afterword was written in 2009.

Budgeting is a process that transforms information into decision. Requests submitted by spending units or generated by central budget staffs are inputted into the process, and allocations to entities, projects and other recipients are outputted. The quality of these decisions depends on the data available to decision makers, as well as on the analytic tools they use to process the information. One of the perennial aims of budget innovation has been to influence the decisions that flow from the process by modifying the classification or content of budget data and by introducing new analytic methods. At one time, most countries classified expenditures by organisational units and items to be purchased. Nowadays, most have economic and functional classifications, and many also classify expenditure by programmes, activities or outputs. As the stockpile of budget information has grown, the means of analysis have multiplied. Innovative countries strive to measure performance, medium-term fiscal impacts, exposure to contingent liabilities and other financial risks, the unit cost of producing government services, the long-term sustainability of the government's fiscal position, the revenue forgone through tax preferences, the distribution of expenditure by region, social class and gender, and other contemporary issues in budgeting.

The surge of data has spurred budget innovators to devise new rules for shaping the decisions that emerge from the process. They want information to be more than available: they want it to transform the way governments go about budget work. They want different information to produce different outcomes. This article focuses on two contemporary efforts to convert information into rules. One is performance budgeting, which seeks to base spending decisions on actual or projected results; the other is accrual budgeting, which calculates expenditure in terms of resources used or liabilities incurred. The first shifts budget decisions from inputs to outputs or outcomes; the second shifts them from disbursements to cost. Performance budgeting and the accrual basis are among the most prominent reforms on the budget agenda. Neither is new, and neither has made as much headway as reformers would like, but both are likely to be promoted within governments and by some international organisations in the years ahead.

Performance budgeting and accrual budgeting are analytic tools that provide information and insights which are not available through conventional approaches. Both can also be framed into decision rules that dictate the way governments allocate resources. One decision rule might specify that a government should spend money to purchase outputs; another might require that the government appropriate funds to cover the cost of goods consumed or liabilities incurred. Although both methods may seem to rationalise budget choice, this article argues that governments should move cautiously in codifying performance budgeting and accrual budgeting into decision rules. It is essential to develop a fuller understanding of these innovations and their implications before mandating that they be the basis of budget decisions. The article also urges, however, that governments incorporate performance and accrual information into the mainstream of data available to policy makers.

The critical difference between analytic tools and decision rules lies in the discretion permitted to politicians and officials when they make allocations. When information is only an aid for analysis, governments may opt to apply or disregard the proffered data, and they may interpret the data as they deem appropriate. For example, armed with data showing that one entity's unit costs are lower than another's, governments may nevertheless provide more money to the high-cost operation. Or, presented with accrual information, they may appropriate funds to cover cash outflows rather than incurred liabilities. However, when information is codified into decision rules, budget makers are required to base allocations on it. To put the difference simply: analytic tools empower budget makers, whereas decision rules constrain them. The former allow full scope for judgment and subjectivity, the latter make budgeting less judgmental and more objective.

The distinction between analytic tools and decision rules may be explained by considering the approaches taken by national governments in incorporating medium-term projections into budget work. As recently as two decades ago, few governments formally projected the future budget impacts of the decisions they made for the fiscal year immediately ahead. Nowadays, however, many governments construct forward estimates or baselines that project expenditures and other budget elements for each of the next three or more years. These projections typically assume that current policies will be continued without change; they thereby provide a basis for the government to forecast the fiscal situation that will ensue if the budget policies already in place are maintained. With this information at hand, governments can estimate the impact of proposed or approved policy changes on future budgets. Using information in this way gives a government a powerful analytic tool to take account of future implications before it acts.

Some governments have gone further by constructing medium-term expenditure frameworks (MTEF) that limit spending in each of the next three or more fiscal years. This "hard constraint" bars governments from taking actions that would cause estimated future spending to rise above the preset limit. When it is used effectively, the MTEF converts projections from analytic tools into decision rules. The MTEF greatly increases the probability that medium-term projections will be used, but it also limits the budget options of the government.

Experience with budget projections and the MTEF suggests the rationale for converting analytic information into budget rules. It also indicates why doing so may not be a good idea. Medium-term projections tend to be ignored by politicians who are pressured by the exigencies of budgeting to focus on the year immediately ahead, even when their decisions adversely affect future budgets. In response, reformers (including international organisations) have campaigned for governments to adopt MTEF-type arrangements that compel them to take account of future impacts before they decide spending levels. The MTEF thus becomes a decision rule that limits the freedom of cross-pressured politicians. But just imposing a decision rule may not suffice to change budgetary behaviour or outcomes. Many – probably most – countries that have a formal MTEF regard it as a technical exercise that is separate from the annual budget process. The rule exists on paper, but is breached in practice. Disappointing experience with medium-term expenditure frameworks and other budget reforms has led this writer to conclude that changing budget rules may not suffice to change budget behaviour.

Over the years, budgeting has evolved through innovations that have introduced new types of information and/or have prescribed new rules. One obvious consequence is that both information and rules have accreted. But this evolution has generated informational overload and decisional complexities. The more information that is provided, the greater the likelihood that some of it will get in the way of completing budget tasks on schedule; and the more rules that are in place, the greater the likelihood that some will be in conflict or be treated as technicalities. Those who would add to tools and rules should be cognisant of a fundamental limitation of budgeting: it is a time-pressured, deadline-saturated process in which making decisions on schedule often is more urgent than getting the analysis right.

With this limitation in mind, Section 1 of this article traces the evolution of budget tools and rules. The key development has been modification in the classification of expenditure data which has transformed budgeting from an insular process whose main task was to finance ongoing operations into an expanded process that contributes to economic stabilisation, programme planning and efficient management. Section 2 seeks to identify criteria for determining when new types of information should form the basis of new decision rules. This is a difficult assignment because budgeting lacks generally accepted standards for estimating and reporting public expenditures. Significant progress has been made in the past decade in devising codes of good budgetary practice, but most of the standards pertain to matters that have long been recognised as essential to good budgeting. Recent codes, such as those developed by the OECD and the IMF, are generally indicative rather than prescriptive with respect to the types of innovative practices discussed in this article. Section 3 discusses performance measurement as an input into budgeting and concludes that it would be premature to base decision rules on these data. Much more work has to be done on linking resources and results before performance measurements can be turned into rules for allocating money. Section 4 concludes that shifting the budget to a full accrual basis would be inappropriate at this time, but that governments should be encouraged to deepen their experience with accruals, especially in balance sheets and other financial reports. The final section briefly points the way to future development of analytic tools and decision rules in budgeting.

1. Classification is the most important decision rule

The history of budgeting is the history of reform. The two cannot be disentangled, because practitioners are basically always tinkering with the machinery of budgeting. They do so by modifying either the classification or the informational content of the budget – that is, they change either the way information is structured for decision or the information available to decision makers. In general, reforms that merely add to the stockpile of data tend to be more successful than those which aim to establish new decision modes. The evolution of budgeting teaches that it is much easier to increase the flow of information than to change the way resource decisions are made.

Changing classifications is hard work that has a high failure rate. But it is essential work because budgeting operates through classifications which both organise information and shape decisions. Half a century ago, Jesse Burkhead observed that "there is an almost infinite variety of ways in which budgetary data may be classified" (Burkhead, 1956, p. 112), and he argued that the search for the ideal classification is mistaken and fruitless because classifications serve multiple purposes in budgeting. In this writer's view, Burkhead's comment is valid only to the extent that classification is a means of presenting budget information; it is not valid, however, when classification serves as the structure for budget decisions. There are many ways to tell the budget's story, but there can be only one way to decide the budget. The government cannot allocate money one day on the basis of organisational units, the next day on the basis of programmes, the day after to regions, and so on. It cannot first set spending levels in terms of the items to be purchased and afterwards in terms of the outputs to be produced. Each of these methods is an appropriate means of displaying the budget, but only one can be the means of deciding the budget.

In almost all countries, the organisational chart is the decision structure. Spending units bid for resources, budget ministers and officials negotiate with those who have political or managerial responsibility for the spending organisations, funds are appropriated to organisations, these organisations spend the money, and financial reports are structured by organisation. Within organisational units, funds may be sub-allocated to particular items of expenditure such as personnel, supplies, equipment, travel, and so on. Over the years, as public expenditures grew, most governments consolidated these "line items" into broad categories. Instead of itemising each type of equipment, the budget lumped all equipment into a single category. Nevertheless, spending units have remained the central decision structure, and their budgets are still compiled by adding up estimated expenditure for personnel, supplies and other items.

Two paths are open to challenge organisations as the key unit of decision. One is to establish specialised classifications for particular types of decisions; the other is to replace organisations as the basic structure. The first is often successful, the second rarely succeeds. The first one works because it retains the organisational structure; the second fails because it attempts to uproot that structure. The most prominent example of a specialised decision classification is the capital or investment budget which allocates resources to projects rather than organisational units. It is important to note that the capital budget coexists alongside the budget for current expenditure, which is still decided by spending units. Another widespread approach is to segregate the budget by source of revenue (general fund, trust funds, and other earmarked revenue) with somewhat different decision rules for each source. In effect, a government has multiple budgets, each with its own classification and decision rules.

Over the years, governments have added many classifications. It is quite common to classify expenditure by economic category (consumption, transfers, subsidies, investment, etc.) as well as by function (agriculture, health, education, transportation, and so on). Some governments classify expenditure by geographic units or by socio-economic groups. The common feature of these classifications is that they provide supplemental information; they do not displace classification by spending units. They are a means of displaying data, not of making expenditure decisions. After the budget has been decided, the government disaggregates spending by these supplemental schedules. The United States government publishes more than two dozen special classifications in a budget document that is aptly called *Analytical Perspectives*.[1] The document provides data on federal grants to states and cities, spending on research and development, tax expenditures and other special categories. Many national governments have similar presentations which supplement the main decision structure. In the language of this article, they are analytic tools, not decision rules.

In contrast to these specialised classifications, some reforms have taken the second path: they have sought to establish an entirely new decision structure in place of organisation-centred budgeting. The most important of these initiatives has been programme budgeting, which was first introduced in the United States during the 1950s and has been attempted in many developed and developing countries. Although programme budgeting comes in many versions, its core idea is that expenditures should be grouped and decided in terms of governmental objectives, not according to the organisations spending the money. All activities contributing to the same objective should be placed in the same programme, regardless of the organisational entity to which they are assigned. To do so, governments seeking to budget by objectives construct a programme structure which is supposed to serve as the basis for formulating the budget. For example, to safeguard citizens against crime, many governments maintain a police force, a prosecutor's office, a court system, a parole or probation agency, and prisons. Each of these is managed by a different entity, but all would be grouped in the same programme because they share a common objective. A programme structure would enable a government to analyse the budgetary impact of more vigorous law enforcement on the courts and prisons. It also would enable a government to trade off among the different elements of the law enforcement programme. The government might decide that allocating more funds for police patrols would reduce the incidence of crime and thereby enable it to spend less on prisons.

Because it groups similar activities together, programme budgeting would seem to be a sensible means of decision, superior to systems that allocate resources on the basis of organisational structure and items of expenditure. In fact, however, governments have had great difficulty implanting a true programme budget. With few exceptions, governments that claim to have a programme budget use it to display spending decisions that have already been made. Having decided how much each spending unit should be allocated, they reclassify expenditures by programmes. Quite often governments label organisational units as programmes and pretend to have programme budgets. When this occurs, the only thing that is programmatic is the label.

The disappointing record of programme budgeting is due to many factors. Arguably, the most important is that it stirs up conflict over government objectives, generating protracted strife over the objectives of programmes. To take one example among many: suppose schools have nurses on duty to deal with routine medical problems and to teach students proper hygiene. This activity may legitimately be classified as serving both health and education objectives. Government ministries fight over the proper classification because it affects the resources they receive and their control over the activity. To mitigate conflict, governments either abandon programme budgeting or turn it into a supplemental presentation.

In line with the argument advanced here, programme budgeting also fails because it cannot dislodge organisations as the basic decision units in budgeting. Organisations and programmes are fundamentally antagonistic bases for structuring budget allocations. In the former, similar functions are grouped together regardless of the objectives they serve; in the latter, activities that serve the same objective are grouped together regardless of the organisation in which they are located. The former are structured for efficient provision of goods and services, the latter to facilitate the analysis of policy options. As sensible as it is to budget for objectives, governments cannot disregard the financial needs of the organisations that provide public services.

Organisations have another important advantage: they are a means of accounting for public funds. One of the difficulties faced by governments when they try to implement programme budgeting is determining who is responsible for the use of public funds. Governments usually solve this problem by classifying programmes within organisations, which robs programme budgeting of its essential purpose.

Organisations and programmes are compatible classifications when the latter serve only as instruments of analysis. Programme budgeting and other innovations have provided many national governments with much more information on objectives and policies than they had a generation ago. They have more data on the effectiveness of programmes and on the outcomes ensuing from them. Often, however, available data are not used in budgeting. The underutilisation of analytic data has more to do with the time compression and rigidities of budgeting than with the failure to implement programme budgeting. When decisions have to be made under tight deadlines, and almost all budgeted resources are claimed by past commitments and ongoing activities, there is not much space in the process for analytic work.

The survival of organisations as the basic decision unit imparts a vital message for performance budgeting. The path to better performance in government runs through the departments and agencies that produce public services. If they are mobilised to perform, performance budgeting has a foothold to spawn better results: more output and improved outcomes. The essential task of performance budgeting is not to produce better measurement but better organisations. Information is an instrument of analysis; organisations and those who work in them are the wielders of these instruments.

2. Criteria for establishing new budget rules

Budget rules determine how spending decisions are made and reported. Some rules, such as annuality and comprehensiveness, have been accepted practice since the emergence of modern budgeting more than a century ago. Some are of recent vintage and rely on new techniques such as the medium-term expenditure framework (MTEF). In general, the older the rule, the more widely it is applied. Some rules are inherently country-specific and include the forms and schedules on which spending units bid for money. Many rules are formal and are codified in budget law and manuals, but some of the most important ones are informal, such as the conduct of negotiations between the finance ministry and spending entities. In every country, a vast body of rules dictates the compilation of the budget by the government and its review by the legislature. Many rules pertain to the implementation of the budget and determine the scope for virement and other modifications of the purposes and amounts of expenditure. Most rules are procedural but some, such as those which constrain fiscal aggregates, are substantive.

Although rules have accreted, stability is important in budget procedure. Having routine procedures that recur with little or no change year after year stabilises budgetary roles and relationships and drains the process of much of the conflict that inheres in the competition for limited resources. Frequent changes in procedure complicate the tasks of calculating expenditures and resolving conflict. Nevertheless, changing circumstances and the development of new techniques make it appropriate for governments to modify budget practices from time to time. The two innovations discussed in Sections 3 and 4 have the potential to introduce new budget rules. The case for performance budgeting and for accrual budgeting rests in part on new forms of information processing – performance measurement and accrual accounting – as well as on new conditions facing budget makers, such as rising expectations and fiscal pressures. Before examining these reforms, it would be useful to specify criteria for assessing the appropriateness of proposed changes in budget rules.

One seemingly logical criterion must be discarded. While it might seem sensible to reject proposed rules that would bias budget decisions, it should be apparent that all significant changes in budget rules have the potential to alter budget outcomes. Rules matter because they affect the behaviour of those who exercise authority in budgeting. The essential purpose of new decision rules is to produce allocations that differ from those that would otherwise occur. Performance budgeting aims to give more money to activities that produce wanted results and less to those that do not. Accrual budgeting intends to make governments more cautious in taking on long-term commitments that may have a negligible impact on the current budget but would adversely affect future ones.

Occasionally new rules are substantive: they purposely change the decisions that emerge from the process. Europe's Stability and Growth Pact is of this sort, as are rules that require a balanced budget or some other predetermined fiscal outcome. Most new rules, however, are procedural: they modify the way decisions are made but do not dictate any particular outcome. Performance budgeting changes the focus from inputs to outputs; accrual budgeting requires that spending be measured on a cost basis rather than on a cash basis. The following paragraphs specify a number of criteria for assessing these and other procedural changes.

2.1. Government's ability to complete its budget responsibilities

Formulating the budget is one of the few tasks that every government must complete, regardless of how difficult the choices or deep the conflicts. Often, new procedures are introduced in disregard of their effect on budget work. They overload the process, require more information than can be handled in the confined timetable, and ultimately fall into disuse because they get in the way of formulating the budget. Zero-based budgeting (ZBB), which was popular in the United States and some other countries a few decades ago, illustrates this problem. It multiplied the number of decision points for government, requiring additional information and analysis for each decision. While ZBB had laudable intentions, it was unworkable and had to be discarded by governments that made earnest efforts to implement it.

Formulation of the budget may also be impeded by reforms that stir up budget conflict. This appears to be one of the unavoidable side effects of programme budgeting, for it requires that policy makers agree on objectives in addition to deciding the amounts to be spent. It also impels them to review a broader range of options than is normally considered in formulating the budget. Politicians and managers often fight harder over the purposes of expenditure than on the amounts allocated. Friction over the programme structure retards efforts to budget on the basis of objectives. A similar problem sometimes besets governments which embrace performance budgeting and become entangled in protracted argument over the definition of outputs and outcomes. Getting the definitions right becomes more important than getting the government to perform.

2.2. Availability and use of information

Effective implementation of budget rules depends on information. If the government is called upon to budget for tax expenditures or contingent liabilities, it must have reliable data on these transactions. Many governments do not. In this writer's experience, reformers have rarely taken account of the cost, availability or use of the requisite data. Reformers assume that once the requirement is in place, the government will take appropriate steps to inform itself. Things do not always work out this way. Quite a few governments that have been pressured to maintain an MTEF lack reliable projections of future revenue, spending or economic conditions. Similarly, governments that nominally have a performance budget may have insufficient data on the outputs they produce or the social outcomes deriving from public policy. It is not reasonable to expect a government that accounts for public finances on a cash basis or lacks timely, audited financial statements to produce credible accrual-based budgets.

In building robust budget institutions, it would be logical to prepare the way by developing necessary information resources first and establishing rules afterwards. Would-be reformers should study the sequence by which Australia made forward estimates the centrepiece of budget policy. As recounted by John Wanna and associates (Wanna *et al.*, 2000, pp. 319-322), the development of forward estimates as a decision rule proceeded in a series of steps over several years. At first, the estimates were internal projections used exclusively by the Department of Finance and Administration in its budget work. They were not deemed sufficiently reliable for public dissemination. However, before long, the Department realised that it would have a stronger case for budgetary discipline if others had access to the forward estimates, and it upgraded them for publication. Once they were public, government leaders decided to use them to frame medium-term expenditure decisions.

The high cost and limited availability of new data are serious impediments to budget innovation in developing countries. But the issue affects all countries because major reforms add to the informational burdens of those who bid for or allocate resources. Far-reaching reforms may be more successful when the government purges some old informational requirements to make room for new ones than when it layers new data on the old. When Australia made forward estimates the basis for policy and fiscal decisions, it eliminated much of the line-item detail that previously dominated budget decisions. And when New Zealand adopted output-based budgeting, it removed almost all mention of inputs from the budget, appropriations act and supporting documents. In many countries, by contrast, budgeting is an amalgamation of multiple waves of reform, each of which has deposited its residue of informational requirements.

When governments add budget rules, they facilely assume that the new information will be used. This assumption leads to the overproduction and underutilisation of budgetary data. For example, requiring governments to compile data on contingent liabilities does not itself assure that they will regulate these financial risks. Even if they were required to publish the data in the budget, governments may lack the incentive or the opportunity to make effective use of the data.

2.3. Relevance of budget rules

New budget rules must make sense to those who are supposed to produce the data or use them. Often they do not make sense, and they come to be regarded as a technical exercise – one of the many chores that must be done to get through the annual budget cycle. This has been the fate of many of the reforms prescribed by international financial institutions for developing countries. It is highly likely that this fate will befall accrual budgeting if it is adopted by governments that do not understand it and have no plans to use the information in managing public finances.

Innovative rules acquire relevance when they are integrated into ongoing budget practices and are not hived off to the periphery of the process. Australia made a success of forward estimates when they became the central instrument for setting budget policy. In many countries, however, an MTEF is irrelevant because it stands apart from the annual budget. Relevance is promoted when governments decide in advance how new rules and the resulting information will be applied. It is often assumed that requiring a particular practice or report suffices. Innovations in budget practice that are not viewed by practitioners as useful do not survive.

2.4. Enforcing the rules

Budget rules are not self-enforcing. Just because a procedure is mandated in law or regulation does not mean that it will be applied. In budgeting, as in other activities, there are numerous ways to sabotage unwanted innovations. When budget rules are deemed important, the means of enforcement should be built in from the outset. In some countries, enforcement is assigned to the audit office or to a legislative committee, such as the Public Accounts Committee in the United Kingdom. In other countries, courts have become involved in enforcing budget rules.

The reforms discussed in Sections 3 and 4 diverge in terms of enforcement. When the accrual basis is embedded in accounting rules and auditors are armed with independence and resources, failure to comply with the rules may result in qualified financial statements and impaired access to capital markets. With rare exception, government pronouncements on performance are not systematically audited. Citizens and interest groups have little recourse when results are misstated or disregarded. For performance budgeting and accrual budgeting to take root, it is essential that governments have formal procedures for reviewing reported results, including accepted standards for measuring outputs and outcomes and for reporting costs and liabilities.

2.5. Learn from past efforts that failed

The spread of budget rules has been propelled by stories of successful innovations in *avant-garde* countries. Relatively little attention is paid to how the reforms were introduced, the obstacles that had to be surmounted, the special conditions that enabled success, and the features that did not work out quite as expected and were discarded along the way. When it comes to emulating other countries, failure is usually a better teacher than success. But who knows or cares about reforms that were launched with much fanfare only to be abandoned with barely a notice? Australia's ambitious strategy to thoroughly evaluate all programmes was accorded much publicity, but no announcement was made when the strategy was terminated. The United Kingdom's "Next Steps" initiative, which led to the creation of more than 100 agencies with broad operating independence, is well-known around the world, but the retaking of managerial control by ministries and central agencies during the Blair regime is hardly known. Sweden is rightfully regarded as an innovative country, but it is hard to find information on why its results-budgeting initiative of the 1980s barely got off the ground. Even more important than absolute failure is the necessary tinkering to take a reform from blueprint to practice, to get a promising concept to work within the demanding realities of budgeting.

Performance budgeting is a case study of repeated failure. The concept was introduced in the United States shortly after World War II, but it disappeared with hardly a trace. Governments attempting performance budgeting today would learn much by studying why this American innovation, and many others like it, lapsed into obscurity. Why did a reform that is so sensible survive for no more than a few years, and why is a new version invented every decade or so? What are the political, organisational and informational prerequisites for making a success of performance budgeting? Addressing these types of questions would shed light on the conditions needed for performance-based innovations to work.

2.6. The architecture of reform matters

Governments that move to performance budgeting or accrual budgeting often have a broader reform agenda that may include lengthening the time frame of budgeting, undertaking programme evaluation, changing the format of the budget, and other innovations. Quite often the various initiatives are disconnected from one another, giving rise to confusion and reform fatigue. Whether innovations are intended to be decision rules or analytic tools, it is important that the government link the pieces together so that those who have to make them work understand how they are connected.

The two reforms discussed in Sections 3 and 4 illustrate this problem. While they are typically depicted as separate innovations, both performance budgeting and accrual budgeting require reliable attribution of costs to activities, including apportionment of indirect and overhead costs. But when each reform is entrusted to a different entity, each entity may define and measure costs differently, leading to inconsistent rules and widespread confusion. The problem occurs when innovation is an analytic tool, but is significantly more damaging when it is promoted as a new decision rule. The solution, which is rarely achieved, is to pay attention to the overall architecture of reform, so that performance budgeting and accrual budgeting are designed as one set of innovations rather than as discrete changes.

2.7. The internationalisation of budget rules

Not long ago, budget rules were specific to each country. Although they were influenced by practices in other countries and there was an active exchange of ideas, governments charted their own course. This situation is now undergoing change, as international organisations recommend or dictate country practices. The rules are strongest with regard to fiscal outcomes, but they also pertain to other budget practices. The European Commission has an elaborate set of rules, including the close review of annual budgets and multi-year spending plans of member countries. The IMF has issued a "Code of Good Practices on Fiscal Transparency" and has converted its government finance statistics (GFS) to the accrual basis. Although it will take considerable time, one should not be surprised if international organisations were to devise rules for measuring and reporting programme results. Once rules are established to account for expenditure, it is only a short distance for them to migrate to the making of expenditure decisions. This has been the path taken by the accrual basis, which is moving from a rule that pertains to financial reporting to one that covers budget decisions as well.

It is important that international organisations be mindful of the distinction between analytic tools and decision rules and, except where there is compelling justification, that they leave rules to the discretion of national governments. It also is important that they distinguish between good and best practice, internationalising practices which have been implemented in a broad swath of countries, not only in the most advanced ones.

3. Performance budgeting

Performance budgeting is easy to explain but has been hard to implement. The basic idea is that governments should budget for actual or expected results (typically labelled as outputs and outcomes) rather than for inputs (personnel, supplies and other items). When deciding the budget, governments should be informed of the services that public agencies will provide and the expected benefits and social conditions that will derive from spending public funds. As appealing and sensible as this idea is, putting it into practice has been exceedingly difficult. Governments have many things on their minds when they allocate resources; performance is only one preoccupation and usually not the most urgent.

While it appears to be simple, performance budgeting comes in as many varieties as there are governments that have applied it. Each government has its own approach, and each has distinctive definitions and methods for feeding performance data into the stream of budget work. The many approaches can be aligned along a spectrum ranging from the loosest concept to the most stringent, with numerous shadings in between. Loosely defined, any system that provides information on the volume of outputs, the activities of government agencies, their workload, indicators of demand or need for public services, or the impact of expenditure qualifies as a performance budget. Strictly defined, only the budget systems which formally link increments in spending to increments in results would qualify. Under the first definition, many governments could claim to have performance budgets; under the second, few could. With such a wide range, one may justifiably argue either that performance budgeting has been truly successful or that it has dismally failed.

The difference between the two definitions corresponds precisely to the distinction drawn in this article between analytic tools and decision rules. If all that performance budgeting does is inform policy makers, it serves as an aid to analysis though, like all analytic instruments, it risks falling into disuse. On the other hand, if it is deployed to decide budget allocations, performance budgeting functions as a rule that can be stated in the following form: the government should consistently allocate resources on the basis of evidence or of reasoned expectations of results. To do so, each increment in expenditure should result in an increment in results, defined as a greater volume of output or additional improvement in social conditions.

Both versions of performance budgeting depend on information concerning the services or results of public expenditure. Their data requirements overlap but are not identical: those deriving from the stringent version are much more demanding. For most analytic purposes, it suffices to disaggregate data to the programme or activity level; for budget decisions on marginal results, data on cost and results must be attributed to discrete units of output or results. Lacking robust cost accounting systems, most governments cannot allocate costs so as to connect incremental resources and results.

For all versions, the dependence on information explains why governments have invested in measuring performance. It is not feasible to budget for performance without measuring it, but it is feasible to measure and not budget for performance. In many countries, defining and compiling data on performance is not only the first step, but the last one as well. As discussed below, analysts and managers often engage in heated and protracted argument over the definition of outputs and outcomes, leaving insufficient opportunity to apply the data in the budget practices.

It is technically feasible to measure and budget for incremental results, but few governments have actually done so. Although they may want to budget for performance, governments must take other considerations into account when they set spending levels. Foremost is the necessity to pay for past commitments as well as for ongoing activities and the operating costs of government departments and agencies. In drawing up the budget, policy makers must also be mindful of political promises, interest group demands, and the overriding need to complete budget work by curtailing conflict over objectives and resources. When all powerful claims on resources have been satisfied, not much is left over to allocate on the basis of results, and performance is crowded out altogether or recedes to the margins of the budget.

Progress has also been hindered by lack of a strong performance ethic in public management. To anticipate an argument that will be elaborated later in this section, the government cannot budget for performance if it does not manage for performance. Managers and rank-and-file civil servants must care about delivering good services and improving the efficiency of operations, and they must pay attention to the outcomes that flow from government policies. They must be willing to take a hard look at what works and what does not, and to reallocate resources from less effective to more effective activities. If they are not willing, no dose of performance data will make much of a dent in their agency's performance. This argument has far-reaching implications, for it portends that the reform of budgeting must be part of a larger transformation of government.

3.1. Analytic tool or decision rule?

The principal theme of this sub-section is that most governments would do well to deploy performance budgeting as an analytic tool because few have the capacity to ground budget decisions on it. Governments usually fail when they conceive of performance budgeting as the key instrument for allocating resources. Failure often leaves governments with a robust supply of relevant information that can enhance public policy. It is important, therefore, to consider both the opportunities and impediments for applying performance information to budget decisions.

The notion that the government should purposely spend money to purchase results has considerable appeal. It is reasonable to expect that the government is informed of the increase or decrease in outputs or of the changes in social conditions that are expected to flow from its decisions. For many budget issues, it is technically feasible to link incremental resources and results in the manner called for by the strict definition of performance budgeting. In fact, a small number of governments operate this type of budget, but it is definitely beyond the reach of all but the most innovative. Few governments have both the political will and the necessary data to link increments in resources to increments in results.

One government that has the requisite conditions is Sunnyvale, a small city in the state of California in the United States, which has operated a true performance budget for approximately two decades. Sunnyvale's approach, which in this writer's judgment is among the most advanced in the world, presents policy makers with a series of options in each major area of public activity. For example, in budgeting for fire services, the city allocates money so that response time from receipt of an emergency call to arrival of fire equipment on the scene should be no more than 7 minutes, 20 seconds. Before taking this decision, city officials consider alternatives that would lengthen or reduce response time by spending less or more money than the amount agreed in the budget. In this example, outputs have a qualitative dimension and are not defined solely in terms of volume.

Although it is two decades old, the Sunnyvale model lies at the cutting edge of performance budgeting. It illustrates the potential for deploying this reform as a decision rule that drives budget allocations. Doing so would transform budgeting into a process for allocating resources at the margins. Indeed, this is almost always the question that confronts budgeting: should government spend a little more or a little less? But there is one big difference: Sunnyvale explicitly decides more or less in terms of marginal changes in outputs or outcomes. This has the effect of making performance budgeting the key rule for deciding how much to spend on each government activity.

Transforming performance budgeting into a decision rule would require at least the following capabilities:

- The government would need information and expertise to disaggregate activities or outputs into standardised units.
- It would then allocate costs to these units.
- And it would acquire capacity to measure results contributed by each unit.

These are truly challenging tasks, for few governments have robust cost accounting systems that enable them to measure marginal costs by distinguishing between fixed and variable costs as well as between marginal and average costs. It is also essential to allocate costs among the units producing outputs and other benefits. Without reliable cost measurement and assignment, Sunnyvale would have no legitimate basis for determining that the amount budgeted would enable the fire department to respond within 7 minutes, 20 seconds. Without more detailed knowledge, one can only imagine the large amount of analysis and measurement that underlies Sunnyvale's budget decisions. Inasmuch as the unit cost of producing the next increment in results usually differs from the unit cost of producing the previous increment, it has been necessary for Sunnyvale to develop tools of marginal analysis for government.

Governments which embrace performance budgeting as a decision rule face another handicap. When it appropriates money, the government usually acquires the entire output of each spending unit for a fixed sum. Except in entities financed by trading income, the amount spent by the government does not vary if fewer or more outputs are produced. The Sunnyvale fire department receives the same appropriation whether it responds to 50 fires or 500. This critical difference between public sector budgeting and commercial budgeting is one of the main reasons why it is not normally advisable to define performance budgeting as a decision rule. Most large businesses have variable budgets: the resources available to operating units vary automatically with the volume of goods and services they produce. If they produce more, they have more to spend. For innovative governments, such as Sunnyvale, it would be necessary to shift from fixed to variable budgeting. This poses difficult questions pertaining to appropriations as legal limits on expenditure.

Additional considerations weigh against deploying performance budgeting as the basis for budget allocations. One is that results are not a sufficient guide for spending decisions. In some situations, poor results may compel the government to spend more, while favourable results may enable them to spend less. In order to budget for results, governments require a deeper understanding of programmes and options than is provided by output and outcome measures. Moreover, when the government is the sole or dominant supplier of an essential service, it may be compelled to spend even when favourable results are not forthcoming. Few governments have the option to close low-performing public schools.

Sound budgeting is as much a matter of political and managerial judgment as of results measurement. These judgments are especially important when the concept of performance moves from outputs to outcomes. There is rarely a linear connection between the amounts spent and the outcomes that ensue. For this reason, the strict version of performance budgeting emphasises outputs, not outcomes. This was the path taken by New

Zealand when it reformed public finance in the early 1990s, and it is the path taken by governments such as Sunnyvale.

In assessing the suitability of performance budgeting for decisions, it is essential to keep in mind that governments finance ongoing organisations, not just programmes and results. This is why organisational units have survived as the main classification scheme in budgeting. As will be elaborated below, organisational performance is defined not only by substantive results but also by its capacity to innovate, its responsiveness to clients, and the morale and skills of its workforce.

The foregoing arguments lead conclusively to the finding that, in all but exceptional circumstances, performance budgeting should be regarded as analytic input into the budget process. The impact of performance information on the budget will vary from one cycle to the next, as well as among programmes within each cycle. A sensible way of thinking about performance information comes from the United States Office of Management and Budget (OMB) which has made significant progress implementing the Program Assessment Rating Tool (PART) that evaluates approximately one-fifth of all federal programmes each year through a menu of questions covering four dimensions of performance: programme purpose and design, strategic capacity, programme management, and programme results. The responses are weighted into an aggregate score for each programme, which is then used together with other information by the OMB to recommend budget allocations. The OMB cautions in its guidelines that "program performance will not be the only factor in decisions about how much funding programs receive. However, the Congress and the President, equipped with information about program performance, can consider performance to a greater degree in their decision making.....".[2] In sum, PART is an analytic tool, not a decision rule.

3.2. Measuring performance

Over the years, governments have invested more effort in measurement than in any other feature of performance budgeting. As already noted, measurement has been the only step in many countries. Efforts to measure the activities and results of government expenditure date back many years. One of the earliest was launched more than 70 years ago when Herbert Simon (a future Nobel Laureate in Economics) teamed with the head of the International City Managers Association to devise a measurement scheme based on the concept that "the result of an effort or performance indicates the effect of that effort or performance in accomplishing its objective" (Ridley and Simon, 1938, p. 2[3]). Since then, thousands of articles and reports have been published, each providing its own language and approach. Perhaps because of the large volume of such studies, management guru Donald Kettl has observed that "measuring government performance is like the weather. Everybody talks about it...but there is no consensus on how to do it" (Kettl, quoted in Osborne and Plastrik, 2000, p. 249).

Because definitions and measures have not been standardised, most governments invent their own, striving to produce the right measurement system for themselves. The novelty and inflated importance of the task often generate interminable argument over whether a particular measure is an output or an outcome, a target or an indicator, a goal or an objective, an end outcome or only an intermediate outcome. In this writer's view, something is amiss when, after decades of research and experience, governments struggle with basic concepts, as if ordinary words such as outputs and targets are so obscure that they need their own dictionary. Protracted argument conveys the impression that measurement is an end in itself; getting government to perform better is secondary to getting better measures.

In the measurement industry, relatively little forethought has been invested in how the new data are to be used in managing government and allocating resources. It is assumed that once data are available, they will be used. Judging from past experience, this is an unwarranted assumption; the more likely action is that they will be ignored. Especially when the aim is to influence budgetary behaviour, it is important to think through the means by which such measures might be invested with greater relevance. To the extent that budgeting entails choices at the margins, it would be sensible to measure performance in terms of the different results that would ensue from different budget allocations. If this were done, the tools of analysis would be aligned with the structure of budget decisions. In fact, however, most performance measures are snapshots: they display outputs or outcomes under only one policy. Although they may yield useful insights, snapshots do not shed light on what budget makers need to know about performance. From the vantage point of politicians and managers, the key performance questions are: what difference will it make if governments adopt this policy option rather than another one? And what difference will it make if spending is raised or lowered? For example, how many more children might complete schooling because the budget is subsidising hot lunches? How many more would continue on to secondary education if the school were staffed with guidance counsellors? As these questions indicate, it is feasible to frame performance measures in terms of the differences in outputs or outcomes that would result from changing the amounts spent.

The next few paragraphs suggest one approach for focusing performance measures on the issues facing budget makers. It is not the only feasible approach, but it is set out here because it fits in well with budget practices in many countries, though the approach itself is not yet used in any country. The core idea is for the government to construct a baseline of the services that would be provided if current policies (including budget allocations) were continued without change. This services baseline would parallel the expenditure baseline that is widely used to prepare and analyse budgets. The expenditure baseline is an essential component of the MTEF; it enables governments to project future spending under current policy. The baseline is usually updated annually (or more frequently) for changes in prices and other economic and programme variables. Once these adjustments have been made, any change in spending – defined as a variance from the baseline – must be the result of policy change. A similar baseline would project the types and volumes of services for the next year or the medium term. Linking the two baselines would greatly enhance the utility of performance measurement as a tool of budget analysis by showing how changes in spending and services are linked.

Many technical issues would have to be resolved in constructing a services baseline, but these are not inherently more difficult than those that arise in estimating baseline expenditures. Both the expenditure and services baselines would rely on assumptions about prices, workload and other variables; both would require rules for estimating future amounts; and both would rely on procedures for adjusting the projections and measuring policy changes. In much the same way that it estimates the spending implications of policy changes, the government would estimate the service implications of these changes. In effect, this is what Sunnyvale must do to compile its annual budget. How else could it estimate the impact of spending levels on response time in the fire department?

The purpose of suggesting the services baseline is not to recommend a particular course of action, but to urge that much can be done to strengthen performance measurement as an analytic tool. Change-oriented performance measurement is relevant because it focuses on the issues governments deal with when the budget is being formulated. Some might object that a services baseline entrenches incrementalism – the tendency to consider only marginal changes – in budget work. The objection is valid, but half a century of warring against incrementalism has left budget reformers with nothing but failure. The most fruitful path to successfully deploying performance measurement is one that recognises and exploits incrementalism's hold on budget decisions.

3.3. *Managing for performance*

Both as a decision rule and as an analytic tool, performance budgeting is effective only when the managerial culture is supportive. Previous waves of reform assumed that budgeting drives management; if the budget is oriented to results, government entities will be managed for results. This premise was grounded on a simplistic notion: government entities need money to operate. Therefore, if the money they receive is conditioned on performance, they will be motivated to perform better. This reasoning is flawed in this writer's view, and dooms performance budgeting to failure, for it does not recognise that budgeting is shaped by the managerial context within which resources are spent and services provided. If managers do not care about results or if employees are indifferent to how well they perform, installing performance budgeting or similar techniques will hardly make a difference. One of the most important lessons from half a century of disappointment is that budgeting cannot be transformed in isolation from the management practices and culture in which it is embedded. Only when they manage for results will managers be able to budget for results.

One corollary of this theme is that it is necessary to measure or otherwise gauge the performance of public organisations. Good performance is not manna from heaven; in every instance, it has the fingerprints of organisations that are doing their job and producing results. Focusing only on outputs and outcomes ignores fundamental questions about how results materialise. Why do some organisations perform well and others poorly? What are the characteristics of high-performing organisations? How can organisations improve results? These and similar questions have a common answer: public agencies have to be organised, motivated, managed and financed to perform the tasks expected of them.

Some governments have attempted to build organisational characteristics into performance measurement. New Zealand has one of the most interesting systems, for it distinguishes between the government's role as a purchaser of the outputs of state entities and its role as owner of the agencies. There is a tension between the two roles that pulls the government in opposite directions. Its interest as a purchaser is short-term: the government aims to buy outputs for the current or next year at a low price. Its ownership interest is long-term: the government is concerned with the capacity of public agencies to respond to future demands and changing conditions, and it is impelled to sell outputs at a sufficiently high price so that agencies can invest in training, research and development, and other actions that capacitate them.

In New Zealand, the purchaser role overwhelmed ownership, with the result that inadequate attention was given to organisational health. The balanced scorecard, which was in vogue a few years ago, attempted to redress this imbalance by treating outputs as only one of four sets of interdependent performance measures. The other three pertain to internal processes and practices, staff quality and morale, and customer needs and satisfaction. In calling attention to this approach, this writer's aim is to encourage governments to think in organisational terms when they invest in performance budgeting. As an analytic tool, performance budgeting works only when the tool is wielded by agencies that know how to use it and are motivated to perform.

4. Accrual budgeting

To assess the accrual basis, it is necessary to distinguish between *ex post* reporting of financial results and *ex ante* specification of revenue and expenditure policy. While it may be appropriate to prescribe the accrual basis in financial reporting, extension of this principle to budget statements raises critical questions that must be addressed by each country through its political-administrative machinery. It is essential to standardise financial statements, but it may still be appropriate for countries to establish their own budget conventions. Thus, the case for accrual budgeting must be made independently of arguments used in support of accrual accounting.

The recent development and dissemination of public sector accounting standards have impelled many national governments to accrue assets and liabilities on the balance sheet, as well as income and expenses on operating statements. However, few governments systematically accrue revenues and expenditures in the budget. The short list of countries that have full accrual budgets contains Australia, New Zealand and the United Kingdom. Other countries have adopted accruals for certain types of transactions. These countries include Iceland, Sweden and the United States. All these countries differ from one another in applying accrual principles to the budget. Some of the countries set aside money for depreciation or a capital charge, others do not. Some book all taxes due as current revenue; others recognise revenue when it is received. These and other differences indicate that accrual budgeting is still in the testing stage and that it would be premature for all but the most *avant-garde* countries to shift their budgets to this basis.

All of the national governments that have implemented accrual budgeting have two distinguishing characteristics. They are regarded as among the best-managed countries in the world, and they generally give public managers broad operating discretion. These characteristics may be necessary preconditions for accrual budgeting. Strong management is essential because the accrual basis adds to the complexity of financial management and requires both skill and probity in valuing assets and liabilities. Operational discretion is also important to enable managers to efficiently use available resources. Without appropriate discretion, managers are likely to regard accruals as technical entries that have no bearing on the resources available for expenditure.

4.1. Reporting and budgeting

The disparity between the wide application of accrual accounting and the limited implementation of accrual budgeting suggests that the factors which have induced governments to present their financial statements on the accrual basis are not as compelling in determining how governments go about estimating future revenue and expenditure flows in the budget. Financial statements are subject to audit; budgets are not, though it is possible that they will be in the future. Financial statements are a means of communicating the government's condition to interested outside parties; budgets traditionally have been a means of communicating within government. The fact that some cutting-edge governments have embraced accrual budgeting indicates that the traditional differences between the two types of statements may be narrowing. But the two types of statements still serve different purposes, and the methods suitable for one might not suit the other.

The distinction between financial reporting and budgeting bears directly on the central question of this article: when should a particular form of information be cast as an analytic tool or a decision rule? Prescribing the accrual basis for financial statements gives a government valuable insights that may enhance the formulation of budget policy. With current information on assets and liabilities, a government can more clearly assess how changes in budget policy would impact its future financial condition. But as long as the budget itself is not on the accrual basis, these insights are only analytic tools, even though they are mandated for financial reports. However, if the budget were put on an accrual basis, this would become a decision rule for estimating the receipts and expenditures expected for the next or subsequent financial periods.

The fact that many governments report but do not budget for accruals indicates a preference for treating information on assets and liabilities as aids for analysis rather than as categories for decision. This is exemplified by the latest reforms in France. Much of the literature on the accrual basis, however, ignores the differences between reporting and budgeting and assumes that what is appropriate for the former also suits the latter. For example, a report published in 2003 by the Asian Development Bank devoted more than three-quarters of its 85 pages to accrual accounting, but then argued that if it were applied only to financial reporting, accrual information may not be taken seriously. The budget is the key management document in the public sector, and accountability is based on implementing the budget as approved by the legislature. If the budget is on a cash basis, that is going to be the dominant basis on which politicians and senior civil servants work. Financial reporting on a different basis risks becoming a purely technical accounting exercise in these cases (Athukorala and Reid, 2003, p. 51).

No claim is made here that accruals add value to budgeting; rather, the case rests on the value that would be subtracted from financial reporting if the budget were on a cash basis.

It should be noted that even when both reporting and budgeting are on the accrual basis, they may show different financial results either because they apply different accounting rules or because they value things differently. For 2005, the State of Queensland in Australia reported a budget surplus of approximately AUD 3 billion, but the balance sheet reported an AUD 18 billion increase in net worth. This increase was due principally to revaluation of existing assets, not to the accumulation of additional assets during the financial year. The difference between the balance sheet and the budget is justified because one measures financial stocks and the other measures financial flows. A much stronger case can be made for applying accruals to stocks, because they provide a full accounting of an entity's assets and liabilities, rather than applying accruals to flows, which measure financial transactions during a fixed time period. The accrual basis would transform the budget from a statement of flows to a statement of fiscal impact. In fact, one of the aims of those who advocate accrual budgeting is to turn the budget into a fiscal impact statement.

Before endorsing this transformation, it would be useful to consider the evolution and purposes of budgeting and how accruals might affect budgetary practices. Modern budgeting emerged in Europe more than two centuries ago as a means of planning and regulating the cash flow of government during a fixed period, typically a single fiscal year. Budgeting supplemented appropriations, which were already on the cash basis, and restricted the amounts that the government was authorised to spend. Because it is inherently a political statement, the budget had its own country-specific rules and conventions. The fiscal balance was calculated as the arithmetical difference between cash received and cash paid out during the financial year. This calculation only covered accounts and funds that were included in the budget; it did not include off-budget or extrabudgetary items.

Operating within their own rules, budgets were subject to manipulation, as opportunistic politicians sought to project or produce fiscal outcomes that suited their interests. In many countries, the manipulations were marginal, such as adding a bit to revenue by selling assets, or subtracting a little from expenditure by delaying certain payments. Although they were not good practice, the manipulations enabled cross-pressured politicians to muddle through from one budget year to the next. In some countries, however, manipulations became so common and significant as to undermine the integrity of budget accounts. Whether marginal or major, these practices highlighted deficiencies in cash-flow budgeting.

During the past two decades, several factors have converged to challenge cash-flow budgeting. One has been the internationalisation of accounting rules and the auditing of government financial reports. The IMF shifted its government finance statistics (GFS) to the accrual basis at the start of the 21st century, and the International Public Sector Accounting Standards Board (IPSASB) has been busy promulgating accrual-based rules for public entities. In addition, various international organisations have co-operated in shifting the system of national accounts (SNA) to a modified accrual basis. A second, related, influence has been the rapid spread of fiscal rules which constrain budget options and outcomes. Effective enforcement of these rules depends on objective information concerning the government's fiscal performance. Moreover, without accounting standards, these rules would provide politicians with fresh incentive to manipulate the timing or recognition of various transactions to make the government's fiscal position appear more favourable than it actually is. Finally, the successful conversion of pioneer countries such as New Zealand to the accrual basis has spurred other countries to follow suit.

In business firms, the budget is an internal document that is not bound by accounting rules. Each firm can prepare its budget in the format and on the basis that fits its interests. However, government budgets are not internal documents; they are presented to parliament for approval and are one of the major instruments for informing citizens of public policies and priorities. Arguably, citizens should have transparent, tamper-proof statements of the government's budget plans that comply with accepted accounting standards and are not manipulated for political advantage. Despite these considerations, cash-flow budgeting has several compelling advantages. It is better understood by citizens and the government than accrual budgeting; it may be less prone to manipulation; and it may provide a more reliable indicator of the government's near-term fiscal condition.

Shifting to the accrual basis transfers budgetary power from elected leaders to technical experts. Cash is the everyday currency of private and public transactions. Governments take in cash and spend cash, and the amounts reported are actual rather than assumed. Accruals are grounded on complex assumptions that can befuddle experienced politicians. One should not be surprised if technocrats get into the habit of soothing the concerns of ministers, assuring them that "these are only technical entries that do not affect the resources you really have to spend." One entry adds money to pay for depreciation or a capital charge; another entry withdraws an equivalent amount of money. In some instances, this new form of double-entry budgeting might change political or managerial behaviour. In most, it will not.

One of the reputed advantages of accruals is that they are less subject to manipulation than cash. Under accruals, the government does not increase its net worth by selling assets for cash, nor does it improve its fiscal position by accelerating tax collections or delaying bill payments. But under the accrual basis, governments can manipulate fiscal estimates or results by changing assumptions about interest rates or tax arrears, adjusting discount rates, revaluing assets, or altering some of the myriad assumptions made in the course of accruing revenues and expenditures. It is often much harder to detect manipulations that are buried under layers of assumptions than those linked to cash transactions.

Finally, cash is sometimes a more reliable indicator of an entity's current financial condition. As the accrual basis becomes embedded, accounting authorities produce more rules which increase the variance between cash flows and accrued results. In recent years, the International Public Sector Accounting Standards Board (IPSASB) has issued more than 20 accrual-based rules for public sector entities, and more can be expected in the years ahead as new financial instruments are devised or new conditions arise. In some circumstances, cash may be a more accurate indicator of fiscal performance. It is well known that the shares of companies whose reported earnings are depressed by negative accruals tend to outperform companies whose earnings are boosted by accruals. This "accruals anomaly" (the term applied to the phenomenon in finance studies) indicates that investors who pay attention to cash earnings will do much better than those who focus on reported earnings.[4] Although one should be wary of generalising from business accounting to government finance, the clear implication that cash is a useful measure of financial performance does pertain to public entities.

4.2. Accruals as an analytic tool

Accruals warrant a prominent place in financial reporting because they provide insights into government finance that are not yielded by cash alone. The three most salient claims for accruals are that they provide better measures of the government's current fiscal condition and of long-run sustainability, and encourage managers to operate efficiently. Each is important, and each warrants close review.

When the government's fiscal condition is measured in cash, it is likely to be incomplete and subject to manipulation. Cash accounts do not include depreciation of assets and can be made to appear more favourable by manipulating the recognition of transactions. The shorter the time frame, the greater the scope for manipulation. In a one-year budget cycle, the government need only defer expenditure or advance tax collections by a few days (or weeks) to produce more favourable outcomes. In a medium-term frame, shifting from one year to another may make little or no difference. Yet even on an annual basis, there is often little difference between cash and accrual accounting. In New Zealand, for example, for the 2004 financial year, there was less than 0.8% variance between revenues recognised on the cash and accrual bases. The variance was also very small for current expenditure, with expensing of depreciation under the accrual basis largely offset by deferring recognition of capital expenditure. In fact, in some circumstances, the accrual basis yields a lower deficit (or higher surplus) than in cash accounting.

It may be argued that New Zealand has an elevated degree of probity in public finance and does not purposely manipulate transactions to improve cash flows. Countries lacking this ethic are likely to show much larger variances between cash and accruals, as would countries which do not efficiently maintain public infrastructure or have significant leakages in tax collections. All this may be valid, but it leads this writer to the conclusion that countries (such as New Zealand) which are best prepared for accrual budgeting get rather little out of it; and countries that need it the most because they have the greatest variances between cash and accruals (such as those which finance deficits through asset sales) probably lack both the technical skill and the political will to operate accrual budgets.

Governments can guard against the manipulation of accounts in a cash system by establishing rules concerning certain types of transactions. Some governments treat income from asset sales as a means of financing rather than as a cash inflow, while some exclude savings due to timing adjustments from baseline projections. It may be argued that these rules introduce accrual-like rules into budgeting, yet they do so within a cash framework. In other words, the government avoids both the cost of moving to accrual budgeting and the principal distortions of cash budgeting.

The second claim shifts the focus from the short (or medium) term to long-term fiscal sustainability. The key concern is that governments that budget on a cash basis tend to ignore the accumulation of liabilities that will be paid in the distant future typically for pensions and health care. But accounting rules significantly diminish the utility of accruals as indicators of long-term fiscal soundness. While they provide for governments to recognise future payments for their own employees, accounting rules preclude the recognition of liabilities for social security and other non-employee benefits.[5] Whatever the rationale for including one type of liability and excluding the other, the result is that accrual-based statements do not provide sufficient insight into the government's future fiscal position. Some well-run national governments have supplemented official financial statements with long-term fiscal sustainability studies which do include social security and other liabilities excluded from accrual accounts. The United Kingdom Treasury publishes an annual long-term fiscal forecast, and the government of Australia publishes an intergenerational report every five years. These sustainability analyses can be conducted regardless of whether the budget is cash-based or accrual-based.

The third claim is that accrual budgeting establishes conditions for managerial efficiency and accountability because it budgets all the costs associated with carrying out particular activities or services. Managers are accountable for all costs, including those paid out of other accounts (such as employee pensions and the imputed cost of accommodation in public buildings). Operating accounts are charged for the depreciation of physical assets and (in some countries) for the capital invested by the government in the entity. Capacity and incentive to manage costs depend on managers having broad discretion to spend operating funds as they deem appropriate. When managers lack operating freedom because the funds they spend are earmarked for designated purposes, making them responsible for full costs is counterproductive, for they are charged for matters over which they have no control.

At present, few national governments give managers sufficient operating discretion to make effective use of accruals. Those governments that do risk complications when managers take money appropriated for depreciation and spend it on other items instead. This has occurred in Australia which, in contrast to some other countries that have accrual budgets, makes cash appropriations for depreciation. In the countries that do not, depreciation and some other accrued charges are regarded as technical matters that have little bearing on how public funds are managed.

Thus far, there is little evidence that accrual budgeting has made much difference in managerial behaviour. It can be argued that accrual accounting and budgeting work only when they are accompanied by performance management and budgeting. Without these management capacities, it is prudent for countries to continue to upgrade their existing cash-based systems. In other words, accrual budgeting may only be ripe for the small cohort of best-managed governments. Many countries would achieve greater progress by improving cost allocation and measurement systems, broadening managerial discretion, and enhancing the quality of performance measurements than by moving to accrual budgeting.

In line with the earlier discussion, countries that have adopted accrual budgeting claim that it has strengthened short-term fiscal performance. But programme managers rarely use accrual budgeting to manage operations. Although it has strongly endorsed accrual budgeting, the Asian Development Bank has also concluded that accrual "information does not necessarily change results." Drawing on New Zealand's experience, the ADB found that the improvements achieved by government were primarily due to political will. A less sophisticated system could have achieved a great deal in the presence of that political will, and an even more sophisticated system would achieve very little if the political will to use it were not present (Athukorala and Reid, 2003, p. 51).

This conclusion has profound implications for the central issue of this article. The essential purpose of new decision rules is to compel changes in budgetary behaviour. But if the changes sought depend on the will of those who manage the budget, the new techniques serve only as analytic tools.

5. Concluding remarks

Neither performance budgeting nor accrual budgeting is ready for widespread application as a decision rule. Both have unresolved issues and are costly to implement. In performance budgeting, the key issue is the extent to which resources should be linked to results; in accrual budgeting, the issues are much more complex and pertain to the valuation of assets, recognition of revenues, treatment of depreciation and capital charges, and other unresolved questions.[6] The few countries that have adopted accrual budgeting have taken different approaches; their experiences should provide a firmer basis for assessing accruals in the future.

Although they are distinct innovations, performance budgeting and accrual budgeting share a dependence on robust, results-oriented management and full cost attribution. Because these qualities are absent in most countries, the suitability of performance and accrual systems is limited. It is not surprising, therefore, that the countries which have good performance-based management are most likely to have adopted features of accrual budgeting. For the vast majority of countries, performance budgeting and accrual budgeting suffice as analytic tools. This is a second-best solution that promises greater gains in budgeting than would be forthcoming from the pursuit of cutting-edge innovations.

Afterword

The two instruments discussed in this article are not the only ones that can be cast either as analytic tools or decision rules. Just about every significant innovation in budgeting faces a similar choice. The main contemporary innovations that have been defined as rules are baseline projections of the future cost of current policies, medium-term frameworks that limit authorised future spending levels, and fiscal rules that constrain key budget aggregates.

Some innovations, however, have not been elevated to decision rules. As noted in the article, this has been the fate of programme budgeting, which survives in some countries only as supplemental information. A similar fate has befallen the tax expenditure concept, which provides useful information on revenue forgone by government. As initially conceived, it was hoped that the government would trade off between tax and direct expenditures, or set a limit on aggregate tax expenditures. In the trade-off model, if the government spent more on tax expenditures, it would have less to spend on direct programmes. In the aggregate model, the government would limit the total volume of tax subsidies each year, in the same way that it limits total direct spending. Neither version has progressed.

In a similar vein, some national governments have explored the feasibility of establishing a regulatory budget that would limit the total cost imposed on firms and households by regulations. A more radical idea, proposed by Herbert Stein (1989), called for governments to budget resources in shares of GDP. Governments would decide the percentage of national output allocated to health, national security, and each of the other functions of government. Stein argued that this scheme would eliminate the incentive for governments to shift expenses from public to private entities. Although it certainly is useful to be informed of the share of GDP spent on each national objective, establishing this procedure as a decision rule is impractical.

As new budgeting methods are devised, governments will confront the "rules *versus* tools" issue. One can anticipate a slew of instruments to deal with fiscal risks arising out of guarantees issued by government, as well as new methods to measure long-term fiscal sustainability. In these and other innovations, advanced governments will first use the tools to enrich the supply of information, but will then move to codify some methods into rules.

Notes

1. The *Analytical Perspectives* for the fiscal 2007 budget is a document of 400 pages. It is published by the United States Government Printing Office together with the main budget documents.
2. PART instructions and results are published on website of the Office of Management and Budget, *www.omb.gov.*
3. This book was drawn from monthly articles published in 1937 and 1938.
4. The seminal study on this subject is Sloan (1996).
5. Under generally accepted accounting principles, a liability is recognised when an event has already occurred, a future payment is probable, and the amount can be reliably estimated.
6. The main issues are presented in Blöndal (2004).

References

Athukorala, S.A. and B. Reid (2003), *Accrual Budgeting and Accounting in Government and Its Relevance for Developing Member Countries*, Asian Development Bank, Manila.

Blöndal, Jón R. (2004), "Issues in Accrual Budgeting", *OECD Journal on Budgeting*, 4:1, pp. 103-119.

Burkhead, Jesse (1956), *Government Budgeting*, John Wiley and Sons, New York, United States.

Osborne, David and Peter Plastrik (2000), *The Reinventor's Fieldbook*, Jossey-Bass, San Francisco, California, United States.

Ridley, Clarence E. and Herbert A. Simon (1938), *Measuring Municipal Activities: A Survey of Suggested Criteria for Appraising Administration*, The International City Managers Association, Chicago, Illinois, United States.

Sloan, R.G. (1996), "Do Stock Prices Fully Reflect Information in Accruals and Cash Flows about Future Earnings?", *The Accounting Review*, 71:3, pp. 289-315.

Stein, Herbert (1989), *Governing the $5 Trillion Economy*, Twentieth Century Fund, New York, United States.

Wanna, John, Joanne Kelly and John Forster (2000), *Managing Public Expenditure in Australia*, Allen and Unwin, Sydney, Australia.

403

ISBN 978-92-64-06087-6
Evolutions in Budgetary Practice
Allen Schick and the OECD Senior Budget Officials
© OECD 2009

Chapter 15

Off-Budget Expenditure:
An Economic and Political Framework*

This paper, originally presented at the 1981 meeting of the OECD Working Party of Senior Budget Officials, discusses the fundamental purposes of budgeting and explores how off-budget expenditures weaken a government's financial control. The paper gives insights on many aspects of budgeting that are still relevant today: the transformation of the public sector, the interface with the private sector, the scope and size of government, the role of regulation, the emergence of new organisational forms, and the use of performance objectives and long-term planning.

---

* This article was originally written in 1981, when Allen Schick was a senior specialist in the Congressional Research Service, United States. The text was published in the OECD Journal on Budgeting, Vol. 7, No. 3, 2007, when Allen Schick was Visiting Fellow, Governance Studies, The Brookings Institution, Washington DC, and Professor, School of Public Affairs, University of Maryland, United States. Boxed comments were made in 2009.

A sense that government expenditures are out of control pervades contemporary budgeting. This feeling is not confined to critics of enlarged public spending but is shared by government officials in many developed countries. Budget officials hold to this view most intensely; they see the process which they command as unable to control the trend in government spending. Their best efforts are of little avail against the forces that dictate fiscal outcomes.

Evidence of weakened budget control is plentiful. Governments habitually announce their determination to curb public sector deficits and to hold spending increases to the growth in gross national product (GNP), only to have these objectives aborted by economic and political realities. Total expenditures and the amounts spent on particular programmes often exceed the levels authorised in the budget. For many programmes, the budget has been transformed from an instrument for making government financial decisions into a process for estimating the costs of decisions made by other means. Worse yet, major expenditures are undertaken without any cognisance of them in the budget. The budget no longer controls: *force majeure* rules public finance.

> The sense that national governments were unable to exercise effective financial control was one of the key factors that led to the first meeting of senior budget officials under OECD auspices in 1980. During the previous two decades, public expenditure in the OECD community had increased an average of more than half a percentage point per year relative to GDP. In the subsequent three decades, public spending stabilised in most OECD countries or increased only slightly as a share of GDP. Many innovations have been implemented to strengthen financial control. Most governments of OECD countries have extended the time frame of budgeting from a single year to the medium term or longer, most operate under rules that limit the deficit or other fiscal aggregates, most have shifted financial statements from the cash to the accrual basis, and most have devised means of measuring outputs or outcomes. Despite these accomplishments, the adequacy of financial control persists as an issue for budget officials. One major concern, discussed elsewhere in this collection, pertains to the long-term sustainability of public finance; another pertains to the inherently difficult task of linking resources and results.

Inadequate financial control affects not only the amount of expenditure but its propriety as well. Fraud and abuse have become widespread concerns in many OECD countries, and the controls that once guarded against the misuse of public funds seem incapable of restoring trust to public expenditure.

The erosion of financial control has seriously weakened the effectiveness of government budgeting. The primary function of budgeting, upon which other critical uses are predicated, is to ensure that public funds are spent only for authorised purposes. Without reliable financial controls, the budget cannot be used for other important government functions such as managing the economy, improving administrative efficiency, and formulating public objectives and priorities. If actual expenditures do not conform to the levels specified in the budget, or if the real spending decisions are made outside of the budget framework, it is of little value for the government to go through the rituals of deciding what should be in the budget. Only when it controls spending can the budget be effectively applied to larger political, economic and management purposes.

When modern budget systems were introduced (in the late 19th century in some European countries; in the early 20th century in the United States), reformers gave highest attention to the imposition of financial controls. Toward this end, accounting practices were standardised, budget staffs were organised and empowered to review the activities of spending ministries, rules for the handling of public funds were elaborated, and audit procedures were developed. By the 1950s, budgeting in various OECD countries had progressed to the point where the basic requirements of financial control were deemed to have been satisfied. It was possible, therefore, to orient budgeting to more ambitious purposes such as economic stabilisaton and programme planning. Planning programming budgeting (PPB) and other advanced budget techniques reflected this shift in emphasis from financial control to policy formulation.

Budget makers are no longer confident that the controls they operate are adequate to the conditions of contemporary government. Every budget brings fresh confirmation of their lack of control. They must constantly remake their budgets in response to changes in economic conditions and other factors beyond their control. Rather than the budget controlling expenditures, spending controls the budget.

No single factor accounts for the attrition in budget control. Weak economic performance, the indexation of government expenditures, expansion of entitlements and other legal claims on public funds have all taken a toll. This article examines one of the factors in the loss of budget control: off-budget expenditures. In order for the budget to be an instrument of financial control, it has to be the process by which financial decisions are made and enforced. Off-budget expenditures violate this condition and thereby impair budgetary control.

Strictly defined, off-budget expenditures refer to financial transactions that are not accounted for in the budget. Rather than being a complete statement of public expenditures, the budgets of most countries exclude certain governmental activities. Off-budget expenditures can apply to direct spending by government ministries, but they are more likely to involve special transactions such as the activities of public enterprises, credit provided or guaranteed by government, or subsidies channelled through the tax system. Because of their special characteristics, these types of activities are often excluded from the regular accounts.

From the perspective of financial control, a mechanistic definition of off-budget expenditures does not suffice. The key issue is not whether an item happens to be entered in the budget, but whether its expenditures can be effectively controlled through the budget. Many of the off-budget expenditures have characteristics that would impair their controllability even if they were nominally brought within the budget's scope. In addressing the problem of off-budget expenditures, one should focus on the factors that facilitate or impede budget control, not on the accounting issue alone. (It might be appropriate if these transactions were designated "extraordinary" expenditures, but this term is applied in some countries to different purposes.)

Yet one must also be wary of broadening the off-budget concept to cover any expenditure that escapes effective budget control. Although governments typically exercise weak control over entitlements, indexed programmes and payments on the public debt, these generally are not classified as off-budget expenditures. Perhaps the most useful definition of off-budget expenditure is one that considers both the extent to which an activity is accounted for in the budget and its controllability. As used in this paper, off-budget refers to various classes of transactions that are often (but not always) excluded from the budget and are difficult to control through ordinary budgetary processes.

> Although definitions have not been standardised across countries, it may be useful to distinguish between extrabudgetary and off-budget expenditures. Extrabudgetary expenditures are similar to ordinary expenditures, but are excluded by law or practice from budget accounts. Off-budget expenditures have characteristics, such as those discussed in this article, that distinguish them from regular expenditures.

Off-budget expenditures pervade contemporary governments. They are neither aberrations of the budget process nor occasional deviations from established norms. Although they are sometimes used to escape budget control, off-budget practices are normal incidents of modern governments. They flourish where government actively seeks to manage the economy, redistribute resources, promote investments and pursue a broad range of social objectives. Off-budget expenditures are most likely to occur in mixed, interventionist economies where the boundaries between the public and private sectors are blurred and where the government attempts to influence private behaviour with incentives and sanctions.

1. The transformation of the public sector

To understand the contemporary problem of off-budget expenditure, it is necessary to take account of the transformation of national governments from providers of public services into purchasers of services provided by others and redistributors of income. This transformation has proceeded in all OECD countries, though not to the same extent everywhere. Although the traditional service role (for example, the protection of health and safety) continues, it consumes a declining portion of the government's budget. A much larger share is disbursed to various private or quasi-governmental spenders.

At one time, governments operated in a simple two-stage expenditure process. First the national legislature voted appropriations for agencies; then the agencies spent these funds on their own operations. This arrangement applied to almost all of the public sector though, of course, agencies also spent some of their funds to purchase goods and services from private vendors. The budget was essentially an accounting for government administration, and it covered virtually all of the financial activity of government. In these circumstances, "comprehensiveness" emerged as one of the cardinal principles of budgeting. Since the budget was spent on agency operations, it was not difficult to satisfy the comprehensiveness rule. The main violations occurred in the treatment of extraordinary income (earmarked revenues, bond proceeds and development assistance) and extraordinary expenses (capital improvements, development projects and spending out of special funds). In many countries, the budget was divided into ordinary and extraordinary accounts, but by annexing the special funds to the budget, it was possible to display the full financial activity of the government. The chief problem was not the incompleteness of the budget, but the preferential status of the extraordinary items.

This simple budget arrangement no longer prevails. Nowadays, the budget is dominated by transfers from government to "third" parties. Most of the budget goes to contractors or enterprises, subnational governments, and recipients of transfer payments. This transformation of the public sector occurred much later in the United States than in most OECD countries. Yet even in the United States, more than 75% of the national budget is distributed to outsiders; the percentage is surely higher in various OECD countries.

When the public sector spills beyond agency boundaries, comprehensiveness no longer offers a useful criterion for determining the scope of the budget. After all, when the scope of the public sector is uncertain, the composition of its budget cannot be fixed with precision. In effect, contemporary governments have inherited budget practices designed for a self-contained public sector, but ill-suited for the interactions that regularly occur between public and private entities.

In place of the two-stage budget process, there now exists a third stage in which appropriations nominally made to public agencies are disbursed to parties on the margins of government. But more has been changed than the locus of final expenditure; the relationship between the public and private sectors has also been altered. By offering financial inducements, governments pursue public objectives through private actions. In so doing, the social costs are no different than if the funds had been directly spent by government agencies. Thus, financial accounts confined to items conventionally reported in national budgets would not show a full picture of the costs imposed on society by government.

2. Guidelines for determining off-budget expenditures

As long as governments spent primarily for their own operations, comprehensiveness provided an operational rule for determining the proper scope of the budget. Now that governments influence private behaviour in myriad ways, a new rule is needed to determine what should be included in the budget (or in a broader process that might supersede the budget for making financial decisions). The rule applied here is frequently used in economic analysis: any cost that serves the same public objectives as a direct expenditure should be included in the government's accounts. This "substitution" rule would enable government to consider costs borne by society, not only those charged to its own agencies.

Consider, for example, a government objective to relieve congestion at certain airports. It could pursue this objective in a number of ways, some of which would be on budget and some off budget:

- It could appropriate funds to the aviation ministry for the expansion of airport facilities. This direct expenditure is conventionally included in public budgets.

- It could authorise a public enterprise to borrow funds for expansion and to cover debt service with user charges. The extent to which these transactions were accounted for in the budget would depend primarily on the status of the enterprise.

- Alternatively, the government could raise airport fees to discourage use, thereby relieving congestion without new facilities. The fees would normally be recorded as receipts in the budget.

● Rather than raising revenues to discourage use, the government might lower them to subsidise expansion. For example, it could extend tax credits to private airport operators who would invest in new facilities. In conventional budgeting, these credits reduce receipts but would not be recorded as expenditures.

● Instead of tax credits, the government could offer loans (at market or preferential rates) to airport operators. The budget treatment of these loans varies greatly among developed countries. In some instances, loans are converted into grants or repayment is deferred because the borrowers are unable (or unwilling) to repay them.

● A variant of direct loans would be for the government to guarantee loans made to airports by private institutions. Because it is a contingent liability, the guarantee is likely to be off budget, though outlays pursuant to default would be entered in the budget.

● Rather than offering financial inducements, the government could limit use of the airport, thereby obviating the need for expansion. The regulatory costs would not appear in the budget.

This illustration pertains to the use of physical assets, but it could be applied to income transfers and many other public objectives as well. Whenever government has the option of relying on indirect action (through "quasi" public or private entities), it can shift from direct to off-budget expenditure. Clearly this option generally is not practicable for the conduct of foreign policy or the maintenance of armed forces, but it applies to the bulk of public activity.

The airport illustration shows that off-budget expenditures can be measured in a variety of ways. In a narrow sense, off-budget expenditures can be limited to "government costs" such as direct expenditures or credit provided at concessional rates. A broader definition would encompass all financial costs imposed on society by government, whether or not the goverment bears the costs. According to this "social cost" definition, any government policy or action that uses resources, or compels their use by others, would incur off-budget expenditures, even if no funds were actually spent by the government.

The broader "social costs" approach has several advantages. Inasmuch as interest in off-budget expenditures arises from concern that ministries and governments might conceal the true cost of their policies, it would be inappropriate to disregard the means by which governments shift costs from themselves to society. In terms of the substitution principle discussed earlier, social costs provide a fuller measure of government options than can be gleaned from a consideration of government costs. If the budget were confined to government expenditures, public officials would have an incentive to shift costs from government to society. But if all substitutes for direct expenditures were defined as costs, decision makers would be indifferent on aggregate economic grounds to the form that the costs would take.

Yet, one must be mindful of the real difficulties of devising an expanded resource allocation process to encompass social costs. Not the least of the virtues of conventional budgeting are the ease of accounting for direct expenditures and the political agreement that can be obtained concerning programme costs. Once government ventures beyond its own accounts, however, it encounters technical and political problems in estimating social costs. In lieu of cash outlays, government needs proxy measures for the costs of its policies, and these often entail value judgments.

As a practical matter, governments are unlikely to convert from direct-expenditure budgeting to comprehensive social-cost accounting. They are likely to extend budget

The distinction between analytic tools and decision rules (see Chapter 14) sheds light on the budgetary treatment of social costs. Analytic tools inform budget makers by supplementing the data they have when allocating resources; decision rules define or limit the way budget resources are allocated or accounted for. From an analytic perspective, it is highly useful to estimate the costs imposed on households and enterprises by government officials. Information on these social costs can spur governments to devise more efficient policies. But applying a decision rule to social costs (for example, by including them together with direct expenditures within a fiscal limit or expenditure target) would transform the budget from a statement of government expenditures into a measure of the impact of government policies on firms or households.

coverage only to those costs for which agreement can be secured, while treating other costs in auxiliary presentations rather than in the core budget.

For the most part, this paper deals with government costs. However, in order to provide a broad treatment of the off-budget problem, at various points the analysis is applied to both government and social costs.

3. Choosing among budget options

When governments can operate through direct expenditure or by off-budget means, they often take the latter course. It is convenient and logical to suppose that they behave in this fashion to escape budget controls. From the standpoint of a public official, it would seem costless to shift to society the burden of performing a public objective rather than to show it in government accounts. The natural incentive to behave this way is stimulated when government operates under political or legal limits on expenditures or deficits. In these circumstances, it is possible to abide by the limits while spending (or borrowing) more through off-budget instruments. In the United States, evidence of this behaviour comes from state governments that authorise public corporations to issue revenue bonds outside the debt limits established in their constitutions.

Several considerations suggest, however, that more fundamental forces are at work than budgetary expediency alone. For one thing, until recently, budget control was not very stringent in most OECD countries. Why should governments try to evade controls which do not restrict their freedom of action? Moreover, the growth in off-budget expenditure has been concurrent with the growth in direct expenditure. It appears that, although the various forms of expenditure are substitutes, they are all subject to the same forces that have expanded the scope and reach of the public sector.

In seeking cause and effect for the rise in off-budget expenditure, the focus must be shifted from economics to politics, from the aggregate effects of government policy to the distributive outcomes. The various spending instruments available to government differ in the incidence of the cost and in the distribution of benefits. When public officials choose among the options, they are deciding how costs and benefits are to be apportioned in society.

The cost of direct expenditure is borne by taxpayers as a whole; the cost of tax credits, by contrast, is apportioned among all taxpayers other than those receiving the credit. Where public enterprises are required to cover their expenses internally, users pay the costs; when enterprises have access to "soft" loans, the cost is shifted to taxpayers or to other borrowers competing for available funds. In the case of regulation, the costs might be internalised (borne by those directly subject to the regulation) or externalised (shifted to third parties).

Just as the distribution of costs varies with the option used, so too does the distribution of benefits, for what is a cost from one perspective is a benefit from another. Direct expenditure for airport expansion benefits air travellers; fees that discourage airport use benefit persons who travel on expense accounts; tax credits assist airport operators in acquiring physical assets; loan guarantees help marginal borrowers who might otherwise be shut out of the market or be compelled to pay higher interest costs.

The conclusion can be drawn that distributive politics, not budgetary evasion, is the principal consideration in selecting the instrument of government policy. The process of selection is not simply one of analysing the economic consequences, but one in which the potential beneficiaries and losers vigilantly seek to influence the decision. The changing composition of the public sector means not only that government spends more on outsiders, but that these outsiders have become parties to the budget.

Consider again the two-step expenditure process outlined above. An agency seeking appropriations deals directly with central authorities (the finance ministry, a legislative committee, or a cabinet subcommittee, for example). The process tends to be insular; government officials negotiate with government officials and reach agreement on the budget. But when a third step is added to the expenditure process (for example, the transfer of funds from ministries to outside entities), the making of a budget is opened to outside influence. Enterprises manœuvre for loans and subsidies; taxpayers press for various preferences; lenders seek guarantees and borrowers look for below-market loans; subnational governments demand assistance in meeting their own expenses; and interest groups petition for new regulations.

When deciding among the available policy instruments, governments respond to and often negotiate with these outside claimants. Among the arguments used by these outsiders is that it is costless for government to assist them through off-budget expenditures. The arguments are quite familiar to anyone who has served in a central budget role: borrowers claim that loans are costless because government does not have to advance any of its own funds; enterprises promise that, with an adequate infusion of public money, they ultimately will be able to return a profit.

The magnitude of off-budget expenditures attests to the political potency of these arguments. Yet when government chooses among policy alternatives, it does more than apportion costs and benefits; it is also defining its scope and role, and the relationship between the public and private sectors. This side-effect can be shown by comparing direct subsidies and tax expenditures. A tax expenditure represents income forgone by government. From the perspective of the beneficiary, it has the same value as a direct subsidy. But the two forms of expenditure are not politically equivalent. Spending through tax expenditures reduces the relative size of the public sector; direct expenditures enlarge the public sector. Thus, every trade-off between these two policy instruments entails a political decision concerning the scope and size of government.

When examining the various policy alternatives, therefore, it would be appropriate for public officials to consider macropolitical issues (the role of government) in addition to micropolitical questions (who pays and who benefits). Although it is difficult to design and operate, an off-budget expenditure framework is essential for considering these issues.

4. Types of off-budget expenditure

Before assessing the effects of off-budget expenditures on control of the budget and finances, it is necessary to identify the main off-budget practices. This is not an easy task because there is no limit to the types of off-budget expenditures that can be contrived. Off-budget expenditures can be classified into four categories, distinguished from one another in the type of expenditure.

An updated list of major off-budget expenditures would include public-private partnerships (PPPs), which rely on private financing of infrastructure investments and other public projects. Countries differ in the extent to which they resort to PPPs, the financing arrangements, the government guarantees and other contingent liabilities, and the budget status of these mechanisms. But all PPPs have off-budget characteristics because construction expenses (and, in many arrangements, operating costs as well) are removed from the budget, typically in exchange for government guarantees. As discussed by Paul Posner *et al.* (2009), many national governments have taken steps to provide data on their long-term exposure to PPP contracts.

These four categories are:

- forgoing revenues through preferences to taxpayers (tax expenditures);
- providing credit to private borrowers (direct and guaranteed loans);
- imposing private costs on private parties (regulation);
- direct expenditure by entities that are excluded from the budget (public enterprises).

4.1. Tax expenditures

Tax expenditures are the revenues forgone by government because of its deviations from its basic tax structure. For government, a tax expenditure is a loss in revenue; for a taxpayer, it is a reduction in tax liability. The term suggests that revenue losses have expenditure and subsidy effects similar to those of direct expenditures. The term was introduced in the United States in the 1970s and has gained currency in other OECD countries, though terms such as tax reliefs, tax aids and tax subsidies are also used.

Tax expenditures take various forms, such as exclusions from income, special tax rates, credits against tax liability, deductions, and the deferral of tax payments. The common element in these techniques is that they reduce tax liability and government revenues.

The concept of tax expenditures has provoked intense ideological controversy. Some reject the term because (they argue) it connotes that all income belongs to the government unless it is returned in the form of tax expenditures. Others insist, however, that the term merely indicates that a government can accomplish public objectives by forgoing revenues and that it therefore ought to regard tax expenditures as alternatives to direct expenditures.

This ideological dispute is linked to the issue of whether tax expenditures entail social costs. Every tax expenditure is by definition a cost to government. A tax expenditure also incurs a social cost if it induces private expenditures that would not otherwise be made. Many tax expenditures change private consumption or investment; some, however, reduce taxes without stimulating additional expenditures. For example, if a firm has already planned for the purchase of equipment, an investment credit might provide it with higher after-tax income without generating additional investment. Those who reject the concept of tax expenditures would not impute any social cost to the investment credit since it leaves society in exactly the same position it would have been without any tax. Those who endorse the concept would regard the investment credit as a social cost since it produces a different distribution of income than would prevail in the absence of the credit.

Because a tax expenditure is a cost to it, a government can face the issue without trying to resolve the ideological question. The basic issue for government is whether a particular objective is to be pursued through tax incentives or direct expenditures. The trade-off between tax and spending methods involves economic considerations (which is the more efficient course of action?), macropolitical questions (should the activity be conducted in the public or the private sector?) and micropolitical questions (who benefits and who bears the costs?).

Tax and direct expenditures are not pure substitutes. They can lead to quite different distributions of social resources and social costs. These differences, more than the evasion of expenditure controls, account for the widespread use of tax expenditures. If tax expenditures were to leave everybody no better or worse off than would direct expenditure, taxpayers would be indifferent as to the course that government follows. Taxpayers are not indifferent because tax expenditures promise a better deal than they expect to get through direct expenditure.

Tax expenditures are a function of tax burdens. Where tax rates are high, tax expenditures also tend to be high. The simplest way to curb tax expenditures (other than through credits of fixed value) would be to lower the basic tax rates. Conversely, when tax burdens rise (whether because of inflation, economic growth or discretionary policy), tax expenditures also rise. High tax rates have a political as well as an arithmetic link to tax expenditures. Where tax burdens are high, taxpayers have greater incentive to seek relief than if the burden were lower.

4.1.1. Budgeting for tax expenditures

In order for tax expenditures to be used in budgeting, they have to be measurable. But the measurement of tax expenditures is much more problematic than the measurement of direct expenditures. Value judgments cannot be avoided, and these are likely to vary among OECD countries. A classification of tax expenditures that comports with the practices in one country might be unsuitable for international comparisons. In general, the concept of tax expenditures can be more appropriately used to analyse tax and spending policies within than between countries.

In almost three decades since this article was written, governments of OECD member countries have made enormous strides in defining, measuring and reporting the revenues forgone through tax expenditures. Thirty years ago, few OECD countries published comprehensive statements of tax subsidies; now most do. Some national governments have established procedures for reviewing tax expenditures, and a few have promulgated rules that regulate the volume of these preferences. The current status of tax expenditures in the OECD community is discussed in the excellent paper prepared by Joseph Minarik for the 2008 annual meeting of senior budget officials (OECD, 2008).

The problem begins with definition of the "basic tax structure". It is generally agreed that "structural" elements of a tax system should not be recorded as tax expenditures, while "programmatic" features should be. Most tax subsidies do not pose any difficulty; they are intended for a particular social objective and can be classified as deviations from the normal structure. Some exclusions or preferences are not so clear cut, however. The United States practice is to exclude deductions for dependents from the list of tax expenditures. On this basis, the United Kingdom child tax allowances might be regarded as structural elements, though the recent substitution of child benefit payments for these allowances suggests that they should be treated as tax expenditures. On the other hand, the United Kingdom Treasury has suggested that mortgage interest relief be considered part of a progressive tax structure and not just a subsidy for housing. Because countries differ in their tax structures, comparisons of tax expenditures in OECD countries would be of questionable value unless they were put on a uniform basis.

Since tax expenditures are not actual outlays, the amounts "spent" are notional; that is, they are based on assumptions and estimates as to how taxpayers would behave under particular conditions. The United States practice has been to estimate the revenue loss of each tax expenditure separately, disregarding the interdependencies among the various items. The virtue of this approach is its simplicity; it is not necessary to consider the extent to which the curtailment of any particular tax expenditure might spur taxpayers to use others. Moreover, this approach assumes that a retrenchment in tax expenditures would not result in changes in the basic tax structure. For both political and economic reasons, this is not a tenable position. Total tax expenditures cannot properly be computed as the sum of all the separately estimated tax expenditures.

Estimates of particular tax expenditures also must be hedged with qualifications. Since the value of any tax expenditure depends on the extent to which taxpayers avail themselves of the opportunities provided by the tax system, the estimates are based on assumptions about private behaviour, not on firm appropriations. These assumptions tend to be grounded on past behaviour and cannot confidently take into account changes that might ensue from inflation, economic growth, or other new conditions. The estimates are especially questionable when they are applied to changes in government tax policy – paradoxically the very instances when they are most needed. In the late 1970s, official United States estimates of the revenue loss that would ensue from a reduction in the taxation of capital gains proved to be wide of the mark. Apparently the lower rates spurred increased sale of assets, substantially offsetting the expected revenue loss.

The foregoing considerations lead to the conclusion that efforts to construct a comprehensive and authoritative "tax expenditure budget" should proceed cautiously. A survey in 1976 found only two countries (Germany and the United States) that published tax expenditure budgets. Since then, other OECD countries including Canada and France have developed tax expenditure budgets. These budgets, which purport to set forth all revenue losses, are of more value for public relations than for analysis. They can encourage public officials to make simplistic decisions. In 1979, for example, a leading member of the United States Congress filed legislation to establish a single limitation (as a percentage of GNP) on combined direct and tax expenditures.

A more appropriate use of tax expenditure data would be to assist government officials to gauge the total input of public resources into a particular activity such as housing or education. They would then be prepared to trade off between direct and tax assistance or to vary the mix of the two. Yet trade-offs are hampered in many countries by the fact that different sets of officials are involved in the making of direct expenditure and tax policies. In the usual case, the finance ministry is the dominant voice in tax matters while the functional ministry has a lead role in shaping direct programmes. Thus, a trade-in of a tax expenditure for a direct expenditure (or *vice versa*) might redistribute political power as well.

Fiscal experts do not agree on the value of comparing direct and tax expenditures. Some believe that it is impossible to fully compare the two types of expenditure, while others insist that the principal gain from the tax expenditure concept is to facilitate such comparisons. Regardless of the arguments, these comparisons have become much more prevalent since the mid 1970s, though they have been incorporated into the basic budget routine in only a few countries.

Trade-offs can be made even in the absence of a tax expenditure budget. The shift from child tax allowances to direct benefits in the United Kingdom has already been mentioned. In a similar move, the Netherlands now provides family allowances in lieu of child tax relief. New Zealand substituted higher cash payments for families with dependent children for tax subsidies in 1972, while Germany followed suit in 1977 and Austria in 1978. Trade-offs in the United States have tended to be less formal. In the late 1970s, Congress faced demands for assistance to parents of college students. One proposal would have provided tax credits to help offset tuition payments; another would have made direct grants to low-income students. The budget committees juxtaposed the two proposals (which had been advanced under separate auspices) and showed that if both the tax credits and the direct payments were enacted, the cost to the treasury would be far greater than the advocates of either proposal intended. This analysis contributed to rejection of the tuition tax credit.

Trade-offs appear to be most formalised in Canada where a new (and not fully tested) "envelope" system requires ministers proposing tax expenditures to offset the revenue loss with reductions in direct expenditures. The great virtue of the system is that it sensitises ministers to the reality that tax relief is not costless. Yet a one-for-one trade-in poses two problems. First, even when the tax and direct expenditures are estimated to be of equal value in the year that the trade-in is made, the costs to government might diverge from this pattern in subsequent years. Second, presumably the trade-in system should also allow ministers to increase direct expenditures by curtailing the tax expenditures in their sectors. But, as noted earlier, this exchange would lead to growth in the relative size of the public sector.

4.1.2. *Distributing tax expenditures*

Tax expenditures entail not only revenue losses but private benefits. The distribution of tax benefits is not likely to be the same as the distribution of direct expenditure. The reasons for this difference include: 1) the incentive for those who would benefit more from tax preferences to pursue this course rather than seek direct assistance, and 2) the likelihood that different government officials (with different perspectives and constituencies) would be in charge of tax and direct spending decisions.

The main reason, however, for the differences between the two forms of assistance is that the value of most tax expenditures depends on tax liability. A dollar of deductions or exclusions is three times more valuable to a taxpayer in a 60% marginal tax bracket than to one taxed 20% at the margin. Since higher income taxpayers tend to be in higher marginal brackets, tax expenditures tend to be much more valuable to them than to lower income persons. Moreover, expenditures are generally "open ended", the limit (in most cases) being full tax liability. Thus, the higher the tax that would otherwise be paid, the greater the potential value of the tax expenditure.

A study in the United States found that tax expenditures in 1977 and 1978 amounted to 8.2% of adjusted gross income for all taxpayers, but 22.2% of adjusted gross income for taxpayers with more than USD 50 000 in income. Further, tax expenditures ranged from 30.2% of "full taxes" (the sum of actual taxes and tax expenditures) for middle income taxpayers to 41.6% for those in the highest income class. Significantly, tax expenditures provided less percentage reduction in tax liability for middle income taxpayers than for those in the lowest or the highest income categories.

It is technically feasible to hold the value of a tax expenditure constant across all income classes and to retain the progressivity of the basic tax structure. One possibility would be to substitute credits against actual tax liability for deductions from taxable income. Another approach would be to allow deductions at a fixed percentage rate for all taxpayers rather than at marginal tax rates.

Although techniques are available for mitigating the redistributive effects of tax expenditures, they tend not to be used much. Obviously a "neutral" tax expenditure system (that is, one that does not impair the distribution of burden in the basic tax structure) would offer less incentive for seeking tax benefits rather than direct benefits. There is reason to believe that one of the underlying purposes of tax expenditures is to counter the high marginal rates in countries with progressive tax structures. For various political reasons, governments and voters need to believe that their country has a highly progressive tax structure. However, high "real" rates are not politically or economically acceptable; hence, governments resort to tax expenditures. As a result, effective tax rates tend to be more proportional than the nominal rates. The difference between the real and nominal rates represents the discrepancy between the type of tax system society believes it ought to have and the one it is willing to have. This discrepancy reflects a common condition in modern democracies: the clash between egalitarian values and the unequal distribution of economic power.

The United States has moved to improve the progressivity of a few tax expenditures by making them "refundable" (or "nonwasteable"). In these cases, if the value of the tax expenditure exceeds tax liability, the taxpayer receives a direct payment from the treasury for the excess. Refundable tax expenditures virtually erase the boundaries between direct and tax expenditures and can give rise to new off-budget practices.

4.1.3. Controlling tax expenditures

Tax expenditures are not as amenable to budgetary control as are direct expenditures. A comparison of the two types of expenditure would help to illustrate the lack of control over tax expenditures.

Consider a government decision to assist investment in a particular area. One course of action would be to issue grants to firms that make the desired investment; another would be to reduce the tax liability of these firms. When it proceeds by direct grants, government typically formulates detailed rules setting forth eligibility requirements, application procedures and other administrative prerequisites for obtaining a grant.

Moreover, government officials review the applications for grants and can turn them down if they are not convinced that the funds would be spent for the intended purposes. They can also require periodic reports by grantees and can audit the investments to determine whether they are being properly made and recorded. A further element of control comes through the appropriations process, by means of which the government limits total spending for the programme.

A tax incentive, by contrast, is likely to be open ended, with the amount of expenditure dependent on the behaviour (and skills) of taxpayers rather than on direct government decision. A firm would not have to satisfy any application procedure, nor would the expenditure be reviewed by government officials in advance. Tax incentives usually operate unilaterally, with taxpayers making their own determination as to whether they are eligible for the relief. While some portion of the tax returns would be audited, the likelihood is that most would escape serious review.

This illustration enables us to identify some of the reasons for the comparative lack of control over tax expenditures. These transactions tend to be encumbered by fewer administrative rules than are applied to direct expenditures. Government programmes are often criticised for red tape, delay and cumbersome procedures; tax expenditures avoid these problems, but only because government control is looser.

Tax expenditures are also subjected to weaker political control. Many tax advantages are established on a permanent basis. Unlike regular appropriations, there is no periodic review by the legislature. Because they are deemed to be permanent features of the tax structure, tax expenditures often continue in practice without examination of their effectiveness. Political control also is impaired by the "invisibility" of these expenditures. Although estimates of their cost might be published when they are introduced, in subsequent years, tax expenditures are absorbed into aggregate revenue forecasts.

There is widespread belief that, once implemented, tax expenditures are more difficult to terminate than direct expenditures. This proposition lacks empirical support, but it reflects a feeling that tax expenditures escape effective government control.

In assessing the impact of tax expenditures on fiscal control, one must be mindful of their implications for the tax system as a whole. The proliferation of tax subsidies has complicated the tax structures in most OECD countries. It is difficult for ordinary taxpayers to determine whether they are paying more or less than the law requires, and for tax officials to monitor compliance with the laws. In addition, these incentives erode the tax base and compel governments to levy high marginal rates in order to obtain needed revenues. Marginal rates in most countries would be significantly lower if tax expenditures were curtailed. The 1981 Netherlands "Budget Memorandum" comments that taxpayers increasingly "resort to deductible items to counter the increased pressure observed in the tax bands and to mitigate the feared increase in the burden of taxes." It further notes that one of the reasons for "the scale of the fraudulent practices is … the level of taxation and the increase in the tax burden over the years." The Swedish government's 1980/81 "Budget Statement" came to a similar conclusion, that "deductions are being abused more and more and contribute to a systematic erosion of the progressive tax system."

Tax expenditures will not be effectively controlled unless they are perceived by the public and by government as the functional equivalents of direct expenditure. Clearly, such is not the case at present. For the most part, tax expenditures are seen as the retained income of taxpayers, not as a grant from government. Under these circumstances, it is quite understandable that they are not subjected to the same measure of control as is commonly expected of direct expenditures.

The foregoing considerations lead this author to the conclusion that a tax expenditure budget is likely to be more useful for economic analysis than for budget practice. One should be wary of pushing the tax expenditure concept to the point where it is treated in the same manner as direct expenditures. Notional budgets can provide useful supporting material but they cannot be decisional budgets for controlling and managing public resources.

4.2. Government loans

When governments spent public funds solely (or predominantly) on their own operations, the budget deficit (or surplus) was an accurate measure of their participation in the credit markets. This condition no longer prevails; in addition to paying for their own operations, contemporary governments finance outside activity. When they do so through direct grants, the transactions are usually recorded as budget expenditures, but when they lend money to others, the expenditure is often off budget.

During the 1960s and 1970s, government loans have become a major means of assistance to various groups. Governments make loans to public enterprises, business firms, homeowners, subnational governments and others. They also guarantee private loans, and they buy and sell debt instruments (such as mortgages, debentures and promissory notes). Because these credit transactions are often excluded, the budget tends to misrepresent the government's impact on economic activity and on the allocation of resources.

If credit assistance were fully accounted for, government economic policy in the 1970s would have probably been found more expansive than intended. Credit activities in many OECD countries appear to have shifted capital from investment in plant and equipment to investment in housing. The growth in credit programmes, many observers contend, has contributed to inflation in recent years.

The failure of government budgets to fully report credit activities is partly due to the fact that budgets were once deemed financial statements rather than expressions of economic policy. Accounting and economic criteria differ, especially as they relate to the treatment of government lending. Because budgetary concepts and practices were developed for different purposes than are now called for, new budgetary methods to deal with credit activities have to be devised.

The problem can be illustrated by reference to the treatment of government loans in the United States budget. When the government lends money, the loan is recorded as an outlay, on a net basis – new loans minus repayments. This treatment is a compromise between accounting and economic concepts. From an accounting perspective, the loan should not be regarded as an outlay since the government's financial condition is not altered by it; the government is merely exchanging one asset (money) for another (a promise of future repayment). Indeed, loans are not recorded on business profit-and-loss statements and appear as assets on their balance sheets. However, from an economic standpoint, the loan should be recorded since the government will have to increase its own borrowing or have a smaller deficit. Moreover, a case can be made for reporting loans on a gross basis (that is, the full amount of new loans) since this represents the full scope of government activity, though it might overstate the economic effect of loans.

The disparity between economic and accounting criteria has opened the door to off-budget practices. Here, too, the United States experience illustrates the problem of handling credit transactions in the budget. When a government agency makes a loan, it receives an obligation (such as a mortgage or a note) from the borrower. The agency can pool these "loan assets" into new obligations which it sells to the Federal Financing Bank, a government agency whose transactions are excluded from the budget. The income from this sale offsets the original loan, thereby reducing the budget outlay to zero, even though the government must still borrow (or reduce its surplus) to finance the loan.

While this particular practice is an intentional evasion of budget control, most off-budget credit activities have a more legitimate purpose. One of the most prevalent off-budget practices is a government guarantee of private indebtedness. Guaranteed loans are generally excluded from the budget because they represent contingent rather than direct liabilities of government. But guarantees can affect the level and distribution of economic activity.

> Contingent liabilities are off-budget expenditures in almost all OECD countries. Although contingent liabilities take many forms, their common element is that the government is liable if a specified event occurs. Loan guarantees are a prominent form of contingent liabilities, as are crop insurance, farm price supports, explicit or implicit government obligations to indemnify households or enterprises against losses due to natural disasters, bank failures, changes in exchange or interest rates, and many other contingencies. Some governments append estimates of contingent liabilities to budget documents or other financial reports.

Government loan programmes can impede economic stabilisation because the amount of lending tends to fluctuate more widely than direct expenditures and can deviate significantly from the budgeted level. In recent years, efforts by the International Monetary Fund to require countries to reduce their deficits and public sector borrowing as a condition of assistance have also been impeded by loan practices in some countries.

4.2.1. The cost of government loans

One of the reasons why credit assistance is popular is that public officials often believe (or pretend) that it is costless. Direct loans, the argument runs, do not cost government anything because they are repaid. On this ground, direct loans are often preferred to grants in which the government does not recover any of its expenditure. An even stronger claim is made for guaranteed loans in which the government makes no outlay except in case of default. Government can make a profit by charging a premium for its guarantee.

Yet there is no such thing as a "free" loan. When the government makes or guarantees a loan, it also influences the availability of credit to other borrowers. Under certain conditions, it can significantly raise the cost of credit to those who cannot borrow from public sources or it might force some borrowers out of the market.

4.2.2. Direct loans

The cost of a direct loan depends on the terms under which it is made. When it charges an interest rate below its own borrowing cost, a government provides a direct subsidy which is paid for by taxpayers. But even it if charges the same rate as it pays, a government might bear higher interest costs because of the additional borrowing that it must undertake. If a government has a USD 25 billion deficit in its own operations, but must borrow USD 50 billion in order to finance both the deficit and the loans it is making, it probably would have higher interest charges than if it only borrowed for its own needs.

Even when government charges its full cost, a direct loan usually provides more favourable terms than a borrower can obtain privately. A government generally pays lower interest rates than other borrowers, and it normally passes these savings on to those who borrow from it. A borrower who can get the same terms privately would have little reason to come to government for credit assistance. These borrowers almost always pay below-market rates, and they are thereby accorded preference over those who must seek credit on less favourable terms. Those who borrow from private sources not only pay more but they also might find it more difficult to obtain credit.

Although the declared purpose of many credit programmes is to assist marginal borrowers who might otherwise be unable to obtain credit, they often provide funds to borrowers who would otherwise be willing and able to borrow at market rates. It is difficult to design a credit programme targeted exclusively to those who would be shut out of the market, and there is reason to believe that government officials do not really want to do so.

Interest rates on government loans are usually not standardised. Interest on direct loans is more often determined by the amount of assistance to be provided to borrowers than by the cost of money to government. It is common for governments to charge concessional rates below their own borrowing costs. The interest rate can be regarded as a measure of the borrower's political power and of the value attached to the programme by government.

The cost of these loans is affected by fluctuations in interest rates. If, as often happens, the interest rate for a loan programme is fixed, the value of the loan (and the cost to government) will vary with subsequent changes in market rates and in the government's own borrowing costs. Thus, the cost of credit programmes can rise automatically and uncontrollably without government action.

Some loans have features which make them virtually indistinguishable from grants. Some, for example, have forgiveness provisions that cancel all or part of the debt. Others can be converted to gifts if it becomes evident that the borrower is unable to repay. In still other instances, governments extend credit to marginal borrowers with little prospect of repayment. Sometimes loans are carried on the books long after the borrower has defaulted because the government lacks procedures for writing them off as bad debts. In sum, governments may prefer to label assistance as loans rather than as grants in order to conceal the true costs.

4.2.3. Guaranteed loans

Unlike direct loans, guaranteed loans require payment out of the treasury only in case of default. The guarantee is excluded from the budget because, as noted, it is a contingent liability. However, any payments necessitated by default would be budgeted as outlays. Loan guarantees are not the only form of contingent liability. Governments sometimes guarantee the price enterprises wll receive for their output, or pledge to pay the difference between market prices and the cost of production. These and other contingent liabilities are also excluded from the budget.

Loan guarantees transfer risk from private lenders to the government. This means that two of the credit market's key functions – evaluating the credit worthiness of borrowers and the element of risk – are not adequately performed. Rather than being concerned about the borrower's ability to repay, lenders are primarily interested in whether the guarantee is sound. The task of evaluating risk and credit worthiness thus must be performed by government or not at all. Governments, however, might be unprepared or unwilling to assume this role. A rigorous examination of the financial condition of marginal borrowers might bar them from obtaining the assistance that loan guarantees are intended to provide them.

Guaranteed loans can reduce the possibility of default or bankruptcy by giving marginal borrowers access to credit. It may, therefore, enable these borrowers to disregard market signals and to continue inefficient practices. Nevertheless, governments can condition loan guarantees on the adoption of efficiency-improving changes. Thus, in the United States, loan guarantees to New York City and the Chrysler Corporation required these borrowers to implement cost savings and other changes as a condition of assistance.

Guaranteed loans reduce the cost of credit for borrowers. Sometimes the subsidy is explicit, as when the government agrees to pay the difference between the market interest rate and the rate that lenders participating in the programme are permitted to charge. In most cases, however, the subsidy is implicit: the borrower is able to obtain credit at a lower rate than would otherwise be possible.

The value of a guarantee depends on the risk of the loan. Marginal buyers usually have to pay a "risk premium" (above-market interest rates) in order to obtain private credit. Thus, the greater the risk, the higher the subsidy provided by the government guarantee. In cases of extreme risk, borrowers might not be able to obtain any credit without government assistance.

Loan guarantees raise the cost of credit to unassisted borrowers. But in periods of tight credit, the main effect might be to reallocate credit from some borrowers to others. In effect, borrowers who lack guarantees subsidise guaranteed borrowers.

In the United States and elsewhere, guarantees tendered in the late 1970s have differed from older loan programmes. In the past, loan programmes guaranteed small loans to numerous borrowers. For example, 97% of the loans guaranteed by the United States government in 1950 went to help families purchase their homes. In these types of loans, the risk of default was pooled among a large number of borrowers, each of whom paid a premium to cover possible default. Some recent loan guarantees (such as for energy development), by contrast, have entailed very large loans to very few borrowers. The risk is concentrated – not shared – and default by a major borrower can compel the government to spend large amounts of money. Moreover, guarantees often go to venture or financially troubled enterprises where the risk of default is higher than in the older types of loan programmes.

4.2.4. *Controlling loan programmes*

The problems and costs of direct and guaranteed loans have prompted a number of countries to consider credit policies in terms of the overall condition of the public sector rather than in terms of the budget. One approach has been to limit the borrowing undertaken by the public sector. This method is used in the United Kingdom which establishes a public sector borrowing requirement (PSBR) in tandem with the annual budget. The PSBR includes nationalised industries and imposes a single limit on public sector borrowing. The PSBR concept is also used in Australia, where it includes net borrowing by state and local governments and by public enterprises. Italy, under pressure from the IMF, has adopted an "enlarged public sector" concept that encompasses all levels of general government and certain public enterprises. In the United States, where the concept of the public sector is not widely used, control has been sought through implementation of a credit budget which sets annual limits on total direct and guaranteed loans, as well as limitations on individual credit programmes.

Since 1992, the United States has included the "subsidy cost" of direct and guaranteed loans in the federal budget. The subsidy cost is the estimated net present value of all future cash flows of direct and guaranteed loans, using a discount rate equal to the interest rate paid by the Treasury on debt of comparable maturity. The estimated subsidy cost is budgeted as an outlay, along with other expenditures.

Integration of credit transactions into the budget process requires more than information; it also means that credit is seen as a policy instrument that can achieve the same objectives as direct expenditures. This level of integration appears to have been successfully attained in Japan which has a fiscal investment and loan programme (FILP) that covers virtually all of the credit activities of the government. The FILP has been designated "the second budget" not only because of its size (almost half of the general account budget) but also because it is considered to be as important to the economy as the regular budget. The FILP is presented to the legislature in tandem with the budget. It sets forth the supply of funds to public corporations, local governments, government-affiliated agencies and various other institutions.

The advantage of a combined statement of the public sector deficit and borrowing cannot be doubted, but this approach can introduce some problems. Enterprises with standby lines of credit to the treasury can "crowd out" spending on public services by government agencies. This predicament has confronted the United Kingdom in the late 1970s. Perhaps the point to be made is that information on public sector borrowing is not a substitute for financial control. Aggregate controls on credit can be effective only when particular loan programmes are controlled as well.

If governments are to control their budgets and manage the economy, they must be able to control the credit they extend to others. This is often difficult to accomplish because the amount of loans can depend as much on the behaviour of borrowers as on the current policies of government. In many cases, the amount of credit authorised for a particular programme is open ended, and eligible borrowers do not have to compete against one another for available funds. In other cases, government has little choice but to provide needed credit to public enterprises or to weak industries.

4.3. Government regulation

Regulation can be an effective substitute for direct expenditures. If a government wants to curb the pollution of rivers and streams, it could appropriate funds for the construction and operation of sewage treatment facilities. Alternatively, it could provide loans or tax preferenes to firms that invest in pollution control practices. These types of expenditure would be recorded in government accounts, though not all would appear in the budget. Still another option would be to order polluters to stop discharging effluents into the waters. Except for the administrative expenses of government agencies, the costs of these and other regulations would not be reported in government accounts.

Through regulation, it would be possible to shift the costs of achieving many public objectives from public budgets to private ledgers. If stringent spending or budget limitations were imposed, government might resort to regulation in lieu of direct services. The costs to society would be no less, and might be a great deal more; they would show up in the costs of production, in the prices paid by consumers, and in other adverse effects on the economy.

Concern about the costs of regulation appears to be much greater in the United States than in other OECD countries.

> On reflection, I do not think that the statement that the United States has greater concern about the cost of regulation than other countries was valid 30 years ago. It certainly is not valid today. The volume of social, environmental and economic regulation has increased worldwide. OECD countries have developed policies and tools to address the costs and benefits of regulation based on OECD analysis, principles and evaluations carried out by the Working Party on Regulatory Management and Reform and the Group on Regulatory Policy.

This might be due to the fact that regulation is more pervasive in the United States than elsewhere. In other countries, public enterprises operate services (such as railroads, telecommunications and utilities) that are provided by regulated industries in the United States. The prevalence of regulation in the United States might also be due to its legalistic political culture and a tendency to define rights and obligations through laws and rules.

During the 1970s, regulatory activity increased significantly, and social objectives were emphasised (such as protection of the environment, the health and safety of workers, and automobile safety). This new type of regulation has proved to be costlier and broader in its impact than older economic regulations that dealt with rates, services and entry into markets. The new "quality of life" regulations are not confined to a single industry; in many cases, the jurisdiction of the regulating agency extends to most of the private sector. But despite its jurisdictional breadth, the agency usually has a narrow regulatory objective. It is not called upon to weigh the value of its objective against competing ones or to consider the effects of its regulations on particular firms or industries.

It should not be surprising, therefore, that some of the regulations promulgated in the 1970s were extremely costly. According to some estimates, as much as 4% of GNP has been diverted to satisfy regulatory requirements. While the estimates are based on questionable assumptions and have been disputed by critics, there is little doubt that the costs of regulation have been very high.

Only a small portion of the costs of regulation are accounted for in the budget. Regulatory agencies are usually quite small, and their expenses ordinarily are not a major consideration in the preparation or review of the budget. The costs of administering thousands of regulations do not add up to one per cent of the United States budget. It has been estimated that compliance with regulations costs the private sector USD 20 for each dollar spent by the United States government.

The direct costs of compliance include the specifications mandated by government regulators. There is a tendency for government agencies to prescribe specific designs or technologies, leaving the affected industry with little incentive (or discretion) to select the most efficient course of action. Moreover, once established, regulations often continue in effect long after their original purpose has been served.

Some critics claim that the "opportunity costs" of regulation may be much greater than the directly measurable ones. Excessive regulation, it is alleged, impedes innovation, diverts capital from productive investment to satisfying government requirements, diminishes risk-taking by entrepreneurs and dampens competition. According to this view, the full cost of regulation includes lost employment and production, higher prices, and a reduced ability to compete in world markets.

4.3.1. Controlling government regulation

As the costs of regulation have escalated, so too have requirements that regulatory agencies consider the costs and benefits of their actions. The trend has been toward broader requirements: President Ford called for the examination of the effect of regulations on inflation; President Carter ordered analyses of economic impacts; and President Reagan directed full cost-benefit analyses of regulations.

It would seem ironic that the United States, which has had only limited success in applying cost-benefit analysis to its own budget, would undertake the much more difficult task of analysing the effects of regulation on the private sector. The measurement of the effects of regulations cannot avoid difficult value questions, and the more ambitious the analysis, the more controversial and problematic are the findings likely to be.

The unstated but often primary purpose of regulatory analysis is not to obtain the precise measurement of costs and benefits but to slow down the issuance of regulations. By requiring agencies to prepare formal analyses before promulgating regulations, government hopes to sensitise them to the fact that regulations are not costless. Regulatory analyses encourage agencies to consider less costly alternatives and sensitise them to the added costs of securing marginal improvements in benefits.

The United States has established a regulatory review process in the White House. The purpose is to ensure a broader consideration of costs and alternatives than might be undertaken by the agency issuing the regulations. The White House group can stop, or more likely seek to modify, regulations that it considers too costly. The Reagan administration has intervened more forcefully in the regulatory process than previous administrations did.

A novel cost control scheme has been proposed in the form of a regulatory budget. The regulatory budget would list the costs of government regulation much as direct expenditures are accounted for in the regular budget. Some have suggested that the regulatory budget be used to limit the costs that each agency would "spend" by means of regulation. The concept of a regulatory budget, however, would have to gain broader acceptance before it could be applied in this manner.

> Although the concept of a regulatory budget has made little headway, many governments have undertaken comprehensive or piecemeal review of regulations. Despite these efforts, the volume and cost of regulation continues to trend upward.

4.4. Public enterprises

Conventional budgeting coexisted with an organisational structure in which government operations were the responsibility of ministries and departments. Appropriations to these "core" agencies accounted for the bulk of public expenditure, so that the same agency spent public funds and operated public programmes. These agencies were organised into a cabinet structure which, in parliamentary regimes, exercised collective control, and in presidential systems functioned in a more hierarchical manner. There was little ambiguity as to what constituted a public entity.

Mixed economies do not have neat organisational structures. Governments have contrived a seemingly endless variety of organisational forms in response to particular needs and conditions. Governments set up autonomous agencies outside the cabinet structure or corporations that combine public and private characteristics. In some enterprises, the government holds some or all of the stock; in others, all the stock is privately owned. In some, the officers and directors are appointed by the government; in others, appointments are made by the corporation or its stockholders. In some, employees are covered by civil service rules; in others, they are deemed to be private workers.

Because public enterprises combine elements of public and private organisations, it is difficult to classify them into neat categories. Some are more public than others; some are only nominally public and have all the essential attributes of private organisations. There are so many types of public enterprises, even in the same country, that it is hard to classify them into a few categories.

An OECD working paper (April 1981) reported that "the most difficult aspect of defining the public sector is deciding what makes an enterprise 'public'." The paper noted that while some countries define public enterprise solely in terms of ownership, others add other criteria such as the degree of control exercised by government or the circumstances under which the enterprise became public. The confusion over definition is reflected in the system of national accounts (SNA) devised by the United Nations. The SNA bases the distinction between private and public "on whether the ownership and/or control of an enterprise rests in the public authorities or private parties" but it does not indicate whether ownership and control are joint or alternative criteria. The OECD paper concluded that variations in country definitions of public enterprise are impediments to international comparisons for the public sector.

Many countries have attempted to classify their public enterprises in terms of the control exercised by the government. For example, Sweden distinguishes between public enterprises and government-owned business companies. The government-owned business companies are independent legal entities subject to government regulation. Government exercises control principally through its role as shareholder. The public enterprises are government agencies, though they have more freedom in fiscal and personnel matters than ordinary agencies. These enterprises have no independent borrowing authority; all long-term capital is supplied by the central government.

Japan has a more elaborate classification, dividing its more than 100 public corporations into nine categories depending on the source of financing and the degree of government control. At one extreme are corporations that receive all their capital from the national government and have their budgets approved by the Diet (parliament). At the other extreme are corporations that receive some public financing but enjoy a great deal of autonomy.

Despite the varied forms, it is rare that a public enterprise is subjected to the same financial controls as are applied to core agencies. One of the main reasons for the establishment of state enterprises is to free them from the budget controls applied to regular agencies; it should not be surprising, therefore, that they enjoy considerable fiscal autonomy. Even when they are in the budget, public enterprises tend to have a great deal of freedom, if only because they have their own source of revenues. Moreover, many enterprises are authorised to borrow from the credit markets or from the treasury.

Paradoxically, while enterprises are located on the fringe of government, they do not conduct only fringe activities. In OECD countries, public enterprises run heavy industry, high-risk technologies, communications and transportation, and the production and distribution of energy.

Over the past 30 years, many governments have privatised state enterprises, but it is a rare country that has no public enterprises. Although it is now widely accepted in the OECD community that commercial goods and services can be more efficiently provided through markets, governments still are impelled by political forces and economic conditions to operate businesses and to sometimes retake control or ownership of previously privatised enterprises.

These operations are so vital to modern economies that governments cannot remain bystanders if major enterprises encounter financial difficulty or if their policies or performance diverge from the national interest.

But governments have a great deal of difficulty in deciding whether and how to intervene in the affairs of their enterprises. A considerable amount of confusion arises out of the combination of public and private characteristics in the same organisation. Governments frequently establish conflicting norms for their enterprises. They want enterprises to be run efficiently and to serve important social objectives. They want the railroads, for example, to cover their operating costs, but governments also insist that service be provided to many communities regardless of cost. Governments want factories to operate without subsidies, but bar them from dismissing employees and impose costly work rules.

The clash between social and economic objectives can be submerged when public enterprises are growing and showing a profit. But governments frequently turn failing industries over to enterprises, and the conflict between social and economic values leads to zigzagging policies. The inability of the enterprises or the government to maintain a steady course can produce outcomes that nobody wants. Many enterprises are disciplined neither by the market nor by the government budget; they live in perpetual crisis and turbulence. Governments, however, cannot isolate themselves from the problems of their enterprises; the enterprises' financial ills become the government's concern. With or without effective budget control, government must supply the grants and credits to keep the enterprise in business.

4.4.1. Controlling public enterprises

The International Monetary Fund has identified three phases in the financial relationship between governments and enterprises. Enterprises are often established at "arm's length" from the government, with a great deal of discretion. They are purposely given autonomy to insulate them from political influences and to ensure their efficient operation. At a later time, however, the government feels impelled to intervene, either because it is dissatisfied with the enterprise's performance or because the enterprise comes to it with pleas for assistance. Government intervention is not a permanent solution, for it tends to further impair the efficiency of enterprises. In response, therefore, governments seek to set performance objectives, returning to the arm's-length relationship. But, unable to dictate the operations of enterprises, governments might not be able to achieve the level of performance they seek.

The argument for establishng public enterprises outside the normal budgetary framework is that they can thereby be operated in a more businesslike manner than would be possible under government control. Thus, the law establishing the Australian Industry Development Corporation provided that "the corporation shall act in accordance with sound business principles … and … shall not provide finance … or participate in a particular enterprise unless the Board considers that the enterprise … will be carried out in an efficient manner and in accordance with sound financial principles." The law further specified that the corporation "is not subject to direction by or on behalf of the Australian Government."

Once they are vested with political autonomy, public enterprises can maintain their privileged status as long as they stay out of financial trouble. Indeed, enterprises that internally finance their own expenses and have independent access to capital markets often escape any serious scrutiny by government agencies. However, if an enterprise experiences financial difficulty and has to rely on the government to cover its expenses or for investment funds, then the government can recapture some of the political control it yielded in establishing the enterprise. But at this stage, the government may have no viable option other than to provide the needed financing even if it cannot fully control how the funds are spent.

A penetrating analysis of the problems faced by governments in controlling their public enterprises was issued by Canada's Royal Commission on Financial Management and Accountability in 1979. The commission observed that "the Government must find that delicate balance between excessive control – which would frustrate the purpose of a Crown Agency – and no control, which would be a denial of the Government's involvement and responsibility in the enterprise."

There is no easy way out of the dilemma facing governments in their relationship with enterprises. As the boundaries between the public and private sectors erode, one can expect enterprises to become more prevalent and more important. Governments cannot ignore the impact of enterprises on their budgets, but neither can they impose tight fiscal control over these entities. The trend seems to be to incorporate enterprises into the public sector budget, but not necessarily to control them by means of the budget. In terms of the enterprises, the budget is more an information tool than a means of making and enforcing financial decisions.

5. The problem of control

Off-budget expenditures weaken budget control. This statement has two meanings that lead to different policy conclusions. First, a government's capacity to budget its expenditures has been impaired by the removal of these items from the budget. The obvious remedy would be to return the off-budget expenditure to the budget, thereby restoring the budget's status as a comprehensive process for handling the government's funds.

Second, the statement can mean that the government's capacity to control off-budget expenditures has been weakened by their special status. Here the concern is not restoration of the budget's lost prominence, but an overall weakening of the government's control of its finances. The appropriate remedy, from this point of view, might be to control off-budget expenditures by off-budget means.

Much of the literature on budget control wells out of the first conception of the problem. It assumes that a sound budget is the purpose of government, and that having a comprehensive budget assures financial control. This author would challenge this budget-centric premise, and argue instead that placing off-budget items in a comprehensive account might amount to little more than a bookkeeping improvement. To understand why this might occur, it is necessary to examine how off-budget practices affect government operations.

Off-budget expenditures impair budget control in three ways: they entail a loss of political control, financial control, and internal control.

Political control refers to a government's capacity to dictate the objectives for which the expenditure is made and to enforce its decisions. Political control is strong in line ministries and weak whenever the actual spending is done by outsiders. Within government, command and control processes are well developed. Ministries generally spend funds on the purposes for which the appropriation was made. Despite universal misgivings about bureaucracy, government agencies generally abide by the dictates of higher authority. But when funds are transferred to outsiders, political control is attenuated. A minister does not have the same leverage over an enterprise (even one nominally under his/her jurisdiction) as over a line agency. The minister is likely to have even less say over the behaviour of an entrepreneur making private use of tax credits or guaranteed loans.

Financial control over off-budget expenditures is often weak because, unlike direct expenditures, they tend to be open ended. The amount spent by government (including the social cost) is not usually fixed in appropriations but determined by the behaviour of the beneficiary. Tax subsidies depend on the extent to which taxpayers avail themselves of the opportunities provided by government. Enterprises often have a line of credit to the national treasury. The cost of regulation varies with the response of those affected by it. The cost of subsidised loans depends on interest rates.

Moreover, since government exercises only weak political control over off-budget spenders, even when limits are fixed on these expenditures, they might not be enforceable. The United Kingdom's unfortunate experience with state enterprises shows how ineffective political control can lead to a loss of financial control.

Internal control refers to the fidelity of spenders to the rules and procedures established by government for the handling of public money. When formal budget systems emerged in the Continent and in the United States in the late 19th and early 20th centuries, adherence to these rules was enforced by external control – that is, central budget personnel, auditors and others policed the financial activity of agencies and required approval before obligations were incurred. Their massive expansion and ambitious policy objectives have forced modern governments to rely on internal control. The agency spending the funds has first-instance responsibility for ensuring that the expenditure is proper, for an approved purpose, and in accord with government regulations and its own rules.

Internal control depends on the basic norms of behaviour, more on attitudes than on rule books. Internal control is firmly implanted in many government ministries around the world, though occasional scandals are a reminder that breaches still occur. But the norms have not been internalised by external spenders. They have their own values and objectives, and these often run counter to those of the government. It should not be surprising that much contemporary fraud and waste in public programmes are concentrated in off-budget expenditures.

The growth of off-budget expenditure produces what might be labelled "the paradox of control". As this paper argues, off-budget expenditures have resulted from the transformation of the public sector from one in which spending was done within government to one in which spending largely occurs outside government. Not the least of the reasons for this transformation has been the striving of government to strengthen its control of the economy, the distribution of income, investment policy, and the supply of goods and services. The paradox is that, in its effort to extend its control over the private sector, government has surrendered a good deal of its control over the public sector.

Restoring off-budget items to the budget would not accomplish much in the way of political control, financial control, or internal control. The budget would be more comprehensive, but this could be deemed salutary only if fundamental changes were made in the relationship between government and outside spenders.

This relationship operates through incentives rather than command and control. By extending credit, changing tax liabilities, chartering independent enterprises and other activities, government "hopes" that the affected parties will behave in accord with its expectations. However, incentives involve not only the expectations of government but those of the recipient as well. And these may be at variance with those of government.

A comprehensive budget process, in sum, might make for a better budget, but not necessarily for more control. If the latter is the pre-eminent objective, governments should devise new methods of control, leaving to secondary consideration the question of whether these controls should operate through the budget process.

6. The problem of planning

The problem of control leads to a second paradox. With the rise in off-budget expenditures, governments sense a heightened need to plan their programmes and finances beyond the next fiscal year, but the efficacy of these plans diminishes as governments transfer funds to outside spenders.

When governments spent primarily on their own operations, they felt little need to plan ahead for a number of years. They could prepare for the future through the normal programming activities of government agencies. But with the transformation of the public sector, government is interested not only in what it is doing, but in what others (principally the outside spenders) are doing as well. The emergence of national planning has, in fact, been concurrent with the developments described in this paper. There has also been, in

> This section on planning is badly out of date because it does not reflect the widespread introduction of medium-term expenditure frameworks (MTEF). In contrast to 30 years ago, most governments now establish fiscal constraints for the next 3-5 years rather than only for the year immediately ahead. These constraints are enforced through regular budget rules and procedures. MTEF systems vary greatly in effectiveness and in the extent to which they are fully integrated into the regular budget process.

most OECD countries, the emergence of multi-year financial plans, such as the public expenditure survey committee system devised in the United Kingdom.

These plans (national, sectoral and financial) attest to the futility of planning when government control is weak. The paradox is that, as the future becomes less certain, the felt need for planning increases; but as the future becomes less certain, the reliability of the plans decreases. Plans are quickly overtaken by unexpected events, especially those outside government control.

Strong planning cannot coexist with weak budget control. But the failure of planning has not diminished the yearning for more effective plans. In response to the control problem, planning now takes two different paths. Indicative planning (such as has been pioneered in France) abandons control in favour of information and consultation. It informs various sectors (particularly the off-budget ones) of government expectations in the hope that, once informed, they will act in a way that makes it possible to achieve the plan's objectives.

The other course is to use planning as an instrument of control. Governments recognise their lack of short-run budget control and try to compensate for this deficiency by establishing a planning process – in effect a multi-year budget process – to strengthen their control over future budgets. The United States is moving in this direction, as are Canada, the Scandinavian countries and the United Kingdom. But one must question whether future budgets will merely accommodate to the lack of control or be used to devise and implement realistic plans and objectives.

7. The path to control

Governments everywhere are troubled by attenuation of control over their budgets. They perceive that off-budget expenditures often escape effective control and they assume, therefore, that placing these transactions in the budget will lead to the restoration of control.

Before stretching their budget processes to encompass off-budget expenditures, governments should contemplate what might be gained and lost from this move.

The notion that off-budget items ought to be incorporated into the budget is predicated on the concept of the budget as a resource allocation process. National budgets have been moving in this direction for more than a generation; in most OECD countries, finance ministries have shifted from expenditure control to economic management. But this is not the only purpose served by government budgets.

Contemporary budgets excel as instruments of managerial control. They define the programmes to be conducted by ministries and allocate resources for these purposes. They set the operational objectives of ministries and limit the amounts that may be spent on various activities. As instruments of management, budgets can effectively control only where managers can. Extending the budget to off-budget expenditures would be of no avail if government does not dictate the programmes or policies of the off-budget spenders.

Budgets cannot be all things to all users. The skills and data appropriate for managerial control are not the same as those essential for fiscal control. Governments, therefore, must decide whether to use their central budget process for the one purpose or for the other. They must, in effect, choose between using the budget to allocate government costs or to allocate social costs.

Understandably, governments try to avoid choosing one or the other course. They want both types of control. Further, they sense that surrendering the managerial functions of the budget would weaken their macroeconomic capabilities as well. The old budget predicament of "the parts *versus* the whole" would come back to plague them if they settled for a "big picture" budget process.

Perhaps governments will succeed in expanding the budget's scope without losing their hold on the budget itself. This author's view is that not all the off-budget expenditures discussed in this paper equally warrant inclusion in the budget. Not all are equally suitable for trading off with direct expenditures. Governments need many paths to control, not only the one that eventuates in a budget decision. The United States, for example, is experimenting with a credit budget which, though annexed to the regular budget, involves different allocation decisions. Regulatory costs similarly might be "budgeted" for in a separate process. Public enterprises might have their own decision and control procedures. These distinct processes might be linked by an umbrella (rather than omnibus) resource allocation process or by a public sector planning process. The budget would then be but one component of the larger process. It would continue to operate as an instrument of managerial control, but broader control would be sought by other means.

References

OECD (2008), "Tax Expenditures in OECD Countries", GOV/PGC/SBO(2008)8, OECD, Paris.

Posner, Paul, Shin Kue Ryu and Ann Tkachenko (2009), "Public-Private Partnerships: The Relevance of Budgeting", *OECD Journal on Budgeting*, Volume 2009/1.

ISBN 978-92-64-06087-6
Evolutions in Budgetary Practice
Allen Schick and the OECD Senior Budget Officials
© OECD 2009

Chapter 16

Budgeting for Fiscal Space

Fiscal space refers to the financial resources available to a government for policy initiatives through the budget and related decisions. The term excludes money allocated in the previous budget and continued in the next, but does include funds that become available through reallocation, incremental resources generated by economic growth, borrowed funds in excess of current revenues, and additional revenue from increases in taxes. Although the term was initially devised for low-income countries, it has useful application in developed countries as well. In developing countries, fiscal space is an estimate of the growth-enhancing investment in physical and human capital that a government can finance with borrowed funds without prejudicing the long-run sustainability of its fiscal position. In this context, fiscal space justifies allowing cash-short governments to borrow for productive expenditures that have a strong prospect of being repaid through the additional revenues produced by an expanding economy.

This paper focuses on the concept of fiscal space for OECD member countries. In this setting, fiscal space pertains to the way governments go about allocating resources. As a process, fiscal space may be regarded as being as old as budgeting itself, or as a fundamentally new way of making budget decisions. It may be regarded as an old concept because budget officials in all countries routinely estimate the "room" available for new expenditures or the "gap" between projected revenues and expenditures. Budget officials typically make these estimates early in each cycle and update them during formulation of the budget. In most countries, the process is largely informal; it is not codified by budget rules. Nevertheless, the practice is ubiquitous because it informs political leaders and budget officials of the amounts that may be spent through new decisions. They need this information to review spending bids and policy initiatives, and to set the budget aggregates.

In a formal sense, however, the concept of fiscal space deviates from the aims of past budget reforms. It recognises that budgeting is inherently incremental and that most decisions focus on marginal adjustments in programmes and expenditures. In compiling budgets, governments rarely treat spending on existing and proposed new programmes in the same way, nor do they ordinarily undertake a comprehensive review of expenditures. As Wildavsky argued almost half a century ago, incremental behaviour enables governments to complete budget work in a timely manner by reducing conflict over resources and by reducing the number of decisions that must be made. After decades of unsuccessfully trying to uproot budgeting's incremental tendencies through bold innovations such as programme budgeting and zero-base budgeting, some governments have begun to formally incorporate incremental norms into the construction of the budget. Two of the most popular contemporary innovations – baseline projections and medium-term expenditure frameworks (MTEF) – build incrementalism into the routines of budgeting. Baseline projections use the current level of expenditure as the starting point for compiling the next budget; an MTEF allocates resources to spending units in terms of changes to the baseline. Fiscal space reinforces these incrementalist reforms by focusing budget work on the new resources available for allocation. If budgeting is unavoidably incremental, the fiscal space argument runs, it makes sense to formally structure the process so that it deals with the resources for which decisions will be made.

The prospect of a more constrained budget environment in the decades ahead also has spurred interest in fiscal space. Governments are not concerned about fiscal space when there are sufficient resources to finance ongoing problems as well as significant policy initiatives. They do pay attention to fiscal space when the budget is tight and when spending priorities are crowded out by insufficient resources. Population ageing in most OECD countries and a concern that economic growth may be less robust than in the past indicate that fiscal space may shrink or possibly vanish in the years ahead. The loss of fiscal space gives rise to the possibility that budgeting will become a decremental process that allocates losses rather than gains. If this were to occur, budgeting will likely become a more contentious process, and politicians will have difficulty financing policy initiatives.

From this perspective, the budget predicament of high-income countries shares some common traits with the situation that confronts low-income countries. Because resources are scarce and demands are elastic, both groups of countries have incentive to structure budget decisions in terms of the space available for allocation. But not all scarcities are alike. There are observable differences between governments that have incremental funds for programme enhancements and those that lack sufficient resources for existing programmes. For developing countries, fiscal space means the capacity to finance productive investment with borrowed money; for affluent countries, space is the increment available to expand programmes.

This paper deals with developed countries. Hence, the concept of fiscal space presented here is inextricably linked to incrementalism in budgeting. Section 1 reviews the factors that contribute to the shrinkage of fiscal space, including pressure on both the revenue and expenditure sides of the budget. Section 2 considers methods for protecting or enlarging fiscal space through adjustments in spending commitments to free up incremental resources and through changes in the way budgets are prepared and expenditures managed. The concluding section reflects on how budgeting may be recast into a process for explicitly allocating scarce fiscal space.

1. The shrinkage of fiscal space

In all highly developed countries, the national government has vastly more money to spend than it had half a century ago. In almost all, however, the government has narrower budget options than it once had. Spending more but having less to spend undermines incremental behavior and underlies the contemporary interest in fiscal space. The volume of space depends on four variables: the extent to which existing programmes claim incremental resources, the propensity of a government to tax, its propensity to borrow, and the performance of the economy. All four factors may now be less favourable than during the post-war spurt in government spending, which is why budget options appear to be more constrained. Each variable is considered in the paragraphs that follow.

1.1. Public expenditures

Contemporary governments have less to spend because public expenditures are sticky – that is, they do not readily respond to changes in political conditions or national priorities. A decision to spend money one year usually is a decision to spend in future years as well, even where there is no legal requirement to do so. When a government launches a new programme, it also ignites political and bureaucratic pressure to continue or enlarge that programme. Groups form to protect their interests, administrative entities are established and staffed to run the new programme, and the programme's expenditures are incorporated into the "base" when the room for incremental expenditure in future budgets is estimated. Often, the new programmes are protected against price increases, thereby increasing their claim on future resources.

If expenditures were not sticky, budgeting would not be incremental. A government could treat new and old claims alike, and broaden its discretion to the full amount of expenditure. Stickiness has a positive side, for it stabilises government, gives citizens clear expectations of the services that will be available in the future, and diminishes conflict over resources. It would be a mistake, however, to regard expenditures as perfectly sticky. Much of the political craft of budgeting involves adjustments at the margins. These sometimes entail programme terminations, but they more frequently amount to shifts within programmes. These shifts are often below the "radar" of budgeting; they are implemented unilaterally by spending units and are not brought to the attention of central budget makers. This tactic has the advantage of reducing the risk that shifts might lead to a loss of resources.

Expenditures tend to be sticky even for programmes that do not perform well. In fact, a government may consider it necessary to augment resources when results fall short of expectations. For example, governments frequently supplement the budgets of troubled schools, either in response to parental demands or in the hope that the additional funds would enable them to improve. Of course, expenditures for successful programmes are also sticky, as supporters exploit their performance to extract more money from the government.

The problem for contemporary governments is not only that expenditures are sticky but that they are so very large, much larger as a share of GDP in member countries than they were when the OECD was established nearly half a century ago. Table 16.1 shows that, although countries differ significantly in the relative size of the public sector, all member countries have experienced a progressive increase in government spending. Several powerful trends account for most of this rise. One is the shift in risk from households to the government; related to this is growth of the entitlement state which has transformed more than half of national expenditure in most OECD countries from discretionary budget decisions into spending mandated by permanent law.

In industrial countries, the government has become the holder of risk for society. The government indemnifies workers for loss of jobs, seniors for retirement, patients for illness, and families for various losses of income. In some countries, citizens and enterprises are compensated for losses due to natural or human-made disasters, farmers are protected against the risk that the market price of commodities will fall, depositors against the risk of default by financial institutions, exporters against changes in currency values, and so on. Some important risks still remain in private hands, but in all advanced countries the public budget is exposed to risks taken by the government.

The pooling of risk through government action has certainly contributed to economic and personal well-being, even though it has sometimes opened the door to moral hazard. A bigger problem is that a government rarely has a reliable estimate of the risk it is taking, nor does it provision for downstream costs in the budget. When these come due, sometimes only years later, the government has no choice but to make good on its obligations.

Table 16.1. **Year-to-year percentage change in real GDP**[1]
Annual average, selected periods 1960-2000

	1960-68	1968-73	1973-79	1979-89	1989-2000
Australia	5.0	5.5	2.6	3.4	3.2
Austria	4.2	5.9	3.0	2.1	2.5
Belgium	4.5	5.6	2.4	2.2	2.2
Canada	5.6	5.6	3.9	2.9	2.5
Denmark	4.6	4.0	1.5	1.4	2.2
Finland	3.9	6.7	2.4	3.6	2.0
France	5.4	5.9	2.8	2.4	1.8
Germany	4.2	4.9	2.4	2.0	1.8
Greece	7.3	8.2	3.3	0.8	2.1
Iceland	4.1	7.6	5.3	3.2	2.5
Ireland	4.2	4.8	4.9	3.1	7.4
Italy	5.7	4.6	3.5	2.4	1.6
Japan	10.5	8.8	3.5	3.8	1.8
Luxembourg	3.1	6.5	1.3	4.3	5.6
Netherlands	4.8	5.3	2.6	2.0	3.0
New Zealand	3.1	5.1	0.0	2.0	2.5
Norway	4.4	4.1	4.6	2.7	3.2
Portugal	6.6	7.4	2.9	3.3	2.9
Spain	7.5	6.8	2.3	2.8	2.7
Sweden	4.4	3.7	1.8	2.2	1.7
Switzerland	4.4	4.5	−0.4	2.1	1.1
Turkey	5.8	5.5	4.5	4.0	4.1
United Kingdom	3.1	3.2	1.5	2.4	2.2
United States	4.5	3.3	3.0	3.0	3.1

1. This table only includes countries that were OECD members throughout the periods covered.
Sources: Data for the periods 1960-68 and 1968-73 are drawn from OECD Historical Statistics 1960-1983; data for subsequent periods are drawn from OECD Historical Statistics 1970-2000. The two data sets are not consistent; hence the data reported here are not strictly comparable across all periods.

Many of the biggest risks facing contemporary governments are in the form of entitlements, which give the eligible persons a legal right to payment from the government. Typically, entitlements are open-ended; they establish a formula for payment, but do not limit a government's exposure. A government must make room for them in the budget when the event or condition triggering the entitlement occurs. Governments can enlarge space in the budget for priorities by curtailing entitlements, but doing so may ignite strong protest. Quite often, bold efforts to trim entitlements end up as marginal adjustments that have little or no effect on near-term budgets, but may create space in distant budgets.

The prognosis in almost all developed economies is that demographic trends will compel national governments to allocate a rising share of their budgets to entitlements established in previous generations. Not only will these expenditures be sticky, but much of the increment available for allocation will also be sticky. The challenge for future governments will be to "unstick" a sufficient portion of expenditure to maintain budgeting as a genuine allocation process.

1.2. The propensity to tax

When space is insufficient to finance programme ambitions and past commitments, governments are tempted to look at the revenue side of the budget. Obviously, spending could not have grown so much during the past half century if governments had relied only on the increments supplied by economic growth. In fact, all governments of OECD countries raised tax rates and expanded the tax base during that expansionary period. They boosted tax revenues in good times because voters wanted enhanced services, and they boosted them when fiscal space was inadequate because expenditures were sticky. Table 16.2 compares government revenue as a share of GDP at various points during the past 40 years. With revenue in the OECD area rising from 28% of GDP in 1960 to 37% in 1990, the data suggest that governments had ample space for budgetary initiatives.

Table 16.2 reveals, however, that the rate of expanding budget space through sizeable tax increases has ended in many OECD countries. In a few, revenues have actually declined as a share of GDP, as governments have purposely reduced their fiscal space in a determined effort to shrink the relative size of the public sector. In most countries, revenues have remained stable for an extended period, suggesting that the government faces political resistance to tax increases as well as pressure to maintain existing programmes. Although it is hard to generalise across the OECD area, because member countries have different tax policies, it is reasonable to conclude that most countries now finance policy initiatives through economic increments and cutbacks or efficiency gains in existing programmes. These actions purchase fiscal space for the budget cycle immediately ahead, but do not significantly alter the long-term imbalance between revenues and expenditures.

Tax policy is never fully at rest. Governments endlessly tinker with rates and rules, sometimes to add or subtract revenue, often to adjust the burden on particular sectors or activities. The extent to which future adjustments affect fiscal space will depend on citizen

Table 16.2. **Current receipts of government as a percentage of GDP**[1]
Annual average, selected periods 1960-2000

	1960-67	1968-73	1974-79	1980-89	1990-2000
Australia	25.6	27.7	28.7	31.6	32.2
Austria	35.8	40.3	43.1	46.4	47.6
Belgium	30.1	35.2	43.9	46.6	46.8
Canada	27.8	34.8	36.8	39.3	–
Denmark	30.1	42.5	45.2	52.0	54.3
Finland	30.8	35.0	41.7	44.8	50.7
France	37.2	38.8	40.7	45.5	46.5
Germany	36.1	39.5	44.0	45.1	45.3
Greece	23.6	26.7	29.1	32.8	41.8
Iceland	30.3	33.4	35.9	41.4	36.6
Ireland	27.2	33.9	35.9	41.4	36.6
Italy	29.7	30.6	33.5	36.8	43.9
Japan	20.4	20.9	24.6	30.6	30.5
Luxembourg	34.2	36.3	50.1	–	44.9
Netherlands	36.4	35.8	51.0	55.2	47.8
Norway	36.2	45.4	48.4	50.3	51.4
Portugal	19.5	23.0	27.6	35.0	37.7
Spain	18.6	22.5	25.7	34.0	38.0
Sweden	37.5	47.9	54.4	59.4	57.3
Switzerland	23.6	26.6	32.7	34.1	–
United Kingdom	32.6	38.1	38.9	40.9	37.8
United States	27.0	29.8	29.7	31.0	–

1. This table only includes countries that were OECD members throughout the periods covered. New Zealand and Turkey have been excluded because of lack of data.

Sources: Data for the periods 1960-67 and 1968-73 are drawn from *OECD Historical Statistics 1960-1983*; data for subsequent periods are drawn from *OECD Historical Statistics 1970-2000*. The two data sets are not consistent; hence the data reported here are not strictly comparable across all periods.

sentiment and political preferences. In some countries, voters will prefer to hold on to promised benefits or to expand governmental responsibilities, even when doing so compels higher taxes. In others, future fiscal space will be constricted by strong resistance to any increase in the tax burden. Countries with relatively high levels of taxation may face conflicting pressures. On the one hand, the high tax rates may indicate political support for a large government role; on the other hand, high tax rates may establish a ceiling on the capacity to generate additional revenue. Countries with an elevated dependency ratio due to ageing populations will likely be pressured to boost taxes. They may find it more expedient to spread the cost among consumers and income earners than to impose benefit cuts on those already receiving payments from the government or scheduled to do so in the next ten years or so.

Budgeting is a process of marginal adjustment to enlarge short-term space. On the tax side, there are numerous opportunities, such as raising "sin" taxes and making small adjustments in other revenue sources. Countries with relatively high levels of tax expenditures may consider it expedient to enlarge budget space by curtailing these subsidies. Governments may also ease budget pressures by relying more heavily than in the past on non-tax income such as fees for public services. In the long run, however, the impact of revenue policy on fiscal space will depend on two key variables: the propensity of governments to make big rather than small adjustments in tax burdens, and the performance of the economy. The worst scenario for future budget makers is one in which the economy stagnates and political leaders lack the will to generate additional revenue; the most favourable scenario is the reverse. Though unlikely, it would enable the governments of OECD countries to recreate the golden age of expansion.

1.3. Deficit budgeting

Fiscal space can be enlarged by adding borrowed funds to the resources produced by current revenues. In fact, many OECD countries borrowed heavily during the post-war growth spurt to finance investment as well as current expenditure. Evidently, the surge in revenue did not fully cover burgeoning public expenditures. Governments had a propensity to borrow because of a far-reaching shift in fiscal doctrine from the balanced budget norm to active demand management. As has often been noted, the governments of OECD countries came to regard balancing the economy as more salient than balancing the budget. The accumulation of public debt was considered prudent because governments would repay their obligations out of the dividends of economic growth.

In those halcyon years, fiscal space was rarely a problem, though governments routinely were pressured by steeply rising demands. When the economy was buoyant, a government acquired ample space from the surge of revenue into its coffers. When the economy weakened, the government created space by justifying deficits that would narrow the gap between potential and actual output. Two factors converged in the late 20th century to undermine the case for deficit financing. One was the looming demographic tide that would impose enormous budget costs on future governments; the other was a shift away from flexible fiscal policies to fixed targets that constrain budget deficits. Most of the early targets were political statements that lacked enforcement and were frequently ignored. Nevertheless, the targets were useful political messages; they signaled to spenders that the high-growth era was drawing to a close and that future budgets would be constrained.

Accommodating targets have been replaced in many OECD countries by preset rules, such as the Stability and Growth Pact (SGP) which limits the annual budget deficit and public debt of euro-zone countries to a fixed per cent of GDP and authorises the European Commission to sanction countries that breach the limits. The original SGP was rigid: its limits allowed no exceptions, regardless of economic circumstances or demands on the budget. Whatever its virtues, rigidity impaired a government's capacity to adopt stimulative budget policies during cyclical weakness in the economy. Moreover, the limits blocked counter-cyclical adjustments through the budget's built-in stabilisers. In 2005, the EC revised the SGP to allow some flexibility when warranted by economic conditions. Arguably, the changes have vitiated the rules but, in this writer's view, the appropriate test of their effectiveness is whether they constrain fiscal outcomes, not whether they absolutely bind politicians. To the extent that they have narrowed the fiscal space available for budget allocation, the rules have had a pronounced impact.

Outside the European Union, countries generally have taken a more flexible path that relies on political accountability rather than imposed limits to strengthen fiscal discipline. This fiscal responsibility approach requires a government to establish multi-year targets for selected aggregates (such as the primary balance or public debt as a share of GDP), to update the targets periodically and explain changes to them, and to report fiscal outcomes. This self-enforcing rule aims to make political leaders accountable for fiscal results, but it does not bar them from running up deficits. In contrast to fixed rules which are most constrictive when the economy is weak, the fiscal responsibility concept constrains the budget when the economy is strong and deficits are receding or have disappeared. When the economy is faltering, a government can fulfil its fiscal responsibilities by explaining why it has eased the constraints. The penalty for fiscal irresponsibility is that voters will turn the government out of office.

Fine-tuning fiscal rules so that they distinguish between different economic conditions is exceedingly difficult. One approach, which was popular during the growth era but subsequently fell into disuse, is to separate out the portion of deficit due to economic weakness while requiring that the budget be structurally balanced. Structural rules were abandoned because they were difficult to enforce and may have contributed to the upward creep in public expenditure, tax burdens and public debt. It appears that there is no perfect time for enforcing fiscal rules. When the economy is robust, a government has plenty of money to distribute via tax cuts and spending increases; when the economy is weak, the government must spend more than it has.

Although they may have limited effectiveness, fiscal rules do shrink budget space. Whether in the form of fixed limits or fiscal responsibility procedures, the rules bespeak a more constrained budget environment, a sense of constraint and a need for government to be more prudent. Inasmuch as the effects of fiscal rules depend on political will, the fact that government leaders are less willing to spend in excess of revenue reduces the space available for allocation. Table 16.3 confirms this conclusion, for it shows lower net borrowings by OECD countries during the past decade.

1.4. Economic performance

The final element in assessing fiscal space is the performance of the economy. High growth rewards a government with incremental revenues which (due to tax elasticities) generally rise faster than GDP. Of course, the reverse holds when the economy weakens, leaving a government with a shortfall in revenue. Expenditures also fluctuate with shifts in economic conditions, though not to the same extent as revenues. With revenues and

Table 16.3. **Net lending of government as a percentage of GDP**[1]

Annual average, selected periods 1960-2000

	1960-67	1968-73	1974-79	1980-89	1990-2000
Australia	1.4	1.9	−3.4	−3.3	−2.2
Austria	0.6	0.8	−2.0	−3.2	−3.0
Belgium	–	–	−5.8	−10.7	−4.2
Canada	−0.7	0.9	−2.0	−4.8	–
Denmark	1.5	2.9	0.5	−2.1	−0.6
Finland	2.3	4.1	5.0	3.6	−1.2
France	0.5	0.6	−0.9	−2.3	−3.5
Germany	0.8	0.2	−3.0	−2.1	−2.9
Iceland	2.9	0.9	−8.4	−9.4	–
Ireland	−3.4	−3.6	−9.2	−11.0	−0.5
Italy	−1.8	−4.8	−9.2	−11.0	−6.9
Japan	–	1.0	−3.4	−1.5	−3.5
Luxembourg	2.4	1.7	2.9	–	3.0
Netherlands	−0.7	−0.3	−2.0	−5.1	−2.6
Norway	4.0	4.3	2.5	5.2	3.8
Portugal	−0.2	1.5	−5.3	−5.5	−3.9
Spain	–	0.4	−0.7	−4.4	−4.0
Sweden	3.3	4.4	1.3	−1.6	−2.9
United Kingdom	−1.1	−0.4	−3.9	−2.3	−3.1
United States	−0.5	−0.6	−1.5	−3.4	–

1. This table only includes countries that were OECD members throughout the periods covered. Greece, New Zealand, Switzerland and Turkey have been excluded because of lack of data.

Sources: Data for the periods 1960-67 and 1968-73 are drawn from *OECD Historical Statistics 1960-1983*; data for subsequent periods are drawn from *OECD Historical Statistics 1970-2000*. The two data sets are not consistent; hence the data reported here are not strictly comparable across all periods.

expenditures moving in opposite directions, the budget has automatic stabilisers which enlarge fiscal space in good times and shrink it in bad times.

Budgeting is a temperamental process. When the economy is strong, budget makers tend to allocate resources in the expectation that favourable conditions will continue. The opposite tendency prevails when the economy is weak. To the extent that economic performance has trended downward in recent decades, it has diminished the amount of space that governments have allocated. Table 16.4 isplays economic growth trends for OECD countries; it shows that, while all countries experienced cyclical variations in performance, growth spurts have been weaker than in the past.

In forming expectations about the future, potential performance carries more weight than predictions about how the economy will actually perform. An economy's potential rests on two main variables: the size of the workforce and its productivity. In most OECD countries, future workforce growth will be significantly lower in the decades ahead as their populations age and older workers retire. Most of the gain in output will have to come from rising productivity, which is extremely difficult to predict. It is highly probable that productivity gains will be uneven over an extended period and that GDP growth also will be uneven. Fiscal space will expand and shrink in response to economic developments, and budget policy will adjust to swings in performance. It is not feasible to predict exactly how the economy will perform in the future, but demographic trends will make it difficult for OECD countries to match past results.

Table 16.4. **Current disbursements of government as a percentage of GDP**[1]

Annual average, selected periods 1960-2000

	1960-67	1968-73	1974-79	1980-89	1990-2000
Australia	20.4	22.1	30.2	33.8	31.7
Austria	29.3	33.4	40.0	46.2	48.1
Belgium	39.1	33.9	46.6	54.9	50.3
Canada	25.8	31.6	36.9	42.6	–
Denmark	25.1	35.0	43.2	54.2	55.6
Finland	24.3	27.5	33.8	39.0	50.9
France	33.0	34.8	38.9	45.8	48.2
Germany	30.2	34.1	42.2	43.8	44.2
Greece	19.7	22.4	28.0	39.2	46.1
Iceland	21.3	24.1	25.6	29.5	–
Ireland	26.7	32.8	40.0	47.4	35.6
Italy	11.1	13.0	38.7	44.3	48.7
Japan	13.7	14.6	21.7	26.3	28.4
Luxembourg	28.7	30.6	41.3	–	38.7
Netherlands	32.3	41.1	49.1	56.3	49.0
Norway	29.0	37.2	42.1	42.8	45.5
Portugal	17.5	19.1	29.1	36.5	39.1
Spain	14.5	19.0	23.6	34.3	38.8
Sweden	29.6	38.5	49.5	59.2	59.0
Switzerland	19.0	22.0	29.2	30.3	–
United Kingdom	30.8	33.4	39.8	42.0	39.6
United States	26.3	29.7	30.7	33.9	–

1. This table only includes countries that were OECD members throughout the periods covered. New Zealand and Turkey have been excluded because of lack of data.

Sources: Data for the periods 1960-67 and 1968-73 are drawn from OECD Historical Statistics 1960-1983; data for subsequent periods are drawn from OECD Historical Statistics 1970-2000. The two data sets are not consistent; hence the data reported here are not strictly comparable across all periods.

2. Protecting and enlarging fiscal space

Fiscal space is a variable quantity that is enlarged or decreased by government action. As discussed in the previous section, past expenditure decisions greatly narrowed the options open to future budget allocators. The task facing contemporary budget officials is to expand fiscal space so that expenditures reflect the policies and preferences of the government.

An essential step is to guard against revenue or spending actions which have only modest impact in the year(s) immediately ahead but balloon in future years. When the current budget is tight, politicians may be tempted to structure revenue losses and expenditure increases in ways that claim little space in the current budget but pre-commit future space without regard for downstream demands on the budget. Many costly entitlements have this characteristic, especially when payments are deferred to later years as is often the case in government-financed retirement benefits. Many types of programmes can be designed to shift fiscal impacts beyond the time horizon of the budget process. Future space can be consumed by deferring necessary maintenance on government facilities, launching numerous projects but extending completion over a period of years, awarding public employees small pay increases in the current year and much bigger ones each of the next several years, booking fees for issuing government guarantees as current revenue but ignoring the claims that will arise in case of default, and other bookkeeping tricks.

Even when they do not shift costs to future budgets, politicians act in ways that reduce future space. Whenever an ongoing programme is established, it reduces the room for maneuver in future budgets. Several instruments are available for protecting space, ranging from procedures that inform policy makers of downstream consequences to procedures that limit current actions. Baseline projections of the future costs of current policies merely inform budget makers, but when linked to medium-term expenditure frameworks, they limit spending decisions to the amounts that can be accommodated within each year's framework. A variant on this approach is to require that any expenditure increase or revenue loss due to new budget decisions must be offset by spending cuts or revenue increases.

New procedures have been introduced or proposed to protect future space. One is to apply the accrual basis to liabilities that come due beyond the year(s) for which budget decisions are made; another is to account for the estimated present value of future revenue or spending changes as a cost in the current budget. Accruals and present-value estimates can be incorporated into fiscal rules which limit the gap between revenues and expenditures. For example, if a policy change was estimated to add 100 million to the present value of future expenditures, that amount would be expensed in the budget and included in enforcing limits on the deficit. It would be feasible for a government to implement this procedure without shifting the entire budget to the accrual basis. However, enforcing this rule would compel the government to extend its fiscal horizon well beyond the 3-5 years of a medium-term expenditure framework. This issue is taken up in the final section, which discusses changes to the budget process.

2.1. Enlarging fiscal space

Governments that encounter shrinking or inadequate room for policy initiatives have introduced numerous reforms to expand their opportunity for manoeuvre. Reforms that have sought to depose incremental norms have always failed, for reasons mentioned earlier in this paper. Accordingly, the adjustments considered here focus on marginal changes in revenue and expenditure policy that would expand the increments available for allocation.

Assuming that increases in tax rates are off the table, the most appropriate course for a government might be to review and prune tax subsidies that diminish its revenues. This option should be the most attractive for countries which forgo significant amounts of revenue through tax expenditures, but these might well be countries in which beneficiaries of tax subsidies are the most effectively mobilised to protect their interests. Nevertheless, it is worth the effort, not only to generate additional revenue, but also to curtail distortions in economic activity caused by undue provision of tax expenditures. In the trade-off between more tax breaks or higher tax breaks, national governments with insufficient budget space would do better by curbing subsidies than by raising already-high rates in order to finance burgeoning expenditure commitments.

On the expenditure side, the most obvious option for enlarging space – reallocation from less to more effective programmes – usually is exceedingly difficult. Every national government has experienced occasional bouts of reallocation: terminating or curtailing major programmes and shifting the funds to other issues. But these bouts are episodic, provoked by fiscal crisis or by major changes in political sentiment and leadership. These reflections are not formally built into the routines of budgeting but are driven by the opportunities of the moment. Quite frequently, however, proposed reallocations fail because they provoke opposition from multiple sources: programme beneficiaries threatened with loss of services, agencies which do not want to surrender coveted activities, politicians discomfited by the prospect of angering voters, public employee unions determined to protect jobs. Explicit reallocation is difficult, even when it is based on evaluative findings and other evidence.

Budgeting is incremental because major reallocations are rare. At the margins, however, there are frequent shifts of resources as new opportunities emerge and old ones recede. These shifts generally are not explicit – they do not overtly pit programmes against one another in a competition for scarce funds. Nor do these shifts take money away from spending units. Instead, they are implicit, and savings are retained by the affected agency. Sometimes these adjustments are made unilaterally by the agency and not even brought to the attention of the central budget office; at other times, the adjustments are agreed in formal budget negotiations. They may be initiated by the spending agency under conditions that significantly lower the risk of losing resources. One objective of the medium-term expenditure framework is to encourage ongoing reallocation and to broaden its scope. But this aim has often been thwarted by faulty implementation of MTEFs.

Four reallocation tactics warrant brief mention. One is to increase budgeted levels by less than the expected rate of inflation. In this situation, programmes and agencies get nominal allocations at the previous year's level or a bit higher, but not enough to compensate for price changes. Recourse to this ploy has been impeded in recent decades by indexation of various programmes and by adjustment of baseline projections for estimated price changes. This issue shall be further discussed in the concluding section below.

Second, marginal reallocations can be financed by reducing agency operating budgets by an amount equal to expected or average gains in productivity or efficiency. These adjustments, which typically range between 1-2% of operating expenditure, are subtracted from either the agency's base budget or from baseline projections. Programme expenditure and transfer payments are exempt from these enforced cuts. Although the amounts saved are small and often are below actual efficiency gains, they stir considerable resentment and can be difficult for small agencies which have little flexibility in managing their budgets.

Third, some governments have experimented with "sunset" rules which automatically terminate programmes or subject them to review according to a fixed schedule, such as every five or ten years. The idea is to require an explicit decision by the government to continue each programme. In practice, sunset provisions have modest impact on minor programmes which have little visibility or political support, but rarely affect the fortunes of large programmes.

Finally, governments can resort to across-the-board cuts to open space for new budget allocations. Singapore, which imposes a 5% cut, puts the savings in a common pool which is allocated through annual budget decisions. This form of cutback is used from time to time by budget officials to close a projected gap between revenues and expenditures. The new version is deployed to make money available for allocation. Consequently, agencies can win back some of the enforced savings by bidding for additional resources.

2.2. Shifting risks and costs

The space created by the various ploys discussed here reinforces incremental tendencies. The ploys do not significantly alter the government's fiscal position. Far-reaching efforts under way in some countries would create budget space by shifting either risk or expenditures from the public treasury to private hands. It was noted earlier that the modern state has become the holder of significant risks for society. Recently, there have been some efforts to reverse this trend through a variety of approaches that offload risk. The most prominent initiative involves retirement benefits which increase in cost as the number of pensioners rises. Traditional defined-benefit plans place the full risk on the government: it must pay promised benefits regardless of the financial condition of its social insurance funds or the longevity of eligible recipients. By converting all or a portion of payments to defined-contribution schemes, governments shift a sizeable fraction of the risk to recipients. Some governments have gone further and introduced private retirement accounts, usually with a guaranteed minimum payout. A few have adopted a scheme devised by Sweden which adjusts payments at retirement for changes in life expectancy. These types of risk-shifting moves are likely to accelerate in the decades ahead as governments are burdened by the costs of supporting an ageing population.

The best way to avoid risk is to be cautious in taking it on. Because a risk taken one year usually comes due in later years, it can be regarded as costless. It would be prudent for governments to wall off decisions on whether to accept risk from an assessment of potential exposure. Ideally, the assessment should be carried out by an independent office or a central agency, not by the entity tendering guarantees or other risks. Governments can induce a more cautious posture by provisioning for risks in advance or by sharing risks with other parties. A rarely tried mechanism would be for a government to purchase reinsurance when it takes actions that expose it to potential losses. It also can purchase insurance for destabilising events, such as natural disasters which burden national budgets by depressing GDP and public revenues and by compelling the government to pay for reconstruction, even when it does not have a legal obligation. But such insurance may be viewed as a bad deal by politicians because the premiums eat into current budget space.

Governments can shift costs by privatising activities or by financing them privately. Public-private partnerships (PPPs), typically for major construction projects, have become a popular arrangement for shifting upfront construction costs or operating expenses to private entities. In exchange for hiving off these costs, governments may guarantee operating performance. For a road construction project, a government may guarantee a minimum volume of traffic or toll revenue, with the government compensating private investors for shortfalls. In this arrangement, the government reduces near-term expenditure but adds medium- to long-term risk. If PPPs are not diligently crafted with prudent assessment of risks and carefully drafted contracts, a government may gain budget space but undermine the control of future budgets.

Some governments have gone beyond PPPs to sell existing assets and book the income as current revenue. This tactic is open to governments that operate on a cash basis; they can disregard the unpleasant facts that the income is non-recurring and that the increase in budget space is ephemeral. A government determined to invent space by liquefying assets can create novel financing instruments, such as securitising future streams of revenue. This imprudent tactic, which has the same effect as pre-spending future budget space, is never appropriate, even when the government is short of revenue to maintain existing services.

Two different conclusions can be drawn from the foregoing discussion. If the objective is to produce increments for budget allocation, a government has an array of marginal adjustments that give it more fiscal space. If, however, the aim is to transform budget choices, few OECD countries have the political resources to vastly expand fiscal space through fundamental changes in revenue or spending policy. As demographic pressures intensify, more governments may feel compelled to question established revenue and spending policy.

3. Adjusting budget processes

The conduct of budgeting affects the space available for allocation. This concluding section considers how the process might be adjusted to protect and enlarge space. Key adjustments pertain to the role of the budget office, the time frame of budgeting, the construction of baseline estimates, and incentives for marginal reallocations.

The primary role of the central budget office should be as guardian and allocator of fiscal space. Performing these tasks requires that it have the macroeconomic and programme analytic skills to estimate available space and the impact of proposed or adopted policy changes. The budget office would manage the baseline, extend its data and decisions to future years, provide incentive for spending units to propose and implement policy changes, inject evaluative and performance evidence into budget work, and seek opportunities to expand the space available for allocation. Budgeting, in short, would be the key process for identifying, deciding and financing policy innovation. To be positioned for these tasks, the central budget office would have to abandon some traditional responsibilities, especially the close monitoring and control of expenditures. If it does not offload control functions, the budget office will lack the time, skills, disposition and credibility to manage policy change.

Many central budget offices in OECD countries have already transitioned from control to costing and reviewing policy initiatives. For some, the changeover has been difficult because they no longer are certain of how they fit into the overall financial management framework of government. Modern budget offices realise that it is not viable to intervene in the details of expenditure, but are unsure of which tasks they should perform and which should be devolved to spending agencies. For example, they may be ambivalent about whether programme evaluation and performance measurement – two useful inputs into the policy process – should be led centrally or by line agencies. They may also be anxious about the leverage which is surrendered when they let go of the instruments of control. Having surrendered some powers but not having yet consolidated new ones, the budget office may be a weak counterpart to spending units which have superior access to information and closer ties to sectoral interests.

To facilitate the transition from traditional responsibilities to new roles and relationships, it would be useful for the central budget office to regard fiscal space as its space – that is, as the portion of the budget on which it focuses. From this vantage point, the budget office has an obvious incentive to expand the space by encouraging trade-offs, expanding available increments, setting aside money in bidding funds or other pools, and taking other steps discussed in the previous section. It also has incentive to protect future space by assuring that trade-offs and savings are accurately costed. This assignment can be a challenging one because spenders have incentive to overstate expenditure reductions and underestimate increases when they propose reallocations. To deter these machinations, the budget office must have relevant data and analyses that enable it to review and correct agency misestimates. Even more important, it must have political support at the top of government to confront agencies. When budget trade-offs are collegially decided by cabinet, the budget office may be overwhelmed by log-rolling ministers for whom spending initiatives have higher priority than protecting future fiscal space.

The budget office's role in protecting fiscal space also is undermined when governments make *ad hoc* spending decisions throughout the year. Nowadays, politicians make *de facto* budget decisions when they meet at international forums, interact with interest groups, respond to a crisis or media attacks, and (in some countries) just about every time cabinet meets. In this writer's observation, *ad hoc* budgeting has become much more prevalent than a generation ago, probably due to heightened mobilisation of political interests, greater pressure on governments to deal with unfolding events, stronger transnational networks, and more openness and transparency in budgeting and other government activities. In a few countries, year-round budgeting has been energised by abundant surpluses which are whittled down by *ad hoc* spending decisions. In some countries, more spending decisions are taken during the period between budgets than during budget season. In several countries, sectoral ministers have "sold" the prime minister costly programme initiatives immediately before the scheduled cabinet meeting, and the proposals were approved without much discussion and without being vetted through the budget process. Whatever the rationale, this practice puts fiscal space at risk by significantly weakening the capacity of the budget office to assess future spending impacts.

3.1. *Baseline estimates*

To allocate fiscal space, the budget office needs two essential types of information: the volume of available space for the next year or longer; and the extent to which that space would be claimed by proposed or adopted changes in revenue and spending policies. Medium-term (or longer) projections of current policy have become standard budget practice in many countries, particularly those that have introduced MTEF-type arrangements. In contrast to traditional "base" estimates which use the previous year's spending level as the starting point for budget work, baseline projections adjust the base for estimated future changes in prices, workload, and other economic or programme conditions.

In baseline budgeting, fiscal space is the difference between projected revenue and expenditure, plus or minus targeted surpluses or deficits. Policy changes are the estimated changes to these projections due to revenue or spending initiatives of the government. For example, suppose that a government estimates that baseline surpluses will be 100 million next year. It then legislates changes in revenue laws that are estimated to reduce the projected surplus to 80 million. In this case, the policy change consumes 20 million of the available space. Re-estimates due to changes in economic conditions or other technical considerations (such as updated estimates of the number of persons receiving payments under existing law) generally are excluded from the computation of policy changes.

It is important to note that national governments differ significantly in how they construct baseline projections and estimate policy changes. Some governments incorporate estimated price changes in the baseline; others do not. Some include only permanent or structural changes in measuring the impact of policy changes on fiscal space; others include all adjustments. The rules for projecting the baseline have a significant impact on both the volume of space and the estimates of policy change, as shown by the hypothetical comparison in Table 16.5.

In this illustration, the country that does not incorporate estimated price changes in the baseline has twice as much fiscal space to allocate than the country which includes price changes. In making budget allocations, country B can opt to compensate spending

Table 16.5. **Comparison of baseline projections**

	Baseline revenue	Current expenditure	Estimated price changes	Projected space
Country A	120	100	10	10
Country B	120	100	No adjustment	20

agencies for expected price changes or it can allocate the money for other purposes. Suppose the government decides to spend 105, which would compensate agencies for half of the projected price increase in this hypothetical case. Country A's decision would be measured as an expenditure cut; country B's decision would be measured as an expenditure increase. Even though the actual expenditure would be identical for both countries, political perceptions would differ greatly. Because of this, country B would likely have far greater difficulty protecting and allocating fiscal space than country A.

There are powerful arguments for and against building estimated price changes into the baseline but, regardless of one's point of view, it should be recognised that baselines are not neutral instruments. How they are prepared directly affects the perceived volume of budget space.

Constructing the baseline and measuring the policy changes are two critical roles of the modern budget office. That office establishes rules for the baseline, updates the projections periodically to incorporate new economic and technical estimates, and measures the budget impact of proposed or approved changes in revenue and expenditure policies. Estimating policy changes is exceedingly difficult for revenue legislation and mandatory entitlements because budget experts must consider how taxpayers and programme beneficiaries will respond to the changes. To make matters even more critical, estimated impacts matter when budget allocations are made, not the actual impacts which only become known after the budget has been decided. In baseline budgeting, erroneous estimates are more relevant in allocating space than what actually ensues in the future.

Because of this, the budget office faces conflicting pressures. From a professional point of view, it must base estimates on specific programme knowledge, an understanding of possible behavioural responses, interactions among programmes and between the policy changes and projected economic conditions, and other variables. From a political perspective, the budget office may feel pressured to produce accommodating estimates that enable policy initiatives to proceed. Ideally, the budget office would deal with these pressures and with the inherent difficulty of projecting an uncertain future by producing a range of estimates. In practice, however, the process of allocating budget space demands that a government have point estimates of the impact of policy changes on revenues and expenditures. Although these estimates are often wrong, sometimes by large amounts, they are the stuff out of which innovative governments allocate budget space.

3.2. *Time frames*

It makes little sense to allocate fiscal space solely in the context of a single fiscal year. Doing so would give politicians and other claimants the opportunity to veil the true impact of revenue and spending decisions by manipulating the timing of policy changes. In one-year-at-a-time budgeting, programme expansions or revenue reductions scheduled to take effect in a subsequent year would have zero impact on fiscal space. When a government looks only one year ahead, it almost certainly will take actions that deprive it of adequate space in future budgets.

There is yet another reason for extending the time frame: fiscal space tends to be relatively narrow in the year immediately ahead and to widen in subsequent years as the economy grows and revenues become more plentiful. Therefore, a government has greater room for maneuver when it considers a stream of years rather than only one. When the reverse occurs and the space narrows (or disappears) in future years, the government has a powerful signal that current policies need to be re-examined.

Governments would not be able to expand their fiscal horizon if they lack contemporary budget tools such as baseline projections, socio-economic models, policy analyses and trend data. The central budget office uses these tools to measure and allocate fiscal space, but other participants in the process use them as well. In contrast to traditional "number crunching" in which the budget office had a monopoly or comparative advantage, it has no special claim of expertise in policy analysis. Anyone with a model or data can estimate the impact of policy changes on future budgets. But although anyone can contribute data and analysis to the policy debate, at the end of the day there can only be one authoritative measure of fiscal impacts, and it is usually the one from the budget office or another central organ.

In advanced countries, budgeting for fiscal space is proceeding along two time frames: the medium term, typically for the next 3-5 years; and the long run, stretching 30 years into the future. The medium term is used for allocation, the long term for analysis of fiscal sustainability. The period of 3-5 years for allocative decisions through an MTEF or similar arrangement recognises the shortness of political terms and the variability of economic conditions. Although it may be desirable to have a longer frame, it may be imprudent to give politicians a platform for pre-spending space too far into the future.

Long-term projections are not used for allocation; rather they analyse whether existing policies are sustainable and equitable across generations. Sustainability focuses on whether extending the revenue and expenditure regime into the distant future will create negative space – that is, a shortfall in resources that would either compel far-reaching policy changes or risk insolvency. Equity focuses on whether future generations will be disadvantaged, compared to the current generation, by a loss in benefits or a rise in tax burdens. It would be desirable to feed long-term projections into ongoing budget work, though one may question whether the budget office should have the main responsibility. Governments that budget exclusively on the cash basis may deem it appropriate to assign long-term work to specialised staff who assess the fiscal position in terms of liabilities rather than disbursements.

3.3. Medium-term expenditure frameworks

The MTEF is at once among the most popular contemporary innovations and among the most misapplied. In blueprint, it is a splendid process for allocating space through policy changes that are costed and decided in compiling the budget. In practice, it often is separated from budgeting and is used to campaign for future spending increases.

The MTEF has two basic features that are relevant to budgeting for fiscal space. First, it has a preset constraint on total spending and (typically) on sectoral or ministerial spending as well. To set the constraint, it is first necessary to estimate the space that will be available for allocation during the next medium-term cycle. Once this space is determined, the constraint is the portion of space that the government intends to allocate. Second, each ministry or sector submits bids for resources consistent with the sub-constraint allocated to it. Any savings proposed by the ministry or sector free up an equivalent amount of resources for allocation. Acting on behalf of the government and, in some countries, with its concurrence, the finance ministry sets the constraint and reviews spending bids to assess whether they are accurately costed and consistent with government policy.

The MTEF accommodates a variety of scenarios with respect to budget space. The standard arrangement may be labeled "positive" space in that the aggregate constraint and sub-constraints have room for expenditure increases. On the other hand, a government may allocate "negative" space, which would be the volume of savings that would have to be achieved in rolling the MTEF forward. When a ministry is allocated positive space, it may enlarge the resources available for policy initiatives by proposing reductions to existing programmes. These arrangements would not be feasible without baseline estimates and central capacity to estimate the budget impacts of savings and initiatives over the medium term. Moreover, the constraints and sub-constraints must be firm; except for compelling reasons, they should not be modified during preparation of the MTEF. Ideally, proposed reallocation should be based on performance indicators, programme evaluations or other evidence of effectiveness.

It is not hard to understand why the MTEF has been a popular innovation. It extends the time frame of budgeting, declutters the process of less significant detail, focuses on the allocation of fiscal and policy changes, and gives spenders some incentive to propose reallocations. More often than not, however, the MTEF is misapplied, with the unintended result that it may put fiscal space at risk. The major deficiency in implementing an MTEF is that it is treated as a separate activity, not as the core process of budgeting. In some countries, the MTEF has its own staff, a separate database, and distinct procedures for compiling out-year estimates. When a government pretends to have two processes for allocation, only one of them totally matters and it almost always is the annual budget process, not the MTEF.

An improperly implemented MTEF can jeopardise future fiscal space. To understand why, it is necessary to note that an MTEF entails spending decisions for each of the next 3-5 years. These decisions are reflected in the aggregate and sectoral constraints discussed earlier. Each year, when a new budget cycle is launched, the MTEF is rolled forward and the decisions made the previous year are incorporated into new baseline estimates. The previous decisions become constraints on how much can be spent in the years covered by a new MTEF. Revisions to these constraints are budgeted as adjustments to the baseline. A government has the option to keep to the baseline or to authorise policy changes that add to or subtract from expenditure. When the MTEF is separated from the budget, the constraints tend to be soft and, rather than being viewed as ceilings on future spending, they are regarded as floors that enable spending units to campaign for higher allocations in the future. Rather than being an instrument that protects fiscal space, the MTEF is transformed into a process that puts space at risk. The only way to avoid this fact is to have hard constraints that are built into the budget and are not regarded as separate projections.

In a medium-term expenditure framework, the central budget office becomes guardian of the country's fiscal space and manager of the policy change process. This is a more political role than the customary one of reviewing estimates. It sometimes places the budget office on a collision course with political leaders and other central actors. If it cannot perform this role effectively, the government may end up budgeting for fiscal space that it does not have.

Reference

Wildavsky, Aaron (1964), *The Politics of the Budgetary Process*, Little, Brown and Company, New York, United States.

ISBN 978-92-64-06087-6
Evolutions in Budgetary Practice
Allen Schick and the OECD Senior Budget Officials
© OECD 2009

APPENDIX A

Annual meetings of OECD Senior Budget Officials: Chronology 1980-2009

Session	Date	Place	Chair	Number of participants	Main topics, titles of papers, authors
1	28-30 May 1980	Paris	Mr Th.A.J. Meys Director General of the Budget Ministry of Finance Netherlands	64	**Expenditure control:** – "The Theory of Expenditure Limitation", *Aaron Wildavsky.*
2	2-3 June 1981	Paris	Mr L.J.C.M. Le Blanc Director General of the Budget Ministry of Finance Netherlands	44	**Country case study:** – "The 1980 Supplementary Budget [of Germany]", *Ullrich Casper.* **Off-budget expenditure:** – "Off-Budget Expenditure: The Economic and Political Framework", *Allen Schick.* **Expenditure control:** – "The Agonies of Decremental Budgeting", *Daniel Tarschys.*
3	3-4 June 1982	Paris	(Workshop on the Control of Off-Budget Expenditure)	32	**Off-budget expenditure:** – "Off-Budget Expenditure: The Economic and Political Framework" (revised), *Allen Schick.*
4	16-17 June 1983	Paris	Mr Ian Castles Secretary Department of Finance Australia	35	**Capacity to budget:** – "Adaptation of the Budget Process in OECD Countries". **Multi-year budgeting:** – "Multi-Year Budgeting and Expenditure Management". **Resource allocation and control:** – "Managing Budgetary Objectives", *Bart LeBlanc and OECD.* – "Managing Entitlements within the Budget Process".
5	28-29 June 1984	Paris	Mr Ian Castles Secretary Department of Finance Australia	43	**Country case studies:** – "Human Resource Budgeting", *Australia.* – "Modernisation of the Public Sector", *Denmark.* – "Policy Review and Budgeting: Some Experiences with the 'Reconsiderations Procedure' in the Netherlands", *Netherlands.* – "Measuring the Effect of Budgetary Policy Changes: Recent United States Developments in Budgetary Analysis", *United States.* **Financial management:** – "Cash Budgeting and Cash Planning".
6	27-28 June 1985	Paris	Mr Jean-Jacques Noreau Deputy Secretary Treasury Board Secretariat Canada	47	**Country case study:** – "Recent Developments in the Canadian Policy and Expenditure Management System". **Capacity to budget:** – "Report on the Capacity to Budget". **Budget office:** – "The Organisation and Staffing of the Budget Office". **Financial control:** – "Effectiveness Auditing as a Budgetary Tool". – "Financial Control of Public Enterprises and Off-Budget Agencies". **Transparency and accountability:** – "The Presentation of Budget Information to Parliament and the Public (design of budget documentation)".

Session	Date	Place	Chair	Number of participants	Main topics, titles of papers, authors
7	9-10 June 1986	Paris	Mr Alan Darling Deputy Secretary Treasury Board Secretariat Canada	38	**Country case studies:** – "Medium-Term Financial Planning in Germany", *Finance Ministry, Germany.* – "Ministry of Treasury", Italy. – "United States Deficit Reduction Legislation (Gramm-Rudman-Hollings)", *OMB, United States.* **Capacity to budget:** – "Report on the Capacity to Budget Study: The Control and Management of Government Expenditure". **Capital budgeting:** – "Capital Budgeting". **Expenditure control:** – "Expenditure Control and Effectiveness and Efficiency of Departmental Management".
8	18-19 June 1987	Paris	Mr Michel Prada Director of the Budget Ministry of Economy, Finance and Privatisation France	39	**Capital budgeting:** – "Capital Budgeting". **Multi-year budgeting:** – "Three-Year Budget Frames in Sweden". – "Structure and Flexibility of Budgets". **Performance budgeting:** – "Performance Measurement and Improvement", *HM Treasury, United Kingdom.* **Expenditure control (human resources):** – "Manpower Controls".
9	13-14 June 1988	Paris	Mr Daniel Bouton Director of the Budget Ministry of Economy, Finance and Privatisation France	50	**Country case studies:** – "The Australian Financial Management Improvement Program", *Budget Office, Australia.* – "Credit Budget and Management", *OMB, United States.* **Intergovernmental relationships:** – "Relationships between Central and other Levels of Government: Some Developments in France", *Budget Office, France.* **Performance budgeting:** – "Measuring Performance and Allocating Resources", *Allen Schick.* **Public-private partnerships:** – "Private Finance and Management of Public Assets and the Consequences for Budgetary Control", *Patricia Brown.*
10	29-30 June 1989	Paris	Ms Inga-Britt Ahlenius Director of the Budget Ministry of Finance Sweden	43	**Country case study:** – "Fiscal Reform: Japan's Experience", *Japan.* **Expenditure control:** – "Use of Budgetary Reserves in Budget Planning and Implementation", *Patricia Brown.* – "Incentives in Budgetary Systems: From Experiments to Structural Changes", *François Lacasse.* **Market-type mechanisms:** – "Financing Public Expenditure Through User Charges".
11	25-26 June 1990	Paris	Ms Inga-Britt Ahlenius Director of the Budget Ministry of Finance Sweden	40	**Expenditure control:** – "The Problems of the Control of Public Expenditures in Belgium". **Multi-year budgeting:** – "Multi-Year Budgeting: Canada, Germany, Sweden, United Kingdom". **Off-budget expenditures:** – "Public Enterprises, Loans and Guarantees: Problems and Practices in Austria, Canada, France and the United States". **Performance budgeting:** – "Public Sector Performance and the Role and Use of Cost Attribution: Canada, New Zealand and Sweden".

Session	Date	Place	Chair	Number of participants	Main topics, titles of papers, authors
12	24-25 June 1991	Paris	Mr Seán Cromien Secretary Department of Finance Ireland	57	**Budgeting for the future:** – "Integration of Longer-Term Information in the Budgetary Process", *Per Schreiner and Mette Wikborg.* **Market-type mechanisms:** – "Framework for Analysing the Redistributive Impacts of Market-Type Mechanisms", *Alain Albert.* – "Mapping Out Market-Type Mechanisms: Concept, Purposes, Classification and Experience". **Transparency and accountability:** – "Accountability Mechanisms for Public Managers: Evolution and Change in New Zealand". – "The Accountability Framework in Government in the Light of Recent Management and Budgetary Reforms: An Australian Perspective".
13	9-10 June 1992	Paris	Mr Seán Cromien Secretary Department of Finance Ireland	52	**Market-type mechanisms:** – "Internal Markets for the Provision of Goods and Services for Use by Central Administrations". – "Markets in Property Rights as Public Management Tools: Fishing Rights in Australia, Canada and Iceland". – "Non-Price Competition, Specialisation, Managerial Autonomy and Cost Control in Hospitals", *D. Fixari and D. Tonneau.* – "Tradable Rights and User Charges in Pollution Control: The Distributive Dimension", *D. Harrison.* – "Vouchers and Market Mechanisms in the Funding of Residential Care".
14	7-8 June 1993	Paris	Mr Laurent de Ryck Director of the Budget Ministry of Finance Belgium	47	**Accrual accounting:** – "Accounting for What?: The Value of Accrual Accounting to the Public Sector". **Budgeting for the future:** – "Progress Report of the Project on Forecasting and Control of the Costs of Transfer Programmes". **Expenditure control:** – "Social Policies: Adjustment, Drift and Equity", *Pierre Strobel.* – "Forecasting the Costs of Social Transfer Programmes for Private Individuals", *André Raynauld and Jean-Pierre Vidal.* **Performance budgeting:** – "Using Evaluation in Budgeting: Impossible Dream?", *Mel Cappe, Harry Havens, Jean Leca and François Lacasse.*
15	26-27 May 1994	Paris	Mr Laurent de Ryck Director of the Budget Ministry of Finance Belgium	48	**Public-private partnerships:** – "Innovation in the Joint Public-Private Provision of Infrastructure: Main Issues and Conclusions". **Budgeting for the future:** – "Report of the Study on Forecast and Control of the Costs of Transfer Programmes". **Budget office:** – "The Role of the Budget Office in Management Improvement: An Assessment of Financial Management Reforms", *Allen Schick.*
16	12-13 June 1995	Paris	Mr Barry Anderson Assistant Director Office of Management and Budget United States	44	**Expenditure control:** – "Managing Structural Deficit Reduction". **Financial management:** – "Assessing Financial Management Reforms", *Allen Schick.* **Intergovernmental relationships:** – "Fiscal Relationships Between Central and Local Governments in Germany and Japan", *Ministries of Finance, Germany and Japan.*
17	11-12 June 1996	Paris	Mr Barry Anderson Assistant Director Office of Management and Budget United States	56	**Budgeting for the future:** – "Budgeting for the Future". **Budget office:** – "Changing Legal and Institutional Frameworks for Budgeting: The Implications for the Role of the Central Budget Office", *Allen Schick.* **Market-type mechanisms:** – "Best Practice Guidelines for Contracting Out Government Services".

Session	Date	Place	Chair	Number of participants	Main topics, titles of papers, authors
18	10-11 June 1997	Paris	Mr Barry Anderson Assistant Director Office of Management and Budget United States AND Mr Paul Gray Director, Budget and Public Finance HM Treasury United Kingdom	62	**Country developments with accruals:** – "Accrual Accounting and Budgeting in the Dutch Government", *Harman Korte.* – "The Development of Accrual Accounting and Budgeting in the United Kingdom", *Andrew Likierman.* **Expenditure control (pensions):** – "Strategies for Reducing Fiscal Pressures of Public Pensions". – "The Chilean Pension System", *Joaquin Vial Ruiz-Tagle and Francisca Castro.* **Management tools:** – "Programme Evaluation". – "Policy Instruments". **Market-type mechanisms:** – "Best Practice Guidelines for User Charging for Government Services".
19	25-26 May 1998	Paris	Mr Hans Reckers Director of the Budget Ministry of Finance Germany	66	**Country review:** – "Budgeting in Sweden". **Role of the legislature:** – "Role of the Legislature in the Budget Process". **Public enterprises:** – "Reforming Public Enterprises", *Adam Smith.* **Market-type mechanisms:** – "Voucher Programmes and Their Role in Distributing Public Services", *Martin Cave.* **Financial management:** – "Modern Financial Management Practices", *Ian Ball.*
20	3-4 June 1999	Paris	Mr Joachim Schwarzer Director of the Budget Ministry of Finance Germany	69	**Country review:** – "Budgeting and Management in Canada". **Expenditure control:** – "Budgeting in a Surplus Environment", *Barry Anderson.* **Performance budgeting and productivity:** – "Integrating Financial Management and Performance Management", *Christopher Pollitt.* – "Measuring Public Sector Productivity", *Ken Tallis, Anne Aaltonen, Brugt Kazemier, Richard Murray, David Caplan and Andy Milne.* **Transparency and accountability:** – "Fiscal Transparency".
21	29-30 May 2000	Paris	Mr Geert van Maanen Secretary-General Ministry of Finance Netherlands	83	**Accrual accounting:** – "Accrual Accounting and Budgeting", *International Federation of Accountants and OECD.* **Budget office:** – "Greater Independence for Fiscal Institutions", *Nicholas Gruen.* **Performance budgeting:** – "The OECD Outputs Manual", *Susan Hitchiner.* **Resource reallocation decisions:** – "Reallocation: Aligning Political Priorities and Budgetary Funding", *Louise Archer, Michael Carnahan, Peder Lundquist, Michael Lund Nielsen, Helena Tarkka, Sirpa Tulla, Jutta Kalabuch, Petros Liverakos, Liam Basquille, John Ming Kim, Peter Saurer, Olivier Kungler, David Morrison, William McLeod, Christopher Johns, and OECD.* **Transparency and accountability:** – "OECD Best Practices for Budget Transparency".
22	21-22 May 2001	Paris	Mr Geert van Maanen Secretary-General Ministry of Finance Netherlands	79	**Country review:** – "Budgeting and Management in the Netherlands". **Performance budgeting:** – "Outcome Focused Management and Budgeting". **Role of the legislature:** – "Can National Legislatures Regain an Effective Voice in Budget Policy?", *Allen Schick.* **Budgeting practices:** – "Does Budgeting Have a Future?", *Allen Schick.* – "A Gender Perspective on Budgeting", *Ministry of Economy, Finance and Industry, France.*

Session	Date	Place	Chair	Number of participants	Main topics, titles of papers, authors
23	3-4 June 2002	Washington DC	Mr Geert van Maanen Secretary-General Ministry of Finance Netherlands	77	**Country review:** – "Budgeting in Finland". **Accrual accounting:** – "Accrual Accounting and Budgeting: Key Issues and Recent Developments". **Budgeting for the future:** – "Time Horizons in Budgeting", *Daniel Tarschys*. – "Investing in Private Financial Assets to Address Longer-Term Needs". **Expenditure control:** – "The Political Economy of Reforming Entitlement Programmes", *Mitch Daniels*. **Governance of agencies:** – "Agencies in Search of Principles", *Allen Schick*.
24	3-4 June 2003	Rome	Mr Richard P. Emery Assistant Director Office of Management and Budget United States	59	**Country reviews:** – "Budgeting in the United States". – "Budgeting in Brazil". **Budgeting for the future:** – "Countering Uncertainty in Budget Forecasts", *Dan Crippen*. **Expenditure control:** – "Reallocation: The Role of Budget Institutions". – "The Role of Fiscal Rules in Budgeting", *Allen Schick*. **Performance budgeting:** – "The Performing State: Reflection on an idea whose time has come but whose implementation has not", *Allen Schick*. **Budgeting database:** – "OECD Budgeting Database".
25	9-10 June 2004	Madrid	Mr Richard P. Emery Assistant Director Office of Management and Budget United States	66	**Country reviews:** – "Budgeting in Denmark". – "Budgeting in Chile". **Accrual budgeting:** – "Issues in Accrual Budgeting". **Budgeting for the future:** – "Incorporating a Medium-Term Horizon to Public Expenditures". – "A Window into Budgeting: Reflections on SBO's Past and Future", *Allen Schick*. **Off-budget and tax expenditures:** – "Best Practice Guidelines: Off-Budget and Tax Expenditures".
26	30-31 May 2005	Paris	Mr Richard P. Emery Assistant Director Office of Management and Budget United States	70	**Country review:** – "Budgeting in Switzerland". **Expenditure control:** – "Sustainable Budget Policy: Concepts and Approaches", *Allen Schick*. – "Public Sector Budget Management Issues in China", *Christine Wong*. **Performance budgeting:** – "Using Performance Information for Managing and Budgeting: Challenges, Lessons and Opportunities", *John Mayne*. **Market-type mechanisms:** – "The Role of Market-Type Mechanisms in the Provision of Public Services". **Transparency and accountability:** – "Communicating Fiscal Issues with the Public", *Jackie Calmes and Peter Gumbel*.

Session	Date	Place	Chair	Number of participants	Main topics, titles of papers, authors
27	4-5 June 2006	Sydney	Dr Ian Watt Secretary Department of Finance Australia	54	**Country reviews:** – "Budgeting in Norway". – "Budgeting in Singapore". **Budgeting for the future:** – "Assessing Fiscal Risks through Long-Term Budget Projections", *Pål Ulla*. **Expenditure control:** – "Design Choices for Fiscal Policy Rules", *Barry Anderson and Joseph J. Minarik*. – "Top-Down Budgeting", *Korea Institute of Public Finance and OECD*. **Performance budgeting:** – "Experiences in Utilising Performance Information in the Budget and Management Processes".
28	31 May – 1 June 2007	Istanbul	Dr Ian Watt Secretary Department of Finance Australia	77	**Country reviews:** – "Budgeting in Austria". – "Budgeting in Turkey". **Performance budgeting/accrual budgeting:** – "Performance Budgeting and Accrual Budgeting: Decision Rules or Analytic Tools?", *Allen Schick*. **Role of the legislature/budget office:** – "Relationship between the Legislature and the Budget Office in the Budget Process", *Paul Posner and Chung-Keun Park*. **Transparency and accountability:** – "Engaging the Public in National Budgeting: A Non-Governmental Perspective", *Susan Tanaka*. **Budgeting database:** – "OECD Budgeting Database: Results of the 2007 Survey".
29	2-3 June 2008	Vienna	Dr Ian Watt Secretary Department of Finance Australia	77	**Country reviews:** – "Budgeting in Australia". – "Budgeting in Greece". – "Budgeting in Russia". **Expenditure control:** – "Budgeting for Fiscal Space", *Allen Schick*. – "Tax Expenditures in OECD Countries", *Joseph J. Minarik*. **Public-private partnerships:** – "Public-Private Partnerships: The Relevance of Budgeting", *Paul Posner, Shin Kue Ryu and Anna Tkachenko*.
30	4-5 June 2009	Paris	Dr Ian Watt Secretary Department of Finance Australia		

OECD PUBLISHING, 2, rue André-Pascal, 75775 PARIS CEDEX 16

PRINTED IN FRANCE

(42 2009 14 1 P) ISBN 978-92-64-06087-6 – No. 56785 2009